Preaching to Convert

Preaching to Convert

Evangelical Outreach and Performance Activism in a Secular Age

JOHN FLETCHER

The University of Michigan Press
Ann Arbor

First paperback edition 2015

Published in the United States of America by the
University of Michigan Press
Manufactured in the United States of America
♾ Printed on acid-free paper

2018 2017 2016 2015 5 4 3 2

A CIP catalog record for this book is available from the British Library.

Library of Congress Cataloging-in-Publication Data

Fletcher, John, 1975–
Preaching to convert : evangelical outreach and performance activism in a secular age / John Fletcher.
pages cm
Includes bibliographical references and index.
ISBN 978-0-472-11915-8 (cloth : alk. paper) —ISBN 978-0-472-02987-7 (e-book)
1. Preaching. 2. Evangelistic work. I. Title.
BV4211.3.F54 2013
269'.2—dc23

2013031517

ISBN 978-0-472-03652-3 (pbk. : alk. paper)

To my sister, Liz,

the wisest person I know,

who teaches me to listen with an open heart

Acknowledgments

More people than I can hope to account for helped me to envision, research, and complete this project. Scott Magelssen, Lance Gharavi, Carolyn Roark, Rob Shimko, Sara Freeman, Henry Bial, and Jody Enders all helped me—as editors and as friends—work through versions of and variations on the book. My present editor, the indispensable LeAnn Fields, has been a dream. She believed in my project more than I did, and her patient support has been a real blessing to me. I am grateful also to the anonymous readers, whose comments and insights on my initial draft were invaluable to me in the revision process.

In addition, a host of friends have all in some way or another (perhaps without their knowing it) been valuable sounding boards for ideas and questions I've pursued: Megan Sanborn Jones, Dorothy Chansky, Patty Ybarra, Patrick Anderson, Rhonda Blair, Ann Haugo, Jean Graham-Jones, Wade Hollingshaus, Marla Carlson, Will Daddario, Joanne Zerdy, Karen Jean Martinson, Mary Karen Dahl, Carrie Sandahl, Shannon Walsh, Maurya Wickstrom, and Laura Edmondson. I have been especially helped by those in the growing circle of scholars researching present-day faith and performance in the United States. Hank Willenbrink and Allan Davis both gave me indispensable help in my work on hell houses; Hank's work on evangelical conversion proved particularly useful to me in thinking through such processes here. Jill Stevenson has been enormously supportive and generous to me. I highly recommend her volume on evangelical performance, which, Lord willing and the creek don't rise, should be published by the time you're reading this. We play in the same sandbox but build different castles, and I am pleased to share the field with such a stellar scholar.

I could not have completed this work without the stalwart support of colleagues past and present at Louisiana State University, including Kristin Sosnowski, Les Wade, Leigh Clemons, Femi Euba, and Mike Tick. I must also give a hat-tip to my students, graduate and undergraduate, over the last few years, all of whom have been admirably patient with Dr. Fletcher as he split time between grading and writing.

I extend thanks to my own professors and academic mentors who guided me and shaped me as a scholar. David Pasto, Judith Palladino, Ruth Charnay, Marsha Keller, and Abigail Keegan at Oklahoma City University all helped to set me on the path to a lifetime of work in the university theater. I write, act, and teach as they taught me to still. At the University of Minnesota, Tim Brennan, Tamara Underiner, and Jane Blocker each made an indelible impression on me. My teacher and dissertation co-chair, Michal Kobialka, modeled for me what it means to question received stances, walk around acquired rationalizations, and push beyond zones of comfort.

My enduring gratitude goes to Sonja Arsham Kuftinec: my adviser then, my friend now, and my mentor always. It was in her seminar on Theatre and Social Change in my first semester of graduate work that I first considered whether those "hell houses" I had heard about might not themselves be a kind of activist performance. She exemplifies the generous, rigorous, passionate, and dynamic nature that I strive to infuse into my work as a scholar, as a teacher, and as a person. She has held me to life more times than I can count. Her work inspires and challenges me. I am grateful that she is part of my life.

I cannot study evangelicals without also interrogating my own faith, and I want to thank the United Methodist pastors who have been my ministers over the past few years: Rev. Susie Thomas, Rev. Dr. Van Stinson, and Rev. Phil Woodland. I especially want to thank the Rev. Dr. Jay Hogewood, whose expertise in biblical Greek and all-around smarts helped me out of philological jams more than once. Moreover, Jay's ministry and friendship were instrumental in helping me be a more committed Methodist. I am also blessed to have at this time a wonderful church group, the Genesis class at University Methodist in Baton Rouge, co-coordinated by two saints on earth, Christine Griffin and Lauren Michaud; the love, prayers, and support of the Genesis class helps to keep me sane.

My thanks, also, goes to the baristas at Garden District Coffee, where so much of this book was written. Their friendliness and sugar-free-skim-vanilla-iced lattes were a boon to me.

Financial assistance from LSU's Office of Sponsored Research Summer Stipend Grant enabled me to travel to the Creation Museum in the summer of 2008. I am also thankful to Texas A&M University's Glasscock Center, particularly the Performance Studies and Queer Studies groups, for funding a visit to College Station in spring 2009 to share an early draft of my work on the Museum as well as some preliminary thoughts about ex-gay ministries (for what became chapter eight). Students in Ashley Currier's Queer Theory seminar gave especially cogent critiques of my work on the Museum that shaped the project's revisions considerably. I am grateful also to countless people in countless evangelical churches, conventions, meetings, and spaces who took time to share a word with me and to show me around backstage, and who without fail showed me hospitality and love.

I am grateful to Robert M. Lee from C. S. Lovett books for permission to use photos from Lovett's *Soul-Winning Made Easy* book. My thanks go to Kensington Community Church for their permission to use a publicity photograph for their "Confessions of a Sinful Church" series. I am also thankful to Answers in Genesis, and Melany Ethridge at A. Larry Ross Communications especially, for securing permission to use the photo of the "dig" site from the Creation Museum. I thank Esther Kim Lee, editor of *Theatre Survey,* and Cambridge University Press for their permission to use parts of my 2007 article on Hell House ("Tasteless as Hell: Community Performance, Distinction, and Countertaste in Hell House" in *Theatre Survey* 48, no. 2 (November 2007): 313–30, Copyright 2007 Cambridge University Press) for my present chapter five.

Finally, I am thankful for my family. My parents, the Rev. Dan and Rev. Juanita Fletcher, taught me that my faith welcomes—no, *requires*—questioning and challenge. Their example of unconditional love provided for me an image of God that I hope to carry throughout my life. Both of them are so brave, strong, intelligent, and passionate. Both of them have taken risks and hits to stand up for me and other gay, lesbian, bisexual, and transgender people within and without the church.

I have dedicated this book to my sister, Liz Fletcher. There are of course the standard reasons for my acknowledging her: the knowledge that I can talk to her about anything, the odd sense of humor only she and I seem to share, the willingness to read my readers' reports before I could work up the courage to look at them. But, quite apart from these blessings, Liz just astonishes me. She has such a depth of spirit, such a broad wisdom, and such a penetrating intellect. A gifted actress and a brilliant clinical therapist, Liz reminds me that theater is the craft of thinking and feeling into the other's shoes—and then making bold (sometimes painful) choices. In her work and in her life, she works miracles. She saves lives. I know she saves mine. She is good faith personified, and I am ever in awe of her.

Last and so precious to me is my partner, Alan Sikes. Alan's mind is so wide-ranging and sharp, his heart so large and fierce and bold. It was Alan who most helped me navigate my first few years of graduate school, guiding me through the thickets of poststructuralist theory, the brambles of spatial historiography. It was Alan who showed me how to be ethical and demanding at once in my scholarship. Though not a believer himself, Alan has supported my faith as strongly as any pastor. He has pressed me to articulate my faith in new and challenging ways, and he makes me a better Christian for it. Throughout my career and this project especially, he's pushed and prodded and nudged when I stall; he's listened and commiserated and advised when I balk. And the sacrifices he's made for this book! He endured hours of listening to Steven Anderson's fundamentalist sermons during long car drives. He's driven me to Grand Rapids, Michigan, so I could attend an ex-gay conference. He accompanied me to the Creation Museum, where we walked from the beginning of the universe to the end of the world together. Alan has been my go-to editor, in-house critic, and emergency ego-booster (sometimes all at once). He is my best friend, the person whose face I most look forward to seeing, whose support and help I seek most often, and whose arms I feel most at peace in. He is a miracle. I thank God I have him.

Contents

Introduction: Tackling You to Change the World 1

1. Performance Activism, Progressive Oversights, and Deep Differences 15
2. Positioning Secular Age Evangelicalism 46
3. Face to Face, Door to Door: Personal Evangelism and the Scandal of Salvation 77
4. Apologies and Apologetics: Meta-Kerygmatic Evangelism 122
5. Hell and Judgement: Houses of Distinction 157
6. Prepare to Believe: Performing the Evangelical Worldview at the Creation Museum 191
7. Staging Church, Marketing the Divine 220
8. Change Is Possible: Exodus and the Opposite of Homosexuality 262

Conclusion: American Grace and Evangelical True Believers 303

NOTES 315

BIBLIOGRAPHY 369

INDEX 389

Introduction

Tackling You to Change the World

Suppose you knew something deeply, utterly true—not just *a* truth but the Truth, a life-changing, capital-T-type Truth. Imagine that you knew with every atom of your being that this Truth could set people free, save them from a certain doom, and lead them into a richer, fuller, life. What would you do? What *should* you do?

If you're Penn Jillette—stage magician, self-proclaimed atheist, and debunker of all things supernatural—the answer is obvious: you tell someone. In a 2008 episode of his web-cast *Penn Says,* Jillette recalls an encounter he had with an evangelical who tried to convert him. It was after a show of his, he explains to his online audience. A man approaches him, complimenting his act and handing Jillette a Gideon Bible, the kind found in many hotel rooms. "I'm kind of proselytizing," said the man apologetically, knowing full well (Jillette guesses) that Jillette is an atheist. "I'm a business man. I'm—I'm sane; I'm not crazy." He looks Jillette right in the eye and proceeds with his pitch. Despite having crafted his public persona as one who resists the theological frameworks, Jillette listens. The man has his say and says goodbye. Jillette ruminates on the encounter thusly:

> I've always said that I don't respect people who don't proselytize. I don't respect that at all. If you believe that there's a heaven and hell and people could be going to hell or not getting eternal life or what-

> ever, and you think that, uh, well it's not really worth telling them this because it'll make it socially awkward. And atheists who think that people shouldn't proselytize—just leave me alone, keep your religion to yourself—ah, how much do you have to hate somebody to *not* proselytize? How much do you have to hate somebody to believe that everlasting life is possible and not tell them that? I mean if I believed beyond the shadow of a doubt that a truck was coming at you and you didn't believe it, if that truck was bearing down on you? There's a certain point where I tackle you. And this is *more important* than that.[1]

This need to reach out, to share a gospel Truth even at the cost of social propriety, serves as the jumping-off point for my project. I propose that evangelicals' impulse to reach out parallels the motivations that animate performances of activism. I have long been inspired by the idea that theater (and performance practices generally) can and should do more than provide entertainment or cultural distinction. I follow a long and diverse tradition of thinkers and artists who draw on performance techniques and insights to inform, convict, persuade, galvanize, revive, shock, enrage, comfort, or disturb audiences in the service of broader social or political causes. My interests encompass a range of performance practices, from narrative dramas mounted in dedicated theater spaces to less formally "theatrical" spectacles like marches, rallies, and protests. Simply put, I study performances that aim to change the world. I examine—and occasionally join—actors driven by the conviction that the world (or at least some part of it) needs changing. A gap exists between what is and what ought to be; another, better world is possible. So vital is this truth, so life-giving, that sharing it, spreading it, and persuading others of it is worth the risk of breaching social proprieties, alienating the powers that be, and seeming, in short, kind of crazy. But how could they, how could I, do otherwise? As Jillette says, how much would I have to hate people *not* to do all in my power to act on my deepest convictions and try to move the world to this better place?

At some point, in other words, I tackle you.

In this book, I write about those kinds of tackles, those transitions from being *for* something to acting on or in the name of something. I argue that examining how evangelicals navigate that transition can shed light on how performance activists (particularly those on the left) do so. Of course, the image of "tackling someone" reminds us that efforts to change the world can involve violation instead of persuasion. The same kinds of deep convictions that prompt the evangelist in the anecdote above to hold a pleasant chat with Penn Jillette also fuel imperialist takeovers or totalitarian repressions in other contexts. World-changing endeavors do not necessarily stem from altruistic motives, nor do good intentions guarantee amiable encounters. Indeed, the very attempt to change someone's mind about religion or other such deep beliefs already introduces a degree of inter-subjective tension: *you are wrong; I am right.* Whether tacit or explicit, such presumptive-corrective subtexts by evangelicals transgress predominant social protocols of privacy and civility. They strain present-day political-democratic values like tolerance and the right to pursue (religious) happiness as one sees fit. They assert that no, in fact, a thousand flowers *can't* bloom. One belief—*my belief*—embodies the Good in a way yours fails to. Evangelicals fascinate me in that their defining impetus—outreach, proselytization, witnessing—puts them in the position of permanent tackler. They make your beliefs their business and intervene accordingly.

What does theater for social change have to do with evangelicalism? First, I am convinced that evangelicals are by nature performance activists. I detail my understanding of *evangelicalism* in my second chapter, but for now let me stress that I do not refer to the activism of religious-right culture warriors around national issues like abortion, gay marriage, or prayer in schools. To the extent I can, I bracket off the partisan culture-war sorties of "religious right" organizations, though certainly these can and should be viewed as activist performances. The "evangelical activism" I study in this project concerns the more basic mission of spreading a gospel message in the hopes that people convert.[2] In this sense, evangelicals have the most venerable, most searching, and most comprehensive discourse about how to proclaim messages and persuade audiences of all the (non-commercial) social activist performers or groups I have ever encountered. Despite wide variation and internal disagreements, evangelicals unite in defining themselves—explicitly, eponymously—by their mission to go out into the world and make disciples. Evangelicals *evangelize.* They seek converts. To do so, they marshal practically every tool, every tactic employed by performance activists the world over: agitprop, street theater, marches, pageants, corner sermons, dances, protests, demonstrations, viral videos—you name it. They likewise wrestle with many of the same problems, conundrums, and frustrations that confront activist performers more generally. How do people change? What tactics facilitate worldview shifts in people? How do activists balance popular appeal and ideological (theological) integrity? How should activists measure the success or failure of their efforts? How do activist groups maintain momentum, passion, and unity? Evangelicals, in other words, operate via a sophisticated technology of activist outreach. I can't be interested in performance activism and *not* study them.

The second factor that links evangelicalism to my interests in activism relates to a cluster of tensions circulating within current conversations on the progressive left about the aims and methods of social change performance practices. I unpack these tensions in the next chapter, but for now let me summarize the situation as a strain between inclusivist and exclusivist tendencies. On the one hand the US progressive left—a group in which I include myself—calls for openness, tolerance, and plural deliberation, stressing these values as basic to any properly democratic (read: rational, just, moral) process or society. At the same time, however, left-progressive groups insist on particular end-point configurations of society, with specific ideas of what justice, equality, and empowerment for all look like. Although the left generally considers these values universal or self-evident, its configuration of justice/equality/empowerment remains singular, leaving out (at least) those who disagree with that configuration. At multiple points and in multiple ways, then, the progressive left's inclusivity imperatives clash with the ineluctable exclusivity of its value claims. I contend that this clash, or more specifically queasiness about this clash, leaves left-progressive activism with limited options when confronting the reality of deep disagreement with its core values. The left may rationalize disagreement with left-progressive values as the result of irrationality, misunderstanding, or immorality (e.g., "If only they had the same information/experience as we did, they would arrive at our conclusions"). Or it may choose to avoid the specter of exclusivity altogether by watering down or withdrawing its strongest claims. Neither of these, I argue, is satisfactory. The former leads to two-dimensional mischaracterizations of opponents, the latter to internecine, more-radical-than-thou squabbles between activists.

Bringing evangelicalism qua activism into this conversation can help. Evangelicals usually *aren't* part of the performance activist conversation in the United States except as the Bad Guys, the forces of oppression, bigotry, or narrow-mindedness that activist performers have to work against. Evangelicals (or "Christians" or "fundamentalists"—there's often very little attempt at nuance or accuracy in such characterizations) get portrayed as naïve and deluded at best or fundamentalist and dangerous at worst. Aside from the blind spot it creates for scholars and activists, I argue that this elision cuts activists and scholars off from a productive case study of others who grapple with many of the same tensions that vex the progressive left. Evangelicals openly affirm an exclusivist (which is not the same as a fanatical or militant) worldview, a narrow path to salvation, that they know will set them at odds with others. But they are compelled by their mission to make that worldview not only known but also (and without adulteration) open and inviting to all people. They must be as broadly inclusive as possible in proclaiming a straight-and-narrow message. Unlike many instances of left-progressive activism, however, evangelicalism confronts this tension head-on, acknowledging it as a central reality of outreach efforts. Moreover, certain aspects of present-day evangelicalism prove surprisingly insightful about and critical of the political common sense that structures available avenues of belief and action in liberal democracies along axes of public/private, secular/sacred, and protected/illegal. Evangelical understandings of and reactions to such constrictive ideological-market logic can, I contend, offer insights for activists on the left similarly caught within neoliberal capitalism. In this book, then, I study the performances (theatrical and otherwise) that evangelicals in the United States use to change their world, to win converts to their faith and worldview. I frame these outreach efforts as modes of activist performance, examining the strategies evangelicals in the United States employ to evangelize, the challenges they face as they do so, and the solutions, innovations, or compromises they create in response to these challenges. In doing so, I wish at minimum to add some dimension to perceptions of US evangelicalism in scholarship about performance activism. My hope is that such a complicated perspective can highlight for scholars and activists areas of tension within left-progressive configurations of "what is to be done."

Lest there be any confusion, I should clarify that I am not myself evangelical. I am a liberal, gay, ex–Southern Baptist, United Methodist, a position that in numerous ways (theological, historical, cultural, and political) sets me well outside the evangelical mainstream. Although I am at points critical of left-progressive values in this project, I launch my critiques of the progressive left as a fellow traveler within the field of radical democratic theory and practice. Furthermore, I can understand the antipathy many of my friends and colleagues have expressed toward evangelicalism. I have personal experience with negative evangelical encounters that in isolation seem to justify the worst stereotypes of conservative believers. I also know, however, that evangelicalism is much bigger and more complex than the wounds I or others have suffered because of it and the damages inflicted by some of its practitioners. I have found evangelicalism, at its best, to be populated by as many activists of good faith and hope as I've encountered in any movement.

But the fact remains: evangelicals—particularly conservative evangelicals—and I believe very different things. No amount of empathy or understanding will mitigate the fact that, on certain issues, we will stand on two sides of a worldview gap. I therefore want to avoid delivering some anodyne plea for rapprochement between progressive-left performance activists and non-left evangelical proselytizers. This book is not a call for the progressive left to extend its signature tolerance to reconcile with evangelicals, inviting them to the table of social justice, as it were. (Conservative evangelicals themselves would be the first to refuse such an invitation on anything more than a contingent basis.) On the contrary, and in the tradition of thinkers like Stanley Fish, Chantal Mouffe, Jacques Rancière, and Wendy Brown, I emphasize that there *is* no common table of social justice, no permanent one, anyway. Activism—performance activism particularly—has no natural configuration, no set of operating procedures or ideal ends so universal or self-evident as to evade the inclusivist/exclusivist conundrum I sketch out above. Insofar as activism of any sort calls for a shift from what is to what should be, from the now to the not-yet, the invitation to participate in that transformation will always seem like anathema to those on the wrong side.

Progressive-left performance activism often frustrates me when it seeks to minimize or deny this fact: people will disagree, and disagree deeply, about core issues, even after good-faith processes of rational reflection and empathic negotiation. Evangelicalism, on the other hand, constantly reminds its followers of the offensiveness and exclusivity of its message. It programs the potential for audience disagreement, opposition, and alterity into every circuit of its outreach technology. Although this expectation of opposition can at times encourage militant, polarizing attitudes from evangelicals, it also opens a new vista of tactics and encounters. In left-progressive activism, encountering audience rejection or opposition often signals the termination point of the activist gesture, the end of an activist performance. For evangelicals, the reality of ideological (theological) difference serves as the starting point, the given circumstances that shape any outreach action. To them, the world is fallen, always yet-to-be-converted by a message that will inevitably seem foolish, counterintuitive, and inflexible. Any single proselytizing encounter or any evangelizing performance plays only one part in a process, the other steps of which the evangelist may never learn and the ultimate success or failure of which is out of any human hands. A seed planted today may yet sprout and bloom in the future—or not. According to evangelical theology, that people convert at all is a miracle, literally an act of God. Believers live under standing orders to participate in the potential miracle of successful activism, making their witness as compelling, winsome, strong, and loving as possible—even and especially to those standing on the other side of deep worldview gaps. Ensuring this means not only deepening one's grounding in evangelical orthodoxy but also learning as much as possible about those operating from other cultural locations, other worldviews. Opposition and invitation necessarily coexist.

Through my examination of evangelical outreach, I hope to underline several vital and all-too-often-overlooked aspects of performance activism. First, even the most universally minded values and agendas will compel a mix of affirmation and antagonism when manifested in performance. Any concrete realization of notions like *justice* or *salvation* robs those values of the generality that enables so many different agents to unify around them simultaneously. Fine, previously hidden distinctions appear and expand once a particular group embodies one and not another definition of an ostensibly shared ideal. Second, the gaps between support and opposition are the very stuff of fundamental ideological difference. These gaps aren't reducible merely to misunderstandings calling for clearer definitions, intelligence deficits in need of better education, or moral deficiencies indicative of the need for (perhaps) empathic encounters or (in extreme cases) warfare. The differences I refer to stem from incommensurable worldviews, wholly different modes of perceiving, interpreting, and operating within social reality. Finally, activism within a schema of liberal democracy—and certainly activism within the spirit of radical democracy—requires a difficult alchemy of mind-sets and goals. Activists must juggle (at least) deep recognition of ideological difference, deep devotion to their own convictions, and persistent efforts to persuade or convert others into adopting those convictions. If I might risk saying it, attempting this combination requires something like love, a desire to see even enemies or anonymous victims as neighbors in need of a soul-saving truth. I do not suggest that evangelicals accomplish this complicated task perfectly or consistently. But in the struggles, frustrations, and even failures of many evangelicals, I see a model for the best kinds of activist encounters that performance on the progressive left might offer.

Though my ultimate goal involves contributing to ongoing conversations about activist performance, my immediate task requires close focus on evangelical outreach practices in their own terms. I arrange my exploration into four main sections, each two chapters long. In the introductory section (chapters one and two), I lay out the groundwork for my study. Chapter one concerns the definition and current state of activist performance scholarship. There I argue that, for the most part, "activist performance" as currently studied refers almost exclusively to left-progressive activism. Performances for social change that emerge from and are expressive of the aims and ideals of the progressive left (e.g., making material resources and civil rights available to ever more and more kinds of people) receive the most attention and enjoy the greatest degree of critical generosity. Performances that advocate different or oppositional points of view tend to be ignored or caricatured. After examining the reasons for and consequences of this tendency, I pose the challenge of reading non-progressive activisms with as much good faith as scholars usually extend to left-progressive ones. I frame my study of evangelical outreach as one such good-faith attempt.

In the second chapter, I chart out a working description of evangelicalism by triangulating perspectives from history, sociology, and theology. I position US evangelicalism as an essentially contested but nevertheless living entity currently struggling with the twenty-first-century reality of an increasingly pluralized, decreasingly "Christian" social world (a reality Charles Taylor christens "the secular age"). Within such a system, evangelicals have to reposition themselves as one option among many while also insisting on the exclusive "rightness" of their position in comparison to all others.

In the second section (chapters three and four), I focus mainly on personal evangelism, small-scale attempts to inspire a conversion in another person. In chapter three I look at what I call the *kerygmatic* mode of personal evangelism, where the focus is on blunt proclamations of the gospel message. I specifically examine the "soul-winning" tradition of door-to-door gospel sharing, the "Four Spiritual Laws" presentation innovated by Bill Bright and the Campus Crusade for Christ (aka "Cru"), and the stop-strangers-on-the-street dialogic evangelism promoted by Ray Comfort in his "Way of the Master." These evangelism models stress the need to create a micro-scene of crisis (or opportunity) in which prospects get confronted with a straightforward decision for or against conversion. They differ, however, in terms of just what this decision consists of and what affect ought to accompany it. They also take differing stands about how easily or how often conversion should occur as a result of the micro-scenes they stage.

In chapter four, I examine what I call *meta-kerygmatic* evangelisms. These models call on evangelists to move beyond simple proclamation, altering the evangelist's role from one of *confronting people with the Truth* to *persuading others of the Truth.* I focus on Jim Henderson's "Ordinary Attempts," Greg Koukl's conversational apologetics, and Greg Stier's "ideavirus" approach. Each of these draws in part from the work of theologian Francis Schaeffer, who counseled evangelists to spend time understanding the worldview of non-Christian people. Only after entering into non-believers' worldviews and understanding them empathically, Schaeffer argues, can Christians hope to present a compelling idea of what Christianity means. For the evangelists I study, such meta-kerygmatic methods might involve careful listening, rhetorical savvy, or even simply not acting like a know-it-all Christian stereotype.

In the third section (chapters five and six), I zoom out to study two examples of large-scale, more traditionally "theatrical" evangelical performance forms. Chapter five focuses on immersive walk-through dramas known variously as "hell houses" and "judgement houses." In such productions, local church groups mount various everyman characters who confront worldly choices (Sin or don't sin? Convert or don't convert?) and then face the eternal consequences of those choices (heaven or hell). Infamous for their often gruesome staging, turn-or-burn messages, and ripped-from-the-headlines plotlines, these dramas sometimes figure as exemplars of evangelical backwardness and hatefulness. I argue, in contrast, that they are best understood as community-based productions that accomplish vital work for the producing communities even as they strive to reach the unconverted. They center a community both on the task of evangelism and on the work of ideological distinction from the non-Christian world.

Chapter six examines the Creation Museum, a multi-million-dollar combination of science museum and discovery-fun-center based around a strictly young-earth creationist viewpoint. As is the case with hell houses, the Creation Museum often serves as Exhibit A for critics' case that evangelicals are anti-intellectual reactionaries bent on brainwashing the masses into their doctrine. I contend that the Museum engages in a more complicated maneuver, embodying a mode of evangelistic preparation focused on worldview analysis. That is, the Museum stages the conflict between "secular science" (i.e., evolutionary theory) and "biblical reality" (i.e., young-earth creationism) not only as a battle of evidence but as a battle of religious preconceptions.

In the final section, I examine, first, how various evangelical churches have re-imagined weekend worship services as performances aimed at attracting new members. Specifically, I study the church marketing movement, which counsels churches to view themselves as commercial enterprises striving to win customers. The Sunday service, in this view, becomes a live, multimedia advertisement for the Christian life. I analyze how this philosophy of worship has led to some of the main currents in evangelical churches today, the seeker-sensitive service aimed at unchurched people and the multisite service that essentially reproduces the church service across a number of satellite venues. As successful as such models have been (especially in the case of megachurches), they have also inspired a great deal of criticism from other evangelicals. The attractional worship service raises deep questions about the meaning of church, prompting many evangelicals to ask whether the impulse to grow has led to a watering-down of the substance of faith.

In chapter eight, I zero in on a wholly individual type of conversion: ministries that aim to help people who have same-sex attractions (i.e., gays, lesbians, and bisexuals) alter their desires and life patterns into more godly (i.e., heterosexual) paths. This so-called ex-gay movement (a name not used by the ministries themselves) finds it necessary to chart a middle path between more stringently homophobic views from the evangelical and fundamentalist right and more accepting or affirming views from the left. Complicating this task is the growing consensus among mainstream mental health professionals (bolstered by stories of "ex-gay survivors") about the ineffectiveness or even harm of "gay cure" ministries altogether. Evangelical sexual orientation change efforts thus find themselves reformatting their work away from the realm of medical treatment that "cures" same-sex attraction and toward a path of life-discipline in which a person "manages" same-sex attraction, living not as gay or lesbian but as a Christian living with same-sex attractions. This highly nuanced position provokes still more resistance from right and left. In my conclusion, I return to the challenges of a secular age of pluralized belief positions, examining how this context makes not just evangelicalism but any strongly committed belief position more challenging.

I aim for a "good faith" rendering of the evangelical events I study, striving to attend to the distinctiveness of each one's motivating theology and manifested strategies in terms that the practitioners themselves would recognize as fair, even if presented from an obvious outsider. To accomplish such a critically generous reading, I prioritize understanding how those who design and implement various modes of evangelism view their own actions. In particular, I inquire into the theological and worldview systems they call upon to ground, rationalize, and evaluate their outreach. I then look at how these understandings relate to other evangelical approaches to similar subjects and practices, for instance, comparing and contrasting one strategy of door-to-door proselytization to another. I recognize that, as a non-evangelical writing primarily to other non-evangelicals, even my best descriptions carry an inevitable degree of distortion. Emic (insider) accounts of any practice of evangelical outreach often *endorse* as well as *describe* that practice, whereas I attempt to stick to the latter task alone. Ideally, however, I aim for my descriptions of evangelical practices to be accurate enough that practitioners themselves would largely concur with their presentation. I then put these descriptions into conversation with more mainstream (i.e., non-evangelical) scholarship about evangelicalism from sociology, anthropology, ethnography, religious studies, and political theory. In most cases I rely on my own firsthand experience of these performances, bolstering and complicating my experience by incorporating secondhand accounts of the same or similar performances. For some sources (e.g., Steven Anderson's door-to-door soul-winning technique) I have to rely on video- or audio-mediated records such as YouTube or podcasts. I also consult writings by the ministers and believers who devise, practice, and/or promote the outreach modes I study.

A word on my sources is in order. I am by training a theater historian. My disciplinary bias is to identify, categorize, and interpret evidence. Historians prefer our evidence hierarchized, neatly segregated between primary versus secondary texts, peer-reviewed versus popular scholarship, etic (outsider) versus emic (insider) descriptions, and objective/neutral versus subjective/biased interpretations. In most cases, scholars prefer the latter member of each pair. The reality of evangelicalism, however, is such that clear separations are difficult to observe. Let me attempt an analogy: many people in the United States know that evangelical America produces parallel cultural institutions that seek to match and compete with secular culture. Investigate contemporary Christian music (CCM) in any depth, for example, and you will discover hitherto unsuspected genres like Christian heavy metal or Christian hip-hop, each boasting its own superstar artists. A similar kind of parallel institution exists in scholarship. Amid how-to guides for ministers, introductory materials for general audiences, and inspirational meditations for believers, evangelical publishing houses like Baker, Eerdmans, Zondervan, and IVP produce a great many works of evangelical scholarship. A host of peer-reviewed scholarly journals of, by, and for evangelical believers complements this discourse. This parallel scholarly culture operates on the margins of secular-academic respectability, in part because its contributors decline to observe one of the key distinctions dear to many religious studies scholars, what Lance Gharavi calls the difference between *doing* religion and writing *about* religion.[3] Doctrinaire scholarship in religious studies keeps itself scrupulously on the "writing about" side. Evangelical scholarship, however, largely assumes that its authors and audiences share evangelical convictions, much as (in Gharavi's argument) theater scholars—and here I would add, *especially scholars of activist performance*—assume that they write to and for audiences who *produce* theater (or performance activism) as well as *describe* it.

Fair warning: I use works of evangelical scholarship extensively throughout this book. Sometimes such of-by-and-for-evangelicals studies serve as my primary texts, the very subjects I analyze. At other moments, I employ these works as reliable secondary texts simply because they provide the most sophisticated historical or critical assessments available on a particular topic. True, when consulting such works I sometimes have to note and account for interpretive slants that I recognize as warped by the gravitational fields of the authors' religious convictions and agendas. In fairness, though, I find comparable warping in many ostensibly "neutral" works on religion, works that can sometimes dwell more on the author's distance from faith than on the beliefs and believers being studied. Scrupulous non-belief can in some instances operate as a de facto faith-based agenda. In any case, I do my best to mark sources I use as evangelical or otherwise for readers—with the proviso that many of the interlocutors I draw on straddle the about/doing distinction, much like crossover music groups who win both Grammies and Dove Awards.

I should also mark that this investigation mobilizes the first person to perhaps a greater degree than is standard in scholarship. At times I mine my own experiences as an evangelical to guide my navigation and interpretation of encounters and performances that non-evangelicals would likely find utterly bemusing. I know from firsthand experience what it is to evangelize. I know what it means to see the world around me in terms of Eternity and afterlife where everyone will face judgement and be divided (to draw on imagery from Matthew 25) into the sheep, who are destined for heaven, and the goats, who are destined for hell. While my current faith practice does not view the world through such an apocalyptic lens, I still carry imprinted on my psyche the imperative to evangelize, to act in expectation that God will greet me at the gates of Heaven with the question *Whom have you brought with you?* To a certain extent, this drive to bring others into the salvific fold, to share the worldview that can make everyone's life better, informs my enduring interest in activism even now. I thus hold my connection to evangelical outreach closely throughout my study as a reminder to myself and (at times) for my readers that the drive to spread the Christian gospel is not necessarily an alien or irrational motive. As I will relate in the next chapter, such a good-faith, critically generous perspective on non-progressive activism contrasts with most scholarship about performance activism, which focuses almost exclusively on left-progressive agents pursuing left-progressive goals. Since this latter perspective informs my own scholarship, it behooves me to highlight and trouble areas in which left-progressive critical assumptions might lead to a tendentious reading of evangelical subjects. I hope, then, for my occasional foray into the first person to index both my sense of estrangement from some evangelical practices and my empathy for evangelical impulses.

That said, I recognize how first-person perspectives can limit as well as illuminate. This book is scholarship, not autobiography, and I strive to keep my firsthand experience as a light to shine occasionally on my subjects and not as a beacon to attract attention for itself. Moreover, as immersive an education as my life as a preacher's kid in the Southern Baptist Church provided, evangelicalism in the United States today is much broader and more diverse than my singular perspective would ever allow. I know evangelicalism now as a scholar much more deeply and broadly than I ever knew it as a practitioner. This scholarly perspective helps me to see movements, trends, and vocabularies circulating now that make today's evangelicalism significantly different than the Baptist faith of my youth. Despite the limitations of the first person, however, I keep it as a tool to mark the simultaneous strangeness and familiarity I locate in evangelical outreach.

A final caveat: even with my firsthand experience and scholarly research, I cannot pretend even to have scratched the surface of this community of communities. I am sure that for every practice I study, for every example I analyze, I will have readers who can recall a dozen other evangelical practices. For every movement or trend in US evangelicalism I reference, some readers will likely have experienced others I leave untouched. I could write a whole other volume, just as long, covering wholly other kinds of evangelical performance. Such future volumes are essential. I am especially, painfully aware that my work here focuses primarily on "traditional"—that is, mainly white, middle- to upper-class, English-speaking, non-Pentecostal/charismatic—evangelicalism in the

United States. This traditional configuration, the evangelicalism of my youth, is increasingly the minority in the world at large and in the United States particularly. The future of evangelicalism—arguably the future of Christianity—rests in the non-white, non-European world, in mainly Pentecostal and charismatic manifestations of faith that claim the devotion of believers from beyond the colonial Church. Evangelicalism in the United States is only now coming to an awareness of this new reality. But a theater-studies-inflected examination of this new order and traditional-evangelical reactions to it will have to wait. Better still, I hope that my partial study of evangelicalism here might inspire other theater and performance scholars to study these other believers. As I will argue (following Charles Taylor's arguments), the secular age we live in is not defined by unbelief but by a multiplicity of beliefs. Learning how to live and act within this age requires us to learn how to listen to our fellow believers more fully.

CHAPTER 1

Performance Activism, Progressive Oversights, and Deep Differences

Writing in the *Chronicle of Higher Education* in 2005, critical and legal theorist Stanley Fish recalls a reporter asking him "what would succeed high theory and the triumvirate of race, gender, and class as the center of intellectual energy in the academy. I answered like a shot: religion."[1] A glance at recent publications from superstar critics on the progressive left confirms Fish's prediction. Alain Badiou writes about Saint Paul as a paradigm for revolutionary ethical commitment to a truth.[2] Slavoj Žižek recuperates elements of the Christian tradition, seeing in Paul's reformation of Christian doctrine a metaphor for anti-capitalist revolution.[3] Jürgen Habermas, having engaged in a lengthy dialogue with then Cardinal Ratzinger/now Pope Benedict, argues that democratic societies must engage with faith as an active and ineluctable force in culture.[4] In his stinging response to "new atheist" writers like Richard Dawkins, Sam Harris, and the late Christopher Hitchens, Terry Eagleton mounts a thorough, passionate apologia for what he calls "the richest, most enduring form of popular culture in human history."[5] None of these critics identifies as a devout person of faith—quite the contrary. Yet each of them, some of whom are avowed atheists, argues that faith deserves careful attention, especially by critical thinkers on the left.

I have predicated *Preaching to Convert* on a similar conviction, that the study of religious faith (US evangelicalism specifically) has something to offer the politically minded progressive left. In this chapter, I make a case for what that "something" is, for why left-progressive activists—performance activists and their critics especially—should attend to the outreach strategies of a group they normally identify as opposed to left-progressive activist projects. I outline the disciplinary subtext of my overall argument, the explanation of why I frame this project primarily as a contribution to activist theater scholarship rather than, say, as a piece of religious sociology or cultural studies. My task involves several steps. First, I define some key terms, situating myself as an activist performance scholar in relation to other scholars of performance activism. Next, I argue that, as lively and diverse as the conversation about activist performance is, the discourse largely stays grounded in a particular (left-progressive) set of ideological assumptions about the proper course of social change. Acts or agents whose ideological orientations fall outside of the left-progressive project, such as conservative evangelicals, generally get categorized as doing something other than activism, usually something nefarious that justifies or necessitates (left-progressive) activist response in the first place. Drawing on recent assessments of left-progressive politics by scholars like Stanley Fish and Wendy Brown, I criticize activist performance scholarship's partiality as a problem in that it fosters critical solipsism, betrays the philosophical tenets of radical democracy, and colludes with a regime of knee-jerk toleration that constrains political possibility. I end by returning to and reframing the left's current engagements with faith, situating my own study of US evangelicals as part of that corrective trend.

Working Definitions and Heuristic Tangles

Since I join a conversation already in progress among scholars, activists, and scholar-activists about activist performance, I offer some working definitions to chart my entry into the discussion. Basic terms come first. I use *theater* to refer to formal, conventionalized practices of staging performances in spaces built and recognized as venues for such productions. In the present-day US milieu, *theater* usually describes rehearsed productions (often enhanced with elements of spectacle) of scripted plays that distinguish performers from spectators. I use the adjective *theatrical* when discussing activities in or out of literal theaters that incorporate elements specifically related to theater and its practice (e.g., spectacle, literal scripts, imitative or character-based performance, rehearsals). I take my cue from performance studies theorists like Richard Schechner in defining *performance* more broadly, beyond the imitative or spectacle-oriented presentations in formal theater auditoriums. Given that *to perform* combines the senses of both *presenting* (for an audience, in accordance with a planned, rehearsed, or ritualized pattern) and *doing*, performance can encompass not merely formal theater but practically any discrete expressive act directed toward and for the benefit of someone else. Schechner introduces a helpful rule-of-thumb distinction between asserting that an event or action type *is* performance and studying that act *as* performance.[6] In studying evangelical outreach, I aim for the latter. I do not seek to establish or modify definitions of theater, activism, evangelism, or religion to make one fit into the category of the others, nor do I study plays that deal with religion in general or evangelicals specifically.[7] Rather, I analyze phenomena like door-to-door evangelizing, open-air preaching, museum displays, worship liturgies, and even schemas of conscious self-presentation *as* performances. That is, I view instances of evangelical outreach as specially designed and enacted events performed for the benefit of an audience.

To see an act as *designed* is to recognize it as the product of conscious choices rather than as a mundane or spontaneous happening. At least some degree of forethought or effort goes into decisions about performance variables. My role as performance analyst thus involves accounting for elements such as location (Is it in a church? Is it on the street? Is it public? Private?), genre (Is it a one-on-one encounter? An open-air sermon? An interactive display?), scheme (Is there a tight script? An open scenario with improvisation?), audience (Is it directed at a specific audience? What kind? What responses does it invite?), performers (Does the production involve live agents? Does it require specially trained people? Certain types of people?), and theatricality (Does the act resemble everyday life, or is it clearly set apart? Are theatrical elements like lights, costumes, sets, and props used, and if so to what end?). Focusing on the *enacted* element of outreach highlights the fact that, however elaborate or rudimentary the plan, the actual encounter with the audience may play out in ways that realize, fall short of, or exceed the producers' designs. A transactional element, a never totally predictable interchange between (at minimum) performer and audience, inflects how a performance unfolds, making each iteration of even the most strictly rehearsed script slightly different. Such a realization is important, for the performances I examine seek to produce specific effects through the transactions they initiate, namely, a fundamental change in the world-and-life-views of their audiences.

Of course, almost any designed-enacted performance can be said to aim for some effect beyond the mundane transmission of everyday information. Performance communicates, yes, but it is not solely a matter of information transmission. Performance-makers consciously attempt to generate extra- or meta-communicative consequences, such as emotional affects (e.g., a tragedy that aims for sadness, pity, and fear), practical spatial effects (e.g., an intervention where activists physically shield others from violence), or particular responses from audiences or institutions (e.g., an advertisement that aims for increased product sales). In discussing *activist performance* (or *performance activism*), I name a special type of performance in which the intended extra effects consciously align with the advancement of broader social or political agendas. These agendas may embody specific goals, such as those of a political group like People for the Ethical Treatment of Animals, or of a particular initiative, such as repealing a sales tax increase. Alternately, the agendas may be relatively diffuse, such as a desire for world peace or community pride. I intend *performance activism* as an umbrella term, shorthand for a host of other popular and scholarly terms that each touch on some aspect of the kind of performances I study. A partial list of these might include the following: political theater, theater for social change, direct action, agit-prop, committed theater, street theater, radical performance, people's theater, community (or community-based, or community-engaged) theater, grassroots theater, participatory political theater, theater of the oppressed, agitational performance, choreographies of protest, acts of intervention, and applied theater/drama.[8] As this sampling suggests, the diversity of strategies, agendas, histories, and theories about how performance and theater strive to change the world interrupts any homogeneity that a single term might otherwise imply. *Performance activism* names not a unified entity but an untidy tangle of traditions and visions.

Disentangling this skein describes the work of multiple volumes. For the present, however, I will unpick these knots of crisscrossing practices into a few artificial-yet-useful threads. I take my cue from Jan Cohen-Cruz, who helpfully divides the last forty years of activist performance into three roughly chronological phases. As she notes, these phases overlap, the styles and strategies that characterize one phase occasionally cropping up, reborn, in a subsequent phase.[9] I use her tripartite division, then, not as a model of chronological development but as a jumping-off point for delineating what I will call three concurrent strands that make up the bulk the performance activism tangle: the oppositional-agitational, the community-based, and the facilitated-deliberative. I offer these distinctions as a heuristic; they do not work as absolute divisions (indeed, many combinations and overlaps exist), but they approximate reality enough to serve my purpose.

The oppositional-agitational performance strand refers to practices with overt, precise agendas for social change, such as to end the Vietnam War, desegregate the bus system, or increase funding for AIDS/HIV research. In this thread, activists use performance and/or theater to identify and mobilize against wrongdoing by exposing, disrupting, and hopefully changing systems or institutions that activists name as unjust. At one end of the range are formal, "theater"-type productions whose content and style directly engage specific political issues of their time and place. The agit-prop productions of Irwin Piscator and Bertolt Brecht exemplify early twentieth-century iterations, as do the Worker's Theater pageants and Federal Theater Project "living newspaper" plays of the 1920s and 1930s. At the other end, the agitational-oppositional strand includes non-theater direct actions like protests, demonstrations, marches, and sit-ins. These run the gamut from the highly theatricalized (such as the street performances of the Bread and Puppet Theater) to the primarily utilitarian (like a line of activists blocking bulldozers from demolishing a building). In the latter cases, literary-dramatic elements of plot, character, and staging often fall away, replaced by the "real life" drama of bodies intervening directly into the normal operation of an oppressive process without the relative safety of "it's just a play" conventions. Particularly in the 1970s and 1980s, the oppositional agendas of such protests aligned with a politics of visibility regarding a number of minority identity positions related to race, sex, sexuality, and disability. In the United States, the 1999 protests against the World Trade Organization (WTO) meetings in Seattle marked the rise of a more pluralistic "movement of movements," where multiple performances of opposition from many different groups or movements operate in rough concert to stage massive rejoinders to the exploitative policies devised in international meetings such as the G8, the G20, or the International Monetary Fund. What binds these various performances together is their unambiguously political or activist orientation. Participants in a Living Theater street performance, a Queer Nation "kiss-in," or a Reclaim the Streets block(ade) party generally claim a role of activist overtly, openly labeling their performances as political. They acknowledge and even stress their specific alignment with particular political views or agendas.

Performances in my second strand, community-based performance, often (though not always) take a step back from the baldly political stances of agitational performances. The focus here shifts from directly opposing structures or institutions to working within a community of some sort (usually geographic, but also vocational, age-related, or identity-based) and using theatrical techniques to represent the concerns or membership specific to that community. To borrow Doug Paterson's helpful distinction, if most professional theater produces plays about or at communities, emphasizing a separation between artist and subject, then community performance produces work to, for, and with communities, establishing or building on solidarity between artist and audience.[10] For example, one of the best-known community-engaged theater ensembles in the United States is the Cornerstone Theater Company.[11] Members of its core ensemble, all professional artists, work with and within communities, collecting stories, histories, and impressions of the community from the people they meet. They then write or (most famously) adapt classical works to create plays that reflect the concerns and stories of that community. Finally, ensemble members work with actors drawn from the community (many of whom have little or no theatrical experience) to stage these shows for the rest of the community. Productions like *The Good Person of New Haven* or *The Three Sisters of West Virginia* embody Cornerstone's aesthetic. Unlike agitational performers, participants in community-based performances—those that are not professional artists, at least—often do not envision themselves as activists. Nor do the professional facilitators always strive to mobilize communities in the name of a particular political goal.[12] In many projects, simply giving communities a chance to participate in art or culture becomes an end in itself. Nevertheless, an electric charge, a distinctly political tingle, attends the act of representing community, especially when the bodies and stories put on stage come from people otherwise underrepresented or oppressed.[13] Even with the less directly political versions of community or community-based performance, practitioners affirm something transformative about the act of confronting the difficult realities of painful or conflicting histories, the rough spots, and the divergent visions (hopes, fears) of the community's future.

Practices of facilitated deliberation make up the final strand. Here performance serves as a means to an educational end, deployed as a mode of investigation and reflection upon situational dynamics. The predominant examples of this trend derive from the work of two people: educator Paulo Freire and theater artist Augusto Boal. In books such as *Pedagogy of the Oppressed,* Freire stressed decentering educational authority and making students more active participants both in their educations and in democratic society.[14] Boal, taking his cue from Freire, created an ensemble of theatrical techniques, the Theater of the Oppressed (TO), to realize Freire's pedagogic-liberatory mode. Most TO and TO-based practices involve workshops (facilitated, in Boal's system, by "Jokers") that invite participants to become "spect-actors," able to flip between roles of spectator and performer. Through a number of game-like exercises, the facilitators guide spect-actors into using theatrical techniques such as mise-en-scène, tableau, role-play, and creative dramatics to "stage" moments from their lives and try out interventions that open up other choices and alternative strategies for navigating oppressive situations.[15] As in community and community-based theater, the spect-actor participants generally do not identify their work as activism in the same sense as, say, a WTO counter-protester. Yet Boal is explicit that such workshops are overtly about politics—undoing or outmaneuvering oppression, multiplying choices and possibilities in situations where choices seem limited. The distinction between his work and, say, anti-capitalist agitprop is that rather than imposing an agenda or solution on a situation (e.g., a revolution against capitalism), those affected by oppression devise solutions themselves. Theater operates educationally, in a Freirean manner, to activate the oppressed person's innate ability to think critically about a situation. Boal's "arsenal" of techniques has inspired an ever-growing body of followers and innovators. Such techniques have found a particular home in facilitated workshops set in situations marked by deep-seated cultural or political conflict, encouraging participants both to envision the debates that divide them and to imagine how those debates might be navigated.

As I mentioned above, many groups and artists combine or flit between these strands. The distinctions I've drawn here do not always obtain. Nevertheless, these threads—the agitational-oppositional, the community-based, and the facilitated-deliberative—together form a robust collection of practices and traditions. I have tried to account for as many different varieties of social change performance as I detect operating within activist and scholarly (and activist-scholarly) conversations. I should emphasize the plural *conversations* here. The tangle of activist performance is also a tangle of controversies and disagreements about activist performance. Laced throughout the snarled threads are deep debates and truculent questions about radicality (Does community theater fall short of political meaning?), style (Is narrative—especially realistic—drama staged in theaters doomed to ideological stagnation?), efficacy (What defines activist theater's success or failure? Is that even an important question?), coalition (Can we express values as universal without falling into imperialist humanism?), and strategy (Is activism divorced from a coherent political vision like Old Left Communism inherently self-defeating?). The result is a rich, varied, and self-critical discourse shaped by a wide range of activists, scholars, and scholar-activists.

Meta-Historical Observations and Left-Progressive Reflections

At this point, I suppose I could easily enough argue for needling yet another contentious question into this tangle: *You know what this field needs? Evangelical activism!* The three strands I've drawn out as representative could include any of a number of performances executed from evangelical bases and toward evangelical ends. Framing hell houses as community-based productions. or open-air preaching as agitational-oppositional direct action, for example, would enlarge the tangle and add a few more colors and clashes into the assortment. To a certain extent, I expect this book will do just that. But I would consider my project incomplete if I did nothing more than follow a recipe: take one cup of performance activist discourse and add a helping of evangelicals. I contend that it's not enough simply to add evangelicals into the mix. I mean for my work of viewing evangelicals as activists to provoke pause and reflection about the conversation about activist performance as a whole. In that spirit, then, I offer something of a historiographic critique.

The performance activist tangle I've been discussing metaphorically names an archive, a product of historians in which events and practices are identified, selected, and bundled together with related events/practices into a collection of facts to be interpreted, described, contextualized, evaluated, reinterpreted, revised, and even recombined with other facts or collections. As historians and theorists like Edward Carr or Michel de Certeau have argued, however, archival collections and the facts therein don't simply exist, out there, self-evidently factual and waiting to be collected, interpreted, and so on.[16] Certainly, *events* happen; I do not dispute the materiality of brave risks, noble sacrifices, and inspiring examples within activist performance history. But it takes a historian—or, at least, it is a historiographic operation—to identify signal moments of social change heroism as such, extracting and showcasing the historically significant events to be archived from the undifferentiated noise of event-filled reality. Sometimes the work of distinguishing important events from trivial ones is straightforward. My signaling left for a turn on the way to work this morning, for instance, will not likely find its way into the next edition of *The Activist Theater Reader.* But just as historical and present-day traditions of, say, Asian or African or Native American performance have only recently come into the mainstream ambit of theater and performance studies, so too have more and more diverse varieties of performance activism been identified as such. I emphasize the scholarly agency required here. The tangle of performance activism has grown larger, denser, and more productively complicated not because more and more performance activism has popped into existence but because historians and critics (many of whom are also activists) have brought more and more kinds of acts to the attention of other scholars, arguing compellingly for their inclusion into the larger archive.

In this spirit, I note the absence of a number of acts—not merely evangelical ones—that technically fit the formal definition of performance activism. The point to be made isn't (or isn't only) that the archive needs to grow, incorporating more performance traditions. The need for growth is built into the notion of archives, archives being by nature dynamic and open to addition. My argument is this: as large, diverse, robust, and vibrant as the archive of performance activism already is, whole sectors, entire traditions that appear to qualify as activist performance, are for the most part missing. Furthermore, this absence signals a strikingly narrow—and often invisible—set of ideological parameters around the practices that performance scholars allow into this collection. I refer to activist performances in which the assumptions and initiatives fueling the performance do not align with or are opposed to those on the progressive left. The critical lenses used to arrange and enrich the performance activist archive also function as blinders, blocking from historiographic view a range of acts and performances badly in need of study. In other words, *performance activism* frequently means *left-progressive performance activism*—and nothing else.

Though common enough in scholarly and popular writing, the term *left-progressive* (or *the progressive left*) requires some tying down.[17] In a US context, the progressive left encompasses a range of post–World War II political agendas defined by specific issues of policy or identity. A partial listing of these might include African American civil rights struggles, second- and third-wave feminisms, lesbian/gay/bisexual/transgender/queer (LGBTQ) liberation movements, Asian-American rights, Latino/a rights, workers' rights, disability rights, rights of incarcerated persons, AIDS/HIV activism, eco-activism, the push for socialized services, and restoration of rights and territories of indigenous peoples. Some of these trace a direct lineage to earlier movements such as the 1920s and 1930s workers' rights activism of the Old Left or the Progressive Era campaigns for women's suffrage. In contrast to some of these prior movements (particularly the Marxian Old Left of the 1930s), left-progressive causes tend to eschew adherence to an overarching theory or political philosophy. As performance scholar Baz Kershaw notes, the postmodern skepticism toward unifying authorities and meta-narratives has led to perpetual mitosis of activisms, with more and more diverse political movements on the left splitting, expanding, and dividing again. "Since the personal became political," maintains Kershaw, "the political has found its way into almost every nook and cranny of culture. Identity politics, the politics of camp, body politics, sexual politics—the political is now ubiquitous and can be identified in all theater and performance."[18] The political, he argues, has become promiscuous. Although invigorating, such a ubiquity of "politics" and the resultant plethora of social change movements make sustaining broad-based activist alliances difficult. The left becomes simultaneously larger and looser, less adept at generating the coalitional momentum necessary for far-reaching social change. In place of a unifying, comprehensive doctrine of activism, left-progressive causes move in discrete orbits within a nebula of democratic watchwords like *liberty, rights, equality, justice, inclusivity, diversity,* and *tolerance.*

To bring this nebula of values into sharper focus, I turn to Chantal Mouffe and Ernesto Laclau's seminal 1985 work *Hegemony and Socialist Strategy.* There they offer an influential diagnosis of and prescription for the promiscuously political left.[19] Drawing on Gramscian Marxism, Lacanian psychoanalysis, and Foucauldian post-structuralism, Mouffe and Laclau argue that, pace Old Left Communism, class struggle now lacks the authority to serve as a common denominator issue across movements for empowerment and liberty. Indeed, they contend, in a time of "New Social Movements" based on minority identities and other specific issues, no essential commonality exists to command collective loyalty on anything but a contingent basis. Postmodern politics are thus hegemonic, by which they mean a matter of moment-to-moment tactical determinations. The left's definitive question transforms from *Which theory/cause/agenda deserves universal commitment?* to *Which immediate struggle can diverse movements unite behind for the nonce?*

Mouffe and Laclau's proposal for the left, *radical democracy,* adapts to these new realities while capturing some of the key impulses that have defined left-progressive movements.[20] Radical democracy begins by affirming the good potentials inherent in liberal democratic ideals, focusing particularly on the liberal tradition of innate human rights and the democratic tradition of popular sovereignty. The coincidence of liberty and equality—a combination Étienne Balibar helpfully sums up in the portmanteau *equaliberty* (*égaliberté*)[21]—thus functions as the core promise that liberal democratic systems offer to subjects. Along with a range of other theorists, Mouffe and Laclau argue that this promise remains unfulfilled. Equaliberty continues to exist as the privilege of the few rather than the reality of all, even and especially within the domains of systems that label themselves "democratic." The political goal of the left, then, must be one of radicalizing and pluralizing the liberal democratic ideal, expanding and making real the promise of rights and empowerment for everyone. In practice, activism in service of this goal often consists of locating areas of faux democracy or not-yet-realized democracy, advocating as a remedy some mixture of redistribution (equalizing access to goods, services, and political power across society) and recognition (de-marginalizing, un-forgetting, making more visible and represented particular groups or identities).[22]

Inevitably, though, different activists and groups will diverge in imaging exactly what admixture of redistribution and recognition to work for as well as how to work for it. Mouffe and Laclau's model accepts rather than resolves such progressive-left splintering. The time has passed, the theorists contend, when left-progressive activism could be conceived as a singular Program that collects and cements together the left's disparate pieces. Diversity is the order of the day. Radical democracy therefore manifests as multiple and successive *projects,* discrete moments of protest and challenge where groups across a span of identity-based and ideological positions work in contingent coalitions and incremental steps to hold liberal democratic governments accountable to their promises or perhaps to declare them irreparably compromised and to start over.

The imperative to expand the liberal democratic franchise, combined with the acceptance of diverse and divergent modes of pursuing that expansion, means that pluralism, inclusivity, and tolerance operate within radical democratic activism as meta-values (or perhaps *para*-values) alongside the larger pursuit of equaliberty. Activists in the radical democratic spirit celebrate the fact that a multiplicity of agents work in their own ways toward the same general goal. By eschewing a final arbiter of "what is to be done" and by keeping open space for dissent, the progressive left evades dogmatism at the cost of perpetual factionalism, as different movements and offshoots of movements interpret its ideals divergently. Like *activist performance,* the term *left-progressive* thus hides countless, intense fissures between and within various activist sectors and traditions. For practically every group or movement—or performance activism—someone else claims to be more radical, more efficacious, more relevant, more authentic, more inclusive, or more democratic than another. Still, while such schisms can play out regarding the exact shape of equaliberty, on the whole the progressive left operates under a rough consensus that diversity, equality, liberty, and tolerance within a framework of rational, democratic deliberation offer the best hope for human society.[23] Such diversity is seen as preferable to the alternative of establishing a political orthodoxy to enforce strict membership boundaries and operational discipline.

The Dance of Critical Generosity and Parsimony in Activist Performance Scholarship

To be clear, I do not claim that those who produce or support left-progressive activist performances necessarily agree with or even know about Mouffe and Laclau's arguments. Nevertheless, I find radical democracy a lucid distillation of the principles, schemes, and contexts that seem to characterize most left-progressive performance activists and their critics. The values that Mouffe and Laclau's model highlights—equaliberty, tolerance, inclusivity—can certainly be seen as animating the three activist theater strands I summarized earlier. Oppositional protests and agit-prop plays, for example, insist upon fairer regimes of recognition and redistribution through such visibility tactics (e.g., the LGBT movement's rallying cry, "We're here! We're queer! Get used to it!"), nonviolent civil disobedience (e.g., human blockades of unjust institutions), and peaceful demonstration (e.g., anti-war marches and parades). Whether overtly "political" or not, community-based performances typically emphasize some degree of representational opportunity (you can see yourself or your community on stage) and representational agency (you can influence or dictate how you're represented).

Moreover, the shared endeavor of devising community-based productions often fosters in participants a sense of tolerance. Participants learn to recognize that one person's mental image of a community may be challenged or modified by that of a neighbor, and that the final staged "community" represents a medley of diverse or even conflicting views. The progressive left's faith in the power of rational, mutually respectful dialogue between people underlies practices within the facilitated-deliberative strand. Particularly in cultural contexts defined by violent conflict, theatrical facilitation techniques are often framed as establishing (or at least taking a step toward establishing) the necessary preconditions for peaceful co-existence within a plural and radical democracy: civility, empathy, and a base-level tolerance. I realize the dangers of ordering so diverse a set of practices as "activist performance" or "activist performance scholarship" under a single descriptor (radical democracy, progressive left). I invite swift and fierce rebuke from scholars and activists alike by suggesting such a totalizing umbrella. Nevertheless, for most present instances of activist performance currently studied as such, equality, liberty, diversity, and tolerance function simultaneously as ultimate goals (What kind of world do we want?) and as guiding ethical standards (What actions do we take to get there?). The whole activist performance tangle, in other words, thus fits more or less within a radical democratic basket.

My meta-historical observation about activist performance criticism flows from this insight. To wit: scholarship about activist performance both shapes and is shaped by left-progressive/radical democratic tendencies. Exceptions exist, but in the main, critical studies about present-day performance activism in the United States emerge from left-progressive traditions, deal with left-progressive activist performances, and reflect left-progressive viewpoints. Critics of performance activism are often (though not always) themselves overtly supportive of or even directly involved with the activisms they study. Theater critic Jill Dolan, for example, openly acknowledges her indebtedness to feminist politics in her pathbreaking studies on feminist and LGBTQ theater.[24] Throughout her extensive and influential body of work, Dolan argues persuasively for seeing feminist-inflected scholarship and pedagogy as modes of advocacy and activism. To advocate for adding, say, African American and Latino/a plays to theater course reading lists or university theater seasons aligns with left-progressive arguments that institutions and endeavors more generally ought to promote diverse representations, contravening historical and cultural contexts that privilege white, male representations as "universal" or "good." Academic theater's largest professional organization in the United States, the Association for Theater in Higher Education (ATHE), features a number of focus groups devoted to supporting and sharing scholarly and artistic work of, by, and about particular minority identities. It is a common convention, therefore, for theater and performance scholars who study activism (particularly identity-based activism) to see their academic work as unified with their political convictions. Even in cases where the activist performance does not stem from a particular identity position, or where the critic's identity differs from that of his or her subjects, activist performance scholarship tends toward marked experience with or empathy toward the aims of the activism in question.

Performance theorist David Román claims this simpatico relationship between scholar and artist as a conscious tactic that he calls *critical generosity*. Critical generosity, as Román proposes it, eschews the veneer of objectivity traditionally expected of scholarly or historical works. Instead, the critically generous scholar acknowledges his or her connection with and support of the performances in question, particularly when those performances engage issues close to the scholar's own identity. In Román's case, critical generosity allows him to examine the aesthetics of a number of professional and amateur AIDS benefit or protest performances from the 1980s not in terms of their objective worth as a works of theater but in terms of each performance's specific triangulation of ambition, exigency, and resources.[25] As Román insists, critical generosity does not lock scholars into writing advanced fan mail; the critic is not a publicist. Jan Cohen-Cruz, echoing Román's argument, affirms the need to recognize and explore when, how, and why community-based performances fail.[26] Critically generous scholars can at times deliver the kind of brutal honesty about a project's shortcomings that only a friend can give. An ethic of critical generosity, however, holds that even negative criticisms should stem from deep empathy for and understanding of the activist causes and contexts in question.

Such empathy represents a departure from a tendency in criticism that Eve Kosofsky Sedgwick identifies as the "paranoid stance."[27] By *paranoid* she means a scholarly attitude that takes as its starting point the certainty of large, oppressive systems that operate behind the scenes. At once a way of knowing and a thing to be known, critical paranoia works by anticipating, seeking out, and uncovering evidence of big systemic oppressions (e.g., heterocentrism, patriarchy, neoliberalism) infesting every cultural text or event. Once a single critical option among many, paranoia has in Sedgwick's view acquired obligatory status, imposing a kind of paranoid imperative in scholarship. To be critical is to practice paranoia's strong hermeneutic of suspicion; to fail to be paranoid is to be uncritically credulous.

Sedgwick's objection to paranoia is precise. The problem isn't that Big Systemic Oppressions don't exist (they do). It's rather that paranoia's cynical strategy of anticipation and exposure does not provide the sole or necessarily the best response to oppressive systems. "Paranoia," Sedgwick writes, "knows some things well and other things poorly."[28] Critical generosity embraces one such alternative way of knowing. Faced with an instance of left-progressive political demonstration, for example, a paranoid criticism might examine the event convinced already that, despite its anti-oppressive intentions, a closer look would reveal its inevitable contamination by those oppressive ideologies it seeks to resist. Critically generous scholars do not deny big systemic oppressions, but they refuse to confine the critical act to a simple exposure of hegemonic ideologies. Alongside their subjects, they instead make a leap of faith that another, better world is possible, and that left-progressive performances might have a role in realizing that world. It is criticism, but it is criticism in good faith.

I find critical generosity a useful way of framing my own approach to activist performance. I concur with Román's critique of ostensibly neutral or objective approaches to movements whose politics directly implicate aspects of my identity. In my own work, I follow the convention of noting links between activist causes and my own politics; I provided a detailed self-identification of my ideological and theological orientations not ten paragraphs into this chapter. Yet I want to put some pressure on the assumption of solidarity between the scholar and left-progressive activism that characterizes much research and writing about performance activism. For all its strengths, critical generosity offers a double edge. As diverse, factionalized, and dynamic as left-progressive motivations and movements are, installing left-progressive values and assumptions into the historiographic and critical lenses of activist performance scholarship can impose significant limitations on the critical and political imaginations of theater and performance activist-scholars. Critical generosity toward some necessarily implies critical parsimony toward others.

As an illustration, I turn to a piece I take to be exemplary of research on performance activism, dance theorist Susan Leigh Foster's 2003 article "Choreographies of Protest."[29] There Foster proposes a hermeneutic of embodiment that focuses on the materiality of bodies in non-violent protest. Such an approach, she argues, highlights the high-stakes efficacy of putting bodies on the line or at physical risk in a tactically and even aesthetically aware way. She provides embodiment-based readings of three key protest performances: civil-rights era "sit-ins" at segregated lunch counters, 1980s "die-ins" staged by the AIDS Coalition To Unleash Power (ACT UP), and anti–World Trade Organization protests in 1999 Seattle. Lest there be any doubt about my views, I consider this a gem of an article. Foster rightly won a prestigious award for it from the American Society for Theater Research, and I regularly assign her in my classrooms and cite her in my scholarship. Her work is smart, inspiring, and an excellent example of critical generosity. As such, the piece also fits securely within the historiographic parameters of left-progressive politics that I suggest shape present visions of activist performance.

As a thought experiment, consider the effect of including in Foster's study acts that, though technically eligible as embodied acts of protest, represent views at odds with a battle for inclusivity within the ideological contexts she discusses. In the Civil Rights era, for instance, George Wallace's famous "stand in the school house door" in 1963 surely qualifies as a choreographic protest. There Wallace, as governor of Alabama, physically blocked the doorway of the Foster Auditorium at the University of Alabama in Tuscaloosa in protest of the imminent enrollment of the University's first African American students, Vivian Malone and James Hood. In numerous statements before and after the act, Wallace stressed the symbolic dimension of his act, describing himself as representing (pro-segregationist) Alabamans who resented the forced desegregation of their public institutions.[30] In terms of LGBT rights and AIDS/HIV issues, what about the bright, eye-catching sign protests of Fred Phelps's Westboro Baptist Church? Phelps and his church regularly appear in national news for their protests of funerals of LGBT people (as well as movie stars, politicians, and veterans). These protests feature members of his congregation, including young children, holding up neon-colored picket signs festooned with camera-friendly block-lettered messages like "God Hates Fags," "Thank God for AIDS," or "Matthew Shepherd [or the name of whoever has died] in Hell." Objectionable as his displays are, Phelps consistently and solidly aligns himself with democratic traditions of free speech and unpopular but protected protest. Finally, in reference to the WTO protests, what of the uniformed riot police who stood against the protesters, a spectacle of resistant embodiment not merely utilitarian but also theatrical, intended to frighten, intimidate (the protesters), and reassure (those attending the WTO meetings)? Each of these, I propose, manifests "choreographies of protest" just as much as the left-progressive agents Foster does focus on. Their absence bears investigation.

Understand: I do not fault Foster individually for neglecting these performances. My point is not a gripe that Foster covers A, B, and C events when she could or should deal with X, Y, and Z events. She does not aim at detailing a comprehensive roster of activisms, nor can she be expected to account for every possible application of her critical model.

I also want to avoid the implication that activist performance scholarship must "show both sides," as if feminist critics, for instance, were obligated to give misogynist perspectives equal airtime whenever they write about feminist theory. Instead, I highlight how Foster's view of activism, a view I take as representative of activist performance scholarship more generally, presumptively excludes qua performance activism acts by those not lined up behind the forces of inclusivity. Events X, Y, and Z are not merely neglected; they do not even appear on the radar as activist performances.

To be sure, non- or anti-progressive-left agents do figure in Foster's account—just not as *activists*. Consider, for example, Foster's representation of the Seattle police during the protests. "Robotized in full riot gear," she writes, "faces shielded, bodies encased in black bullet-proof nylon, police offer no opportunity for contact or dialogue. . . . these officers emblematize the anonymous repressive force of the state."[31] They are, for Foster, among "those defending the status quo,"[32] the armed contrast to activists' bodies—and nothing more. The choreography of protest focuses on the anti-WTO activists' movements, their tactical maneuvers and planned reactions to the mechanical ("robotized") wall of repression and oppressive-institutional strength represented by the police. The police matter insofar as activists take their movements into account and respond creatively to them, but the officers' agency is neither choreographic nor activist. Indeed, as Foster portrays it, their intentions and presence aren't even human. Activism as Foster and many other performance scholars construe it refers solely to oppositional direct action against exclusivist institutions and their defenders. Those who represent such views or institutions are by definition not activists.

At the risk of oversimplification, let me aver that the tacit assumption in her article—activism equals left-progressive causes—is endemic throughout scholarship in English on present-day performance activism.[33] To be sure, I am hardly alone in pointing out that activist or politically engaged performance may operate in non-progressive directions.[34] But with only a few exceptions, non-left activist performances remain offstage possibilities while the critical and historiographic spotlight focuses on progressive-left players.[35] A pattern thus manifests by implication, where conferences or collections of activist performance scholarship reference mainly or exclusively those works that affirm left-progressive causes.[36] At other times, scholars define performance activism in such a way as to denote left-leaning projects exclusively.[37] More common, however, is the view adopted by David A. Schlossman (who is himself referencing Steven C. Dubin's *Arresting Images*), that the left represents agendas who oppose exclusionary or unjust institutions, whereas the right represents insiders who defend such institutions.[38] To a certain extent, the very terms commonly in use for the political left and right in the United States install a spatial image: the left *progresses* while the right *conserves.* In describing politics as *movement,* then, it is the left alone that actually moves, whereas the right suffers stagnation or even steps backward.

Devil's Advocacy

An obvious question presents itself: What's wrong with this division? Why should performance activism not specifically name progressive-left movements for democratic values like justice, equality, and human rights? Surely there is something wrong, sacrilegious even, about the notion that police with their batons and pepper spray, Wallace with his racism, and Phelps with his radioactive hatred deserve comparison to ACT-UP, Medgar Evers, or WTO protesters. How, for example, could the Seattle PD in 1999 possibly be considered activist performers? In that situation, they defend an oppressive, exclusionary status quo. In fact, they are Louis Althusser's Repressive State Apparatus incarnated. What they represent isn't *protest;* it is *subjugation.*

Rather than arguing directly that a distinction between left/inclusive versus right/oppressive doesn't work, let me pose a counter-question: What work does this distinction do, and for whom? To begin with, stacking the deck in favor of left-progressive causes lends them the undiluted support and attention of performance critics. Taking a critically generous stance toward left-progressive activism allows scholars to connect their work to left-progressive politics more generally. Scholarship, historiography, and pedagogy in this sense transcend dry, detached scrutinizing to become, as Dolan argues, varieties of advocacy and activism themselves. To be sure, whether or not someone writes a scholarly article about this or that sit-in or demonstration may have little effect on the act itself within the moment. But an act's inclusion within or exclusion from an archive of performance activism, a decision largely made by scholars and historians, can make long-term contributions to the causes the act sought to advance. Historians may, for example, bring to light otherwise invisible or forgotten movements and personalities from left-progressive activism, reminding present-day activists of the diversity and divisions of their predecessors.

Alternately, the scholar might characterize acts closer to the present in terms of a larger left-progressive lens. For instance, Foster's work incorporates the "Battle of Seattle" into a narrative line that includes civil rights and early AIDS epidemic activism. In doing so (and working in concert with a number of other scholars from multiple disciplines), she influences how audiences after the 1999 event view and interpret what happened. She folds what might otherwise be seen as spontaneous and reactionary disorder by malcontents into a narrative of heroic, intentional, and strategically savvy struggles for justice. She helps to grant the WTO protests a degree of legitimacy and rhetorical traction within theater and performance scholarship, inviting other performance scholars to account for not only "classical" instances of social change protest but also the complicated (and still ongoing) "movement of movements" active in the WTO protests. Critical assessments of such performances after the fact—what worked, what didn't, how better to evaluate tactics and outcomes—can participate in the larger activist initiative, inspiring future activist performances while sharpening their effect. The activism-equals-progressive-causes frame also operates more broadly to foster a sense of connection between left-progressive initiatives past and present. Thus "performance activism" can assemble into a single skein a totality of activism (and scholarship about activism) qua a pro-democratic (perhaps radically democratic) fight against the forces of oppression and injustice.

Importantly, however, the coherence of such activist (i.e., left-progressive) struggles depends upon a similar uniformity among "the forces of oppression and injustice." Again, critical generosity toward some necessitates critical parsimony toward others. It does not so much eradicate critical paranoia as displace it—onto "those on the other side" of left-progressive forces. A good-faith left-progressive critical slant in activist performance scholarship can reserve privileges of human agency, benevolent intentions, nuanced contexts, and even forgivable imperfections only for those on the progressive left. Those identified as resisting left-progressive causes mutate into something akin to B-grade horror movie monsters: dangerous, deranged, and one-dimensional. Contrasted with the noble missions of those involved with the long, hard march toward justice, then, the opponents of desegregation, gay rights, or anti-globalization activism figure as evil (like Phelps), amoral (like the police), or at the very least deluded (like Wallace in light of his subsequent conversion/enlightenment).

To return to my earlier counter-examples, it bears emphasizing that Wallace, Phelps, and the Seattle police do not articulate their positions in terms of evil-crazy-unjust-alien-deluded motivations. No one outside of a nineteenth-century melodrama does. Wallace, for example, aligned himself not with "racism" but with a relatively elaborate and (at the time) widespread doctrine of democratic governance called interposition.[39] He framed his action as a stance not against black students but against a federal government that had overstepped its bounds. Now, I have no interest in baptizing the Wallace of the 1960s as some kind of secret anti-racist hero. Even in a context where he was demonstrably not as pathologically dedicated to racism as some of his peers,[40] Wallace's protestations about fighting for states' rights rather than white supremacy carry more than a whiff of disingenuity.[41] A critically generous reading does not discount Wallace's racism, but it does push us to look beyond or beside it. Characterizing his stand in the schoolhouse door as nothing more than a bigot pouting about the advent of justice obscures Wallace's own delicate choreography. Crucially, for example, the actual stand captured by cameras and relayed throughout the country lent credence to Wallace's interpositionist framing of the conflict. He confronted not the two students (they stayed in a car) but the Kennedy administration's deputy attorney general.[42] Moreover, there are indications that Wallace's action, while reprehensible from a left-progressive standpoint, forestalled a more violent response by Alabamans opposed to racial integration. The previous September, Ole Miss endured violent riots by segregationist forces angered at the integration of James Meredith. Keenly aware of the potential for similar violence in Tuscaloosa, Wallace literally stood for (i.e., in place of) segregationist whites, imploring his supporters to stay home.[43] He routed the simmering tensions of that day (tensions, it must be remembered, that he himself helped to create) into the symbolic realm, fixing the locus of attention and unrest on his body as the federal marshals went through the rote (and peaceful) process of removing him bodily from the doorway.

As a counter to ACT UP's die-ins, consider the virulently anti-gay rhetoric of Fred Phelps's Westboro Baptist Church. Phelps and his crew regularly appear in national news for their protests at funerals of queer people (and more recently US soldiers). These protests feature members of his congregation, including young children, holding up neon-colored picket signs festooned with camera-friendly block-lettered messages like "God Hates Fags" or "Thank God for AIDS." Horrible. Like it or not, Phelps ensconces himself firmly within the tradition of unpopular but protected speech. With his acidic rhetoric, Fred Phelps seems even more explicitly, vehemently opposed to gay rights than Wallace was to desegregation. He and his group regularly serve as cautionary examples of where the slippery slope of Christian conservatism ends. Yet, while he is undeniably Christian and conservative, assigning him to the same subset as conservative evangelicalism generally works only at a paranoid remove. In terms of his theology and his activism, Phelps is sui generis, standing well outside of the evangelical spectrum. Similarly, reducing his rationale to "homophobia" or "bigotry" (or "fundamentalism") occludes his grounding in an intricate and in its own way reasoned understanding of Christianity, an understanding whose connections with and contrasts to other understandings by conservative Christians bears closer examination.[44] His displays do not aim at conversion but condemnation. God has judged America; Phelps is merely the messenger of that condemnation. And although his hate speech shocks, he delivers it with scrupulous legality. Phelps's church includes many lawyers, who painstakingly research exactly where he can stand, what he can do—and what police and counter-protesters must tolerate. Indeed, legal injunctions against Phelps and his church found their way to the Supreme Court in *Snyder v. Phelps,* an odd case in which the left-leaning American Civil Liberties Union filed an amicus brief in favor of Phelps's right to protest. In an eight-to-one decision, the Justices ruled that Phelps's speech, though reprehensible, nevertheless deserves First Amendment protections.[45]

Even the Seattle riot police, so obviously the very embodiment of repression, become more complicated upon closer inspection. After all, despite their costuming, the police are human beings, not robots. One can acknowledge that capitalist super-corporations frequently take advantage of state resources to defend their operations while at the same time recognizing that individual officers likely did not imagine themselves as Faceless Enforcers of Economic Tyranny. Indeed, there is no reason to assume officers' sympathy for the World Trade Organization's powerbrokers or toward "globalized capitalism" in general.[46] Tasked instead with keeping the peace, the police confronted a heterogeneous crowd of noisy demonstrators whose plans, ethical orientations, and limitations the officers could not know with the same degree of surety that the activists themselves did. It is one thing to look back at the 1999 riots and declare with a historian's certainty (or perhaps even a participant-observer's certainty) that the majority of demonstrators were committed to nonviolent, peaceful protest. It is another to face down thousands of people, some of whom have announced their intent for civic disruption or even property damage, and have to guess at the best way to respond to the whole with minimal bloodshed.[47] If, as Foster maintains, the protesters enacted a choreography of protest, then surely that dance was not a solo piece but a pas de deux.[48] The police acted as intelligent, complexly motivated dance partners, moving along with the demonstrators, striving to match them step for step.[49]

In none of these cases am I arguing that these non-progressive agents are justified. I have expressed, I hope, my own stances enough so as not to be seen as suggesting a moral equivalency between Wallace, Phelps, and Seattle riot police on the one hand and sit-in protesters, ACT UP, or WTO demonstrators on the other. I would not wish for Foster, Román, Dolan, Cohen-Cruz, Kershaw, or any of the other (mainly left-progressive) scholar-activists whose work I admire to dilute their studies with phony neutrality toward the movements or people they study. Furthermore, I reject a cable-news pseudo-objectivity of reporting "both sides," presumptively assuming an equivalency between dichotomous political perspectives. Scholars do not write from a political no-space; they probe into and write about situations defined by unequal power relationships, contexts in which agents and causes are sometimes rendered unseen or marginal. In such cases especially, it is vital that scholars acknowledge and overcome such structures of invisibility, spotlighting the subjects working against and within such structures. Studying non-progressive groups with critical good faith does not ameliorate my antipathy for the stances they espouse.

But critical generosity toward those whose stances I oppose does force me to sharpen the tools I use to frame and study their performances. After all, if I assert a critical lens like choreographies of protest, acts of intervention, or utopian performatives, surely it is reasonable to expect that these models can productively illuminate ideologically unfamiliar performances and not just those that move me personally. Along with Sedgwick, I sense the limits of my own left-progressive critical paranoia whenever I write about non-progressive agents as if they were nothing more than perfect representatives of big, systemic operations like neoliberalism or heterocentrism. Again—the point isn't that neoliberalism doesn't exist or that it isn't important to seek out and expose its operations. The point is rather, as historian Timothy Burke argues, that "you can't afford to treat communities and groups that you politically oppose, however fiercely, as if their motivations and habitus aren't as complex and historically intricate as any other community or group." Precision and nuance, after all, are scholarly demands, not favors extended only to subjects whose politics a historian finds agreeable. "You have to be curious about everything," Burke insists, "or you might as well be curious about nothing."[50] Such good-faith curiosity calls the critic to more intensive registers of reflexive interrogation. Recognizing my critical generosity toward a subject, I remind myself to take extra care to avoid falling into a mode of credulous encomium ("It's good because it happened!"). Recognizing my critical alienation from or even antipathy toward a subject, on the other hand, demands that I avoid demonization. To do otherwise not only threatens scholarly sloppiness but constitutes a betrayal of the radical democratic vision I claim to endorse.

Democratic Disagreements

To explore this point, I turn again to Chantal Mouffe. In her work subsequent to *Hegemony* (particularly *The Democratic Paradox*), Mouffe complicates the image of activism as a hard-but-sure march toward a more perfect union, with equaliberal superheroes batting back avatars of oppression and exclusion. For Mouffe, the fundamental struggle within liberal democracies concerns not equaliberty versus totalitarian invaders from the outside; it concerns the struggle over what *equaliberty* means in the first place. Mouffe identifies liberal democracy as the shotgun marriage of two different political philosophies: the liberal tradition of human rights and individual autonomy on the one hand and the democratic tradition of equality between rulers and ruled on the other. These traditions jar with each other, each disrupting the other's tendency toward mob rule on the one hand or anarchic individualism on the other. This philosophical conflict manifests in concrete disputes. Inevitably in liberal democratic politics, a democratic (i.e., majority) sentiment will contradict an individual or minority's understanding of human rights. Liberal democratic systems lack any preset formula for resolving those contradictions. Thus liberal democracy by nature operates paradoxically. Its divergent political traditions generate perennial, tectonic clashes about how to co-articulate liberalism and popular sovereignty. Yet, argues Mouffe, the democratic paradox isn't a problem to be resolved but the central mechanism of any healthy democratic society. Conflicts over the realization and interaction of liberal and democratic ideals turn the crank of liberal democracy's engine. These conflicts keep constituent concepts like rights, autonomy, equality, and empowerment open to challenge and revision, protecting them from calcifying into the inflexible doxa of any single segment of the populace. The absence of conflict—consensus—signals for Mouffe a threat to politics.

A range of other political theorists echo Mouffe's point. Michael Walzer points out that, for all the progressive left's fondness for diversity, democratic systems really require only one kind of difference to function as such: ideological difference. A society may be homogeneous in terms of race, age, sex, income, or any other identity factor and still qualify as democratic so long as there exists some substantive disagreement that requires debate and (ultimately) voting. If no one disagrees, or if disagreement means nothing, then it is reasonable to ask whether a democracy exists at all, no matter how heterogeneous the society otherwise appears.[51] To a greater degree than Mouffe or Walzer, Jacques Rancière emphasizes the depth of these necessary disagreements. He builds his vision of democratic politics around the notion of *dissensus*. Politics, in Rancière's theory, describes ever-so-rare instances of social disagreement in which a group not included as a player in the democratic game (what Rancière calls "a part with no part") interrupts the appearance of plenary order, demanding that the entire democratic game reformat itself around the previously excluded part. Rancière stresses that dissensus does not name a simple case of groups who just need to communicate clearly to discover they are saying the same thing. Genuinely democratic contentions name conflicts between incommensurable views on the very question of who counts as a legitimate player in the democratic game.[52] Though his brand of politics describes a scenario more all-or-nothing than what Walzer and Mouffe envision, Rancière joins them in warning that an absence of disagreement—or a regime that minimizes substantial disagreement—ceases to be democratic at all.

I acknowledged earlier that the tangle of progressive-left performance activism hosts any number of fierce disagreements and ongoing debates. To suggest that left-progressive groups or activists minimize disagreement risks a swift and heated rebuke from veterans of such conflicts. Nevertheless, despite the left's real and admirable recognition of divergent expressions, I contend that the progressive left remains marked by a degree of deep consensus. A big-picture ideological coherence exists that captures and shapes most if not all micro-level divergences. When Mouffe, Walzer, and Rancière discuss essential disagreements, they mean primarily divergences between one big-picture coherent ideology and another. Such disagreements concern not so much matters of policy application but rather issues involving philosophical starting points. Questions about such issues arise over not merely how best to realize or protect X human right—a matter of parliamentary policy—but whether X qualifies as a right (or if its bearers qualify as human) in the first place—a matter of political axiom. When I describe even the progressive left as a coherent entity, I mean that its constituent groups tend to accept roughly similar sets of answers to such axiomatic questions. At this level—the level of common assumptions—the left's ideological orientations distinguish it from groups that operate from wholly different sets of assumptions.

The upshot is that the progressive left's commitment to radical democratic values means that it cannot be all things to all people. It excludes as well as includes, refusing to tolerate as well as extending toleration. For example, it may seem as if radical democratic theory argues solely for expansions of rights, protections, and empowerments. Responding to questions like "Is X a right?" or "Is X human?" radical democracy will, at first glance, tend to default to the affirmative. But if human rights and civic participation really have no preset shape, if the forms of liberal democracy's constituent concepts actually are contestable, then we must recognize that democratic contests do not guarantee only those outcomes that accord with left-progressive goals. Liberal democratic politics is not a one-way air valve that only allows expansion—more rights/powers for more and more types of people—and never contraction or restriction. The horizon of political possibility extends in every direction, not solely toward more radical and plural realizations of equaliberty but also toward narrower and more bounded configurations.

Choosing the more radical/plural direction necessarily means rejecting the opposite path. Such rejections do not imply a betrayal of liberal democratic promises. Even the most radical, inclusive vision of society requires limits, decisions about the application of ideals that deny some possibilities. No government could operate without setting boundaries around the rights or sovereignty accorded to its denizens. Infants do not sign up for selective service. Pets do not pay taxes. Foreign exchange students visiting the United States do not vote in US elections. Of course, alongside these relatively unobjectionable limits are areas of extreme debate: drivers' licenses for undocumented workers, marriage and adoption rights for same-sex couples, First Amendment protections for corporations, or civic personhood for fetuses. Such discussions are precisely the kind of fundamental contests Mouffe posits as intrinsic to liberal democratic systems. Labels like left and right, progressive and conservative, or even radical-democratic fail to predict exactly how political agents will engage such discussions. A left-progressive view, ostensibly committed to pluralizing and deepening liberty and sovereignty, balks at certain extensions (e.g., fetal personhood) even as certain conservative views will insist on them. The lessons need to be underlined: it is not anti-democratic to consider or debate limitations to the democratic franchise, and radical democratic and left-progressive stances absolutely traffic in such limitations. Mouffe's analysis thus reveals two traps to avoid when studying political actors from opposing camps. On the one hand, critics of activism have to avoid viewing the political field as a pro-wrestling match with good guys and bad guys in a knockout, winner-take-all battle.[53] On the other hand, activists and critics have to beware of the danger of irenic consensus, a politics aimed at little more than blunting the edges of ideological disagreements. Tolerance, ostensibly an indispensable pretext for radical democratic politics, can itself become a problem.

Of late, a number of theorists have argued that the progressive left suffers precisely from a surfeit of tolerance discourse.[54] That is, the left's meta-values of tolerance and diversity as well as its underlying fear of a constraining orthodoxy have displaced and muffled its ultimately *intolerant* drive for maximized equaliberty. Wendy Brown, for example, traces how tolerance began its career as a political stopgap measure, a better-than-general-warfare agreement to attempt nonviolent interaction rather than mortal combat. It functions, properly, as a precondition for civic interaction. Yet recently, Brown notes, tolerance has shifted from being one among many necessary preconditions for liberal democratic governance to operating as an endpoint goal, the sine qua non guiding principle for civic and political life. In Brown's evocative comparison, this shift transforms the activist impulse, turning the "I have a dream" of Martin Luther King Jr. into the plaintive "Can't we all just get along?" of Rodney King. Or perhaps the two merge: *I have a dream . . . where we all just get along.* What's wrong with getting along? Nothing, except that, as a final goal for any activism that calls itself radically democratic, simple comity offers (in Brown's words) a "terribly thin vision of membership, participation, and social transformation."[55]

Nor are calls for tolerance as irenic as they seem. Stanley Fish explains that the appeal for inclusivity only appears passive when in fact it conveys normative force. "The imperative of keeping the marketplace of ideas open," he observes, "means that some ideas—those urged with an unhappy exclusiveness—must either themselves be excluded or be admitted only on the condition that they blunt the edge of their assertiveness, and present themselves for possible correction."[56] Although later in the piece Fish specifically references faith-based ideas as exemplary of passions that brook no compromise, political theorist Lucas Swain notes that numerous activist positions offer similarly absolutist claims that simply aren't open to debate.[57] Activist ideals in particular often function not as requests for justice, freedom, and so on, but as *demands.* Many of the major heroines and heroes of activist movements past (e.g., Stanton, Luxemburg, Parks, King, Chávez, Gandhi) might qualify as intolerant or "unreasonable" in that they are moved by political convictions that they refuse to modify or privatize in the name of tolerance. But within a regime where tolerating differences becomes more important than choosing between them, Brown concludes, "the morally passionate citizen becomes strangely intolerable."[58]

For critics like Brown, Rancière, Žižek, and Badiou—all of whom operate from positions of passionate opposition to neoliberal capitalism—normative tolerance functions as a systemic circuit-breaker, protecting exploitative political and economic systems (they specify the current combination of liberal democracy and globalized capitalism) from potentially disruptive challenges from activist quarters. As long as passionate (i.e., intolerant, exclusivist) beliefs remain unacceptable, so long as agitational impulses and movements get quarantined to the private/personal sphere, the predominant system remains immune to criticism. Activism limits itself to palliative measures (proposing incremental half-reforms rather than wholesale revolution) and strictly personal politics (encouraging ever-increasing but systemically insignificant proliferation of lifestyle possibilities instead of a unified movement).[59] Meanwhile, having inoculated itself against the danger of deep disagreement, liberal-tolerant society finds itself ill-equipped to deal with the reality of fundamental differences within its population and in international politics. Cultures resistant to the normative-tolerant pulse of Judeo-Christian, capitalist-democratic culture become not opponents to engage qua equal participants but "different" subjects to be exoticized as beautiful-but-inscrutable objets d'art, infantilized as primitives incapable of "getting" tolerance, or vilified as terrorists to be isolated and destroyed. Deep differences from the ideals of radical democracy—an opposition to gay marriage, for example, or an ardently pro-life position—often get interpreted not as viable positions but as the result of mental or ethical deficiencies. Those who hold such views are perhaps undereducated (acutely irrational), unreasonable (chronically or intransigently irrational), or evil (pathologically immoral).

Activism, Evangelicalism, and Holy Envy

None of this is news to evangelicalism. The complex criticisms of left-progressive solipsism and normative tolerance regimes I have spent this chapter elaborating represent well-worn arguments for many conservative evangelicals in the United States today. Throughout its mass media, the evangelical right (a group that has considerable but not complete overlap with US evangelicalism in general) regularly bemoans the double standard of "liberal tolerance." Evangelicals Josh McDowell and Bob Hostetler, for instance, criticize what they call "the new tolerance," in which every lifestyle, every act, every expression, every permissive policy seems allowable, even praiseworthy, except for disagreement regarding the praiseworthiness of said lifestyle, expression, act, and so on.[60] In their interpretation of this tolerance regime, any intolerance of left-progressive cultural values and political agendas—or even a perceived failure to celebrate such values/agendas sufficiently—becomes the worst kind of crime, proof positive that the disagreeable person represents a nascent (or full-blown) theocratic fascist. Asserting a religious basis for a refusal to endorse or tolerate an aspect of left-progressive politics automatically invalidates the one making the assertion. The only allowable motivations for values in the public sphere are "neutral" or "reasonable" or "scientific"—never religious. Conservative evangelicals, in this line of thinking, exist as a harried group constantly under threat from left-progressive thought police. Now, to many readers, the notion that representatives of the majority religion in the United States are in fact a persecuted minority may seem patently silly. Yet a discourse of left-wing coercive tolerance runs throughout US evangelical subcultures, painting the picture of an inordinately powerful anti-Christian bias that emanates from left-progressive bastions such as secular academia, the entertainment industry, and certain sectors of government.[61]

I do not want to underestimate the extent to which certain forces on the political right promulgate and manipulate the image of left-wing bias and liberal indoctrination by Hollywood, the press, and secular universities to partisan advantage. Nor do I consider it necessary or productive in this venue to entertain the legitimacy of a vast, anti-religious conspiracy. This being said, it remains true that many of McDowell and Hostetler's allegations about toleration—sans conspiratorial subtext—actually jibe with the criticisms from secular theorists I have related above. Moreover, evangelical criticism of tolerance emerges from wider and more heterogeneous sources than just the politically aligned sectors that McDowell and Hostetler represent. A number of evangelical academics, for example, take pains to extend and respond to many of the criticisms from secular scholars and theorists that I have outlined above, contributing to the ongoing conversation in political theory about the proper makeup of pluralized democracies.[62] These critiques reinforce the same basic diagnosis that critics like Fish and Brown make: the culture of tolerance exerts constraining effects that delegitimize certain classes of deeply held beliefs.

I do not want to imply concord where none exists. Despite their concurrence, evangelicals and left-progressive theorists remain ardent opponents on multiple issues. Conservative evangelicals in the United States are hardly well known for devastating criticisms of the free market. And all too often, actions by various Christian figures (e.g., pastors burning Qur'ans, marches against same-sex marriages, religious talk-show hosts blaming natural disasters on victims' sins) resemble object lessons for, not against, promoting robust tolerance regimes within a strongly secular governments. It seems odd, then, to suggest that evangelicalism offers the progressive left hope for navigating the conundrum of tolerance. Yet, as I mentioned in my opening paragraphs, critics on the progressive left have begun to turn their attention to religion, finding in it aspects they admire. Why is faith, and Christianity in particular, suddenly so popular among political theorists on the left, theorists who in many instances disclaim any religious affiliation or beliefs? In her survey of various (ostensibly secular) engagements with faith, Ola Sigurdsen proposes a rationale I find compelling enough to quote at length:

> The main reason seems to be that theology and religion significantly aid radical thinking in keeping politics radical in an age of post-politics. If religion has been the "other" of modernity, it is perhaps not surprising that philosophers of very different stripes—post-secular secular philosophers or post-religious secular philosophers—have taken up reading religious texts as a way of trying to find alternatives to a certain version of modernity, especially those who stand in radical traditions such as Marxism or Psychoanalysis. Even if they prefer to read the theological classics for their form rather than their content as such, all the same it gives them the opportunity to achieve a critical distance from current accounts of modernity. Especially in more radical traditions, as exemplified by Žižek, Agamben, Badiou and Eagleton, there is a growing dissatisfaction with contemporary politics and also a growing dissatisfaction with the more traditional liberal solu-

> tions of the distinction between different spheres of life, such as they have come to be defined by modern secularism.[63]

Sigurdson's thinking here parallels Fish's arguments. Religious belief figures as an indigestible bit of bone in the grist of liberal democratic discourse, stubbornly refusing to submit to protocols of tolerance or schemas that compartmentalize commitments into public and private boxes. For a number of critics, then, certain expressions of faith serve, mutatis mutandis, as examples of how left-progressive activisms might live out their moral passions (or, as Badiou might say, how they might act in fidelity to the Event) in a world inimical to the public performance of conviction.

A similar hope—that faith might assist left-progressive activism—informs my present project. I investigate US evangelicalism in the spirit of what theologian Krister Stendahl calls "holy envy." A former head of the Harvard Divinity School and a leader in interreligious dialogue, Stendahl offered three guidelines for engaging with faiths not your own. First, he said, you must listen to practitioners of the unfamiliar-to-you faith rather than to critics of that faith. In a sense, the remaining chapters of this book each represent attempts to "listen" to activists following a set of beliefs very different from those animating left-progressive activism. I will largely take as a given that most (though not all) of my readers will differ from my subjects in terms of belief on issues like the afterlife, universal origins, and sexuality. Though I often mark my own distance from my subjects' beliefs, I strive to focus mainly on giving as thorough and nuanced an account of those beliefs as I can rather than on whether those beliefs err. Very often, a closer investigation reveals that evangelicalism itself embraces a considerable and contentious diversity of views on a particular topic where left-progressive critics too often assume evangelical homogeneity. Where possible and appropriate, I highlight that internal diversity of views.

Second, Stendahl counsels, you must be careful not to compare your best to their worst. Very often, the image of evangelicalism that the progressive left holds comes mainly from the worst examples of faith-based expressions. A pastor on a viral YouTube video calls for gays and lesbians to be rounded up and locked forever behind high walls. Another minister announces plans to burn copies of the Qur'an. Sleazy televangelists fill the late-night airwaves promising riches and physical health in exchange for cash. All of these bear witness to beliefs I find repellent. But I cannot overstate how little resemblance these spectacular examples have to evangelicals in general. Indeed, some of the harshest critics of such worst-case specimens are themselves evangelical Christians profoundly embarrassed and dismayed at having their faith so represented.

Finally, Stendahl challenges, when engaging with those of differing faiths you must make yourself open to what he calls *holy envy.* That is, you must strive to find something in the other's faith-practice to admire even as you preserve the awareness of deep differences between your faith and the other's faith.[64] Like the left-progressive critics I cited at the beginning, I locate in evangelicalism something to be admired: its commitment to promulgating (non-coercively) its worldview convictions in the face of cultural disinterest and resentment. Such a commitment demands not only faith in what one affirms but also transparency about what one resists, a careful balance of tolerance and conviction. And there is this: I detect something more in evangelicals than cold zeal for the Right and True. I am also convinced of, even moved by, the sincere concern for others that moves most of my subjects to risk their own encounters with people beyond their own faith. The Truth they wish to share is, after all, Good News, spread not just out of duty but out of joy and a deep conviction that the News can save souls. In even the most extreme and ostensibly unloving examples of outreach I examine, I find at least a spark of love for the enemy, a desire to see the enemy converted rather than defeated, and a faith that such a miraculous transformation may happen.

In a time of cynicism and diminished hopes, in a time of partisan polarization, in a time of desperation and apathy, I am envious of evangelicals' faith in activism.

CHAPTER 2

Positioning Secular Age Evangelicalism

What's going on with evangelicalism?

Consider two perspectives on faith in the United States, one from an evangelical minister and one from a sociologist of religion. In the spring of 2009, Michael Spencer, an evangelical pastor and blogger known as "the Internet Monk,"[1] posted a three-part series—part argument, part manifesto—entitled "The Coming Evangelical Collapse."[2] There Spencer sounds a grim alarm: "I believe we are on the verge—within 10 years—of a major collapse of evangelical Christianity." Evangelicalism in the United States, he asserts, has doomed itself to marginality. Over-identification with partisan issue-mongering, failure to articulate a core theological orthodoxy, and an unproblematic adoption of numbers-based market mentalities for ministry have hobbled evangelicalism's ability to present a compelling case to a culture increasingly disaffected with Christianity. As a result, he predicts, church membership will shrink by half, seminaries and parachurch groups will close, and popular intolerance of Christianity will grow. "This collapse," he contends, "will herald the arrival of an anti-Christian chapter of the post-Christian West." Spencer's challenge sent shock waves throughout evangelical media. The *Christian Science Monitor* picked up an abridged version of his argument for their March 2009 issue (later naming it one of the top ten stories of 2009), and it subsequently saw widespread distribution via the Drudge Report. Soon, blog entries, radio shows, and podcasts lit up as pundits, pastors, bloggers, and readers began asking tense questions around Spencer's theme: "Is evangelicalism collapsing?" "How long has the collapse been coming?" "Can it be prevented?" "How do we survive the evangelical collapse?"[3] As I will touch on later, Spencer's article participates in an ongoing trend in evangelical discourse reacting to an ostensible twilight of orthodox US Christendom (i.e., evangelicalism).

Such dire predictions stand in seeming contrast to the other assessment, which I take from Peter S. Berger, one of the more venerable scholars in the sociology of religion. Reflecting on his four-decades-plus career, Berger recently summarized his scholarly journey in terms of a reversal.[4] At the beginning of his work studying the phenomenon of religious belief in a modern context, Berger, along with other sociologists of religion, confidently predicted that religion of all sorts would decline as the twentieth century progressed. Evidence-based scientific processes and rationalistic political procedures, he thought, would displace superstition and faith-based prejudices as surely an oven melts ice. Since that time, however, he and his field have rejected this "secularization thesis." "As one looks over the contemporary world," relates Berger (writing here with Anton Zijderveld), "it's not secularization that one sees, but an enormous explosion of passionate religious movements."[5] In contrast to early assessments of religion's inevitable retreat in the face of encroaching secularity, Berger finds that there now exist more, and more varieties of, religious faiths active in the world. In other words, he argues, modernity doesn't secularize; it *pluralizes*. Moreover, and in contrast to his early predictions, this plurality alters but does not extinguish faith.

Do the assessments of Berger and his colleagues—not secularization but plurality—mean that evangelicals err in predicting decline and collapse? Are Spencer and his evangelical brethren crying wolf? After all, Spencer is hardly the first evangelical to prophesy the decline of Christianity. Doomsday predictions and jeremiads against backsliding form a subgenre of Protestant discourse as venerable as fire-and-brimstone sermons. And to many of my readers, the notion that evangelicals suffer from a lack of influence in US culture and politics likely seems laughable. What better way to galvanize the masses than by painting the big red devil of "coming collapse"?

Two observations are in order. First, whatever the *actual* status of faith in US culture, evangelicalism (or at least a significant portion thereof) sees itself as weathering an unprecedented existential crisis. To a large extent, this *sense* of crisis influences evangelical outreach even more than non-evangelical sociologists' studies do. I concede that some people (particularly on the partisan religious right) mobilize this crisis mentality toward political ends, but I would caution against facile readings of evangelical mind-sets that reduce them to little more than ideological manipulation by conservative elites. On the whole, I see little evidence that evangelicalism's anxiety about its future is feigned or consciously overblown. Spencer himself, for example, was known for resisting the over-alignment of evangelicalism with the religious right.[6] His was a call away from cynical politicization; to read his work as partisan fear-mongering is to ignore his specific position in evangelical thought.

The second observation I want to make concerns the consonance between Spencer's diagnosis of evangelicalism's place in culture and Berger's plurality thesis. Spencer's particular warning departs from apocalyptic scenarios of his forebearers. He predicts *collapse*, not *extinction*. For Spencer, the coming world is post-Christian not because Christianity disappears altogether—it does not—but because it loses a level of authority and respect long considered a given in US culture. To survive, it must compete—and compete not only with non-religious scientific materialism but also with an ever-increasing number of alternative faith positions. Because evangelicalism seems so slow to react effectively to this new world, Spencer contends, evangelicalism collapses not in the face of secularity but in the face of plurality.

To characterize this religious plurality, this need to compete, I turn to philosopher Charles Taylor's massive work, *A Secular Age*. There Taylor traces a profound shift in Western cultures whereby non-belief in religiously transcendent dimensions of existence acquires legitimacy as an available position for subjects to take. He rejects with Berger et al. the "subtraction theories" whereby secularity conveniently displaces or replaces religious faith. Faith, he argues, does not disappear completely, and likely never will.[7] Nevertheless, within Christendom—the European and New World cultures once dominated by Christianity—something has changed. Over the past half-millennium, it has become possible *not* to believe, to profess non-belief in any supernatural or transcendent reality, in a way that was once, and very recently, unthinkable for most people. But this possibility heralds neither the wholesale extinction of religious belief per se nor the dawn of a new era of nonreligious rationalism. Viability of non-belief does not necessarily translate into its monopoly or even popularity. Instead, Taylor identifies a secular age defined not by the hegemony of irreligion but by a terminal plurality of faith in which belief of any sort, including non-belief, become available choices in an increasingly diverse array of options. Plurality is the condition of Taylor's secular age, a state where belief is an option rather than an assumption.

This secular age poses the challenge to evangelicalism that Spencer identifies, for although faith in general diversifies, specific identification with a normative mode of Christianity (e.g., evangelicalism) does decline. Indeed, one of the signatures of the current secular age in the West as Taylor sees it is a popular distancing from or sense of alienation toward formal Christian institutions and identities. Taylor cites the growth of "a gamut of intermediate positions" between professed atheism (still a minority identification in the United States) and commitment to a formal Christian creed. Such intermediate positions include both non-Christian religious identities and "believing without belonging" professions. People might affirm parts but not all of a particular church's orthodoxy, or they might combine tenets of multiple faiths that more doctrinaire participants would consider impossible.[8] Either case poses challenges to evangelicalism, for which innovations outside of the truth of the Gospel generally spell doom.

Yet, as Taylor, Berger, and a host of other critics argue, secular age plurality poses problems not only for evangelicals anxious about the loss of dominance but also to twenty-first-century human societies that profess democratic ideals such as tolerance and freedom of religion. Faith-based differences can produce profound, passionate, and even deadly conflicts within and between cultures. Denied the deus ex machina (machina ex dei?) of a rationalism-only secularity that might conveniently trump fundamental conflicts between faith-based belief systems, culture finds itself desperately in need of tools for imaging and navigating a world defined by multiple and perhaps incompatible faith commitments. Berger's latest work with Zijderveld, for instance, promises in its subtitle to explain "how to have convictions without becoming a fanatic."

Thus stated, Berger and Zijderveld's project resonates with the challenge that I argue faces left-progressive politics. How can activist endeavors remain definite and uncompromising in their goals without lapsing into oversimplified representations of their encounters with those who believe otherwise? In the previous chapter, for instance, I observed that criticism about activist performance nearly always assumes a left-progressive cast to activism. This tendency at once casts left-progressive activists and critics as the sole authentic standard-bearers for democratic values while forgetting that "the other side" often imagines itself as fighting for similar values. The challenge's core question might as easily be reversed: how can activist endeavors remain open and inclusive without diffusing the momentum of singular conviction? As I noted previously, the danger of lionizing tolerance as the sine qua non of the left occludes the ways in which any politics must articulate exclusivist dimensions. A purely tolerant left becomes an entity that includes and accepts rather than one that stands for or against particular values. In concert with a range of critics, I suggest that investigating faith—particularly decidedly non-left-progressive evangelical Christianity—might assist the progressive left in navigating this conundrum. Evangelicalism after all represents a movement with exclusivist convictions that nevertheless strives to make itself available and appealing to those who do not share those convictions. But exactly what is evangelicalism? So often in scholarly and popular discourse, *evangelical* functions as a rough synonym for the forces of exclusion, intolerance, anti-liberalism, anti-democracy, and basic backwardness that radical democracy fights against. In this chapter, then, I'd like to dissolve the partisan haze surrounding evangelicalism, isolating my own understanding and specific focus here.

A truism of writing about evangelicals warns that defining *evangelicalism* constitutes the most difficult step. As several scholars have quipped, outside of particular pundits and academics, there's no such thing as a card-carrying evangelical. No official evangelical denomination or ecclesiastical authority exists empowered to dictate evangelical orthodoxy. Nor is *evangelical* the first label of choice for many Christians so identified. Even so, researchers looking for a clear idea of what evangelicalism is confront a surfeit of definitions. Countless agents and entities offer competing statements of belief, manifestos, traditions, guides, books, articles, sermons, podcasts, *Complete Idiot's Guide to . . .* , debates, and practices, each of which proposes slightly different and not-quite-compatible definitions for what evangelicalism really is. Settling on any description of evangelicalism invites inevitable reproach from critics within and without evangelicalism, who will certainly take issue with the given definition as overly generous or overly tendentious. Historian Donald W. Dayton famously urged a moratorium on the term, "in the hope that we would be forced to more appropriate and useful categories of analysis."[9] In a similar vein, Jon R. Stone finds most attempts at description too imprecise. Even gestures toward complexity, such as calling evangelicalism "kaleidoscopic," he argues, evoke interesting images but tell scholars very little of value.[10] Stone suggests seeing evangelicalism as, at best, a set of temporally contingent coalitions among church and parachurch groups,[11] defined mainly in terms of other groups or trends they react against.

Most vehement in arguing against *evangelical* as a term is D. G. Hart. In his trenchant critique of evangelical historiography, Hart contends that evangelicalism does not actually exist except as a sock puppet constructed and propped up for the convenience of academics, religious right celebrities, and statisticians. Beyond the "constructed phenomenon that academics, journalists, and parachurch leaders endow with great meaning," he argues, lies only a loose collection of dissimilar church traditions and organizations who but for the term *evangelical* would not be seen as close associates.[12] Everyone would be better off if the term were dropped altogether. Never have so many cared so much about something that might be nothing.

As my book's title indicates, and alongside the majority of church historians, theologians, and evangelicals, I believe that something called evangelicalism does exist.[13] Constructed it may be; nevertheless, the term carries positive force in denoting a distinct sector of belief and practice within US Protestantism. Millions of people in the United States—not just academics and pundits—affirm an affiliation with evangelical beliefs, even if they call themselves "born-again" or "Christian" rather than evangelical. I take seriously Hart's and Dayton's criticisms, though, in acknowledging that evangelicalism offers no entity, identity, or institution so certain or solid as, say, the Roman Catholic Church or the Church of Jesus Christ of Latter-Day Saints. These entities provide a clear historical object, a finite set of doctrines, and a coherent identity. By contrast, evangelicalism alternately resembles a historical trend, a sociological movement, and a theological inclination depending upon which disciplinary lens one uses to bring it into focus.[14] I abandon hope for an exact definition in favor of a rough triangulation, then, by reviewing historical, sociological, and theological approaches to evangelicalism.

I complement this trio of approaches with the understanding of evangelicalism as an essentially contested concept.[15] I draw the notion of essentially contested concepts from the work of W. B. Gallie, a mid-twentieth-century political theorist who was vexed by the fact that certain critically indispensible words like *democracy* or *art* seemed to lack a consensus definition. Every proffered definition, Gallie found, inspired credible and discordant counter-definitions. Moreover, the struggle between definitions could not simply be dismissed as unimportant. The terms Gallie offers as examples carry appraisative as well as descriptive force. To call something democratic, artistic, or evangelical is not merely to describe but to judge and value, though the valence of that judgement depends upon one's historical-cultural perspective.[16] Rather than jettisoning such terms as unworkably vague, Gallie proposed installing ongoing dissention about their meaning as part of their essential definition. Fierce debate about what *democracy* is, then, partially defines *democracy* in any particular time or place (or between eras). To ignore this ongoing contest is to miss a core aspect of democracy itself. Gallie insists that describing a concept as essentially contested does not rob the term of any descriptive power whatsoever. To be essentially contested is not to be indistinct or chimerical. Democracy is not monarchy, art is not economics, and evangelicalism is not Catholicism or liberal-mainline Methodism. But no final authority delimits exactly where and how evangelicalism ends and, say, fundamentalism or liberal theology begins. Any definition or description of an essentially contested concept, then, must attend not only to the general array of features endemic to the concept but also to the specific debates about the relationship between those features.

I keep the reminder of evangelicalism as an essentially contested concept close at hand, like a talisman, in the hopes of warding off some of the more serious shortcomings inherent in the task of generalizing so complex and heterogeneous an entity as evangelicalism. Indeed, I would prefer to keep such generalization largely confined to this chapter. The bulk of my work in future chapters deals with very specific sectors of evangelicalism: singular events, individual agents, and distinct strategies. I pose case studies of evangelical outreach tactics and conversations, not a comprehensive overview of all evangelicalism. Readers should not assume that, for instance, Ray Comfort's "Way of the Master" mode of evangelism (which I discuss in the next chapter) necessarily mirrors the methods of the evangelical congregation down the street. Evangelical readers will doubtless spot numerous differences between their own beliefs and those of the people and groups I write about. Some evangelicals may find their own distinctive identities and modes of outreach missing from my study. Nevertheless, each of my case studies exists within a larger field of evangelicalism in the United States, a field that requires some critical specificity. To that end, I paint a picture of evangelicalism here that is as representative of the majority of US evangelicals and as well-supported by etic and emic accounts as I can make it. As I move into an overview of evangelicalism from historical, sociological, and theological perspectives, however, I ask that readers keep in mind evangelicalism's essentially contested, heterogeneous status, even in those instances in which I neglect to insert qualifiers like "most" or "generally" before blanket characterizations of evangelicalism and of evangelicals. No single description of evangelicalism, even my own triangularization here, stands as unexceptionally true. It can, however, provide a starting place for a more detailed exploration.

History

Distinguishing evangelicals as a historical force within Christianity proves tricky. Both *evangelism* and *evangelicalism* stem from the Greek root *euangelion* (Latin *evangelon*), meaning "good news." In most forms of Christianity, this good news—the gospel—refers to God's act of incarnation (birth and life), passion (suffering and death on a cross), and resurrection in the person of Jesus. Since most Christian traditions advocate some effort at proclaiming or bearing witness to the good news thus understood, most varieties of Christianity can be thought of as generically evangelical. Not every evangelizing entity, however, is evangelical in the sense I and other scholars mean. Historian David Bebbington (writing about British evangelicalism) notes that the term *evangelical* functioned through most of its history as a fairly neutral adjective, meaning "of the gospel."[17] Only in the nineteenth century did it earn widespread status as a noun naming a particular group of revivalist Protestants.

Within current religious historiography, *evangelicalism* typically names any of a number of disparate movements and traditions within Protestantism from (at least) the eighteenth century onward. In the main, such trends emerged as reactions or revivals, attempts to reinvigorate or break away from an orthodox form seen as dead or constraining. In the United States, the key evangelical movements prior to the nineteenth century include those growing out of the First and Second Great Awakenings. Revivalists like Jonathan Edwards and John Wesley consciously broke with established denominational structures to reinvigorate and popularize worship. Through tireless campaigns of preaching, teaching, and writing, these and other preachers worked to spread their understandings of the gospel, winning many converts and planting long-standing church traditions (e.g., Presbyterianism and Methodism). By the early 1800s, when these groups began to be called evangelicals, US religious life consisted of multiple, diverse strands of revivalist Protestantism. These strands, argues historian George M. Marsden, blended features from previous US Protestant iterations, particularly the intellectualism of Calvinist traditions (such as Presbyterianism) with the highly emotional-experiential focus of pietistic traditions (such as Methodism).[18]

Throughout the nineteenth century, sectors of this diffuse evangelicalism within the United States and Great Britain began to flow along parallel channels, reacting against certain elements of post-Enlightenment modernity. Continental European trends in biblical scholarship, collectively known as the higher criticism, caused a sea change in how the Bible was read and interpreted. Combining methods and insights from philology, archeology, and literary criticism, higher critics portrayed the Bible not as a unified document of congruent propositional truths but as a patchwork quilt made up of multiple, conflicting traditions and contributions.[19] Higher critics began calling into question previously solid assumptions about the authorship, integrity, and authenticity of certain biblical books and beliefs.[20]

Shocked at the suggestion that the Bible spoke with numerous, fallible, human voices rather than with a single, perfect, divine one, nineteenth-century evangelicals countered with a stricter understanding of the Bible as the literal, complete Word of God, free from any kind of error or contradiction in any of its accounts or statements.[21] Crucial to this view was the insistence on the literal truth of miracles such as the virgin birth and Christ's resurrection. Such a view found its harshest test in the rise of naturalistic science, particularly Darwinism. Darwin's evolutionary account of life's origins were seen by some (though not all) evangelicals as challenging the integrity of biblical creation narratives—and thus the integrity of Christianity itself. Increasingly, being for an inerrant, infallible view of the Bible meant being against Darwinist theories (and perhaps science more generally). Gradually, these pro-literalist, anti-Darwinist varieties of evangelical thought began emphasizing the need for believers to set themselves consciously apart from and against worldly culture. In contrast to concurrent, turn-of-the-century "social gospel" movements, these evangelicals taught that Christians were to live differently, separately even, from the rest of culture.[22]

By the early twentieth century, such reactions had attracted a roughly coherent group of believers within and without major Protestant denominations. This group produced a number of statements that asserted their views, most notably a series of essays called *The Fundamentals,* which variously attacked modernity's vices, such as higher criticism, Darwinism, and ecclesiastical capitulation with sinful culture.[23] In a 1920 article in a Baptist newspaper, editor Curtis Lee Laws christened as "fundamentalists" those who not only affirmed but agreed to "do battle royal" for the Fundamentals.[24] Early fundamentalists found their most articulate spokesman in J. Gresham Machen, who in 1923 argued cogently that the fundamentalist view and what he termed the liberal church represented not merely opposing poles of the same faith but two utterly distinct faiths. Co-existence was impossible; truth cannot abide falsehood and error.[25]

Theologian Robert E. Webber characterizes this early twentieth-century evangelical phase as anti-intellectual (distrustful of science and higher learning), anti-social action (separatist rather than socially or politically engaged), and anti-ecumenical (refusing to ally with other Christian groups).[26] Such strident positions—and the penchant for labeling those who disagree not merely different but heretical—generated considerable friction within denominations and culture at large. These tensions reached a popular breaking point in the 1925 Scopes Trial, where John Scopes, a high school biology teacher in Tennessee, was tried for teaching evolutionary theory. The case attracted national attention, with Clarence Darrow from the ACLU defending Scopes and popular religious speaker and occasional presidential candidate William Jennings Bryan arguing for the prosecution. Though the fundamentalists' side technically won the case, the publicity around their cause (and particularly around Bryan's occasionally embarrassing defense) cost the fundamentalists much in terms of popular support, cementing a stereotype of fundamentalists as backward, anti-intellectual, and intolerant.[27] Fundamentalist takeovers of key denominations subsequently failed, and many fundamentalists broke away to found splinter denominations and new seminaries.[28]

Yet the fundamentalists did not disappear after the Scopes embarrassment. Over the next few decades, their numbers grew, though thanks to their anti-social orientation their national influence remained minimal. This changed, however, in the post–World War II era, when a wave of young evangelists, theologians, and seminarians began to step back from some of the more separatist influences of fundamentalism. Most articulate about this shift was Carl Henry, whose 1947 work *The Uneasy Conscience of Modern Fundamentalism* castigated fundamentalists (with whom he identified) for disengaging with culture. "Whereas once the redemptive gospel was a world-changing message," laments Henry, "now it has narrowed to a world-resisting message."[29] Henry complemented his attend-to-society arguments with work in the newly founded Fuller Seminary, which quickly became a respected center for new evangelical thought.[30] These relatively rarefied efforts at academic levels paralleled the popular ministry of evangelists like Billy Graham, who began a preaching career marked by an emphasis on outreach—winning converts—over orthodoxy. He won the enmity of many fundamentalists in 1957 by accepting an invitation to hold a crusade in New York City made by the (non-fundamentalist) Protestant Council of Churches. His willingness to work with non-fundamentalists and his refusal to secure fundamentalists' approval for his ministerial decisions marked him as something new on the evangelical field.[31] This new break coincided with the rise of entities still active in evangelicalism today: organizations like the National Association of Evangelicals, parachurch ministries like Campus Crusade for Christ, and periodicals like *Christianity Today*.[32]

It is this conscious movement away from strict fundamentalism—keeping fundamentalist beliefs but reshuffling them to prioritize outreach and a cultural engagement (even some degree of ecumenism)—that defines the tradition initially called neo-evangelicalism. In Webber's view, neo-evangelicalism challenged the signature tendencies linked to fundamentalists. Where fundamentalism was (and, according to some, often remains) anti-intellectual, anti–social action, and anti-ecumenical, neo-evangelicalism took steps toward reviving (or articulating) a distinct intellectual tradition, sought actively to engage culture (without merging with it), and tentatively made overtures toward other faiths.[33] My use of *evangelicalism* in this project refers specifically to the inheritors of the neo-evangelical breakaway from what was perceived as fundamentalist separatism and toward outreach-motivated engagement with culture.

To be sure, outside of a few high-visibility examples, this break manifested as a loosely defined trend rather than a conscious social movement. As Jon R. Stone notes, the decades that followed the initial splits by Henry, Graham, and others featured a series of temporary and shifting evangelical coalitions made up of diverse celebrity-based, denominational, educational, political, and parachurch movements. These coalitions operated by cycles of splintering and rapprochement, mainly over issues such as ecumenism (e.g., Can evangelicals participate with Roman Catholics in mission efforts?) or doctrine (e.g., Are Pentecostals evangelicals? May women serve as ordained ministers?). Nevertheless, by the time that candidate-and-then-president Jimmy Carter garnered attention for his explicit self-identification as a born-again Christian in the mid-1970s, the evangelical trend had cemented its existence as a distinct force in US religious life.

The 1970s, 1980s, and 1990s witnessed a degree of evangelical mainstreaming, as evangelicalism grew, diversified, and popularized.[34] Accounting for all of the last few decades' changes would exceed the limits of my present task, but I will briefly note three developments. First, subsequent to Carter, evangelicalism began aligning strongly (though not uniformly) with the partisan right. Groups such as the Moral Majority, the Christian Coalition, and Focus on the Family, along with pundit-pastors like Jerry Falwell, Pat Robertson, and Pat Buchanan, defined a deep, disciplined, and extremely effective base for the Republican Party: the religious right. The religious right's raison d'être seemed to be waging a culture war, identifying and battling various threats to traditional—that is, conservative Christian—values, mainly Communism, sexual immorality (homosexuality), and abortion. Though the religious right does not by any means represent all evangelicals—and I stress here that I do not use *evangelical* and *religious right* (or *conservative Christian*) synonymously—its influence was such that, today, it is difficult to disentangle evangelicalism from conservative partisan activism.[35]

Concurrent with the growth of the religious right, a sizable segment of evangelicalism began exploring various mass-market techniques, repackaging their messages and reorganizing their institutions along market-research lines. Webber characterizes this trend as an extended experiment with pragmatism, where evangelicals appropriated many of the features of popular entertainment media.[36] Contemporary Christian Music (CCM) mimicked secular and mainstream music, and church services began replicating conventions of large-scale rock concerts. Christian television and movies took cues from mainstream, secular entertainment media to create Christian variants on popular niche entertainment genres (children's superhero shows, adult romances, etc.).[37] Finally, and perhaps most significant for my purposes, evangelicalism has diversified as it has grown. During the 1970s and 1980s, groups and traditions like Pentecostalism that were previously unconnected to (or even opposed by) evangelicals began to be counted, and to count themselves, as part of the evangelical mainstream.[38] Historically Black churches, once vilified by conservative white evangelicals in the South, heard and at times accepted overtures to unite with evangelicals in parachurch or religious right initiatives.[39] Most profound, however, is the growing awareness of the massive shift of evangelicalism from the Christian West (i.e., the United Kingdom and North America) to the Global South and East Asia. I address this latter shift later in this chapter.

Present-day evangelicalism retains many of its earlier, fundamentalist roots. Though few groups proudly claim the label *fundamentalist* (and not all of these are evangelical),[40] there remain sectors of evangelicalism that expend considerable effort marking points of departure from other groups that outsiders might assume to be evangelical as well. Indeed, the very question of what one must believe—or what one can get away with believing—and still remain "evangelical" itself serves to define various positions within evangelicalism. A recent evangelical anthology, *Four Views on the Spectrum of Evangelicalism,* features four prominent theologian-scholars discussing precisely this issue. Each of the writers hails from a different sector of present-day evangelicalism (fundamentalism, confessional evangelicalism, generic evangelicalism, and postconservative evangelicalism), and each stakes out different sets of essential and limit-point beliefs.

R. Albert Mohler Jr., representing "confessional evangelicalism," helpfully borrows the mathematical imagery of "sets" to characterize these positions. Sets, Mohler explains, describe collectives of items, objects, or ideas that maintain coherence as a collective. Sets may be described as centered, bounded, or center-bounded. That is, a set of objects may identify (1) a common center of core beliefs around which the objects orbit (centered); (2) parameters beyond which objects/ideas may not go and still remain a member of the set (bounded); or (3) some combination of center and parameter that maintains set coherence (center-bounded).[41] The contributors to the book generally agree that evangelicalism as a set is at least centered. What boundaries exist, and how sharp-edged those boundaries may be, however, serve to distinguish—at least as a rule of thumb—tendencies toward or away from the fundamentalist end of the spectrum.

Kevin T. Bauder, writing for the "fundamentalist" tradition, declares that evangelicalism has both a clear center and hard-edged boundary.[42] The other contributors affirm progressively fuzzier or more porous boundaries. In my work here, I retain the idea that the term *fundamentalist* indicates an emphasis on the existence and enforcement of boundaries. Evangelicals on the fundamentalist end of the spectrum will tend to embrace processes of distinction and orthodoxy-policing, processes that may lead them to separate not only from non-evangelicals but also from evangelicals who do not similarly separate from non-evangelicals. I use *fundamentalist* in a strictly denotative sense to describe an indistinct zone of evangelicalism, not as a pejorative naming narrow-minded militancy. Not surprisingly, fundamentalist evangelicals approach the endeavor of outreach and witness differently than their less fundamentalist cohorts. Many of these ongoing historical differences presage conflicts between and within evangelical outreach initiatives that I will discuss later in the book.

Sociology

Just how many evangelicals are there in the United States? Simple to pose but thorny to answer, this question has inspired a miniature library of articles and books. Beneath a hard-science exterior of numbers, percentages, and statistical formulae, quantitative sociological efforts to measure evangelicalism depend on navigating some of the same uncertain definitional waters as historians do. Like historians, sociologists disagree about precisely how best to characterize such a diffuse group. Different ways of defining evangelicals yield radically different indexes of evangelical strength and form. In their review of various methods of measuring evangelicals, sociologists Conrad Hackett and D. Michael Lindsay note that the number of US evangelicals may waver between 7 and 47 percent, depending upon the definitional criteria used to identify evangelicals.[43] They list three main methods used to define evangelicals within quantitative surveys: affiliation, identification, and belief. I use their tripartite division as a guide for my overview here.

Affiliation-based measurements of Christians straightforwardly inquire about respondents' denomination (e.g., "Which church do you attend?"), cross-matching that denomination with a particular category of religious belief. Among the more popular affiliation-based categorization schemes is the RELTRAD classification system, innovated by Brian Steensland et al.[44] Using data from the General Social Survey (GSS),[45] Steensland et al.'s RELTRAD organizes religion in the United States into several major categories: Roman Catholicism, Protestantism, Judaism, "Other," and "Religiously Unaffiliated."[46] RELTRAD further subdivides Protestantism into three distinct faith families. The first is mainline Protestantism. This family includes many of the more venerable Protestant traditions in the United States such as the Episcopal Church, the United Church of Christ, the United Methodist Church, the Presbyterian Church, the Disciples of Christ (i.e., Church of Christ—Disciples), the Evangelical Lutheran Church in America (ELCA), and the American Baptist Church. Next is evangelical Protestantism, which includes the Southern Baptist Convention (the largest Protestant denomination), churches in the Pentecostal tradition (including the Assemblies of God), and a large number of denominationally unaffiliated (or loosely affiliated) congregations. Finally, and somewhat controversially, there are historically black Protestant churches, sometimes known collectively as "the Black Church." An umbrella term for a diverse array of African American denominations such as the American Methodist Episcopal Church, the American Methodist Episcopal Zion Church, and the Church of God in Christ, the Black Church shares some theological features with both mainline and evangelical Protestantism while foregrounding African American racial identity centrally and explicitly in ways that the other two groups generally do not.[47]

Hackett and Lindsay note that RELTRAD yields an evangelical population of around 27 percent of the US population.[48] But RELTRAD's affiliation-based methods have their share of detractors, calling into question the accuracy of that measure. Assigning non-evangelical identity to mainline denominations, for example, neglects the fact that many mainline churches have significant numbers of believers who identify with evangelical beliefs. Within systems like RELTRAD, for instance, members of the mainline United Methodist Church are ipso facto non-evangelical, no matter what they may believe or how they may self-identify. Black Protestantism poses a still more vexed question for affiliation-based studies. In RELTRAD as well as in Robert D. Putnam and Bruce E. Campbell's study, race trumps affiliation.[49] Thus, Barack Obama's one-time minister Jeremiah Wright, a pastor in the liberal-mainline United Church of Christ tradition, counts as a Black Protestant rather than as a mainline Protestant, as does Obama himself. RELTRAD-type categorizations thus put Obama and Wright into the same category as popular religious right televangelist T. D. Jakes, whose own affiliation (he is a pastor in the Oneness Pentecostal tradition) would otherwise identify him as evangelical.[50] The "none" and "unaffiliated" categories pose yet another problem for affiliation-based surveys. Increasingly, many US Christians gravitate toward congregations that eschew or downplay denominational affiliation. RELTRAD accounts for this by measuring the monthly church attendance of respondents identifying as "nondenominational" as "no denomination." Any such respondent who reports attending church at least once a month or more counts automatically as evangelical Protestant.[51]

In contrast to RELTRAD's affiliation-based measures, identity-based surveys bypass complicated denominational cross-matching in favor of direct inquiry. The Gallup Poll, for example, asks a standard, yes-no question: "Would you describe yourself as a born-again, or evangelical, Christian?" This question regularly yields one of the larger numbers for evangelicals in the United States, 40 percent or more each year from 1997 to 2007.[52] To be sure, such a high percentage can prove eye-catching (e.g., "New poll finds nearly one-half of US citizens call themselves evangelical!"), lending news stories about evangelicals extra weight. Yet the high number is in part an artifact of the question's looseness. Since the question declines to define what *born-again* or *evangelical* means, a poll based only on this question could conceivably capture Roman Catholics, Eastern Orthodox, or liberal Protestant Christians.[53]

Both identification and affiliation measurements seem to reinforce D. G. Hart's criticism of evangelicalism as a concept. The category, he argues, describes a group "so immense that many Americans cannot help but be an evangelical if they answer pollster's questions a certain way or belong to a church that historians and sociologists somewhat arbitrarily identify as evangelical."[54] As my historical survey above indicates, however, some sectors of evangelicalism are not so neutral about who counts as evangelical. For those sectors, both affiliation and identification are too subjective to serve as criteria for what is to them not merely a social group but a marker of authentic, lifelong Christian commitment. They would argue that proof of this commitment, and therefore of evangelical identity, is to be found not in one's church membership or response to a general poll question but in more specific measures of faith and practice.

Enter the Barna Research Group, the brainchild of researcher George Barna and perhaps the lead polling organization of, by, and for evangelicals. Barna takes an exacting approach to measuring evangelicals, basing their schema on reported behavior and professed beliefs rather than denominational affiliation or self-labeling. Barna distinguishes between "born-agains" and "evangelicals." The labels are the Barna Group's creations. Neither category uses a person's self-identification as a criterion for inclusion; one may self-identify as evangelical and yet only be considered born-again by Barna. To be counted as "born-again," people must affirm that they have made a lasting, personal commitment to Jesus and that they believe that they will go to heaven when they die because they have confessed their sins and trusted Christ as their savior. By Barna's measure, roughly two in five US citizens count as born-again Christians.[55] For Barna, *evangelical* refers to a more restricted category within the born-again group. To be evangelical, born-again Christians must affirm a particular set of truths drawn from statements of faith from the National Association of Evangelicals: that faith remains important in their life, that they have a responsibility to share their faith with others, that Satan exists, that salvation comes through grace rather than works, that Jesus lived without ever sinning, that the Bible is completely accurate in its teachings, and that God is the omniscient, omnipotent creator and ruler of the universe.[56] Barna notes that such "nine-point evangelicals" (the two born-again points plus the seven evangelical points) are relatively rare, typically encompassing less than one in ten US citizens. Significantly, for Barna, these true, nine-point evangelicals contrast starkly with the 38 percent of people who *claim* to be evangelical.[57] Much of the Barna Group's work involves investigating the discrepancies between self-proclaimed evangelicals and authentic evangelicals, often citing deficits in the percentage of born-agains affirming the seven evangelical-specific questions as evidence of wavering orthodoxy among US Christians.

Which one of these methods is right? Which one gives the most accurate picture of the number of US evangelicals? Surprisingly, and perhaps frustratingly, the answer appears to be "all of them." Hackett and Lindsay's study finds that most of the various measurements are valid so long as the definitions being used remain consistent.[58] Studies that copy RELTRAD's affiliation-based schema find numbers comparable to RELTRAD's study. Studies that replicate Barna's more exacting criteria—and that use similar criteria, of course—find comparably small numbers of US evangelicals. Works critical of evangelicalism and what it ostensibly represents can tout the Gallup Poll's 40-plus percentage measurement as evidence that the United States is trapped in evangelical clutches. So, too, can politicians on the religious right ground their authority in Gallup-level measurements of evangelicalism. Evangelicals convinced that the United States is drifting away from authentic Christian faith, on the other hand, can cite the vanishingly small percentages generated by Barna-type surveys. Each of these actions is both accurate and inaccurate.

Given such complexity in measuring evangelicals statistically, even the most impressive sounding numbers should summon a degree of caution in scholars. Sociologist Christian Smith, in his own review of such survey strategies, warns against what he calls the factual survey fallacy: "the general belief that public opinion surveys accurately and adequately represent the views of ordinary people." He points out that survey research "does not merely tap into and report 'objective realities' that exist out in the real world, but itself helps to create and organize that 'reality.'"[59] In reporting on evangelicals, for example, the Gallup Poll modifies the raw data it collects in answer to its self-identification question by excluding Catholics and non-whites. Explaining this latter filter, Gallup reporter Frank Newport explains that Black churchgoers historically support Democratic platforms, so for Gallup to include them along with white evangelicals (who largely support conservative or Republican platforms) would disrupt its political data.[60] Thus, to a certain extent, Gallup's image of evangelicals as Republican relies on survey methods that preemptively exclude a majority-Democrat group from being evangelical in the first place. The poll partially creates the reality it purports only to measure. I would add, in concert with Smith, that acknowledging the constructed nature of survey research—or the constructedness of evangelicalism itself—invalidates neither evangelical surveys nor the group/concept they aim to measure. Constructedness does not imply unsoundness. There are stronger and weaker constructions, more and less useful tools that might be differently applied to different ends. Smith's warning reminds us not to read or apply the results of any quantitative study of evangelicalism facilely. Even scientific and self-consistent measurements begin with contestable assumptions about the nature of an essentially contested concept.

Theology: Four Concepts

Perhaps even more than is the case with historiography or sociology, settling on a consensus definition of evangelical theology seems a doomed endeavor. Broadly, evangelicals operate within the bounds of orthodox Christianity as outlined by the fourth-century Nicene Creed (though they do not necessarily affirm the Creed formally).[61] That is, along with Roman Catholics, mainline Protestants, and Orthodox traditions, evangelicals commonly profess the existence of a single creator God, who exists as three coexistent expressions of the same Godhead: the Trinity of Father, Son (Jesus), and Holy Spirit. In the Christian story, God became incarnated as a human, Jesus Christ. Christians are taught that Christ was born of a virgin (Mary) and that he lived a sinless life, was crucified, died, and rose from the dead, subsequently ascending into heaven to rejoin the Father. In place of the corporal Christ, God currently dwells with believers and the Church as the Holy Spirit, and Christians in general affirm Christ's eventual return (though the exact nature of this return is a matter of debate). Some traditions would be satisfied in affirming the Nicene Creed as a satisfactory expression of their core theology. Others, evangelicalism included, consider the Creed's statements a necessary but insufficient portrait of orthodox Christianity. In the main, evangelical theologies depart from those of other Christian traditions based on their additions to and priorities within the beliefs laid out by the Creed.

Such evangelical modifications to Christian orthodoxy have, especially over the last century, led to a pattern whereby evangelicals separate themselves from other Christian traditions via schism and condemnation. They draw theological lines in the sand between allowable variation and intolerable heresy and then, unsurprisingly, discover themselves alone on the orthodox side of the line. Thus, evangelical theology might be defined negatively: it is *not* Roman Catholic, Eastern Orthodox, or liberal-mainline (evangelical discourse often links the two adjectives) Protestant. Evangelicals occasionally disagree about whether or not such non-evangelical groups qualify as Christian at all; particularly within more bounded-set strains of evangelicalism, the level of Christian recognition one extends to, say, Roman Catholics, is itself at times seen as a litmus test for orthodoxy. In fact, one of the perennial contests essential to evangelicalism relates to tensions between theological orthodoxy and theological openness. To what degree and in relation to which issues may evangelicals disagree and still be evangelical (i.e., Christian)? In the main, when evangelicals talk about Christians, they mean evangelicals like themselves. Importantly, however, evangelicals tend to eschew a coherent creed or statement of belief that would define once and for all just what "evangelicals like themselves" means. The coalitional and essentially contested aspects of evangelicalism make various statements of evangelical theology, at best, suggestive and partial.

Pinpointing a specifically evangelical theological core thus presents a vexing problem. Among the more successful attempts at synthesis (in terms of its acceptance by a wide range of evangelical scholars and ministers) is David Bebbington's fourfold characterization of evangelicalism's theological hallmarks. Evangelicalism, he argues, is Christianity that emphasizes *biblicism, crucicentrism, conversionism,* and *activism.*[62] As Bebbington himself emphasizes, these describe something of a lowest-common-denominator set of theological tendencies across much—though not all—of evangelicalism. Each of these points marks a zone of intense controversy as much as it does an area of concord. They are representative clusters of common evangelical concern, not proposals in a manifesto or commandments on a list. Different segments of evangelicalism interpret and prioritize these hallmarks differently.[63] Nevertheless, Bebbington's quadrilateral has gained traction across a broad cross-section of evangelical thinkers and pastors. It remains a useful rule of thumb for distinguishing evangelical areas of focus. I will briefly review each of his four hallmarks in turn.

Biblicism refers to evangelicals' high regard for the Christian (i.e., Protestant) Bible as the inspired Word of God. In theory, this belief traces back to Martin Luther, who emphasized *sola scriptura* ("scripture alone") as one of his major reformations to Roman Catholicism. Where Church teaching contradicts the clear doctrine expressed in scripture, scriptural readings ought to predominate. Today *sola scriptura* remains a rallying cry for many Protestants, marking their distance from the Roman Catholic magisterium. For evangelicals, however, *sola scriptura* implies not just a matter of authority or non-Catholicism but a mode of reading. Drawing on the nineteenth-century traditions of biblical literalism and commonsense readings, evangelicals today typically revere the Bible as the actual Word of God, a stance many evangelical traditions call having a high regard of Scripture or, more simply, being "Bible-believing."[64]

For evangelicals, Bible-believing involves viewing scripture as *inspired*, that is, God-breathed, uniquely revelatory, and a source—the source—of authority. In delineating what this inspiration means, most branches of evangelicalism affirm that the Bible is *infallible* in that its presentation of theology is sufficient, coherent, and utterly authoritative. *Sufficiency* here means that the Bible requires no outside tradition, creed, or ecclesiastical body to amend, clarify, or repair its message. Indeed, in the evangelical view, no such extra-biblical source has the power to do so. The Bible stands over and apart from the teachings of the church, the experiences of Christians, and the influence of culture. Scripture corrects and directs tradition, reason, and experience—not the other way around. Since the Holy Spirit guides the reading of scripture by believers, evangelicals argue that Scripture communicates its messages to any of the faithful clearly. The individual believer-interpreter, not church traditions or catechisms, thus serves as the preferred model for determining belief.

Evangelicals further define the Bible as *plenary* in that it is canonically completed, closed to subsequent addition or modification.[65] Most (though not all) evangelicals will further regard the Bible as *inerrant:* without contradiction or counterfactual claim in any truth statement on any subject—theological, historical, or cosmological.[66] Evangelicals understand scripture as *self-authenticating* and *self-interpreting*. That is, for evangelicals, the Bible does not merely contain or point to God's utterances or ideas; it *is* the Word of God. While careful not to deify scripture (they consistently deny charges of "Bibliolatry"),[67] evangelicals hear scripture as God's clear, self-consistent, unmediated voice. To qualify or criticize any part of the Bible equates to critiquing God. Whereas Episcopalians or Methodists might consult scripture in relation to tradition (How have previous Christians or Church Fathers viewed this issue?), experience (What does the active Spirit of God counsel about this issue?), and/or reason (What does God-given intellect or God-guided scholarship tell us about this issue?), evangelicals emphasize the *sola* in *sola scriptura.* The plain-sense meaning of scripture—when properly interpreted—outweighs human considerations or processes. If scripture seems to be at variance with human reason, then human reason must submit to the clear teaching of scripture. As an old evangelical saying avers, "God said it, I believe it, that settles it." Many evangelical pastors would be loath to suggest that the Bible speaks with anything other than a unified, consistent voice about any topic. Confronted with a *seeming* tension (e.g., why do the four Gospels contain discrepant accounts of Jesus's death?), a pastor might explain via reference to the differing scriptural contexts (e.g., each relates a partial account that may be blended with the others into a coherent whole) or, in extremis, to the lack of access to the "autographs" (original texts) of scripture or to the inadequacies of human understanding. Whereas non-evangelical Christians might read the Bible along with other texts or in conjunction with other considerations to discern what God is saying to them, for many evangelicals the Bible simply *is* God's plain, clear word. Un-clarity or confusion about the Word stems from human misunderstandings, not from deficiencies in scripture.

Biblicism, however, does not imply absurdity. Evangelicals are quick to discredit straw-man portrayals of "Bible-believing" as brutish literalism. When the speaker of Song of Solomon 4:1 tells his lover, "Your eyes are doves," no evangelical hermeneutic would deny the operation of a poetic metaphor. Biblicism recognizes (and requires that readers recognize) distinctions of genre and narrative conventions. Poetry is not law. Parables do not relate historical events, nor is historiography intended to be metaphorical. Nor is it the case that evangelicals are encouraged simply to flip to random Bible verses and assemble a meaningful message in some religious Dada exercise. Inerrancy doctrine as affirmed in most evangelical traditions resembles a complex, nuanced conversation about interpretation based on certain common assumptions, not a set of hard-and-fast rules and official interpretations.[68]

Biblicism inflects evangelical life and thought in ways both obvious and subtle. Bibles play a larger material role in evangelical church services than is the case elsewhere in Christianity. In many evangelical churches, individual believers are often expected to have their own Bibles and bring these with them to every service. As the pastor delivers the sermon, parishioners turn to the verses being read to follow along, make notes, and underline key terms or phrases (all at the instruction of the minister). Church activities for children and young adults prioritize verse memorization and biblical literacy. Churchgoers learn songs about the Bible ("The B-I-B-L-E / Yes, *that's* the book for me!") and may recite pledges of allegiance to the Bible at church camps.[69] Evangelical teaching counsels that all Christians, young and old, should read and pray over the Bible daily. Biblicism also affects the rhetorical structure of evangelical discourse. Within much evangelical scholarship and preaching, arguments are judged in part based on how extensively they cite specific scriptures as support. Works of evangelical scholarship, for example, regularly contain separate indexes detailing a work's various scripture references, with the tacit assumption that even a work of scholarship is trustworthy in proportion to the frequency and range of the author's biblical references.

Biblicism also provides some sense of structure to evangelical theology. Biblicism gives evangelicals a standard—at least in theory—by which to distinguish essentials of doctrine from *adiaphora* (non-essentials, beliefs neither required nor prohibited). Evangelicals recognize that the Bible speaks clearly about some points of doctrine, like the resurrection of Jesus, while remaining silent on other points. Ostensibly, the essentials of faith—the center and boundaries that define the evangelical "set"—would follow wide, clear, and consistent scriptural direction. Evangelicals typically resist innovations of doctrine or policy at odds with the plain sense of scripture, such as blessing same-sex unions or endorsing non-creationist accounts of life's origins. Yet, as in all things evangelical, dissention exists about just what the plain sense of scripture is. In his polemical study criticizing biblicism, Christian Smith argues for the operation of what he calls Pervasive Interpretive Pluralism (PIP) in evangelical hermeneutics. Eschewing extra-biblical traditions or creeds that would establish particular readings of scripture, evangelicals inevitably disagree—and disagree profoundly—about the proper meanings of certain passages and therefore about which beliefs qualify as essential or adiaphoric. In Smith's view, strict biblicism cannot work since the Bible as a text remains perpetually (pervasively) open to multiple exclusive interpretations.[70] Evangelicals who defend biblicist views of course offer a number of well-worn rebuttals to Smith and other such critics.[71]

Determining the validity or viability of biblicist views is not my role here. I will point out, instead, that evangelical dissentions regarding interpretive readings and the doctrinal conclusions that emerge from them still play out in a biblicist register. That is, evangelical disagreements about issues like gender roles or life's origins revolve around considerations regarding what the Bible *really* says about the ordination of women (does Paul forbid *all* women or just those in the church he's writing to?) or creation (does Genesis describe a literal six days or is it a metaphor for evolution?), not whether it is acceptable to bracket biblical mandates as outdated or whether doctrines about gender or universal origins need extra-biblical clarification. This perspective is essential to appreciating the complexity of many intra-evangelical tensions about cultural issues. To a left-progressive outsider, for example, evangelical debates about homosexuality can resemble a melodrama where tolerant, loving individuals (people who *really* get Jesus's message of love for all) battle forces of homophobia and ignorance (people twisted by their own lack of empathy or understanding). For biblicist evangelicals, however, the issue concerns not merely homosexuality per se but also fidelity to the authority of God's Word. As I will explore later in chapter eight, managing the juggling act of sexuality and biblicist faith proves especially complicated for Bible-believing evangelicals who themselves identify as same-sex attracted.

Crucicentrism names the fact that evangelicals tend to focus on Christ's crucifixion as the central event of the Christian story. In technical theological terms, evangelicals typically approach the crucifixion as an act of penal substitutionary atonement by God, through Christ, on behalf of humanity. Within the schema of substitutionary atonement, humans are hopelessly fallen. Both corporately (through the original sin of Adam and Eve) and individually (through their own acts), they have broken the divine law of God. At the Final Judgement, God will—*must,* actually, in accordance with God's perfect nature—find them guilty. Humans' sin irrevocably condemns them to an eternity in Hell, a place of everlasting torment and separation from the perfect, holy God. Against this charge humans can offer no defense. No matter how good or admirable people are, no matter how seemingly insignificant their sins, humans remain stained by their guilt in the eyes of God. Christ's sinless life, however, allows him to transfer human guilt and its penalties to Himself. On the cross, Christ assumed the weight of all human sin and its consequences, removing the guilt from any human who invests belief in the efficacy of that act and reconciling humans with their creator. Jesus essentially stands in for humanity in the Court of the Final Judgement, justifying humanity in the eyes of the Judge. Christ's act of sacrificial substitution thus enables atonement (literally *at-one-ment*) with God.[72] While evangelicals, along with other Christian traditions, venerate many aspects of the Christian story—for example, Christ's birth (Advent), the Last Supper (Eucharist), Christ's resurrection at Easter, or Pentecost (the investment of the Holy Spirit on the believers at Antioch)—evangelical theology places the crucifixion at the center of the faith. The substance of substitutionary atonement theology (e.g., the reality of sin, Hell, and judgement) forms the bedrock of evangelical life and work.

Conversionism refers to the evangelical emphasis on the importance of an individual conversion experience, a distinct moment in which one makes a conscious decision to become a Christian.[73] For many evangelicals, this decision involves a two-step process (though believers may experience these as a single act): (1) repentance, turning away from an old life of self-sufficiency to a new one defined by submission to Christ's grace, and (2) profession, formally (and, ideally, publically) affirming belief in and acceptance of Christ's sacrifice on the cross as the only salvation from the penalty of sin. As I will explore in greater detail in the next chapter, exactly how conversion occurs remains a matter of considerable debate within evangelicalism.[74] But evangelicals remain united that personal conversion (as opposed to, say, communal or ethnic salvation) is essential.

Anyone who converts is understood to have been "born again" or "saved," spiritually renewed and indwelt with the Holy Spirit, though different evangelicals may differ about their preferred term of self-identification. In salvation (the theological term is *justification*) the guilt of human sin disappears, washed away (to use the evangelical idiom) by the blood of Jesus. Those so saved have their names written in the Book of Life (a heavenly tome consulted to determine whether or not someone will receive eternal life in heaven). Evangelicals tend to imagine conversion as a discrete, one-time event experienced by someone intellectually capable of appreciating it. It is not the case, for instance, that one is a Christian simply by virtue of being raised as an evangelical or by attending evangelical churches. No human action—no amount of being good, attending church, feeding the hungry, or following the Ten Commandments—can suffice to save someone from hell. Only Christ's grace, received by sinners in conversion, can save. Most strands of evangelical theology insist that conversion is a possibility only within the bounds of a human's lifetime prior to Christ's return. Both an individual's death and the Second Coming of Jesus (i.e., the Final Judgement) represent an end to the invitation God extends to humanity. After either of those events, individuals cannot take advantage of Christ's atonement and are doomed to an eternity of torment in hell.[75]

So central is the doctrine of conversion to evangelicals that nearly every aspect of their churchgoing life includes a plea to those listening to convert. Sometimes referred to as an "altar call," this invitation generally comes at the end of any church service, with the pastor making an appeal for those who wish to be saved to come down to the front and pray as the congregation sings or the instruments play an invitational hymn. Altar calls often occur even in cases where the sermon's theme or service context seem unrelated to conversion topics. I have even attended funerals where, at the graveside, the evangelical minister makes an altar call to the mourners. While some (even some evangelicals) might consider such a choice in poor taste, I suggest seeing it instead as evidence of how central conversion is to the evangelical life of faith. Conversionism underlines the fact that, for evangelicals, the primary question in human existence concerns whether or not they have received Christ's gift of salvation. Even those who consider themselves already saved should examine themselves carefully in order to confirm that they have, in fact, converted and aren't simply fooling themselves. To be sure, evangelicals see the Christian life as much more than conversion. But conversion remains the sine qua non for believers. No subject, no circumstance, and no consideration outweighs the ultimate concern of salvation.

Stemming from the evangelical focus on conversionism is Bebbington's final hallmark, *activism.* Bebbington initially uses the term to mean attempts to persuade others to convert, which I have thus far been calling *evangelism.* Subsequent interpreters have extended Bebbington's original meaning to include *missions* more generally. An extremely complicated term throughout Christianity, *missions* as a concept involves both activism as Bebbington means it and interventionist gestures into culture more generally (i.e., activism as I discussed it in the previous chapter). In his influential text about Christian (not just evangelical) missions generally, David J. Bosch helpfully distinguishes between *mission* in the singular and *missions* in the plural. The former, he says, refers to the *missio Dei,* God's mission in a Christian context: "God's self-revelation as the One who loves the world, God's involvement in and with the world, the nature and activity of God, which embraces both the church and the world, in which the church is privileged to participate." Missions in the plural describes the *missiones ecclesiae,* the "missionary ventures of the church" in which the people of God participate in the *missio Dei.* Critical to such endeavors is evangelism, which Bosch defines as "the proclamation of salvation in Christ to those who do not believe in him, calling them to repentance and conversion, announcing forgiveness of sin, and inviting them to become living members of Christ's earthly community and to begin a life of service to others in the power of the Holy Spirit." Yet missions are more than simply evangelism. They involve presenting what Bosch calls

"God's 'yes' to the world," which impels the church to engage "the realities of injustice, oppression, poverty, discrimination, and violence" since for Bosch "salvation also has to do with what happens to people *in* this world."[76] Thus expanded, evangelical *activism* accounts for Christianity's tendency to be involved in cultural or political movements beyond mere evangelism, standing up for issues they see as aligned with God's mission as well as reaching out to invite the lost into communion with God through Christ. Certainly, with the advent of the religious right in the United States, such conservative or right-wing activism seems at times to account for the totality of evangelicalism's activity in the world.

Though this larger sense of missions remains important, I focus in this project primarily on the evangelistic aspect of missions. For most evangelicals, evangelism qua witness to the lost lies at the core of all mission activity. Such an emphasis affects how evangelical traditions think of missions (and the related phenomena of mission trips or missionary activity) more generally. For example, if a congregation of the United Church of Christ (a liberal mainline tradition) were to "go on a mission trip" or "do missions," most likely it would pursue a project consisting primarily of social justice activism, for example, providing medical assistance to those in need or helping to build houses for Habitat for Humanity. Rarely if ever would such UCC missionaries consider bundling an overt pro-conversion message into their actions (though they might be ready for and open to queries about their religious identity). For them, the act of helping others is their evangelism, their living out of the gospel of Christ.[77]

By contrast, an evangelical congregation on a mission trip would inevitably include some pro-conversion message, either along with or even in place of social action. "Missions" in an evangelical context means at least—and perhaps exclusively—the presentation of the gospel and invitation to convert. For evangelicals, the question isn't whether one should "do good works" like helping the needy *or* evangelize by spreading the Gospel. Rather, evangelicals argue that the ultimate good that anyone could do is to share the gospel and perhaps be a vessel through which the Holy Spirit inspires a conversion. From an evangelical perspective, even the most effective feed-the-hungry or clothe-the-needy program (and many evangelicals are quite active in such programs) is ultimately useless if the people being served fail to convert, and so they die in their sins. For evangelicals, missionary imperatives unfold within the framework of biblicist, crucicentric, and conversionist convictions. *Activism* thus means, primarily, evangelistic outreach to the lost.

Useful as I and many evangelical scholars find Bebbington's quadrilateral of biblicism, crucicentrism, conversionism, and activism, I stress that these four concepts serve as guides best used in conjunction with other considerations. A number of other faith traditions—the Church of Jesus Christ of Latter-Day Saints, for example, or the Jehovah's Witnesses—could align at least minimally with some or all of Bebbington's criteria. But, while debate persists (among evangelicals) about whether such groups are properly Christian, few would make the case that they are evangelical. Theological orientation contributes only part of what makes evangelicals evangelical. For this reason, I rely on a triangulation between theology, history, and sociology in order to locate present-day US evangelicalism.

Summary

With this rough triangulation in place, I can now establish more clearly what I mean and don't mean in this project by present-day US evangelicalism. From a historiographic standpoint, I mean mainly traditions that hearken back to the mid-twentieth-century neo-evangelical break with fundamentalism. Of course, this names less a coherent group than a multivalent, ever-shifting array of engagements with a central conundrum: how can the church remain faithful to doctrinal fundamentals (as defined by the US fundamentalist tradition) while participating in a meaningful, conversion-focused outreach? Sociologically, the group I investigate is both popular and elite. By most statistical accounts, the number of self-identified or self-affiliated evangelicals numbers anywhere from a fifth to a third (or even a half) of US citizens. A considerable discrepancy persists, however, between the number of people who describe themselves as evangelical when pressed to consider the question (e.g., those the Barna Group identifies as "born-agains") versus the number of people who actually believe in a set of key evangelical beliefs (e.g., those Barna labels "evangelicals"). As a group—insofar as one can speak of evangelicals as a single group—evangelicalism exists in the tension between such popular (wide, shallow) affiliation and elite (narrow, deep) orthodoxy.[78] Theologically, US evangelicalism covers an ever-widening range of positions, but I will follow Bebbington's lead in focusing particularly on evangelicalism's interest in (and debates about) biblicism, crucicentrism, conversionism, and activism. As I have mentioned, the last of these four hallmarks concerns me most.

This triangulation allows me to make a few broad-stroke clarifications to block out what I *don't* mean. First and foremost, evangelicalism does not equal social conservatism, the political/religious right, or the entirety of Christian fundamentalism. Some sectors of evangelicalism do advance strongly partisan positions and political activism, though not all of these positions are right-wing. Many other evangelical sectors sideline politics, or they "render unto Caesar what is Caesar's," observing a degree of separation between their faith practices (worship, discipleship, outreach, service) and partisan preferences (voting, politicking, social activism). Evangelicals are renegotiating what it means to be a Christian in a non-Christian world, many times concluding that the intensive politicking of the Moral Majority and Christian Coalition detracted from the more fundamental goal of "making disciples." Though many self-described fundamentalists are evangelical, others (fundamentalist Roman Catholics, for example) would not be. And most of evangelicalism defines itself against the appellation *fundamentalist,* rejecting that term's orthodoxy-focused doctrines of separation in favor of an emphasis on activism. Many of the outreach techniques I study are responding to the aftereffects of the turn-of-the-millennium culture wars over issues like abortion, gay marriage, and evolution/creationism. I focus primarily on those aspects of evangelical practice more concerned with winning converts to Christianity rather than winning a partisan battle over, say, which science textbook to adopt. To be sure, many of my subjects relate directly to partisan culture-war battlefields. I can hardly examine the Creation Museum of Answers in Genesis, for instance, without wading a bit into national debates about evolution. But, as I elaborate in chapter six, to see the Creation Museum as nothing more than an expensive bit of artillery lobbed at pro-evolution/anti-creationism forces is to misread it. Winning souls and strengthening the faithful in their beliefs so that they may ultimately win souls are more important for Answers in Genesis than winning the culture war (or, rather, winning the creation/evolution culture war is a means to the end of widespread evangelization).

I should also reiterate that my study of evangelical outreach should not be mistaken for an ethnographic study of evangelicalism or evangelicals per se. To the extent I can do so, I restrict my investigations to the *activism* (qua outreach) aspect of evangelicalism. Though evangelicals hold that outreach to the lost is commanded of all Christians, in practice few evangelicals engage in such activism regularly. For that reason, my case studies engage the work of a relatively elite selection of evangelicals, just as a study of left-progressive performance activism would deal with a select subset of theater artists. A spokesperson for Exodus International, for instance, will naturally have thought longer and more deeply about issues of sexuality in the church and in culture as a whole than the average evangelical. None of the specific practices, performances, or philosophies of outreach I study can stand without qualification for evangelicalism as a whole. Evangelicals disagree with other evangelicals over core evangelical values, including mission and witness to the world. The evangelicals who produce yearly "hell houses" may harbor deep reservations regarding Ray Comfort's Way of the Master school of outreach. Door-to-door "soul-winners" like Steven Anderson may think the entire ex-gay movement's efforts to convert homosexual people utterly ill-advised even as the latter group rebukes Anderson's anti-gay rhetoric as un-Christian.

Since my focus is so restricted—evangelical outreach, not evangelicalism in general—I leave relatively unaddressed vast swaths of present-day US evangelical life, belief, and practice. Struggles with ethnicity and race, for instance, command a growing percentage of evangelicalism's intellectual and spiritual energy. Certainly, many of the churches and groups I study include Latino/a, Black, and Asian American evangelicals, and some of the outreach movements I address (particularly urban megachurch seeker-sensitive worship services) make special efforts to target nonwhite populations. But, by and large, like evangelicalism overall, the groups I study are predominantly white—for now, at least. Demographic trends in US evangelicalism, mirroring trends in the US population overall, point to an increasingly non-majority white future for Christianity in the United States. I also follow the lead of most sociologists of religion in not including "the Black Church" within the generic evangelical category, even though many predominantly Black churches espouse evangelically consonant theologies and engage in outreach to the lost. I share the skepticism of critics who judge the "Black Church" label as overbroad and dismissive. Yet neither am I comfortable with a remedy that would lump historically black denominations into a Protestant subset whose own history includes a degree of ethnic exclusivity. Most evangelical churches and denominations are today critical of overt racism, and many churches are taking proactive steps to diversify racially. Yet, to their shame, many of the major evangelical denominations (particularly the Southern Baptist Church) inherit a legacy of under-engagement with or even overt resistance to racial justice movements of the civil rights era and beyond. Historically black denominations exist at least in part because of their having been effectively cast out of predominantly white denominations (and not just evangelical ones, of course). Only now, and only with a great deal of effort, are some of these denominations and churches working to rectify the lingering effects of such interracial violence. Books can be written—have been written, are being published—about such efforts and the histories behind them. Such an accounting, however, lies beyond the scope of my project here, though I hope that my work can contribute to future projects that explore interracial evangelical outreach efforts more specifically.

I also exclude from this study Christian evangelicalism as it manifests in the world beyond US borders. To be sure, such exclusion is both brutal and artificial. It is brutal because focusing on the United States means bracketing-off the vast majority of evangelicals currently living. It is artificial because within a globalized, mass-mediatized, hypertexted world, neat geographic boundaries segregating the United States from the world beyond increasingly exist only as quaint fantasies. I ignore for now the multiple interactions between US and non-US evangelicalisms, encounters in which churches, organizations, and individuals in Old Christendom (the United States and Western Europe) shape and are shaped by encounters with the relatively young Christianities of the two-thirds world. These interactions pose a different species of productive crisis for evangelicalism (and US evangelicalism specifically) than the existential one I address in this project. To wit: while US evangelicals fret about the survival of the evangelical Church in a secular age, for most other evangelicals the world over this is simply a laughable threat. If *secular* means "without faith," the world is light-years from any secularity. Global/glocal evangelicalism's question isn't *Will faith survive?* but *What is Christianity becoming?* and *How will Old and New worlds coexist?* To be sure, this crisis calls for a wide-ranging study of how such global/glocal evangelical questions manifest in outreach and encounter performances in the United States and abroad. This present book, however, is not that project. That being said, however, I cannot keep the global status of evangelicalism out of my conversation completely. Particularly in my later chapters, my examination of certain ostensibly US-based practices ends up confronting distinctly multicultural challenges.

For the present, however, I concentrate on how certain debates about evangelical outreach play out against the backdrop of a particularly US-based sense of existential crisis among evangelicals, a crisis I approach in terms of the secular age. My fascination with evangelical outreach relates to how evangelicals engaged in outreach so often display a clear-eyed assessment of the twin challenges of the secular age. First, they (and here I mean the specific evangelical groups and agents forming the focus of my study) recognize the necessity of confronting the fact that people believe very differently from themselves. Evangelicals have a technology of ideological alterity, by which I mean a relatively sophisticated (which is not necessarily the same as *accurate* or *effective*) means of imagining or characterizing differences of conviction in people. Evangelicals have a healthy sense of how deep differences run. The evangelicals I study recognize that differences of belief aren't simply the rational conclusions of dryly intellectual arguments but the results of fundamental sets of presuppositions about how the world works, presuppositions that actively resist assaults against them. Moreover, although evangelicals by and large believe non-evangelicals to be in error, I am impressed by how so many of them work to move beyond simplistic explanations for why such error persists. It's one thing, for example, to assert that humanity's sinful nature leads astray from the path to Christ; it's another to investigate how exactly that straying occurs and how it might be stopped or resisted.

Second, despite the depth of the differences that separate them from or oppose them to others, the evangelicals I study refuse either to leave those differences untouched or to see non-believers as mortal enemies to be eradicated. They believe deeply in the epistemological and ethical superiority of their own beliefs, and that belief prevents them from simply accepting or submitting to schemes of interaction that would force them to mute or marginalize those beliefs. They cannot regard beliefs as simply a private matter. In fact, their beliefs compel them to evangelize, to strive to convince others to adopt their beliefs. Yet they also recognize that whether or not their efforts succeed, whether or not a prospect converts, evangelicals cannot simply give up. They are called to persevere in witness, to keep trying, following the example set by God, who (in evangelical understandings) went to extraordinary lengths—incarnation, death, and resurrection—to reconcile God with humankind. Confronted with a culture increasingly shaped by calls for tolerance as an end unto itself, evangelicals insist on a degree of intolerant exclusivism. That is, they recognize and embrace the singular, normative dimension of the values that animate them. They know that their message will alienate them both from those who disagree and from those who would prefer not to be bothered. Yet they strive to make their exclusivist message, about how things ought to be, compelling and even popular. They want their version of the Truth to catch fire and spread, believing that (A) it is the command of God that they do so; and (B) that adopting the Truth will improve the lives of converts. In the chapters that follow I turn to close, good-faith readings of various evangelical modes of living out these convictions. I begin with perhaps the most widespread type of outreach: personal evangelism.

CHAPTER 3

Face to Face, Door to Door

Personal Evangelism and the Scandal of Salvation

A young man, mid- to late twenties, dressed in a suit and tie, climbs the porch steps to knock on the door. As the door opens, the man introduces himself: "Hi, I'm Steven Anderson; I pastor Faithful Word Baptist Church." Provided the person does not shut the door at that point, Anderson politely inquires whether the homeowner goes to church and, if so, where. Anderson briefly acknowledges the homeowner's answer before launching his key question: "Listen, more important than going to church, though, if you were to die today, are you one hundred percent sure you're going to heaven?" He pauses, poised to direct the conversation down any of several paths depending upon the response. On this occasion, the man in the doorway gives a relatively uncertain "Yeah, I think I'm going to heaven," which for Anderson's purposes might as well be "No, not at all." The homeowner now confirmed as unsaved—an evangelical *prospect*—Anderson pivots to his primary presentation: "OK, could I just take a couple of minutes to show you how you could know that one hundred percent, for sure?"[1]

In this chapter, I focus on the form of evangelistic outreach perhaps most stereotypically associated with evangelicals in the United States: the personal encounter, the one-on-one pitch, variously referred to as personal evangelism, witnessing, soul-winning, and missions work. For simplicity's sake, I will align these different modes under the single rubric of *kerygmatic* evangelism. In Christian thought, *kerygma* refers to preaching or proclaiming the core gospel: God came to earth as Jesus, lived a sinless life, died in place of sinful humanity, and rose bodily from the dead, acts that open the door for humans to be reconciled with God. The overtures I study here are kerygmatic in that they structure themselves around the more or less straightforward presentation of that narrative, trusting the power and import of that story (or, properly, the Holy Spirit's working through that story) to inspire a change in the prospects they approach. I would venture to guess that most people growing up in the United States, particularly in the Bible Belt, have been on the receiving end of some form of personal evangelism, whether announced by a knock on the door, a Bible tract pressed into the hand while strolling through the mall, a message bellowed through a bullhorn on a busy sidewalk, or even an intimate (perhaps unasked-for, perhaps even embarrassing) testimonial by a friend or personal acquaintance regarding their own salvation. A provocative, potentially offensive subtext threads through all of these: *You're wrong—badly, desperately mistaken—and I'm right. I have something you need, even if you don't realize you need it.*

As I have discussed, the audacity of such a statement intrigues me as a scholar. Still, I admit to a degree of irritation when I find myself the target of such evangelistic audacity in my non-research life. In part, I register unsolicited solicitations as yet one more quasi-commercial pitch, one more voice pestering me to invest in the latest commodity—in this case a commodity that often comes soaked in a political ideology (and theology) I find foreign, even offensive. *How dare you suggest my deepest, most personal convictions are (A) any of your business, and (B) disastrously wrong, even evil?* On a deeper level, though, my discomfort stems from a sympathetic embarrassment. For much of my childhood and youth, I *was* one of those earnest evangelists intruding on people's privacy to gently suggest that their most intimate beliefs are at fault. I can still picture my twelve-year-old self working up the courage to wrench a casual conversation with a friend or acquaintance away from neutral topics and toward matters spiritual—or, worse, approaching a complete stranger and asking how they think they'll spend eternity. I recall how uncomfortable I was, how fully I realized the violations of social norms and personal space I was committing. My research into kerygmatic evangelism indicates that my adolescent anxiety is commonplace among erstwhile evangelists. Books and curricula aimed at training believers in interpersonal evangelism focus considerable time on the theme of "overcoming fear," that is, working up the courage to ask complete strangers about the fate of their soul. Yet I also remember my nagging conviction that any personal uneasiness was a small price to pay for the chance to participate in the salvation of someone's eternal soul. If you're tackling someone about to walk off a cliff, fretting over bruises (your own or the other person's) seems small.

In this chapter, I examine three kerygmatic strategies of personal evangelism: the soul-winning door-to-door pitch represented by ministers like Anderson, the softer and more positive "witnessing" approach of the Campus Crusade for Christ (also known as "Cru"), and the confrontational street evangelism of Ray Comfort's Way of the Master technique. In studying these approaches I examine both recorded instances of the approaches in action as well as the considerable how-to manuals and instructional materials that unpack and justify the particular strategies and theologies underlying them. I devote most of my attention to analyzing the soul-winning, as its structure and assumptions form a basis upon which (or against which) the other approaches build and react. The usual caveats regarding scholarship on evangelicalism apply. None of the methods I study can be said to hold a monopoly within US evangelicalism, nor can I claim to provide a comprehensive accounting of extant evangelistic strategies. Neither, however, have I chosen marginal or obscure approaches. Soul-winning, witnessing, street evangelism, and conversational evangelism are, if not ubiquitous, at least familiar across a broad cross-section of the US evangelical spectrum. Each claims adherents who interact, overlap, and at times conflict. Comfort's Way of the Master, for example, bases itself largely on a critique of evangelistic techniques that begin with "God loves you and has a wonderful plan for your life" (i.e., the "First Spiritual Law" in Campus Crusade for Christ's signature pitch). Evangelistic approaches tend to be reactive, highlighting features—preferred tactics, theological emphases—that distinguish them from other strategies. Yet, true to the essentially contested dynamic of evangelicalism generally, these mutually reactive strategies persist alongside the counter-movements they inspire. Approaches multiply but rarely disappear altogether. Anderson's soul-winning strategies, for example, echo those of mid-century evangelists. Yet, even as some evangelists caution that such old-time religion techniques seem out-of-date, the soul-winning strain of personal evangelism continues alongside the latest evangelistic innovations from the Campus Crusade for Christ.

None of the techniques I cover here obviously resembles performances in traditional theatrical settings; most demand an interpersonal intimacy at odds with the shared spectatorship of a sizable audience. Yet of all the outreach methods I address in this book, the personal encounter most closely exhibits a straightforward, climactic dramaturgical structure. In his widely used textbook on play analysis, *Backwards and Forwards,* Daniel Ball characterizes (Western) drama in terms of stasis and intrusion. For Ball, a play's dramatic action takes off the moment a force or agent intrudes upon an otherwise static situation, disrupting stability and challenging other agents within the situation to react. The intrusion thus provokes a response, which in turn provokes a counter-response, which spurs yet another response, and so on. These reaction/counter-reaction ("trigger/heap" in Ball's terms) cycles continue until the intrusion is expelled or assimilated and a recuperated stasis (or a new stasis) installed.[2] Ball's stasis-intrusion-(new) stasis model basically echoes the core structure of the kerygmatic personal evangelism encounter.

Of course, most guides to personal evangelism warn against treating encounters as scripted lest the evangelist seem insincere or rehearsed. Even so, such guides also typically outline a step-by-step series of overtures and responses that operates as an open-ended script for intruding into (and hopefully transforming) someone's spiritual status quo from oriented toward sin or self or false gods to Christ-oriented. The intrusion scenario is essentially improvised; even the evangelistic approaches that use illustrative scripts (the Way of the Master, for instance) stress that in actual encounters evangelists must keep themselves open to a range of responses. But for the most part personal evangelism remains a highly structured improv, the evangelist's responses always geared to redirect the flow of the encounter back to unpacking the significance of the transformative intrusion. Training in personal evangelism highlights the need to maintain this through-line as well as tactics for redirection, with the evangelist always guiding prospects toward the climax of (ideally) conversion. The strategies I address here differ mainly in terms of how they manage the initial intrusion of the evangelistic encounter, how they navigate its aftermath, and how they imagine the end-point stasis toward which the encounter arcs. All of them, however, recognize fully their intrusiveness as such; they each acknowledge the fact that the imperative to witness puts Christians in an unusual position, one that might prove costly in terms of interpersonal regard or comfort levels.

Behind the problem of crafting just the right kind of evangelistic intrusion lies the question of just what the "right" kind of intrusion means. For most kerygmatic strategies, rightness encompasses two interrelated concerns. First, evangelists ask whether the technique in question is *biblical.* That is, can the evangelist demonstrate scriptural precedent for the conversational strategy being used? Second, evangelicals ask whether the strategy is *effective*. Does it produce results, that is, converts? Of course, for many evangelists the two criteria—biblical orthodoxy and practical efficacy—are so intertwined as to make no sense as distinct factors. In their view, the biblical mode of evangelism functions as the most effective one, and vice versa, both because the Bible's strategies for evangelism consist of examples from the most effective evangelists in history (i.e., Jesus and the apostles) and because God prefers to work through orthodox rather than heterodox methods.

Thus, most every technique of personal evangelism claims some degree of biblical grounding, even to the point of claiming plainly and neutrally to be "doing what the Bible says to do" or following "the Way of the Master." As is the case with missions in general, personal evangelism draws its authority from Jesus's final words to his followers in Matthew 28:19–20a (a command known as the "Great Commission"): "Therefore go and make disciples of all nations, baptizing them in the name of the Father and of the Son and of the Holy Spirit, and teaching them to obey everything I have commanded you." Nevertheless, the efficacy factor inevitably arises for evangelicals because the Bible never defines a singular correct method of how one should make disciples. Both the gospels and the epistles of the Christian Testament contain numerous and diverse examples of Jesus and his followers preaching to passersby on the streets (Acts 17), going out two-by-two to neighborhoods and towns (Mark 7:6), striking up conversations with strangers (John 4:1–26), and holding intimate, late-night dialogues (John 3:1–21)—to say nothing of instances where evangelism follows theophany (Christ appearing in transfigured glory before Saul on the Damascus road in Acts 9) or miracles (healings, exorcisms, etc.). At some point, then, evangelists must choose one among the many available scripts for staging an effective, transformative intrusion into another's spirituality.

Theological Performatives

But what exactly is this spiritual transformation? What is the new stasis that the drama of evangelism seeks to produce? Evangelicals peddle a complicated product. On the one hand, evangelical theology more or less uniformly promotes salvation as a gift. Protestant ministers of all stripes take pains to impress upon their audiences that heaven can't be earned or won through any human effort. Only God saves. But the command of the Great Commission is not to "facilitate salvation" but to "make disciples." And being a disciple, one whose life is lived under the discipline of wholesale orientation to Christ, bespeaks more than a one-time pledge. Salvation may be free, but discipleship involves work and sacrifice, fear and trembling, blood, sweat, and tears. Although not often discussed overtly as such, the salvation/discipleship distinction (theologically speaking, the relationship between *justification* and *sanctification*) haunts evangelical outreach efforts generally and personal evangelism strategies specifically. Is it possible for someone to be technically saved (i.e., they made an authentic commitment once) and not be a disciple (i.e., they have not lived up to that commitment)? Or, more cynically, can personal evangelism be described as effective or biblical if its climax creates salvation (i.e., *justification,* a transition from "hell-bound" to "heaven-bound") but not discipleship (i.e., *sanctification,* a life lived with Christ as ultimate concern)? Or does justification presuppose a degree of sanctification? Evangelicals differ on this question, both in terms of possible answers to it and in terms of the question's importance or legitimacy.

Most evangelical sectors, however, affirm the necessity of some kind of conversion experience, normally imagined as a discrete moment of transition from (at least) unsaved to saved. Whatever they may name this moment—*being saved, turning to Christ, giving your heart to Christ, surrendering your life to Christ, receiving Christ as Lord, accepting Christ as savior, believing on him,* and *trusting in him* are among the more popular phrases—evangelicals view authentic conversion as a transformative act of divine power. It is something God does, not something humans do. Human action prior to (and in some strands of evangelicalism subsequent to) conversion cannot hinder or strengthen the transformation itself. A vile, God-hating murderer who sincerely professes faith in Christ at the point of death is no less saved than the walked-down-the-aisle-at-age-six Christian who spends eighty years feeding the poor and hungry. Conversely, even the most ascetic saint, the most generous caregiver, or the most selfless hero is doomed to hell without a specific, intentional decision for Christ. The transformation that is salvation is a sine qua non of evangelical Christianity. More often than not, evangelicals view this transformation as occurring through a particular utterance: a formal, verbal statement of commitment or surrender, a profession of faith offered to God in prayer. Perhaps the most common such statement in personal evangelism is "the sinner's prayer," which might be described as the ideal denouement to the evangelistic drama in which the unsaved prospect explicitly converts. Countless variations on the prayer exist. Anderson recommends the following: "Dear Jesus, I know I'm a sinner. I know I deserve to go to hell, but I believe that you died on the cross for me and rose again. Please save me right now and give me eternal life. I'm only trusting you, Jesus, Amen."[3] The prayer synthesizes a number of complex theological actions, *confessing* one's sin and hellbound fate, *affirming* the core tenets of the Christian gospel, *exhorting* Christ to save, and *professing* a whole-self trust in Christ's saving power. For some evangelicals, these acts necessarily involve *repentance*—a turning *from* the previous state of non–trust/belief and *to* the trust/belief in Christ's saving power. Whether such repentance is implicit in authentic belief or explicit and separate from simple belief is a matter of contention between various evangelical sectors.[4]

Formally, most evangelicals would deny that any particular verbal recital is essential for salvation. The actions of confession, exhortation, belief, and so on, matter more than any literal words. But in practice, saying the words takes on a great deal of importance. In his study of hell houses, theater scholar Hank Willenbrink recalls a conversation with a hell house producer in which the producer, an evangelical, became concerned that Willenbrink claimed a Christian identity (Roman Catholic, in his case) yet denied ever having specifically uttered the words "I take Christ to be my personal Lord and Savior." Willenbrink's protestations that he had been baptized and confirmed in the (Catholic) Church proved unpersuasive to the hell house minister. *Had Willenbrink been saved? Had he literally uttered a formal profession of belief in Christ?* Only after Willenbrink assured him that in fact he does speak words to that effect in reciting the Nicene Creed at each Mass did the producer seem mollified. Struck by the evangelical insistence upon a particular act of profession, Willenbrink helpfully offers the idea of the "theological performative" to describe this utterance that performs the pivot from unsaved to saved.[5] Willenbrink uses *performative* in the tradition of J. L. Austin's speech act theory. For Austin, a speech act occurs when a statement, rather than merely referring to reality (a constative utterance), alters or creates reality by virtue of its being spoken (a performative utterance). The sentence "Kendra is a Christian" is constative. It refers to a reality (Kenda's Christianity), and the assertion may in theory be judged as accurate or inaccurate, true or false, by comparing it to this reality. Kendra's saying something like "I place my trust in Christ," on the other hand, is performative. Her utterance in the appropriate context performs her act of investing trust. Provided Kendra means what she says (i.e., that she is not joking, acting, or otherwise speaking ironically), she accomplishes the transition from unbeliever to believer by uttering those words or their equivalent. The key criterion of performative statements concerns not validity but efficacy, not *Is it true?* but *Does it work?* or *Is it effective?*

I use Willenbrink's notion as a useful term for the desired outcome of the kerygmatic evangelism scenario, albeit with a few qualifications. First, although speech act theory highlights the agency of the speaker situated within a speech context, evangelical theology generally de-emphasizes human agency in the working of salvation. The sinner's prayer is not a magic spell that creates salvation via the force of the proselyte's belief. At most, evangelicals view the theological performative as the speaker's opening her heart's door to Christ's knock. But it is Christ and Christ alone who knocks, enters, and reshapes the home He finds. That humans hear a knock at all, that they experience the option of opening a door to Christ—these are gifts of grace from the Holy Spirit, whose power enables any evangelistic endeavor to succeed at all. Insofar as believers participate in their salvation, it is only to the extent that a drowning person reaches out and clings to a life preserver thrown out to her (and even here some evangelicals would protest that this illustration grants too much agency to humans).

Second, evangelicalism would take issue with speech act theory's logocentrism. Though many evangelical sectors promote particular prayers or formulaic sayings that articulate the core tenets of belief, they also stress that the words of the profession have no inherent power. One may in fact be saved entirely without words (confessing belief internally or privately, for example). *Repentant belief,* not words, is the hallmark of salvation, though anyone who is saved ought to be able freely to profess their belief explicitly.[6]

Finally, in contrast to poststructuralist theorists like Jacques Derrida or Judith Butler, evangelicals would insist that the force or authority of the theological performative derives not from networked chains of performative citations but from a single source: God. Without God's power infusing, animating, and responding to a sinner's prayer, even the most sincere entreaty or profession of faith is mere noise. Of course, as Willenbrink points out, sociologists of religion might observe that a sinner's prayer enacts a number of performative effects quite apart from any theological reality. Conversion might initiate, for example, a formal personal alignment with another worldview, an alignment that may produce real reactions from the speaker's immediate social circumstances (family members who recoil in horror, church members who rejoice, etc.).

Without denying the importance of such nonspiritual effects, I largely bracket a consideration of those sociological functions here, focusing instead on the theological transformation that evangelicals desire conversion to realize.

Soul-Winning with Steven Anderson

The pastor in my opening paragraph, Steven Anderson, exemplifies the first kerygmatic approach I examine, soul-winning. Broadly speaking, soul-winning describes a dedicated missions activity organized and supervised by a local church in which members go in pairs or small groups out at a particular time to a particular place, such as a neighborhood, an apartment complex, or a residential section of town. There the soul-winning pairs move door-to-door, knocking, inquiring, and if possible taking the people they meet through the steps of salvation. Members of Anderson's small congregation, Faithful Word Baptist Church in Tempe, Arizona, plan and track their soul-winning activities via a large map posted on their sanctuary wall that illustrates where they have been and where they have yet to go. They follow a systematic plan for canvassing their local households with door-to-door encounters. Apart from worship services and Bible studies, soul-winning functions as the central congregational activity of Faithful Word. On any given day of the week, at least some members are knocking on doors, working systematically through the map of Tempe/Phoenix over and over again, holding some version of the conversation I referenced at the beginning of the chapter.[7] Anderson even offers classes in Spanish and German (both of which he himself speaks) to his parishioners so that members can reach out to non-English-speaking populations in the area.

Soul-winning also bespeaks a particular mode of navigating the intrusion and aftermath of the one-on-one evangelistic encounter. A "just the facts, ma'am" approach, soul-winning strips the encounter down to a simple, more or less formulaic pitch. After a brief introduction ("Hi, I'm Steven Anderson . . .") the evangelist poses a simple icebreaking question ("Do you go to church?") before advancing directly to the key inquiry ("If you were to die tonight, are you completely sure you would go to heaven?"). From there, soul-winning initiates a form of theological diagnostic, probing the prospect to detect any issues regarding the prospect's salvation and underlying beliefs. Should this diagnostic determine unsaved status, the evangelist leads the prospect through the core evangelical doctrines of sin, hell, Christ, and salvation through a series of Bible passages, each buttressed by explanation. All of this culminates in the evangelist's posing a stark decision to the prospect for or against committed belief in Christ as savior and Lord. Ideally (from the soul-winner's point of view), the encounter concludes with the prospect making a formal commitment to Christ (a theological performative).

Though many Christians engage in personal evangelism, "soul-winning" tends to bespeak a particular subset of evangelical tradition; it carries the connotation of quaint, old-time religion hearkening back to backwoods revival preachers and big-tent evangelists. Here the aim involves salvation, pure and simple: leading people to the point of professing faith in Christ. It often implies a conservative theology. Such is the case with Anderson, who identifies as an Independent Fundamental Baptist (IFB).[8] Less a formal denomination than a loose affiliation of like-minded congregations, the IFB's theological stances position it solidly in the fundamentalist end of the evangelical spectrum. As is the case with most evangelicals, Anderson basically affirms a Christ-centered, cross-centered, Bible-centered, outreach-centered theology. He reveres the Bible as the inerrant, infallible Word of God, meant to be taken more or less in its plain (English) sense. Unlike most evangelicals, however, Anderson holds that only the King James Version (KJV) of the Bible from 1611 (the version with *thee* and *thou* prose) preserves the unadulterated Word in English.[9]

Even by fundamentalist evangelical standards, Anderson espouses extremely conservative social views, especially regarding gender and sexuality. For instance, Anderson regularly preaches that homosexuals ("queers," as he calls them) are not merely sinners or sexual addicts; they are reprobate, sociopathic rapists who ought to be executed by the government, like Leviticus commands.[10] Men ought to keep their hair short, women ought to wear only dresses, and children ought to be homeschooled and constantly monitored by parents until marriage. Anderson won minor media notoriety in 2009 with a sermon in which he declared that he prays that God would kill Barack Obama. "Break his teeth, O Lord," he preached, here quoting Psalm 58:6 (one of the "imprecatory Psalms" in which the speaker calls on God to curse his enemies).[11] Other evangelicals have roundly condemned his anti-Obama rhetoric.[12]

Despite his extreme fundamentalism, I include Anderson in this study because of the centrality of evangelism to his ministry and theology, a centrality that distinguishes his fundamentalism from that of other, more totally separatist systems. To Anderson, Christianity concerns salvation above all. That is, the answer to the question he poses at the start of his soul-winning pitch—*If you died tonight, are you completely sure you'd go to heaven?*—outweighs every other consideration or criterion of belief and action. This is not to say that fundamentalist beliefs about the Bible, culture, and gender roles do not matter. In Anderson's view, any authentic Christian will affirm similarly strict, KJV-only beliefs as he does, and his sermons regularly and vociferously castigate those who stray from this straight and narrow path (i.e., other Christians and churches, especially those claiming to be Baptists). But these concerns exist separately from and subsidiary to the core issue of salvation. Belief in the primacy of the King James Version, in the reprobate status of homosexuals, or in the patriarchal structure of the heterosexual family—none of these by itself or in combination establishes salvation. People can believe in all of these things technically and still find themselves burning in hell after death.

The attribute that matters for Anderson (and for the soul-winning tradition in general) is belief on Jesus as savior and Lord.[13] The latter bespeaks a combination of *conviction* regarding the authenticity of Christ's divinity, earthly life, death, and resurrection and *trust* invested in the efficacy of Christ's work to forgive and save sinners from Hell, a combination generally articulated through a profession of faith. Though not all soul-winners so quibble over prepositions, the underlying distinction between purely rational knowledge that does not save and transformative, convicted trust/dedication that does holds across most of evangelicalism. Orthodox lifestyles flow from convicted, trusting commitment to the Savior Jesus. But the lifestyle itself does not save. Good works, regular churchgoing, and a pious attitude—all of these should flow from being saved, but they themselves do not save. Only the commitment of belief—the act of "being saved" by Christ—makes someone Christian.

Anderson, while fiercely intolerant of human wickedness, suspends this intolerance in the service of sharing the gospel with unbelievers. For him, the Christian's prime duty involves spreading the gospel through soul-winning and not through public condemnations or right-wing political action. And for Anderson, soul-winning requires that he present a persona quite distinct from his pulpit persona. In the pulpit, Anderson regularly launches vehement attacks on groups or individuals he views as ungodly—the better to train his flock of mature Christians. But all of this rhetoric disappears in his encounters with evangelistic prospects. There, he is not teaching Christians but evangelizing the lost. For this reason, his demeanor is calm, personable, and friendly—a sharp contrast to his pulpit persona, which can be vicious, sarcastic, and hectoring.

To the uninitiated, Anderson the soul-winner, Anderson on your doorstep, Anderson giving you the gospel—none of these seem particularly "fundamentalist," intolerant, or offensive. Anderson intends this effect. "You're there [on doorsteps] because you love them," he explains in a sermon on soul-winning, "so you ought to be nice and kind."[14] The goal is winning souls, not replicating Fundamentalist Baptist beliefs.

Soul-Winning from Diagnosis to Conversion

The doorway scenario I related earlier comes from a YouTube video Anderson provides, "Basic Soul-Winning Demonstration Video," in which he reenacts a typical door-to-door visit. In addition to this video demonstration, I will draw on the podcast of a sermon of Anderson's, "Soul-winning Training."[15] Complementing these sources, I consult two soul-winning guides that represent the broader theological tradition of soul-winning that Anderson participates in. As is the case with many evangelical pastors, pinpointing the theological heritage informing Anderson's methods proves difficult. In contrast to more connectional denominations, the IFB has no official procedure for training its ministers (beyond general guidelines, e.g., males only). Pastors may have little or no formal education in theology or biblical history, relying largely on a lifetime's worth of indoctrination in a more or less distinctively "Baptist" culture of biblicism to define and unify their hermeneutics and doctrines. In several sermons, Anderson refers to his time at Hyles-Anderson Bible College, a small Independent Baptist institute founded by IFB pastor Jack Hyles.[16] Hyles-Anderson espouses roughly similar views to Anderson's (e.g., KJV-only-ism, strictly defined gender roles). Like Anderson, the college insists on its students' adopting a regular practice of systematic soul-winning in the surrounding communities.[17] Although Anderson now distances himself from Hyles-Anderson (Bible colleges being as unbiblical and corrupting, ultimately, as any other college experience),[18] his own ministry echoes the college's strong soul-winning focus as well as many of Hyles's own recommendations for soul-winning.

Hyles rose to prominence during the mid-twentieth century explosion of evangelistic activity and literature in the United States. This explosion produced a small library of how-to manuals on soul-winning, including one by Hyles himself.[19] Among the more striking of these is a 1959 booklet by evangelist C. S. Lovett, *Soul-Winning Made Easy (The Encounter Method)*.[20] A painstaking, step-by-step explication of the soul-winning pitch (complete with illustrative photographs), Lovett's book underlines the dramaturgical aspects of the soul-winning encounter. Though they date from nearly half a century prior to Anderson's ministry, Hyles's and Lovett's guides outline and expound upon the same basic soul-winning approach Anderson himself uses. I use them as bolsters to an explication of Anderson's own technique.

Winning a clear decision, argues Lovett, depends upon the evangelist's ability to control the evangelical conversation. Lovett insists upon—and Anderson exemplifies—the importance of establishing and maintaining a driving momentum, dispensing with chitchat in order to get right to the point. In the soul-winning tradition, most introductions are brief. The soul-winner does not typically pretend to be anything other than an evangelist. Anderson, for instance, starts with a straightforward identification of himself as representing a local church in the soul-winning demonstration video. In his own how-to-soul-win guide, Hyles emphasizes that soul-winners on visitation must be neat, clean, amiable, and complimentary.[21] If going two-by-two (which Hyles and Anderson both recommend), only one does the talking; the other essentially runs interference and offers silent, prayerful support.[22]

Inevitably, the evangelist pivots from introduction to diagnosis: Is the prospect saved? Here the soul-winner faces a dilemma similar to that of the sociologists trying to determine the number of evangelicals. Most evangelists realize that a bald-faced question along the lines of "Are you a Christian?" will likely fail to elicit useful information.[23] Prospects may mutter "yes" out of guilt or a desire to get rid of the questioner. Or they may think of themselves as Christian due to their having been raised in a Christian family or by virtue of their occasional church attendance. Soul-winners are less interested in whether the person considers him- or herself Christian and more interested in whether or not the person is actually saved. Hyles, in fact, counsels soul-winners to seek out ways to "get them [prospects] lost"; that is, turn the conversation as soon as possible to the exploration of the fate of their eternal soul.[24] Soul-winners presume, in other words, that prospects need to hear the gospel. The possibility that prospects are already believers is rarely acknowledged, and even then the assumption is that any authentic believer will welcome the chance to review the basics of conversion. The classical diagnostic question is something along the lines of "If you were to die now, are you completely sure you'd go to heaven?" Any hint of uncertainty on the prospects' part—*I hope so, I think so, I guess so*—signals the need for the soul-winner to launch the pitch. Even the "right" answer to this diagnostic question ("Yes, I'm absolutely sure") merely obliges the soul-winner to follow up with an orthodoxy check ("Could you tell me *how* you know?") followed if necessary by a gentle correction ("Could I take some time to show you what the *Bible* says about being saved?"). Lovett recommends that the orthodoxy diagnostic be followed by asking prospects' permission to continue with the "right" answer to the questions: "Could I share with you . . . ?" With this permission thus granted, the soul-winner begins the formal pitch.

In the soul-winning tradition, the structure of the evangelistic pitch centers on the Bible. Specifically, the evangelist walks the prospect through a series of specially selected verses, pausing to emphasize the significance of each one before moving on to the next. Different strategies recommend different verses (for example, "the Roman Road" strategy uses a series of verses taken entirely from Romans). Regardless of the exact texts chosen, the mini-Bible lesson always addresses a few key areas: humanity's sin, the consequences of sin, the redeeming work of Christ, and the assurance of salvation.

First, the evangelist has to establish the sinful state of all humans, generally through a verse such as Romans 3:23 ("For all have sinned, and come short of the glory of God") or Romans 3:10 ("There is none righteous, no, not one"). Here a soul-winner might follow this broad statement with a miniature exercise to prove to prospects that this description of the *all* and the *no one* includes the prospects themselves. The exercise draws on some of the Ten Commandments to pose questions such as "Have you ever told a lie?" or "Have you ever stolen anything?" To the prospects' inevitable affirmative (*yes, I've told a lie*), the soul-winner lightly asks if this lie doesn't in fact make them a liar. ("How many lies do you have to tell before you become a liar?" asks Anderson in the video). Stealing, similarly, makes one a thief. Adultery and murder are also popular tests, as soul-winners can quote Matthew 5:28 to establish that looking on a woman "to lust after her" equals committing adultery, and hating your brother equates to murder (1 John 3:15). The tone here isn't one of holier-than-thou judgement. The innocent, question-and-answer format—*Isn't it the case that . . . ?*—shifts the agency of judgement to the prospect rather than the soul-winner. The soul-winner further blunts the sharp edge of judgement by averring that they, too, are imperfect sinners. Everyone is.

With prospects thus (ostensibly) convinced of their sinful status, the soul-winner's next step involves establishing consequences of sin: an eternity in hell. Soul-winners have a plethora of verses at their disposal to explain the punishment for sin. Common choices include "The wages of sin is death" (Romans 6:23a); "But it is appointed unto man once to die, but after this the judgment" (Hebrews 9:27); or "And death and hell were cast into the lake of fire. This is the second death. And whosoever was not found written in the book of life was cast into the lake of fire" (Revelation 20:14–15). "But," soul-winners insist, "God loves you and does not want you to burn in hell. He provides a way out." At this point the soul-winner deploys verses like John 3:16 ("For God so loved the world that He gave His only begotten son that whosoever believeth in him shall not perish but have everlasting life"); Romans 6:23b (". . . but the gift of God is eternal life through Jesus Christ our Lord"); or Romans 5:8 ("But God commendeth his love toward us, in that, while we were yet sinners, Christ died for us"). Here Anderson pauses to review the essentials of the Christ story. Jesus Christ, son of God, born of a virgin, lived a sinless life and was arrested, beaten, and crucified. Anderson explains:

> Well, when he was nailed to the cross, the Bible says that he would bear our own sins on his body on the tree. Every sin you've ever done. Every sin I've ever done. When Jesus was on the cross, it was as if he had done it. So he was being punished for murder, for stealing, for lying. He never sinned, but he bore our sins on his own body. They took his body, buried it in a tomb. [His] soul went down to hell for three days and three nights. What happened three days later? ["He rose again," answers the prospect] He rose again.[25]

As any first-year seminary student would recognize, Anderson's summary glosses over several semesters' worth of theological thought and debate regarding the dynamics of salvation (let alone redemption, salvation, propitiation, justification, sanctification, and atonement). Yet, for the most part, soul-winners like Anderson steer clear of theological jargon. Nor do soul-winners so much as nod to the centuries-long, marvelously complex discourse about the meaning and import of the Christ event that continues to play out within Christendom. Debate regarding salvation and belief effectively does not exist. Instead, the soul-winner pares the Christian story down to a simple, cause-and-effect narrative presented in down-to-earth, there-it-is-right-there-in-front-of-you terms.

From here, soul-winning centers the locus of dramatic agency on the prospect. Though Christ died for everyone, Anderson cautions, not everyone is going to heaven. What is the difference, he asks, between those who live eternally in heaven and those who burn forever in hell?

John 3:18 provides his answer: "He that believeth on him [Jesus] is not condemned: but he that believeth not is condemned already, because he hath not believed in the name of the only begotten Son of God." Belief, Anderson stresses, is all that is required to receive the gift of eternal life from God. Anderson then expands on the idea of salvation as a gift, emphasizing that, once granted and received, the gift of salvation through belief on Christ is non-rescindable. But just as the gift is not won through human effort, neither is it imposed by divine fiat or acquired automatically. One must consciously, freely, decide to believe.

Thus the soul-winner reviews the steps so far with a question-and-answer series that doubles as a quasi-profession of faith: *Do you believe you've sinned? Do you believe that if God were to judge you right now you'd be condemned to hell?* Again, the soul-winner reinforces the biblical basis for every point, every conclusion. "According to what I showed you here in the Bible," Anderson asks in his demonstration video, "if you were to ask Jesus to save you right now, would he do it?" With this summary, the soul-winner sets the climactic scene of the evangelistic encounter: Christ (God in human form) who suffered and died out of love for humanity desires to spend eternity with you—but God withholds, waiting upon the belief of the person. You're a sinner, doomed for Hell, but Christ died to make you right with God. He will save if asked, and *he's asking right now.* Here soul-winning guides often suggest quoting Revelation 3:20: "Behold, I stand at the door, and knock: if any man hear my voice, and open the door, I will come in to him, and will sup with him, and he with me." Lovett recommends personalizing this scenario: *If a friend were knocking on your door and asking to come in, what would you say?* Lovett notes that the prospect's almost automatic answer—"Come in"—"prepares him to utter the same words to the Lord."[26] All that remains is to pose the question to the prospect as such: *Will you let God in? Will you ask Christ to save you?*

Should the prospect indicate openness, the soul-winner initiates a two-person prayer. "Let's pray together," Anderson suggests (preferring this to "Can I pray with you?"), and then, assuming an attitude of prayer (bowing his head, straightening his shoulders, closing his eyes), he launches directly into a "repeat after me" prayer—the sinner's prayer, in fact. Should the prospect resist the pressure to pray with a flat-out refusal at this point ("No, I don't want to pray with you"), Lovett recommends, first, complimenting the prospect for being honest. Then his script has the soul-winner re-frame the dramatic scene one more time. "Now I didn't ask to come into your heart, did I?" Lovett's evangelist asks.

"Then you're not refusing ME, are you? . . . You are actually refusing the gift of Eternal Life. When you refuse to let Christ come into your heart, you are refusing the gift. That's clear to you, isn't it?"[27] At that point, the soul-winner still relates what prospects *could* pray ("You don't need me around to do it") should they decide to become saved. After that, the encounter ends with the person's fate in God's hands.

Soul-winning instruction guides, however, tend to present such refusals as the exception rather than the rule. "If you've done everything right up to this point," Anderson explains, "99% of people are going to pray with you. You may not be doing a thorough enough job if you're not getting that percentage. If you really present it, usually they're thrilled to be saved." Lovett and Hyles similarly recommend a soul-winner-led prayer that gently but firmly pushes prospects into responsiveness. Lovett's technique emphasizes the "terrific psychological pressure" that the soul-winner's actions and words can have in pressing for a prayerful response:

> Lay your hand firmly on the subject's shoulder (or arm) and with a semi-commanding tone of voice, say to him: "Bow your head with me." Do not look at him when you say this, but bow your head first. Out of the corner of your eye you will see him hesitate at first. Then, as his resistance crumbles, his head will come down. Your hand on his shoulder will feel the relaxation and you will know when his heart yields.[28]

As noted, the prayer enacts the theological performative of conversion, professing belief in the core doctrines of the gospel (human sin, hell, and Christ's salvific intervention) and entreating Christ to save. Though Hyles recommends letting prospects create their own prayers, soul-winning generally counsels an "I say/you repeat" sinner's prayer delivered bit by bit.

Assuming that the prospect follows the soul-winner's lead, all that remains is the denouement, a quick check-in to ensure that the performative was accomplished properly. "You meant that, didn't you?" Anderson recommends asking, following this with a review of the gospel basics (e.g., *You understand that you're saved now, right? That your salvation can never be taken away?*).[29] Hyles suggests a follow-up prayer that emphasizes the assurance that Christ has responded to the prospect's entreaty.[30] The encounter concludes with an invitation to the local church and a polite farewell. And then it's on to the next door.

The Gospel as Central Player

Let me resurface momentarily from the deep dive into the soul-winning process to take a quick breath and re-orient on the activist model at work here. Soul-winning operates from the assumption that the kinds of transformations it desires unfold through live, interpersonal encounters with individuals, an assumption not that alien to secular activist performers. Soul-winning departs, however, from non-evangelical activism in that its performances focus purely on the transmission of information, the straightforward, point-by-point narrative of How Things Really Are. The plain presentation of the gospel message takes priority over all other considerations and must repeat itself in more or less the same fashion regardless of context. In a way, the gospel—not the soul-winner or the prospect—is the main focus. For most soul-winners, a physical Bible functions as a crucial tool in making the pitch. Soul-winners do not merely preach at prospects; they incorporate the prospect into a two-person mini-Bible study. Most of the action in soul-winning encounters consists of locating and reading scripture out of the soul-winner's Bible. Lovett recommends using a pocket-sized New Testament (King James) with signature verses tabbed and underlined in red. "With these," Lovett writes, "you can swiftly turn to your references with a single motion of the hand." Such dexterity proves essential, he argues. "Sometimes a delay in seeking a verse allows Satan to get in a question that will throw you off the target. Your plan and the turning of the pages of the Testament should move with clock-like precision."[31] Hyles likewise recommends a small New Testament, reasoning that a larger Bible might prove intimidating to prospects.[32] He suggests drawing a "map" of scriptures to be used in the testament to assist in turning from one to the next.[33] In his video, Anderson uses his own, complete KJV Bible, flipping to each verse in turn as necessary.

Like Hyles and Lovett, Anderson has his prospect read verses with him, following up with simple questions that reinforce vital points. "'For the wages of sin is death,'" reads Anderson, pointing to the verse (Romans 6:23) so that the prospect can see. "So what's God's punishment for sin?" he asks. "Death," the prospect responds obediently. In theatrical terms, the soul-winner casts the prospect into a line-reading role. No passive audience member, the prospect becomes a fellow Bible reader who discovers the (plain, clear) answer to (straightforward) theological questions along with the evangelist. While sharing verses of scripture, Lovett advises soul-winners to move side by side with the prospect, holding the

". . . I'D LIKE TO READ YOU 4 VERSES AND EXPLAIN . . ."

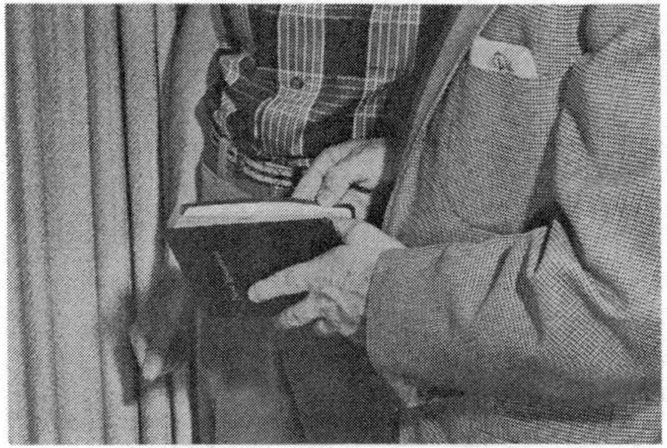

TABS LOCATE THE REFERENCE INSTANTLY

AT THE RIGHT MOMENT YOUR TESTAMENT IS QUICKLY PRODUCED FROM ITS PLACE OF CONCEALMENT.

YOUR TESTAMENT HELD IN FRONT OF THE SUBJECT CONFRONTS HIM WITH GOD'S WORD.

Instructions on using the Bible from Lovett's *Soul-Winning Made Easy (The Encounter Method)* (Baldwin Park, CA: Personal Christianity, 1959), 31–32. Reproduction permission thanks to C. S. Lovett Books.

"NOW LISTEN CAREFULLY FOR THIS IS THE LORD SPEAKING . . ."

"THAT DOOR IS THE DOOR OF YOUR HEART"

Closing the deal, from Lovett's *Soul-Winning Made Easy (The Encounter Method)* (Baldwin Park, CA: Personal Christianity, 1959), 43. Reproduction permission thanks to C. S. Lovett Books.

Bible in front of the both of them. "This suggests," he explains, "that the discussion is between [the prospect] and God and removes you from the scene."[34] Anderson's soul-winning video demonstrates a similar blocking pattern, his Bible held out in front of the prospect, confronting the prospect not with himself but with the (plain, perspicacious, authoritative) Word.

Lovett and Anderson both use their Bibles as props to illustrate particular doctrinal points. Explaining the concept of Christ's sacrifice as a gift, Anderson closes his Bible:

> If I said, "Dave, I'm going to give you this Bible as a gift. Now you give me five dollars." Is that a gift? What if I said, "Dave, I'm going to give it to you for free, but I need to you to go wash my car"? If you have to do any work for it, it's not a gift. But if I just gave the Bible to you [*hands Dave his Bible*]. Whose Bible is that now? It's yours. Can I come back any time that I want and just take it away from you? [*Dave shakes his head*] What if I come back a few months from now and you've done something really wrong to me. Could I just come back like this [*takes Bible back*] and take it away? That would make me what?—a thief and a liar![35]

Lovett, who recommends a comparable bit of Bible blocking for that doctrinal point, suggests reinforcing other points with the physical Bible, such as tapping on the Bible when talking about Christ's knock on the prospect's heart's door.[36]

As central a part as the Bible plays in the scenario, soul-winning tends to avoid what many might consider the most obvious objection to soul-winning tactics: skepticism regarding biblical authority. The soul-winning scenario depends upon the prospect's going along with the soul-winner's question-and-answer dialogue, verse-by-verse exposition, and point-to-point logic (e.g., one lie makes you a liar, any sin condemns you to hell, repentant belief saves). Almost inevitably, soul-winning instructions advise evangelists to avoid getting drawn into debates about biblical authority or complex theology. Confronted with a question about the morality of God in the face of disasters, for instance, soul-winning guides advise either gentle deflection or outright evasion. Anderson warns his congregation to avoid "foolish questions and contentions." When someone asks him, for example, "Who was Cain's wife?" or "What do you think of the nation of Israel right now in the news?" Anderson demurs. "Let's get back to that," he suggests that soul-winners say. "Let me finish up what

I'm saying here because I don't want to lose my train of thought." Usually, Anderson explains, prospects will go "Oh, OK," allowing the soul-winner to continue. "By the time you're done getting that person saved," he concludes, "they've forgotten all about their question."[37] Hyles advises a similar line: "That's a good question, and I will tell you what we will do. I'll make a note of it and we will discuss it when we get through."[38] Lovett takes an even stronger position, insisting, "Regardless of the charge a person makes against the Word—IGNORE IT AS THOUGH IT HAD NOT BEEN UTTERED."[39]

Soul-winning's reluctance to engage skepticism seems at first to confirm the stereotype of fundamentalist evangelicals as blinkered anti-intellectuals plugging their ears at the first sign of critical questioning. Without defending Lovett's "just ignore it" or Anderson's "just hope they forget about it" tactics, though, I point out that soul-winners ground these responses in rationales entirely unrelated to intellectual cowardice. Soul-winners avoid engaging in detailed debates, first, because they generally see soul-winning as a distinct endeavor from apologetics (reasoned defense of the faith) or theodicy (a specific defense of God's benevolence in the face of evil). Soul-winners are in the business of sharing the gospel to save people from hell—full stop. Their focus is the gospel story as laid out in the Bible, not on their own rhetorical powers or theological acumen. Questions about this or that minor doctrinal point, warns Lovett, present an all-too-tempting opportunity "to show off how much you know," upstaging the gospel with the soul-winner's own expertise.[40]

Second, soul-winners approach their task fully aware that some people they encounter will simply not be open to that gospel. They might be bitter about Christianity or religion in general, or they might profess belief in a wholly different set of beliefs. Lovett counsels soul-winners to be attentive to the distinction between *reluctance* and *resentment* in their prospects. Reluctance—reluctance to accept that one is a sinner, for instance—can be gently overcome; resentment, however, bespeaks a completely closed mind. In such a case, Lovett recommends stopping the soul-winning presentation, giving a sincere compliment, and ending the encounter.[41] For Anderson, such dead-end conversations include engagements with militant members of what he refers to as "cults"—faiths like Jehovah's Witnesses, Roman Catholics, and Mormons (he also includes Pentecostals) that teach very different doctrines from that of the IFB. At issue, Anderson specifies, isn't whether the soul-winner might lose a theological grudge match with a "cult" member but that the argument detracts from the task at hand:

> You know that if you want to argue doctrine with these people, you're going to eat their lunch, right? Because you've got the truth. But wait a minute. It's unprofitable. It's vain. And a lot of times you can eat up forty-five minutes or an hour like that going back and forth with one of these cult members, one of these members of a false religion. And all the while there's somebody down the street who wants to hear the gospel, that would have gotten saved and would have listened to you. And you're spinning your wheels with someone who's not going to get saved.[42]

At most, Anderson argues, soul-winners should make two solid attempts to break through such deep resistance with Bible verses. After that, they are to give a pleasant "Have a nice day" and be off. Arguments with such members distract from the soul-winning mission and create negative feelings.[43] Anderson does not preclude debates or engagements with "cults," but in general such activities fall beyond the bounds of soul-winning. "Winning an argument does not equal getting someone saved," he argues.

Beyond the pragmatic reasons for avoiding debates or defenses of theology, the soul-winning approach's reticence stems from a strong version of evangelical biblicism. This biblicism rests on a particular notion of what *reading* or *interpreting* the Bible as a text involves. The Bible is not merely a book of propositional truths to be affirmed or disconfirmed, proven or disproven. It is the *living* Word of God, an active circuit charged with the Holy Spirit's dynamic power. To read the Bible—particularly the gospel message—is to tap into that power, exposing oneself to the divine current. Evangelicals commonly cite Isaiah 55:11, "So shall my word be that goeth forth out of my mouth: it shall not return unto me void, but it shall accomplish that which I please, and it shall prosper in the thing whereto I sent it." For many evangelicals, the idea of God's word never returning void means that the gospel possesses an agency entirely separate from that of the evangelist. Evangelism's transformative potential flows not from the charisma of the soul-winner but from the wellspring of power that is God's Word. God can work through even an inept or insincere presentation of the gospel. In soul-winning, the evangelist just gets out of the way, figuratively and literally, to confront prospects with the living God present in and through the Bible.

Such biblicism grounds Lovett's vociferous insistence that evangelists resist the temptation to defend scripture against prospects' incredulity. In a startling analogy, Lovett presents a staged photograph of a masked intruder confronted with a homeowner holding a gun. He explains:

> If an intruder attempted to enter your home you might protect your family with a gun. You would not say to him though, "This is a Colt .45, it holds six bullets and when I squeeze the trigger a process of combustion takes place and discharges a lead pellet from the barrel which will lodge in your abdomen and kill you!" NO—you wouldn't defend or explain your gun—you would use it. Weapons are not defended, they are used.[44]

In a time where strong religious belief often gets linked to violence, Lovett's firearms illustration conjures the most frightening stereotypes of faith-based militancy, suggesting perhaps that anyone who questions the Bible equals a home intruder deserving of being shot. This is of course not Lovett's point. His metaphor focuses not on the challenger's character but on the weapon's efficacy. He takes pains to emphasize that those who challenge a soul-winner's presentation are challenging not the evangelist but the Holy Spirit. "He [the Holy Spirit] is continually affirming the truth to their hearts even as you speak," Lovett advises. "The fact that men refuse to acknowledge the Bible does not reduce its effectiveness. It remains forever, 'Sharper than any two-edged sword,' [Hebrews 4:12] and it is the voice of God speaking to men's hearts whether they like it or not."[45]

Thus is soul-winning as promulgated by Lovett, Hyles, and Anderson perhaps the most purely kerygmatic mode of outreach I cover in this book. For them, the task of witnessing consists entirely of staging what they see as the central biblical story. They incorporate prospects into that staging through body position, interactive dialogue, and physical action. And they conclude with a climactic scene in which the prospect feels fully the weight of the decision before them: accept the Divine Story (manifested literally in the physical Bible in front of them) or reject it with full awareness of the consequences. This is bare-bones activist performance: a simple message, strongly presented, with no conversational window dressing. Yet it is also very close to a rote sales pitch for goods or services. Despite his protestations to the contrary, Anderson does in some ways resemble the classic image of a door-to-door salesman running through the same routine no matter what greets him at the door. For Anderson and other soul-winners, the pitch carries an undertone of threat. His "product" isn't (or isn't merely) the latest innovation in home cleaning or kitchenware; it's the rescue from an eternity of torment—a hard sell indeed.

Campus Crusade and God's Wonderful Plan

The soul-winning encounter sets the basic pattern of most personal evangelism pitches. For many Christians, however, the classic soul-winning model's intrusive bluntness and whiff of brimstone proves off-putting. I turn now to one of the most widespread variations on the soul-winning pitch, the Four Spiritual Laws approach promulgated by the Campus Crusade for Christ (CCC), a parachurch organization founded in 1951 by Bill and Vonette Bright.[46] Bill Bright was an Oklahoma native, a salesman and would-be radio performer who while living in Hollywood in the late 1940s came under the influence of evangelist Henrietta Mears. Mears's teachings convinced Bright to re-invest in his childhood faith and commit himself wholly to Christian ministry.[47] Mears also steered him toward ministry on college campuses, a focus that only became stronger in conjunction with the growing Cold War mentality of the 1950s. Bright operated from the twin conviction that secular colleges served as a hotbed of anti-Christian, pro-communist recruitment and that a strong Christian (read: evangelical Protestant) presence on those campuses could counter that influence. By converting souls and creating disciples in universities through his Crusade, Bright sought "to win the campus today and change the world tomorrow."[48] Although the anti-communist subtext faded as the Cold War ended, CCC's evangelistic emphasis—sometimes but not always associated with elements of the political Christian Right—has remained constant. Today, the CCC—recently renamed "Cru"—describes itself as an organization dedicated to sharing the gospel and creating laborers for Christ.[49] Alongside organizations such as the Inter-Varsity Fellowship (IVF) and the Fellowship of Christian Athletes (FCA), the Cru has become a common evangelical fixture on university and college campuses, with branches at over a thousand schools.[50] Today, roughly a decade since Bright's passing, Cru has well-established international offshoots and remains one of the largest parachurch evangelical organizations in the United States.

While the CCC broke ties with fundamentalism in the 1950s (largely over Bright's refusal to repudiate Billy Graham), the same old-time fundamentalist soul-winning strategies that feed into Anderson's technique inform Bright's own evangelical approach. Bright tempered the basic pitch, however, with a dose of culture-friendly know-how, reworking the soul-winning presentation into simple, non-archaic language. Drawing on his own background in sales, Bright borrowed many principles of effective evangelism from commercial advisers like Frank Bettger (who had written a popular book on successful selling)[51] and Bob Ringer. The latter, a salesman and believer who spoke at a 1957 Crusade conference, impressed upon Bright the dangers of "presentation fatigue," counseling that the best salespeople stick to a consistent pitch. Inspired, Bright devised a slick, consumer-friendly version of the soul-winning presentation: the Four Spiritual Laws. The "Laws" represent Bright's packaging of evangelical doctrine, not a formal theological principle. They summarize the gospel and are scripturally based, but they are not in and of themselves scripture. The Laws read as follows:

1. God loves you and offers a wonderful plan for your life.
2. All of us sin and our sin has separated us from God.
3. Jesus Christ is God's only provision for our sin. Through Him we can know and experience God's love and plan for our life.
4. We must individually receive Jesus Christ as Savior and Lord; then we can know and experience God's love and plan for our lives.[52]

Though they address the core gospel points of soul-winning—human sin, sin's consequences, Christ's sacrifice, and the need for conversion—Bright's Laws envelop this doctrine in a warm, positive glow. Whereas Anderson's if-you-died-tonight pitch sets the focus on the afterlife, Bright's "wonderful plan" introduction bespeaks a temporal encounter with God's love as an end in itself. Positive reinforcement—reconciliation with God—replaces the threat of punishment; hell gets no mention in the standard CCC presentation. Since the positive love of God had defined his ministry, Bright reasoned, starting with an affirmation of that positive love made sense.[53]

Aside from these positive-reinforcement alterations, however, the tract's doctrinal progression more or less mirrors the soul-winning pitch I described earlier. Bible verses about sin, consequences, Christ, and salvation buttress each law, accompanied by down-to-earth explanations of each verse and point. Bright devised some drawings—simple enough so that evangelists could sketch them out for prospects—that illustrate the theological concepts. For instance, in explaining the second law about the separation between sinful humans and holy God, Crusade evangelists would draw a chasm with "Holy God" on the one side and "Sinful Man" on the other. Arrows pointing toward God's side extend from the human side, but they come well short of reaching God. Presenting the third law about Christ's atoning sacrifice, evangelists would then draw a large cross (labeled "Jesus") bridging the gap, with an arrow from God to humans drawn alongside it. In the final law, the need for human decision to receive Christ, Bright's recommended illustration consists of two circles with a representation of a chair or throne in it. In the left-hand circle, a large letter *S* (for *Self*) sits on the throne while a letter *J* (for *Jesus*) sits outside of it. In the right-hand circle, *J* sits on the throne at the circle's center, while *S* sits at the foot of the throne in submission to Christ. Standard questions about the illustrations help to frame the decision scene, e.g., "Which circle represents you? Which do you *want* to represent yourself?" Again, and in contrast to Anderson's soul-winning pitch, the CCC presentation's climax, the stark choice facing the prospect, involves not "avoiding hell" but "living a Christ-centered existence." A typical sinner's prayer along with a recommendation to join a local church completes the presentation.

By 1959, Bright had honed his presentation and translated it into a tract, a small, thin (generally pocket- or wallet-sized) booklet complete with iconic versions of Bright's illustrations. In the subsequent decades, the Four Spiritual Laws booklet went on to become one of the most widely produced evangelical tracts.[54] With some minor modifications, the booklet remains a favored tool in CCC's arsenal. Like any tract, the Four Spiritual Laws booklet can operate autonomously, left in public places for strangers to pick up and read—again demonstrating an evangelical faith in the potency of the gospel message apart from direct human effort. Yet, to a greater extent than other evangelical tracts, the Four Spiritual Laws function as a script for a live encounter between an evangelist and a prospect. Bright and his staff eventually urged CCC evangelists to let the booklet structure their own evangelistic pitches, recommending that evangelists literally read through the booklet along with prospects rather than improvise around the booklet's script.[55]

Performing Witness through Script and Testimony

Since Bright's time (he passed away in 2003), Cru has continued to honor the Four Spiritual Laws presentation even as it has in many respects moved beyond purely kerygmatic strategies. In the mid-1990s, for example, the organization revised the booklet into a new tract called *Would You Like to Know God Personally?* The four-step theological content and signature graphics remain the same (i.e., God's plan to know you personally, humanity's condition, Christ's sacrifice, humans' response), but the revised framing avoids calling the principles "laws." Cru's current evangelistic emphasis now stresses combining such approaches with relational and holistic strategies similar to those I study in the next chapter.[56] Nevertheless, the organization continues to promote the Four Spiritual Laws (and Four Laws–derived) presentations as proven (if slightly old-school) guides for one-on-one encounters. An article about the Four Laws entitled "The Compass," a discipleship curriculum developed by Cru Press (Cru's publishing arm), suggests a number of possible uses for the booklet. Shy or rushed disciples can, of course, simply hand the tract out to friends or strangers. "The things this booklet talks about changed my life," the article suggests saying by way of introduction, drawing on phrases Bright himself reputedly used. "If you are interested I'd love to talk to you about it. Would you like a copy to read yourself?"[57] Better still, however, would be a personal presentation of the Four Laws, either by memory or (best) by the "classic Crusade" approach of just reading the book along with them.

The Compass curriculum's developer, a branch of Cru called Centerfield Productions (now organized under Cru Press), even provides a "Four Laws Script"—essentially an annotated edition of the *Four Laws* booklet—that directs the Cru evangelist in guiding prospects personally through the tract.[58] The Script's annotations include three categories of instruction: *do this, say this,* and *write this [into the booklet].* Around the framework of the *Four Laws* booklet, the Script adds sample dialogue and graphical exercises to enhance points or transition between laws. For example, in lieu of drawing out the illustrations of the two circles (one with Self as center, one with Jesus as center), the Script suggests writing into the booklet numerical percentages—0 percent and 100 percent—next to the printed illustration while explaining, "It all boils down to this question: Who is this person [i.e., the circle on the left] trusting to pay the penalty for their sin? Themselves. So they have 0% of their sins forgiven. And who is this person [on the right] trusting to pay the penalty? Jesus. So they have 100% of their sins forgiven."[59] Other suggestions involve replacing the generic "you" of the laws with the prospect's own name (e.g., "God loves Barbara and offers a wonderful plan for her life") and recommending particular (more or less well-known in evangelical circles) allegories to explain, say, divine judgement.[60]

The script concludes with an elaborate flowchart to guide evangelists through prospects' varied responses to the "Which circle would you like to represent your life?" question—the climax of the Cru script. For those who express a desire to change, the flowchart has the evangelist initiate a mini-review, asking them *why* they want to live a Jesus-centered life and re-explaining laws 2 and 3 (sin and its consequences) for those who answer incorrectly or uncertainly. From there, the flowchart asks how one might move from living in the Self-centered circle to living as a Jesus-centered circle (i.e., law 4 about receiving Christ). Once prospects can correctly articulate the doctrinal logic of sin, separation, and salvation, the flowchart points to the last line of recommended dialogue: "Let me continue to read this booklet to clarify what it means to go from the left circle to the right circle." Actually, this last response (i.e., finishing reading the booklet and reciting the sinner's prayer) functions as the presentation's endpoint regardless of the prospect's answers. Even for those who reply negatively to the chart's initial question, declining the invitation to join the Jesus circle, the flowchart recommends thanking them for their honesty and continuing with the rest of the presentation just in case they should someday wish to convert. Those identifying as already living in a Jesus-centered life likewise hear the same sinner's prayer conclusion as those who don't. The flowchart explores *how* to get from climax to denouement, but it does not envision any but a singular ending.

The staff and authors of Cru recognize the pitfalls of a standardized, formulaic presentation. "Just remember," the Centerfield guide warns, "that if it sounds like you are reading a script, you're not doing it right."[61] Those who feel awkward about reading a booklet out loud, the guide continues, should attempt to memorize the presentation and deliver it at their own pace. Moreover, it cautions, almost every evangelistic situation lends itself to the Four Laws approach. Disciples must develop increased sensitivity to setting and audience, an ability to discern what a particular prospect might be open to hearing. Why, then, have a script, a standard pitch, at all? Centerfield's guide argues that having a standard pitch provides a solid base, a clear and proven template upon which to build. It *works,* providing confidence for the presenter and clarity for the prospect. Just as Anderson urges soul-winners to step aside and let the Bible (that is, the Holy Spirit via the Living Word) do the work of conversion, so too does Cru recommend that disciples sideline their own egos and submit to the proven standard of the Four Laws approach. The Four Laws, which *summarize* but *are not literally* the Word, become the focus of the Cru presentation, a script in which both the evangelist and the prospect (by answering questions and reading along with the evangelist) participate. The Four Laws' clarity also helps Cru maintain a degree of control over its doctrine. Most Cru participants, after all, are disciples in training rather than fully trained disciples. Cru's curriculum aims at young adults on college and university campuses, people for whom confident public speaking and interventional evangelism do not come naturally. The Four Laws presentation and booklet enable young Christians to get their feet wet in spreading the gospel person-to-person.

The classic Four Laws approach, like soul-winning, tends to encourage evasion or demurral ("Let me finish reading this, and we'll get back to it") regarding truculent responses or difficult-to-hostile questions. Again, I suggest this tendency has less to do with any inherent fear of deep thought on the part of evangelists and more to do with the driving impulse to deliver the message (which, like Anderson, Cru evangelists see as imbued with divine agency for transformation) and the simple fact that the Four Laws is designed partially with neophyte evangelists in mind. Advanced apologetics requires a step or three beyond just-starting-out evangelism.[62] That said, I conclude this section with a strategy that Cru has long advised for evangelists to use in circumventing argumentative resistance to the Four Laws presentation: the personal testimony.

A common fixture in evangelical churches, the testimony is a brief (three- to five-minute) expository monologue that relates the story of one's conversion. The structure follows a roughly dramatic (in Ball's scheme) outline: what life was like prior to conversion (stasis), what led you to receive Christ (crisis-intrusion), what life is like now (denouement/new stasis). Numerous online testimonies exist. Centerfield's "Compass" curriculum dedicates a lesson to personal testimonies (or, as they call them, "personal stories")[63] Their instructions divide the testimony into five parts. In "the opening," evangelists should try to communicate a "word picture" or theme that encapsulates what their life revolved around prior to their conversion. The next section expands upon this theme, describing pre-conversion life. Storytellers, however, should not "dwell on how bad you used to be or glory in past sin," warns the guide, "Share only the details that relate to your theme, and give enough details to show your need for Christ."[64] Neither should pre-Christ narratives criticize or even mention other denominations. The focus is on the gospel, not on intra-Christian strife. The crux of the presentation, the conversion story, comes next. At stake here is not merely relating the details of one's personal decision but ensuring that the raw instructions on how anyone might come to Christ (i.e., enact a theological performative) get communicated. The fourth step, "Your Life After Christ," emphasizes the positive changes that manifest the spiritual transformation of conversion. "Emphasize the changes in your character, attitude, and perspective," advises Centerfield, "not just the mere changes in behavior." Nor should stories paint an overly rosy post-conversion picture. "We still struggle as Christians. Life is far from perfect, isn't it? But what makes it different for you now?" the guide says. "Be honest, and God will use your personal experience regardless of how 'unspectacular' you may think it is."

Particularly important, here and throughout, is avoiding "Christian-ese," terms or language that function as ecclesiastical jargon that the uninitiated might find off-putting. Specifically, the guide recommends avoiding terms like *saved, sanctified, sin, justified, atonement, wonderful, joyful, peaceful,* and *happy*. The final section, the closing, consists of a statement that wraps up the story, relating the narrative again to the central picture/theme. "You could close with a verse, but don't throw one in to sound spiritual," cautions the Centerfield guide. "Use it if it is meaningful and relates to the story you've just told."[65] A worksheet with question prompts follows to assist storytellers in constructing their testimonies. And it is a construction—a carefully crafted monologue to be prewritten, edited, and rehearsed. Like the Four Laws pitch, testimonies should not *seem* scripted, but (keeping in mind that the guide aims at relatively inexperienced Christians) the guide stresses that practiced testimonies can help the evangelist stay on task, a quality that both glorifies God (as it retells the miracle of God's intervention) as well as appeals to listeners.

Of course, though glorifying God is important to Cru evangelists, testimonies tend to be valued more for what they add to an evangelism encounter. The personal drama of conversion, scrubbed clean of Bible verses, overt doctrine, and Christian-ese language, can powerfully complement the positive-yet-absolutist feel of the Four Laws. Moreover, Cru evangelism recognizes that personal testimonies enjoy a degree of relative immunity to skepticism. As one CCC training manual explains, "Although people can try and argue about the veracity of Christianity's claims (e.g., the historicity of the resurrection, the reliability of the Bible), no one can argue with what Christ has done in your life."[66] Turner quotes Bright himself as acknowledging the millennial preference for stories, that "this generation is more open to an emotional approach, whereas another generation was open to a logical approach."[67] In concert with the Four Laws approach, the personal testimony functions as a softer, gentler conversion pitch. It avoids mention of hell, focusing instead on the positive effects of a Christ-centered life.

Of course, today Cru relies on more than just the Four Laws and personal testimonies in its outreach. The organization hosts a number of websites and publishes several discipleship curricula that draw on, synthesize, and devise a wide and expanding range of evangelistic techniques.[68] If the Four Laws proves not to a chapter's liking, Cru offers an ever-growing variety of alternative presentations or summaries of the gospel message. Cru Press operates as something of a "research and development" adjunct to the organization's ministry, blending administrative know-how with field experience in ministry to create constantly evolving tools, training curricula, and ministry directions for Cru and for local churches.[69] Indeed, so varied and complex are these resources that I could produce a lengthy study of nothing more than the ongoing Cru arms race of evangelistic techniques, a never-ending battle between outreach and secular apathy that encompasses everything from modifications to the Four Laws booklet to Facebook-based ministry activities and conversation-starter YouTube videos.

For now, however, I have restricted my examination to the signature interpersonal approach that has defined—and continues to shape—CCC's public face for the past half-century. This face highlights the classic CCC emphasis on the positive, personal benefits of a relationship with Christ. Its message culminates not in the crisis Anderson poses but in the opportunity to take advantage of a great deal.[70] Yet for some critics, Cru's well-meaning step away from the turn-or-burn harshness of Anderson brings the organization's ministry dangerously close to a self-centered commercial sales pitch. Christianity becomes less a necessary, life-saving resolution to humanity's eternal crisis and more an enriching philosophy that boasts plenty of satisfied customers. For many evangelicals, such an approach purchases attractiveness at the cost of doctrinal integrity. Indeed, for the third evangelist I study here, Ray Comfort, the Campus Crusade for Christ may have ceased to offer the authentic gospel at all.

"Hell's Best-Kept Secret": Ray Comfort's Way of the Master

If the Campus Crusade for Christ represents a softer, gentler version of the soul-winning pitch, Ray Comfort's Way of the Master (WotM) represents a step in the opposite direction. A native of New Zealand, Comfort describes himself as growing up in a largely secular-Jewish household (his mother was Jewish). Upon converting to Christianity in the early 1970s, Comfort began a street-preaching ministry and gradually gained international attention for his evangelistic approach and signature sermon presentations, "Hell's Best Kept Secret" and "True and False Conversion." In the late 1980s, Comfort accepted an invitation to relocate to the United States, where he founded his current ministry, Living

Waters Publications. Thanks to endorsements won from a wide range of evangelical leaders and to his own immense output of books and media, Comfort today enjoys a reputation as one of the most recognizable Christian evangelists in the United States.

Living Waters sponsors a wide variety of offshoots, including a School of Biblical Evangelism, annual national conferences, evangelical training workshops, a successful television series called *The Way of the Master,* and an ever-growing array of apologetic and activist ministry initiatives.[71] Comfort's theology and evangelical approach have inspired a number of other evangelical individuals and groups who follow approaches basically patterned after Comfort's Way of the Master, including Last Words Ministry (*Last Words Radio* podcast), Trisha Ramos ("Fish With Trish" ministry), and Todd Friel (*Wretched Radio* and *Wretched* television series).[72] Perhaps most famously, former child star Kirk Cameron continues to works closely with Living Waters, co-hosting the *Way of the Master* television series and co-authoring several of the Living Waters books. Comfort generally declines to align with any formal denomination or evangelical sector, maintaining Living Waters as simply a biblically based ministry.[73] The Statement of Faith for Living Waters outlines a relatively generic conservative-evangelical theology (touching on biblicism, crucicentrism, activism, and conversionism) with some reformed tendencies. In terms of culture-war politics, Comfort stakes out some decidedly right-wing culture-war positions, sponsoring a number of initiatives, for example, dedicated to criticizing evolution, atheism, and abortion. His politics are both more mainstream "religious right" than Anderson's and more pronounced as an aspect of his overall ministry. Like Anderson, however, he does not endorse parties or politicians. In every endeavor, Comfort's driving impulse of evangelism shines through; even his anti-abortion interventions (most recently a pro-life propaganda film offered for free online)[74] inevitably segue into the standard Way of the Master evangelistic pitch.

At first glance, the WotM approach can seem like little more than a more dialogic version of Anderson's soul-winning. After an amiable introduction, WotM evangelists pose the standard, arresting question (*If you were to die tonight, are you absolutely sure you would go to heaven?* Or *Do you think you're a good person?*) before proceeding to a diagnostic (*Why? What makes you so sure?*). Then, should prospects give an unsatisfactory answer, evangelists move on to discussions of human sin and its consequences, urging prospects to a conversion experience through prayer. Some surface features distinguish Comfort's method from classical soul-winning.

Rather than going door-to-door with Bible in hand, Comfort's preferred method involves stationing himself on public walkways and engaging passersby. Comfort stresses that effective evangelism must appeal first to people on a "natural" level before moving to spiritual matters. To that end, Living Waters offers a wide range of attention-getting conversation starters (e.g., brain-teasers, "surveys," jokes) as well as props, from "trillion-dollar bills" to optical illusion booklets to pennies stamped with the Ten Commandments. Such devices, many of which have no obvious religious content, function to catch the attention of strangers on the street and build a minimal level of rapport. Way of the Master training teaches evangelists then to turn the conversation to the initial pitch question. From there, the pitch proceeds as a quasi-Socratic conversation built on pointed, yes/no or otherwise obvious-answer questions from the evangelist and predictable answers from the prospect. Comfort's technique does not rely on the evangelist's having a Bible. Aside from the Ten Commandments (which WotM evangelists memorize), most doctrinal points regarding sin, damnation, and salvation get paraphrased rather than quoted chapter and verse. Comfort's is therefore a much more person-to-person encounter, with the evangelist focused directly on the prospect rather than on a Bible.

Beneath these surface details, however, the WotM technique evinces a significant shift in theological and dramaturgical emphasis. Anderson's evangelistic pitch arcs toward a climax in which the prospect must decide whether or not to believe on Christ. Much of Anderson's presentation, then, focuses on the significance of that decision, reinforcing how simple belief on Christ establishes the prospect as permanently, indelibly rescued from Hell. Such arguments for the eternal security of the believer coupled with the definition of conversion as pure belief (and not any kind of action) drive the theological sense of Anderson's gospel. The Campus Crusade for Christ's signature tactics, the "Four Laws" presentation and the personal testimony, both foreground God's "wonderful plan"—the necessity of putting Christ at the center of one's life and the benefits (temporal and eternal) that flow from living in accordance with that plan. The Way of the Master, by contrast, takes as its point of departure a stringent critique of the underlying theology behind Anderson's style of soul-winning and the CCC approach. Comfort elaborates this criticism primarily through his two signature sermons, "Hell's Best Kept Secret" and "True and False Conversions," messages that initially won him his fame. Living Waters and its related ministries inevitably link to these sermons (usually in audio format) or reprint them in their books, framing them as starting points for understanding the Way of the Master.[75] Comfort's own writings regularly draw on arguments and analogies from these talks, and they undergird his entire evangelistic approach.

Both sermons rehearse a similar story of discovery. After some years working as a street evangelist in the 1970s, Comfort recalls, he began to suffer from what he called "evangelical frustration":[76] the conviction that a majority of people who recited the sinner's prayer with him soon fell away from the faith. Using the gospel of "God loves you," Comfort found he could elicit from a prospect a sincere, even tearful profession of faith. But more often than not, these ostensible converts eventually reverted to lives lived as if the profession of faith had never happened. Their conversions appeared not to stick. Liaising with other evangelists, Comfort discovered that his observations seemed to hold across most of evangelicalism. The gospel message—God's love and Christ's sacrifice as saving humans from Hell—simply lacked an essential staying power. Comfort eventually latched on to a statistic (one he claims was reported in the magazine of a major national denomination) that suggested that 80 to 90 percent of converts fell away from the faith.[77]

The Wonderful Plan versus the Painful Truth

Comfort diagnoses the problem as a lack of actual repentance on the part of the prospect. To be sure, soul-winning evangelism can produce a *kind* of repentance, a momentary turn toward God through the sinner's prayer. But such facile affirmation, Comfort argues, does not constitute the kind of life-changing turn away from sin, the spiritual rebirth and new life that define authentic conversions. Yet the fault, he finds, lies not with prospects; they are just mouthing the words they've been manipulated into saying. Evangelists (Comfort includes himself) bear the guilt. Modern evangelism, he argues, fails because it undervalues the gift God offers. Evangelists present forgiveness and salvation without establishing for prospects the reality of guilt and damnation. A fan of analogies, Comfort draws a parallel between God's law and civil law. "Imagine," he urges, "if I said to you, 'I've got some *good news* for you: someone has just paid a $25,000 speeding fine on your behalf.'" Such good news, he explains, would likely seem like foolishness or even offense. After all, you don't think that you've committed any traffic violation. But what if, Comfort continues, you were informed that police had clocked you going driving 55 miles an hour "through an area set aside for a blind children's convention" where the clearly marked speed limit was fifteen miles an hour? What if, further, you learned that a $25,000 fine awaited you for your flagrant, dangerous violation? Hearing then that someone had stepped in and paid that fine for you would legitimately come as good news.[78] Absent the realization of their sinful state and its consequences, Comfort argues, prospects can't be expected to receive the message of salvation with a shrug at best and an offended rejection at worst. Too many evangelical approaches, he laments, seek to sidestep the uncompromising harshness of the reality of human sin. For Comfort, a simple "no" to the gospel invitation is less troubling than an easy "yes."

Though he stops short of naming names, Comfort's criticism specifically targets Bill Bright's opening line, "God loves you and has a wonderful plan for your life." First, Comfort argues, "Never, ever, would I approach someone and say, 'Jesus loves you.' Totally unbiblical; there's no precedent for that in Scripture."[79] Indeed, for Comfort, it is simply not the case that God loves everyone. Comfort's theology follows a more Reformed path than does Anderson's or Bright's.[80] In this system, God's primary attribute is not *love* but *holiness.* God is by definition the righteous antithesis of sin and sinfulness. Since humans are after the Edenic Fall consumed by sin, all humans stand as wretched, filthy sinners from God's perfect perspective. Bible passages about God's love, in this view, refer exclusively to God's elect—that subset of humanity that has been pre-selected as saved by Christ's atoning sacrifice on the cross. God loves *those* sinners, just as Christ's sacrifice ransoms *those* sinners. But God does not—definitionally cannot—love unrepentant, reprobate sinners, nor does Christ's sacrifice apply to such non-elected humans. True to his desire not to divide the body of Christ, Comfort does not stress his Reformed leanings explicitly (as doing so would alienate non-Calvinists).

The bulk of Comfort's criticism of the "Four Laws" approach instead stresses how the "wonderful plan" approach proves ineffectual, even dishonest. Christianity's eternal rewards may be sweet, Comfort observes, but earthly life remains fallen, pain-filled, and inimical to Christians. Espousing Christianity does not magically make worldly stresses and tribulations vanish. Indeed, Comfort warns that authentic Christianity—a life lived wholly in the service of Christ—guarantees hardship insofar as it invites worldly scorn and demonic resistance. Comfort affirms that Christianity offers help in facing troubles, giving Christians hope and strength to endure trials. Yet faith is not a get-out-of-misfortunes-free card. Evangelistic pitches focused on God's love and wonderful plan, Comfort concludes, can actually hurt evangelistic efforts by creating a set of impossible promises. In one of his favorite analogies, Comfort imagines the gospel as a parachute offered to two passengers on a plane. The first is told that wearing the parachute will improve the flight. Donning the parachute, however, he suffers discomfort. The parachute chafes and weighs heavily. He can't sit properly in his seat with it on. The other passengers snicker to see him wearing it. Embarrassed, uncomfortable, and frustrated, the man doffs the parachute and throws it on the floor. "Disillusionment and bitterness fill his heart," Comfort says, "because, as far as he was concerned, he was told an outright lie." The second passenger also dons a parachute, but he's been convinced by a different rationale. He's been told to put it on because he'll be required to jump out of the plane at 25,000 feet. That man wears the parachute gratefully, unmindful of the weight, the discomfort, or the other passengers' attitudes. "His mind is consumed," Comfort explains, "with the thought of what would happen to him if he jumped without that parachute."[81] The parachute of the gospel thus only becomes meaningful to the lost if they internalize the threat of the crash (hell).

From Comfort's point of view, authentic conversion relies upon repentance. Authentic repentance in turn depends upon a deep realization of about what one turns away from and why one turns away from it. Evangelism thus has to *convict* before it *converts*. People must realize that they are sinners, and they must feel sadness and horror at the reality and consequences of such a state. Comfort thus boils the Way of the Master down to a simple, four-step process: Relate, Create, Convict, and Reveal.[82] Way of the Master evangelists *relate* to prospects via one of the many attractor devices described earlier. They then *create* a connection between the non-spiritual intro device/conversation and spiritual topics. From there, evangelists *convict* prospects using the Law, that is, the Ten Commandments, before *revealing* to them the saving grace Christ offers.

Inspired Convictions and the Affect of Repentance

Of these steps, *convicting* receives the most dramaturgical weight in a WotM presentation. Media ministries related to or inspired by Living Waters typically devote considerable airtime to "on the street" encounters between evangelists and random prospects (sometimes called "fish").[83] While the *relate* and *create* steps—clever ice-breakers, eye-catching props, and introductory small talk—differ from encounter to encounter, practically every such video or recording highlights the same basic "Good

Person Test." There evangelists pose a series of questions about whether prospects have broken the Ten Commandments, that is, told a lie, stolen anything, hated someone, used the name of the Lord in vain (e.g., as an expletive), or lusted after someone they aren't married to. Each "yes" from the prospect prompts a "So that makes you what?" from the evangelist, who then underlines prospects' status as (respectively) lying, stealing, murdering, blaspheming adulterers. Now, as I mentioned above, Anderson's soul-winning approach also uses the Ten Commandments as a tool to demonstrate prospects' sinful lives. Yet in soul-winning the Ten Commandments test is a minor step, a brief illustration. Anderson even cautions against hammering people down with guilt by going through commandment after commandment.[84] Comfort, by contrast, wants people hammered down by the weight of their own guilt. The barrage of questions—not just one or two of the commandments but five or six—as well as the sin upon sin upon sin conclusion variously bemuses, embarrasses, angers, and distresses the prospects filmed. Provided the prospects don't simply walk away in irritation, the evangelist then proceeds to ask whether God would judge them guilty or innocent by God's Perfect Standard. Should prospects protest that God is good and forgiving or that God would not send people to hell just for lying occasionally, the evangelist reframes the situation in legal terms, casting God as the good and fair judge and the prospect as the convicted criminal. Do judges in civil courts, the evangelist asks, randomly forgive convicted criminals? Convicted murderers? Convicted thieves? If the judge did so, wouldn't that mean that they aren't a good judge? What if the criminals protest that they committed the crime only once or that they have done lots of good things in addition to the crime? Does that mean they aren't guilty and don't have to pay the penalty? By this point in the videos, the prospects who have stuck around long enough for this conclusion are often subdued, even weeping.

The Way of the Master's pitch thus consists of a series of upsetting leading questions with distressing conclusions. Comfort's approach, in fact, functions as a guilt trip. The evangelist does not directly heckle or berate prospects; she simply poses straightforward questions and underlines their (unquestioned) significance. The Law convicts, not the evangelist. Comfort's theology highlights Romans 2:15, which describes God's law as being written on the human heart. In this view, the Ten Commandments are not some alien standards imposed by a foreign God from an ancient time; they are distillations of universal moral standards hard-wired into the circuitry of personhood. *Conscience* thus functions as the evidence of the Biblical Law's existence and power. "The word 'conscience' (*con + science*) means 'with knowledge,'" Comfort explains, "Whenever we sin, we do so 'with knowledge' that what we're doing is wrong."[85] Humanity's sinful nature, however, inspires people to snuff out the light of ethical knowledge. The evangelist's challenge, then, consists of helping prospects to let this inner light shine, exposing their status as sinful beings. Asking someone if they've ever told a lie (or stolen something or hated someone or lusted after someone) provokes guilt. This guilt, Comfort maintains, is a reliable indicator that the Law of God is active within prospects, fighting to break through the willful ignorance of prospects' sinful lives. In WotM encounters, Comfort and his protégés look for that moment where their guilt trip lands, a turning point signaled most often by tears.

But not just any tears will do. The affect of true repentance, Comfort argues, is precise and easily confused with other, non-salvific emotional reactions. Producing tears per se in listeners proves all too easy. The evangelism of "God loves you," he observes, will inspire weeping in some simply because their lives have lacked love. To them, the image of a God exuding warm, non-judgemental affection fills an emotional hole in their psyche. But it doesn't cultivate authentic conversion. Comfort recalls an early experience in which his message of love and God's wonderful plan caused a woman to weep. "Unbeknown to me," he laments, "her tears were not tears of godly sorrow for sin, but merely an emotional response to the need of a father's love."[86] The woman subsequently fell away from the faith, feeling betrayed (in Comfort's view) that the emotional high of God's love flagged in the face of life's inevitable trials. Neither, cautions Comfort, should evangelists aim at instilling fear. Hell is real, but unlike Anderson's approach, the WotM features no lengthy descriptions of the Lake of Fire and eternities of torment. Fire-and-brimstone sermons can inspire someone to walk down an aisle and say a sinner's prayer, to be sure. But the soil of fear-filled conversion proves just as thin as the soil of lovelorn conversion. A man may convert out of fear, Comfort maintains. "But in his heart, he thinks God is harsh and unjust, because the law hasn't been used to show him the exceeding sinful nature of sin. He doesn't see hell as being his just desert, that he deserves hell."[87] Salvation in that case works as someone's taking advantage of a loophole in the ludicrous statutes of a divine tyrant. It produces deep-seated resentment, not contrition and certainly not gratefulness or dedication. The kind of tears Comfort looks for and the quality of emotion his technique aims for stem from the deep, dawning realization that one actually is guilty and deserving of hell. Prospects must not merely be *told* they are sinners; they must *realize* their blameworthiness and *accede to* God's judgement and sentence. Only then, Comfort argues, does the "good news" of Christ's atoning sacrifice mean anything. Only then can people authentically repent, turning away from a life they recognize as corrupted. Only then do people acquire the abiding sense of humble gratitude that fuels a life of discipleship and evangelizing.

For all his voluminous instructions to evangelists, Comfort devotes very little attention to the exact structure of a theological performative. He largely eschews traditional "sinners' prayers." If prospects have arrived at a state of authentic conviction, then words seem almost like an afterthought. At that point, prospects need only be encouraged to confess their sins, forsake their sinful life, and place their trust in Christ, clinging to him as—well, as a passenger on a crashing plane might cling to a parachute.[88] The clinging—the life of discipleship—comes not from the parachute itself but from the passenger's utter certainty in the plane's crashing and in the chute's ability to save.

In his many recorded encounters, Comfort proves himself a consummate WotM evangelist. Marshaling an affable, self-deprecating manner and disarming Kiwi accent, he manages the transition from genial chitchat to sad-but-true revelation deftly. He projects a sense not of a stereotypical fundamentalist screaming "sinner!" but of a doctor compassionately explaining a complex terminal diagnosis, gently recognizing and shutting down the patient's defensive denials and rationalizations. Years of experience make him well-nigh unflappable; even in the face of vituperative resistance or outright mockery, Comfort maintains a slightly funny, slightly sad manner, urgently pressing home the news that *you have sinned and are subject to divine judgement.*

Not surprisingly, though, very few of Comfort's numerous filmed WotM encounters appear to end in conversion. Steven Anderson, in a video clip entitled "Epic Soul-winning FAIL" lashes into Comfort for just this reason. He doesn't quote scripture. He doesn't have a Bible. His methods produce no obvious fruit.[89] For Anderson, Comfort's relative lack of "success" (i.e., winning converts) demonstrates that his methods are both heterodox and ineffective. From Comfort's view, the soul-winning style that Anderson practices yields facile, transient, and ultimately false conversions, whether through fear of hell, joy at the loving God, or the plain desire to get this annoying salesman off of your porch as quickly as possible. The difference also indicates the divide between the two evangelists' theologies. For Anderson, God's salvation is for all people, offered freely and accepted easily. Discipleship (that is, sanctification), if it follows at all, exists as a separate process from salvific justification. As a door-to-door evangelist, Anderson's duty consists of encouraging salvation—belief on Christ—and saving people's souls. Comfort, however, sees justification and sanctification as much more intertwined. Belief without repentance—without the deep-down, soul-wrenching realization that *I have sinned and am wretched before God*—has no power. He sees his duty as producing authentic converts, people who have undergone a permanent reorientation. Naturally, such converts will represent a minority. Comfort preaches to anyone and everyone, but he reserves salvation (or, rather, preaches that God reserves it) as the prize for only a few.

Of course, one could say that Comfort's whole technique garners fewer converts simply because it aims, practically, at people who at least on some level really do believe in the image of God as judge and the Ten Commandments as the standard. The tearful conviction so central to his technique relies on Comfort's faith in the existence and power of the Law of God written on every human heart. You have to feel guilt and acquiesce to Comfort's schema of the Just Wrath of the Holy God for the Way of the Master to do its work. Many people undergo the WotM good-person test and do not care. Others flatly reject the fairness of eternal punishment for temporal sin. Still more deny a supernatural basis for the conscience that Comfort insists evinces the Holy Spirit. Like Anderson and the CCC, Comfort generally does not take pains to defend the legitimacy of the biblical law or of the inspired dimension of guilt and conviction. His typical response to someone who questions the reality of Hell exemplifies his approach: "That doesn't matter. You still have to face God on Judgment Day *whether you believe in it or not.*" After all, he continues, an eighteen-wheeler truck bearing down on you don't pause to verify that you acknowledge their existence before smashing you.[90] Comfort doesn't seek to prove the theological underpinnings of his pitch; he simply asserts them as so, knowing that some prospects will accept them (or that, on some level, they already accept them) and some will not.

Conclusion

To a certain extent, a take-it-or-leave it approach underlies all three of the kerygmatic modes I have reviewed here. All of them consist of simple presentation: here's the Gospel. It's yours to accept or not. Anything beyond that presentation risks alienating prospects, diluting the gospel, or wasting time with someone who would never convert in any case. It is the live-evangelism equivalent of mass mailing, a high-investment, minimal-return shotgun strategy. Unlike a mass mailing, however, concerns about efficiency contribute only a bit to Anderson's and Comfort's strategies. Their presentational format instead reflects their wholesale faith in the transformative power of the Word of God (Anderson), the Wonderful Plan (Bright), or in the Law (Comfort). Their evangelism is pure kerygma, simple presentation of the gospel, because in their view this simplicity is sufficient for the Holy Spirit to work. Their strategies are geared to introduce life-changing epiphanies in the lives of strangers. Anything more than this constitutes both a waste of time and a heterodox departure from the Bible's script.

These approaches restrict the parameters of the performance to the literal time and space of the evangelistic presentation itself. The same script—the kerygma of the gospel—operates basically unchanged regardless of the rest of the performance. Aside from stressing some general guidelines of comportment (e.g., don't be disheveled, angry, or hectoring), these approaches recognize only one responsibility for the evangelist: get the message across. Anything that does or does not happen afterward is between the prospect and God. Provided the message gets proclaimed, the prospect assumes the full weight of acting on or rejecting the gospel. Comfort's theology provides him with a theological explanation for such outcomes—*they'd never believe anyway.* Similarly, Anderson's soul-winning approach stresses the need for discerning open prospects. Confronted with unbelief, Anderson simply moves on, thinking ahead to the next, hopefully less obstinate prospect. If evangelists are doing their jobs correctly, then prospects are confronting not Christians but God. Rejecting an evangelical overture constitutes a rejection not of the messenger but of the message—the Holy Spirit itself. Evangelists can essentially wash their hands of responsibility for how or if the message lands home.

At first glance, such hit-and-run tactics seem distant from most forms of secular, left-progressive performance activism. Feminism, anticapitalist, or queer performance activisms, for example, have very few direct parallels to door-to-door, hi-how-are-you-are-you-saved proselytism. The closest secular analogue might be partisan canvassing during a campaign, where volunteers knock on doors or make cold calls to gauge support, increase awareness, and persuade or inspire likely voters. Like some of the kerygmatic modes I relate here, such canvassing often relies on quasi-formulaic scripts delivered with a minimum of personal embellishment. Also like kerygmatic evangelism, canvassing as such rarely gets framed as a mode of performance activism. Such small-scale, play-and-repeat encounters lack the mass spectacle of a parade or demonstration. They possess little of the disruptive, direct-action riskiness that accompanies civilly disobedient protests. From an ideological perspective, door-to-door (or on-the-street) encounters also bear an uncomfortable resemblance to crude salesmanship.

The resemblance is undeniable. Kerygmatic evangelism is indeed conformist. It demands activists' subservience to the message/cause being promulgated. In fact, the pure promulgation of the message trumps any consideration of performance medium. That is, evangelists' faith in the transformative power of the gospel leads them to view the human elements of evangelism largely as a matter of minimization. *Stay out of God's way. Don't make this about yourself. Stay on message.* By contrast, signature examples of left-progressive activist performance tend to focus on the activists themselves: the civil rights activists being arrested for sitting at a counter, the ACT UP protesters blocking a street with their prostrate bodies, or the diverse mass of WTO protesters bravely approaching (or retreating from) a line of uniformed riot police. Against such stirring examples of sacrifice and bravery, a serially repeated presentation of similar messages seems cheap ("Occupy Wall Street has a wonderful plan for your life. May I tell you about it?").

Without downplaying the value of high-spectacle choreographies of protest, however, I submit that kerygmatic evangelists' relatively unexceptional acts offer a rejoinder to the assumption that mass-producing a message or position necessarily cheapens the message and the messenger. For evangelicals, clarifying exactly what the gospel message is and spreading it as widely as possible through interpersonal contact signify respect for the message and the cause. Kerygmatic evangelism represents the "ground game" of evangelical activism, the unromantic grind of communicating a coherent message again and again and again. The discipline behind kerygmatic evangelism may be conformist, but such conformity is very stuff of ideological consistency within members of a cause or social movement. Indeed, Anderson's tiny church's intensive door-to-door efforts in his city evince a notion of activism as a consistent discipline of outreach, not just as a singular, once-in-a-while mass event.

As I reflected in the first chapter, the current progressive left has found it difficult to achieve such consistency over long periods. A well-earned postmodern suspicion, endemic to many left-progressive groups, of master narratives and capital-T Truth makes the notion of submitting to message discipline somewhat obnoxious (though many historical left-progressive activist movements demanded a high degree of discipline from members). From left-progressive perspectives, investing any particular message with an evangelical level of divine authority and power reeks of unthinking submission to authority (though, again, many historical left-progressive activist causes have drawn rhetorical and spiritual sustenance from religious sources). But such distaste for controlled messages and consistent methods of presenting those messages can hinder the long-term durability of activist causes. So too can a focus on high-visibility spectacle ignore the indispensability of less visible, less romantic, and more disciplined activist actions such as lobbying, canvassing, letter-writing, and fundraising. My study of kerygmatic evangelists makes me wonder what a left-progressive cause or movement would look like whose members mirrored the commitment, zeal, and discipline demonstrated by dedicated evangelists like those in Anderson's church, active Cru groups, or Way of the Master followers. I would venture to say that such a widespread "church" of left-progressive activism has not existed in the United States since perhaps the days of Old Left communism. Like evangelicalism, such a view asserted (and in some present forms still asserts) a life-altering truth, a way of viewing the world that presents listeners with a stark choice: unite or be damned. The Old Left's communist message is a gospel of sorts: good news, harsh realities, and strict demands all in one. And although its ultimate focus is not supernatural, its adherents would hardly deny that the news that "you have nothing to lose but your chains" carries a power, a convicting truth, greater than the charisma of its individual advocates. Such a powerful, disciplined, and message-driven activism seems distant from the progressive left of today. This distance on the one hand marks a wariness of the pitfalls that such message-centered movements present (i.e., the potential for totalitarian or cultish excess). Yet the example of interpersonal evangelists raises the possibility that this protective distance from excess is also something of a loss, a rejection that activist ideals or visions of alternative worlds might be compelling enough to demand the same degree of disciplined evangelism as that advocated by Anderson, Bright, and Comfort.

For most other evangelicals, however, the kerygmatic formats I have studied here continue to define the baseline for personal evangelism even today. Some of the core features they exhibit—trusting solely in the power of the Word and the Spirit rather than in human skill, maintaining a proper attitude while evangelizing, and knowing when to back off or end the presentation—all inform most other evangelism forms I will study. Likewise, some of the tensions between these approaches—which is best/most biblical: leading with love or leading with guilt/fear? A hard sell or a soft sell?—recur in nearly every area of evangelical outreach. Even with their internal differences, however, the kerygmatic personal evangelism modes form enough of a singular entity to inspire a host of techniques in reaction to them. Such reactions are the focus of my next chapter.

CHAPTER 4

Apologies and Apologetics

Meta-Kerygmatic Evangelism

For the approaches I reviewed in the previous chapter, evangelistic effectiveness depends upon the miraculous power of the gospel message. Those strategies stress that the Holy Spirit, not the evangelist, works to convict and persuade prospects through kerygma, the plain proclamation of the gospel message of sin, sacrifice, and redemption. In this kerygmatic mode of interpersonal evangelism, the evangelist does little more than point to this message and get out of the way. If prospects voice doubt with the Word so proclaimed, the evangelist ignores the complaint, defers to a future conversation (which may not ever occur), or, in Comfort's case, resorts to quick-fire rhetorical tricks designed to steer the conversation back onto the straight, narrow trajectory of guilt-conviction-repentance-conversion. "It doesn't matter if you believe," responds the Way of the Master evangelist. "It's true in any case. So, are you a good person?" Should a prospect refuse such a redirection (as is frequently the case), the conversation stalls, Comfort clucks his tongue regretfully, and the prospect walks away unconvinced. End of play.

Although I do not want to rely too heavily on a simplistic analogy of soul-winning encounters as theatrical productions, I note that, if kerygmatic evangelists were seen as theatrical producers, just about any theater-trained observer would critique them for harboring a constricted view of how performance communicates. As any intro to theater course will teach, the effects of a performance exceed the time-span of the show and the space of the stage. Audiences start gathering information about a production long before the curtain rises. The marketing for a show creates a first impression of the play (comedy or tragedy?), the company (well-established or little-known?), and the venue (high-class? small-town?). The front-of-house environs—the location of the space, the décor of the lobby, the price of the tickets, the dress and manner of other spectators—further shape the spectators' horizon of expectations. The theater house itself communicates a level of professionalism or ramshackle amateurism before the first performer actually appears. These and other pre-show communications influence an audience's reception of the production itself. People watching the local middle school's production of *Oklahoma!* bring different expectations and apply different aesthetic standards to that performance than they would were they attending a high-profile revival on Broadway. Theater artists know that the performance of the play itself—while possibly the most prominent element of the production—relies heavily on these extra-theatrical communications.

Of late, a number of evangelicals have begun to resist the self-contained, confrontational mode of interpersonal evangelism and its simple reliance in the efficacy of the gospel plainly presented. These evangelicals call for increased attention to their prospects' horizon of expectations, the contexts and backgrounds surrounding and shaping any evangelistic encounter. The audiences for evangelical outreach, as it turns out, often do not prove amenable to purely kerygmatic techniques. Randy Newman, an evangelist with a long tenure working with Campus Crusade for Christ, recalls an occasion of sharing a Four Spiritual Laws approach with a prospect. Having taught multiple seminars on the art of evangelistic booklet presentation, Newman found himself caught up short when his prospect stopped him after hearing the first spiritual law ("God loves you and has a wonderful plan for your life"). The prospect asked some simple questions: "What do you mean when you say the word *God*? . . . What do you mean when you say the word *love*? And, most importantly, how do you know all this is true?"[1] Newman found himself stymied. He realized this person's questions weren't smoke screens to disrupt the gospel presentation. "I know the difference," writes Newman, "between an honest inquirer and a truth-avoider." This prospect represented the former. The standard CCC response ("That's a good question. How about we come back to that when I'm done reading the booklet?") simply wouldn't do. The prospect's questions demanded answers not covered in the booklet, answers whose explanation would create a scenario very different from the declarative, linear thrust of traditional evangelism.

Evangelicals like Newman stress that Christians have a responsibility not only to perform the gospel authentically on evangelistic stages but also to attend to the theological context that surrounds and shapes prospects' responses to any singular evangelistic pitch. Though they retain faith in the transforming power of God's word, such evangelists emphasize that all outreach scenarios unfold within specific cultural situations. Post-Christendom, twenty-first-century Western culture, they argue, poses considerable challenges to the smooth operation of the proclamation-reception model that informs confrontational approaches. To acknowledge these challenges, they argue, is not to deny the miracle-working power of the Holy Spirit, but it is to suggest that proclamation alone does not suffice. A powerful message is necessary but not sufficient to create converts. Something beyond or before that message must complement its proclamation. I call these approaches *meta-kerygmatic* in that they emphasize accounting for and moving beyond the pure proclamation of the gospel.

In this chapter, I examine a few of these meta-kerygmatic counter-approaches as interventions into the formulaic dramaturgy of the confrontational evangelisms I studied in the previous chapter. In contrast to the race to conversion that defines much of confrontational evangelism, these techniques slow down. They acknowledge and even delve into rather than dodge the objections or hang-ups that prospects may harbor about the gospel. And while all of them desire the eventual conversion of unbelievers, none of them aim explicitly for or judge their success on the production of a theological performative. Theirs might instead be called a form of *prevangelism* (or *pre-evangelism*), an intentionally incomplete evangelistic scene opening a way toward or planting a seed of an eventual relationship with Christ. I begin by examining a direct reaction to confrontational evangelism, Jim Henderson's Doable Evangelism approach. From there I turn to the renaissance of conversational apologetics apparent in Greg Koukl's Ambassador Model and Greg Stier's Dare 2 Share viral evangelism approach.

Apologies for Ugly Evangelism

One of the most obvious examples of meta-kerygmatic evangelism responds directly to the negative blowback created by kerygmatic evangelists' tactics. An example: in the spring of 2005, an associate pastor of an evangelical church in Santa Ana, California, Josh Matlock, led a group of parishioners onto local campuses armed with postcards to hand out and a message to share with passersby. In place of a "turn or burn" message, an invitation to God's wonderful plan, or even a clever introduction to a Ten Commandments test, the messages Matlock's church passed out read, "Apology #1: We're Sorry for Our Self-Righteousness and Hypocrisy." A week later, the church repeated its actions with "Apology #2: We're Sorry for Our Endorsement of Slavery." Each subsequent week saw the congregation issuing another apology. "We're Sorry for Our Mistreatment of Homosexuals." "We're Sorry for the Medieval Crusades." "We're Sorry for Saying the Earth is Flat." Matlock claims to have distributed 2,500 such cards, each with a copy of the apology and an invitation to a "free event" at the church. "Bring friends, neighbors, acquaintances, enemies, siblings, strangers who are college age," read the invitations. "We are serious about our need to confess to you. It is not a joke." The free event of course was a church service featuring a sermon series about the week's confession.[2]

Since Matlock's initiative, multiple congregations across the country have taken up the "Confessions of a Sinful Church" strategy. Kensington Community Church, a multisite church (see chapter seven) based in Troy, Michigan, sponsored their own "Confessions" sermon series in 2008, with apologies for "judging you," "being too political," "shutting out homosexuals," and "discriminating against Muslims."[3] Their promo video features a pastor interviewing people on the street, asking not "Are you a good person?" but questions such as "When you hear the word *Christian* or *evangelical Christian,* what's your first impression?" "Where do I start?" laughs the passerby, who then proceeds to voice a series of views echoed by other interviewees. Christians are hypocrites. They are judgemental. They mean well but come off as hateful. They are nosy. They are bigoted. They aren't like Jesus. And the pastor, hearing this, responds simply and humbly. "I think you've nailed it," he says, "wanting to communicate love but not coming across that way. I just want to say to you, man, I feel like I've blown it. I feel like I've been a part of that. Sorry for that."[4] The trend continues, and a web search for "confessions of a sinful church" reveal any number of variations on this theme in churches around the country.

Such encounters unfold light-years from the confrontational strategies of Anderson, Comfort, or the classic Campus Crusade for Christ. Instead, these public confessions of ecclesiastical sin seem more attuned

Kensington Community Church co-founder and lead pastor Steve Andrews holds up a sign for his church at a local football game. This image is the cover art for Kensington's 2008 message series, "We're Sorry." Reproduction permission thanks to Kensington Community Church.

to the (non-evangelical) public's negative reaction to evangelical Christianity in general. What good is the message if no one listens to the messenger? Many of the meta-kerygmatic evangelists I study here are keenly concerned that evangelicals' reputation does not predispose audiences to hear the gospel proclaimed. Perhaps the most exemplary and influential evangelical work along these lines is the bestselling 2007 book *UnChristian: What a New Generation Really Thinks about Christianity . . . And Why It Matters,* by Barna Group researchers David Kinnaman and Gabe Lyons. Through a series of quantitative and qualitative surveys and interviews, Kinnaman and Lyons canvass thousands of "Outsiders"—people in the United States not belonging to a Christian faith—for their views on present-day Christianity. The authors focus mainly on demographics they name "Busters" (born between 1965 and 1983) and "Mosaics" (born between 1984 and 2002), with a special emphasis on respondents aged sixteen to twenty-nine.[5] From these interviews, they conclude that US Christianity faces a crisis of public relations, a failure of effective Christian witness. They find that among Outsiders, the three most common perceptions about "present-day Christianity" are *antihomosexual, judgemental,* and *hypocritical,* followed by a list of negatives like "old-fashioned, too involved in politics, out of touch with reality, insensitive to others, boring, not accepting of other faiths, and confusing."[6] While not the only perceptions Outsiders have (they are mixed with some positive associations), these findings contradict the self-image most Christians have of their own outreach efforts.[7] Christians see themselves as projecting sincere love and Christ-like concern. To Outsiders—especially Busters and Mosaics—Christians often seem consumed by a salesperson's drive for commissions, overly eager to re-route every encounter, every conversation, into a so-aren't-you-bothered-by-your-imminent-damnation pitch. The people in Christians' audiences—Outsiders—simply aren't getting the impression Christians believe they display.

Nor, argue Kinnaman and Lyons, can Christians blame Outsiders' negative impressions on stereotypes circulated by an ostensibly anti-Christian popular media. Most Outsiders, they report, develop their sense of Christianity from firsthand experience with real-life Christians. Many Outsiders recount having been members of churches themselves or maintaining friendships with committed Christians. These personal experiences, which some Outsiders found actively hurtful, substantiate the ambivalent-to-negative attitudes of a majority of twentysomethings toward the church.[8] Outsiders gather firsthand evidence of Christianity's antihomosexual, judgemental, and insincere (or faux-sincere) elements. Not surprisingly, Kinnaman and Lyons conclude, many young adults enter their twenties identifying as Christian but enter their thirties having drifted away from faith. Outsiders are not so much *unchurched* as *de-churched,* dissuaded from a lifetime of Christian discipleship in part by the poor examples of Christian disciples.[9] Kinnaman and Lyons warn that, unless Christianity in the United States recognizes and addresses these trends, their witness will continue to lose or even repel younger generations.

The perceived hemorrhaging of young ("emerging adult") people within US Christian churches is a widespread theme in current evangelical discourse. Attention to catching and keeping the devotion of teenagers and those in their twenties has become something of a synecdoche for evangelicalism's faltering more generally. *UnChristian* joins a growing library of books within and without evangelicalism dedicated to investigating the phenomenon of generational falloff, speculating on its implications, and suggesting solutions.[10] While the diagnoses of the core problem differ slightly, the recurrent conclusion is threefold: Christianity (read: orthodox evangelical Christianity) is in trouble, Christians bear some of the blame, and evangelicals must rethink their approaches to evangelism if they are to help fix the problem. One of the leading evangelical voices engaged in such a rethinking is Jim Henderson.

All You're Really Doing Anyway: Doable Evangelism and Not *Preaching*

Each week on the public radio program (and podcast) *This American Life,* host Ira Glass explains that the producers take a theme and present a variety of stories around that theme. For the week of November 9, 2009, the theme was "Bait and Switch," focusing on instances in which a lure into a decision, a situation, or a lifestyle turns out to be a ploy—a lie, really—in which what gets delivered differs from what was initially offered. One of the segments concerns the bait-and-switch tactics that some Christian groups use to lure in unsuspecting "lost" people. One of the correspondents, Dave Dickerson, had been raised as an evangelical, and he recalls participating in a number of Campus Crusade for Christ events that used the tactic. There he handed out fliers for a luau advertising "free drinks"—but no mention that the drinks were non-alcoholic or that the event was sponsored by an evangelical group. Those attending got an evening packed with lamentably wholesome party games punctuated with occasional speeches from CCC members about how Christ had changed their lives. Dickerson also got trained to conduct "surveys" (a long-standing CCC strategy) which would begin with innocent inquiries about spiritual beliefs and turn into a seemingly spontaneous invitation to a local church or CCC meeting. Dickerson recalls experiencing such tactics as nonstarters. "The false pretense was supposed to make [evangelizing] easier, was supposed to give us cover so that we didn't seem religious," he tells Glass. "And it wasn't fooling us. So it seemed both false and didn't really help."[11]

To counterpoint Dickerson's experience, Glass turns to Jim Henderson, an evangelical pastor with over twenty-five years of experience in the ministry. Henderson, in his blog about the interview, recalls not being surprised: a show about bait-and-switch tactics? "*Of course they thought about Christians.*" Henderson serves as one of the foremost critics of traditional evangelistic approaches in the United States. He has written extensively on the failures of traditional evangelism and counsels churches in (his words) "helping Christians learn how to not be jerks." In the interview, Henderson acknowledges that "bait and switch" does perhaps describe a lot of contemporary evangelical approaches (including some I touched on in the previous chapter). "I told Ira," he explains in his blog, "that when I was in my evangelism heyday, Bait and Switch techniques were for sissies. Instead, we went straight at people cold turkey. No Bait and Switch for us—it was All Switch and no Bait." After hearing about Henderson's alternative evangelical tactics, however, Glass concluded that Henderson's approach seems more like "all bait and no switch"—a description Henderson endorses.[12]

Henderson's own testimony retells how in the mid-1990s he "resigned" from witnessing. "I knew," he writes, "I could never go back to the same old programs, the contrived joviality, or the fake evangelistic caring."[13] He did not leave the faith. The message of saving grace through trust in Christ remains true and powerful for him, and he affirms that Christians have a duty to be witnesses for Christ in the world. But the predominant models of spreading the good news, he argues, do not work. "Evangelism isn't normal," he contends. "It's a program, a presentation, a memorized script. It's formalized and structured, and as a result, Christians have to work up a lot of nerve just to do it."[14] Very few people are gifted with the ability to go door-to-door, stranger-to-stranger, and deliver the hard-but-true news of how sinful the prospect is and how necessary it is for the prospect to convert. Fewer people still actually respond positively or permanently to such pitches. Echoing Kinnaman and Lyons's research findings, Henderson maintains that confrontational, just-the-message evangelism projects an ugly picture of committed Christianity. "If evangelism-by-frontal-assault works," he writes, "then let's all start carrying large signs that say, 'You are lost! You are bad. You are an idiot! Ask *me* for help!' Like it or not, that's often how we appear in the eyes of the people Jesus misses most."[15] Kerygmatic evangelism rarely gets done, argues Henderson, and when it is practiced, it too often backfires.

In 2000, Henderson founded an organization called Off The Map dedicated to rethinking what effective outreach to the lost might mean. First and foremost, the group decided, the words evangelicals use to describe non-Christians had to change, especially the term *lost.* "I came to the conclusion," relates Henderson, "that for the most part, using *lost* as much as we did generally made us [evangelists] meaner people. It made it harder for us to connect with 'lost' people." Believers, he observes, typically only use the term among themselves, behind the backs of "lost" people.[16] Henderson and his colleagues at Off The Map lean more toward terms like "missing persons," "outsiders" (which he draws from Kinnaman and Lyons), or "the people Jesus misses the most."[17] The main difference from *lost,* Henderson explains, lies not in the fact that *outsider* is necessarily kinder or more inclusive; he admits that the term only underlines the other-ing tendencies in evangelistic approaches. Yet in such transparency lies the appeal. "My contention," he relates, "is that if Christians want to create these divides, we at least should own up to them and say the word to outsiders' faces."[18] No false bait allowed. Off The Map subsequently inspired a number of related ministries, most notably Henderson's current organization, Jim Henderson Presents, and a related organization called Doable Evangelism, led by evangelist Randy Siever.[19]

In their work leading evangelism workshops with congregations around the country, Henderson and Siever typically ask the local church they visit to arrange an "Interview with Three Lost People." That is, they ask that churches find a few people in their local community who do not attend church and invite them in for a public interview between them and the visiting Doable Evangelism minister. All church members attending the session must agree to a compact ("the Off The Map Pledge of Kindness"): *no evangelizing.*[20] The interviewer asks the guests to talk about their experiences with Christians, especially instances in which someone Christian tried to convert them. The interviews proceed with the guests sharing their stories and taking questions (or even accepting apologies) from audience members. Henderson and Siever have made several of these interviews available online for churches to use, and Henderson has a book/DVD combo to explore the issues around these interviews.[21]

The "stop trying to convert and start listening" ethic embodied in the public interviews encapsulates Henderson and Siever's overall approach to changing the evangelistic paradigm. In his initial book outlining his approach, *Evangelism Without Additives* (originally published as *AKA "Lost"*), Henderson alternates manifesto-type argument (e.g., why traditional outreach is both awkward and ineffective) and exercises in his alternative mode, small activities that challenge readers to put into practice a better sort of evangelism. His exercises resemble similar prompts in more traditional evangelistic how-to literature, but their trajectory diverges from that of the traditional model. "This week," he suggests in one exercise, "ask someone this question: 'How are you?' . . . When the person begins to answer, actually listen. Don't interrupt with your own story. Spend a few minutes being unusually interested in the person, and leave it at that. Don't witness, preach, or say anything religious."[22] Other prompts barely go beyond this simple task. Go somewhere and observe people for a while. Ask questions. Make small talk. Practice normal (i.e., non-religious) conversation.[23] Take pauses to notice and investigate small, significant moments in yourself and others.[24] Interact (lightly, non-religiously) with people around you that you'd normally not.[25] All of his instructions repeat his command not to advance the conversation beyond simple listening and exchange. Henderson repeatedly counsels readers to avoid the standard overtures of evangelism like the "if you died tonight" question.[26] He warns them to cleanse their dialogue with Outsiders of evangelical jargon, even providing a list of banned words and phrases.[27]

For a work advancing a significant criticism of evangelical outreach, many of Henderson's replacement exercises less resemble new scripts for witnessing and are more like remedial lessons in socialization. To a certain extent, Henderson argues precisely that present-day Christians need such lessons to purge them of the traditional evangelical falseness that makes sharing faith into a contrived, uncomfortable chore. The evangelists I wrote about in the previous chapter each picture outreach as a distinct scenario removed from the normal flux of life. In their approach, evangelism consists of interrupting the random flow of everyday existence with a crisis of faith, a life-or-death microdrama where the prospect meets Eternity itself. From Henderson's perspective, Christians have to unlearn the false interaction scripts of traditional interpersonal evangelism. They must stop imposing on or interrupting normal life with a crisis melodrama. Indeed, Henderson concludes, "We [evangelicals] need to lose our fascination with drama. Once we give ourselves permission to *not* do something dramatic, we begin to see the people who have been there all the time."[28] This is a major distinction between Henderson's evangelism and the kerygmatic models. Anderson, the classical Campus Crusade, and Comfort all call on Christians to be poised to turn an everyday situation into confrontation with the Word of God, a sacred (as in removed-from-the-ordinary) encounter that transforms. Henderson, by contrast, insists on dissolving the distinction between holy epiphany and ordinary interaction.

In this spirit, Henderson christens the small actions of engagement and listening that he champions "Ordinary Attempts." The *ordinary* emphasizes that they are simple efforts at honest engagement with people already in a Christian's life rather than specially created scenarios thrust upon unsuspecting neighbors or passersby. He calls these acts *attempts* to distinguish them from *accomplishments,* "so no extra credit is awarded for succeeding and no demerits are given for failing." Ordinary attempts are essentially "free attention giveaways"[29] characterized not by a close-the-deal drive toward conversion but rather by what Henderson calls "nonmanipulative intentionality." "It's fine to want your friend to know Jesus and to even attempt to persuade him or her to consider Jesus," he clarifies. "But it's not fine to pressure, coerce, or steer your friend. Human beings don't like to be manipulated, but we are receptive to influence."[30] Confrontational evangelism—springing the crisis of are-you-going-to-hell (or even do-you-want-God's-wonderful-plan) on people—fails to influence. It disconcerts. It upsets. It alienates. It produces, in sum, the negative stereotype of evangelicals that defines so many Outsider impressions. To combat that stereotype and to undo the habits that nurture it require that Christians re-learn how to create and sustain actual, authentic relationships.

Of course, Henderson's Ordinary Attempts do not ignore spiritual issues. Some of his prompts encourage conversation along spiritual lines, though the intention is purely to gather information, not to maneuver someone into a conversion script. He even recommends conducting an informal spiritual survey of strangers. Unlike the Campus Crusade surveys mentioned in *This American Life* that end with a segue into the Four Spiritual Laws, Henderson's four-question survey concludes by asking, "If Christians would listen, what would you tell them?" and "Has anyone ever tried to 'save' you?" After listening politely and without comment to the answers, Henderson instructs readers to "say 'thank you' and let him or her go without doing any preaching."[31] At the heart of nonmanipulative intentionality, he emphasizes, is the imperative *not to preach*—an abstention from kerygmatic performance. Asking for someone's opinion about spiritual things or about Christianity means that you—the Christian—must resist the urge to correct them, to point them to the straight and narrow. Nor should Christians verbally acknowledge that they are doing anything outside of ordinary, open interaction. At most, Henderson recommends praying for Outsiders—but without their knowing it. Often, an evangelical's "I'll pray for you" can be interpreted (and is sometimes delivered) as a passive-aggressive threat (i.e., "I hope you admit how wrong you've been and realize how right I am"). Henderson thus stresses the need for "praying behind their backs"—directing thoughtful, spiritual attention to Outsiders—all without their knowing about it.[32]

These small, ordinary attempts comprise what Henderson calls Doable Evangelism (thus the name of Siever's spinoff organization Doable Evangelism). In contrast to the extraordinary and therefore vanishingly rare efforts that make up traditional (kerygmatic) interpersonal outreach, doable evangelism involves infusing one's day-to-day interactions with spiritual intention and awareness. It describes a discipline of interest in and concern for others separated from the need to close the deal with a confirmed conversion. The ordinary attempts of doable evangelism work, he argues, because they shed the manipulative subtext of kerygmatic interactions. They aren't about chatting in order to turn the conversation to "if you were to die tonight" questions; they're about chatting in order to demonstrate concern for another person. Doable evangelism also works, writes Henderson, because it is, well, *doable.* It requires no superhuman zeal or divine audacity; it necessitates no disruption of the flux and flow of everyday life. Ordinary attempts are, instead, "all you're going to do anyway," so they are already preferable to the soul-winner's model.[33]

All Bait, No Switch

Clearly Henderson, Siever, and their colleagues traffic in a different set of standards for what efficacy of outreach means than those that Steven Anderson holds. A more traditional evangelist would likely concur with Glass's skeptical conclusion that doable evangelism is essentially "all bait and no switch." It's so ordinary that it makes no apparent difference except to perhaps make evangelists more pleasant people to engage in conversation. From the crisis perspective of Anderson or Comfort, such mundane civility in the face of imminent damnation represents an inexcusable crime, like waving cheerily at someone about to walk off a high cliff. Certainly, they would concede, some minimal politeness may be necessary just to get people to listen, but such niceties are preludes to the nitty-gritty of evangelism, not the thing itself. Siever disagrees mightily. The notion of "pre-evangelism," Siever explains, depends upon a model of conversion entirely focused on a one-moment-in-time transition from "saved" to "non-saved" brought about by the verbal proclamation of the gospel. Using a combination of Bible verses and statistical research, Siever counters that the singular-conversion model need not be normative and that it often does not match the experiences of actual Christians. People's decisions to become disciples, he points out, most often occur over a long period of time—months or even years—rather than as the result of a single presentation.[34] The decisions come not only from verbal proclamations but also from meaningful, positive interaction with Christian disciples. Ordinary attempts are not therefore "pre-evangelistic"; they are evangelism par excellence.[35]

Henderson complements Siever's argument by challenging the unilateral quality of transformation presumed in the kerygmatic conversion model. Traditional interpersonal evangelism, he argues, assumes that only the prospect needs changing. Not so, contends Henderson. He finds that such an assumption results in manipulative intentionality, a compulsion to "close the deal" with every customer, that inevitably comes off as false or condescending. Authentic conversion—really participating in the transformation of another's faith—requires authentic connections between those already converted and those not converted. In his more recent work Henderson in fact calls on Christians to be "connectors" instead of evangelists, even suggesting that connectors might replace evangelists in the coming decades. "Here's why," he explains, "Evangelists have *speaking* skills; connectors have *listening* skills. Evangelists *win* people to Christ; connectors *woo* people to Christ. . . . Finally, evangelists count *conversions;* connectors count *conversations.*"[36]

Henderson illustrates his point by citing two evangelists, Beth and Kirk, who excel at making connections. Kirk, a pastor, schedules 25 percent of his professional hours "hanging out" at a Starbucks, just making conversation with people there. Beth and Kirk don't just love the people they connect to, Henderson maintains; they *like* them. They like people so much that they refuse to ruin their connections with sales-pitch tactics that would strain that connection. Yet their ministries have resulted in outsiders making commitments to Christ, people who otherwise would never tolerate, let alone be persuaded by, a soul-winning presentation. What changes, Henderson argues, is the "power of like." "Kirk and Beth," he concludes, "have discovered that *when people like each other, the rules change.*"[37] Henderson reinforces this conclusion by sharing a youthful experience in which he found himself involved with a drug culture due to the passive influence of a friend he liked. The rule-changing influence of authentic connection, he warns, can flow either way.[38] In a Christian context, the price for authentic connection is the evangelist's need to arrive at the climax of conversion in every encounter with "lost" people. Only by giving up the obligatory scene of the sinner's prayer, letting go of the compulsory dramaturgy of the soul-winning pitch, can the evangelist hope to create a real connection to another.

As they would likely admit, Henderson and Siever are neither the first nor the only evangelicals to call for non-confrontational outreach. Many of their arguments recapitulate those of previous evangelicals who have sought to reimagine evangelism along more interpersonal, everyday lines. The late 1970s and early 1980s, for example, saw the rise of "lifestyle evangelism" and "friendship evangelism" as popular trends in several Christian circles. These terms refer to non-confrontational modes of witnessing in which believers live a life that exemplifies the appeal of Christianity while forming meaningful friendships that (hopefully) naturally produce opportunities to share faith. In his seminal (and popular) 1981 book on lifestyle evangelism, evangelist Joe Aldrich describes his approach as "incarnational/relational" in contrast to "proclamational" or "intrusive/confrontational" models.[39] Much of what he and other lifestyle/friendship evangelists recommend tracks closely with Henderson's and Siever's doable evangelism. Like them, Aldrich recommends Christians take care not to initiate unwelcome or intrusive proselytizing overtures, choosing instead to cultivate an appealing, day-to-day witness that leads non-believers to be curious about what makes their Christian neighbor tick. Yet Henderson and Siever strike a more reformist tone than Aldrich. They do not offer Doable Evangelism as merely the latest, more effective form of outreach for reaching cynical-secular postmodern outsiders. Their methods of ordinary attempts, outsider interviews, and praying behind people's backs primarily target the evangelist herself. Siever and Henderson promote a discipline of un-learning the lifestyle of evangelical culture that in their view produces Christians who—

despite the best of intentions and a sincere desire to live out the Great Commission—end up repelling the very people they are trying to reach. It is basic training in interpersonal skills for Christians, a training necessary (in Henderson's and Siever's views) for the continued health of the evangelical enterprise.

A Step beyond the Front End of Evangelism: Apologetics

Henderson and Siever focus, as they say, on "the very front end" of disciple-making processes.[40] Insofar as their approach calls for resisting formulaic, close-the-deal evangelism and engaging in authentic exchanges with unbelievers, few evangelicals would disagree. Even the kerygmatic soul-winners of my previous chapter would protest that they follow the spirit of these recommendations. But Doable Evangelism parts company with most other approaches in its assertion that Christians should stay at that front end of evangelism and (at least for a time) not advance to more directed or persuasive communication. For the soul-winner, an evangelistic conversation that does not contain the literal gospel message fails to qualify as an evangelistic conversation at all. To them, a "free attention giveaway" sans gospel is no more evangelism than smiling warmly at a stranger on the sidewalk is environmentalism. The strand of personal evangelism to which I turn now, conversational apologetics, might be seen as occupying a middle way between the pure proclamation of soul-winning and the pure incarnation of Doable Evangelism. Like the latter movement, conversational apologetics notes the need for preparatory work before someone can really hear the gospel message. Unlike Henderson's approach, however, interpersonal apologetics proceeds from the assumption that Christianity necessarily includes an element of disruption, a sense of ill fit with the non-Christian world. A Christian's job, in this view, involves making that difference-from-the-world both appealing and unmistakable. It operates as a nudge beyond the nonconfrontational bonhomie of ordinary attempts while rarely entering fully into the realm of overt proclamation.

Apologetics per se is nothing new. Evangelicals have long understood that Christians must be willing and able to defend their faith. They cite 1 Peter 3:15, for example, which commands, "Always be prepared to give an answer to everyone who asks you to give reason for the hope that you have." The word translated *answer* here is the Greek *apologia* (defense), and Christians have historically embraced the term *apologetics* as a polemic justification for faith in the face of skepticism or heresy. Traditionally, apologetics named erudite defenses by Church Fathers against (initially) Greek and Jewish detractors of Christianity and (later) justifications of faith by major theologians. It described the work of elite scholars producing learned treatises of philosophical and theological rigor. Ensconced within hegemonic Christendom, the average Christian rarely needed to (let alone enjoyed the education necessary to) engage in such rarefied discourse. Why defend what everyone around you more or less already believes? Christian belief has rarely been static or homogeneous. During Christianity's periodic (and often violent) schisms, a kind of apologetic awareness—a basic knowledge of and advocacy for the distinctive beliefs of one's side—perhaps accompanied struggles between Orthodox and Catholic, Catholic and Protestant, Calvinist and Arminian, and so on. In addition, colonial projects in the early modern era on produced "discoveries" of primitive peoples following native, non-Christian faiths; such populations and their religions became the object of overseas missions. But rarely did the average post-Reformation Christian growing up in Western Europe or the United States see the need for formal defenses of their religion.

Throughout much of the nineteenth and twentieth centuries, in many parts of the United States (most notably the Bible Belt) this hegemony of faith essentially defined the cultural backdrop. To tap into personal anecdote for a moment, I experienced this hegemony firsthand, growing up in a series of small, rural towns in Oklahoma and Louisiana. Until I entered high school in a larger city, I can't remember ever encountering someone who was not to my knowledge some flavor of "Christian" (though a few of these were from my perspective rather exotic, like Jehovah's Witnesses or Mormons). I knew, of course, that Hindus, Buddhists, and Muslims existed, but for the most part these remained theoretical realities occasionally discussed in social studies classes or by a visiting missionary who had served abroad. The saturated, internet-linked plurality of the secular age, however, makes such a cloistered upbringing if not impossible, then more difficult to sustain.

To an extent undreamed of in my childhood, demographic, political, and technological shifts have multiplied the number and variety of faith positions that US citizens encounter in person or electronically every day. Hindus, Buddhists, and (especially) Muslims are now no longer fantastic notions; they are here-and-now, right-down-the-street, or at least talking-on-this-channel/website people whom even the most sheltered Southern Baptist has to acknowledge. Not only are more kinds of faith present in popular culture and everyday life, but with the recent popularity of "new atheists" like Christopher Hitchens, Sam Harris, and Richard Dawkins, various strands of atheism and agnosticism have cropped up to challenge the basis for religious belief altogether. Not content simply to not believe in the supernatural, some of these new atheists have taken on a sort of evangelical fervor themselves, actively arguing for the benefits of a secular outlook.

Perhaps more sobering for evangelicals than either non-Christian faiths or proselytizing atheists, however, is the demographic one *USA Today* article deems the "So Whats." As reported by several religious belief surveys, this "So What" segment of the population evinces scant interest in any spiritual orientation or issue. They do not wonder about life after death. They are not concerned with finding a deep or transcendent direction to their lives. They don't lament the decline of religion in the United States. Religion—or even focused opposition to religion—simply does not exert much attraction for them. The So Whats are not atheists in the Dawkins/Hitchens vein so much as they are (in the words of atheist blogger Hemant Mehta) "apatheists."[41] They are neither overly threatened by nor especially attracted to or nostalgic for religion. To be sure, bona fide So Whats—those registering no religious identification—represent a minority (less than 10 percent) of the US population. But researchers are discovering an uptick in So What-ish sentiments, a general caring less about religion, even among the religiously identified. All three trends—increasing religious plurality, a more articulate and evangelical atheist sector, a growing segment of people who feel no religious compulsion at all—characterize the new religious landscape of the secular age. To repeat Charles Taylor's thesis, the secular age signals not *unbelief displacing belief* but *diversification of available belief/nonbelief positions.* The secular age renders the assumptions of purely kerygmatic evangelism problematic.

One of the main reactions to this secular age within evangelicalism has been a renaissance of apologetics as a necessary component of effective outreach. A 2008 *Christianity Today* article about the resurgence of apologetics notes the unprecedented popularity of big-name apologists such as Josh McDowell, Lee Strobel, and William Lane Craig.[42] Craig, a philosophy professor at Talbot Theological Seminary in California, is particularly known for elaborating erudite cosmological arguments for theism. He balances his work as a scholar with a side career as a professional debater and speaker. His public debates with popular atheists have drawn audiences of hundreds, with thousands more watching and responding to his performances online.[43] Concomitant with the fame of superstar apologists is the spread of apologetics training programs for churches, especially youth groups. "The apologetics resurgence," says evangelist Sean McDowell, "has been sparked ultimately by teens who are asking more questions about why people believe the things they do."[44] No longer is apologetics seen as purely the domain of scholars like Craig. "Apologetics is not a peripheral discipline for Christian egg-heads," argues apologetics professor Douglas Groothuis. "It's right at the center of the kingdom of God."[45]

The Presupposition of Total Truth: Schaefferian Apologetics

Although the turn to apologetics among evangelicals stems from a number of sources, most of the major streams of the apologetics renaissance trace their sources back to the influence of Francis Schaeffer (1912–84), a US theologian perhaps most famous for founding a Christian retreat in Switzerland, the L'Abri Fellowship.[46] Broadly fascinated with the influence of Christianity on historical and contemporary art, literature, and music (and vice versa), Schaeffer promulgated a vision of conservative evangelical Christianity as resistant to the assumptions and values of post-Enlightenment modernity. Though he himself largely stayed aloof from direct political engagement, Schaeffer's vision influenced major figures in the Christian right of the 1980s and 1990s. He and his ideas appear ubiquitously throughout the work of apologist evangelicals I discuss in this chapter.

At the core of his approach is an argument about epistemology. In one of his signature works, *The God Who Is There* (initially published in 1968), Schaeffer traces the history of what he considers the decisive feature of modern life: the dissolution of belief in absolute, communicable truth.[47] He identifies Hegel as originating a basic skepticism toward absolute truth, exchanging what Schaeffer calls an "antithetical" view of truth (i.e., that which is true cannot be false, and vice versa) for a "dialectic" view (i.e., truth and non-truth do not exist stably but merge into a synthesis). In Schaeffer's view, this philosophical innovation represented a sharp departure from centuries of Christian (and, prior to that, classical) thought about the nature of reality and human interaction with reality. He sees Hegel's philosophical view spreading outward through the late nineteenth and early twentieth centuries, infusing the realms of art, music, general culture, and ultimately theology. The result, he concludes, is that Western culture has lost the willingness and ability to distinguish reliably between truth and falsehood, right and wrong.

Schaeffer proposes that modern culture has instead fractured formerly unified epistemological processes. He deploys a "two-story" metaphor for diagnosing modernity's bifurcated epistemology. In the "upper story," Schaeffer locates the modern realm of *meaning*. Here, humans operate on the basis of deep convictions and affective passions—*faith,* in other words. The ground for such convictions, however, lies not in evidence, logic, or reason (such being anathema to the upper-story values) but on a "leap of faith," a spiritual-philosophical gamble of whole-self conviction that eschews direct relation to material (scientific or historical) reality. Humanity as imagined on this story resembles a shade, free-floating and insubstantial. On the "lower floor" Schaeffer locates a realm of *reason* trafficking solely in cold, empirical facts. While such pure naturalism proves invaluable for the sciences, it falters when directed at more value-based, immaterial matters like love, art, or justice. Its significance is restricted to soulless calculations of brute survival—or brute destruction.[48] Humans in this realm, observes Schaeffer, can be little more than machines.[49] For Schaeffer, this split vision of truth condemns humanity to a state of despair and pervasive pessimism. Since humans are inextricably *within* and *of* reality, he reasons, the split view of reality denies them an essentially unified view of themselves and their world. Within this fissured existence, the world (i.e., life, humanity, selfhood) can be either meaningful but not verifiable or verifiable but not meaningful. Living according to the rules of either story leads to moral, artistic, philosophical, and spiritual dead ends: destructive nihilism, empty mysticism, and resigned apathy. The bulk of his book consists of his readings of various (Western) mid-century philosophers, artists, writers, and theologians whose productions exemplify for Schaeffer the history and consequences of this anguished split.[50]

By contrast, Schaeffer maintains, Christianity embodies the unified system par excellence. It has historically wagered its existence upon absolute truth—meaning and reason indissolubly linked—faithfully communicated to and by humans.[51] The Christian system refuses a binary or dialectical distinction between meaning and rationality, and therefore cannot take refuge on either floor. Nor does it need to. As a faithful expression of the unified nature of the really-real, Christianity alone satisfies humans' need for deep meaning grounded in material, historical reality. It has no need to keep itself cloistered on the second floor of free-floating belief. Schaeffer is adamant that Christianity, as far as it can be verified scientifically and historically, ought to be so verified. Christianity, as far as it can be logically and rationally assessed, should so meet challenges of logic and rationality. "It [Christianity] is prepared," writes Schaeffer, "to face the consequences of being proved false and say with Paul: If you find the body of Christ, the discussion is finished; let us eat and drink, for tomorrow we die."[52] Either God created the universe as we know it—or not. Either God intervened materially into a lost world in the person of Jesus Christ—or not. Either Christ lived a perfect life, died for humanity's sins, and rose from the grave—or not. If not, then Christianity, along with any unified system of meaning-truth-significance, is an exploded proposition.

Yet rather than serving as a beacon for a lost and despairing world, Schaeffer laments, present-day Christianity has itself fallen into the two-story trap. As he interprets things, nineteenth-century biblical historians (particularly the German higher critics) sought initially to lend Christianity the full support of historical and archeological evidence for its claims (e.g., Christ's life, crucifixion, and literal resurrection). These historians surrendered, however, to the naturalist presupposition that miracles could not happen. Within the bounds of such assumptions, the Bible's accounts of supernatural events (the Creation, the worldwide flood, the life and passion of Jesus) must be either explained by non-supernatural science or discounted as superstition and myth. No miracles—no divine intervention into mortal life—equals no Christian story. Unwilling to either challenge this naturalist presupposition or to declare the faith defunct, Christianity retreated fully from the lower story of truth to the upper story of meaning, ceding the epistemological and cultural authority of science and history to secular culture.[53] In this Faustian bargain, Christianity secures its survival by agreeing to refrain from making verifiable truth claims. *Sincerity* replaces *verity* as the marker of Christian orthodoxy. Christian faith morphs, then, into a soft mysticism with no ambition beyond a subjective, non-rational, and incommunicable persuasion. As such, it languishes as an unpersuasive persuasion. Christianity has ceded its right to popular appeal and broad relevance.

To many present-day evangelicals, Schaeffer's portrait of a compromised Christianity struggling within a truth-averse culture captures the malaise of the secular age perfectly. His prescription for curing this disease similarly resonates. Christians, he urges, must rejuvenate a vision of Christianity as a—as *the*—complete, unified system of truth. The Christian faith must breach the self-imposed quarantine of the second story and assert its proper status as what Schaefferite evangelicals Nancy

Pearcey and Charles Colson call "total truth."[54] It must argue not just for its affective appeal but also for its material, historical validity, refuting the idea that Christianity has no purchase on lower-floor procedures of verification or relevance. Evangelism, he argues, must embrace an apologetic mission.

Yet not just any apologetic will do. It is not enough simply to declare Christianity as total truth. No matter how comprehensive and sophisticated the case Christians make, the appeal to truth will fail in a modern setting. Classical apologists, Schaeffer explains, largely enjoyed the benefit of sharing with those they spoke to a basic faith in absolute truth. Though they had to struggle to convince people of the content of that truth, they could more or less rely on the assumption that their audiences believed that Truth existed, that it was the opposite of falsehood, and that the distinction between Truth and falsehood could be demonstrated. Modern culture, however, does not recognize absolute truth as a coherent concept. Christians can argue all they like about the truth of Christianity; to a world alienated from the very idea of total truth, such an argument might as well be a series of clicks and whistles. Modern-day apologetics, Schaeffer maintains, must meet people where they are, entering provisionally into their assumptions about life and reality. Apologetics must, in other words, become *presuppositional* in orientation.

A brief word here on twentieth-century apologetic schools is in order. As sub-discipline within Christian scholarship and theology, apologetics recognizes that a broad spectrum of approaches for asserting and defending the Christian faith exists. I lack the space here to describe this spectrum fully.[55] Two of the main players in the last century or so, however, have been evidentialism and presuppositionalism. Evidentialist apologetics attempts a neutral presentation of facts to support the Christian faith. Josh McDowell's popular *Evidence that Demands a Verdict* (in its several editions) and Lee Strobel's *The Case for Christ* exemplify this approach. In those works (and their multiple respective spin-offs, e.g., *The Case for Faith, The Case for the Resurrection, The Case for the Creator*), the Christian faith story (i.e., Christ's birth, life, death, and resurrection) constitutes a factual, verifiable reality that can be judged true by any impartial inquirer. Defense of the faith consists mainly of an objective presentation and examination of available evidence, the weight of which will ostensibly support Christian conclusions, since only Christianity presents the Truth. The apologist's role involves providing skeptics with the relevant evidence, bolstered by logical reasoning, to "win" the case for Christianity. To that end, popular evidentialists use legal (McDowell) or journalistic (Strobel) models of proof and accumulative argument to validate the historical and scientific underpinnings of the Christian story.[56]

Presuppositionalists, by contrast, hold that humans primarily operate not on the basis of evidence neutrally gathered and assessed but on the basis of pre-rational assumptions about life, truth, and values. This view attributes belief in Christian truth to pre-rational assumptions about epistemology, ontology, and theology.[57] Belief in the Christian God functions as the foundation of all legitimate rationality, and no one can hope to bracket that fact for the sake of a "neutral" discussion with unbelief. Appeals to evidence will fail, from the presuppositionalist perspective, without the realization that humans read all "evidence" through the lens of their own preconceptions.

Given the reality of multiple and incommensurate truth systems, a presuppositional approach would seem at first to replicate Schaeffer's dismal portrait of modern truth, stranding everyone on their own island of truth-assumptions. Such a view would appear to snuff out the possibility of evangelism altogether. How can you even speak to, let alone persuade, people who hold baseline assumptions utterly at odds with your own? Yet, Schaeffer insists, his entire project strives to demonstrate that "when we get to those holding the concept that there is no such thing as objective (or universal truth), we can still keep talking."[58]

Presuppositionalists preserve a few loopholes in their scheme that save them from hopeless relativism. First, presuppositionalism diverges from a superficial resemblance to postmodernism by affirming a strong claim that absolute, objective, and knowable truth exists. This truth, not surprisingly, is precisely reflected in the basic presuppositions of Christianity. Alone among all presuppositional sets, then, the Christian system possesses accuracy, self-consistency, and durability. Its ground-level assumptions about reality, life, and morality faithfully reflect That Which Is. Second, presuppositionalists maintain that the structure of reality itself testifies to the unique coherence and validity of the Christian system. Cornelius Van Til, one of the prime innovators of presuppositionalist thought, strongly identified Christianity with universal laws of logic, particularly the law of non-contradiction (A is not non-A). In this view, any rational system that follows basic logical precepts essentially "borrows" its rationality from the divine largesse that is the sensible universe. Similarly, every apprehension of passion or deep meaning draws, consciously or otherwise, on the wellspring of Ultimate Meaning that is God. The facts that humans can reason at all, that they have any sense of right and wrong, and that they can communicate with some degree of intelligibility testify to the miraculous power of the Creator. Attempts to construct a world of reason or morality without God (or, alternately, attempts to imagine God disconnected from reason and morality) lead to contradictory, incoherent, or nihilistic dead ends.

Faith in the fallibility of all but the Christian system thus justifies the presuppositionalist apologetic and defines its method. Christianity is *true*—reasonable and meaningful both—in a way that no other system is. Yet declaring that true-ness outright convinces no one but the already converted. The starting point for modern apologetics, Schaeffer urges, must therefore be the dysfunction of non-Christian presuppositions. Since non-Christian presuppositions ultimately jar with the flux of the created universe, no one can actually live consistently and faithfully by them.[59] Lower-story rationalists who live as if humans were nothing but biological machines eventually run up against their non-machine-ness, the whole that transcends the sum of its physical components and processes.

Upper-story subjective-spiritualists, by contrast, find themselves observing rationally based laws in order to live and thrive. If followed consistently to their logical conclusions, Schaeffer maintains, modern, non-Christian presuppositions about life lead to empty outcomes. Thus no one outside of a few artists or philosophers ever try to live consistently with non-Christian presuppositions. Most people instead live in a state of psychic-intellectual-spiritual tension, sensitive on some level that their picture of reality does not work but unable or unwilling to perceive why. Schaeffer's presuppositional apologetic consists of guiding people into an awareness of this "point of tension," removing the defensive structures ("roofs") that people erect to shield themselves from confronting this tension head-on.[60] Only after people come to grips with the unworkability of their non-Christian presuppositions can they truly hear and receive the Christian message. The work of modern evangelism, Schaeffer argues, must therefore devote attention to *pre-evangelism,* which he calls "no soft option."[61] Apologetics has to focus not merely on rebutting anti-Christian attacks but on singing the eternal message in tones the modern ear can hear.

Putting a Stone in Their Shoe: Greg Koukl and Tactical Apologetics

One of the most in-demand evangelical apologists in the Schaefferian tradition today is Greg Koukl. Koukl founded Stand To Reason, an evangelical think tank-cum-training organization dedicated to helping Christians articulate and defend doctrinaire biblical stances in a non-Christian, pluralized culture. He is at the forefront of the apologetic renaissance in US evangelicalism, publishing a popular guide in 2009 called *Tactics: A Game Plan for Discussing Your Christian Convictions.* Like Henderson, Koukl stresses the value of paying attention to everyday interactions with others, listening carefully to what others say, and inviting them to share more of their beliefs. Also like Henderson, Koukl steps back from the blunt proclamationism of Anderson or Comfort. His preferred method, he explains, "trades more on friendly curiosity—relaxed diplomacy—than on confrontation."[62] Nor does Koukl adopt the always-be-closing, get-them-to-a-decision mentality of the soul-winner. In fact, he writes, "My aim is never to win someone to Christ. . . . *All I want to do is put a stone in someone's shoe.* I want to give him something worth thinking about, something he can't ignore because it continues to poke him in a good way."[63]

With such pebble-planting, Koukl takes a deliberate step away from the nonmanipulative intentionality of Henderson and Siever. He has an overt intention, and he espouses certain kinds of manipulation in order to fulfill it. The irenic metaphor of "relaxed diplomacy" rests on Koukl's more fundamental, Schaefferian conviction that even casual, everyday encounters with nonbelievers rehearse a spiritual warfare between incompatible and mutually antagonistic belief systems. Whether the nonbeliever realizes it or not, such encounters are clashes, opportunities for competition between worldly and biblical Christian (read: evangelical) perspectives and assumption sets. Yet Koukl's preferred metaphor for Christians engaging in such clashes isn't *warrior,* one who battles to the death, but *ambassador,* one who negotiates and persuades. Koukl promotes what he calls the Ambassador model of conversational apologetics, training Christians to bring Schaeffer's tension points gently but surely to the surface of conversation.

At the heart of his model are "tactics," which he describes as "the orderly hands-on choreography of the particulars" of conversations with non-Christians.[64] Tactics consist of rhetorical maneuvers for leading nonbelievers into articulating what they believe, probing those beliefs for logical fallacies or contradictions, and then gently exposing those problems as such to the nonbeliever. Like Newman, Koukl recommends operating mainly by posing questions in friendly conversation rather than making statements. For example, the "Columbo tactic" as he calls it (after the fictional detective played by Peter Falk) consists of a number of all-purpose questions that allow the evangelist to gather information ("What do you mean by that?"), reverse the burden of proof ("How do you know that is true?"), and even suggest a conclusion ("Have you ever considered . . . ?").[65] The Columbo tactic forces the evangelist to listen, puts the nonbeliever on the defensive, and ideally prevents the evangelist from seeming judgemental or hypocritical while still poking a few holes in the nonbeliever's ideological armor.

Like Schaeffer, Koukl assumes that ultimately all non-Christian belief systems will manifest terminal flaws. Koukl devotes considerable space to reviewing typical flaws of non-Christian or anti-Christian stances. To the "postmodern" critic who claims "there is no Truth" or that "Truth can't be known," for instance, Koukl recommends asking whether such an assertion is itself a Truth and, if so, how the critic's no-knowable-Truth system can tolerate, let alone rely upon, such a contradictory foundation.[66] Christian ambassadors thus train to expect such flaws in non- or anti-Christian belief systems, listen for them in conversation, and lightly highlight those flaws (preferably in the form of a question) so that they become for the non-believer a "point of tension," a dissonance in their non-Christian belief system that potentially could cause them to reconsider and perhaps become more open to Christian avenues of thought.

Where Henderson's Ordinary Attempt evangelism gives lessons in remedial sociability, Koukl's ambassador approach teaches the art of polite argument. It's the "how to influence people" counterpoint to Henderson's "how to win friends." Of course, as Koukl and other conversational apologetics teachers note, ambassadorial tactics do little more than recycle classical lessons of rhetoric and argumentation. Maneuvers like reversing the burden of proof, exposing fatal worldview contradictions, and exploding logical fallacies prove so effective in conversation not thanks to some infusion of miraculous power but because most people (Christians and non-Christians) simply aren't trained to think through and defend their beliefs in such a systematic way. Koukl even finds it necessary to caution readers against misusing the power of effective conversation. "The temptation will be strong to use your tactical skill like a club," he cautions, "Don't give in to that urge."[67] Tactics, he argues, should only operate within a larger context of concern for the spiritual well-being of others. "They are not meant to belittle or humiliate those who disagree with you so you can gain notches in your spiritual belt," he argues.[68] Ambassador-evangelists are not culture warriors, nor should tactical apologetic conversations flare up into heated political debates. If any participant in the exchange gets angry, Koukl warns, you've lost.[69]

Koukl pushes apologists to locate and highlight areas of common ground and agreement as well as points of tension.[70] Yet some tension is necessary. Ambassadors cannot be all bait and no switch. In contrast to both Anderson and Henderson, Koukl rejects the idea that contention and argument detract from the evangelistic enterprise.[71] Apologetics, though not itself inherently salvific, can participate in the Holy Spirit's process of turning someone toward Christ. It is, in the Schaefferian sense, pre-evangelistic. Most Christians, Koukl ventures, are not gifted harvesters of souls. Very rarely, he believes, does a singular close-the-deal encounter lead to a lasting, authentic commitment. Most Christians, though, can be gardeners, tending and attending to those around them who might be growing toward faith commitments.[72] And, if nothing else, Koukl's evangelistic mode requires that Christians do attend, and attend carefully, to those around them who believe differently. He demands that Christians move beyond both the easy out of the singular, take-it-or-leave-it kerygma and the all-bait-but-no-switch banality of friendship evangelism.

How to Sneeze: Dare 2 Share and Viral Evangelism

Evangelist Greg Stier likewise charts an evangelism of active attention, incorporating elements of both ordinary friendship and tactical apologetics. Having converted to the faith after being raised in "an inner-city family of violent body builders,"[73] Stier served as a pastor in an Arveda, Colorado, church throughout the 1990s. After the Columbine High School massacre occurred in nearby Denver, Stier was struck by the need to change the lives of youth. He resigned his church position to dedicate himself full-time to youth ministry, specifically the "Dare 2 Share" ministry he began during his pastorate. He now serves as president of Dare 2 Share Ministries International (D2S), which describes itself as a non-denominational organization dedicated to "mobilizing teenagers to relationally and relentlessly reach their generation for Christ."[74] Today D2S operates with a multi-million-dollar budget and provides resources, curricula, and training opportunities to youth pastors throughout the United States and beyond. Stier himself has published a number of books on evangelism (particularly youth-oriented evangelism) and serves as a popular speaker to churches and parachurch organizations.

Theologically, Stier and D2D maintain a solidly evangelical alignment, affirming biblicist, crucicentric, conversionist, and activist tenets as central to the Christian life.[75] Stier's ministry focuses on the activist component: encouraging and equipping Christian teenagers to share their faith with other teens. And by *share,* Stier means verbal proclamation, not lifestyle evangelism. He quotes evangelist Bill Hybels (whom I'll discuss in chapter 7) on this point: "Far too many Christians," Hybels writes, "have been anesthetized into thinking that if they simply live out their faith in an open and consistent fashion, the people around them will see it, want, it and somehow figure out how to get it for themselves. . . . Let's be honest: That almost never happens."[76] Though Christians are supposed to offer living testimonies to a life transformed, Stier says, the biblical imperative to evangelize requires that Christians literally speak the gospel to others. In one of his books, *Outbreak,* Stier introduces the notion of viral evangelism, where the gospel message, which he describes as an "ideavirus," spreads like an epidemic.[77] As virulent and contagious as the good news is, he argues, believers cannot rely on passive transmission. For the gospel to go viral, Christian carriers have to *sneeze,* that is, initiate overt disruptions of everyday life that are unmistakably evangelistic.[78]

Stier's model of a "sneeze"—his core advice to youth about how to share the gospel with friends—more or less resembles the soul-winning pitch of Anderson, Campus Crusade, and Comfort. Once viral evangelists find themselves in a conversation about spiritual things (perhaps sparked by a question such as "Do you know for sure you're going to heaven after you die?"), Stier counsels Christians to share the kerygma using his signature presentation crafted around the acronym GOSPEL:

> God created us to be with Him.
> Our sins separate us from God.
> Sins cannot be removed by good deeds.
> Paying the price for sin, Jesus died and rose again.
> Everyone who trusts in Him alone has eternal life.
> Life with Jesus starts now and lasts forever.[79]

Stier urges Christians to use these statements as a guide, a framework for personalization and elaboration, rather than as a script to be recited exactly.[80] After the GOSPEL presentation, he advises, Christians should ask whether the presentation made sense and, if so, whether the person is ready to put her trust in Jesus as savior right there.[81] Nothing here deviates significantly from the soul-winner's standard, just-the-facts declaration of evangelical truths (perhaps spiced-up with a personal testimony or illustration). Nevertheless, and in line with meta-kerygmatic evangelists like Henderson, Schaeffer, and Koukl, Stier argues that simple declarations or polished GOSPEL presentations by themselves will likely not work. A truly contagious sneeze, he explains (apologizing for the unpleasantness of his metaphor), only spreads a virus to people in close proximity. "If we expect to start an epidemic of evangelism," he writes, "we must be near the uninfected."[82] Near, he specifies, indicates not merely proximity but also cultural intimacy. His viral evangelism depends upon close, long-term contact between Christians and non-Christians, the kind of contact born of authentic relationships rather than (à la Anderson or Comfort) brief encounters with strangers on porches or street corners.

Like other meta-kerygmatic evangelists, Stier underscores the reality of a theological landscape defined by postmodern preference for non-exclusivist pluralism. Relating a skit he once created for his youth group, Stier allegorizes the present-day evangelism field as a crowded Starbucks. In this hypothetical spiritual coffee shop, customers stand in line to order any of a wide variety of religious flavors: a "Carmel Cult Latte," an "Atheist Americano," a "Tai Chi Chai," or a "Mormon Frappaccino" ("decaf only," he specifies). The only drink not on the menu? *Venti Jesus.* "Your actualized, open-minded barista," he explains, "was open to giving you a quasi Jesus (Jesus with a shot of something else) but not a straight-up Jesus." Pure, unadulterated, triple-shot Jesus, he explains, would eradicate a customer's desire for any other drink, ever, as well as convincing them to recruit others to try the Venti Jesus. "And if that happens too often," he concludes, "then Spiritual Starbucks is out of business for good."[83] The insistent exclusivism of Christianity runs counter to the postmodern mind-set of *That faith works for you. Here's what works for me.* Yet too often, Stier contends, the present-day church in the United States has either capitulated to such wishy-washy relativism or assumed a pose of harsh intransigence: "This is the truth. Take it or leave it."[84] Both approaches, he argues, get Christians nowhere. Echoing Schaeffer's apologetic prescription, Steir writes, "If we [youth leaders] want to energize our students to evangelize their world, they must know their world." Straightforward, propositional truth statements, he argues, do not wash with the people of this world. They prefer compelling stories, personal, narrative accounts of values and beliefs. To be sure, Stier clarifies, Christianity is certainly the one, only, exclusively true story on the menu, but Christians cannot depend on that truth to shine through on its own. "Because there are so many belief systems," he argues, "we must present the good news about God's love through Christ as an exciting, life-altering story that just happens to be true instead of a theological treatise that cannot be false."[85] Christianity must advertise itself in the idiom of secular-age plurality. Its draw is not (or not only) its truth but (also) its positive, transformative effect manifest in the lives of actual Christians.

Stier's view of the postmodern climate shapes the presentational techniques he recommends. Anderson and Comfort, both convinced utterly of the self-sufficient power of the Word, find it appropriate to confront perfect strangers with the Truth of the gospel, trusting in the Holy Spirit to pierce the cloudy membrane of postmodern relativism. Although Stier affirms his faith in the power of the gospel, his viral model of evangelism proposes a subtler, more adaptive mode of cultural-ideological infiltration. His evangelistic method echoes elements of Henderson's and Koukl's approaches while taking both a step further. Like Henderson, Stier stresses the need to develop authentic, long-lasting relationships with prospects. Similar to Koukl (and in contrast to Henderson), Stier emphasizes the need for Christians to become better at the art of directed conversations. But Koukl's recommendations are, as Koukl himself specifies, *tactics,* on-the-spot reactions to one-time conversations with strangers.[86] Stier's overall approach is strategic rather than tactical. In one of D2S's current initiatives, "THE Cause" (so called because evangelism is not just a cause but THE cause for Christians), Stier encourages evangelists to frame their relationships with non-Christians in terms of a long-term plan: Pray, Pursue, and Persuade. Stier advises Christians first to pray for non-Christian prospects (something like Henderson's "praying behind their backs"), asking God to open opportunities to build relationships with them. Once a relationship blossoms, Christians move on to *pursuit,* which involves finding ways to introduce spiritual topics into everyday conversation, learning about what the prospect believes and where they are coming from, theologically. As spiritual conversations with the prospect get deeper, evangelists move to *persuasion,* introducing tactical and apologetic elements (similar to Koukl's recommendations) to conversations with the ultimate aim to get the person to (in the plan's words) ABC: Accept Christ as savior, Belong to a church, and Commit to a life of evangelism.[87] Where a soul-winning or street-preaching approach concentrates these steps into a single encounter, Stier's pray-pursue-persuade model bespeaks a longer timeline for initiating spiritual change.

Like Cru in the present day, Stier's organization takes a comprehensive approach to training young evangelists in its evangelism strategy. Stier's ministry aims first at motivating students to evangelize, giving them what he calls "passion fuel" to share their faith with others, and D2S sells a youth-group training curriculum, "Deep & Wide," that emphasizes the importance of the Great Commission.[88] For youth motivated to share the gospel, the D2S site hosts lengthy lists of "spiritual segues," conversational transitions and lead-ins to spiritual topics, including a long series dedicated to helping teens link popular culture items (everything from *Glee* to rickrolling) to faith-oriented chats.[89] For youth leaders, D2S hosts a number of on-site and online workshops for training youth in effective evangelism.

Integral to this training is Stier's conviction (a Schaefferian one) that evangelism requires Christians to familiarize themselves with the theological presuppositions of various non-Christian perspectives so that they can present the gospel in terms non-Christians will understand. He dedicates almost a third of his *Dare 2 Share* book to explaining various kinds of non-Christian faith/non-faith positions. He constructs the entries as personal profiles of a fictional adherent to the position, such as "Bailey the Buddhist," "Jenna the Jew," "Andy the Atheist," or even "Erin the Evolutionist." He even includes an entry for "Tara the Typical," roughly analogous to the "So What" demographic of young people who do not espouse any strong religious belief. Each profile begins with a narrative encounter between Stier and the profiled person ("I was walking along when I met Marty [the Mormon] . . ."), followed by a basic description of the position's beliefs.[90] The entries go on to list common misconceptions that evangelical Christians may harbor about the position, such as the mistaken belief that "Mo the Muslim" is a terrorist or that she can't be Caucasian.[91] He follows these up with "three interesting facts" about the faith, a list of "things we probably agree on," and "things we probably disagree on." The rest of the profile concentrates on conversational overtures, including possible conversation starters ("What do Wiccans believe about Christians?"),[92] general tips for "pursuit" and "persuasion" conversations (e.g., "Christians sometimes come across as superior to agnostics, so be sure to maintain a respectful and gracious attitude"),[93] and even a compliment to use ("I've got to appreciate the unflinching boldness that you show in declaring yourself a Satanist in a nation where the average person describes himself as a Christian. You have a lot of courage to do that!").[94]

Granted, Stier's brief, formulaic profiles hardly qualify as complex representations of non-Christian theological positions. Yet, even as it is important to recognize the distortions that actual Muslims, Jews, or "evolutionists" would find with the D2S entries, I emphasize that Stier's profiles offer a marked departure from other evangelical representations of non-Christianity. A casual internet search, for example, will soon uncover evangelical representations of Islam as a necessarily violent or terrorist faith, stereotypes that fuel anti-Muslim sectors of the religious right.[95] Other evangelical strains, particularly those with more fundamentalist or bounded-set leanings, often routinely label as a "cult" any number of non-Christian faith groups, including many that consider themselves Christian, such as Roman Catholics, Pentecostals, and Mormons.[96] Insofar as Stier's profiles include a nod toward "common misconceptions" and engage in a comparison/contrast rather than a pure heresy hunt, his descriptions take on a degree of nuance that non-evangelical perusals might otherwise miss.

Stier's Dare 2 Share approach to other faiths also diverges from how kerygmatic presentations of the previous chapter deal with other faiths. Though they caution against wasting time on purely uninterested or belligerent audiences, Anderson and Comfort offer tips on navigating soul-winning or Way of the Master interactions with adherents to other faiths. Comfort's massive guide to evangelism, for example, contains a number of outreach recommendations and sample dialogues for use with atheists, Mormons, Buddhists, and other non-Christian faiths.[97] Yet his suggested interactions take the form of complete scripts in which the evangelist pitches out a few "facts" about the prospect's belief and then railroads the conversation into the WotM "good person test." Similarly, Anderson provides a YouTube video on how to witness to someone adhering to a non-Christian faith (Anderson will only go so far as Pentecostalism; nothing so exotic as Islam or atheism trespasses onto his radar). His technique, though, consists mainly of leading the prospect in co-reading a series of specific Bible verses that counter what he perceives as Pentecostalism's major doctrinal error (i.e., believing that salvation requires repentance rather than simple belief—Anderson's usual bête noir).[98]

Both Comfort and Anderson, in other words, view other faith/non-faith positions as little more than a detour in the mental flowchart of the gospel presentation. They acquire just enough knowledge of other positions to figure out exactly where the other position detours from the straight and narrow. Once that diagnosis is made, they deploy a pat response designed to reroute the conversation back onto the well-worn path. True to their theological convictions, soul-winning and Way of the Master street preaching rely not on a Schaefferian apologetic but on a bare restatement of the central kerygma. Entering into the theological perspective of unbelievers, in their view, makes no sense. The driving force of kerygmatic personal evangelism isn't the false faith of others but the uncompromising truth of God's law and grace. The power of the Word will, they trust, overpower any un-Christian presuppositions, and if it does not, then that is either the person's choice (Anderson) or God's choice (Comfort). Stier's profiles of other theological positions, by comparison, emphasize conversation: here's how to start a conversation with a Hindu person. Here are questions to ask. Here are conversational routes to avoid. Like Koukl, he encourages listening, and like Henderson he sometimes counsels that evangelists should *only* listen—at least at first. The temporality of personal evangelism changes, stretching beyond a singular encounter with a relative stranger into a deepening set of authentically friendly relationships.

Conclusion

To be sure, D2S's approach is no innocent exercise in ecumenical tolerance. None of these approaches are, not even Henderson's Ordinary Attempts. The end goal in every case involves the prospect's conversion to the one, true faith, not interreligious understanding where everyone comes away enlightened. Like Schaeffer, and indeed like Anderson and Comfort, meta-kerygmatic evangelists hold that, deep down, everyone really *does* know God, that the human conscience, the human mind, and the human spirit all testify to the existence and activity of the Christian-biblical deity. Evangelism and apologetics are in this sense custodial, clearing away (through the help of the Holy Spirit) the obstacles that block a person's knowing and choosing Christ. Where Henderson, Koukl, and Stier differ from Anderson and Comfort is in their recognition that the obstacles between God and humanity involve not merely sinful pride but also the negative witness of Christians, the cultural context of religious plurality, and the challenge of postmodern epistemology.

The meta-kerygmatic evangelists I have reviewed here address these challenges directly, though differently. Henderson and Siever insist on at least a temporary moratorium from confrontational evangelism, recognizing that non-Christian audiences may in some cases need and deserve to hear an apology from representatives of the faith for boneheaded or unloving witnesses past. For Henderson, an embodied witness of Christian love—plain old human friendship, really—must supplant the manipulative salesmanship of traditional confrontation. Since, in Henderson's view, only friends really persuade others in any case, Christians must first and foremost learn to be friendly. Koukl, by contrast, advocates an articulate rationality to create a crack in the defenses of listeners' anti-Christian presuppositions, a crack through which the Holy Spirit may enter. The barriers his ministry seeks to overcome stem from a widespread cultural reticence to articulate beliefs persuasively at all. For him, the lessons of classical rhetoric can help believers bypass their own reluctance while demonstrating to unbelievers internal problems with non-Christian belief systems. Even for him, however, such tactical apologetic encounters avoid "closing the deal." Stier, finally, echoes elements of both Henderson's and Koukl's approaches in his more comprehensive Dare 2 Share model. For him, authentic friendships come first, followed by spiritual conversations that involve some informed apologetics.

All of their approaches, however, would likely seem too gradualist to soul-winners like Anderson or street preachers like Comfort. The approaches of Henderson and Koukl, for example, do not get to the literal presentation of the Good News at all, and even Stier's system puts such presentations off. From a more confrontational evangelist's perspective, these approaches are less meta-kerygmatic than *non*-kerygmatic, hardly evangelism at all. In bowing to cultural pressures (*Maybe we need to deal with people's emotional and rational barriers before going into John 3:16*), meta-kerygmatic evangelists seem to take a step back from a trusting faith in the power of the Word to change the human heart. Delayed approaches also dilute the sense of impending danger, the hellfire that awaits unrepentant sinners, so essential to the dramaturgical tension of soul-winning and street preaching. Nothing about the postmodern world, after all, makes the reality of Judgement any less real.

Nevertheless, even the meta-kerygmatic approaches share a sense that the activist message, the truth to be shared, carries a power. In fact, far from watering-down faith in the gospel message, meta-kerygmatic evangelists might better be seen as holding an especially grand sense of the gospel as truth. Whereas Anderson's soul-winning microdrama can present the gospel as little more than a free pass on damnation,[99] a Schaefferian approach insists on the gospel as a *worldview*. It is not a truth; it is *the* truth, "total truth," a comprehensive, internally consistent lens for seeing all of life and culture. As such, the gospel need not exist only as an eschatological exigency plan to be called upon when hellfire threatens. It is rather a way of living that can and should exert its own intellectual and affective pull provided it is given enough space to be seen and experienced. As such, the gospel's total truth operates subtly. It lacks an epiphanic ability to shatter competing preconceptions all on its own (or, rather, it *has* that ability but is rarely experienced as such). In this life, in a secular age, total truth must compete with counter-truths and falsehoods tricked out as truths.

To a greater extent than even the kerygmatic evangelists, then, Henderson, Koukl, and Stier insist on the need for evangelistic training. Schaefferian evangelists have to be both deeply rooted in the total truth of the gospel and attuned to the primary modes of falsehood that attempt to pass themselves off as just-as-true. For these evangelists, simple proclamation has its place, but that place is rarely if ever at the opening of an evangelical encounter. Or, to put it another way, meta-kerygmatic evangelism aims at something beyond merely "Well, I told them the truth; whether they accept it is between them and God." Although all of the meta-kerygmatic evangelists I relate here would aver that God ultimately does determine the outcome of evangelism, they insist that humans' role in God's salvific process goes beyond mere declaration. They want to *convince* audiences of gospel truth, defend it, provide an *apologia* for it, and not just utter it in front of the unchurched. Committing to this persuasive process means letting go of the all-in-one, always-be-closing encounter of the soul-winner or the Way of the Master follower. Interpersonal activism in the meta-kerygmatic mode is better conceived as a long, slow, often incomplete process of mini-encounters: ordinary attempts, free attention giveaways, listening sessions, apologies, and—at most—a question or comment to "put a stone in the shoe" of the listener.

In my previous chapter's conclusion, I asked what a secular left progressive kerygmatic evangelism (and thus a secular progressive left gospel) might look like. As I mentioned, I think it unlikely that feminist or environmental or anti-racist activists would readily adopt something like Anderson's door-to-door or Comfort's on-the-street formulaic presentations. Yet such left-leaning movements have—fairly or not—accrued a similar kind of reputation problem in the public eye. Like some evangelists, left-leaning activists are often seen as living out a pushy and intrusive stereotype. They are often framed as confrontational and off-putting in their insistence on a singular, *I'm-right-and-you're-wrong* truth. Could it be, then, that performance activists on the progressive left could benefit from adopting something like a meta-kerygmatic tactic, a more subtle and stopping-short-of-proclamation type of activism?

Such a project touches on recurring questions for left-leaning causes regarding just what counts as "activism." Consider, for example, the standard question posed to feminist, anti-racist, environmental, and other left-progressive activists: *What can I do to help* . . . with its unspoken subtext of . . . *that won't prove too taxing or brand me as a radical?* Does buying compact fluorescent light bulbs count as environmental activism? Is it feminism to not buy products from a company that runs sexist ads? Can you strike a blow for racial equality by watching *The Color Purple* on Broadway or donating to the NAACP? On the one hand, labeling such minor market decisions as activism (or as "activist performances") invites the scorn of "authentic" activists, providing easy examples of hipster conformism begging for some radical leftist critic like Slavoj Žižek to come along and eviscerate them. None of these involves significant risk or sacrifice. None of these would be read by an outsider as "activist." None of them touch on the larger systems of power and historical legacies that produce and sustain sexism or racism. None of these, in other words, spread the gospel. They miss the left-progressive "total truths" of capitalism, anglo-hetero-patriarchy, colonialism, or privilege.

Yet, whether or not such tiny acts qualify one as an activist, it is the case that a life lived in observance of a feminist, anti-racist, or other such left-progressive total truth might very well include actions or decisions like those I mentioned. Moreover, such acts might constitute first steps toward a more involved and system-engaged activism—especially if someone asks something like *Why are you buying those light bulbs?* Small acts may not be activism, but neither are they *not* activist. That is, they might be rightly seen as micro-activist performances, infused with an activist spirit and expressive of a set of deeper convictions. The meta-kerygmatic evangelists draw attention to the fact that activism—and even activist performance—can be a way of life, the accumulation of small acts, tiny interpersonal encounters, performed in service of a larger truth. The danger always exists that such small acts ("all you're really doing anyway") might *replace* rather than express a deeper or more substantial commitment to a cause. But, as Henderson, Koukl, and Stier would insist, such acts can also communicate—and even communicate more compellingly, in the long run, than a straightforward proclamation.

Keeping that possibility in mind, I turn now to evangelistic modes that engage in more overt proclamations—and that do so on broader scales than do the interpersonal encounters I have related thus far.

CHAPTER 5

Hell and Judgement

Houses of Distinction

It's 10:30 at night, the day after Halloween 2003. I'm standing in line outside of the Freedom Assembly of God Church in Tallahassee, Florida, to watch the congregation's first annual Hell House.[1] It is my first Hell House as well, and I am a little uncertain just what to expect. News reports and word of mouth about large-scale productions in Texas and Colorado have painted lurid pictures of fundamentalist Christian versions of traditional haunted houses, where demons and temptations replace ghosts and axe murderers. Having read such reports carefully, I brace myself to absorb shocking, graphically staged scenes of "sin" and its consequences: gay people dying of AIDS and burning in hell, black-clad, Columbine-style gunmen mowing down Christians in schools, and blood-soaked abortions featuring vacuum-cleaner noises and bowls of raw meat meant to resemble fetuses. Signs posted on the walls beside me warn that the production is not intended for children under thirteen. This is *R*-rated evangelism, a turn-or-burn sermon promising to shatter my postmodern cynicism and shake me to my core.

Today, almost a decade after my first experience with them, Hell Houses and performances like it have gained in popularity. Every year, hundreds of congregations across the country mount such dramas—often but not exclusively as Christian alternatives to Halloween—to confront unsaved audience members with the reality of spiritual warfare and the necessity of being born again. The Hell House Outreach script and format devised by Colorado pastor Keenan Roberts remains the most well-known iteration. Since the 1990s, Roberts and his New Destiny Christian Center have produced a yearly Hell House production for their local community as well as making their script and format available for purchase. For $299, any church group can buy Roberts's Hell House Outreach Kit, which includes a video of a typical production, a sound-effects CD, and a massive *Hell House Outreach Manual.*[2] The *Manual* serves as a combination how-to guide, resource book, and production script. Though Hell Houses hold pride of place as the most famous (or infamous) outreach drama, a host of similar performance forms play out all over the country; Judgement House, Tribulation Trail, Revelation Walk, Rapture House, Final Exit, *Scaremare,* and *The 99* represent only a few of the better-known local and regional offerings.[3] Most of these parallel Roberts's model, presenting elaborate episodes of humans making sinful choices on earth and experiencing the consequences for unbelief after death.

These dramas draw widespread notoriety for their in-your-face evangelizing. Roberts modifies his script every year, emending his core, seven-scene script to incorporate scenes that grapple with various major culture-war topics, such as a nightmarish same-sex wedding or an in-vitro fantasy about an aborted fetus's dreams of her future life. For every such issue, Roberts asserts a perspective that seems to reinforce the most extreme stereotypes of fundamentalist Christianity. In Hell House's moral universe, rave parties always lead to gang rapes, gay people inevitably get AIDS, Wiccans engage in human sacrifice, and abortion doctors revel in sadistic butcheries. Such scenes make for irresistible fodder for local and national news media. Hell Houses (i.e., versions of Roberts's particular type of drama) have been featured on public radio's *This American Life* as well as in a popular documentary film by George Ratliff.[4] While the latter two sources focus with a degree of documentary neutrality on local congregations who produce Hell House, most press treatments highlight the controversy and criticism Hell House events inspire. Such representations have won Roberts and other such productions condemnation from critics left and right, evangelical and otherwise. The show has been castigated as "pornography for the soul," "simplistic theology," and "spiritual violence."[5] Secular theater companies in New York and Los Angeles have added to the mass mockery, producing tongue-in-cheek versions of Roberts's script for non-evangelical audiences to marvel over and laugh at.

In recent years, scholars of religious studies, rhetoric, and performance have offered more complex analyses of Hell House and dramas like it. Jason C. Bevins and Brian Jackson each explore Hell House's use of fear as a rhetorical motivator (the *argumentum ad baculum*) and as a reflection of US cultural anxieties.[6] Performance critic Ann Pellegrini provides an excellent, non-paranoid reading of how the Colorado Hell House productions generate a distinctively evangelical "structure of feeling."[7] Allan Davis and Hank Willenbrink take Hell Houses and similar events as the object of their master's and doctoral theses.[8] Jackson and Willenbrink both underline how Roberts's drama ghosts previous rhetorical and theatrical genres such as the hellfire sermons of Great Awakening preachers like Jonathan Edwards and medieval European morality plays. Bevins situates Hell Houses and similar events alongside other expressions of "scary Christianity," such as apocalyptic Christian fiction like *Left Behind* and alarmist Christian criticisms of popular music. Pellegrini usefully articulates the approach these and other studies take when she argues that "cultural critics need to move beyond simply analyzing—and lambasting—the overt content or theology of Hell Houses (what Hell Houses *say*) and focus instead on the affectively rich worlds Hell House performances generate for their participants (what Hell Houses *do*)."[9] My present contribution to this conversation, which builds upon my previous research on Hell House,[10] parallels Pellegrini's approach. Like her, I strive to put these dramas' obvious elements of shocking imagery and moralizing narrative into conversation with the worldviews and outreach strategies of the evangelicals who produce these shows. *What do these dramas do?*

The most straightforward answer, from the producers' standpoint: Hell House and its cousins strive to create converts through fear. They manifest, in graphic detail, the infernal consequences of denying salvation. Like the interpersonal evangelisms I explored earlier, these performances stem from that favorite eschatological ice-breaker: *If you died right now, do you know for sure that you'd go to heaven?* The fear and uncertainty that this question inspires fuel their dramaturgy. The belief in the evangelistic power of afterlife anxiety justifies, in the producers' minds, the extreme production choices: the realer the fear, the more potent the outreach. What do these dramas do? They try to scare people into heaven. Roberts himself reinforces this impression. "Fear is a great motivator," he insists. "We are not communicating fear for fear's sake; we are communicating reality and truth. We're saying, 'You're living in a burning house, and it's about to crash down on you.'"[11] For evangelicals like Roberts, hell is a reality that unsaved people rightly should fear. If twenty-first-century culture has rendered people numb to the terrors of the Eternal Pit, then (from Roberts's perspective) they likely need Hell House's "in-your-face, high-flyin', no denyin', death-defyin', Satan-be-cryin', keep-ya-from-fryin', theatrical stylin', no holds barred, cutting-edge" approach to evangelism to shock them out of their complacency.[12]

To acknowledge that this mode of outreach traffics in fear, however, represents only a starting point to a more thorough exploration of its operations. In this chapter, I want to complicate the image of Hell House, Judgement House, and other such events as little more than garish (amateurish, fundamentalist, effective/ineffective) scare tactics. I agree that they strive to frighten, but I see important differences in how specific performances craft the fears they stage and whom they want to frighten. Most writing about these kinds of evangelical dramas—including my own—has tended to describe events like Judgement House, Tribulation Trail, Rapture House, and Hell House all as basically the same kind of theatrical and evangelistic "doing," as variants of a single "hell house" genre. I now argue otherwise. Although these performance forms share certain elements of structure and theme, I maintain that each operates as a distinct evangelistic strategy grounded in different assumptions about the gospel to be proclaimed and the audience that needs to hear it. Each functions, then, as a different activist response to the challenge of the secular age. Rather than embarking on a comprehensive survey of these forms, then, I focus in detail on the two most popular specimens: Roberts's Hell House Outreach and the Judgement House dramas devised by Tom Hudgins's New Creation Experiences.

Dramaturgical Similarities

These dramas could be described as representatives of a singular genre, though the name "hell house" fits less well than something like *interactive eschatological theater.* Fear-based, afterlife-focused evangelism from the pulpit and from the stage is nothing new, of course. Medieval European morality and cycle dramas commonly featured cavorting demons intent on drawing mortals into fiery hellmouths. Eighteenth-century pastors painted vivid portraits of the burning torment that awaited the unsaved. Jackson notes that such fire-and-brimstone sermons in the United States declined as the nineteenth century wore on, and evangelists like Dwight L. Moody (1837–99) eschewed purely fear-based appeals.[13] Most scholars and journalists trace the modern-day renaissance of theatrical fear-based evangelism to Jerry Falwell's New Thomas Road Baptist Church in Virginia (later incorporated into Liberty University). Bevins writes that one of Falwell's ministers in the early 1970s saw a drama, *A Scream in the Dark,* that convinced him that fear could play a role in outreach initiatives.[14] In 1972, Thomas Road Baptist premiered *Scaremare,* a yearly haunted-house-type event with an evangelistic twist. As historian Ethan Blue describes the show, having attended a production in 2005, *Scaremare* (now fully under the auspices of Liberty) largely resembles a standard haunted house, replete with threatening figures (not particularly sins) lurking creepily or jumping out to startle audiences. A brief evangelistic pitch and invitation concludes the experience.[15]

Although *Scaremare* is likely the earliest and longest-lived example of the dramas I focus on here, I do not assert any linear genealogies in which Falwell directly inspires Judgement House, Hell House, *The 99,* and the rest. My research into and conversations with these dramas' producers suggest that these shows developed more or less autochthonously, drawing variously from a cluster of generically conservative-evangelical rationales such as providing a Christian Halloween alternative, matching the sight-and-sound culture of young adults, or fighting secular culture "fire" with a bit of hellfire. The notion of adapting the haunted house format to do evangelical work is not, after all, a difficult leap, and one hardly needs to be a Roberts follower or *Scaremare* alumna for the idea to seem attractive. Evangelical outreach strategies often circulate as memes, with one minister or church member hearing about how this or that other congregation did X type of activity and getting excited enough to attempt their own version of the idea. Along these lines, my research suggests that interactive eschatological theater is even more widespread and varied than Roberts's yearly Hell House Kit sales figures tell. For every famous or franchised drama I have encountered, I have heard many more anecdotes of homebrew "hell houses" and "judgement houses" that students, friends, and colleagues recall watching or participating in as children and teens. Vast collections of scripts, photographs, and videos of such local iterations doubtless sit stacked at the back of church closets across the Bible Belt, awaiting discovery and study by future historians and critics.

For the present, I restrict myself to characterizing relatively well-known, standardized forms that market themselves to local churches. In terms of staging, interactive eschatological theater shares with secular haunted houses a degree of similarity to what Richard Schechner calls environmental theater.[16] That is, they typically occur in non-theater spaces and depart from the static performer/audience conventions that characterize most modern Western performances. The dramas unfold in spaces that have been altered to create labyrinthine pathways through a succession of rooms, each redesigned as a discrete setting and host to a particular scene. Some congregations transform their church building's classrooms and meeting areas (though not, generally speaking, the sanctuary). Other churches, sometimes in partnership with neighboring congregations, rent off-site properties with lots of open space (e.g., empty department store buildings), erecting a maze of walls and flats to create rooms and hallways. Still others, as I will explain, offer self-contained, portable structures that local church groups may rent and erect in their communities. The unusual layout requires audience members to process from scene to scene in small groups, led from room to room by cast members who sometimes play characters and sometimes merely guide. As is the case in haunted houses, environmental theater conventions deny attendees the relative comfort of passive spectatorship. These shows *promise* to ignore fourth-wall conventions. They guarantee that shocks and surprises (crashing noises, blinding lights, even in some cases sharp smells) will shake up anyone daring enough to brave the experience.

Of course, such shows want the visceral unease of the haunted-house-type walk-through to translate into transformative unease about the afterlife. Thematically, all of the dramas deal with eschatological themes; that is, they concern the moment of death and the immediate consequences after. Scenes of human life on earth culminate in an afterlife sequence of varied structure, complexity, and duration, where characters experience the consequences for their earthly choices. All of them make the conversionist point that faith in Christ, not "being good," guarantees entry into heaven. To reinforce these points, these dramas end with a straightforward evangelistic pitch delivered in a space distinct from the rest of the performance, an "invitation room." Plain-clothed church representatives assure audience members that the scary or theatrical parts of the presentation have ended. The audience then either absorbs a mini-sermon by a minister or gets invited to sit individually at counseling tables where a church volunteer engages them in a one-to-one conversation about the evangelistic themes of the evening. Audience members generally have the option of receiving Christ for the first time (i.e., "getting saved") or rededicating their lives.[17] These nondramatic afterpieces typically include some opportunity for audience members to register their responses to the show, leaving comments or (more often) marking whether they have made a first-time commitment or recommitment to Christ.

I approach all of these productions as specimens of community-based performance. As I mention in chapter 1, *community-based* denotes a performance that emerges from, reflects, and to a significant extent aims at a particular group of people—in this case the community of believers who purchase, adapt, and stage the drama in question. Viewing these dramas through a community-based lens emphasizes a few key features. First, I stress that although each of the dramas I examine relies on scripts written by someone not of the producing community, each of them allows for a degree (often a considerable degree) of adaptation. Churches who purchase the Hell House Outreach Kit, for example, tailor the script and its presentation to their community's values. They may leave out scenes, rewrite dialogue, or add new elements as they see fit. Even with more "set" scripts like Judgement House and *The 99,* the drama changes based on the identity of the church community producing it. To a greater extent than is the case with mainstream, secular play productions, then, no two productions of these dramas are exactly alike.

Second, I argue that these dramas that ostensibly focus on outreach to the lost in fact engage in a great deal of "preaching to the converted." Scholars of community-based theater call attention to the fact that a community's process of staging its values necessitates a measure of self-examination by that community. To a greater extent than would be the case in a church's production of *Godspell,* for instance, a church involved in adapting and staging a Hell House must address dramaturgical and staging questions via direct reference to its evangelistic philosophy: *Does the abortion scene reflect our values? Is heaven as important to stage as hell? How graphic should we get to balance sobering truth-telling with loving invitation?* Moreover, despite the desire to appeal to unchurched audiences, many of these types of performances in fact draw audiences from neighboring church communities. Their dramaturgy often depends upon audience members' having some prior familiarity with evangelical doctrine in order to "work." Yet instead of seeing this as a failure of outreach or activism, I argue that such preaching to the converted tunes in to the wavelength of a different set of fears than "Are you going to hell?" With that question in mind, then, I return to my first experience with Hell House.

Hell House

Back to the night in Tallahassee: at this early point in my hell house research, my horizon of expectations is still narrow. I know little more about what I'm going to see beyond a vague idea of conservative evangelical shock theater. I am alone, my partner electing to wait in the car rather than endure (yet another) sermon in the service of my critical hobby. He has seen the same news reports I have. Some preteens in line ahead of me chatter nervously among themselves. "Will it be scary? I hear the devils jump out at you." "Will you chicken out?" Their fear echoes my own unease. Just how extreme will this be? Will the actors somehow know that I'm not a Pentecostal evangelical but a liberal, gay United Methodist? Scarier still—and this is what the long-buried Southern Baptist preacher's son part of me really fears—what if this Hell House *works*? Converts me back to the straight and narrow? Vivid childhood memories of Sunday-school lessons on the eternal suffering of hell where the Worm Does Not Die come flooding back. Can hell still scare me? Staring at the church doors, I start to question my scholarly resolve. The tour finally begins, and a young woman with a flashlight beckons us into a dimly lit room. As the first actor appears—a teenaged demon-masked guide with a breathy, raucous laugh that telegraphs "I'm evil!"—I breathe a silent sigh of relief and realign my expectations. *Amateur theater I can handle,* I tell myself.

Over the next thirty minutes the demon guide leads our group down the church's darkened hallways and into various Sunday-school rooms, each cleared out and refurnished to represent a particular locale. The guide corrals our group into a taped-off spectator area, and a miniature scene unfolds before us. The scene ends, we are guided into the next room, and the process repeats. My initial fears of shock-show depictions of AIDS deaths, abortion clinics, and school shootings thankfully proved unfounded. Instead, the Tallahassee production focuses on familiar, domestic squabbles that escalate to soap-opera proportions. The actors, mostly young adults and their parents, throw themselves into their roles, making up in volume and raw energy what they lack in technique. In a living room, a mother and daughter scream tearfully at each other about the daughter's drug abuse, premarital sex, and (inevitable) pregnancy. At a slumber party, preteen girls unwittingly invite satanic influences through Ouija boards and a Harry Potter DVD. In each such scenario, our demon guide detaches from us, crossing the fourth-wall line to whisper into the characters' ears, urging them to reject Christian concerns:

"It's just a Harry Potter movie," he oozes to the preteen at the slumber party. "Everyone's seen it. You want to fit in, don't you?" Every scene builds to a climax in which the characters succumb to the demon's influence and suffer immediate, generally awful consequences. The demon then rejoins the spectators, cackling at the characters' misfortune and rehashing exactly where they went wrong.

Other scenes illustrate the various dangers of heeding demonic temptations. We see, for instance, a scene in which characters choose to drink and drive, which in turn leads to an impressive (and expensive) car wreck tableau complete with victims spattered with stage blood and sprawled over demolished junkyard vehicles. Between rooms, we pass a man handcuffed to a computer, who raises his shackled hands and rattles his chains at us. "I'm addicted to pornography!" he wails. We enter a dance club in which an unsuspecting girl, already endangering herself (we are told) by attending such a party in the first place, accepts a drug-laced drink from a stranger. A morning-after scene follows in which the guilt-ridden girl, urged on by demonic whispers, rejects Jesus ("Where were you when I was abused as a child?" she screams at a picture of Christ) before slitting her wrists. The demon guide hoots with sadistic glee at this ("What a solution!"), punctuating each scene with quips to urge us on ("There's so little time and so many people to kill!").

Finally, the guide invites us to tour the ultimate consequence: hell itself—a red-tinged affair with pounding hard-rock music, dry-ice smoke effects, and a slow strobe light. Amid the haze and twenty-five-watt lighting effects, a demon, presumably Satan, perches on a large black throne. Decked out in an oversized monster mask and a pair of Halloween creature gloves, the Lord of Darkness claws the air in a sinister invitation. In front of him, a group of middle-aged women with fright wigs, dark makeup, and black jogging suits beckon to us in charming Deep South accents: "Come join us!"

After about thirty seconds of this, a door on the far side of the room flies open and a preteen angel bursts in (I'm reminded, surreally, of a scene from *The Best Christmas Pageant Ever*). "Wait!" she declares, "You don't have to be in hell!" The devils recoil, and the angel leads us into an unadorned room just outside of the Eternal Pit. There, clad in boxer shorts and bleeding red paint from multiple wounds, a young man hangs from a cross propped up against the wall.

Enya plays on a small boom box plugged in nearby.

"Jesus died for your sins," explains the angel, who drops to her knees as "Jesus" groans and expires. His is the starkest, goriest scene of the evening. We then file into a brightly lit church classroom where a plain-clothed minister greets us, assuring us the frightening scenes of demons screeching at us are over. He recapitulates the drama's themes—the tragedy of sin, the reality of hell, the gift of salvation—and asks us to pray ("every head bowed, every eye closed") and indicate by raised hand whether we wished to give our hearts to Christ. On the way out the back door hangs a large poster board with Sharpie markers, where we are invited to sign our names under various columns ("Made commitment to Christ," "Recommitted my life to Christ"). I head back out to my partner in the parking lot.

Analyzing Fear

Thus ended my first live Hell House experience: not really scary, not overly offensive . . . and curiously unconvincing as an advertisement for how great Christianity is. Granted, I came in with no small amount of skepticism, but I was hard-pressed to imagine an unbeliever making a decision to convert based on this performance. True, the script explains that being a Christian involves not going to hell, but at no point did the production propose that making Christian choices led to any kind of better life here on earth. I was struck, on the contrary, by how awfully alone all the young human protagonists were, how cut off they were from any meaningful support, human or divine. Parents screamed at them, friends belittled them, technology corrupted them, strangers drugged and raped them, and demons tormented them. Nothing in the imagery presented suggested that Christianity would ameliorate the situation or that God or other Christians had any presence or influence in the mortal world. Indeed, the only representation of a heavenly alternative lay in the bloody arms of a dying, teenaged Christ. I wondered how anyone besides someone already indoctrinated into the evangelical narrative about the terrors of hell and the rewards of heaven would find Hell House's message compelling enough to convert.

My subsequent interview with the youth pastor in charge of the Tallahassee production confirmed my suspicions. I learned that of the five hundred or so people who had seen the Tallahassee Hell House, only twelve made first-time confessions of faith.[18] Though no comprehensive studies on Hell House efficacy exist, my research suggests that Tallahassee's statistics are not out of the ordinary; the people who simply watch the show and leave substantially outnumber those who choose to convert.[19] In his *Manual,* Roberts boasts of a conversion and/or recommitment rate of one in four or even one in three audience members, which he describes as "overwhelming percentages that just about any church in the world would welcome enthusiastically."[20] Exactly how Roberts calculates this success rate is questionable, likely relying on anecdotes and self-reports by churches. Furthermore, Roberts's statistics tend to blur first-time commitments of brand-new converts with "recommitments" by backsliding Christians into a single figure of people "won to the Lord."

Beyond Roberts's own reports and those of his more ardent fans, many other evangelicals question the wisdom and efficacy of his gorier-than-thou approach. "The Holy Spirit doesn't like to work that way," argues Baptist theologian and pastor Russell D. Moore. "How many people do you know who came to know Christ through a Halloween 'Judgment [*sic*] House' or 'Hell House'?" he asks readers. "If you know one, you're outpacing me, and everyone I've ever talked to about this." In its morbid focus on demonic torments, Moore maintains, Hell House emphasizes the wrong parts of the gospel, which after all is about grace more than judgement, love more than fear. And when it comes to fear Moore deems Hell House as simply "not scary enough." It could not be. No mortal effort, let alone the amateur efforts of "teenagers in plastic devil masks," could ever accurately represent "the anguish of the damned walled off from relationship with God."[21] Amy K. Hall, a blogger with Greg Koukl's Stand to Reason organization, expands on Moore's points, noting that the haunted-house-style terror of "falling into the hands of twisted and sadistic evil" differs qualitatively from the eschatological terror of an unrepentant sinner's facing the Holy God. Hell Houses, Hall writes, are "confusing the two kinds of terror in people's minds and inadvertently promoting the idea that God's judgment is likewise twisted and sadistic rather than being a righteous, just expression of His authority as our Creator and Judge."[22] Similar to Ray Comfort's criticism of soul-winning, these authors argue that salvation through fear means nothing unless accompanied by a repentant awareness of God's holiness and humanity's sin. By emphasizing disconnected scenes of shock-show horror, Hell House seems to transmit the message not that God redeems repentant sinners but that God uses Hell to cruelly punish innocent victims.

Still less does Hell House's bag of bloody tricks impress those outside of the faith. Blogger Tom Farr recalls seeing some version of the Christian haunted house similar to Hell House: "It was a fun experience if you loved the thrill of getting scared . . . but I know I walked away from that thing my first time (before I had come to faith), having prayed a prayer that I didn't understand or take seriously. I just wanted out." Particularly disturbing for Farr was the fact that the performance crafted a world where most of the characters simply suffered awful fates and went to hell, each situation presented without even a hint of Christ's compassion or saving power. "The darkness won," he writes. "Sure, Jesus shows up in the end, but it's too late for all the people we just saw. Where's the hope in that?"[23] A number of comments on Moore's and Hall's entries echo Farr's sentiments, adding that Hell House's haunted house aesthetic can invite the wrong kind of reaction from the wrong kinds of audiences. Hell Houses "provide mock-worthy fodder to universalists," warns one commenter. "I used to be one, and we used events like these to point out the ridiculous lengths those who believed in hell went to scare people into faith in Christ."[24] Another commenter reflects, "Doctrines of God's holiness, judgment and hell are deep and complex beliefs." Events like Hell House, he notes, fail to communicate this complexity and therefore "give skeptics one more reason to write off Christians as judgmental, emotion-driven, superstitious, manipulated sheeple."[25] To be fair, a few commenters took issue with the criticisms of Hell House, citing their own local productions and the conversions as proof that some people do come to the Lord thanks to these events. Even here, however, such endorsements came with qualifications. A visit to a Hell House can play an important part in outreach, insists one youth pastor, but only when it is contextualized within a comprehensive, Spirit-filled ministry. "God forbid I take these students to hell house and leave it at that," he writes.[26] So the question remains: how can a ministry so dedicated to matching and bettering the shock and awe of secular entertainment fail more than it succeeds in reaching its target audience?

Performance theorist Baz Kershaw offers a useful means of analyzing why the Hell House format seems so ill-equipped for outreach. Writing about grassroots activist theater in the United Kingdom, Kershaw adopts Elizabeth Burns's work about theatricality to theorize that community-focused performance engages two sets of conventions: rhetorical and authenticating.[27] Rhetorical conventions refer to how a production's format and identifying practices create a particular stage reality, calibrating audience members' horizon of expectations so that they may distinguish a tragedy from a farce, or a third-grade recital from a Broadway musical. Authenticating conventions refer to those signs presented in the performance that link the staged reality to the audience's local reality. Hell House draws upon the rhetorical conventions of the generic haunted house: a guided walk-through of a space that has been adapted to present scenes that are meant to provoke shock and fear. The authenticating conventions that Hell House mobilizes, however, refer to a restricted notion of reality: specifically, the evangelical worldview of fallen humanity and eventual judgement. In order to "work," Hell House relies on an audience of people willing to buy into (authenticate) the picture of reality that Hell House presents. For those who do not already believe in demons or God or the evangelical definition of sin, Hell House offers at best a kind of curious fantasy world, an inauthentic reality vulnerable to ridicule.

Indeed, the Hell House format and script tend to invite mockery if removed from a community that does not endorse an evangelical theology. As I mentioned earlier, two notable productions of Roberts's Hell House by secular groups have occurred. In 2004, a Los Angeles–based group calling itself "The Youth Group" (the creation of writer-actor Maggie Rowe and Jill Soloway) purchased one of Roberts's Hell House kits and mounted a production, apparently attempting to follow his suggestions to the letter. Marketed for its camp value and starring comedians like Bill Maher as the demon guide and Andy Richter as Jesus, the production became a hit as a showcase of how backward and bigoted evangelical fundamentalists were.[28] In the fall of 2006, I watched a *Hell House* mounted by Les Freres Corbusier, a New York City–based theater company known for avant-garde stagings. Under the direction of Alex Timbers, the New York production eschewed parody, playing Roberts's script "as is"—sans overt irony—in all its gory grandeur. Freres even brought Roberts himself out during dress rehearsals to give comments and pointers. Accounts of the production hailed its camp entertainment value as well as its "authentic" representation of the more extreme strands of fundamentalist Christianity.[29] Although both productions preserved Hell House's rhetorical conventions (the script and setup), neither the two companies nor their target audiences subscribed to the set of assumptions that the script presented. Abstracted from its intended community, the Hell House's earnest, shock-show warnings about the horrors of gay marriage or rave parties could be nothing other than laughably offensive, indicative of little more than the backwardness of small-town evangelicalism. Even in "straight" Hell House productions, nonbelievers tend to leave unconvinced. "I don't believe in this," said one spectator at a Detroit-area (and non-ironic) Hell House. "I don't think any hocus-pocus show is going to change my beliefs."[30]

Of course, evangelical Hell House producers are quick to point out that they themselves do not measure efficacy merely in terms of how many people convert after each show (though Hell House producers regularly cite Roberts's 20 to 30 percent figure). Recall that evangelical doctrine stresses how God, not humans, accomplishes the work of conversion, and God may choose to change someone's heart weeks, months, or years after a Hell House production. Evangelicals often quote Isaiah 55:11 to this end, in which God says, "so is my word that goes out from my mouth: It will not return to me empty, but will accomplish what I desire and achieve the purpose for which I sent it." Like the soul-winning interpersonal evangelists, Hell House producers invest the "truth" they present (Hell is real, Christ can save you from eternal torment) with a persuasive power that overrides purely rational assent. The core message of Hell House, in the producers' minds, is the gospel kerygma; it is God's message, not humans'. Any promulgation of that message, satirical or sincere, carries the divine imprimatur and transmits the Holy Spirit's life-changing power. For this reason Roberts responded to both secular productions with good humor. Commenting on the Brooklyn production, he insists that "though their intentions were to harm the message and the ministry by trying to humiliate it and make fun of it . . . it still took the exposure of 'Hell House' to new levels. I believe the message is what is sacred. The method is not."[31] Even if after-show tallies of the newly converted fail to match the one-quarter success rate Roberts promises, producers aver that God's transformative work surely continues beyond the invitation room. And, of course, convert counts are not the whole point. The Tallahassee pastor whom I interviewed, for instance, insisted that even one new conversion to the Lord justifies the whole endeavor.[32]

Dramaturgy of Distinction

Nevertheless, although Hell House producers insist that they are in the business of bearing witness to the lost, the events they produce actually do quite a bit of preaching to the converted. In this sense, I argue, Hell Houses may enjoy a great deal more success as activist performances than a surface reading might suggest. In theater studies, "preaching to the converted" recalls David Román and Tim Miller's insightful article of the same name. In response to criticisms of gay, lesbian, bisexual, and transgender performances as overly directed to LGBT audiences, Román and Miller assert the value of community-specific performances that emphasize and celebrate the core values and shared hopes of a given community. "If 'the converted' exist," they argue, then, the very term "the converted" needs to be "understood as a dynamic assembly that both individually and communally enters into the space of performance to sustain the very state of conversion."[33] More recently, Jill Dolan has built upon their argument, christening the affect generated by such rejuvenating, community-focused events as "utopian performatives." In the utopian performative, Dolan contends, a performance enables members of a community to suspend inner conflicts, the better to engage in an imagining in common, in which activist communities may unite, at least for a time, around a utopian image of the world as it should be.[34] Nevertheless, christening a community-based, activist production like Hell House as a utopian performative seems inappropriate. Hell House, after all, does not stage the community of faith unified and strong in the face of adversity. Indeed, it doesn't represent the community of faith at all (save for occasional forays into heaven). If anything, Hell House appears to generate a *dystopian* performative, seeking to foster not rejuvenation and inspiration (imagine what we could accomplish) but fear-induced transformation of character.

In evangelical practice, however, preaching to the converted does not necessarily imply inspiration and goodwill. As a child, I heard countless evangelical pastors preach revival sermons. Some of the speakers did excite joy and hope, spinning tales of the paradise to come that were so sweet I still grin to remember them. Yet many other preachers I heard took the "hard-sell" approach, painting vivid pictures of the constant threat of eternal fire and the demons that lay waiting in alcohol, gambling, rock music, and dancing. (Homosexuality was not yet on my cultural radar screen.) We heard that we were to flee all temptation, to refuse to be "yoked" to unbelievers, to seek first (and only) the kingdom of God: all because, the preachers warned, the Day of Judgement was approaching. The sky could rip open at any moment. Jesus and his heavenly hosts could return as unexpectedly "as a thief in the night," ready to separate the wheat of the church from the weeds of the world. Do your best, those preachers urged, to distinguish yourself from the weeds, lest you be thrown on the fire along with them. Though producing an affect diametrically opposed to Dolan's utopian performative, such jeremiads nevertheless succeeded in reviving the audience's sense of themselves as the Christian community. We drew close to our core beliefs not out of excitement about the beliefs per se but out of a need to pull back from the doomed, dystopian world. Such pronounced separatism recalls sociologist Anthony Cohen's work in *The Symbolic Construction of Community*. There he argues that two gestures comprise every expression of community: an inclusive gesture that takes in and mutes differences, and a discriminatory gesture that demarcates a boundary between those within and outside of the community.[35] It follows, then, that some performances of community generate utopian inclusiveness, celebrating the bonds that hold members together. Likewise, however, other performances highlight the exclusive nature of the community, the features that alienate it from other communities or from the world in general.

Pierre Bourdieu's theories can further clarify the mechanisms of communal exclusivity. In *Distinction,* Bourdieu suggests that social groupings in late capitalist society depend upon taste—that is, on group members' abilities to discriminate among different behaviors, styles, and attitudes in order to distinguish those of their own class from those of other classes.[36] Such class distinctions, however, come under stress when the class in question engages in "cultural proselytism," expanding its ranks by reaching out to a wider culture.[37] In such cases, a group's mechanisms for distinguishing itself from the rest of society conflict with its impulse to popularize. As a group seeks more members, it redefines itself in terms of a taste more palatable to more people. The distinctions that give it coherence thus become less definite.

A similar tension can be seen within secular-age evangelicalism. Evangelical authors Bruce Shelley and Marshall Shelley explain, "[Evangelicals'] life in the Christian *community* calls for their loyalty to the Word of God. . . . But at the same time their *mission* in the world demands that they try to influence a secular society, which usually means identifying with [that society], accommodating and compromising."[38] Compared to the large-scale socioeconomic classes that Bourdieu studies, the issue of whether one is a member of a particular church may seem like a casual, completely voluntary affair. For hard-sell evangelicals, however, active membership in a church community does not qualify as a casual preference. To be an evangelical in the hard-sell sense involves subscribing to a comprehensive worldview defined by a constant awareness of the connection between present, material actions and future, spiritual consequences.

Hard-sell evangelicalism directly engages what Bourdieu calls *habitus*—the structured and structuring cognitive apparatus by which a subject perceives and interprets reality in the course of generating a particular lifestyle.[39] As a discriminatory mechanism, taste forms an integral aspect of habitus. Hard-sell evangelicalism mandates a fundamental change in a subject's habitus, a wholly new way of seeing reality in terms of the fallen state of the earth and of imminent judgement. This new habitus necessarily translates into a lifestyle, a way of moving through the world, that is distinctively evangelical. This lifestyle in turn structures, reinforces, and perpetuates the evangelical tastes that contribute to it. The danger facing Christian evangelists, argue Shelley and Shelley, is that in connecting to the world to change the world, evangelicals might lose touch with the features that distinguish them from the world. They explain:

> To the eye of faith, this world is an empire; its capital city is heaven; its emperor is Jesus Christ. But the Lord Christ has not yet subjected the world to his law, educated it in his ways or united it in loyalty to himself. To achieve all this he has set throughout his empire colonies. . . . In the colony, citizens carefully nurture the stories, values and customs of the homeland. They wisely introduce their young ones to a lifestyle that the surrounding culture neither understands nor respects.[40]

Hell House shores up the boundaries between the world and the heavenly colony by deploying a tactical tastelessness, staging those evangelical doctrines, preferences, and actions that the nonconservative evangelicals find intolerable or unappetizing. More precisely, Hell House asserts an evangelical *counter*taste, "a lifestyle that the surrounding culture neither understands nor respects" to set them apart from the sin-filled world. "We are not going to soften our approach," Roberts insists in the face of criticism. "We will continue to be bold."[41] That this countertaste manifests itself through a dramaturgy of demonization is no accident. "In matters of taste, more than anywhere else," writes Bourdieu, "all determination is negation, and tastes are perhaps first and foremost distastes, disgust provoked by horror or visceral intolerance ('sick-making') of the tastes of others."[42]

In that light, the "doing" of Hell House concerns not only promoting the love of Christ to unbelievers but also provoking in believers a properly Christian attitude of distaste for the world in general. Hell House represents twenty-first-century culture as, in the words of one Texas Hell House actor, "the worst the world has ever been," replete with demonic traps disguised as harmless self-indulgence.[43] The "real-life" scenes escalate each of those indulgences into melodramatic horror. Rave parties inevitably turn into date rapes. The morning-after pill induces bloody miscarriages. Wicca meetings end with human sacrifices. Homosexual lifestyles result in grotesque AIDS deaths. And what makes these evils so insidious is that they mask themselves as popular, everyone-else-is-doing-it fads: It's just one little drink. Wiccans aren't really Satan worshippers. God wouldn't hate me because I'm homosexual. It's just a Harry Potter DVD.

To these siren calls from twenty-first-century culture, Hell House stages a grisly *au contraire.* Hell House enables conservative evangelical communities to renew their sense of being the colony of heaven on earth by staging a core aspect of the evangelical worldview: beneath its feel-good facades, the world without Christ is irredeemably hellish. "We don't need Jason and Freddy to scare people," explains one Detroit-area Hell House performer. "It's scary enough out there."[44] Though they aim at the outside world, Hell House productions serve the producing communities first and foremost. Within a movement increasingly at ease with consumerist culture, Hell House seeks to galvanize a "colony of heaven" defined by its unease with the material world.

Hell House's significance, I argue, does not lie in its use of distasteful imagery per se but in the example it provides of how distastefulness itself functions in the life and performance of community. Hell House suggests that discriminatory elements are necessarily present in any expression of community, especially in the performances of activist communities that work against or within a hegemonic status quo. Embracing discrimination as an aspect of community runs against the grain of much current thinking about community performance. Dolan's utopian performative, for instance, highlights the lowering of divisive barriers in order for spectators to connect to a deeper sense of unity. But, notwithstanding such moments of communal magic, not every performance of community need share that mystic affect. The rhetorical attractiveness of Dolan's model (who wouldn't want to experience something called a "utopian performative"?) can occlude the fact that communities must be at least as discriminatory as they are inclusive or they cease to operate as distinct communities at all. Even the most pro-diversity imaginings of a world-that-could-be must functionally exclude those dedicated to achieving a fundamentally different world. A gay-friendly utopia, for instance, inescapably alienates people who believe LGBT people to be sick and/or immoral. Rather than view such discrimination as a necessary evil, though, I submit that it behooves activists and performers to claim discriminatory countertastes as a tactic, even an ethic, of an activist community. Although Hell House can be faulted for the bigotry of its dramaturgy, it remains true that imagining what a community ought *not to be* is at least as important as imagining what it is or should be. Therefore, performances of countertaste can serve as a complement to Dolan's utopian performative, balancing Román and Miller's rejuvenating sermons to the converted with the occasional fire-and-brimstone revival.

In this sense, I suggest that the Brooklyn Hell House of Les Freres Corbusier worked better than its producers thought. They sought to match Roberts's staging as closely as possible, drafting a surface reproduction rather than a parody of a "real" Hell House production. In capturing and re-presenting such a community-specific text in a decidedly un-evangelical DUMBO warehouse space to (mainly) non-evangelical audiences, however, Les Freres Corbusier ended up replicating the same distinguishing function as "legit" Hell Houses do. Only instead of showing evangelicals how awful the secular world is, it showcased for (ostensibly non-evangelical) New Yorkers just how horrifying (non-New York) evangelicals are. In no sense interested in creating Christian converts, the company instead produced a kind of exotic display of "real" or "authentic" evangelical America. It reinforced for its New York audience the bad taste of (and a degree of disgust toward) those scary-but-sincere evangelicals out in the hinterlands of fly-over country.[45] Pellegrini, writing about her experience of the New York production in comparison with Roberts's original, wonders what would have changed had the Brooklyn company done outreach to evangelical audiences, "a kind of reverse missionizing." She suggests that such encounters might have revealed areas of overlap between evangelical and "hipster" worldviews.[46] I might agree—with one proviso: I cannot help but think that the Hell House producers are more sincerely interested in altering the worldviews of their non-evangelical audience members than Corbusier was in reaching, let alone convincing, any evangelicals.

Judgement House

It is Halloween weekend, 2009, at the Amite Baptist Church in Denham Springs, a small town just outside of Baton Rouge. I'm standing with a dozen or so other audience members at the gates of heaven and hell, in something like the check-in desk of eternity. In front of our group, positioned behind a central podium, stands an older man in a white robe. Addressing us all like a pastor giving a sermon, he intones a straightforward gospel message about sin, its consequences, Christ's sacrificial death on the cross, and the possibility of redemption. After hitting these standard points, he bends over a thick book with enormous pages sitting on the stand before him: the Lamb's *Book of Life.* "In this book," he explains, "are recorded all the names of the redeemed, those who have chosen to accept Jesus as their sin-bearer. Some of you have made preparations for this day." He sweeps his gaze across the audience. "But some of you have not."[47] He calls a name, "Matthew," and a high-school-age boy—an actor—steps forward nervously. The man (Saint Peter, or perhaps some unnamed angelic secretary) thumbs through the Book, searching for Matthew's name. Will he find it? Will Matthew go to heaven?

By now I feel like a seasoned connoisseur of interactive eschatological drama, no longer bracing myself for assaults on my liberal sensibilities but cataloguing choices and variations in format. This night I am watching a Judgement House, the second I've seen in person (the first almost five years before in Tallahassee). The staging conventions are familiar enough: a small group led by a guide through a series of church rooms refurbished to resemble various spaces. The actors reflect the mix of ages and talent levels standard for such dramas, and, as usual, all of them seem devoted to the task at hand. I know that beyond this afterlife anteroom wait the standard hell, heaven, and invitation spaces.

But this event is no Hell House. Instead of a succession of disconnected, blood-soaked shock scenarios, the performance unfolds more like a standard play with non-traditional staging. Each scene functions as an episode within a coherent narrative drama about a handful of stable characters—in this case Matthew and his friends—living in the same setting. For most of the evening, the style remains within the bounds of fourth-wall realism. The guide accompanying us from room to room is neither demon nor spirit but only a church volunteer in a Judgement House T-shirt. The malevolent spiritual entities infesting the Hell House world remain invisible here. The plot of this Judgement House production, *59 Minutes,* concerns a group of teens associated with a local church. In the first scene, set in a hospital morgue (complete with a funky astringent smell), our guide informs us that the characters we are about to meet have died, three teenagers in a senseless act of violence and one adult from a heart attack. The rest of the narrative unfolds in flashback, reviewing the last hours before these characters' deaths and spotlighting the choices that define their eternal fate. In subsequent scenes we pick up bits of their stories and relationships leading up to the inevitable death and, after that, the judgement.

In one early scene set in a church foyer, Matthew, a Christian, converses with Jennifer, a friend of his who attends his church. Jennifer reminisces about her deceased father, mentioning that he was a Christian and reflecting how nice it would be to see him in heaven. An adroit personal evangelist, Matthew gently presses her as to why she has not yet become a Christian. Jennifer cites a need to live her life—go to college, travel Europe, see the world—whereas becoming a Christian would mean giving all of that up, moving to Africa to become a preacher's wife. Disabusing her of such mistaken ideas about Christianity, Matthew shares with her the gospel and urges her not to put off salvation. Jennifer accedes, and he leads her in a sinner's prayer.

In the same scene, we meet Jake, who declares himself uninterested in church and impatient with his churchgoing mother. "I want to live my life to have fun," he complains to his worried mom, "not to please God or anyone else." Matthew invites him to hang out with the church youth, but Jake rejects him and storms off.[48] Other scenes present parallel plotlines about the adults in the church community, including a lawyer who (as we see) discounts the need for a personal relationship with Christ, assuring his wife that he attends church regularly and gives more money than anyone. After he leaves, our guide informs us somberly that, unbeknownst to him, he was about to meet his maker. None of us knows, she warns, how much time any of us has. Sure enough, soon after the conversion scene, our guide cautions us that the next scenarios will be noisy, scary, and heartbreaking. The teens whose stories we've been following, our guide informs us, have all been killed by a random act of violence, and the lawyer has suffered a fatal heart attack.

This is a markedly different experience, a far different affect, than Roberts-style dramas seek to provide. Where Hell House traffics in gross-outs and jump-scares, Judgement House privileges *clarity of message.* In every scene, at least one character relates a basic evangelical gospel pitch: all have sinned, the wages of sin is death, Christ's sacrifice can save us, acceptance/profession is necessary. After each scene, our group pauses between rooms so that the guide can reiterate to us the salient points of the previous situation (e.g., "Did you hear the excitement in Jennifer's voice when she accepted the simplicity of God's plan for her life?") and underline the salvific choices available to the characters. Hell House presents a fire-and-brimstone harangue; Judgement House provides a set of extended Sunday School lessons. Indeed, one of the boys in my audience group reacts more or less as if he's in a particularly boring class, snickering at the melodrama and acting out his ironic distance from the pathos playing out before us.

In addition to didactic (and repetitive) evangelistic clarity, Judgement House dwells on the tragic impermanence of life, how tomorrow is never guaranteed to anyone. Having forewarned us of the (random, unexplained) massacre of the teens we've come to know, our guide ushers us into a room where the characters' bodies lie in a carefully posed pile beyond a barrier of yellow "crime scene" tape. Off to one side, bystanders (more teens) wail in sorrow as sirens blare and red emergency lights flash. This is about as close as Judgement House gets to a Keenan Roberts–style tableau of terror, and even here the focus seems more about producing *pity* than *fear.* The accompanying scene underscores this preference for pathos over horror, showing us the lawyer, post–heart attack, unconscious and dying in a hospital bed. A heart monitor chirps steadily in a corner, and his wife sits by his side, weeping. "Why did this happen?" she wonders aloud, reflecting that only this morning she had promised her children that they would see their father. "How could I have known?" A doctor enters and breaks the news to her that her husband will not last much longer. With the pastor of the church arriving to offer comfort (and, of course, the gospel message), the wife ushers in her young children to say their final good-bye to their dad. The heart monitor slows and stalls on a dead note, and the family cries in sorrow. Shaking her head sympathetically, our guide again takes over, commenting how sad the whole situation is and reminding us that no one is guaranteed a tomorrow. Again—Judgement House aims for tears rather than visceral disgust or bone-chilling horror.

Fear does eventually come into play, however, as the guide leads us into the next scene: Judgement. Back to the Book of Life: Saint Peter (or whoever it is—the performances I've seen are vague about such potentially iffy theology)[49] finds Matthew's name, praising his Christian witness and welcoming him into heaven. Assisted by another white-robed figure (an angel?), he beckons the boy into the doorway on his right, a portal festooned in white and pastel tulle. Matthew walks through, praising God. The man at the podium calls Jake forward, frowning at the book and informing the boy that, because he never gave his life to Christ, he died a sinner and is destined for Hell. "I don't care!" Jake yells, "All my friends are there!" His tone changes from defiance to panic, however, as figures in dark clothes (still much tamer than any Hell House demon) step forward, seize hold of him, and drag him through the left-hand portal. Next, Peter calls Jennifer, the new convert. Finding even this neophyte Christian's name in the Book of Life—salvation is a matter of giving one's life to Christ, not a function of time served—Peter sends her after her friend through the heaven door. Finally, Peter calls the lawyer's name. "I guess this is heaven," the man says confidently as he steps up to the podium. He knows where he's going. He's gone to church all his life and put lots of money in the offering plate. Yet, though Peter checks and rechecks the Book, he fails to locate the man's name. You see, the robed figure explains sadly, being a Christian isn't a matter of sitting in pews or coughing up cash. It is all about your answer to the question *Have you accepted Christ as your savior?* The man, alas, never did so, and now, at his final judgement, it is too late. The door on Peter's left-hand side yawns once more, revealing menacing darkness. The man screams as the black-shirted figures grab him and drag him through the gate to hell.

The scene continues after the lawyer's departure. As the hell mouth closes, Peter selects a sheet of paper from beside the Book and announces the next three names—not characters this time but names of people in our audience group. As I expect, mine is one of the names called. My eye, however, picks out the too-cool-for-school teen in my audience group. As he hears Peter read out his own name, the teen's jaw drops and the blood drains from his face. His friends all take an unconscious half-step away from him, tittering with uneasy schadenfreude. The people Peter calls are told to step forward. We do so. "It is not yet your time," Peter intones, fixing us each with a stern gaze, "but if it were, would I find your name in this Book?"

The Hell scene we are led to after this is relatively tame, basically a hot, dark room with some ambient moaning. Compared to Roberts-style scenarios, this inferno boasts few inhabitants. Gone are the horn-and-pitchfork devils of Hell House; the *Judgement House Training Manual* explicitly forbids such stereotypical portrayals.[50] A pale man in a three-piece suit—Satan, we take it—laughs evilly as a thin young man in black, besmirched with soot, laments that he's in agony and begs us to tell our unbelieving friends about the reality of hell before it's too late. Heaven, our next destination, is by contrast an elaborate affair. Judgement House does not skimp on paradise. Smiling figures in white mill about, enjoying their eternal bliss. Angelic song plays from hidden speakers ("I Can Only Imagine" by the Christian band MercyMe is a favorite in such scenes). At the head of the room, directly in front of us, is a throne upon which sits a grinning, middle-aged Jesus (longish hair, beard) welcoming us. The two teens from the Judgement scene enter, enraptured at the heavenly glory, and meet Jesus, who gives them each great bear hugs. "There's someone here," Jesus tells Jennifer, "who's been waiting to see you again." Another middle-aged man enters, smiling. Jennifer turns to see him. "Dad!" she cries, rushing to him.

After this, our audience group files into the church's sanctuary, and we take our seats on the front pews. One of the church's pastors stresses for one last time the you-never-know-when-you'll-face-judgement themes of the drama. He asks us to pray ("every head bowed, every eye closed"), raising our hands in turn if we need prayer, want to give our lives to Christ, or want to make a recommitment. I do not peek to see if the call-out from Peter had any effect on the teen I noticed earlier.

Analyzing Judgement

Though often presented as a variant of Roberts's Hell House Outreach, Judgement House—typically printed as Judgement House™—in fact predates Roberts's Hell House outreach, having been started in 1983 by Tom Hudgins, a pastor in Clearwater, Florida. As Hell House has gained fame and notoriety in the media, Hudgins's ministry, New Creation Experiences, Inc., found it necessary to clarify Judgement House's distance from Roberts's outreach.[51] In general, Judgement House eschews the in-your-face controversy Roberts sometimes seems to crave. The culture-war elements of abortion and homosexuality so dear to Roberts have no place in Judgement House scripts. Nor does Judgement House position itself as a haunted house, a Halloween alternative, nor even as a fear-based event at all. To be sure, its themes revolve around a degree of anxiety about death, but the quality of this fear more resembles an insurance commercial ("you'd best prepare for inevitability") than a moralizing psycho-slasher flick ("transgress and suffer gruesome consequences"). Instead Judgement House's strategy involves posing (and posing, and re-posing) to audiences the gospel message and the central evangelistic choice: *Will you be saved?* Every scene, and every speech by the guides after each scene, presents the kerygmatic gospel message. Even the hell room—which, the *Training Manual* stresses, is *not* the focus of Judgement House[52]—features dialogue with explicit instructions on how to be saved. Now, Roberts would doubtless claim that the salvation of the lost is Hell House's goal as well, but whereas he views fear as a means to that end, Judgement House views it as a distraction.

Judgement House does resemble Roberts's outreach, however, in that it operates partially as a commercial endeavor. As a franchise, Judgement House requires a greater degree of loyalty and dedication from its respective franchisees than Hell House. Churches spend more than twice as much ($599 as of this writing) to become "Covenant Partners," signing agreements that affirm the church's doctrinal integrity (as matched with

Judgement House's own statement of faith), honest evangelistic intentions, and compliance with Judgement House's production strictures.[53] In exchange, churches get *The Judgement House Training Manual,* the rights to produce one Judgement House script (an unlimited number of performances for one year), and a required training session with a Judgement House professional, who travels to the covenant church for an intensive production workshop. With the exception of the script, the *Manual* covers similar ground to the *Hell House Outreach Manual.* It outlines sample budgets, production timelines, artistic and technical roles, publicity recommendations, set- and costume-building instructions, and more. It explains how to set up and run the walk-through using a clever system of "Door Knockers"—people stationed at every room-scene's door giving coded raps to warn and cue the actors to set up and begin just as audiences enter.[54] Judgement House's website sells T-shirts that churches can purchase and re-sell (at a suggested three-dollar markup) as part of their own productions.[55]

Judgement House offers about a dozen different scripts, each a singular narrative consisting of up to nine scenes. I previously watched one of these, *Land of the Free, Home of the Brave,* performed by a church in Tallahassee (not the same as the one that produced the Hell House) in 2004. *Land of the Free* traces the tale of three friends as they grow up, join the military, and perish in battle. In a series of scenes, we witness their childhood, follow them through high school, see them during their time volunteering for and serving in the armed forces, and watch as each dies on the battlefield (the conflict is vague and unnamed). All of them then appear before the Peter figure in the judgement scene, moving on to either hell or heaven from there. As was the case in *59 Minutes,* the different characters represent various standard points on the continuum of Christian life and potential: a long-term Christian, a last-minute convert, and a stubbornly unsaved person. *Land of the Free* appeals specifically to patriotic pro-military themes (though these are more muted and generic than one might expect).[56] Other scripts touch on different specific challenges. *Web of Lies,* for example, engages the temptations and traps of the internet, *Collision* deals with the perils of drunk driving, and *Found Faithful* adapts a "real life" story of a cancer victim whose witness led others to Christ.[57]

The last few scenes of any Judgement House script inevitably feature the same three scenarios of judgement, hell, and heaven. Each of these incorporates standard Judgement House tropes. At the gates, St. Peter calls out audience members by name. In the low-key hell sequence, the

"Damien" character begs the audience to tell their friends about hell. During the heaven scene, a friendly Jesus reunites characters with their deceased Christian relatives. Even the invitation room features specific directions for different roles. The pastor's "every head bowed, every eye closed"—a common pastoral instruction during the invitations of evangelical worship services—becomes the scripted signal for church volunteers ("Encouragers") to take people aside for one-on-one prayer or evangelizing (i.e., posing diagnostic questions, pushing gently for a decision, leading people in a sinner's prayer if necessary).[58] Everything about the production, every scene, every step, aims at its evangelistic ends.

In that sense, Judgement House would seem to address and transcend the criticisms that evangelicals like Moore, Hall, and Farr level at Hell House and shock-fear-based evangelism. In downplaying hell, avoiding controversy, and emphasizing sound doctrine and kerygmatic clarity, then, one might expect Judgement House to succeed where Hell House perhaps falls short. From a strict perspective of theatrical criticism, however, Judgement House's pure evangelistic focus introduces its own pitfalls.

Judgement House productions face the same challenges as a Hell House: a limited budget and inexperienced performers charged with matching and bettering the allures of secular pop culture. Yet Hell House's dramaturgical simplicity—basically a series of noisy, scary, gory tableaux vivants—proves oddly ideal for amateur realization (to say nothing of ironic spectatorship). Conveying the cartoonish villainy of demon guides or the pain-wracked screams of dying abortion patients, after all, requires little in the way of theatrical finesse. Making the exposition-heavy dialogue of a Judgement House script compelling and believable, on the other hand, poses a significant challenge to raw young actors. Without the shrieks and cackles and blood-spattered scenarios—and, it must be said, without the culture-war shout-outs and controversial, I-can't-believe-they're-doing-that audacity—Judgement House has to rely on its audience engaging actively in the lives and fates of its characters. This is, to put it mildly, no mean feat. Actors, directors, designers, and playwrights train for years to master the difficult magic of dramatic engagement in psychologized, slice-of-life styles. Judgement House adds to these standard theatrical hurdles the complications of Sudden (hard-to-swallow) Melodrama and Constant Presentation of the Gospel. Each scene thus attempts an uneasy combination of believability (*Character X is a person just like you!*), pathos (*How sad character X is to hear of her son's unexpected death!*), and sermonizing (*If only X's son knew that all have sinned and fall short of the glory of God, etc.!*). Neither sufficiently bad-offensive to be notorious nor well-executed enough to be admirable, Judgement Houses simply do not seem to offer much in the way of innovative or effective evangelism.

Of course, such a dismissal underlines the importance of a critically generous lens, of suspending the standard theater critic questions of aesthetic polish to probe a community-based performance's actual intents. Specifically, I argue that, similar to the Hell House case, appreciating Judgement House's operation depends upon asking how it preaches to the converted. More accurately, I maintain that Judgement House emphasizes preaching *with* the converted. Beyond the dramatic script realized by actors, designers, directors, and support personnel, Judgement House productions play out a parallel series of actions unique to its evangelical endeavor. As I describe above, a plain-clothes guide accompanies each audience group, ushering us from one scene to the other and reiterating the various plot points and spiritual themes of the script. Unbeknownst to audiences, however, another church member, what Judgement House calls a Prayer Walker, walks with us. A Prayer Walker embeds with audience groups, going with them through each scene, charged with doing nothing except praying silently and earnestly throughout the production for the members of her audience group by name. A complicated set of transactions between the registration desk, the Guides, the Door Knockers, and the Prayer Walkers ensures that copies of a list of every person in the audience group (a list created as audience members register to see the production) get passed to the Guide and to the Prayer Walker, who keeps the copy hidden, consulting it only as necessary to identify and pray for people in the group as the Holy Spirit moves her to do so. Outside of the Judgement scene, the Prayer Walker surreptitiously hands the list to the Door Knocker for that scene, who in turn hands the list to the Peter actor, enabling the coup de théâtre in which various audience members (those the Prayer Walker marks as particularly needful of or receptive to the incident) hear their names called.[59]

Here I reach the limits of strictly dramaturgical analysis. From a purely secular analytic perspective, this kind of behind-the-scenes prayer has little significance. The audience is unaware of the presence or action of Prayer Walkers; such prayer has no obvious semiotic or phenomenological effect on unaware spectators. Even I, confident as I was in my grasp of the dynamics of these kinds of performances, knew nothing of the Prayer Walkers accompanying me—praying specifically for me, noting that I should be one of the names Peter calls forth in Judgement—until I read the *Training Manual* and realized just how vital these figures are to the ministry. The *Manual* (as well as, presumably, the training sessions required of all Covenant Partners) emphasizes that prayer in general must saturate every aspect of the production. Aside from locating and tapping the technical expertise necessary to build sets, find costumes, and run lights, the *Manual* mandates that Judgement House directors recruit "Prayer Warriors," people charged with doing nothing but praying for the cast, crew, and audiences for the run of the show. The *Manual* even includes standardized prayer cards (including the name of a particular person and a sample prayer) that Warriors can fill out and use to guide their prayers.[60] Each evening before the first group, everyone involved in the production—from actors to Door Knockers to registration table workers—must attend a prayer and praise session, orienting them toward the task of ministry.[61] Every room has a "Room Director" charged with coordinating the efforts of each room/scene's actors, including acting as a Prayer Warrior for the room itself by praying with the cast before and between audience groups.[62] Prayer Walkers circulate in and out of audience groups throughout the run. "Exterior Walkers"—Prayer Walkers not embedding into audience groups—patrol the outside of the performance areas all evening long, literally surrounding the space with prayer.[63] Encouragers wait for audience groups in the invitation room to pray with and for people in need.

To be clear, prayer and prayer teams are hardly unusual features of evangelical ministries. Hell House, for example, encourages churches to solicit people to pray for the success of the production. But Judgement House incorporates acts of secret (to audiences) prayer into the structure of the performance itself in a way other productions do not. The website foregrounds this "bathed in prayer" aspect of Judgement House as a distinguishing feature of the ministry for churches considering becoming Covenant Partners. "The first thing you will learn about a Judgement House presentation is that prayer is the most essential ingredient required for success," boasts the site. "Something we found," relates a testimonial, "was that the very first time we produced a Judgement House presentation, our church family changed. Young kids in a drama scene with a more mature person as their door knocker would come together and pray between scenes!"[64] These and other such prayer moments shape the "doing" of Judgement House. Prayer Walkers, Prayer Warriors, prayer rooms, and the like function not as authenticating conventions—incidental features for evangelical audiences to recognize—but as rhetorical conventions, definitional attributes of the Judgement House dramatic form. A Judgement House stripped of the saturated prayer factor (e.g., an ironic or secular production of *59 Minutes*) would in some vital way fail to be a Judgement House at all, resembling instead a satirical staging of a mawkishly churchy play.

I am proposing, then, that prayer operates performatively—it enacts, it changes reality—in Judgement House performances. What exactly does prayer do? Addressing this question purely from a secular, objective view proves tricky; to do so would depart drastically from the understandings of the community itself. I could argue, for example, that Judgement House's prayer-saturation creates or enhances a sense of communal solidarity. The praise-and-prayer services before each performance are literally instances of preaching to the converted, and as Román and Miller argue, such performances reconnect the community of activist performers to the stakes and ends of their efforts. Sociologists who study activist social movements often cite participation in specific social networks, the sense of working together with like-minded people, as an important catalytic step in turning an individual into an activist.[65] Insofar as Judgement House consciously creates a cooperative community resolutely focused on saving the lost through a joint endeavor, it fits social movement theory's models for individual mobilization. On the Judgement House website, the "What is Judgement House?" page seems to echo this sense of unity and activation:

> Our Covenant Partners annually report that aside from SEEING PEOPLE ACCEPT CHRIST, the Judgement House presentation:
>
> 1. UNIFIES THEIR PEOPLE
> 2. REFOCUSES THEIR OUTREACH MINISTRY
> 3. ENRICHES THE SPIRITUAL LIVES OF ALL INVOLVED
> 4. CREATES AND SUSTAINS A PRAYING CHURCH[66]

That Judgement House "transforms the host church or community" serves as another "Why Judgement House" selling point. "Since our inception in 1983," the site claims, "more than 3,000 CAST MEMBERS have accepted Christ as their personal Savior."[67]

Yet I also know that the church community itself, the people who produce Judgement Houses, would insist that their prayers do more than create a sense of energized focus (though they would affirm this effect at least). To pray is not merely to entreat God to action; it is to open oneself to being transformed or used by God. It invites the Holy, the Miraculous, into the performance as co-performer (or, rather, co-*director*). Prayer Walkers choose whom to pray for, whose names on the list to mark for calling out in Judgement, via the movement of the Holy Spirit. The performative act of prayer in Judgement House involves submitting to the greater-than-you mission and transformative potential of the performance. For Judgement House participants, however, submission accompanies *protection.* Although Judgement House performances disallow demon guides and pitchfork-wielding devils, the producers definitely see their work as unfolding amid a scene of spiritual warfare. The Prayer Warriors' cards, for instance, encourage the Warriors to pray that God will "keep Satan far from them as they go about your work in this production of Judgement House."[68] The *Manual* recommends restricting pre-show access to the dressing rooms of actors playing the roles of Satan, Jesus, and Damien (the tortured soul in Hell). These actors "will be primary targets for spiritual warfare," the *Manual* explains. "They will need this [pre-show] time for prayer."[69] Even a role as seemingly mundane as staffing the registration desk gets special attention. "Make sure your registration workers attend the group prayer and praise time," cautions the *Manual.* "This area is also very vulnerable to Satan's attacks, but is often overlooked in the rush to get ready for the guests arriving for the first tour."[70] It lies beyond the purview of my project to speculate about the anti-demonic efficacy of prayers offered for ticket-takers. But the special attention accorded to star performers and front-of-house volunteers alike, the prayer that affirms and unites them all as warrior-activists for Christ, consolidates the overall sense of the production as not just a Really Big Show but as corporate worship. Judgement House literally casts the Divine as a participant, a silent partner who accompanies cast, crew, and audience. To an even greater extent than the Hell House, the Judgement House format exemplifies Miller and Román's sense of preaching to the converted. The subtext of saturated prayer draws every participant into a charged evangelistic encounter, one that has the potential to change audience and producers alike.

Conclusion

As I have mentioned, aside from formal Hell Houses and Judgement Houses, I have seen a number of home-brew, off-the-beaten-path productions along the same basic lines. In south Louisiana, for example, one can find a production called *Final Exit.* Devised by local pastor John

Neel, the production consists of a traveling pre-fab set that churches (or groups of churches) may rent and (along with Neel's help) produce. Its script largely follows Roberts's Hell House model, though it features more scenes and specializes in what Neel calls "extreme reality," meaning gory, violent set pieces.[71] In contrast to the Tallahassee Hell House, the *Final Exit* I watched (in Baker, Louisiana) never passed up an opportunity for full-on gruesomeness. As "spirit guides" (*Final Exit*'s version of Hell House demons) led my audience group to the abortion scene, for example, I noted a transparent plastic sneeze shield set up between the stage and the audience. The abortion doctor, as per Hell House's standard, was portrayed as a brutal, dirty sadist wielding a vacuum cleaner against a shrieking victim/patient. Not only did he have a bowl of hamburger meat soaking in red-colored corn syrup, however; he cackled and threw the "fetus" pieces at the audience so that they splattered against the pane. *Final Exit*'s Christ on the cross was by far the grossest set-piece I have ever seen on any stage: a drooling, naked mass of wounds from thorn-crowned head to nailed feet. As is the case with other such productions, the energy behind the production at times translated into garbled stagecraft. Many actors' lines, though loudly and lustily bellowed, were frequently unintelligible. The gospel-message voice-over playing over the crucifixion scene was inaudible, hopelessly upstaged by the spectacle of the (totally uncontextualized) torture victim before us. Like many of the other productions I have seen (the professionally acted Freres Corbusier *Hell House* being an exception), I wondered how anyone could be moved, let alone transformed by this production. To be sure, the production animated a particular evangelical community, but what effect could it possibly have on the not-already-converted?

Yet here I must take care not to underestimate how my own positions as an outsider, as ex-evangelical, and as regular critic of evangelical theology and practice conspire to set my experience of these shows far apart from that of the average attendee. I have watched audience members accompanying me through various productions weep with sorrow at depictions of the crucified Jesus I found laughable. The Judgement House's father-daughter reunion scene, which to my eye was telegraphed well in advance and maudlin in execution, inspired a deep gasp of surprise and tearful joy from spectators near me. And, though I have cast considerable doubt on claims of mass conversions after such productions, I cannot deny that some people at least truly experience the event as life-changing. Certainly the producers and cast believe in such transformative potential, taking specific steps (in the case of Judgement

Houses) to build into the structure of the show reminders to be themselves open to transformation.

And I must admit, the energy and ingenuity driving many of these productions stuns me. The challenge of staging a multi-site, environmental-theater, audience walk-through with a rotating cast of hundreds is considerable by any measure, even for seasoned theater artists. These communities make such shows happen with little or no formal training in design or construction. And they occasionally produce amazing things. For instance, the technology behind *Final Exit*'s transportable labyrinth of temporary walls to define different rooms and hallways—computer magnets to hold the walls together—was unconventional, effective, and in its own way brilliant. Off-putting as it was for me, the bloody Christ effect was likewise a special effects success, achieved by a flesh-colored wetsuit, heavily distressed and soaked in red corn syrup. Neel gushed proudly about these innovations, going on to express pleasure at how hard his cast worked and how realistic the gore was. And then he pulled out a picture of a grinning toddler, informing me soberly that this was a little girl whose mother decided against having an abortion after seeing the show.

I did not know what to say to that. I still don't. Certainly my own political and theological convictions set me apart from—against, actually—what I see as the vicious anti-abortion sentiment of *Final Exit*. As is the case with any number of the more extreme hell house– or judgement house–type imagery, I have difficulty affirming fear as a means of persuading the non-believer or reviving the already-converted. As Bourdieu was fond of pointing out, academics rely heavily on their own mechanisms of distinction. Despite my commitment to critical generosity I have peppered my argument here with indicators of my own sense of distinction from evangelical stances and practices (e.g., *amateur theater I can handle*). Alongside my dis-taste for its theology, however, I do find myself admiring—and, again, envious of—the faith that these productions have in the transformative power of theater (or, properly, in the ability of theater to serve as a conduit for the Holy Spirit's life-changing power). I have a host of reservations about the idea of a pregnant woman's being so profoundly affected by a shock image I find offensively at odds with reality (doctors are not sadists; women terminating their pregnancies are not victims). But I find it moving that the producers expect that their productions can have an effect so profound.[72] "Amateur," after all, attests etymologically not to poor craftsmanship but to love—a sincere passion for the power of theater to convey a life-changing message.

I know of few activist performances from the secular progressive left that imagine, let alone boast of, a transformation in their audiences as striking as those Roberts, Hudgins, Neel, and other practitioners attest to. Their productions are, from the producers' perspectives, not merely well-done acts of theater; they are the Word of God manifested spectacularly. The dramas performed are not just stories about God; they are (thanks to the saturation of prayer) platforms for the Divine to enter in and change the hearts and minds of audience members. Such an invocation seems at first glance to set these productions far apart from most left-progressive examples (though, as I have mentioned, many left-progressive agents have aligned their messages with supernatural purposes, e.g., Martin Luther King Jr.). Still, I have participated in left-progressive community-based and Theatre of the Oppressed productions myself. I know that these processes, while not religious, often invoke or engage something like a secular spirituality. The act of sharing and receiving (and ultimately re-playing) another's story in a TO workshop, for example, often takes on a kind of sacred aura. Performing a community-engaged show for the community itself can similarly weave a spell of unity that *feels* magical (similar to Dolan's utopian performative). Productions that engage social or political causes regularly reference a shared acknowledgment of grand abstractions—justice, equality, fairness—that nevertheless have real effects.

None of these ideals, of course, carries the same valence of agency, personality, or divinity that God does for the evangelical productions I have related here. I imagine that some left-progressive activists might recoil a bit at the suggestion that, for example, *The Laramie Project*'s inspiring meditation on shared humanity has much in common with Judgement House's invocation of God. The latter production, one could say, obviously excludes and, well, *judges,* while the former offers an invitation open to all, even extending a modicum of pity and understanding to Matthew Shepard's killers. Yet such a reading overlooks how even the *Laramie Project*'s join-hands-together aura accompanies worldview messages that many evangelicals might find difficult to endorse. While no evangelical I know of condones Shepard's assault or murder, some decry what they see as the Tectonic Theatre Company's coercive message of tolerance or even acceptance of homosexuality. These critics particularly take issue with *The Laramie Project*'s inclusion in high school curricula.[73] My point is not that the play's critics are correct but that their voices trouble the notion that the play's meditation on tolerance somehow escapes the possibility that some people or groups might disagree (and that they might disagree without necessarily being supporting a Fred Phelps–type anti-gay bigotry). Hell House and Judgement House, by contrast, have no illusions about the fact that their portrait of reality does and will alienate some. Though they are invested in converting those who disagree with them, "not offending" simply isn't part of their agenda. Moreover, as an instance of "preaching to the converted," hell house and judgement house events reinforce the kind of ideological-theological distinctions that define someone as a believer in the first place, even and especially if this distinction invites unrest from the converted.

CHAPTER 6

Prepare to Believe

Performing the Evangelical Worldview at the Creation Museum

I confess: I was taken aback by how *professional* it looks, this Museum, how slick. Past experience with conservative evangelical productions led me to expect something like hell houses: an earnest but awkward attempt at "science," a sincere but threadbare facsimile of a secular discovery-center. But here in July 2008, as my partner and I walk through elaborate portico at the entrance to the Creation Museum in Petersburg, Kentucky, I decide that my preconceptions need re-aligning.

A tall rock face, festooned with fossils and glass-enclosed displays, lines either side of the entry hall, which then opens onto a large foyer dominated by a jungle motif accented with lighting and ambient jungle sound effects. Beside us towers a two-story waterfall stocked with live gar and turtles.[1] Above the waterfall sits a life-sized diorama in which brown-skinned children sporting rough-spun shifts frolic beside two baby tyrannosaurs. Across from this group, a massive sauropod swings its long neck to and fro above our heads, placidly munching fake ferns. Beyond the waterfall we find a planetarium and a book store, behind the sauropod a 3-D theater. The lower level boasts yet another movie theater, a well-stocked fossil display, and a coffee shop. And straight ahead, a smiling, uniformed volunteer waits to take our tickets at the entrance to the main Museum tour. This, I realize, is no local church effort whose reach extends its amateur grasp. This is no-expenses-spared, state-of-the-art edutainment aimed at competing with—and bettering—the best family-oriented science museums that secular culture has to offer. This Museum wants a national audience. "Prepare to Believe," reads the Museum's motto. And while it didn't change my views on evolution, the Creation Museum certainly convinced me of the seriousness of its aspirations.

Built to the tune of twenty-seven million dollars in 2007, designed by a small army of artists and special effects experts, and stuffed with information from theologians and scientists working for evangelist Ken Ham's young-earth creationist group Answers in Genesis (AiG), the Creation Museum represents a pinnacle achievement of creation science. To evangelicals invested in a literal interpretation of Genesis, the Museum brilliantly testifies to the solid foundation of creationist beliefs in a six-day divine creation, six thousand-year-old universe, and specially designed (not evolved) human beings. To those skeptical of creationism's status as science—a view that includes the vast majority of credentialed scientists[2]—anti-evolutionists' influence threatens the legacy of the Enlightenment itself, promising a renaissance of superstition over rationalism, delusion over critical thinking, and theocracy over secular democracy. From this latter viewpoint, it is difficult not to see the "Creation Museum" as a contradiction in terms, more a temple to ignorance than a showcase of science and inquiry.

Although I endorse scientists' efforts to challenge anti-evolutionist[3] claims to scientific validity,[4] I write not as a scientist but as a theater scholar. My fascination with the Museum stems less from its notoriety among scientists as a bastion of anti-intellectualism and more from the role it plays in evangelical strategies of survival and outreach in the secular age. Within the atmosphere of existential threat that partially characterizes present-day US evangelicalism, the state of the anti-evolutionist movement often serves as a bellwether for evangelical health more generally. On this score, evangelicalism seems to be in trouble. The creation-evolution war, although far from ended, has not gone well for anti-evolutionists over the last few decades. Anti-evolutionists' efforts to maintain hegemony (How can we prevent Darwin from being taught?) have gradually become ever-more-harried struggles for legitimacy (How can we ensure that some kind of creationism is taught alongside Darwin?). Subsequent to the Scopes trial in 1925 (which anti-evolutionist forces won), courts have consistently ruled against anti-evolutionist influence over public school curricula.[5] Conservative evangelicals view creationism's dwindling authority as but one more symptom of a deeper evangelical malaise, a tragic cultural and political shift away from Bible-based foundations.

Given the beleaguered state of US evangelicalism in general and anti-evolutionist movements specifically, the Creation Museum's audacious subtext—*We exist, and are stronger than ever*—takes on a revivalist fervor. In this chapter I argue that AiG's Creation Museum represents a shift both in the scale and the strategy of conservative evangelical self-performance in the face of waning evangelical power.[6] Departing from the evidentiary battles that have characterized the evolution/creation debate, AiG draws upon the performative power of museums to define artifacts of study, a nineteenth-century commonsense understanding of science, and a presuppositionalist apologetic tradition to restage the evolution/creation struggle as a competition of *worldviews* rather than of *evidence.* Welding the young-earth creationist cause to evangelical identity in toto, then, the Museum (re)defines evangelicalism in terms of a winner-take-all war of worldviews with the evolution/creation struggle as the prime battlefield. In terms of activism, the Museum, in concert with AiG's related outreach initiatives, exemplifies a trend toward tactical retrenchment along Schaefferian lines. Faced with the secular authority of the naturalistic scientific worldview, Answers in Genesis urges evangelicals to embrace (what they present as) an equally well-founded and sophisticated apparatus of Creation science—a biblical worldview. The "Prepare to Believe" slogan, I argue, speaks not primarily to unbelievers but to evangelicals, with the emphasis on *preparation* as an integral component of secular-age outreach.

Museum Performatives

A word about how Museums perform is in order. I join critics like Barbara Kirshenblatt-Gimblett and Valerie Casey in approaching museums[7] as sites of performance in which disciplines (mainly art, anthropology, history, and science) produce themselves through spectacular, consumer-oriented acts of display.[8] That is, museums do not merely house objects self-evidently important to art, history, anthropology, or science; they act as mechanisms by which artistic, anthropological, historical, and scientific discourses define themselves by identifying their objects of study. Museums thus contribute to the creation, exploration, and refinement of what constitutes knowledge in various fields. In doing so, they charge themselves with tasks of object selection, arrangement, and presentation strikingly similar to the tasks of theater artists. "Exhibitions are fundamentally theatrical," notes Kirshenblatt-Gimblett, "for they are how museums perform the knowledge they create."[9] Three features of museums' theatricality concern me here.

First, as Kirshenblatt-Gimblett argues, museums' acts of display performatively (re)create objects as artifacts.[10] A pot (alternately, "a fossil" or "a piece of rock strata") in its original context exists only as a pot. But a museum's act of displacement (removing the pot from that context) and re-situation (placing the pot in a room, under a spotlight, attended by a caption, alongside other implements) grants the pot a grander metonymic significance. The simple pot now stands in for an era, a location, or even an entire culture. It ceases to be merely an object and becomes an *artifact.*

Second, museums arrange their objects-cum-artifacts into an ordered narrative, "an intelligent train of thought," that simultaneously acknowledges and co-creates the defining narratives of a particular discipline.[11] Art museums, for example, select and arrange pieces into groups in conformity with official narratives of movements, eras, or artists. These historiographic or taxonomic groupings themselves then contribute to the ongoing discourse of significance within art criticism.

Finally, twenty-first-century museums increasingly experience tension between their dual roles as sites of cultural/scientific authority and sites of display. Michael M. Ames goes so far as to call museums "compromised institutions, caught between their twin desires for both authenticity and the spectacular."[12] At present, museums are tourist attractions as well as educational centers, competing with numerous other destinations for spectators' money and attention. Economic competition pushes museums to seek out ever-more-spectacular draws, designing installations that "give greater attention to the visitor's perceptual and aesthetic experiences in the context of other consumer experiences" and presenting their key narratives "with the theatricality of a theme park or Hollywood film."[13]

The Creation Museum recognizes and accepts the challenge to be both authoritative and entertaining, blending its truth claims with market-savvy elements to rival those of secular cultural offerings. Its publicity materials, for instance, boast that while individual exhibits had input from paleontologists, geologists, cosmologists, and biologists, the Museum's overall "storyline" (i.e., the main walk-through tour) was designed by a former Universal Studios theme park designer, Patrick Marsh. "Patrick brought with him the vision of making the museum more than stuffy exhibit halls filled with bones and fossils," explains the Museum's own history book. "To effectively present a message, [an exhibit] must be designed and developed as 'edu-tainment.'"[14] Indeed, as the description I related at the start of this chapter demonstrates, the Museum blends some *Jurassic Park* with the Smithsonian.

Yet Marsh and the other designers never let the dazzle factor impinge upon the Museum's presentation qua museum. Despite the robot sauropods and life-sized dioramas, the Museum successfully presents itself as "science museum" and not as "Six Flags Over Eden." It mobilizes all of the semiotic delivery systems—the *rhetorical conventions,* to use Baz Kershaw's term—that spectators might use to identify a location as a science museum.[15] Aside from the specific offerings I study here, the Museum offers a number of features standard to any well-stocked discovery center or modern edutainment-oriented museum. It boasts multiple movie theaters, including a 3-D show with audience-interactive elements. Its gift shop brims with books (all carefully filtered for a young-earth-creationist message), dinosaur toys, posters, and Museum-related knick-knacks. A petting zoo and nature walk are situated just outside of the Museum proper.

Nor does the Museum simply traffic in thin creationist propaganda or theme park fluff. A genuine fascination with scientific facts—numbers, statistics, models, and so on—inflects every display. The Museum dedicates whole rooms to its impressive fossil collection, with each piece captioned by a mass of raw paleontological data (e.g., what animal this fossil is from, what we know about this animal and how, what the fossil tells us about life in the animal's environment) leavened with young-earth-creationist doctrine (i.e., that the fossil formed during the Flood thousands of years ago rather than by other causes millions of years ago). The Museum even features a large planetarium whose show mixes standard astronomical fare (constellations, the solar system, the movement of heavenly bodies) with a creation science–themed take on certain vexing cosmological problems (e.g., "gravitational lensing" explains how light from stars billions of light-years away reaches earth when the universe is less than ten thousand years old).

Space limitations prevent me from delving too far into any of these elements. Suffice it to say that from a lay perspective, the Museum looks like a science museum, sounds and smells like a science museum, is arranged like a science museum, has all the attractions one expects from a science museum, markets itself as a science museum, and costs as much as any discovery-center-type science museum. In what follows, I focus on the Museum's primary attraction: the walk-through tour of the main exhibit hall.

The Artifact of Investigation

Past the portico, beyond the smiling volunteer ticket-taker, the Museum's walk-through begins.[16] Museum-goers expecting more spectacular re-creations of young-earth scenarios such as those in the foyer find they have to wait. For at least the first third of the tour, the Museum steers away from such explicitly anti-evolution portrayals. Instead, the walk-through initially presents visitors with a life-sized diorama display of a present-day fossil dig at the Grand Canyon. Two scientists, one older and one younger, hunch on a dusty outcropping of rock against a brilliant blue sky of a panoramic Canyon vista, frozen in the act of brushing dirt away from the partially excavated skeleton of a medium-sized dinosaur (a *Utahraptor*, according to captions). On television screens placed around the room, the scientists on whom the mannequins are based speak to the audience on looped videotape. One identifies as a creationist, the other as an evolutionist. Both present their different "reading" of the *Utahraptor* remains. The creationist (the older one) tells patrons that he sees the remains and the layers of strata that make up the Grand Canyon itself as evidence of a massive flood that inundated the earth, destroyed most life, laid down rock layers, and carved out the Canyon's features—all on the order of about four thousand years ago.[17] The evolutionist (a younger man) explains that he interprets the dinosaur as having lived and died tens of millions of years ago and that the Canyon itself came about over a similarly epic timescale.

Already, museological performatives come into play; indeed, in this display I locate the Creation Museum's definitive critical maneuver. The first artifact the Museum creates and offers up for consideration is not the dinosaur, but the *scientists*. More specifically, the scientific investigation of evolution/creation becomes in this display an artifact for consideration. In creating what Kirshenblatt-Gimblett calls an "in-situ" display that constructs the appearance of an object or person's "original context," the Museum's designers have detached and re-contextualized the very debate over creation and evolution.[18] The diorama's design of the scientists' "original" context scrubs the debate clean of rancorous history or present political contexts—or of any historical or cultural details at all. Two scientists of equal stature and equal anonymity amiably discuss how they each interpret a simple set of bones on which they are both

"The Dig" display at the Creation Museum. Photo courtesy of Answers in Genesis.

working. Departing notably from the attack rhetorics characteristic of both sides of the debate at large, this first display introduces the creation/evolution struggle as an object amenable to calm, rational inquiry. Why, the dig site display asks in its irenic way, do different scientists see the same evidence so differently?

The next phase of the tour addresses that question through a series of side-by-side picture-and-caption displays entitled "Same Evidence, Different Starting Points." An extended crash-course in how evolutionary theory and young-earth creationism differ, the picture displays each tackle a different origins question (e.g., How did fossils form? Where do animals come from?), showing how two different "starting points"—"autonomous human reason" and "God's Word"—each explain the evidence. Like the dig site, these comparisons project calm even-handedness, avoiding straw-man attacks or overt comparative critique. They merely explain generalities of the two alternatives they've established, supplementing the "God's Word" point of view with references to specific Bible verses. The even-handedness gradually fades, however, as the displays shift to black-and-white photographs of people in various states of confusion and distress. The Museum captions suggest that how we interpret present-day human suffering also has to do with whether we see suffering through the lens of human reason or the Bible. "Why is there suffering?" "Where do we go when we die?" "Why are we here?" In its inability to answer these questions, imply the captions, autonomous human reason falls short.

The tour narrative then moves into a history of the writing and transmission of the Bible, beginning with a room full of several life-sized diorama scenes featuring ancient Jewish prophets (Moses, David, Isaiah) and apostles (Paul) scribing verses onto parchments. Since these inspired beginnings, the Museum's wall displays explain, the Bible has been the site of nearly constant attack and defense. A text-heavy wall display recounts various historical points of challenge against biblical authority. The adjoining room renders some of these battle points in life-sized dioramas. On one side, a mannequin of Martin Luther (heroic proponent of evangelicals' *sola scriptura* biblicism) nails his Ninety-five Theses onto the Wittenberg door. On the other side, stylized two-dimensional figures in a cartoon courtroom re-create the 1925 Scopes trial.[19] A chart on the wall depicts a descending timeline, indicating a flagging reverence for biblical authority in US culture.

The next phase of the tour takes spectators through a nightmarish, claustrophobic "Culture in Crisis" space—basically a hallway redecorated as a run-down urban scene adorned with red lights, plastic rats, graffiti ("Modern World Abandons the Bible"; "Today Man Decides ~~Truth~~ Whatever"), newspaper clippings of tragic headlines, and anecdotes of apostates (the story of evangelist-turned-agnostic Charles Templeton gets special attention). This bombed-out alleyway soon opens into a cul-de-sac of sorts dominated by a huge facade of a dilapidated church building. A massive wrecking ball hangs from the ceiling at an angle, frozen in the act of smashing through the church's walls. Stamped on the ball are the words "Millions of Years." Across from this scene of destruction, several television screens each play a looped, live-action video of domestic crises: a teenage boy looking at porn, a young girl getting a positive pregnancy test, a false minister preaching the rapprochement of evolution and the Bible.

Prepare to Believe? Fundamental Assumptions, Inerrant Citations

For an institution whose motto stresses belief, these initial displays present little in the way of convincing evidence to an impartial observer. Nothing here would likely persuade a lay skeptic, let alone a pro-evolution scientist, that the biblical account as given has any kind of special appeal or that the evolutionary viewpoint suffers from a fatal flaw in its explanations of fossils and biology. More important for my argument here, scientists who are critical of the Museum's brand of creationism would likely balk at endorsing the initial display's presentation of the creationist and the evolutionist as equally qualified scientists, or of creationism and evolution as similarly legitimate scientific theories. Judith Butler (drawing on Jacques Derrida) reminds us that, in order to "work," a performative gesture depends upon successfully citing an authorizing entity. "By the power vested in me by the state . . ." says the minister at a wedding, drawing her authority *to wed* from a network of state and local authorities.[20] Museums ground themselves in the authority of a relevant discipline (art history, anthropology, science) even as they shape and contribute to that discipline. Like most anti-evolutionist institutions, however, AiG and the Creation Museum do not enjoy the endorsement of the vast majority of scientists—quite the opposite. The Museum's performative gesture of definition ("*This* is what science is") should therefore fail insofar as the gesture relies upon the encomium of mainstream science for its authorization. Yet I maintain that the Museum succeeds. How?

One possibility is that the Museum accesses its authority as a museum illegitimately, masking its lack of mainstream support through slickness of presentation. Many secular reviews of the Museum imply as much. According to such an allegation, the Museum makes a false claim that it enjoys the support of a substantial number of scientists. The detail and polish of its "science museum" conventions thus constitute a disguise, a clever copy of marketing and design cues from other edutainment facilities. It features professional-sounding speakers with science degrees from respectable institutions, suggesting that these isolated scientists represent a much larger number of supporters. The Museum in this view acts as a creationist wolf in scientific costume, stealing citational sustenance for its performative assertions from the reserves of legitimate scientists and science museums.

Though I do not consider this argument compelling, it should be noted that such an act of deceit is not without precedent in the creation/evolution wars. The Intelligent Design (ID) controversy serves as both a recent example of anti-evolutionist duplicity and a useful contrast with the approach that AiG takes. Initially presented as a secular criticism of evolutionary hegemony by proponents such as the Discovery Institute and biologist Michael Behe, ID argues that certain biological structures and mechanisms display such sophistication that natural selection alone cannot account for them.[21] Instead, ID posits that such "irreducible complexity" points to the active intervention of an intelligent designer (though not necessarily a deity). For a time, ID made serious claims to scientific respectability, promoting itself as a valid, secular-but-open-to-faith competitor to evolutionary theory. In 2005, however, a district court in Pennsylvania heard and rejected arguments that ID qualified as a non-religious, scientific theory.[22] Influential to the court's decision was evidence that distinctly Christian anti-evolutionist organizations had surreptitiously orchestrated the push to promote ID theories' inclusion into science classrooms as a "wedge" to allow religious creationism to regain a foothold in public schools.[23] Expressing dismay at such duplicity, the court ruled that ID constitutes de facto religious creationism and that it fails to meet the standards of legitimate science.[24]

As damaging as the Dover affair has been to the ID movement, I do not see any evidence of mendacity in the Creation Museum or in AiG. Simply put, the Museum has little interest in engaging, let alone filching authority from, secular evolutionary scientists. The lack of detail or rebuttal in the presentation of evolutionary theory is telling in this respect. Creation science literature, including that of the ID movement, typically overflows with exacting criticisms of specifically pro-evolutionary arguments for biological evolution or long-term geological development. Critics of creationism often complain that its interlocutors have little to offer other than shotgun rebuttals stuffed with outdated or far-fetched bits of scientific-sounding factoids.[25] But very little in the Museum dwells on criticism of traditional anti-evolutionist hot-buttons like radiocarbon dating of rock strata, fossils of transitional species, or the irreducible complexity of certain biological structures. Indeed, many of the Museum's initial exhibits (A diorama of Martin Luther? A video drama about internet pornography?) make no attempt to appear as "science" at all.[26]

Who or what, then, authorizes the Museum to (re)define the act of scientific investigation? As is the case with hell house, I argue that the Creation Museum preaches to the converted, specifically to those conservative evangelicals already predisposed to young-earth creationism. The citational reservoirs it draws on are theological, not secular-scientific. The specific quality of this doctrinal fuel, however, requires some specification. Answers in Genesis, the umbrella organization behind the Creation Museum, espouses solidly evangelical beliefs with a special emphasis on a strictly literalist biblicism. The six days of creation outlined in the first chapters of Genesis, according to AiG, describe the literal events of six twenty-four-hour days. Adam and Eve were literally the first human beings, created by God uniquely (i.e., unlike all other creatures) in God's image. Subsequent to the Fall and the Expulsion from the Garden of Eden, most of the world was destroyed by a global flood whose survivors included the inhabitants of Noah's Ark. The earth is thus no older than the timescales literally described by the Bible. In such a view, of course, accounts of biology, geology, physics, and cosmology that subscribe to or support Darwin's theory of natural selection cannot be true.

Within the evangelical spectrum, Answers in Genesis stakes out a particularly hard-line stance. Not all *creationism* is anti-evolutionist or even evangelical. Most Christians may be described as generically creationist insofar as they believe in a God who somehow created (or who continues to create) the universe in which life developed. Such Christians (among them many scientists) often do not see any problem with affirming that mainstream scientific theories of cosmological development, geological history, and biological evolution adequately describe the mechanisms by which God creates. A considerable cross-section of evangelicals takes this view, arguing that a properly interpreted scripture does not jar with scientific accounts of universal origins.[27] The more rigorously one affirms biblical inerrancy, however, the more detailed and less flexible one's creationist views tend to become. So-called young-earth creationists represent the strictest, most fundamentalist view. For them, the Genesis account is utterly literal, with the entire universe coming into existence at God's behest in six twenty-four-hour days and a global flood wiping out most life sometime after. Young-earth creationists insist that biology, geology, and cosmology align to produce a universe no older than about ten thousand years (the preferred number is six thousand or so) based on a literal reading of listed genealogies of Adam's descendants, a stance that separates them from the relatively more moderate claims of Intelligent Design.[28] Curiously, as many scholars have noted, a strict young-earth creationism has historically qualified as a minority view among believers, even anti-evolutionist believers.[29] Only recently has this most fundamentalist branch of anti-evolutionist creationism achieved such widespread support and publicity.

Answers in Genesis and the Creation Museum promote an unabashedly young-earth creationist standpoint consistent with a strict understanding of the Bible as inerrant. All along the tour route I have described so far, the Museum's designers have inserted nods to this viewpoint for Bible-believers to recognize and affirm.[30] The "Same Evidence, Different Starting Points" displays, for example, traffic in a rhetoric of neutrality, fairly and objectively comparing the "secular" and "biblical" explanations for various phenomena. But to an evangelical affirming a strictly inerrant/infallible view of scripture, the two sides never actually compete. One explanation is scripturally supported while the other is not: end of debate. To a believer in inerrancy, the Bible's assertions—doctrinal, historical, scientific, and moral—serve as the unassailable criteria for right and wrong, accuracy and inaccuracy. As such, the Bible judges the fruits of human reason and science, not vice versa. For such Bible-believing Christians, the options offered—the Bible or human reason—present a Hobson's choice: plainly, only one side is viable. For the target audience, then, the artifact these initial exhibits create is not so much the debate between equally valid scientific viewpoints but the confrontation between two incommensurate belief systems, only one of which is correct. It is thus *biblical authority* and not *scientific authority* that fuels the Museum's performative definition of science.

Doxological Science and the Christian Worldview Apologetic

But this is not to say that the Museum, on its own terms, relinquishes a claim to science altogether. It merely defines *science* in such a way as to render it compatible with biblical inerrancy. Indeed, its definition of science seems broad enough to include, at least in theory, both evolutionary and creationist viewpoints. What, then, is *science* according to the Museum? To judge from the initial display, science is something like "a reasonable investigation of evidence." Evidence (the bones of a dinosaur, for example) presents itself plainly and equally to all investigators. Reasonable people (the two scientists presented at the top of the tour, investigating the same set of bones) may disagree reasonably about the results of such investigations so long as they are able to base their conclusions in the evidence presented.

Such an idiosyncratic rendering of scientific investigation actually enjoys a long history within evangelicalism and fundamentalism. Historian Theodore Dwight Bozeman points to the long-standing influence of a particular understanding of science popular in late eighteenth- and nineteenth-century US religious culture. This understanding, which Bozeman christens "doxological science," blends the influence of Francis Bacon as transmitted through the writings of the Scottish School of Common Sense with certain evangelical assumptions about revelation.[31] From Bacon and the Scottish philosophers, doxological science stressed strict induction of general laws from the plain evidence of the senses. One does not, in this philosophy, begin with wild hypotheses ("guesses") and deduce predictions; one examines evidence, arranges it into its natural categories, and very cautiously inducts what general truths about nature this evidence straightforwardly suggests.

Three features of the doxological science tradition inform the Museum's understanding of science, binding it to inerrancy doctrine. First, doxological science viewed investigations of the natural world (God's general revelation to humankind) as inseparable from investigations of the Bible (God's special revelation to humankind).[32] Any proper scientist or theologian will, in this view, be naturally invested in both varieties of investigation. Second, the inerrant quality of God's revelations mandated that proper inductive conclusions about scripture align seamlessly with conclusions about nature. Finally, any apparent discrepancy between scripture and science most likely bespeaks a human fault in either the theologian or the scientist; one or the other may be misreading the plain evidence due to the distorting influence of a preconceived idea or theory. The faith in the readily apparent status of evidence and an emphasis on the role of preconceptions and the consequences of their distortions explain the Museum's extended inquiry into why the two scientists in the first display would disagree. Mobilizing a commonsense definition, the Museum presents *science* as the straightforward investigation of evidence to produce reliably true propositions about nature.[33] As a result, creationism and evolution become not alternative modes of investigation but alternative lenses for interpretation ("starting points"), one of which (evolution) distorts reality, as can be seen plainly from its divergence from biblical truth.

This strategy bespeaks an apologetic stance that distinguishes Answers in Genesis from other anti-evolutionist organizations. Historically, anti-evolutionist forces have tended to prefer evidentialist approaches. The tactic of "overwhelm with neutral evidence" (i.e., the shotgun blast of factoids that supposedly undermine evolutionists' cases) continues to characterize many anti-evolutionist sorties. Though by no means eschewing facts or research, AiG bases its apologetics not on neutral evidence but "starting points," aligning it with presuppositional apologetics—or, more accurately, with what has come to be called *worldview apologetics*. Presuppositionalism draws on the tradition of evangelical thinkers like Cornelius Van Til and Francis Schaeffer to argue that defense and spread of the Christian gospel depends upon appreciating the reality of competing systems of presuppositions. All the evidence and sound argumentation in the world, they argue, will not convince someone operating from presuppositions that support conclusions different from those that the evidence points to. For presuppositionalists, "neutral" facts do not exist, since the selection and interpretation of facts unfold within the context of presuppositions. Even the most compelling Christian case for proving God's holiness, humanity's sin, and Christ's sacrifice would fail to convince someone for whom the idea of "sin" has no traction or for whom "God" is purely myth.

Although presuppositional apologetics in its pure form holds something of a minority position among current evangelical apologists, an attenuated presuppositionalism known as "worldview analysis" currently enjoys widespread appeal across evangelicalism.[34] Like presuppositionalism, worldview analysis posits that people's decisions about theology, morals, and politics stem from a pre-rational grounding in a "worldview" (from the German *Weltanschauung*). Though the notion of a worldview is not new to philosophical thought, evangelical thinkers like James W. Sire and David Naugle have tailored the idea to serve as a means of conceptualizing ideological alterity. It is somewhat analogous to concepts like ideology or social frame. They systematize a range of contemporary ethical, theological, and epistemological positions into a discrete set of different worldviews to label modes of thinking that depart from a "Biblical Christian" norm.[35]

Training in worldview analysis involves two main steps. First, worldview training equips Christians with a solid, consistent idea of the "Biblical Christian" (i.e., Bible-believing evangelical) worldview, shoring up believers' theological and intellectual faith in Christian presuppositions. Second, worldview training introduces a detailed taxonomy of alternative, competing worldviews (secular humanism and postmodernism are common favorites), characterizing these non-Christian views in terms of the worldview's presuppositions about truth, divinity, ethics, afterlife, and so forth. With feet firmly planted in the biblical-Christian worldview, Christians can confidently engage with nonbelievers.[36] Evangelical publishers and organizations currently produce a wide range of sermons, podcasts, workshops, and curricula, all designed to equip evangelicals—especially younger evangelicals—with a worldview-based vision of Christianity and its intellectual/theological competitors.

The most elaborate of these, sponsored by organizations such as Worldview Academy or Summit Ministries, offer multi-week preparatory camps aimed at college-bound high-schoolers or even "worldview semesters" for college credit. In these programs, students read summaries and primary documents representing a range of alternative worldviews under the guidance of professional worldview analysts. Analyzing the "postmodern" worldview, for example, students might learn about thinkers like Jacques Derrida or read bits of Michel Foucault. They might examine specimens of popular culture—movies, music, websites—to look for evidence of postmodern presuppositions and stylistic markers. Worldview analysis teachers train the students to identify and pick apart such alternative worldviews from an evangelical perspective, ostensibly immunizing them against the predations of anti-religious college professors.[37]

On its face, a worldview apologetic might seem to reinforce an isolationist stance appropriate to the most exclusivist strains of fundamentalism. As critics from other apologetic traditions often point out, presuppositionalism can all too easily erect a high, rationality-proof wall between Bible-believing Christians and practically everyone else, making any effort at interaction or outreach moot. Worldview analysis seeks to sidestep this pitfall by emphasizing the potential for worldview conversion; worldviews are starting points, not inescapable prisons. Nevertheless, like the Schaefferian presuppositionalism that informs it, worldview apologetics insists upon the exclusive epistemic superiority of Christianity—and not just any Christianity but a specific configuration of evangelicalism—over all other worldviews. It simply isn't possible, from a worldview analysis perspective, for a properly trained worldview evangelist to reason her way out of commitment to the biblical Christian worldview. Similarly, the Museum's worldview comparisons—the biblical and "human reason" starting points—presume a conclusive victory for the biblical/young-earth creationist worldview. Such separatist and exclusivist elements reinforce other fundamentalist indicators about the Museum: its young-earth stringency, its strict inerrancy doctrine, and its relative disinterest in debating opponents.

Nevertheless, and in concert with Schaeffer, worldview analysts insist that outreach, not insularity, defines their focus. Reinforcing Christians' sense of worldview, they argue, ought not lead to withdrawal from the world—quite the contrary. Worldview analysis trains Christians so that they may better and more effectively interact with, and expose the incoherence of, non-Christian views. Indeed, "worldview" currently functions across a wide range of evangelical discourse as a sort of folk critical theory, a vocabulary for imagining those with whom Christians disagree. Those holding non-Christian worldviews figure in worldview discourse not (or not only) as threats to Christian belief but as targets, potential believers who have only to see the error of their ways in order to find new life in Christ. Yet pure argument or neutral evidence, in presuppositionalist or worldview-based thinking, does not exist. In order for any persuasive overtures to work, Christians have to know exactly how "the other side" thinks and why. Worldview analysis thus sets before Christians the challenge of systematic, even scientific (in the commonsense vein) investigation of unbelief. The books, workshops, and curricula that categorize alternative worldviews also include intensive training on how Christians might interact with and persuade people operating from alternative worldviews. Apologetics (defense of the faith) thus blends into evangelism (presenting a winsome case for the faith). Only by solidly and confidently articulating their own (correct) worldview can Christians engage non-Christians on the unbelievers' own terms, leading non-Christians into an exploration of the consequences of living life according to their incoherent, non-comprehensive worldview (a practice called *apagogy*—argument by *reductio ad absurdum*). In other words, and despite appearances to the contrary, the Creation Museum's worldview-focused outreach positions it solidly in line with the flow of mainstream evangelicalism.

This evangelical goal of innovative, even risky outreach to secular culture underlies AiG's mission. In fact, according to AiG's founder and leader, Ken Ham, evangelistic outreach justifies the existence and design of the Creation Museum itself. In his book *Why Won't They Listen?* Ham outlines the basics of what he calls "creation evangelism." Why, he asks, are churches today struggling for members? Why does culture seem so resistant to the Christian message?[38] By way of answer, Ham diagnoses what he sees as a cultural divide, a difference in worldviews that aligns with the side-by-side "Starting Point" presentations of the early part of the Museum tour. Ham paints a picture of culture (here he means culture in the United States, Great Britain, and Australia) as it used to be, based on a rock-solid foundation of belief in God's Word. Over the course of several generations, Ham contends, humanists and liberal Christian ministers have introduced and expanded fractures within that foundation, incorporating "millions of years" of development and evolution into a creation narrative that the Bible insists only took six days.

As the foundation of "God's Word" erodes, a new foundation, human reason, takes its place. In a domino effect of unbelief, doubts about Genesis inspire doubts about the inerrancy of scripture as a whole, which in turn produce doubts about the salvation narrative of Christ, which then produce doubts about Christianity itself, and which ultimately undermine the notion of moral absolutes altogether.[39] As a result, Ham concludes, present-day culture unsurprisingly adopts a view of Christianity as alien and nonsensical. Why should this generation believe in the Christian message, Ham asks, when it lacks the common ground of belief in scripture—when it doesn't share the Christian worldview—that previous generations of evangelists could assume? Ham's solution: "You can't change the system from the top down," he writes, "when it has changed from the bottom up."[40] Evolutionism's attack on the inerrancy of Genesis (and therefore of all scripture, and therefore of Christianity itself) produced the foundational problem. Thus the first step toward reaching a world now alien to Christian thought involves restoring faith in Genesis's literal account. Crucially, this restoration must begin not with culture but with Christians. In Ham's view, most Christians have drifted away from the historical faith in a literal creation. Indeed, he argues, humanism alone could not have so successfully broken the Christian foundation had not Christians themselves become lax in accommodating non-literal interpretations of Genesis.[41]

Here, then, is another crucial performative gesture present in the Museum's first phase: by defining *science* as commonsense investigation of evidence, both creation and evolution become not competing scientific approaches but representatives (artifacts) of competing worldviews. True to the worldview apologetic, the Museum proceeds by apagogy, demonstrating that the worldview animating evolution—secular, naturalistic humanism—fails as a coherent, comprehensive set of epistemological and ethical presuppositions when taken to its logical extremes. Through the "Battle for the Bible" section, the Museum furthers this argument, showing how faith in human reason leads to an increased irreverence for God's Word. Straying from such traditional Bible-belief snowballs into a wrecked culture (the "Culture in Crisis" alleyway and cul-de-sac) full of hurting people bereft of any explanation for why they're in pain and separated from any hope of easing that pain.

The negative case against secular human reason completed, the walk-through switches tone. The rest of the Museum's displays dedicate themselves to solidifying for Christians a biblical worldview (according to AiG), reaffirming the Genesis account as literal, sound history and installing that account into a narrative line that connects creation to Christ. Creation Museum designers structure the last phase of the walk-through tour around Ham's hermeneutic of the "Seven C's of History." This approach divides young-earth history into seven eras, each marked by a turning point in human-divine relations recounted in the Bible.[42] The first four of these—Creation, Corruption, Catastrophe, and

Confusion—are retold in the first eleven chapters of Genesis. The last three—Christ, Cross, and Consummation—reference events recounted in the Christian New Testament.

After viewing the "Culture in Crisis" displays, spectators walk through a star-speckled "Time Tunnel" to a widescreen theater, where they watch a film portraying the creation of the universe (complemented by sonorous narration of the relevant passages from Genesis). The next room, dedicated to the "wonders of creation," returns to the familiar tropes of natural history museums, depicting various fascinating bits of information about life on earth (nature being the general revelation of God's grandeur). The tour path then takes spectators into a lush, immersive jungle, the prelapsarian Garden of Eden, punctuated by mannequin scenes of, for example, Adam naming the animals, Adam and Eve meeting for the first time, and of course dinosaurs and other animals peacefully coexisting with humans.[43] A massive Tree of Life dominates the scene, branching out above all of the Creation era's exhibits. At this point, the rhetorical conventions of "science museum" have given way to those of "history museums." The dioramas in this section are no longer even ostensibly artifacts of creation science (no evidence of any sort gets offered to support literal life in a literal Eden); they are articles of faith, reminders for believers.

The winding path through Eden narrows into a darkened, somber passageway punctuated with intimate scenes of the Serpent and of Adam and Eve sharing the forbidden fruit featured behind glass.[44] The hall then opens up into a "Cave of Sorrows," a gray room with photographs representing various different aspects of the fallen world: a wolf growling over a newly killed carcass, a woman giving birth in pain, a mushroom cloud, African children starving, and Holocaust prisoners. The next part of the tour, "Corruption Valley," echoes the prior Eden path, but this time the dioramas depict scenes from a post-Fall world, such as a blood sacrifice, a man struggling to grow seeds in a thorn-infested garden, an animatronic (and decidedly predatory) dinosaur, and Cain's murder of Abel. To an even greater extent than the six-day creation itself, the Fall of Adam and the world's subsequent corruption play a central role in AiG's creation evangelism. The "Cave of Sorrows" in many ways mirrors the misery displayed in the "Culture in Crisis" room. Crucially, though, the sorrows depicted in the cave have been re-situated into the explanatory matrix of the Christian worldview. Why is there suffering? Because of the Fall of Man. Human suffering becomes another artifact, this time indicating the ongoing consequences of Adam and Eve's original sin.

That the Museum offers up such a grim, blunt explanation of human suffering might seem surprising for an institution dedicated to asserting the appeal of Christianity. But, to AiG, such brutal, simplistic honesty advances the apologetic task of contrasting the Christian worldview, which like any proper worldview offers answers to human questions, with the secular humanist worldview, which offers nothing. Christianity's willingness to grapple with difficult questions about pain and suffering, argues AiG, is a strength too many Christian churches overlook.

In a sermon entitled "Demolishing Strongholds: Evolution in Popular Culture," AiG spokesperson Carl Kerby echoes Ham in his criticism of present-day, ineffective evangelistic techniques.[45] Kerby sees Christian evangelism failing because all too often the Christian message gets sold as little more than a consumer-friendly product: become a Christian because "Jesus loves you and has a wonderful plan for your life."[46] Such a get-Jesus-and-have-a-better-life message holds little appeal, argues Kerby, because anyone can see that the world is as harsh and full of pain for Christians as it is for unbelievers. To the world's pressing, central question—*Why would a just God allow suffering?*—Christians must provide meaningful answers, and all too often they cannot.[47] The Museum therefore highlights the fall (the second C, "Corruption") not as a historical event to be substantiated as proof of creationism (indeed, they make no attempt to offer extra-biblical substantiation for it) but as a theological explanation for human suffering. Humans suffer, in this logic, because Adam's sin introduced death into God's otherwise perfect creation. By contrast, secular worldviews remain willfully ignorant of the real reasons for strife in this world, denying the moral authority of the One Who Defines Morality and responding to corruption and suffering with more corruption and suffering. Rather than make the argument that creationism is good science, the Museum suggests that evolution is *bad religion,* an inferior worldview.

Such theological explanations soon get seasoned with some commonsense science. With the scene of a talking, robotic Methuselah ("Can you guess how many centuries old I am? Six? Seven? No—nine!"), the tour skips several hundred years after the Fall to "Catastrophe," which focuses primarily on the Flood (God's judgement) and the Ark (God's mercy). Visitors walk through a life-sized, incredibly detailed re-creation of "about 1%" of the Ark in mid-construction.[48] Noah and his sons (animatronic mannequins) saw wood, pound nails, and paint pitch on the massive edifice. Several scale models painstakingly show how the Ark might have looked and how the interior could have been structured to hold two of every kind of animal—provided large animals like the dinosaurs were very young.[49] Here the dioramic re-creations largely cease as the Museum switches back to a more "science museum" semiotics, with text-based presentations of key points of Flood geology.

The prime player among the disciplines that contribute to young-earth creation science, Flood geology (or "catastrophism") holds that the Global Flood accounts for practically the entire body of geological and paleontological evidence that most scientists maintain points to a billion-year-old planet.[50] Fossilization, sediments, and continental drift all receive attention, complete with professional-sounding (at least to the ears of the faithful) explanations of how Noah's flood accounts for them. The final walk-through area deals with "Confusion" (i.e., the Tower of Babel), re-creating various pieces of ancient culture, art, and statuary and explaining how the Babel event accounts for the diversity of human languages and cultures. The tour ends with a final film, *The Last Adam,* which gestures toward the last three C's: Jesus' advent (Christ), his sacrificial death and resurrection (Cross), and his imminent return (Consummation).[51]

Preaching to the Converted

Like the Museum's initial displays, nothing in this final section of the tour would likely convince someone not already a believer operating from a strong young-earth worldview. Earlier, I described the Creation Museum as preaching to the converted, drawing again on Tim Miller and David Román's rejuvenation of this phrase. Responding to the "preaching to the converted" criticism often leveled at queer artists (i.e., that they perform exclusively for LGBT audiences), Miller and Román point out that the charge dismissively and inaccurately homogenizes an audience of "the converted" into passive receptacles for whatever propaganda the preacher/performer wishes to feed them. Using Miller's own interactive performance practice as an example, they argue that all performance, and especially community-based performance, is more complicated than the one-way model of speaker/hearer suggests. In cases where a community of spectators attends a performance that purports to be by, for, and about people and viewpoints of their own community, audience/performer interactions take on a heightened charge, with audience members constantly checking a performance's presentation of the community's identity and beliefs with their own understandings of those beliefs.[52]

Miller and Román's reminder about the heterogeneity even of "converted" audiences takes on special relevance in relation to the Museum's engagement with evangelical culture. I should first reiterate the diversity of fundamentalist, evangelical, and creationist communities that patronize the Museum.[53] AiG presents but one sermon among many others, one specific alignment of creationism, evangelism, and Bible-believing among a smorgasbord of other theologies. As evangelical culture typically flourishes outside of the regulatory structure of formal denominations, and thus beyond the purview of unifying (and border-defining) creeds, evangelicals are used to encountering and evaluating for themselves multiple, overlapping, and conflicting messages. Such instability, however, only underlines the need for and utility of preaching to the converted. Miller and Román argue that *conversion* isn't a one-time event. "If 'the converted' exist," they write, "then 'the converted' needs to be understood as a dynamic assembly that both individually and communally enters the space of performance to sustain that conversion."[54] Miller and Román offer "preaching to the converted" as a productive, even necessary activist tactic, a practice of reminding members of the activist community (in this case, Bible-believing evangelicals) of the content and stakes of their struggle, re-energizing them with new strategies and renewed passion.

Evangelicals hardly need a reminder about the power of preaching to the converted, of course: as their own saying attests, "You preach to the choir to get them to sing." Evangelicals affirm that every human has an innate sense of God and God's law; this existential given in fact forms the basis of communicative bridges across presuppositional divides in apologetics. Worldview analysts, however, acknowledge that a comprehensive, fully articulated worldview doesn't come into being on its own, nor can Christians maintain their worldview's integrity without frequent renewal. In this sense, seeing the Creation Museum as a kind of activist preaching to the converted reframes my reading of its motto: "Prepare to believe." The focus, I find, is not on *belief* per se but on *preparation*. The Museum equips its patrons with a clarified worldview—a refined "starting point"—with which to view science, evolution/creation, and evangelism itself.

With this presupposition solidly in place, the Museum advances its anti-evolution argument not by out-evidencing evolution but by outworldviewing it. By donning the semiotic clothing of science museums, mobilizing the authorizing force of inerrancy doctrine, and substituting a commonsense definition of science, the Creation Museum successfully resituates evolution as a nonscientific, morally troubled worldview formally on par with (and sensibly inferior to) young-earth, biblically literalist Christianity.

Of course, the power of this redefinition flows not merely from the logic of its argument but from the tactile-aural-visual experience within which the Museum couches its sermon. In her keen reading of the walk-through experience, performance scholar Jill Stevenson underlines how the Museum's performative work operates at sub- and pre-conceptual levels. Drawing on conceptual blending theory, Stevenson analyzes how the immersive, sensually rich experience of the dioramas, displays, movies, and presentations create a space that invites believers to "live in" the dual, oscillating frames of (young-earth creationist) biblical truth and secular/evolutionary science.[55] The AiG interpretation of the entire debate, the sermon it delivers to its converted, thus consists not merely of words and ideas but affects of comfort, strength, and completeness that reinforce the performative authority of the Museum's young-earth creationist views. Certainly, evolutionists and other anti-creationists would take issue with the Museum's sermon, but what of it? Their contribution to the Museum's performances consists only of two things: (1) outside the Museum, a discourse of condescension—or even sarcastic attack—on the Museum by pro-evolution science pundits and militant atheists; and (2) inside the Museum, a single, anonymous wax mannequin crouched over a *Utahraptor* fossil, preaching amiably to the converted about his godless interpretations.

Teaching to the Converted

The scope of AiG's sermon extends beyond the Museum's walls. In addition to maintaining a vast repository of articles on creation science available across a wide range of websites, AiG has developed a library of books and educational materials aimed at conservative evangelical institutions and home schools. All of these materials replicate a strictly biblicist worldview, incorporating much of the Museum's materials and displays into their pages. The organization also offers a number of prepackaged curricular programs for Vacation Bible Schools. A staple of church life in the United States, Vacation Bible Schools are weeklong day or evening camps for children (kindergarten through middle school is standard, though some extend classes for adults) run by local church volunteers during the summer months. VBS programs usually offer a daily, age-specific schedule that blends worship, Bible lessons, crafts, games, refreshments, and music. VBS appeals of course to the church's own younger members, but often the emphasis is on evangelism to new audiences; children and families are often encouraged to bring friends to each day's offerings.

Though some congregations create their own programs, increasingly churches purchase prefabricated VBS curricula from denominational or parachurch resources. Typically, these programs operate around themes that establish an aesthetic milieu (e.g., "renaissance fair" or "superheroes" or "cooking show"). Program packages provide basic curricular materials like booklets, instructional manuals, clip art, banners, CDs of original music, and branded merchandise, but the major effort for realizing the theme lies with the creativity of local churches. Each VBS is in a sense a miniature, quasi-theatrical production not unlike a hell house or judgement house; congregational volunteers redecorate the church space to fit the VBS theme, often creating costumes and characters appropriate to the theme and setting. Since 2008, AiG has joined the VBS market, devising attractive program packages around yearly themes such as *Gold Rush* (a frontier setting), *Egypt File* (a vaguely *Raiders of the Lost Ark* adventure feel), and *IncrediWorld Amazement Park* (an amusement park-cum-zoo).[56] Though each of these boasts a distinct look and feel, the underlying pedagogical thrust hews closely to AiG's basic imperative of creationist-inflected worldview evangelism.

For example, Answers in Genesis's first VBS curriculum, *Operation Space: A Close Encounter with God's Word* from 2009, blends astronomical discovery themes with a *Star Trek* sci-fi tone. Set directions include tips and floor plans for turning church rooms into spaceship control rooms and other planets (no aliens, though).[57] Costume suggestions outline how to create a cardboard box robot and ray-gun. Snack-time recipes include "Blast-Off Bananas" and "Space S'Mores." The *Assembly Guide* provides scripts for leaders to use in the opening and closing assemblies. The first day's gathering highlights science-y facts about how huge the universe is (using a ruler and yardstick to conceptualize the length of a light-year) and praising God for creating such a big, wonderful place.[58]

The next day's gathering script begins with the leader holding up a Bible. "How did the universe come to be?" the leader asks. "I'll answer that in a minute, but first I need your help. When I point to you, I want you to enthusiastically say 'It's right!'" After a few practice runs (point, *It's right!*, point, *It's right!*), the leader says, "Let's begin. When the Bible talks about: The past . . . It's right!" The leader continues, eliciting "it's right" replies about the Bible's authority on the future, animals, plants, weather, and of course the age of the universe. This is, of course, a demonstration of Schaefferian "total truth," the AiG apologetic base that avers the Bible's trustworthiness on all subjects, not just faith. "Let's go back to our question," suggests the leader. "How did the universe come to be?" Stage directions take over: "*Hold up a child's nonfiction space book that has evolutionary content. These are available at public libraries.*" The leader: "This book says the universe started with a big bang, a huge explosion, billions of years ago." The leader again holds up the Bible. "This book, the Bible, teaches us that the universe was created by God in six days about 6,000 years ago. If you hear something that doesn't agree with the Bible, which should you listen to? You should listen to the Bible because it's right! Because the Bible is God's Word, only the Bible is perfectly right on every single thing it talks about—that's why it's the absolute authority."[59] Even the closing assembly skits, a five-part serial *Star Trek* parody, feature intrepid space explorers battling an evil mad scientist who wields a "Bible-blasting" gun to destroy all copies of the Bible in existence. He fails, of course, because (as the characters quote), "Heaven and earth will pass away, but God's Word will never pass away!"[60]

A similar emphasis on inerrant scriptural authority, especially as manifested through young-earth creationism, defines the curricula of AiG's other VBS programs. Like *Operation Space,* other themes include lessons that mix Bible stories, relatively neutral factoids about nature, and AiG-specific items about, such as how dinosaurs didn't entirely die out, how evolutionist accounts of life's origins get the order of creation wrong, or how the Grand Canyon's structure could be explained by a global flood. In marketing their programs to churches, AiG highlights its uniquely apologetic thrust. "What makes an Answers VBS program different from any other Vacation Bible School?" asks AiG's *IncrediWorld* website. "Two words: real life." The blurb goes on to reference AiG's own research about the evangelical crisis of young people leaving the church. In light of that situation, the ad declares, "We need to show [children] God's Word connects to every area of our lives and is as relevant today as it was thousands of years ago."[61] The 2012 *IncrediWorld* program (where lessons about animal facts coincide with literalist teaching about creation and Noah's Ark) even devotes an entire day to teaching grade-schoolers about worldviews (e.g., "Put on your Bible glasses!").[62]

To some readers, AiG's VBS programming as I have described it might inspire horror. *How awful that this creationist organization is brainwashing children with fundamentalist pseudo-science!* To be sure, AiG's VBS program does not take any collaborative-education, free-inquiry pedagogical cues from Paulo Freire. Like the Museum itself, AiG's VBS lessons are unidirectional, not participatory or open. The teachers have The Truth, and students are to absorb it, just as the scientific model the Creation Museum espouses mandates that scientific inquiries arrive at conclusions comfortably set within strictly predetermined boundaries.

Lest it be at all unclear, let me state that I do not endorse AiG's biblical hermeneutic or scientific stance. That said, I would resist the notion that Answers in Genesis commits a crime by creating lessons and displays that teach its deeply held truths. Neither the Creation Museum nor the Vacation Bible School qualifies as a cult, capturing hapless victims and violently forcing them to alter their deepest beliefs under threat. There is no bait and switch operating in any of AiG's programs; no one goes to the Creation Museum thinking that it will be the Smithsonian. And castigating a Vacation Bible School for religious proselytization is like criticizing a restaurant for serving food. Recognizing profound disagreement with the Creation Museum's narrative or *Operation Space*'s didacticism is a thing distinct from demonstrating instances of physical or psychological harm. After all, within the AiG frame of minoritarian persecution—*We are harried true believers amidst the philistines*—it is secular education that does the brainwashing, poisoning innocent children with idea that belief in supernatural realities is ridiculous.

Conclusion

Still, as I have indicated, AiG's particular blend of hard-line anti-evolutionism and worldview apologetics is difficult even for many conservative evangelicals to endorse. Answers in Genesis purchases the organizational clarity of sharpened boundaries at the cost of evangelicalism's bigger-tent flexibility. The Museum and, to a lesser extent, the VBS programs restrict possible configurations of the Christian-evangelical worldview to exactly one, obliging evangelicals who consider themselves "Bible-believing" in any sense to buy into AiG's all-or-nothing argument about young-earth creationism. Many evangelical groups view the Museum as a foolish distraction, an embarrassing mis-investment of time, money, energy, and reputation. Christian writer (and physics professor) Karl

Giberson, for instance, laments, "The ideas on display in the Creation Museum are thoroughly at odds with contemporary understandings of both the Bible and science."[63] Giberson points out that a host of Christian naturalists and scientists have themselves dismantled the scriptural and empirical bases that AiG recycles and repackages. Other sectors of evangelicalism, though critical of evolution, seem less invested than AiG is in christening creation science as either the shibboleth of evangelical commitment or the culture-war sword to fall on. Certainly, Ken Ham's resistance even to anti-evolutionist fellow-travelers like Intelligent Design only exacerbates the internal fractures that plague US evangelicalism. Furthermore, AiG's stance further polarizes an already polarizing debate about whether religious belief and scientific sophistication can co-exist, echoing dichotomizing (and reductive) arguments by overtly anti-religious intellectuals like Sam Harris or Richard Dawkins.[64] Giberson, an advocate of reconciling faith and science, joins Ham's alarm at the loss of evangelical youth. But where Ham attributes such defections to secularism as evidence of a fatally eroded biblical Christian worldview, Giberson fears that young Christians leave the faith because they are taught a fragile worldview structure utterly dependent upon exploded scientific and theological concepts. Such a "thin and brittle" structure, Giberson argues, "can withstand little more than the most superficial challenge; a modest bit of education will demolish it."[65]

Far from being demolished, however, Answers in Genesis's programs appear poised for growth. The organization has just announced its 2013 VBS theme (a medieval setting), and it has just (as of this writing) finalized a land purchase for "The Ark Encounter"—a whole new theme park featuring a fully realized, life-sized replica of Noah's Ark as its centerpiece.[66] The debate about creationism within evangelicalism and without will likely continue for some time. I submit, then, that even non-evangelical critics of and participants in cultural struggles can benefit from examining Answers in Genesis's worldview apologetic. Both anti-evolutionists and evolutionists find it galling that they have to explain why their opponent is wrong.

But the truth is, argues National Academies of Science spokesperson Jay Labov, anti-evolutionist creationists are currently quicker to accept the hard necessity of outreach. They realize how outlandish their beliefs can seem from a secular or postmodern perspective, and they task themselves with the job of knowing those antagonistic worldviews from the inside out so as to outmaneuver them. Anti-evolutionists, Labov suggests, are therefore proving more adept at popular outreach than evolutionary scientists, for whom the utility of evolutionary theory and (for many) its distinction from religious inquiries is so obvious as to require no justification.[67] Labov stresses the need for scientists to articulate more clearly what actually constitutes scientific practice (e.g., how *un*certainty, even controversy, can be science par excellence) and to be more watchful about how scientific discourse can drift into quasi-religious conclusions about the destiny of humankind.

Here Labov echoes scholars like Michael Ruse and Mary Midgely, who caution that evolutionary theory can occasionally encourage nonscientific attitudes that themselves seem to calcify into philosophical worldviews. Ruse, for instance, distinguishes between *evolution* (the theory that life originated in a common biological ancestor and developed over time via natural selection) and *evolutionism* (the philosophical faith that human beings and institutions develop progressively and inevitably from lesser to greater complexity and goodness). While evolutionary scientists since Darwin have resisted evolutionism and progressivism, Ruse notes, progressivism often tends to creep into evolutionists' writings.[68] Moreover, he reasons, scientists cannot isolate themselves completely from their cultural presuppositions. To communicate their findings, scientists must use language and metaphor, systems that inevitably refract "facts" through culturally specific lenses.[69] Mary Midgely, writing earlier, makes a similar claim:

> Symbolism, then, is not just a nuisance to be got rid of. It is essential. Facts will never appear to us as brute and meaningless; they will always organize themselves into some sort of story, some drama. These dramas can indeed be dangerous. They can distort our theories, and they have distorted the theory of evolution perhaps more than any other. The only way in which we can control this kind of distortion is, I believe, to bring the dramas themselves out into the open, to give them our full attention, understand them better and see what part, if any, each of them ought to play both in theory and life.[70]

In designing and mounting its multimillion-dollar worldview apologetic, the Creation Museum brings one version of this drama of science and faith out into the open. Though I disagree with the legitimacy of both its theology and its science, I underline the degree to which the AiG engages the worldviews of both its allies and its opponents, shifting its strategies of display and communication accordingly. The Museum challenges evangelicals to see the drama of the evolution/creation debate anew, to reconsider the identity and motivations of its key players, and to reframe the definition and stakes of the central conflict. In a way, the Museum enacts a Schaefferian meta-kerygmatic evangelism on a grand scale. It accepts the "Total Truth" of its young-earth-creationist worldview and fully expects that the intellectual and affective consistency exerts its own appeal. As self-evidently true as young-earth creationism is to AiG, however, the organization realizes (laments, even) that for many others, this self-evidence does not obtain. Evangelicals cannot simply *insist* on the truth of the gospel and expect postmodern secular audiences to agree automatically. Like Henderson, Koukl, and Stier, then, AiG insists that evangelicals have to train themselves not only in the basics of (young-earth creationist) Christian faith but also in the basics of non-evangelical resistance to that worldview.

Similar to Labov's warning to scientists about the need to listen to anti-evolutionists' arguments and—for lack of a better term—*evangelize* about the "total truth" of non-creationist theories of universal origins, I would pose to left-progressive performance activists the challenge of listening to their opponents. In his book *The Righteous Mind,* moral psychologist Jonathan Haidt inquires into the bases for ethical decision-making, focusing especially on how "liberals" and "conservatives" (his terms) in the United States each tend to base their sense of right and wrong in different sets of considerations. Fascinated by the gap in moral worldviews, Haidt performed survey research that asked liberals and conservatives to imagine how their opposites might navigate various moral scenarios. How do conservatives think that a "typical liberal" thinks, and vice versa? He then compared respondents' answers to these hypotheticals to data in which liberals and conservatives addressed the same scenarios from their native points of view. He found that, in general, conservatives and moderates were better able to accurately predict how liberals would behave in a given situation. Liberals, and especially those who identify as "very liberal," were not so adept at guessing at the mind-sets of their conservative cohorts.[71] Though I would not go so far as to call the Creation Museum's characterizations of non-creationist or postmodern worldviews accurate, I stress that it is important for those on the progressive left to see that this group, at least, is *trying.* As Labov notes, groups like AiG (and, I would add, many other evangelical groups) are somewhat ahead of their secular, non-creationist, and left-progressive opponents insofar as they adopt as a matter of activism the task of conceptualizing how and why those who disagree with them see the world. They start with the realization of a worldview gap and prepare to engage from that realization.

Haidt's research and Labov's call to scientists echo the trend I detected in left-progressive scholarship back in chapter one. I have very rarely seen activists and scholars on the progressive left attempt a careful assessment of the worldviews of their non-progressive opponents. Instead, those on the progressive left often consider the truths of (left-progressive takes on) justice, equality, freedom, and community to be self-evident to any moral, thinking person. I wonder, then, if something like a measure of worldview analysis might not be a good exercise for the progressive left and/or a productive avenue for left-progressive performance to explore. The benefits would not merely be a fuller and more complicated understanding of political opponents but also a more thorough and articulate grounding in what left-progressives actually believe and why. The exercise might, in other words, enable progressives to accomplish some belief preparation of their own.

CHAPTER 7

Staging Church, Marketing the Divine

The video begins with a young couple pulling into a Starbucks. "So, are you nervous?" the young woman asks. "Because I haven't been to a coffee shop since I was a little girl." The storefront looms in the windshield. "At least you've *been* to a coffee shop," her husband replies.

Searching for a free space in the immense, comically crowded lot, they whisper to each other about the bumper stickers they see. One reads, "Real Men [heart] Java." Another challenges, "Think *this* coffee's hot?" accompanied with a mug spouting hellfire flames. A third decal displays a Starbucks insignia Pac-Man-chomping the Columbia Coffee label.

The pair finally finds an empty space ("So far away!" notes the woman). As they cross the lot to the entrance, they snicker at reserved parking signs at choice spots near the door for "Barista," "Manager," and "Manager's Wife." On the building itself, a sign in clichéd Papyrus font proclaims, "International Anointed First Starbucks of the Northern Valley." They have to try several doors before finding one that opens. Entering, they pass young men sporting "greeter" badges but ignoring the visitors to chat among themselves.

Once inside, the couple finds the restaurant replete with slapdash, mismatched posters touting the benefits of coffee drinking, the gospel of caffeine. The posters' messages lurch haphazardly from touchy-feely ("Let the Aroma of Coffee Fill This Place") to threatening ("Coffee shall be hot or cold. If lukewarm, I will spew out of my mouth") to evangelistic ("How to share Starbucks with your friends: Start a conversation. Bring up coffee and ask them to go to Starbucks with you"). Well-dressed people in line or lounging in chairs eye the couple dismissively and return to their own conversations. A man's voice booms over the speakers, shilling for the restaurant's current drive to make 500 new coffee converts. "Because remember," he concludes, "coffee is good . . ." "All the time!" everyone in the restaurant answers automatically. "And all the time . . ." the announcer responds. "Coffee is good!" complete the patron-parishioners. The visiting couple stands, bemused, not sure what to say or where to go.

A barista finally greets them and asks what they'd like. "I think I just want some coffee," says the man. The barista smiles condescendingly. "You've never been here before, have you?" He grabs a microphone and speaks into it. "Excuse me—if this is your first time visiting with us, would you go ahead and raise your hands? We would love to welcome you." Mortified, the couple awkwardly obeys. The other patrons clap or tip their mugs in toast. "Java-luyah!" they intone. The barista hands the couple lengthy forms to fill out ("We would love to get some information about you"), promising them a "special gift" once they've completed it. They couple protests that they just want some coffee, but the barista insists: form first. Needless to say, by the time the couple completes the form and gets their cup (having endured a coffee testimonial-cum-fundraising spiel), they've decided not to return.[1]

Evangelicals (and former evangelicals) of a certain cast will recognize many of the ham-fisted techniques and embarrassing failures the fictional "International Anointed First Starbucks" practices: the cheesy-manipulative tone, rituals that exclude the uninitiated (e.g., The barista's call-and-response is a play on the evangelical "God is good / All the time / All the time / God is good"), the cliquishness of members, and an overall focus on misplaced priorities. The parody video suggests that churches can be as manipulative and false as the stereotype of a fast-food chain like Starbucks. Yet the video's creator, Richard Reising, is not launching broadside against Christianity for being too much like Starbucks. On the contrary, Reising's company Artistry Labs (formerly Artistry Marketing) designed the video, titled "What if Starbucks Marketed like the Church? A Parable," to assert that Christian churches are *not enough* like Starbucks. The problem Reising spotlights is not that churches market themselves but that so many churches market themselves badly, flubbing the tasks of product branding, consumer research, employee ethos, and customer care that (in his view) Starbucks executes so well. Like any Starbucks, Reising argues, churches should invest time and interest in seeing themselves through strangers' eyes. Good intentions are insufficient. Effective marketing—effective *outreach,* that is—requires such empathy, especially about main weekend worship service.

Reising works as a church marketing consultant. A former industry advertiser who decided in the 1990s to devote his talents to ministry, he specializes in helping congregations to identify and organize around a distinct identity, an ethos they can capture, focus, and advertise through design—a brand, in other words. Evangelists' drawing on business advertising strategies to inform outreach is nothing new, of course; recall the salesman's influence on Bill Bright's Four Spiritual Laws presentation. Reising and other present-day church marketers go a step further, however. They argue that a marketing mentality should guide not just discrete activities of a church like mail-outs, newspaper ads, or websites (i.e., the traditional purview of marketing); it should instead shape a congregation's whole identity.

Such an admixture of secular commercialism and *missio dei* troubles many evangelicals. Is the gospel—is *Christianity*—nothing but a product to be branded, prepackaged, and offered to a target market? Few, least of all Reising, would make such a claim. Yet in a secular age, churches can hardly afford to ignore the shifting tastes of the people they wish to reach. Not surprisingly, much of Reising's own marketing to churches (the Starbucks video is a case in point) involves convincing congregations to think of themselves as vendors. In a series of blog posts about his Starbucks video, for example, Reising explains that if marketing involves the sum of the functions involved in moving goods from producers to consumers, "The sum of everything your church does to connect Christ with your members and the outside world is marketing."[2] Any mission-oriented church that seeks to win disciples, in other words, must necessarily engage in marketing.

Reising's focus on churches, and specifically church services, as outreach mechanisms frames this chapter. Thus far I have dealt with evangelical outreach efforts that the average evangelical would consider extraordinary. Every Christian carries the charge to spread the Good News, but efforts like proselytizing conversations, hell house productions, and Creation Museums all require a step beyond the daily routines of faithful living. Reising's video, however, reminds his potential clients how Christians engage in outreach simply by virtue of producing a weekly, public service in a sanctuary space. The weekend (generally Sunday morning) service operates as a major outreach—perhaps *the* major outreach mode—for most evangelical congregations. In this light, Reising warns, "every single church out there is currently marketing whether they know it or not—there are just some doing a great job, and some doing a not-so-great job."[3] A business venture that declines to connect with its customer base will falter. A congregation that ignores how those outside of the church view it similarly risks failure.

Though not all evangelical churches sign on to Reising's gospel of marketing, the questions he raises about church services play a central role in secular-age debates about the vitality of evangelicalism in general. Are evangelical churches declining in part because their services are too stodgy? How might churches compete with other popular culture events? Or are people turned off by the McDonaldization of megachurches? Is there a hunger for old-fashioned spirituality, some holy authenticity rising above a sea of Six-Flags-over-Jesus mediocrity?

In this chapter, I focus on a recent evangelical shift in the philosophy of worship design that argues that church services themselves can and should operate evangelistically as outreach to the lost. I locate this trend itself, variously called "worship evangelism" or "attractional worship," within a larger body of evangelical thought, particularly the Church Growth movement and its offshoot, the church marketing movement. As their names suggest, these movements embrace a mind-set in which successful missions involve being fruitful and multiplying; the will of God, in other words, involves congregations growing ever larger and planting more churches. I examine in depth the paradigmatic attractional worship production shaped by this school of thought: the seeker-sensitive service. Innovated by Rick Warren's Saddleback Church and Bill Hybels's Willow Creek Church, seeker services redesign the conventions and structures of the traditional church service around the preferences and prejudices of an unchurched/dechurched public ("seekers"), creating an experience of church designed to be especially welcoming to those generally uncomfortable with Christianity.

In doing so, however, seeker services summon the skepticism of those who wonder how a congregation can praise God while taking so many cues from Mammon. Many evangelicals question whether adopting a customer-centered, high-emotion taste of Christianity clarifies or adulterates the Christian message. Such debates about market-informed worship evangelism become all the more important given the statistical prevalence of "megachurches," super-large urban congregations that in many cases structure their ministries around seeker-friendly models.

As such seeker-friendly megachurches increasingly become the face of congregational Christianity in the United States, critics from within and without the evangelical spectrum raise concerns about the quality of Christianity these churches' worship services promote and therefore the kind of Christian these services help to create.

Performing Service

I break no new ground by describing a church service through a performance lens. Comparing Sunday morning worship to a stage production is a common exercise in college intro to theater courses, and many seminaries offer courses and degrees that blend arts training with liturgical design. A church service, for example, has a dramaturgy, a dramatic movement from music to prayer to sermon to sacrament and offertory. Like a performance, services tap into and mobilize conventions of active and passive audience response, defining the "feel" of the church. Is this "high church," with formal recitations of creeds and scriptures, old hymns accompanied by organ and orchestra, and exegetical sermons inspired by a liturgical calendar? Is this charismatic worship, where a rock band replaces the pipe organ, hands-in-the-air praise-and-worship tunes supplant hymn-book songs, and uplifting personal growth themes characterize the sermons? When do congregants stand, sit, or kneel? Will the pastor speak in tongues? Will the congregants? Is there a bulletin or program to guide newcomers? Are there overhead displays to tell visitors what to do? Is there a worship leader who directs, or do visitors just follow the lead of the regular churchgoers? While mainline and Catholic services often adhere to relatively standard guidelines for worship (e.g., first prayer, then song, then sermon, then offertory, then benediction), evangelical churches vary widely in tone, length, and formality.

Design elements complement and shape the service's action. The mise-en-scène of altar, pulpit, choir, instruments, chancel rail—or the lack of such elements—communicate to congregants key relationships of power and authority between participants. What object enjoys pride of place, downstage center? An altar? A cross? A pulpit? Is the backdrop of the sanctuary "stage" a large cross? An array of huge projection screens? How easy is it to spot the pastor (or pastors) among the people on stage? Is there a choir or a praise band (or both)? Are there pews or movie theater seats? Is the sanctuary more like an auditorium, a black box theater, or a stadium cinema?

The church building itself—its architecture, its location in a community, its size, its recognizability as "church"—also generates a performance field that transmits messages of welcome or hostility to attendees. What part of town is the church building in? Do the people streaming into the church reflect the demographic of the immediate neighborhood? Does the foyer or lobby area resemble the anteroom to heaven? A hospital lobby? A shopping mall? Newer congregations plan and build churches (or, in the case of larger congregations, "campuses") with coherent answers to such questions in mind, answers based most often on up-to-date demographic research about the makeup and preferences of their desired congregation. Congregations in older, more established buildings often find themselves having to adapt around the design choices of yesteryear. Reising, for example, relates how he can determine the last time a church had the resources and inclination to care about structural outreach by looking at the typeface on the church building's signs.[4]

Yet any church must do more than reach out. Services and sanctuaries do not exist merely to attract and keep new members. Churches grow based on the appeal of their ministries, which includes the draw of their services (the feel, the music, the message, etc.). But they survive and thrive based on how well they cultivate durable communities of committed disciples. Even the largest churches provide salaries for a relatively small collection of ministerial and logistical positions. The bulk of any church's day-to-day life relies on the voluntary commitment of its core membership. The worship service is simultaneously the most regular mode of evangelization and the main touchstone for this ongoing community of believers. Worship services manifest the Body of Christ on earth. This means they must actually include worship, directing the praise and entreaties of the faithful toward the Divine.

Communal worship also challenges and recharges Christians, renewing and reviewing core Christian narratives while motivating believers to activate their faith beyond the walls of the sanctuary. It creates occasions for administering sacraments and performing key life rituals (e.g., marriages, funerals, christenings). Sunday worship also serves to solicit and collect believers' tithes and offerings. Problematically, some of these basic worship functions can also be precisely the kind of insider-only, visitor-disorienting elements that Reising urges churches to avoid. Navigating the various functions of church services, then, requires that church leaders balance the insider-directed functions of a faith community (what might be called *discipleship*) with the outsider-directed recruitment activities (*evangelization*).

One more qualification is in order. Services may function as the primary representation of a church to the public, but services do not equal the church. To illustrate: in researching this chapter, I attended the main Sunday morning service of a local evangelical megachurch, Healing Place Church of Baton Rouge. I earned snickers from my small-congregation, liberal Methodist friends when I told them where I was visiting. Among those friends, Healing Place exemplifies growth-obsessed, shallow-conservative, glitzy-gaudy Christianity. And I cannot lie: Healing Place's seeker-friendly service was not my cup of tea. I found the music well performed but a bit doctrine-light, the sermon well delivered but simplistic, and the camera crane that swung out over the congregation to capture audience reactions (projecting these on huge screens behind the pastor) more "late-night talk show taping" than "worship."

To be fair, however, I was likely not among the seekers that service sought nor among the members that church ministered to. Most of the other congregants around me seemed to enjoy the service. And I know many people, people who do not fit any stereotype of shallow-conservative-glitzy-gaudy, who gladly call Healing Place their home. Their reasons have to do with much more than the style of the service. They point instead to the fact that the church gears itself to the needs of (middle-class, heterosexual-with-young-children) families. It offers elaborate, well-equipped programs for kids. It boasts an array of small-group structures that effectively create comfort zones of familiarity and belonging, pockets of small church within the megachurch. The leadership structure provides multiple contact points with members that belie the seeming remoteness of its superstar clergy. And it engages in a great many charitable ministries like food and clothing drives. Behind even the most extravagant megachurch worship services, then, lie hidden infrastructures that make a congregation appealing to its members. Successful churches succeed for reasons that transcend the marketing savvy of their Sunday services or the charisma of their pastors. My focus here on weekend services, then, spotlights only one aspect of what drives congregations.

Church Growth and Church Marketing

Evangelicals define and measure the efficacy of their ministries in different ways, as I have suggested. For some, like Steven Anderson, the evangelist's responsibility begins and ends with delivering the straightforward plan of salvation, explicitly leaving up to God any concerns about whether the prospect actually converts (or stays converted). Other ministries like hell houses judiciously keep numerical track of the number of conversions they can trace explicitly to their productions. Still others, like the Creation Museum, emphasize the need for Christians to absorb and defend precisely the right kind of doctrinal foundation. Through the latter half of the twentieth century, evangelical churches in the United States turned increasingly to quantitative criteria as an index for churches' efficacy. How many adult baptisms did your church perform in the last year? How many new commitments to Christ? What's the average attendance for Sunday School? How many spinoff churches did your congregation start (or "plant," in the parlance of evangelicalism)?

Such questions were the special focus of the Church Growth movement, spearheaded by minister Donald McGavran. McGavran began his career in the 1930s as a third-generation missionary to India. There he became fascinated with the question of why certain churches seem more apt to grow in membership and vitality while other, nearby churches seem to stagnate or falter. His experiences convinced him that "the multiplication of churches nourished on the Bible and full of the Holy Spirit is a *sine qua non* in carrying out the purposes of God."[5] That is, although the mission of the church includes both social service (e.g., feeding the hungry, caring for the poor, and working for justice) and evangelism of the lost, the latter must take precedence as the primary goal for the church. McGavran roundly criticizes perspectives that would direct missionary efforts away from the pure task of making disciples for Christ.[6] In McGavran's view, God desires all peoples to become Christian. God is, for him, primarily "a Finding God," possessed of an overriding concern to go out into the world and bring the lost into the folds of God's church.[7] As God's "finders" on earth, Christians are likewise to prioritize seeking and saving the lost in the world.

Accomplishing this task, McGavran argues, requires that Christians equip themselves with the best information and research on the dynamics and demographics of evangelism they can. Indeed, one of the chief legacies of the Church Growth Movement on evangelicalism is the incorporation of quantitative data gathering and analysis into the task of church outreach. In works like *The Bridges of God* (1955) and *Understanding Church Growth* (first edition 1970), and later as head of the evangelical Fuller Theological Seminary's School of World Mission, McGavran sought to impose rigor and regularity on evangelical metrics of growth. Armed with such research, McGavran asserts, churches can then create and implement targeted strategies for ministry to particular groups of people, ultimately turning the spread of the gospel into a mass movement.[8]

Though today not all parts of evangelicalism embrace Church Growth precepts as such, McGavran's influence on evangelical missions remains undeniable. He shifted the focus of evangelistic training from interpersonal encounters (e.g., door-to-door soul-winning) and mass evangelism (e.g., Billy Graham rallies) to long-term, community-specific strategies for churches. He fomented the still-pervasive notion that, like a living organism or colony of organisms, a church's health was best measured by its growth (in terms of baptized members) and spread (in terms of generating offshoot congregations). Finally, while affirming the importance of presenting the unadulterated gospel to the unsaved, McGavran underlined the indispensability of contextualization, matching a congregation's ministerial profile to the demographic and ideological makeup of its home community.

The 1980s saw the rise of a related trend that enhanced this emphasis on contextual matches: church marketing. Led by ministers like George Barna and continuing today in the work of marketers like Reising, church marketing tackles McGavran's questions about how churches grow as challenges best met by capitalist ingenuity. Church marketing borrows research tools and norms from secular advertising and commercial public relations rather than sociology, anthropology, or Church Growth experts. In his manifesto-like 1988 work *Marketing the Church,* Barna recasts the evangelistic aims of the church in marketing terms. That is, he urges churches to see their ministries through the lenses of product, place, promotion, and price.[9] In his 1992 follow-up, a more workbook-style how-to guide, Barna elaborates on the product the Church offers (or should offer). "We are not selling Jesus," he writes. "Nor are we selling the Bible. . . . We are not focused on promoting our worship services or programs."[10] Barna categorizes a church's programs (preaching, music, classes) and their effects (community support, entertainment, personal fulfillment) as product features and benefits.[11] Such features are nice, but they aren't the main product. "Ultimately," he clarifies, "*we exist to move people into a relationship with Jesus Christ.* That relationship *is* our product."[12] The price for such a relationship, he continues, is not money but "an intellectual and emotional toll: commitment."[13] Church marketing thus involves strategies and tactics for making the product (a relationship with Christ) seem enticing enough that the price (a lifetime commitment) seems worthwhile. And though Barna clarifies that the place for promotions is essentially in Christians' everyday lives, his books focus particularly on how churches can manipulate their programs to better move their product. As with McGavran, growth and spread figure as indices of health, though the animating metaphor is mercantile rather than biological.

Perhaps the most conspicuous and long-lived innovation to arise from the 1980s church marketing boom is the seeker-sensitive service. I use the label *seeker-sensitive* to describe evangelical church services that depart consciously from the look, feel, and flow of traditional or old-time Christian worship, exchanging these for styles deemed amenable to "seekers," a demographic identified and studied via market research. Seekers are distanced from traditional churchgoing but open to experiencing Christianity. Seeker-sensitive services tend to promote a relatively generic, upbeat evangelical message, muting or eschewing altogether markers of denominational specificity, doctrinal hair-splitting, and turn-or-burn sermonizing.

Though a number of churches today can be said to exhibit a seeker-sensitive ethos in their weekend services, most conversations about seeker-sensitive services focus primarily on two congregations: Bill Hybels's Willow Creek Church and Rick Warren's Saddleback Church. Both Hybels and Warren followed parallel paths in building their highly successful ministries, and the innovations in weekend services they developed are widely regarded as paradigmatic of the seeker-sensitive style. Barna himself praises Willow Creek's ministry in *Marketing the Church.* "If I had my way," he writes, "there would be 100,000 Willow Creek Churches in this country."[14]

Let me offer a few qualifications here. Though the go-to examples for seeker-sensitive services (i.e., Willow Creek and Saddleback) involve expensive productions playing before a congregation of thousands, the term *seeker sensitive* is not strictly a synonym for *megachurch.* The latter label describes a church's size as measured by average weekly attendance. I draw here on research from Warren Bird and Scott Thumma, whose authoritative research on Protestant megachurches in the US reserves the designation for any church with an average weekend attendance of two thousand or more.[15] Bird and Thumma report that a majority of megachurches (71 percent in their sample) self-identify as evangelical,[16] and most megachurches formally link to a denomination or like-minded association of churches.[17] To be sure, Willow Creek and Saddleback both qualify as megachurches, and many seeker-sensitive services similarly occur in megachurches. I would even go so far as to assert that most megachurches in the United States today have adopted something like an attractional or worship evangelism focus in some or all of their weekend services.[18]

But not all megachurches have, nor is every congregation that produces a seeker-friendly service a megachurch.[19] I note, also, that not all congregations incorporate seeker-sensitive modes as centrally into their ministerial strategy as the two paradigm churches do. Many congregations produce seeker services merely as a side ministry, a supplement to older, more traditional meetings. I therefore try to reserve the seeker-sensitive label for *services* rather than *churches,* though in most other literature the phrase "seeker-sensitive church" is standard.

Finally, as with most issues evangelical, seeker-sensitive services and the churches that produce them vary tremendously. Services at Joel Osteen's Lakewood Church, for example, focus on different attractions than do Rick Warren's Saddleback services. The seeker-sensitive approach describes a ministry style, not a formal program. Different congregations name and realize that style differently. Today, seeker sensitivity exists as the underlying ethos of a number of church services, especially those in megachurches, but not all of these would necessarily identify as Saddleback/Willow Creek acolytes. That said, the seeker model as innovated primarily by Willow Creek Church and Saddleback Church in the 1980s and 1990s provides a baseline representation of the form. I thus devote time to examining those churches' seeker service styles.

In his study of Willow Creek, sociologist Kimon Howland Sargeant traces the seeker style back to the 1970s, when Chicago pastor Bill Hybels began investigating why his church growth had stalled.[20] Consciously borrowing a page from commercial approaches, Hybels did market research in his community in the hope of discovering what discouraged the average non-Christian suburbanite—what Hybels calls "unchurched Harry" (and his wife, "unchurched Mary")—from attending church. He found, for example, that most non-churchgoers felt that most churches just wanted money, so Hybels resolved to be sensitive to that perception when fundraising. His surveys further indicated that most felt church services were boring, so Hybels decided that Willow Creek's services would spice things up with drama, music, and video presentations.[21] Hybels's research, in fact, suggested that many of the accoutrements of traditional churches, such as crosses, formal attire, liturgies, offering plates, and denominational specificity, alienated people who do not normally attend church. Friendly faces, easy-to-sing songs in contemporary styles, laid-back atmospheres, and nonconfrontational theology attracted them.

Taking those findings to heart, Hybels reformatted his approach to worship services at Willow Creek. Willow Creek became famous in the 1980s and 1990s for holding church services that look to outsiders very little like church. Its sanctuary uses comfortable theater stadium seating rather than rows of pews. Its architecture eschews stained glass, steeples, cross displays, and the like. Its services resemble energetic rock band concerts with video and/or drama presentations, followed by a well-delivered (and video-accompanied) inspirational speech with some biblical and spiritual themes. And, all through the 1980s and 1990s, Willow Creek's new mode of doing church seemed to work beautifully in terms of growth and spread. Willow Creek itself swelled to a membership of thousands, and Hybels founded a Willow Creek Association designed to aid local congregations in replicating Willow Creek's ministry successes.[22]

Just as Hybels was beginning his ministry in the Midwest, another pastor, Rick Warren, set out to plant a new church on the West Coast.[23] With some research, he found that the Saddleback Valley region of Orange County in California displayed the fastest population growth rates throughout the 1970s. Reasoning that such a high-growth region would need new church plants, Warren resettled to the Saddleback area and set about locating and talking to people who did not attend church. Taking his cue from McGavran, Warren asked what kept the unchurched unchurched. What made Christianity unappealing to them? What did they look for in a church community? Like Hybels, Warren and his ministry team created (and now constantly update) a composite identity for his target audience, "Saddleback Sam." "His age is late thirties or early forties," explains Warren. "He has a college degree and may have an advanced degree. . . . He is married to Saddleback Samantha, and they have two kids, Steve and Sally."[24] This, Warren determined, describe the seeker that Saddleback Church should pursue. A seeker-sensitive service, then, reshapes itself around Saddleback Sam's preferences. Music is exciting, accessible, and upbeat. Sermons are story-based, uplifting, and simple (though not, Warren qualifies, *simplistic*). Insider-specific aspects of church life (denominational specifics, fundraising, committee work) get moved out of the casual visitor's view. Like Willow Creek, Saddleback grew to megachurch status and remains one of the most high-profile evangelical congregations in the United States today.

Central to both ministries is the seeker-sensitive service, a tactical production geared to appeal to a specific group of non-churchgoers (both Hybels and Warren insist that they do not target other churches' congregants). Compared to many of the other performances I have explored, especially soul-winning and hell houses, a seeker service can seem Pollyannaish, a "soft sell" Christianity compared to the hard (or harsh) sell of turn-or-burn truth-telling. I would say rather that they shift from deploying an individualistic narrative of salvation that requires a response from prospects (*You are sinful and heading for Hell—what will you do?*) to creating a communal experience of relationship that invites seekers to join it (*This is what Christianity is like—wouldn't you like to be a part of this?*). Warren grounds himself explicitly in the work of McGavran, affirming that God's primary orientation to humanity is not Wrathful Judge but Seeking Shepherd. God wants to find people. God wants people to come to him. More than that, Warren argues, the reality of the Christian life is inherently appealing to humans. People naturally desire what the Church has to offer. The Church's main product—relationship with Christ—is a wonderful, life-giving thing, not just because it gets people out of hell but because it enables people to live fulfilling lives here on Earth. The Church's job, Warren concludes, thus involves getting out of the way of the mutual attraction between God and the unchurched. In marketing language, seeker services ease the flow of goods between providers and consumers. I want to explore two main aspects of seeker services especially geared toward greasing those wheels: music and the sermons.

Words and Music

One of the signature features of seeker-sensitive services is the kind of musical experience they offer. Warren stresses the importance of music choice in seeker-sensitive events, calling it perhaps "*the* most influential factor in determining who your church reaches for Christ and whether or not your church grows." Warren also acknowledges that the choice will likely be controversial.[25] Few areas of Protestant worship prove as volatile as the choice of what music to sing at church. The insider/outsider tension inherent to worship services and churches in general crystallized in the so-called worship wars of the 1990s and early 2000s; debate continues about whether or not the worship wars have even now ended. On the one side are those who advocate the use of traditional hymns in worship. This vision of worship features a congregation singing particular songs together out of a standard (usually denominationally specific) hymnal, accompanied most often by a pianist and/or organist. A choir whose membership is typically open to any congregant supplements the accompaniment and may provide occasional "special music." For those on the pro–traditional worship side, hymns connect the church to its past while grounding the congregation's worship in well-established, strongly presented doctrinal statements. Critics of traditional hymn services, however, charge that the music seems quaint and slow, the lyrics bizarre to outsiders (a sample: "There is a fountain filled with blood / Drawn from Immanuel's veins / And sinners plunged beneath that flood / Lose all their guilty stains"),[26] and the entire affair simply too old-fashioned.

Opposing the hymn approach are supporters of contemporary or "praise and worship" music, a musical style growing out from Pentecostal and charismatic congregations.[27] Worship songs[28] tend to exchange the volunteer choir for a rock band (at minimum: drums and a guitar, preferably with a synthesizer/keyboard) along with lead and backup singers. In larger congregations, these musicians may be professionals hired by the church. Musically, the form resembles popular music—pop and rock-and-roll specifically—more than classical hymnody. Though various strands of popular church music (e.g., gospel choruses) have long been found in US churches, the contemporary worship-song style emerged relatively recently. The early 1970s saw the birth of the Jesus Movement, a group of recording artists newly converted to Christianity who conjoined contemporary popular music styles with sacred lyrics.

Through the 1980s, musician and pastor John Wimber's Vineyard Association of Churches sought to define a "Third Wave" of charismatic renewal in the United States, blending the popular appeal of the Jesus Movement with the spirit-focused, ecstatic worship from Pentecostal traditions. For Wimber, music was not a prelude or ornament to worship but worship itself. "Rather than singing *about* God, we are to sing *to* him, to interact with him," explains charismatic minister Don Williams about Wimber's influence. "Worship is not a spectator sport. It is a dialogue for participants with the living God. Its main goal is relationship."[29] Wimber's formula for such relational worship began with a time of worship music, led into a sermon, and ended with works of prayer, prophecy, and healing in the charismatic/Pentecostal tradition.[30]

Pentecostal and charismatic influences continue to have limited impact in the United States (in stark contrast with their popularity in the rest of the world). Yet Wimber's embrace of (and contribution to) worship songs helped many Third Wave style features gain a foothold in mainstream Protestantism. Wimber's own compositions have found their way into the musical canons of most Protestant churches.[31] Worship songs also inform much of Contemporary Christian Music (CCM), today the fastest-growing music genre in the US recording industry, with many artists garnering appeal beyond Christian audiences.[32] Yet for many on the pro-hymn side, worship songs resemble nothing so much as liturgical Muzak, with second-rate pop melodies and shallow insipidity for lyrics.

The worship wars frequently play out as a matter of generational difference, with the musical tastes of older congregations for hymns clashing with the preferences of younger congregants for worship songs. Music researcher Kenneth Hull, however, presses for a deeper interpretation of the conflict. People get worked up about music in worship, Hull argues, because they recognize how much music matters to the act of worship. Music, he writes, "not only expresses meaning, it forms the listener and participant over time."[33] Hull identifies two key distinctions between the styles. The two differ, first of all, in terms of the modes of their transmission. Hymns are recorded music; they exist as standardized text/music scores reprinted in hymnals and songbooks. Worship songs, by contrast, circulate primarily as "recorded transmission."[34] Their lyrics and music aren't generally written and read; they are heard, picked up, and repeated.

My own experiences as a church accompanist in hymn-based and worship song–based services exemplify this distinction. When playing piano or acting as worship leader in traditional churches, I rely on hymnals, working with the pastor and music directors to select hymns appropriate to the particular service. While a lifetime of churchgoing lends me enough familiarity with hymns in my tradition to play most of them easily, I still read the music printed, ornamenting (or at times simplifying) the score as need be. When I played keyboard in a praise-and-worship band (volunteer, not professional), by contrast, I had to play by ear. Our band had no sheet music, only a set of lyrics and a list of chord progressions. Learning a new song typically involved listening to a recording from the artist and essentially improvising my own accompaniment. As my musical preferences and experiences tended toward the traditional, I was initially unfamiliar with and even dismissive of many of the worship songs our band chose. To my surprise, however, I found the music easy to learn and even fun to play.

Musically, worship songs often feature the same basic (three or four) chord progressions and musical structures (verse, chorus, verse, chorus, bridge/key change, chorus) as many pop songs. Improvising around these progressions comes easily with a bit of practice. The lyrics typically use repetitive adoration/praise lines (example: "How great is our God / How Great is our God, sing with me / How great is our God and all will see / How great, how great is our God").[35] Frequently written with radio-play appeal and crossover potential in mind, the songs are designed to be recirculated in praise-and-worship services. A visitor may not know a particular worship song, but (provided the visitor has experience listening to popular secular music) just about anyone can catch on fairly quickly. They are familiar even when they are new. And for many congregants, the songs our band played were already old favorites thanks to CCM artists' work played on CDs, iTunes, and Christian radio.

Hull notes that worship songs' harmonic familiarity often works against the grain of their lyrics. The song's verses may expound upon the transcendent majesty of the all-powerful God, for example, but the music often puts listeners in the mood of an intimate, even comfortable pop tune about the object of one's affections.[36] Though such an apparent disjunction strikes traditional hymnody advocates as odd or borderline sacrilegious, theologian Robert R. Redman Jr. points out that the effect is intentional. He links the worship songs' emphasis on intimacy (even the songs' sometimes strikingly physical metaphors for spiritual closeness) to Pentecostal and charismatic traditions that emphasize a publically shared, ecstatic encounter with the Godhead.[37] Hull credits this blend of familiar affection and transcendent worship as one of the reasons for worship songs' (and, implicitly, seeker-sensitive services') appeal more generally.[38] Though critics balk at worship songs' personalization, seeker-sensitive worship leaders value such music as a useful bridge between the church and Unchurched Harry or Saddleback Sam. Worship songs can bring God—and therefore Christianity—within touching distance for an audience of religion outsiders.

Hull further suggests that hymns and worship songs each inspire different modes of worship. Hymns work as discrete components that can be slotted into a variety of different services. Often crafted around a particular season (e.g., Christmas songs, Easter songs), theological topic (forgiveness, the glory of God, the wonder of salvation), or segment of the worship service (gathering time, prayer time, invitations), hymns operate as liturgical building blocks alongside elements like the invocation, pastoral prayers, or offerings. Though song leaders and pastors often work to create a degree of thematic consonance and flow between the chosen hymns for a particular service, each hymn begins, plays, and ends as a self-contained mini-event.

Worship songs, as noted above, were developed in part to fit with charismatic praise-and-worship services. In those services, most of the music occurs at the beginning, generally in a block of twenty to thirty minutes. Similarly, most seeker-sensitive services feature a lengthy music session rather than a distinct succession of hymns and prayers. Thanks in part to their musical similarity, worship songs flow into each other like the play list of a gifted DJ, with the ending of one song modulating seamlessly into the beginning of the next one. Prayers or announcements by pastors and worship leaders get accompaniment from the band, folding even these spoken parts into the overall musical block.[39]

Seeker-sensitive blocks generally follow a conventional affective arc of high-energy praise songs first, followed by slower and quieter prayer/adoration numbers, and finally leading into the sermon with songs that personalize worship and ramp the energy back up again for the pastor's entrance. Warren recommends using Saddleback's IMPACT model to capture this musical arc: Inspire Movement (through high-energy, participatory songs), Praise (with joyful/upbeat songs), then Adore (with slower, meditative numbers), and end with Commitment songs (first-person "I Will Follow Him"-type lyrics) that Tie it all together.[40] Thus, while traditional worship services feature a series of distinct meditations, seeker-sensitive services use the worship music block to generate a sustained soundscape of musical affect.[41] Specifically, the seeker-sensitive music production nurtures a sense of thrilling, welcoming intimacy with the Divine.

Seeker-sensitive homiletics (sermon-writing) likewise diverges from standard evangelical practice. As noted previously, biblicist and conversionist impulses in evangelicalism typically require any meaningful sermon to refer directly and extensively to scripture and to include a presentation of the gospel coupled with an invitation to convert. In a standard evangelical sermon format (insofar as such a thing exists), the pastor begins with a scripture passage and expands thematically from there, linking the lessons of scripture to the lives of believers. The seeker-service format, however, operates from the assumption that most secular audiences do not attend services in search of a Bible lesson. "You cannot start with a [Bible] text, expecting the unchurched to be fascinated by it," argues Warren, "You must first capture their attention, and then move them to the truth of God's Word."[42] Warren's how-to guide for seeker-sensitive services counsels pastors to craft sermons around a theme that seekers will recognize as relevant to their own lives. Seeker-service messages thus might boast titles like "Building an Affair-Proof

Marriage," "Keep Calm and Carry On," or "Conquering Financial Worry."[43] Warren recognizes that such self-help-aisle-themed messages might strike believers as shallow pandering. "I have been criticized," he writes, "for using sermon titles for our seeker services that sound like Reader's Digest articles. This is intentional."[44] *Reader's Digest,* he explains, knows exactly how to appeal to the "felt needs" of its readers. A seeker-sensitive, user-friendly church can do no less, provided a "hard-core Biblical message" undergirds the populist connection.[45]

Yet even in connecting worldly themes to scriptures, stresses Warren, seeker services must be careful to make the Bible as accessible as possible for unchurched visitors. He advises choosing modern translations that do not require extensive contextualization or analysis, handing out outlines with scriptures written out for people to take with them.[46] Warren also insists that even seeker services offer an invitation for commitment. Yet the focus for such invitations departs from the hard-sell, turn-or-burn confrontation of Ray Comfort or hell house dramas. On the contrary, as Hybels's and Warren's surveys suggested, the Bible-thumping, Jonathan Edwards–style hellfire approach turns out to be precisely one of the "turnoffs" for nonmembers that seeker services try to minimize. Though not omitting references to hell and salvation altogether, seeker services generally try to highlight the "soft sell" of the Gospel. They tout the benefits of relationship with Christ, the ways that the Christian way of living can lead to personal fulfillment, enabling you to realize "your best life now," as megachurch pastor Joel Osteen's seeker-friendly messages promise.[47] Instead of pointing to the infernal consequences of sin, seeker churches tout the benefits of Christian community. If you reject the Gospel message, Hybels preaches, "You'll miss the reward your heart yearns for. . . . You don't want to miss [God's] compensations because they're . . . soul-satisfying."[48]

Strict Church, Strong Church

Now, it may seem that in promulgating the seeker-sensitive model Warren and Hybels did little more than capitalize on common sense: *More people will come to churches that seem like nice, comfortable places to be.* Yet, in the late 1970s and early 1980s, the notion of a weekend service reworked to appeal to the unchurched ran against the grain of received wisdom about church growth. In 1972, Dean M. Kelley, a Methodist minister and researcher for the National Council of Churches, published *Why Conserva-*

tive Churches Are Growing, a still-influential text in ministry circles today.[49] There Kelley contrasts mainline (i.e., liberal and progressive) churches with conservative congregations, arguing that the latter seem to be outstripping the former in terms of attendance and membership growth. Kelley poses a counterintuitive yet (for many) compelling explanation for this discrepancy. Conservative churches, he asserts, thrive not in spite of their firm, conservative doctrines but because of them. In contrast to liberal churches' focus on irenic ecumenism and social justice, Kelley argues that conservative churches keep their sights on "their essential business: the dispensing of religion."[50] That is, conservative churches prioritize "explaining the meaning of life in ultimate terms," which Kelley sees as the primary sociological function of organized religion.[51] They identify and minister to parishioners' spiritual and existential needs, offering them a solid picture of what it means to be a Christian.

Moreover, Kelley elaborates, the conservative churches successfully couple their clearer sense of meaning with a clearer, stricter set of *demands* for members (indeed, his preferred title for the book was *Why Strict Churches Are Strong*).[52] These churches' strictures—theological/ecclesiological absolutism, intolerance of heterodox views, high barriers to new members, stringent discipline for existing members—make membership in these churches a hard-won, valuable commodity while ensuring that the congregants they do accept and keep are active, committed, and doctrinaire. Liberal and mainline congregations, by contrast, encourage a de facto "lukewarmness" about the church's core meanings and the demands that flow from those meanings. Valuing tolerance over exclusivity, reserve over fanaticism, and dialogue over missionary zeal, the mainline-progressive churches cultivate a membership—and thus a movement—intrinsically weaker than that of more fundamentalist churches.[53] Kelley's argument (now somewhat complicated by subsequent research)[54] continues to provide ammunition for conservative factions in Protestant denominations.[55]

On its face, the seeker-sensitive service seems to value the features that Kelley identifies as the cause for weak churches—consumer-oriented, non-offensive, and casual. Hybels and Warren, however, would very likely agree that a church constructed around nothing but pleasing customers would likely fail. Both frame the seeker service as only one component of an overall church orientation. Warren specifies, for example, that he promotes *purpose-driven* churches, not *seeker-driven* churches.[56] Appealing to unchurched outsiders is important, but Hybels and Warren both recognize that church is more than just outreach.

Seeker services function as but one tactic within a larger ministerial strategy. Behind Saddleback's and Willow Creek's seeker-friendly services are many of the features of high-demand, meaning-intensive membership that Kelley links to strict (and therefore strong/growing) congregations. Anyone can attend a Saddleback seeker service, for example, but those wishing to join Saddleback must profess Christ, undergo an in-depth membership course ("Class 101: "Discovering Saddleback Membership"), be baptized by immersion, and finally sign a Membership Covenant.[57] Doing so transitions a person from being a part of what Warren calls "the crowd" that attends seeker services to being a member of "the congregation." Writing in 1995, Warren estimates that he has about five thousand members: quite impressive (still megachurch status) but a much lower number than the obvious weekend attendance figures for Saddleback's seeker services. Warren in fact claims, "we are not interested in a large membership," pointing out that Saddleback initiates annual membership purges, removing from the rolls those who have moved or who have ceased to participate in the life of the church.[58]

Beyond initial membership, Warren outlines two deeper levels of participation: "the committed" and "the core." Each of these tiers involves taking more in-depth classes and making more formal commitments. "The committed" are those who dedicate themselves to continuing discipleship; they agree to practice having a quiet time every day, to tithe 10 percent of income, and to participate in a small group.[59] Core members take still more classes and make more elaborate commitments to move from discipleship into formal lay ministry, becoming leaders within the larger congregation. The core members "are the secret of our strength," writes Warren. "If I were to drop dead, Saddleback would continue to grow because of this base of 1,500 lay ministers."[60] Warren encourages ministers to set and maintain high expectations of commitments for members in terms of their continued spiritual growth, their service and contributions to the church, and their maintenance of the core community of believers.[61] Behind its high-visibility seeker services, Willow Creek similarly has a thriving infrastructure of continuing discipleship, small groups, lay leadership, and believers' services.

In this light, Saddleback and Willow Creek—as well as any church successfully following their lead—exemplify Kelley's ideal for a strict, growing church. They incorporate marketing techniques not to replace but to supplement their core ministries. Indeed, the thrust of Kelley's argument harmonizes with Barna's and Reising's contentions: *If churches want to grow, they must identify what they want to provide.* Kelley and Barna likewise concur as to what churches' product is. For Barna, the Church ideally provides a relationship with Christ at the cost of commitment. For Kelley, the Church provides a sense of ultimate meaning that compels commitment. The seeker-sensitive service is not the product; it merely advertises some of its features for the benefit of possible consumers. Warren specifies that only committed believers—members of the congregation rather than the crowd—can participate in authentic worship. Since worship is by definition up-reach, not out-reach, the communion of God with Christians, outsiders cannot themselves worship God. But, Warren continues, outsiders can *watch* believers worship. Provided that the believers worship in a way that is recognizable and attractive to such outsiders, the outsiders can be further drawn into commitment themselves.[62] Seeker services therefore stage a version of "worship" for the benefit of those who might find raw worship alienating. The services feature Christians enjoying the product of church—a demanding-but-fulfilling relationship with an Ultimate Meaning—in the hopes that visitors might eventually want to invest in that relationship themselves.

Dispersed Church: Multisite Congregations

By the standards of the Church Growth and church marketing traditions in which they ground themselves, Saddleback and Willow Creek have succeeded wildly. They've continued to enjoy increasing attendance, adapting Sam and Harry profiles as their target demographics have shifted from Baby Boomer to Gen X (and now Millennial). And they've spread, inspiring hundreds of other churches and church start-ups to follow their lead. Most metropolitan areas in the United States (particularly in the South) can now boast at least one church that mounts seeker-friendly—or at least seeker-friendly-inspired—services on the weekend, and at least some of these have achieved Saddleback levels of megachurch success. Of course, megachurch success brings its own challenges. Once a congregation reaches a certain average weekly attendance number, they run up against the limits of their physical facilities. Even megachurch auditoriums can grow only so large before the sheer logistics of welcoming 10,000 or more people to a service overwhelm a congregation's ability to adapt. Simply juggling traffic inflows and outflows between Sunday morning services can prove nightmarishly complicated. Confronting such a crossroads, a church can decide to build a bigger space, creating or acquiring a still bigger campus. Of course, doing so involves hurdling financial or geographic barriers, and in any case erecting larger facilities merely delays the problem since as long the church continues to grow it will eventually hit even a larger space's physical limits. Alternately, a church can branch out, like a business franchise, planting a whole other autonomous church in another part of the community. Yet the Church Growth tradition enshrines constant growth—more attendees—as both the will of God and the mark of missiological success. Starting a whole other church somewhere nearby (i.e., "church planting"), while also a Church Growth goal, does not add to the core church's attendance.

Enter one of the latest innovations for seeker-sensitive services: the multisite church. Rather than building ever-bigger facilities or spinning off smaller, autonomous churches, multisite churches start other campuses ("satellites") of the main church.[63] In a typical multisite setup, each campus begins its main services at the same time. Each hosts its own music ministry (often targeted to the tastes of the seekers in their part of town) and may include campus-specific announcements. At a pre-appointed time, however (perhaps halfway through the service), the live presentation at each campus transitions to beamed-in programming from the home campus or other studio-equipped site. Members of the ministerial staff under the direction of the home campus's lead pastor(s) each take turns delivering the main message for the week. Other models feature satellite campuses that play pre-recorded sermons from the main church. Some (particularly the smaller multisite churches) even feature a live minister delivering a message based on the home service's lead.

Though both Willow Creek and Saddleback have adapted to multisite formats, the paradigmatic multisite megachurch is Craig Groeschel's LifeChurch.tv. The name is not a URL; the church is literally called "LifeChurch.tv," signaling its multimedia, tech-intensive profile. The home location for the church is Edmond, Oklahoma (on the outskirts of Oklahoma City), but in essence LifeChurch.tv "exists" across fourteen campuses, most of which are in Oklahoma but some of which exist in Tennessee, Florida, Texas, and even New York. Across all fourteen campuses, LifeChurch.tv boasts 35,000 attendees on an average weekend, making it the second-biggest Protestant church in the United States, ahead of Willow Creek (23,400 attendees) and Saddleback (22,418) and second only to Joel Osteen's Lakewood Church (43,500).[64] Like most megachurches in the United States, LifeChurch.tv's identity depends heavily upon the personality of its founder and senior pastor, Groeschel. Also like most megachurch pastors, Groeschel heads a large ministerial staff of logistics managers, teaching pastors, campus ministers, and other experts.

LifeChurch.tv, however, also employs a full-time "Innovation Leader"—currently Bobby Gruenwald—who spearheads the church's continuing online and multimedia initiatives.[65]

As its name suggests, LifeChurch.tv's technical savvy under Gruenwald has enabled it to define the bleeding edge of online and social media use in worship evangelism. Beyond its fourteen physical sites, for instance, the church offers regular online broadcasts of its services, a ministry it calls "ChurchOnline." Visitors to LifeChurch.tv's website see a clock counting down to the next service.[66] When the clock hits zero, the ChurchOnline website (linked to the clock on the church's home page) features a video feed of a service side by side with a chat feed. There a church-appointed moderator prompts reactions to the music and message, responds to questions, and follows up with anyone wanting more information or special prayer requests. Amazon.com links to music the band plays are displayed below the video feed alongside invitations to join LifeChurch.tv on Twitter, Facebook, and other such social media.[67] Not surprisingly, LifeChurch.tv—to say nothing of its extensive niche ministries for small groups, children, youth, and other sub-demographics—is extensively involved in multiple web media.

In the summer of 2011 I visited a Sunday morning service of LifeChurch.tv's main campus in Edmond.[68] The physical campus boasted the standard array of de rigueur attractions: a coffee shop in the lobby, branded merchandise for sale in a gift store, smiling greeters galore, and multiple entries to the main sanctuary. The sanctuary itself featured rows of comfy theater-stadium seats (complete with cup-holders). Casually dressed attendees, many obviously regulars, mingled in the lobby to chat with friends and peruse the merchandise, making their way eventually to their seats (often with coffee in hand) as the band warmed up. A bank of large projection screens hung from the upstage wall. Though I didn't notice it at the time, a small digital clock in the back faced the stage, alerting the performers to the synched-up time.[69] At the campus I attended, a rock band started precisely on the hour (LifeChurch.tv prides itself on punctuality), providing a praise-and-worship music portion that more or less followed Warren's IMPACT model. At what I later found out was precisely nineteen minutes and thirty seconds into the service,[70] the service transitioned to the beamed-in potion. The congregation merely had to look up slightly to view slickly produced video messages and advertisements about upcoming church events (e.g., a LifeChurch.tv film festival, an upcoming sermon series).

Groeschel himself soon appeared on screen, an energetic, charismatic guy in short-sleeved shirt and jeans. He greeted the expanded audience (both at the campuses and through ChurchOnline) and launched into his message. Most LifeChurch.tv sermons are part of a two-to-five-week sermon series; each series has its own logo and promotional video (think of a teaser for a movie). The sermon I saw was "Remain," which roughly dealt with how to persevere in life and in the Christian faith in particular. It was part of the "RE" series, which aside from the current topic included talks titled "Remember," "Repentance," and "Renew."[71]

Groeschel proved himself as talented a speaker as any seeker-sensitive megachurch pastor I have seen: gregarious, charismatic, well-rehearsed, and clear. Echoing Warren's recommended homiletic progression for seeker services, the message began with Groeschel taking the congregation through a miniature personal inventory, conveniently printed in congregational handouts. "I wonder how many of you," he asked, "would say that sometimes you can be a little bit unloving? . . . Are you sometimes or often depressed? Are you lacking joy?"[72] He moved from this personal, everyday-life index of feelings to scriptures about God's promise of love, joy, peace, and patience ("the fruits of the spirit") to those who remain connected to the vine, Jesus. At every Bible verse, Groeschel encouraged the congregation to follow along with him on LifeChurch.tv's smartphone app, YouVersion, which features easy-access scripture capabilities in a number of translations.[73] Tiny screens lit up all around me.

He peppered his message with personal anecdotes that illustrated his points, relating stories about a child staying close to her mother and a couple in trouble who kept praying despite their uncertainties. His thesis, underlined often, was that remaining in close relationship to Christ—and, through LifeChurch.tv's many programs, remaining in close fellowship with other believers—can help people persevere through the trials of everyday life. He concluded with a simple invitation to come to Christ along the evangelically familiar lines of *Raise your hand if you'd pray this prayer* [a prayer of salvation] *with me,* adding that ChurchOnline attendees should "click right below me" (i.e., below the video feed frame). Though Groeschel beamed his message in from a remote location, the audience responded largely as if he were actually present, laughing at his jokes, leaning in for his more intimate stories, responding when prompted ("Can I get an Amen?" "Amen!"), and nodding appreciatively when he struck a chord with them. Trained with a bias toward live performance over televised production, I was surprised at how readily the congregants adapted to a purely televised pastor.

The multisite model presents several elegant solutions for the unique logistical problems facing seeker-service-using megachurches. Since attendees at any satellite campuses "count" as attendees for the church itself, multisite churches can grow far beyond the physical limits of their spaces. Churches can explore new locations without risking the same level of investment as a wholly new church plant. Spinoff campuses can still tap into the cachet of the home church (and, often, the star power of the founding/senior pastor or pastors) while in practice relying on local resources to run the campus. Likewise, a community otherwise ripe for seeker-sensitive ministry and interested in starting a new congregation can cut down on financial risk by availing themselves of the greater resources of a multisite network.

Multisite models also allow churches to further tailor their seeker services to diverse member tastes. Saddleback's multisite adaptations, for example, include simulcasting Warren's sermons into multiple separate venues on the main (very large) Saddleback campus. Visitors can choose from a range of different music styles (e.g., old-time hymns, black gospel, and even Polynesian); Warren (who preaches in the central venue with adult-contemporary worship music) beams in his message to these other venues at the appointed time.[74] Satellite campuses of other churches provide the option of "patio services," casual or even outdoor seating where congregants sip lattes and munch on pastries while watching the video message.[75]

Groeschel and LifeChurch.tv see their ministry model not merely as a logistical solution to megachurch problems but as an effective ministerial response to twenty-first-century evangelistic challenges for all churches. Like Warren and Hybels before him, Groeschel promotes LifeChurch.tv's model for general use by ministers. Through their Network program, LifeChurch.tv supports a loose association of congregations beyond its fourteen campuses and ChurchOnline.[76] At no cost, a church in the network may semi-formally align itself with LifeChurch.tv. Network Churches retain ministerial and financial autonomy but commit to using LifeChurch.tv's ministry materials (i.e., sermons and multimedia media resources) at least once a week. They may in return publicize themselves as a "LifeChurch.tv Network Church" and receive access to LifeChurch.tv's archive of sermon videos and associated supporting materials, such as illustrative subtitles for projection, transcripts, outlines, and promotional videos.

The sermon videos are specifically set up to mimic the official campus's formats, with a Network Church providing its own (usually live) music and announcements and then playing or simulcasting a Life-

Church.tv sermon. My parents' rural Oklahoma town features one such Network Church, RawChurch.tv (RAW for Radical, Authentic, and World-changing), which proudly advertises that it offers Craig Groeschel's teachings weekly.[77] Network churches may even pursue formal alignment with LifeChurch.tv, becoming an official campus of the church and submitting to the ministerial, financial, and logistical authority of Groeschel. Congregations unwilling to become formally networked with LifeChurch.tv, however, are still welcome to the church's online resources. LifeChurch.tv's OpenChurch website contains practically the same material available to Network Churches (sermon archives, supporting materials, promotional art and videos, and teaching helps). Anyone is free to use their resources.

Thanks in part to LifeChurch.tv's success, the multisite model is increasingly viewed as a must for any church interested in growth and evangelism. Megachurches are trending increasingly toward multisite delivery. But research on multisite churches from the Leadership Network, a nonprofit advisory resource for ministers, indicates that churches describing themselves as "one church in two or more locations" now outnumber megachurches in the United States.[78] The Leadership Network's survey of multisite churches suggests that satellite churches inject a new energy into the congregation, adding not just numbers but evangelistic impetus. Some satellite campuses, for example, themselves start "grand-daughter" campuses, plant whole new congregations, or even achieve autonomy.[79] Multisite churches also reflect the shift of attractional worship services from Gen X seekers to Millennial seekers, those born into a world of social networking saturation. Paralleling trends in higher education, internet-aware multisite churches maximize the convenience of the church experience—the Christian product—for seekers. Find a LifeChurch.tv campus or Network Church near you! Download worship now! Experience church in the comfort of your bedroom!

Criticisms

Despite their continued growth, seeker-oriented megachurches have inspired a strong current of counter-reaction against them, their ministers, and their philosophy of outreach. Marketing-informed worship evangelism strategies have long endured criticism. From their beginnings, Hybels, Warren, and other new paradigm churches have had to field allegations that they do little but peddle a shallow, consumerist spirituality with glitzy production values. In a 1994 interview with *Christianity Today,* Hybels counters that such charges come from those unfamiliar with Willow Creek's worship. Were his critics to "sit in our auditorium, next to several thousand churched and nonchurched people, and experience our music and drama package," he promises, "they would retract every single word they've ever written about it."[80] Even today, seeker-sensitive ministers regularly have to remind critics not to expect services intended for unchurched seekers to match standards set by believers' worship services.[81] Judging Saddleback, for example, as Christianity Lite on the basis of its seeker services misses the point, insists Warren. The seeker service is only "the tip of the iceberg," he protests. "It's like two percent of the church. What goes on the rest of the week, beneath the surface, is much more revealing of who we are. It's two hundred different ministries. It's more than three thousand small groups. It's six thousand hours of counseling a month. It's all sorts of things that people don't readily see on a Sunday morning."[82]

Yet Warren's tip-of-the-iceberg defense recalls a lesson regularly taught in undergraduate directing and acting classes: *An audience sees only what you, the artist, show it.* A hard truth for directors, actors, and designers to internalize involves the fact that they do not have the luxury of explaining to audiences the beautiful complexity of the backstage, preshow intentions that feed into a production. If a production fails to connect to an audience, artists typically cannot shield themselves behind "Yes, but what I *really* meant to show was . . ." excuses. Audiences judge what they view on stage, and the production team's responsibility includes making sure that its concept translates effectively to spectators not otherwise aware of the team's thought processes. Similarly, for Warren, Hybels, and other purveyors of seeker services to cry foul at accusations of customer-pleasing shallowness is understandable but unconvincing. Seeker services function as the public face of a congregation to the unchurched world, and such services are explicitly designed to be pleasing to that audience. They stage the bill of goods—the soft-sell gospel, the easy intimacy with the Divine, the emotional worship high—that a church sells to the public as Christianity. That people judge the church based on its own self-presentation can hardly be surprising.

Quite a few people, Christian and otherwise, have taken Hybels up on his challenge to judge Willow Creek's services by watching them firsthand. Even though such services represent a statistically thin slice of total evangelical worship productions, visits to Willow Creek, Saddleback, and other megachurch seeker productions regularly figure in popular-press, journalistic profiles of "evangelicals."[83] Such accounts inevitably comment upon the churches' elaborate—and expensive—physical environments. Saddleback Church's home site, for example, occupies 120 "meticulously landscaped" acres, a campus that "has more the appearance of a village than a traditional church."[84] In addition to its many worship venues, educational buildings, and church offices, Saddleback boasts a waterfall, a life-sized replica of Jesus's tomb, and a number of eateries.[85] Willow Creek's main campus also features a waterfall, multiple buildings, two coffee shops, a food court, a bookstore, and a huge central sanctuary.[86] "I feel like I'm in a Christian Nordstrom's," reflects Matt Casper, a self-identified atheist touring Willow Creek and other megachurches with evangelist Jim Henderson. "The colors are monochromatic, the lighting muted, and the chairs incredibly comfortable. I feel like I'm at a trade show or something."[87]

Though physically smaller than Willow Creek and Saddleback due to its multisite setup, LifeChurch.tv's home base similarly features slick, modern architecture, color-coordinated design, and an elaborate lobby (including a special children's entrance to the church equipped with animatronic characters). LifeChurch.tv can adapt its lobby environment to specific events. Every summer, for example, LifeChurch.tv touts an annual summer "At the Movies" series in which it shows family-friendly mainstream films like *Happy Feet,* using them as both a draw for visitors and as a jumping-off point for spiritual conversations. For the 2011 series, in conjunction with *Kung Fu Panda,* the Edmond campus refurbished their lobby with a decorative, generically "oriental" look: a koi pond, a rock garden, red paper lanterns, and even a children's slide installed in a huge walk-in Chinese food take-out box.[88] All of these design touches serve the seeker-sensitive model, removing churches from the stereotypical (and seeker-unfriendly) "look" of classic churches while also providing a wide array of hooks for casual visitors. At the same time, however, the detailed consideration given to display calls attention to itself, highlighting both the immense financial resources the church devotes to appearances and adding hints of profiteering (a bookstore, a coffee shop, a restaurant—in a church?) that recall the moneygrubbing image of Christianity Warren and Hybels both initially strove to disrupt.

Outsider accounts of seeker services frequently note that the "spare no expense" feel of the grounds extends into the services' production values. The latest in theatrical lighting and concert sound bolster the multimedia stage shows. All agree that the music is well-performed and the sermons well-crafted and well-delivered. But, again, the high-class, virtuoso production proves off-putting to some outsiders. Casper (the atheist touring different megachurch services), for example, found Saddleback's musical performances to be "too contrived, too slick, *too* professional. . . . Too much polish and you lose the heartfelt power, you lose the soul of the music, and you're not gonna move anyone."[89] Willow Creek's music, which incorporated a cover of U2's "Beautiful Day," impressed him even less. "Look at that singer's smiling face and listen to those lyrics," he tells Henderson. "'This world holds nothing for me.' How can you sing that and smile?"[90] The music, in other words, seems chosen for its surface features rather than for its substance. Other commentators echo worship-wars criticisms of contemporary praise songs' bathetic musicality and shallow lyrics. Writing about Colorado Springs's New Life Church (the congregation of now-disgraced pastor and former head of the National Association of Evangelicals Ted Haggard), reporter Jeff Sharlet gives a withering micro-analysis of megachurch music:

> Male singers at New Life and other megachurches are almost always tenors, their voices clean and indistinguishable. . . . The drummers all stick to soft cymbals and beats anyone can handle; the guitarists deploy effects like artillery but condense them, so the highs and lows never stretch too wide. Lyrics tend to be rhythmic and pronunciation perfect, the better to sing along with when the words are projected onto movie screens. Breathy or wailing, vocalists drench their lines with emotion, but only within strict confines. There are no sad songs in a megachurch, and there are no angry songs. There are songs about desperation, but none about despair; songs convey longing only if it has already been fulfilled.[91]

Of course, many of these eyewitness accounts come from skeptical if not outright hostile observers. One wonders exactly what kind of service would appeal to a visitor who enters expecting nefarious manipulation. Yet even many "friendlier" critics—other evangelicals—point to potential troubles with seeker-oriented services. The professionalism and rock-concert setup of megachurch praise-and-worship musicians and the super-star status of the senior pastorate contribute to the feeling of *watching* worship—watching the professional/photogenic performers sing, watching the star pastors preach—rather than *participating* in worship. In multisite churches, the added layers of mediation—though clearly for many congregants not a deal-breaker—nevertheless do little to ameliorate the sense of spectatorship rather than participation.

Of course, regardless of what outsider or insider critics think about seeker services' music, the performances clearly appeal to a great many people, proving sufficient to draw crowds in (or, at least, not push them away) weekend after weekend. And "participation" is partially a subjective affair. The charismatic/Pentecostal influence in contemporary worship music encourages an expressive, ecstatic level of congregational singing that emphasizes embodied worship. It matters less, to a certain extent, that the service features a stage full of professional singers rather than a volunteer choir of congregants. At the large-scale seeker services I have attended, simply singing along with a worship chorus often involves raised hands, swaying, and even (in certain songs) jumping up and down—experiences that hardly match any notion of "non-participatory." Compared to that kind of experience, it is the traditional church service's reliance on rote hymn-singing that can seem disengaged and spiritually deadening. The pastors I have watched likewise draw from a rich arsenal of public-speaking techniques (or perhaps large-scale class teaching tricks) to snap congregations out of purely passive auditing: interactive exercises to complete as part of the sermon, prompts for audience activity ("Turn to your neighbor and say, 'God loves you, and there's nothing you can do about it!'"), and good old-fashioned appeals for audience response ("Raise your hand if . . . ," "Can I get an 'Amen?'").

But critics of seeker-sensitive sermons—and there are many—question whether a pleased or moved congregation necessarily translates to a meaningful Christian experience. Do large numbers, polished showmanship, and affective intensity, in other words, necessarily evince quality? Such critics observe that megachurch seeker-sensitive preachers often deliver messages so "Christianity Lite" that they seem more like self-help seminars for business executives than doctrinally solid meditations on the gospel or the Bible. For many evangelicals, the exemplar of such pabulum preaching is Joel Osteen, senior pastor of Lakewood Church in Houston. Known as "the Smiling Preacher" for his perpetual grin and unassuming, folksy demeanor, Osteen leads what is currently the largest congregation in the United States, a church so big it bought and relocated to Houston's 16,000-seat Compaq Center (formerly the stadium for the Houston Rockets).[92]

Thanks to his widely broadcast services and his many (often bestselling) books, Osteen is one of the most well-known evangelicals in the United States today. His services fit the generic seeker-sensitive model perfectly. High-energy, professionally performed praise music transitions at the thirty-minute mark into Osteen jogging onto the stage wearing his wide smile along with a broad-shouldered three-piece suit. Osteen delivers relentlessly upbeat messages, cheery paeans to hope and good old stick-to-itiveness dispensed in a soothing, slightly sing-song tone.[93] He distills the easy-accessibility God of traditional seeker services into a vision of the Divine as an omniscient best friend, intimately invested in helping you to live "your best life now" (the title of his first best-seller).

In Osteen's view, God wants people financially secure, personally fulfilled, and physically healthy—and that's basically it. He scrubs his sermons clean of anything remotely difficult for church outsiders to swallow. Where Warren will occasionally tread into the political realm (hosting conversations with presidential candidates in 2008, for instance), Osteen scrupulously avoids contentious issues and keeps himself well clear of the partisan religious right. Where most seeker-sensitive pastors pass on fire-and-brimstone themes, Osteen eschews even the word *sinner*.[94] "There is no condemnation in Osteen's message for failing to fulfill God's righteous law," writes seminary professor Michael S. Horton. Instead, he continues, Osteen promotes a vision of God as "a buddy or partner who exists primarily to make sure we are happy."[95]

In part, this message aligns with Osteen's theological lineage, an offshoot of the Pentecostal/charismatic movement known variously as the Word of Faith movement, the prosperity gospel, or the health and wealth gospel.[96] As *Time* magazine's profile of him notes, Osteen preaches a "Prosperity Lite": a toned-down, softer-edged version of such messages than one gets from send-your-money-and-get-it-back-tenfold televangelists such as Kenneth Hagan, Benny Hinn, or Creflo Dollar.[97] Where Hagan, Hinn, and Dollar lay out extensive theological underpinnings for their messages (interpreting scripture along the lines of a quid-pro-quo, obedience-for-blessings contract between God and humans), Osteen steers clear of wading too far into any advanced theology.

In fact, Osteen typically references scripture only lightly. True, every sermon features Osteen leading the congregation in a brief, pledge-like recitation about the importance of the Bible, and Osteen peppers his sermons with references to stories of biblical heroes who persevered and were blessed. But most critics judge these gestures to be weak tea. "Despite the cut-aways of an enthralled audience with Bibles opened," writes Horton of Osteen's televised services, "I have yet to hear a single biblical passage actually preached. Is it possible to have evangelism without the evangel? Christian outreach without a Christian message?"

Absolutely not, says Michael Spencer, the late evangelical blogger who wrote "The Coming Evangelical Collapse." Spencer voices one of the strongest condemnations of Osteen in a 2005 post calling on his fellow evangelicals to publically denounce the Lakewood minister (an uncharacteristic move for Spencer):

> Make no mistake about this: Osteen isn't confused about Jesus like many of the prosperity preachers you hear on TBN [Trinity Broadcasting Network]. Osteen is intentionally avoiding irritating language about sin because he wants to keep it positive every week. He is not just avoiding mentioning Jesus, the cross and the Gospel just because he is seeker sensitive. Joel Osteen is preaching the no-Gospel, no-Jesus message *because it's filling the church with thousands of people who want to hear it.*[98]

Now, few critics would tar every seeker-sensitive pastor with an Osteenian prosperity-gospel brush. Indeed, Warren and Groeschel have both expressly rejected God-wants-you-rich theologies.[99] Yet Osteen's low-cost/no-cost advertisement for Christianity seems in some ways like a straightforward précis of the Church Growth and marketing movements' own vision. God loves you and wants the best for you. It is OK to downplay the costs of Christian commitment to better highlight the product's attractive features. High attendance at church means that God has blessed your ministry. For Spencer, and for many other evangelicals, Osteen provides a grim object lesson on the slippery slope of market-based worship outreach. In creating a service in Warren's mold of "church for people who don't like church," Osteen has (according to his critics) gone too far in the non-church direction. Osteen's extremely popular but (for Spencer) dangerously heretical productions undercut the assumption that high attendance and happy, energized congregants who feel close to God necessarily equates to "effective ministry."

Needless to say, Osteen's critics do little to dissuade the 45,000 people who attend his services each week or buy his books. And to be sure, some evangelical criticism of successful seeker congregations like his may originate in ordinary jealousy. Extant seeker-sensitive-using megachurches, after all, represent survivors of a decade-long seeker-sensitive fad that trended through the 1990s. One chronicler of that fad—or perhaps "bubble" is more appropriate—and its aftermath is Sally Morgenthaler, a pastor whose 1998 book *Worship Evangelism* served as a seminal text in turn-of-the-millennium conversations about designing attractional church services.[100] Reflecting on the seeker craze in 2007, Morgenthaler relates her impression of how the worship evangelism approach produced mixed results.[101] The seeker-sensitive/contemporary worship boom, she notes, saw hundreds of new church plants as well as grand attempts at revival at older congregations, all scrabbling to make themselves into the next Saddleback or Willow Creek. By 2000, however, these start-ups had experienced one of two fates. Most failed to reach what Morgenthaler calls "critical mass" of 300 to 400 members; such churches either disappeared or began drifting away from seeker-friendly/contemporary worship outreach models.

By contrast, a few churches using contemporary worship-evangelism models succeeded wildly. Provided they had "1,000 or more [weekly] attendees" and kept their founding pastors, these churches grew exponentially.[102] Yet the kind of growth the survivor megachurches experienced and the kinds of people enjoying their product both changed. Rather than seeing the unchurched being drawn in by seeker-sensitive services and then feeding into deeper levels of congregational membership, these successful megachurches in fact began catering more to experienced churchgoers. The success stories, Morganthaler notes, "were invariably congregations with visionary, talented leaders and the determination to do whatever it took to grow." She continues:

> And these star performers became masters at what the churched wanted. They raised the bar several times over for what could be expected out of a Sunday morning experience, and they worked tirelessly to develop the high quality, practical programs the churched now demanded. Having excelled at making theirs the best churched experience on the market, they were perfectly positioned to absorb the windfall of disgruntled attendees from dwindling mainline congregations and failed, contemporary start-ups.[103]

After the year 2000, in other words, Morgenthaler argues, successful worship-evangelism megachurches grew not so much because their seeker services drew in unprecedented numbers of unchurched Harrys than because they consolidated the already-churched from smaller congregations. Thus, she concludes, the Church faces a conundrum of millennial churchgoing: a few worship-evangelism-focused megachurches continue to expand, but overall statistics in the United States suggest rising percentages of people who do not go to any church.[104]

Subsequent statistical research lends some support to Morgenthaler's argument. Thumma and Bird's in-depth surveys of twelve US megachurches (many though not all of which employ the attractional worship elements I have been investigating here) indicate that the majority of megachurch attendees transfer from other Christian congregations.[105] Only about a quarter of megachurch attendees identify either as first-time participants in a Christian church (6 percent) or lapsed Christians who have returned to worship after several years of non-attendance (18 percent). The remaining attenders (excepting the4 percent who have called the congregation home all their lives) report having transferred to the megachurch from another Christian congregation. Thumma and Bird hasten to note that many of those who switched from extant churches were recent transplants to the area—they switched churches because they had recently moved—rather than "stolen sheep" from neighboring congregations.[106]

Nevertheless, their findings seem to reinforce Morgenthaler's claim that surviving (and thriving) megachurches have tacitly shifted the focus of their appeal from unchurched to churched seekers. Such a shift coincides with a drastic redistribution of church attendance in the United States generally. A comprehensive survey of churchgoing in the United States, the National Congregations Study (NCS), revealed that while most US churches were small, most churchgoers attend larger congregations. "Even though the average *congregation* has only 75 regular participants and an annual budget of $90,000," observe the authors, "the average *person* is in a congregation with 400 people and a budget of $280,000."[107] That is, half the *churches* in the United States report congregations of 75 or fewer attendees. Yet half of all *churchgoers* attend a church with 400 or more weekly attendees.[108] Large churches, and especially megachurches, account for the majority of US churchgoers. This effect becomes more pronounced as the size of the church approaches mega-status. Saddleback, for instance, welcomes more numbers in a single weekend than the average/median church in the United States sees in five years put together.[109] "In a nutshell," the NCS authors declare, "the largest 10% of congregations contain about half of all churchgoers."[110]

Such a statistic in part reflects broad rural-to-urban population shifts, not simply the runaway success of large church outreach programs or the failure of small-church programs. But that shift itself has ramifications for outreach and discipleship schemes. In particular, the NCS authors note that congregational and denominational decision-makers have to navigate some tricky problems about whether to plan more from the perspective of most congregations (i.e., mixing in small, often rural congregations) or from the perspective of most church attendees (i.e., focusing mainly on large, urban/suburban congregations). The de facto focus increasingly defaults to large congregations in urban areas. "Congregations may be opening new doors in America's suburbs," the authors conclude, "but doors are closing in rural communities. There is good reason for worry about the plight of the rural church in America."[111]

In terms of numerical growth, then, large congregations and megachurches in mainly urban/suburban areas appear to be consolidating a monopoly on US Christendom. But what about more qualitative growth metrics? What kind of spiritual experience or religious growth actually happens in a megachurch? A number of prominent voices have raised concerns about whether worship-evangelism-reliant megachurches necessarily meet the needs of the already-churched members joining them. In 2007, for example, Willow Creek made waves by publishing the results of an in-depth audit of its membership, the *REVEAL* study. Through a series of quantitative and qualitative surveys and interviews, the study authors inquired about members' self-perceptions about their spiritual growth, correlating those reports with the respondents' level of involvement in the church's ministries.

To their surprise, the authors found that people's participation in the church's ministries (e.g., Sunday Schools, small groups) did not necessarily lead to satisfactory levels of spiritual growth (as measured by respondents). A significant number of respondents (about 30 percent) reported feeling stalled in their spiritual journeys and said they were considering leaving the church despite their active involvement in church programming.[112] Hybels himself expressed dismay at the study's results, interpreting them to suggest that Willow Creek's ministry model was not working as well as he had assumed. Although Willow Creek provided great programs for neophyte Christians, it failed (in Hybels's estimation) to create an environment in which believers could grow in their faith.[113]

Other researchers see a less alarming picture.[114] The majority of megachurch attendees responding to Thumma and Bird's 2008 survey, for example, self-report general satisfaction with their level of spiritual growth and development.[115] Their research troubles attempts to generalize patterns of active participation in megachurch congregations. They find that attendees adopt a diversity of approaches to the many offerings a large church affords, devising individualized patterns of participation and commitment. Small-group participation, for example, has long been a mainstay of Saddleback-, Willow Creek-, and even LifeChurch.tv-style ministry rhetoric. Seeker-service defenders commonly posit the intimacy and personal touch of cell groups as an indispensable balance to the relatively distant, mass-spectator setup of seeker-sensitive mega-services.

Yet a full 40 percent of megachurch attendees report not participating in such small groups at all.[116]

Asked what attracts and keeps them at their megachurch, respondents list (in descending order) the style of service, the talents of the senior pastor, and the reputation of the church. The kind and quality of member programs, the congregation's denominational affiliation, and the presence of friends and family at the church all rank lower.[117] Thumma and Bird stress, of course, that many megachurch attendees do volunteer for church ministries, do join small groups, and do contribute tithes and offerings. For many megachurch attendees, however, simply attending a weekly service—in most cases a seeker-friendly, well-performed, high-profile service—appears to satisfy their spiritual needs. They seem content, in other words, to remain atop the tip of Warren's iceberg.

Conclusion: Moralistic Therapeutic Deism and Its Discontents

This concern, that megachurch seeker services inspire a discipleship satisfied with the surface features of worship and little else, resonates with a recurrent theme in evangelical warnings about the future of the Church. One of the mainstream scholars most regularly trusted by evangelical thinkers is sociologist Christian Smith. Known for penetrating, sympathetic treatments of religious life (and particularly evangelicalism) in the United States, Smith has provided evangelicals with influential statistical research on the religious beliefs and habits of the next generation of churchgoers. In two books, one about US teenagers (2005's *Soul Searching*) and one about college-age adults (2009's *Souls in Transition*), Smith and his co-authors use a combination of quantitative surveys and qualitative interviews to take the measure of the state and fate of religion in the secular age. Among Smith's findings, evangelicals have especially latched onto his argument that the de facto faith of young people in the United States is what he terms "Moralistic Therapeutic Deism" (MTD). Less a formal creed than a loose collection of common belief tendencies, MTD as Smith describes it consists of five core tenets:

> First, a God exists who created and orders the world and watches over human life on earth. Second, God wants people to be good, nice, and fair to each other, as taught in the Bible and by most world religions. Third, the central goal of life is to be happy and to feel good

> about oneself. Fourth, God does not need to be particularly involved in one's life except when God is needed to resolve a problem. Fifth, good people go to heaven when they die.[118]

This belief structure is *moralistic* in that it mandates a generic "niceness." People ought not harm others. They should work hard, respect people, and practice tolerance toward others' beliefs (provided those beliefs are similarly nice). It is *therapeutic* in that faith is conceived as a practice intended to benefit individuals, bolster them, give them inner peace and happiness, and assist them through difficult patches in life. Finally, MTD is *deistic* in that it recognizes a God but views this God as distant, tolerant, and (most of the time) politely hands-off—that is, until such time as God is needed for therapeutic reasons. Though Smith originally posited Moralistic Therapeutic Deism as a synthesis of the worldviews of many people aged thirteen to seventeen (and, in a more "diluted" way, aged eighteen to twenty-three), a range of evangelicals have taken up MTD as an accurate diagnosis of ecclesiastical malaise generally.[119] To critics of Osteen specifically and of consumer/market-oriented trends in worship design generally, MTD seems to describe perfectly the kind of easy-to-digest version of Christian commitment and discipleship megachurch seeker services sell. Of course, even the most ardent evangelical church marketing advocate would bristle at allegations of peddling MTD rather than the gospel. Certainly Hybels, Warren, and Groeschel manifest in their larger ministries a Christianity that jars with MTD's easygoing, minimal-demand doctrine. Their whole point is to cultivate disciples who resist the lure of do-nothing, self-centered faith.

Yet the accessible, customer-oriented ethos of the seeker service can easily seem all too similar to MTD. Attractional services base their ministry model on providing a free sample of Christianity's appeal. They stage an especially palatable display of features for the Christian product, creating experiences in which Christian spirituality becomes familiar, accessible, and above all convenient for members of a culture all too often distanced from Christianity. The hope is that this free taste will inspire deeper engagements and more formal commitments on the part of the previously unchurched. Yet today, attractional services in the seeker-friendly vein appear in many cases to offer less an easy-to-try *sample* of Christianity for the unchurched and more an easy-to-practice *version* of Christianity—moralistic therapeutic deism with a spritz of Christianity—for the already churched. Given the choice between the total-immersion, slickly produced, and seeker-oriented hour of Christian relationship on the one hand and the high-cost, high-demand, day-to-day strictness of the strong church that may lie beneath that surface, many churchgoers choose the former.

Nevertheless, the market-minded, attractional worship service seems well-ensconced in evangelical life thanks to the continued success of megachurches like Willow Creek, Saddleback, LifeChurch.tv, and Lakewood. Yet this model is hardly the only response that evangelical churches have devised to respond to shifting cultural dynamics. Aside from the many congregations (mainly small, as the NCS indicates) that largely practice some form of "traditional" church services, a number of evangelical counter-movements have sprung up that tackle the challenge of ministry within a secular age differently than the attractional worship service. Many of these movements contrast themselves to the perceived commercialism of the seeker service, striving for more meaningful worship rather than a more popular worship.

The house church or "organic church" movement in the United States, for example, steps back from the perceived impersonality of the large-scale seeker service; in fact, it steps back from conventional church-based worship altogether. Borrowed in part from the tactics of Christians in China who found it necessary to hold tiny, underground services in the relative privacy of their homes due to state restrictions on religion, the organic church movement in the United States embraces the small-group dynamic Warren and Hybels see as essential to meaningful spiritual growth. Organic churches might meet in someone's house, in a coffee shop, or in any other non-church space. Generally led by experienced Christians, house churches feature a bare-bones style of worship centered on Bible study, prayer, and even sacraments.[120] George Barna, once a champion of Willow Creek–style seeker churches, has more recently promoted organic churches as an important alternative practice for reaching a populace turned off by both traditional church stodginess and attractional worship glitziness.[121]

Other evangelical counter-movements seek less to do away with churches than to re-imagine what "doing church" means in light of postmodern culture.[122] The close of the twentieth century saw evangelicalism (and Christianity more generally) struggling to adapt to generational shifts in perspective. A number of Gen-X-focused ministries (typically young-adult services with contemporary music and casual dress) sprang up as part of the market-based church growth models of the late 1980s and early 1990s. By the later 1990s, however, several ministers began expressing dissatisfaction with merely adjusting traditional services to fit younger generations' tastes. Cultural shifts reshaping US life, they saw, transcended merely generational differences. "My big 'aha' moment," recalls minister Todd Hunter, "was when it hit me: Everything I know about church is about Christendom and modernity and the baby boom, and all three of these things are going away."[123]

As evangelicals became more conversant with the meaning(s) of postmodernity—the suspicion of propositional Truth, the preference for juxtaposition and non-linearity, the embrace of openness and uncertainty as productive—several leaders began asking what it might be like for Christian worship not merely to speak to postmodern seekers but to become itself postmodern in form. Gradually, a loose association of (mostly but not exclusively evangelical) ministers formed, eventually christening itself Emergent, or the Emergent Conversation. Congregations taking their cues from the Emergent Conversation and parallel inquiries became known as "emerging churches." Today the name "Emerging Church"[124] describes a range of ministries, services, and churches in the United States and abroad (mainly in the Anglicized world) who consciously open themselves to postmodern modes of worship.

Even more than the seeker-sensitive movement, the Emerging Church comprises not a formal program but a collection of parallel inquiries about what a postmodern church might be like, worship "without the generic wrapper," as Morgenthaler puts it.[125] Since different ministers and emerging churches produce vastly different pictures of wrapper-less Christian worship, synthesizing a list of characteristically "Emergent" worship features makes for a frustrating task.[126] Chiefly, however, emerging churches reject some of the core assumptions and practices of seeker-sensitive worship. Though attentiveness to popular culture plays a role in worship design, Emergent ministries do not take seeker preferences as their starting point, nor do they prize seekers' emotional fulfillment as a worship goal. Seeker-sensitive worship tends to be a highly managed affair, with practically every element of worship devised and presented by a select group of professionals. Emerging services often seek to disrupt a unilateral, polished-product presentation feel in favor of creating a messier, more dialogic and participatory space. Ministers might displace the standard music-then-announcements-then-sermon progression in favor of open mic nights,[127] sculpture and painting,[128] small group discussions, or interactive skits.

Yet, though much less regularly structured than seeker services, Emergent worship tends to value depth and overt doctrinal/theological inquiry over (or alongside) affective engagement. Where seeker services often mask "traditional church" elements, emergent churches pursue what many call an "ancient-future" mode, mining classical creeds and patristic writings and putting them alongside present-day texts. They may borrow and recontextualize ancient Christian practices such as meditation, chanting, silence, and prayer labyrinths, deploying these in worship (typically with a lesson about their original historical contexts) precisely to interrupt twenty-first-century cultural rhythms. Where the point of market-informed attractional worship often involves smoothing out more difficult points of doctrine for seekers to swallow, Emerging Church ministers often highlight difficult juxtapositions between orthodox expectations and secular-cultural mores (especially though not exclusively about commercial culture). Finally, the Emergent movement tends to adopt what it calls a "missional" orientation, emphasizing the expectations that Christians engage in social ministries as a form of evangelism, manifesting the Kingdom of God on Earth through direct assistance for the poor and the oppressed.

Yet for some, the Emerging Church represents just another form of surrender to secular-age tastes. Where seeker-sensitive services warp with the medium of worship to appeal to consumer mentalities, emerging churches alter the message of the gospel to fit MTD-friendly conceptions of a purely non-judgemental God.[129] Such critics point, for instance, to Rob Bell, pastor of one of the largest and most successful Emerging congregations, Mars Hill Bible Church in Grand Rapids, Michigan.[130] In his 2011 book *Love Wins,* Bell launches a biblically grounded yet unconventional argument criticizing predominant ideas of hell, specifically the notion of hell as a literal afterlife location defined by eternal torment for all non-Christians.[131] Though Bell's argument represented neither a departure for him nor a new position within Christendom, the book shocked a wide range of evangelicals. To his many critics, *Love Wins* exemplified the dangers inherent in the Emerging Church. By opening received doctrines (e.g., hell) to postmodern scrutiny and "re-imagining," Bell and other Emergent ministers abandon theological integrity in the name of worldview adaptation.

In practice, of course, evangelical ministers rarely stake out positions as extreme as Joel Osteen's or Rob Bell's. Conversations about church service design—the mediums, the messages, the audiences, the limits—regularly mix and match insights from and warnings about multiple philosophies of worship. As is the case with practically any area of evangelical outreach, few would discount altogether either the need to make the gospel understandable to unsaved people or the dangers of adulterating the message to appeal to the widest possible audience. The never-ending search to find the right balance between *efficacy* and *orthodoxy, evangelism* and *discipleship,* fuels constant innovations as well as constant criticisms between and within congregations. Like faith more generally, evangelical worship is diversifying, providing an ever-increasing range of options for believers. The extent to which evangelicalism generally can encompass such a range remains to be seen.

I return to questions of depth and substance in activist performances, and particularly to how the troubling notion of moralistic therapeutic deism might relate to left-progressive contexts, in my conclusion. For now, I would simply note that evangelicals' struggle between attraction and challenge in their worship services represents familiar ground for activist performers. Indeed, much of Western theater practice has been caught between the twin imperatives of *teaching* and *pleasing.* Given that some degree of pedagogy—perspectives to be gained, consciousnesses to be raised, complacencies to be challenged—by definition informs most activist endeavors, politically engaged theater can rarely present itself as fun evening of happy escapism. Part of the reason why so much activist performance involves preaching to the converted involves the fact that only the converted would consent to a performance where they know they'll be preached to. Efforts like those of Warren, Hybels, and Groeschel to re-imagine a church service as a space of enjoyment, an attractive invitation to outsiders for church life, prompt parallel lines of inquiry about left-progressive activist performance. Left-progressives offer a variety of confrontational direct action performances that strongly assert a clear resistance to or critique of a given authority. They likewise offer many "preaching to the converted" spaces where groups can recharge and reconnect without having to spend all of their time and energy engaging in Anti-Racism 101 or Intro to Feminism. The value of such performances is not in question here. But the attractional worship trend in evangelicalism does pose a compelling question: How many activist performances from the progressive left would pass the Reising's Starbucks test? That is, how open are the progressive left's activist performances to people who aren't already on the same page as the producers in terms of political ideology and/or in terms of familiarity with theatrical convention?

The danger of such attractional performances, like the danger of attractional church services, is that they might make the Truth or Idea they promulgate *too* attractive, too easy. To recall some of Ray Comfort's criticisms of Cru's "wonderful plan" approach, sometimes the affective thrill of a well-delivered or manipulative performance can substitute for an authentic encounter with or conversion to a way of life. To the challenge of this conundrum evangelicalism offers no certain answers. Evangelicals' ongoing conversation about substance versus attraction (or, à la McGavran, the attraction of strict substance), however, is one that nonevangelicals might benefit from.

CHAPTER 8

Change Is Possible

Exodus and the Opposite of Homosexuality

It is mid-June 2009, and I am sitting in an ancillary chapel of the huge Sunshine Community Church in Grand Rapids, Michigan. At the podium is Alan Chambers, president and public face of Exodus International,[1] the largest and oldest evangelical organization dedicated to helping homosexuals find healing (i.e., stop being gay). This day he leads a breakout session of "Love Won Out," a twice-yearly conference of speakers and workshops for conservative evangelical Christians interested in supporting or partaking of Exodus's ministry.[2] I chose his session, "Hope for Those Who Struggle," primarily to hear Chambers himself speak. For those participating in evangelical sexual orientation change efforts (SOCE), Chambers's biography is legend, repeated constantly in Exodus's publicity materials and self-help resources: an early childhood feeling odd and alienated, his youth spent drifting away from the church and his family, a time living as an openly gay man, a path back into God's embrace, and finally his current status as a happy non-gay who serves God full-time with a wife and two children. To people deeply conflicted about how their sexuality can co-exist with their faith, Chambers and other SOCE superstars represent templates of hope. If health, happiness, and wholeness were the destination, Chambers and Exodus know the directions.

The suggestion that evangelical "ex-gay" ministries like Exodus have anything to do with health or happiness invites controversy. Since no mainstream medical or mental health organization currently considers lesbian, gay, bisexual, or transgender (LGBT) identity as anything other than a normal and positive variation of human sexuality, the idea that such identities indicate sickness and need changing, repairing, or curing seems at best ignorant and at worst homophobic. Religious and secular LGBT-affirmative groups often characterize SOCE as a ploy of the political right to grant anti-gay agendas a veneer of compassion while furthering the marginalization of LGBT people.[3] Medical and mental health research consistently undercuts SOCE claims of efficacy, a conclusion echoed by a growing community of "ex-ex-gays" or "ex-gay survivors," who have stories of their own about the incompetence, hypocrisy, or even malignity of SOCE ministries.[4] In pop culture, SOCE and the people who use them appear more pathetic than malicious, for example, the "ex-gay" as comic stereotype: self-righteous, flamboyant, and doomed to succumb to his or her desires. In this light, the claims of Exodus and other SOCE seem little more than spiritual/political quackery, the snake oil of the deceitful swallowed by the desperate.

Listening to Chambers speak, though, I question the simplicity of such assessments. Surely, I think, snake oil salesmen would make their product sound more appealing. Chambers's talk focuses less on "hope" than on "hard truths." Speaking to a gathering of about seventy-five "strugglers" (and one clandestine, happily gay Methodist), Chambers stresses the need to approach any SOCE with "realistic expectations." While his life testifies to the redemptive power of God, for most people *change* and *healing* must mean something aside from his storybook ending of heterosexual marriage-with-2.5-children. Chambers is blunt: "There's no guarantee that you're going to find a wife or a husband. . . . There's no guarantee you will get to a place where you don't experience temptation." Even he, Chambers admits, does not live entirely free from temptation. I can feel the men and women around me deflate slightly as they absorb this. But, he assures them, he experiences his post-gay life as fully changed and fully worth the struggle. Change is possible, he insists, but you must let God decide what change means. The aim, in other words, cannot be heterosexual, nuclear family bliss; you must aim instead for Christ, for being right with God. "The opposite of homosexuality isn't heterosexuality," Chambers says, "It's *holiness*."

Thus far, I have investigated various different performances of evangelical conversion efforts, those aimed at converting unbelievers as well as those geared toward re-converting or strengthening the faithful. Turning my attention toward ex-gay ministries might at first seem like something of a detour into territory I have tried to avoid, namely, the treacherous terrain of partisan culture wars involving the political religious right. To be sure, culture-war battles about LGBT issues do involve activism and do aim at winning ideological converts to their cause; someone might, for example, strive to convince a voter to sign a petition calling for a referendum banning same-sex marriage or forbidding adoptions by same-sex couples. Yet my interest here relates to more personal and long-lasting interventions, namely, convincing people to commit (or re-commit) not merely to a momentary decision or vote but to a whole way of life, a worldview. From the moment I conceived of a study of evangelical outreach, I knew I could not explore how evangelicals spread and internalize their messages of whole-self transformation without talking about the practice sometimes known as *conversion therapy.* Ministries like Exodus engage in what might be the most ambitious—and therefore the most daunting—overtures of all of US evangelicalism. Even in Ray Comfort's Way of the Master, with its insistence upon the convert's profound sense of conviction and repentance as prerequisites for authentic conversion, the performative act of conversion gets collapsed into the singular moment of the encounter with the street evangelist. SOCE ministries also call on a profound repentance, a whole-being turn away from sin. But whereas Comfort expects repentance to come in a breakthrough moment of tearful confession in which the prospect renounces all sin *tout court,* SOCE ministries preach the necessity of a day-to-day, moment-to-moment discipline of turning away from one's most deeply felt desires. And this discipline, as Chambers counseled, knows no ending point. It is lifelong, a moment-by-moment performance of (re)orienting oneself—and especially one's sexuality—toward God.

In framing such daily discipline as performance, I stretch that elastic term in a different direction than I have thus far. Instead of using *performance* to name expressive enactments for an audience, I speak here of conscious habits of thought and action intended to alter or produce a reality: *performative acts.* As I will explain, and as several other critics have noted, SOCE ministries frame gender and sexuality in ways that parallel models propounded by queer theory, which is itself known for viewing gender and sexuality through performative lenses. Judith Butler famously proposes considering gender identity not as the natural radiation from a primordial core of maleness or femaleness (e.g., "Of course she acts like that; she's a woman") but as an artifact, a sense of genderedness built up as the side effect of countless conscious and unconscious performative acts of gender. One's masculinity depends not (only) upon genetics or physiology but (also) on how successfully one "acts like a man"—whatever that may mean in a particular time and place. Queer theorists have since applied Butler's performative model to a variety of identity axes, writing productively about performing race, class, nationality, dis/ability, age, sexual orientation, and religion.

Now, to be clear, Exodus ministers are not queer theorists; SOCE ministries assert (as queer theorists generally do not) an originary, normative standard of maleness, femaleness, and the sexual identities proper to both. Yet the kind of change Exodus proposes for lesbian and gay people (or, as they would prefer, "those who struggle with same-sex attractions") stems from the recognition that the originary model does not work for everyone. By and large, evangelical SOCE ministries teach that "same-sex-attracted" (SSA) people, through no fault of their own, experience "natural" desires at odds with what Nature (i.e., God) actually mandates. Just as the mortal world has departed from God's perfect, original pattern in Eden, so too do SSA people depart from the right model of sexuality and gender. And just as repentant Christians have to live out a life in tension with their sinful desires and in accordance to the divine model, so SSA people must live out their lives "acting like a Christian," faithfully hoping that their lifelong performance disciplines—and God's graceful intervention—manifest as change.

At the same time, Exodus and ministries like it have to perform their share of good old-fashioned outreach to various skeptical audiences. To those outside of evangelicalism, the notion of "ex-gay" ministries seems like a joke. SOCE ministries confront a sizable and growing community of "ex-ex-gays" or "ex-gay survivors," people who experienced unsuccessful or downright harmful engagements with SOCE therapies. Peterson Toscano, for example, spent seventeen years (and $30,000) in therapies like Love in Action, one of Exodus's affiliate ministries, doing his best to remake himself into the heterosexual man his faith and Love in Action preached that he had to be. After awakening from what he calls a "biblically-induced coma," Toscano rejected attempts at a "cure" and instead (and with a great deal of work) embraced a revised, LGBT-affirmative understanding of his Christianity. He eventually created a one-man show about his experience, *Doin' Time in the Homo No Mo Halfway House—How I Survived the Ex-Gay Movement,* and co-founded a website dedicated to helping SOCE veterans like him.[5]

As the multiple testimonials on Toscano's website and others like it demonstrate, Toscano's unsatisfactory experience with SOCE is hardly exceptional. Indeed, Exodus and other SOCE ministries have a continuing history of enduring high-profile defections and repudiations by former leaders and ministers, including Exodus co-founders like Michael Bussee and ex–Love in Action leader John Smid.[6] These firsthand accounts of ineffectuality (at best) and psychological abuse (at worst) only have fueled increasing skepticism from researchers and mental health professionals about the efficacy and even legality of SOCE. Finally, in US popular culture, "ex-gays" commonly serve as easy jokes on television shows (e.g., Neil Patrick Harris's guest spot as an ex-gay minister on *Will and Grace*) and movies (e.g., *But I'm a Cheerleader, Saved*). In such narratives, ex-gays are invariably homosexuals who either pretend to be straight or fool themselves into thinking they can be. Real-life versions of these narratives seem to play out when public figures—particularly on the right—claim to have been cured of same-sex attractions (often after having been caught or exposed in the midst of a same-sex tryst). Ted Haggard, formerly president of the National Association of Evangelicals, famously lost his ministry after being caught in (and admitting to) numerous dalliances with a male sex worker. Reappearing some months later on *Larry King Live,* Haggard's explanation of himself seems comically evasive. Asked if he's gay or bisexual or something else, Haggard answers, "That's a good question. . . . My first therapist said you are a heterosexual with homosexual attachments. . . . My current counselor says you're a heterosexual with complications. . . . I don't think the boxes work for me. I think I have . . . some processes in my life that just don't fit neatly into the boxes . . . And I know that I'm in a process. I am changing."[7] Haggard and others like him become fodder for late-night comedy monologues. My fascination with SOCE ministries begins with the realization of how exquisitely aware they are of their dubious reputation in non-evangelical culture and their status as abusive agents in many LGBT contexts.

Also of interest to me, however, is the delicate relationship SOCE ministries maintain with US evangelicalism more generally. As negative as SOCE ministries can seem from secular or LGBT-affirming perspectives, Exodus and other such entities come under regular fire from more stridently anti-gay forces within the evangelical church. Skeptical outsiders can often miss just how much work Exodus has to do convincing other, more conservative Christians of the right and wrong ways to witness to LGBT people. Of late, Alan Chambers has won attention and even the grudging admiration of at least a few of his critics not only for his gay-to-nongay biography but also for his part in reformatting of the evangelical ex-gay movement in the early twenty-first century. Over the last decade or so, he and other current SOCE leaders have tweaked the image and rhetoric of ministries aimed at treating or healing those who do not wish to be LGBT.

In this chapter, I argue that a close examination of present-day evangelical SOCE ministries—I focus particularly on Exodus—troubles the portrait of ex-gays as deluded or deluding. SOCE ministries like Exodus have lately made strides in modifying their relationship with conservative evangelicalism, justifying (to a degree) their work to the secular mental health establishment, and sharpening their understanding of what constitutes a change to sexual identity. As I explain below, homosexuality functions as a hot-button issue for most evangelicals, polarizing them not merely in terms of partisan culture wars but also in the contexts of disputes within evangelical communities. Kinnaman and Lyons note that a critical mass of non-evangelicals views Christianity as a fount of antigay bigotry. SOCE ministries often find themselves mediating between a secular public convinced that evangelicals hate gay people and a church convinced that taking anything other than a hard-line stance against homosexuality augurs apostasy and the decline of the church. In doing so, SOCE ministries complicate what *conversion* means.

A few caveats are in order here. First, a perfectly neutral term for the movements I study does not exist. While some spokespeople and organizations claim the "ex-gay" model proudly, others (including Chambers and, under his leadership, Exodus) resist the label, preferring "former homosexual" or "person struggling with same-sex desires." Other labels, such as "conversion therapy" or "reparative therapy," carry connotations I do not endorse (e.g., that LGBT identities need conversion) and/or refer to models of change that SOCE ministries do not universally espouse (e.g., that same-sex orientations emerge as malformations of the reparative drive). I settle, then, on the term "SOCE ministry," drawing the acronym SOCE (sexual orientation change efforts) from the American Psychological Association's recent report on such therapies, which I discuss later in this chapter. Since the SOCE umbrella potentially covers multiple divergent, unrelated, and unregulated practices past and present, I add the "ministry" designator to signal my focus on US-based organizations and individuals aligned with conservative evangelicalism. In general, these ministries blend off-the-beaten-path psychological (specifically psychoanalytic) theories and evangelical theology to position homosexuality as incompatible with mental and spiritual well-being.

Though most believe and would argue that living as a gay- or lesbian-identified person (i.e., not being celibate, embracing one's homosexuality as a positive and self-definitive quality) does have negative effects on mental and perhaps even physical health, they currently take spiritual outreach rather than medical intervention as their bailiwick. I exclude here—as do Exodus and most other present-day SOCE ministries—radical or physically coercive interventions (such as exorcisms) as well as gruesome medical aversion therapies from the past (e.g., electroshock, nausea pills, invasive surgery).

Mapping Out US Evangelicalism and Anti-Gay Attitudes

I triangulate Exodus and the current SOCE movement in relation to the range of attitudes about such issues within Christian theology, right-wing national politics, and internecine ecclesiastical struggles. From non-evangelical and/or LGBT-affirming perspectives, the range of evangelical attitudes toward homosexuality can seem quite narrow, beginning with WASP-ish, we-don't-discuss-such-things disapproval and terminating at "God Hates Fags." Within the generally non-affirming stance assumed by most evangelical groups, however, hides a great deal of internal dissention and discussion. Christian scripture castigates same-sex erotic behavior as sinful, yes, but exactly what this means to evangelicals varies. A good portion of secular-age evangelicalism recognizes, for instance, both that conservative takes on sexuality increasingly represent a minority view in US culture at large and that the church's public witness to lesbians and gays has often been repellent. At present, the status of LGBT people[8] figures as a flashpoint of major debates in Christian denominations generally and in evangelicalism especially. Present-day SOCE ministries are obliged not only to account for secular or LGBT-affirmative attitudes; they must also account for and engage this range of views while basing their approach in a view all their own. I pause, then, to map out a rough portrait of the evangelical landscape vis-à-vis homosexuality.

Evangelicalism in the main tends to disapprove of homosexual activity, taking its cue from the handful of verses scattered throughout the Hebrew and Christian Testaments that refer to (or seem to refer to) same-sex eroticism. Arguments asserting anti-homosexuality stances typically build their case on obvious passages like Leviticus 18: 22 and 20:13, in which God commands that Hebrew men should not to lie with a man as one lies with a woman, naming the act "detestable" (or, in the King

James, an "abomination") and calling for capital punishment of any transgressors. Buttressing this straightforward prohibition are a number of other verses and stories, particularly the tale of Sodom and Gomorrah in Genesis 18 and 19 as well as a parallel narrative in Judges 19. Both of these relate instances wherein an unruly mob of male citizens violate hospitality norms, demanding that a homeowner hand over his male guests so that the mob might rape them. Other passages feature the inclusion of words translated "homosexual" or "effeminate" in lists of sinful people (e.g., I Corinthians 6:9, I Timothy 1:9–10).[9] The most extended treatment of same-sex eroticism as such is in Romans, chapter 1, verses 24–28, in which Paul describes the state and fate of pagan humanity:

> Therefore God gave them over in the sinful desires of their hearts to sexual impurity for the degrading of their bodies with one another. They exchanged the truth about God for a lie, and worshiped and served created things rather than the Creator—who is forever praised. Amen. Because of this, God gave them over to shameful lusts. Even their women exchanged natural sexual relations for unnatural ones. In the same way the men also abandoned natural relations with women and were inflamed with lust for one another. Men committed shameful acts with other men, and received in themselves the due penalty for their error.

Evangelical positions on homosexuality begin—and for many evangelicals, end—with these verses.[10] As per biblicist hermeneutics, most evangelical interpretations of these verses tend to presume that disparate passages speak with a single, consistent voice about a selfsame phenomenon and that this phenomenon equates to present-day understandings of homosexuality/homosexuals. In this view, when Paul writes of men and women burning with lust for members of their same gender, he diagnoses the present condition of LGBT cultures. When God calls male-male intercourse an abomination, God explicitly means the sex acts of gay and bisexual men in all times and all places.

Despite this general consensus, evangelicals draw variant conclusions about same-sex behavior and those who engage it. At the extreme, intolerant end of the spectrum stand the more overtly fundamentalist representatives. Pastors like Steven Anderson, for example, conclude from scripture that homosexuals aren't merely sinful but *reprobate*—irredeemably damned.[11] For Anderson and those like him, the Romans passage in particular establishes homosexuality not merely as a sin that leads (as all sins do) to destruction. The people Paul speaks of in the passage first committed idolatry, Anderson insists, worshipping things rather than God. God, in response "gave them over to shameful lusts." Homosexuality, Anderson concludes, is the *punishment,* the sign that God has formally, finally abandoned these people, that they now lie beyond all hope of redemption. Anderson, who often speaks about the danger of "sodomites," summons a host of other verses, including a number of idiosyncratic readings of other texts, to argue further that homosexuals are malicious, murderous, God-hating cretins whom the government should execute (the same conclusion reached by Fred Phelps). Those who treat such dangerous vermin as human—this includes Christians who see lesbians and gay people simply as sinners in need of therapy or loving intervention—commit a grave sin themselves, akin to someone mollycoddling serial rapists.

At the opposite end of the evangelical spectrum stand groups such as Evangelicals Concerned, which adopt LGBT-affirmative stances based largely on alternative readings of the "clobber passages" commonly used, they feel, to denigrate LGBT people. In the main, such interpretations contest the notion that the Bible communicates anything like a present-day understanding of homosexuality or bisexuality as orientations. "There are no homosexuals in the Bible," asserts Evangelicals Concerned founder Ralph Blair. "Ruth and Naomi were not lesbians. David and Jonathan weren't gay. Neither were Jesus and John, the men of Sodom, cult prostitutes, slave boys and their masters, nor call boys and their customers."[12] Blair argues that Levitical laws, Genesis accounts of Sodom, and Pauline references to same-sex eroticism all designate culturally specific practices of pagan worship, inhospitality, or coercive sex—not the actions of consenting adults whose sexuality orients them toward members of their same sex. Within these interpretations, the Bible remains authoritative, even inerrant, but about the morality of two adult women living in lifelong, faithful sexual intimacy the scriptures are as silent as they are about the morality of astronauts.

Evangelicals Concerned and groups like it participate with a larger network of LGBT-affirming groups and sub-groups within Christianity generally. Practically every major denomination—Catholic, evangelical, and mainline—boasts some sub-group, official or otherwise, dedicated to providing a safe space for LGBT people within the denomination. In many cases particular congregations or ministers may formally or publically affiliate with that subgroup (e.g., "More Light" Presbyterians or

"Reconciling" United Methodists). Still other groups strive for a more ecumenical reach, often shaping themselves around welcoming LGBT Christians first and asserting theological or doctrinal specifics only later if at all. I discuss one such group, the Gay Christian Network, later in this chapter. More prominent is the Metropolitan Community Church, founded in 1968 by defrocked Pentecostal minister Troy Perry. Broadly Christian, the MCC primarily defines itself as LGBT-inclusive and dedicated to working toward issues of justice.[13] Local congregations (MCC polity operates congregationally rather than creedally or connectionally) often take on more biblicist stances than do the LGBT-affirming congregations of mainline denominations.[14]

On the whole, however, few evangelical groups formally endorse views as extreme as Anderson's, and LGBT-affirmative readings of scripture remain a distinct minority within evangelicalism. Insofar as any mainstream evangelical view exists, such a view would hew closely to basic "love the sinner/hate the sin" approach based not on the reprobate status of homosexual people but on the normative model of heterosexual marriage. This stance asserts that, in addition to forbidding homosexual relationships, the Bible actively propounds a normative model for sex and family set in Genesis: one man, one woman, monogamously.[15] Since homosexuality, like adultery or fornication, falls outside of this ideal, same-sex behavior constitutes sin, a perversion of God's plan. But it is not unforgivable or necessarily graver than other sins. Such a "pro-family" (pro-*heterosexual* family) stance informs the positions of prominent evangelical denominations such as the Southern Baptist Convention and the Assemblies of God as well as evangelical parachurch groups like Campus Crusade for Christ.

Political "religious right" organizations like Focus on the Family, the American Family Association, and the Family Research Council likewise present their views as pro-family, asserting an interpretation of scripture that presents valuing monogamous (ideally procreative, ideally husband-headed) heterosexual marriages as integral to orthodox Christianity. Within this interpretation, left-progressive stances about reproductive rights, abortion, LGBT civil status, sexually explicit expressions, and women's rights typically get framed as threatening the health or existence of biblical marriage. Within the constellation of interest groups advancing such views circulate smaller, more focused organizations specially aimed at combatting LGBT-affirmative cultural and political goals. Groups like Americans for Truth about Homosexuality (AFTAH) and the National Organization for Marriage (NOM) operate as specialist think-tanks for the religious right.[16] Such organizations serve as watchdogs and first responders to activist advancements on the progressive left around LGBT issues like anti-discrimination laws and same-sex marriage. Their stories, opinion pieces, and research get forwarded to and recirculated by larger, more general groups. These specialist organizations typically foster a picture of LGBT-affirmative groups as nefarious political operatives serving a faceless "homosexual agenda" that seeks to undermine the essential foundations of US culture, especially those espoused and preserved by pro-family, Bible-believing Christians.

Of late, many of the major sectors of the Christian right have seen fit to intensify the anti-gay/pro-family front of the US culture wars. A number of factors contribute to this reemphasis. During the culture wars of the 1980s and early 1990s, the anti-gay religious right could count on a sizable repository of popular antipathy or disgust toward LGBT practices. Times have changed. Mass media offers a growing number of popular and normalized representations of LGBT identities in television shows (e.g., *Ellen, Queer Eye for the Straight Guy, The L Word, Will and Grace, Modern Family*), movies (e.g., *Philadelphia, In and Out, Brokeback Mountain, The Kids Are Alright*), and on stage (e.g., *Angels in America Parts I and II, The Laramie Project, Rent*). Over the last two decades, the LGBT movement has also scored a number of legislative and legal victories over the last twenty years, such as overturning anti-sodomy laws, repealing "Don't Ask/Don't Tell," instituting same-sex marriages and civil unions in some states and cities, and establishing anti-discrimination protocols in various corporations and municipal districts. Public opinion appears to be shifting toward increased support for such initiatives. In 2011, for example, Gallup polls registered a majority of US citizens as favoring the legalization of same-sex marriages.[17] To be sure, anti-LGBT bias remains pervasive in many areas of public and private life; vehemently anti-gay political rhetoric continues to motivate certain subsets of the electorate. Nevertheless, and in general, it has become less acceptable to assert stalwartly anti-gay stances than it used to be.

Conservative evangelical groups at the center and the margins of partisan politics both interpret this large shift toward more tolerance for LGBT people as just one more piece of evidence about the worsening moral-religious state of the nation and the dimmer future for Bible-believing Christians. Keenly aware that overtly anti-gay attitudes are less popular than they used to be in mainstream mass culture, many religious right groups have adopted a defensive posture, recasting their disapproval of same-sex practices as a protected religious expression. In this narrative, anti-discrimination policies and hate-crime laws that include sexual orientation provisions have a de facto effect of chilling pro-family religious expression, essentially forcing pro-family evangelicals (for instance) to mute or hide their moral disapproval of a way of life they consider sinful and harmful. From this perspective, pro-tolerance advocates themselves exhibit a sharp intolerance toward (conservative) Christians. An LGBT anti-discrimination policy, for example, gets framed as promulgating a pro-gay ("anti-family" or "anti-marriage"), anti-Christian attitude. Debating the validity of such arguments falls beyond my present focus.[18] I renew Christian Smith's caveat about the folly of assuming that the strident rhetoric of national religious right pundits, politicians, and attack groups transparently express the views of individual evangelicals. It is not the case, for example, that every evangelical in the United States is as exercised about LGBT issues as an activist like Peter LaBarbera or Tony Perkins is. Indeed, part of the rationale for the persecution narrative involves implicating segments of the evangelical population who normally might not care (or care all that much) about LGBT issues.[19] By framing the issue as a polarized, us-or-them struggle between militant gay secularists and innocent, faithful Christians, organizations like the American Family Association appear desperate to make the issue more central to evangelicals than it otherwise might be.

For better or worse, SOCE ministries have played an integral role in these political maneuvers. Exodus, for example, has historically leaned heavily on James Dobson's right-wing group Focus on the Family for financial and logistical support and publicity. Organizations like Focus in turn use their support of SOCE ministries like Exodus in order to distinguish their stances from the heartless condemnation of people like Anderson or Phelps. Consider, for example, activist Peter LaBarbera's Americans for Truth about Homosexuality. LaBarbera has distinguished himself as perhaps the most vociferous critic of LGBT-affirmative movements within the mainstream religious right. His rhetoric transcends merely being "pro-family"; he is flatly anti-gay.[20] Yet, though he avers his belief that the homosexual movement presents a clear and present danger to Christian values, he bristles at the suggestion that he operates out of irrational bigotry or hatred of gay people. His biography on the AFTAH website insists that LaBarbera "does not fit the liberal caricature of angry 'homophobe'" due in part to his belief that "people [LGBT people] can leave the homosexual lifestyle." This belief, the bio asserts, sets him at odds with Fred Phelps, who questions whether homosexuals can "leave homosexuality behind" (mainly) by "becoming born-again Christians."[21] The AFTAH website provides links to a number of SOCE organizations.[22] AFTAH doesn't *hate* LGBT people, this logic goes; it wants the best for them—the "best," of course, being deliverance from the unhealthy/hell-bound lifestyle of homosexuality and gender confusion. In a time where openly wishing that LGBT people would perish (e.g., via blithe references to AIDS as just punishment for same-sex behavior) invites swift, widespread denunciations rather than silent approval, Exodus and other SOCE grant a minimal plausibility to right-wing and conservative-orthodox claims that they are pro-family and not homophobic, bigoted, or anti-gay.

The result of this long period of politicized, anti-gay rhetoric, suggest critics like Kinnaman and Lyons, is plain: people see evangelicalism's claim of loving all people as hogwash. "Hate the sin/love the sinner" simply failed as effective communication when uttered alongside declarations of AIDS as God's just punishment for gay people. Picking up on such internal critiques, SOCE ministries like Exodus have recently taken up the task of rehabilitating evangelicalism by reforming its interactions with the LGBT community. Returning to this summer's Love Won Out conference, I was surprised at how many of the speeches and support materials aim not at struggling gays and lesbians but at the evangelical mainstream.

Consider the conference's plenary session speeches before the entire assembly of six hundred. There, Joe Dallas, another SOCE superstar, blamed the church for alienating gay people, pointing to anti-gay rhetoric that fabricates lurid details of gay sex practice or to the evangelical failure to respond lovingly to the AIDS epidemic. Dallas urged conference-goers to repent of past antagonisms toward the LGBT community, realizing that most LGBT people have no "agenda" and live perfectly normal lives. Chambers, switching from hard truths for strugglers to hard truths for non-strugglers, listed a series of pro-family arguments and catchphrases that he wants churches to avoid, such as maintaining that homosexuality is a choice or repeating the "Adam and Eve, not Adam and Steve" line. Such sound bites, he warned, are offensive to the LGBT community; they fail to communicate the love that homosexuals need and that Christians are obligated to provide. Echoing arguments from his 2006 *God's Grace and the Homosexual Next Door,* Chambers went on to shatter the common perception of homosexuality as somehow worse than other sins. Non-evangelicals are correct, Chambers said, in calling evangelicals on their hypocritical focus on homosexuality. Nancy Heche, mother of bisexual movie star Anne Heche, spoke of the need for parents to let go of the fantasy that they can control the lives of their children, urging them to demonstrate as much love as they are able while respecting their children's autonomy.

Of course, at the conference and in their printed materials, Exodus rejects efforts to condone homosexuality or reconcile it with biblical teaching; other breakout sessions included tips on combating gay-affirmative theology or resisting discourses of LGBT normalization in public schools. Only the strictest fundamentalist would confuse Exodus with a pro-LGBT movement. Nevertheless, the new SOCE ministries appear to have taken on the role of evangelical conscience, reminding evangelicals that, if the world is to take seriously Christians' claims of loving all people, they must moderate how they imagine and interact with the LGBT community. Without minimizing the overlap between partisan religious right organizations and evangelical churches, then, I want once again to assert a heuristic distinction between *political organizations* on the one hand and *evangelical ministries* (churches and parachurch organizations) on the other. Participating in an AFA-sponsored protest outside of the capitol to urge legislators to vote against a bill legalizing same-sex marriage could certainly qualify as a kind of evangelical activism. But for most evangelicals such a protest would be exceptional, something done apart from the core activities of churchgoing, prayer, Bible-reading, and outreach. In this project, I am most interested in the latter sort of activities as activist gestures, witnesses to a lost world about a more excellent way of life. That evangelical SOCE ministries have and continue to collaborate with partisan organizations is indisputable. SOCE ministries regularly provide a loving-ministerial alibi for flagrantly anti-gay rhetoric and actions. Nevertheless, framing SOCE ministries purely or primarily as patsies of the anti-gay religious ignores the fact that these understand themselves not—or not primarily—as right-wing agents aimed at effecting political changes but first and foremost as gospel ministries aimed at changing people.

This is a crucial distinction because most of the people directly involved with evangelical SOCE ministries, as people undergoing treatment, as people giving treatment, or (as is often the case) as both engage SOCE out of a sense of personal calling rather than partisanship. Understanding this sense of calling—or, rather, a sense of crisis or tension—from the perspective of evangelical faith as such rather than faith as a religious-right façade likewise spotlights the centrality of LGBT issues within organized US Christianity today. Multiple Christian churches and denominations across the ecclesiastical spectrum are enduring intense dissention, even schisms, over the status of LGBT people in the church. Such disagreements unfold most visibly in the mainline denominations.

The Episcopal Church in the United States, for example, famously strained its ties to the global Anglican Communion by ordaining an openly gay and non-celibate bishop, Gene Robinson. For many conservative Episcopal congregations in the United States, congregations that identify in many ways with evangelical theology, this ordination signaled a breaking point. Some of these congregations disaffiliated with the US Episcopal Church to form the Anglican Church in North America (ACNA). Similar breakaway denominations (or sub-denominations) have formed in the evangelical-leaning segments of Presbyterian and Lutheran churches in reaction to shifts in denominational policy such as allowing celebration of same-sex unions in their churches and by their clergy, the ordination of openly LGBT ministers, and the endorsement of antidiscrimination measures.[23]

Such LGBT-affirmative actions function as the presenting conditions, straws that break camel backs, for such splinter congregants who decide to secede. Although LGBT-related debates as such entangle many congregants, the fault lines of such disagreements engage deeper and older tectonic struggles over scriptural hermeneutics and church authority within the denominations. In the eyes of many evangelicals, taking a moderate stance toward LGBT issues bespeaks a divorce from strict, faithful biblicism. That is, reconciling scriptural prohibitions on same-sex eroticism with LGBT identities usually (though not always) requires some degree of conscious attenuation of a purely "plain sense" reading of verses. From the perspective of many conservative churchgoers, any such modification to this biblicist stance is objectionable. When the denomination decides, for example, to ordain women as clergy or allow a diversity of opinions regarding universal origins, many conservatives see their church as taking treacherous steps down a slippery slope to heresy. From this perspective, a denomination that opens its doctrinal doors to female clergy or evolutionary accounts of life's origins (as most mainline churches have done) has already been drifting in the wrong direction, scripturally.[24] For the church to decide to elevate a gay man to the episcopacy crosses a final line. The underlying issue for many mainline churches therefore has as much to do with the question of how much internal disagreement about scripture the church can withstand, how much heterodoxy a church can tolerate, as it does with the place of LGBT people per se.

Evangelical churches face a conundrum similar to that of the mainline churches. The congregational (i.e., autonomous, congregation-by-congregation decision-making) setup of many evangelical churches shields them from the schismatic conflicts of the large mainline denominations. Yet they, too, struggle with where and how strictly they should establish lines between allowable and anathema, welcoming and orthodox. In US Christianity, then, "the gay issue" is almost never merely about LGBT people or LGBT issues; it instead concerns core identity issues about what it means to be a Christian in the first place. Ostensibly Christianity is a matter of having committed one's life to Christ and living out that commitment in witness to the world. But—and this is the central question—can one be said to be living faithfully if one either discounts significant portions of scripture or tolerates those who do so?

Such dissention regarding LGBT issues is not merely an ecclesiastical issue; for evangelicals who experience same-sex attractions, it is a personal one. Quite apart from the private-public struggles of closeted right-wing political activists, evangelicals who subscribe to the pro-family, heterosexuals-only interpretation of scripture face a desperate conundrum of personal identity definition. Exodus spokesperson and SOCE counselor (as well as former homosexual) Joe Dallas characterizes the typical "struggler" who approaches SOCE ministries for help.[25] First, he writes, those who seek out SOCE ministries tend to identify as born-again Christians. This is their primary identity, the self-understanding that matters most to them. Second, they wrestle with a great deal of confusion, frustration, and even anger that their intensive, sincere prayers for deliverance from their same-sex attractions have not so far yielded satisfactory results. Finally, strugglers typically resist identifying as "gay." This is a subtle but critical point. In common parlance, *gay* functions as a simple adjective describing one whose primary attractions are toward those of the same sex. The term describes inner predisposition; if you are primarily or exclusively attracted to members of your same sex, you are gay—full stop. One can be gay (or lesbian) without ever literally engaging in homosexual encounters, and one is definitively gay/lesbian (or at least bisexual) for as long as same-sex attractions persist.

But for strugglers in SOCE ministries, *gay* connotes not a neutral description of sexuality but a positive, affirming embrace of homosexuality as self-definition. Since strugglers' understanding of themselves as evangelical requires that they identify first and foremost with the divine (heterosexual) ideal, they reject calling themselves gay, regardless of the direction of their attractions. They see the term, Dallas explains, as "a positive way of describing something they don't feel positive about."

He continues, "Instead, they identify themselves primarily as Christians, but they feel largely misunderstood by the church, which (they feel), sees them as either the worst or the weirdest of sinners."[26] For people participating in ex-gay ministries, then, the key issue is the disjunction between their evangelical (biblicist) faith and their self-understanding as individuals attracted to members of the same gender.

Exodus and other SOCE ministries thus struggle within a trifold tension, defining themselves in simultaneous relationship to political pressure from the pro-family religious right, anxiety about maintaining evangelical orthodoxy (however one might define it), and Christian imperatives to provide sensitive, culturally engaged evangelical ministry to the lost. Evidence suggests that Exodus has grown increasingly uncomfortable with serving as the (mostly silent, mostly background) character witness for the conservative Christian forces of the culture wars. Many Exodus-affiliated ministers have realized that the interventions they actually offer require a much more involved, nuanced appreciation of the issues than most right-wing political entities allow. Anti-gay rhetoric from the religious right regularly touts stories of former homosexuals who have overcome with Christ—with the strong implication that anyone could if only they cared to. As the session for "strugglers" I related earlier demonstrates, however, Exodus and other SOCE ministries are less sanguine—or perhaps less dismissive—about the challenges of living a life of non-gay holiness.

Ex-Gay Evangelism

Ex-gay evangelism began in the early 1970s, conceived not as a tool of the religious right (which at the time did not exist as such) but as a means of responding to the situation of gay and lesbian evangelicals who experienced a conflict between their sexuality and their faith. Such outreach to counter-cultural movements was a signature of the so-called Jesus movement, a largely evangelical trend toward nondenominational congregations and out-of-the-ordinary ministry projects. Moved by the struggle of Christians with same-sex attractions (as well as the struggles of those people's families), evangelicals like Kent Philpott and Frank Worthen saw an opportunity for ministry and began counseling them. In 1973, Worthen, Philpott, and Mike Riley began a group called Love in Action in California.[27] Similar ministries emerged soon after in other locations, such as the EX-gay Intervention Team (EXIT) and Ex-Active-

Gay-Liberated-Eternally (EAGLE). In 1976 these and other ministry efforts united to form Exodus International, intended as an umbrella organization to help organize and network disparate ministries.

At first these ministries lacked much in the way of a unified, specific approach to homosexuality. Predominant models of Christian counseling in the 1970s-era evangelical church were heavily influenced by an anti-psychiatry stance and an emphasis on the Bible as the only proper basis for diagnosis and treatment. In a series of influential books, for instance, evangelical minister Jay E. Adams launched a broad critique of secular psychotherapy and counseling as operating from an anti-Christian world-view that prioritized self-actualization instead of addressing the problem of sin. Adams proposed an alternative he called "nouthetic counseling" (from the Greek verb *noutheteo,* meaning *admonish, instruct,* or *correct*).[28] Briefly, Adams posits that, apart from organic disorders of the brain, much of what secular psychiatry mislabels as mental illness is in fact the manifestation of habitual sin. Counseling, therefore, should be viewed as a form of ministry, and Christian pastors abandon their rightful duties when they surrender counseling to secular authorities.

Lambasted by many within Christian counseling circles for his misconceptions about psychology, Adams's model nevertheless won a wide following among biblicist evangelicals, and adherents to his views persist (with some modifications) to this day.[29] In nouthetic models, a Christian minister approaches behavioral and psychiatric problems primarily as manifestations of sin (one's personal sin and/or the original sin of the Adamic Fall). Bulimia, for example, might be treated as a form of idolatry, lust, or pride. The counselor uses scripture to confront clients (lovingly) with the biblical reality of their guilt and the hope Christ offers for sanctification and healing. In his 1973 *Christian Counselor's Manual,* Adams specifically addresses the problem of counseling "the homosexual." Flatly rejecting the notion of homosexuality as an intrinsic or genetic predisposition, Adams insists on clarifying to clients that their homosexuality is a sin.[30] Such a confrontation, Adams argues, actually offers hope. Rather than being an intrinsic attribute of self, a permanent reality, homosexuality-as-sin enables clients to deal with their desires and actions as any Christian deals with persistent habits of self-indulgent sin.

For the nascent SOCE ministries, biblical counseling models dictated a prayer-and-Bible-study approach. Soon after Exodus's founding, however, many SOCE ministries were finding such strategies inadequate. Viewing homosexuality purely as a sin (or as evidence of sin) and praying for an authentic Christian conversion and relationship with Christ to initiate healing largely proved unsatisfactory. Men and women still struggled with same-sex attractions, even after numerous admonishments, sincere commitments, and fervent prayers for healing.[31] Such failures were especially painful for strugglers, especially since from biblical counseling and nouthetic perspectives the lack of success implied terminal problems with a struggler's faith and religious identity. Such a conclusion only deepened strugglers' frustration and despair, which led many early adherents to drop out.

In 1979, Exodus suffered the first of what would be many high-profile defections. Michael Bussee, former head of EXIT and an Exodus cofounder, publically left the organization with another Exodus minister, Gary Cooper, after he and Cooper fell in love with each other. Bussee would go on to become (and remain) one of Exodus's strongest critics.[32] In order to present itself as a viable response for struggling believers and their families, Exodus and related ministries needed something firmer than just prayerful wishing; they needed scientific—or at least a passably science-ish—underpinning. Yet by the early 1980s the leading mental health organizations had established that homosexuality was not in and of itself a mental disorder in need of treatment. Looking beyond the mainstream authorities, ex-gay ministries found the work of Elizabeth Moberly, a British psychoanalyst who in 1983 published *Homosexuality: A New Christian Ethic.*[33]

In that slim volume, Moberly embraces psychoanalytic insights and bypasses a traditional focus on the *act* of same-sex eroticism to focus on the *condition* of same-sex orientation. This she frames as a kind of psychosexual immaturity caused by a deficit in socialization. In normal human development, argues Moberly, a child will detach from their opposite-sex parent and receive appropriate same-sex (platonic) affection from their same-sex parent. In homosexuals, this process somehow goes awry (too much opposite-sex attachments; too little or disruptive same-sex attachments). Homosexuals fail to bond with—and receive appropriate love-affection from—their same-sex parent. Instead they become ambivalent toward their own sex, estranged from same-sex peers through a process Moberly terms "defensive detachment."[34] Eventually, reasons Moberly, homosexuals seek sexual connections with members of their same gender in order to fulfill their still-unmet needs for same-sex affection. Same-sex attraction is thus a reparative drive, an attempt to restore or repair relational needs that go awry in early development. (It is from this theory that some SOCE ministries derive the phrase "reparative therapy"; the phrase does not refer to "repairing" homosexuality itself.)

Inevitably, however, the struggler's tactic fails, leading to serial, empty sex encounters and fundamentally flawed same-sex relations.

Wayne Besen, a prominent critic of SOCE, castigates Moberly as rehashing an old-hat, blame-the-parents pseudo-psychoanalysis.[35] While it is true that much of the theory that Moberly uses had been available for a while, her presentation of that theory and her combining it with elements of Christian ethics proved novel and, for the nascent ex-gay movement, extremely productive. Especially in light of the confront-and-be-converted tone of many contemporary Christian counseling schemes, Moberly's theories created space to be both compassionate toward homosexuals and intolerant of homosexuality. Or, to put it bluntly (and in terms Exodus, at least, might dispute), she provides a systematic model for loving the sinner while hating the sin. Moberly emphasizes, for instance, that same-sex attraction is a condition experienced by the innocent, not a choice selected by the immoral. Moreover, she argues that this condition operates as a logical, understandable response to a failure to have common human needs met.[36] Harsh disapproval—anti-gay rhetoric—can thus exacerbate the problem rather than help it. Furthermore, Moberly dismisses as ineffective commonsense "cures" such as simple celibacy or "a good hetero experience."[37] Neither of these, in her view, addresses the underlying cause—an inability to relate to same-sex peers appropriately. Finally, Moberly's theory provides a matrix for addressing the tension LGBT people can feel between their desires and their faith. Indeed, Moberly suggests that, for gay men at least, Christ himself can be the ultimate same-sex-but-nonerotic partner. Developing a relationship with Christ thus furthers a movement away from homosexuality.[38]

Hopefully it goes without saying that that I do not endorse Moberly's schema. Its heterocentrism, outdated theorization, and above all lack of supporting evidence render it laughably inadequate by mainstream mental health standards. At the same time, though, Moberly's model urges a step away from viewing homosexuality as reprobation or willful sin. She makes homosexuals into a kind of person—a neighbor in need of healing and appropriate love—rather than a kind of creature in need of extermination or censure. And, regardless of her argument's flaws, it remains meaningful to many in the ex-gay movement. Tanya Erzen points out that Moberly's theories (as refined through SOCE writers like Joseph Nicolosi, Richard Cohen, Joe Dallas, Anita Worthen, and others) underlie most evangelical SOCE ministries today.[39]

In the decades subsequent to Moberly's publication, a number of ex-gay ministries and organizations have sprung up within and without evangelical churches, most basing their approach on a combination of Christian restoration/healing and a Moberly-esque model of homosexual attraction as a flawed-but-unchosen response to childhood difficulties in gender identification. Most of these ministries operated (or continue to operate) locally, being homegrown outreach programs based in local churches. Some are denominationally specific SOCE ministries with semi-standardized responses and support structures, like Courage (Roman Catholic) or Evergreen (Latter-Day Saints). Other SOCE promote specific programs or curricula and have a more widespread reach, such as Homosexuals Anonymous, Love in Action, the International Healing Foundation, and Living Waters (a division of Desert Stream Ministries).

Alongside these religious SOCE ministries, psychologist Joseph Nicolosi founded the National Association for the Research and Therapy of Homosexuality (NARTH), fashioning the group as a scientific, ostensibly non-religious hub for legitimate (i.e., secular, peer-reviewed, non-anecdotal) research on SOCE. By design, Exodus, International operates as an umbrella entity for specifically evangelical SOCE ministries, though it has in the past maintained links to NARTH resources. Exodus works as spokesperson, clearinghouse, and referral agency, hosting regional and later national and international conferences at which SOCE ministries, strugglers, and other interested parties can network. Exodus does not, however, exert any direct regulative control over member ministries. Characterizing any single ministerial/therapeutic approach as typical is therefore necessarily problematic. Even excepting coercive or aversion-based approaches, a wide range of models exist, each specific to a particular ministry and not all of which operate with Exodus's imprimatur.

While significant differences in duration, intensity, philosophy, and structure make it difficult to generalize about these SOCE ministries, a few commonalities seem apposite. Just about every SOCE, for example, tends to distinguish between attractions, behaviors, and identities, asserting that the former two—attractions and orientations—exist largely outside the realm of conscious control. Discussions within and between SOCE ministries about the etiology of same-sex attractions mirror nature/nurture and even essentialist/constructivist debates about sexuality and gender beyond evangelicalism. Though Exodus generally resists the notion of a genetic basis for sexuality, Chambers contends that conversations about origins are ultimately moot. One can recognize, he argues, genetic predispositions toward a variety of negative behaviors like alcoholism, overeating, or narcissism without ever once thinking that the innate or unchosen status of such predispositions renders them harmless or praiseworthy.[40] Attractions are unchosen, but behaviors and identities are matters more under conscious control.

In his survey of Christian SOCE ministries assembled for the benefit of evangelical ministers, psychologist Sam R. Williams (himself a conservative evangelical) helpfully boils down SOCE philosophies of sexuality into a two-step process: identity *crisis* and identity *attribution*.[41] Crisis comes when evangelical Christians perceive themselves as experiencing same-sex attractions, or even a same-sex orientation. Feelings of guilt, self-hatred, confusion, and anger result from the conflict between one's identity as a Christian and one's deeply felt, unchosen, and (within the evangelical worldview) un-Christian desires. These are the "strugglers" Dallas refers to in his characterization of SOCE clients. They are, in the parlance of SOCE, *ego-dystonic* (as opposed to *ego-syntonic*) regarding their sexuality.[42] Eventually, however, crisis stabilizes as the struggler transitions into identity attribution, in which the struggler settles on a self-understanding—Williams describes this as a "script" or "narrative" of self—that incorporates the tension between self-perception and emotional/erotic experience.

For many, the script of choice is what Williams (following Mark Yarhouse) calls the Gay Explanatory Framework (GEF).[43] In GEF, strugglers reinterpret same-sex attractions/orientations as natural, definitive, and positive. They go from being Christians who experience problematic same-sex attractions to being gay Christians—or, shedding their religious identification altogether, simply gay/lesbian people. Given that most evangelical SOCE see "gay Christian" as at least problematic if not altogether oxymoronic, SOCE ministries strive to provide strugglers with an alternative script, what Williams dubs the "Christian Explanatory Framework" (CEF).[44] Crucially, the CEF does not eliminate same-sex attractions. It merely resituates them into a grander context of Christian living within a fallen world. Same-sex attractions figure here as persistent temptations, tendencies of thought and behavior that it is a Christian's duty to resist. SOCE ministries often borrow the language of alcoholism, describing same-sex attractions as a kind of addiction to spiritually harmful (though carnally fulfilling) behaviors. They are not consciously chosen, they are not consciously or easily changeable, but neither are they destiny. They need not define the person experiencing them. SOCE ministries aim, then, at providing strugglers with a mode of self-definition within a (conservative, often evangelical) Christian Explanatory Framework.

The process for transitioning a struggler from crisis to Christian Explanatory Framework tends to follow a similar pattern across evangelical SOCE.[45] First, the person must reconcile with Christ, finding and receiving love from a welcoming body of Christian worshippers while turning from indulging in same-sex activities. Second, the person must identify and address the spiritual or mental deficit that creates the same-sex attraction in the first place. Depending upon the specific SOCE ministry, this process may involve developing the ability to bond platonically with people of the same sex, learning to take on the gender-normative behaviors attributed to one's biological sex, and/or confronting and re-framing childhood traumas that caused the initial defensive detachment. Finally, and only after the first two goals are met, clients may begin exploring appropriate romantic relationships with the opposite sex, again in accordance with evangelical understandings of God's design for the heterosexual family.

Most long-term SOCE ministries pursue these goals through step-by-step, comprehensive programs that blend individual or group counseling, spiritual interventions, and behavior modification within a structure of peer accountability. In his massive *Complete Christian Guide to Understanding Homosexuality* (co-edited with Nancy Heche), Joe Dallas advocates what he calls the ROUTE model, an acronym for Repenting, Ordering, Understanding, Training, and Enduring. First, strugglers must repent from sinful behavior patterns, cutting off all same-sex activities and indulgences, from sexual encounters with others to masturbatory fantasizing.[46] Next is ordering one's life to enhance "discipline and motivation," establishing behavior and thought patterns that put an evangelical Christian identity and lifestyle at the center of day-to-day existence.[47] Understanding involves identifying the emotional and psychological needs underlying SSA, discovering how one's past can establish patterns of pain or need that homosexual activity attempts to redress.[48] Dallas notes that the key here is less about identifying a singular origin of homosexual attractions and more about equipping oneself to recognize these attractions as understandable-but-flawed attempts to repair childhood traumas. With these recognitions comes the ability to train oneself to notice and identify triggers for same-sex indulgences, avoiding situations that tempt the struggler to stray.[49] Finally, and after a great deal of work, strugglers learn to endure by developing a sense of contentment and pride in one's progress in order to stave off relapse.[50]

In his popular Living Waters program (based heavily on his workbook *Pursuing Sexual Wholeness*), Andrew Comiskey offers a roughly analogous plan that combines teaching Bible-based gender roles, exploring the (Moberly-ish) etiologies of same-sex attraction, and promoting strategies to turn the self away from same-sex erotic fixations.[51] More elaborate programs, such as Love in Action, feature residential living situations in which participants agree to follow strict behavioral codes and minutely planned daily schedules.[52]

Determining how to effect this redefinition differs from ministry to ministry (or therapist to therapist). Some, following Moberly closely, strive to seek out, identify, and work through the childhood issues of defensive detachment or abuse that underlie same-sex orientations. Nicolosi is particularly known for tracing male homosexuality to negative issues between father and son. Erzen, whose ethnography focuses on male clients in a residential facility, notes how participants "proudly understood themselves as the weary survivors of battles with some kind of addiction, abuse, or syndrome" that contributed to their present struggles with same-sex attraction.[53] Describing his experience with SOCE ministries (particularly Love in Action), Peterson Toscano relates how he was led to see his same-sex attractions as a direct result of sexual abuse he suffered as a child.[54] None of these approaches suggests that knowing the root cause of one's SSA magically causes the SSA to cease. Instead, these therapies provide a lens through which to view one's desires, measuring them as maladaptive reactions to an original wound or trauma.

Other organizations take a more embodied approach to rehashing SSA-causing childhood traumas. Journalist Tim Cox, for example, went undercover for a "Journey into Manhood" weekend, a program offered by an organization called People Can Change (PCC).[55] Founded by Rich Wyler in 2000, PCC focuses on how gay men suffer from a "father wound" that inhibits their ability to relate normally (i.e., non-erotically) to other men. The Journey into Manhood program takes place at a wooded campground. For $695, participants (all men) engage in a series of lectures, exercises, and ritual activities that focus on restoring their authentic, masculine selves. Cox, a straight man who had long ago abandoned his Mormon faith, relates his experiences at the camp with a mixture of incredulity and compassion. Well-versed in SOCE philosophies, he registers surprise at finding a program about reasserting manhood to be full of such (literally) touchy-feely events as "holding therapy." In that exercise, participants physically embrace each other in a series of ostensibly supportive-but-non-erotic positions (Cox relates sensing that the person holding him was sexually aroused).[56] Another activity involved participants ritually confessing to each other the ways they had hurt others (especially wives) through their same-sex behaviors. Later, the camp guides led a session of psychodrama in which participants were urged to think of and then stage a memory of being hurt, rejected, or ignored by their parents. In a maneuver that theater scholars may recognize as an echo of Augusto Boal's Forum Theater exercise, participants are then led to intervene into their restaged memories to "take control" and "change the memory." Cox relates this example:

> When Charles, a young evangelical minister from Oregon, recreated the day his father beat his mother because she wanted to buy Charles designer jeans, the Guide told Charles that to take control of his memory he had to remove his abusive father. What ensued was a four-minute wrestling match, where Charles struggled to drag the Guide out the cabin and slam the door shut.[57]

Despite his skepticism at the efficacy of these sorts of activities, Cox notes that several of his fellow participants were deeply moved by the program. For some of the men, the weekend represented the first time that they had ever been able to admit to other people that they felt same-sex attractions. Simply naming their struggle before a sympathetic audience proved a cathartic experience, a way to put into words—or even to *perform* and *re-perform*—a crisis of self that in their everyday lives had to go unuttered.

Of course, evangelicals fold a great deal of Bible study and spiritual work into these mental and psychological investigations. Most evangelical SOCE include a thorough indoctrination into evangelical gender relations. Wolkomir relates group therapy sessions focusing on Bible study in which participants revisit biblical passages on same-sex behavior and gender norms.[58] Such Bible lessons, however, do not merely reiterate scriptural prohibitions against homosexuality. In their published works and public lectures, Chambers and other Exodus leaders spend a surprising amount of time injecting nuance into the traditional readings of anti-homosexuality "clobber passages." True, Chambers admits, the Bible condemns same-sex behavior as an abomination, but that same Hebrew word rendered *abomination* (*toeva*) appears in other biblical contexts unrelated to same-sex behavior. Chambers points to Proverbs 6:16–19, for instance, which labels as *toeva* "haughty eyes, a lying tongue, hands that shed innocent blood . . . and a man who stirs up dissension among brothers."[59] Homosexual behavior is a sin, Chambers agrees, but it is not uniquely awful in the eyes of God, and the evangelical church errs in presenting to the world the impression that homosexuality is the vilest of all possible sins.

Such nuance performs two theological actions at once, distancing Exodus and other SOCE from both LGBT-affirming and fundamentalist positions on homosexuality. Exodus has multiple, well-developed responses to "pro-gay" theology, criticizing it for what they consider a sacrifice of biblical faithfulness at the altar of self. Yet they also speak out against fundamentalist readings that label lesbians and gays as irredeemably damned or reprobate. Strugglers can too easily absorb from the public witness of the church a message that gay people are public enemy number one for Christians. Such "anti-gay" positions, contends Exodus minister Scott Davis, actually have much in common with "pro-gay" theologies. "The error of hatred and the error of acceptance boil down to the same mistaken belief—that the gospel doesn't apply to homosexuals," Davis writes. "Both exclude homosexuals from the gospel by claiming that change is either not possible or not desirable."[60] Against the intensely anti-gay positions of Fred Phelps, evangelical SOCE ministries ubiquitously cite I Corinthians 6:11, a verse directly after one of the major "clobber passages" that lists men who engage in same-sex behavior as "wrongdoers" who "will not inherit the kingdom of God." The very next verse, argue SOCE ministers, is key: "And that is what some of you [i.e., the author's intended audience] were. But you were washed, you were sanctified, you were justified in the name of the Lord Jesus Christ and by the Spirit of our God." This verse above all, they argue, proves that strugglers are beloved of God and that they, like any Christian, can claim the promise of redemption and transformation in Christ.

To be sure, none of these programs seems particularly pleasant from the perspective of someone who does not share their beliefs, such as that homosexuality per se is immoral and unhealthy. From an LGBT-affirmative perspective—a perspective I share—SOCE ministries wrongly apply pathologization narratives to an integral, properly ethically neutral aspect of self. Though their take on same-sex attraction is not as straightforwardly condemnatory as that of Adams's nouthetic counseling models, Exodus ministries still frame sexual attractions as a form of addictive behavior (mental and physical), injecting toxic doses of fear, shame, and stress into the lives of especially vulnerable people. Furthermore, while again less extreme than nouthetic models, Moberly-based SOCE still function within and perpetuate a closed system of self-loathing, where one's same-sex attractions function as a barrier to one's Christian faith and identity. This system in turn fuels larger initiatives to demonize and marginalize LGBT people. The narratives of "ex-gay survivors" attest to people's wrenching struggles with the internalized guilt that SOCE programs can prolong. Understandably, many of these "ex-ex-gays" look back on the energy, time, money, and heartache they expended in such programs as evidence of the damage that SOCE ministries can inflict. And even these objections fail to address darker issues of outright sexual and physical abuse that can occur in these unregulated, unsupervised ministries.

Nevertheless, it would be inaccurate to portray these programs as psychological horror shows of *Clockwork Orange*–style brainwashing. It is not the case that out-and-proud LGBT adults get dragged into therapy and "corrected" to emerge as lobotomized Stepford Straights.[61] As I have suggested, the processes involved in any of these ministries simply require too much individual effort (and money) to succeed without the willing participation of those involved. Today, many of these ministries specifically stress that they do not accept anyone who does not want, fully and of their own accord, to participate.[62] Mainstream evangelical SOCE ministries in the United States, then, do not promote themselves as mandatory treatment regimes to which all LGBT-identified people ought to be subjected. Nor are results as quick or as certain as some sci-fi heterosexualizing machine, even though something like that describes what many strugglers and their families ardently wish for.

APA and the Question of Efficacy

In the mid-1970s, after some controversy, the American Psychological Association (APA) voted to declassify homosexuality as a mental disorder, echoing earlier action by the American Psychiatric Association to remove *homosexuality* from the *Diagnostic and Statistical Manual of Mental Disorders* (*DSM*).[63] Thus, by the time SOCE ministries began appropriating psychological techniques in the early 1980s, the psychological and psychiatric mainstream had ceased to view homosexuality as pathological. Funded research on SOCE largely dried up, fostering an unregulated, marginalized network of SOCE researchers and therapists (both credentialed and otherwise), a situation that remains fairly standard today. Exodus, for example, does not itself provide or enforce standardized therapy but acts as a clearinghouse and figurehead for SOCE ministries who may affiliate with Exodus. "Exodus isn't Starbucks," Chambers explained in a recent public roundtable.[64] The main organization merely connects individuals to local affiliates, making little or no guarantees as to the type or quality of therapy offered.

This lack of regulation in part reflects the fact that no research that meets professional standards has proven that SOCE actually succeed at altering same-sex orientations. Individual ministries often tout success rates, but as none of them perform long-term tracking studies of their clients, the validity and longevity of such "successes" are doubtful at best. In place of solid research, SOCE rely heavily on anecdotes, particularly the evangelical performance genre of the "testimony," in which a convert narrates his or her life prior to, during, and after a conversion event for an audience of the faithful (see chapter three). These narratives follow the established conventions for proselytizing testimonies: a before-my-change, point-of-change, and after-my-change narrative. The Exodus conference, for example, featured several quasi-theatrical biographical testimonies by Exodus and Focus on the Family speakers (complete with slide displays of photos illustrating the narrator's life), all of which echoed Chambers's conversion narrative. They begin with an innocent (and often churchgoing) childhood marred by an instance of abuse or parental alienation. Then comes the awakening of same-sex attractions and the crisis of choice between gay-affirmative and Bible-believing life paths. Most speakers I heard confessed to living "the gay lifestyle" (or "the lesbian lifestyle"), sometimes in combination with drug or alcohol abuse. Each of them, however, eventually encounters a turning point—often by way of a faithful Christian friend or family member—in which they realize clearly and fully that they are called to deny themselves in favor of the way of Christ.

Here a connection with Exodus or some affiliated SOCE ministry enters the story. The "after" aspect of the narrative generally includes admissions of struggle and imperfection coupled with attestations of an overriding sense of contentment and peace. The most successful Exodus testimonies, of course, end with the struggler now happily married to an opposite-sex partner, perhaps even with children or grandchildren (this model fits Dallas, Chambers, and many other Exodus officials). Publicity materials of SOCE highlight similarly colorful biographies of those who have kept with the program, assuring audiences that "tens of thousands" of others exist just like them. Within evangelical contexts, where testimony is an accepted and reliable mode of relating spiritual truths, such bio-shows prove persuasive.

Anecdote, however, fails to pass muster by professional scientific standards. Little better, in the eyes of mental health researchers, are the offerings of ostensibly scientific SOCE entities like NARTH. NARTH's website brims with position statements and white papers written in academic-ese. Throughout the 1990s, NARTH researchers struggled to carve out even a small amount of professional respect. Consistently they failed, hindered by their alignment with politicized religious-right interests, their own tendency to use shoddy (non-peer-reviewed) research methods, and at times by their broadside allegations of conspiracies.[65] Psychological researcher Warren Throckmorton (himself an evangelical with experience in practicing and assessing SOCE) disassociated himself with the organization, led by evidence to different conclusions about SOCE therapies than Nicolosi was willing to admit. Today, Throckmorton serves as a major in-house critic of SOCE. He points out that, despite its pretentions to scholarly legitimacy, NARTH's membership consists mainly of non-professionals. Given that fewer than 250 of NARTH's some 1,000 members are mental health professionals, Throckmorton argues, their aims align more with political advocacy groups than scientific research.[66] Today, Exodus no longer includes NARTH on its list of helpful resources.[67]

By 1997, the APA had begun expressing official suspicion about the legitimacy of "gay cure" techniques.[68] The questions being asked turned from "Do such techniques work?" to "Are they harmful?" and "May APA members ethically practice them?" Facing the possibility of prohibition, SOCE researchers strove to define their standards and moderate their rhetoric. Evangelical scientists like Throckmorton, Mark Yarhouse, and Stanton Jones began producing research that, if not completely compelling, was more acceptable than much of what NARTH was infamous for.[69] In 2000, these researchers managed to hold a roundtable at the APA's annual conference, presented as a neutral discussion about how various therapists holding various points of view about SOCE dealt with clients wishing to change their orientations.[70] That panel and other such professional maneuvers managed to shift the debate away from pure questions of efficacy (though SOCE researchers continued to conduct studies to gauge SOCE effectiveness) and toward other concerns. Specifically, they asked, what role ought faith to have in conceptions of mental health? Do religious convictions constitute a kind of diversity to be respected or a type of prejudice to be overcome? And, when approached by deeply religious clients who feel torn between their faith and their erotic desires, what ought a mental health professional to do?[71]

Such even-handed inquiries, accompanied by the suggestion that SOCE itself suffered from some anti-religious bias in the APA, won SOCE researchers some grudging support. Particularly valuable was the interest of Robert Spitzer, a well-respected psychiatrist who had been instrumental in the original effort to remove *homosexuality* from the *DSM*.[72] Answering some NARTH-associated SOCE researchers' open invitation to see if SOCE really did work, Spitzer initiated his own study, concluding that some evidence existed to suggest that some people do in fact report significant change in their sexual orientations following therapy.[73] His conclusions (and his questionable methodology) won him considerable backlash from his peers, and Spitzer recoiled at the attack.[74] NARTH and various religious right organizations have since used the Spitzer study as proof that "gays can change." Unhappy to see his work used in such a way and convinced, finally, of the methodological flaws dogging the study, Spitzer issued a full retraction in early 2012.[75] Nevertheless, his participation, as well as the sounder research of people like Yarhouse and Jones, helped to move the question of SOCE from the realm of God-blinkered quackery into a legitimate area of professional attention.

Such attention bore fruit in August 2009, when the APA released a comprehensive report by a task force charged with reviewing available literature on SOCE and making official recommendations. Surveying over eighty studies from 1960 to 2007, the task force concludes that SOCE do indeed lack any evidence to support claims of long-term changes to sexual orientation, noting even that some evidence exists to suggest that SOCE may be psychologically harmful to those who attempt it.[76] The report ends with an official resolution reaffirming APA's conception of homosexuality and bisexuality as normal and positive, stressing APA's sole reliance on scientifically grounded therapies and warning psychologists and other mental health professionals not to portray SOCE as empirically supported. These conclusions made national headlines: "Psychologists reject gay 'therapy.'"[77] NARTH, anticipating the report's conclusions, dismissed the task force as flawed long before the report itself was released. Given that many members of the APA task force were themselves LGBT-affirmative, NARTH argues, their views could only be biased. Moreover, NARTH's own recommendations of qualified psychologists to participate in the task force (a list that included Nicolosi himself) were ignored, undermining in their view any hope of the task force's "worldview diversity."[78]

But other SOCE ministries, particularly Exodus, saw within apparent defeat some key victories. The report stops short of calling for an outright prohibition of SOCE. The task force in fact recognizes that, for most people currently pursuing SOCE in the United States, religious faith—especially conservative Christian faith—constitutes an integral element of the person's self-conception of health.[79] Although the APA itself takes no position regarding the validity of any faith claim, notes the report, ethical and therapeutic concerns for the client's right to self-determination require that therapists accompany honesty about SOCE's low likelihood of success with a willingness to explore possibilities for identity development "without imposing a specific sexual orientation identity outcome."[80] In other words, therapists should not only affirm the scientific consensus about mental health (i.e., the non-pathology of homosexuality and the apparent ineffectiveness of most SOCE); they must also respect the legitimacy of clients' religious convictions about what constitutes spiritual health. Moreover, the report distinguishes (as most SOCE do not, the task force notes) *change of sexual orientation,* which does not appear to occur, from *change of sexual orientation identity,* which in fact may happen in some individuals.[81] The role of the therapist, the report suggests, is not to push clients toward one identity (gay or straight) but to multiply possibilities for how the client might peaceably live in accordance with both his or her desires and faith convictions.[82] Thus, while undercutting the SOCE promise of making gay people straight, the report preserves a right for people with same-sex orientations to at least strive not to be gay.

Ascesis and Ex-Gay Identities

No wonder, then, that reactions by SOCE ministries like Exodus expressed approval of the report's respect for faith convictions, for the right of people to live according to those convictions, and for the legitimacy of therapists' supporting people in their efforts to do so (media outlets quoted Alan Chambers ubiquitously).[83] Chambers, of course, stressed in such quotes that he still believes that "change is possible" (which for some time functioned as the motto of Exodus). In truth, though, *not-being-gay* describes the goal of most present-day SOCE more accurately than does *becoming straight.* Better still, as Chambers clarifies, *change* for people going through present-day SOCE aims not at turning hetero but at becoming holy.

Embracing this nuance and communicating it clearly and consistently, however, has proven difficult for Exodus. From the perspective of strugglers approaching SOCE ministries, as well as from the perspective of evangelical and religious right organizations linking to these ministries, the "change is possible" theme communicates a clear message: *these programs turn gay people into straight people.* What else, after all, could "ex-gay" (or "post-gay") mean? SOCE ministries like Exodus have abetted and in many cases continue to foster such an impression. Married couple John and Anne Paulk were for some time the poster couple for Exodus, appearing on the cover of *Newsweek* in 1998 as the model of "cured" lesbian and gay people.[84] In 2004, Exodus produced a number of slick advertisements on television and in magazines and newspapers featuring photos of smiling people (including Alan Chambers and Randy Thomas) with captions like "I questioned homosexuality" and "Change *is* possible."[85] Former Love In Action executive director John Smid recalls (ruefully now) how his organization once created a billboard featuring his picture along with the words "I Used To Be A Homosexual."[86] Recently, however, Exodus and various other SOCE ministries have begun to back off from the change message in light of the solid consensus among mental health professionals that SOCE do not alter sexual orientation in the vast majority of people who undertake such efforts.

Beneath the surface messages promoting (presumably gay-to-straight) "change," "hope," "freedom," or "choosing other than homosexuality," most SOCE now outline more specific and modest expectations. The organization People Can Change, for example, touts that four out of five Journey into Manhood participants experience "significant reductions in same-sex attractions"—but not a complete transformation from homo to hetero.[87] In his books, Dallas outlines four reasonable expectations of intervention: a change in behavior, as the struggler ceases to "act out" on same-sex attractions, gaining control over behaviors (not just sexual encounters but also lusting and self-pleasuring) once experienced as compulsive. Dallas argues that strugglers can also expect their same-sex attractions eventually to decrease in both intensity and frequency (in his list these count as separate expectations). Again, however, Dallas cautions that in most cases strugglers should never expect same-sex attractions to evaporate completely. Nor can they necessarily expect ever to develop heterosexual attractions. Finally, and most importantly, Dallas writes that strugglers may anticipate developing a new perspective on themselves and their sexuality.[88] They internalize the "Christian Explanatory Framework" in which same-sex attractions become seen as temptations to be dealt with rather than self-defining evidences of an unchangeable inner essence (i.e., a "Gay Explanatory Framework").

SOCE ministries almost universally protest that such shifts in attractions, while not necessarily a 180-degree turn from gay to straight, nevertheless represent significant change. NARTH's statement on reorientation, for example, contends that applying such "categorical," 100 percent transformation standard to treatments for depression, grief, or marital distress would be patently objectionable. Does treatment for depression fail if someone's depression recurs at any future point, regardless of the intensity or duration of the recurrence? Though unlike many SOCE ministries, NARTH still insists on the possibility of actual reorientation, they concur with Exodus and other organizations in arguing that *change* must have a broader meaning than absolute, unalterable reorientation.[89] In recent years Exodus, International has quietly muted its "change is possible" theme while simultaneously intensifying explanations of a more generous understanding of change.

Even this clarification, however, poses problems for Exodus. In January 2012, Chambers participated in a roundtable discussion at the annual conference of the Gay Christian Network (GCN). Founded by openly gay evangelical Justin Lee, the GCN structures itself as bridge between the two sides of what it calls "the great debate" about the place of homosexuality in the lives of Christians. "Side A," as the GCN dubs it, espouses an LGBT-affirmative stance roughly along the same lines as Evangelicals Concerned. Lee himself, in his position statement representing Side A, professes a "theologically conservative" understanding of sex as sinful outside of marriage, but he argues that scripture allows for gay and lesbian people to experience fullness of faithful Christian discipleship within monogamous, committed relationships.[90] "Side B" represents the belief that same-sex behavior is prohibited by scripture, full stop. Gay and lesbian Christians—meaning Christians who experience same-sex orientations—should thus commit themselves to a life of faithful celibacy.[91] Both argument statements share solidly evangelical-biblicist foundations, and both lie well to the right of many mainline and left-progressive Christian positions on sexuality. Yet all sides within the GCN affirm that gay and lesbian people can be and are faithful Christians, regardless of which side of the debate they occupy. Moreover, GCN has taken strong stands against SOCE ministries; many of its members identify explicitly as having been harmed directly or indirectly by encounters with SOCE evangelicalism.[92] The GCN operates mainly as an online entity with a website that hosts extensive discussion forums and resources, and it hosts an annual conference. It strives to be a common-ground endeavor for Christians (not just evangelicals, though the membership appears especially to attract those from evangelical traditions).

In January 2012, at the GCN annual conference in Orlando (the current home base of Exodus, International), Lee hosted a roundtable on Exodus. There he invited former Exodus ministers John Smid (former executive director of Love in Action), Jeremy Marks (formerly with Exodus in Europe), and Wendy Gritter (head of New Directions Ministry, which disassociated with Exodus)—and, as a somewhat last-minute announcement, Alan Chambers. The two-plus-hour session makes for some riveting viewing. Smid, Marks, and Gritter each relate their stories of engaging with and then leaving Exodus-type SOCE ministries. Exhibiting general charm and good humor, Chambers himself endured some fairly harsh criticism from Lee as well as from his former associates. Chambers affirmed unambiguously that people can be gay and Christian. He spoke to the good faith of the participants. Most stunningly, Chambers directly stated that over 99 percent of "ex-gays" that he knows still have some degree of same-sex attraction. *Almost no one totally changes from gay to straight.* "Change is possible" no longer serves as Exodus's motto. When asked what it was, Chambers answered, half-joking, "Life is messy."

The GCN panel sent ripples through the ex-gay and ex-ex-gay communities alike. Though many GCN members praised Lee for hosting such a panel, many other members were incensed at his giving Exodus's president such a prominent spotlight. Many felt that information about the panel and about Chambers's participation in particular had been insufficiently communicated to conference goers. To ex-gay survivors attending what was presented as a safe space to be gay and Christian—and specifically safe from the depredations of ex-gay rhetoric—Chambers's participation felt like a deep betrayal. Other critics felt Lee had treated Chambers too softly, allowing Chambers in essence to spout Exodus propaganda without sufficient challenge. From their perspective, Chambers has long been a bad-faith actor, speaking out of both sides of his mouth, appealing simultaneously to GCN critics and to his religious-right funders. Still other SOCE ministries, those espousing views closer to that of nouthetic/biblical counseling models, recoiled at what they considered Chambers's accommodationist rhetoric. Some people insisted that they had, in fact, experienced long-lasting, total transformation of attractions from gay to straight. For others, Chambers's seeming affirmation that gay people can be Christian simply flew in the face of clear biblical teaching.

From secular perspectives, Chambers's admission about not knowing many 100 percent gay-to-straight converts figured as news. Yet, as Chambers and his supporters noted, he was from his perspective repeating a message he and Exodus had been delivering for some time. Exodus's critics were right, however, in noting that Chambers and Exodus have been less than clear about communicating that understanding of change explicitly in all communications. In almost every venue and to almost every kind of audience, Exodus affirms the power of God to change homosexuals. But only with certain audiences in certain situations has Exodus generally taken the time to define the quality of change they expect God to initiate, specifying that *change* does not necessarily mean (in fact, it hardly ever means) a wholesale transformation of same-sex attractions to heterosexual attractions. Of course, explaining such a nuanced take on sexuality proves well-nigh impossible, especially in mass media venues like cable news talk shows. Given the polarizing effects of pro-family religious right discourse (which insists on the reality of a miraculous, gay-to-straight cure) and LGBT-affirmative politics (which are eager to explode such notions), Exodus's position on change can too easily seem either heretical or ludicrous.

I would argue instead that it moves the goals and activities of SOCE processes out of the realm of therapy and into the realm of spiritual or life discipline. Like an addict who might experience a desire for drugs or alcohol regardless of whether he or she partakes, so too (teach SOCE ministries) might the person struggling with same-sex attractions remain forever tempted by homosexual sin. Nevertheless, the life one leads does not have to be chained to a core orientation. SOCE ministries urge strugglers not necessarily to forget or ignore their temptations but to displace those temptations' centrality, putting devotion to Christ above devotion to desires. Characterizing Exodus followers as gay or lesbian people who choose a life of white-knuckled abstinence thus overrules their self-understanding of their conversions. They are Christians who understand themselves as living with persistent same-sex attractions. It is in this sense, then, that SOCE spokespeople like Chambers claim that the opposite of homosexuality is *holiness.*

Although the APA does not endorse holiness per se, their recommendations about SOCE do enable some degree of flexibility in dealing with religious individuals who struggle with same-sex attractions. Throckmorton and Yarhouse, for example, have developed what they call a "Sexual Identity Therapy" (SIT) framework.[93] Their framework is not, the authors underline, "sexual reorientation therapy protocols in disguise."[94] Both authors situate themselves firmly within the mainstream consensus that research supports the non-efficacy of "gay-to-straight" therapies, and both authors strongly recommend "advance informed consent" procedures in which the counselor clarifies the consensus of mental health professionals about homosexuality (i.e., non-pathological) and SOCE (i.e., mainly ineffective).[95] Instead, the researchers seek to integrate into therapy a more embodied appreciation of the role of religious identity in clients' lives, recognizing that at times clients may feel more attached to a faith identity that precludes same-sex attractions than to an identity based on affirming those attractions. In such cases, Throckmorton and Yarhouse argue, therapists can best respond not by discounting clients' faith but by helping clients to negotiate the relationship between their faith and their sexuality, a conclusion that the APA Task Force cites and endorses.[96]

Such SOCE processes bear a striking resemblance to Foucault's writings about *ascesis,* disciplines involving what he calls technologies of self, defined as "the kind of techniques you use in order to recognize, to constitute yourself as a subject of ethics."[97] Foucault invokes techniques of self in his later work (post–*History of Sexuality*) as a way to complement his analyses of techniques of domination whereby bodies and minds are forced into a particular configuration. Ascetic techniques, by contrast, equip individuals with tools by which they may reshape themselves so as to achieve states of happiness or purity.[98] Thinking of SOCE as a mode of ascesis—an art-of-self—troubles images of pathetic repression or deceitful self-righteousness that often characterize people undergoing SOCE. Foucault of course insists that power does not operate by pure repression; it is productive, consisting of the complex interaction of coercion-technologies and self-technologies to create new modes of being and resisting.[99]

Not surprisingly, then, many scholars of SOCE conclude that the ministries end up producing an essentially novel sexual identity, one that oddly resembles the fluid, binary-challenging identity modes called for by queer theory. Indeed, writing about the members of one ex-gay live-in ministry, Erzen asserts that the members of the household who remain undergo a "queer conversion . . . they take on an unstable identity—ex-gay—that resists a binary heterosexual or homosexual definition."[100] Some SOCE groups and spokespeople, such as Parents, Friends, and Families of Ex-Gays and Gays (PFOX), explicitly claim "ex-gay" as an identity, pursuing and often winning protected class status for ex-gays and former homosexuals in local and state laws that already recognize LGBT people.[101] Although Alan Chambers and Exodus as a whole eschew the term "ex-gay," certainly he and other Exodus spokespeople seem to define themselves largely in terms of their ongoing discipline of sexuality and spirituality. Not-being-gay (or, perhaps, being Christian-instead-of-gay) operates less as a telos of psychological intervention but as an ongoing practice of self-creation.

For evangelicals like Smid or the GCN, the distinction between "Christian struggling with occasional same-sex attractions" and "gay/lesbian Christian (who lives celibately)" just feels too disingenuous to sustain. They stress the importance of actually claiming the identity "gay/lesbian" as a neutral descriptor of orientation (wanted or unwanted). At the roundtable, Chambers resisted invitations to identify himself as gay or to commit Exodus to a course of affirming gay/lesbian as an identity for Christian strugglers. But while Exodus seems unlikely at present to rebrand itself as a "Side B" entity welcoming celibate gay/lesbian Christians as such, the organization does appear to be taking some steps away from enshrining the heterocentric ideal of monogamous marriage as the tacit goal of SOCE ministries. In a series of posts on the Exodus website in April 2012 (in anticipation of the next Exodus conference in May), Chambers confessed concern that Exodus has been until now insufficiently cognizant of the situation of people who choose to remain in holy celibacy.[102] Testimonial posts by upcoming conference speakers emphasize the quality of change they understand themselves to have experienced, stressing that simply turning into straights was not ultimately what they needed. "My goal of overcoming unwanted SSA was far too small," writes Bob Ragan, "God had so much more for me."[103]

Over the next year, Exodus continued to distance itself from the SOCE rhetorics of yesteryear. In his June 2012 letter to followers, Chambers declared, "we [Exodus] are no longer an organization that associates with or promotes therapeutic practices that focus on changing one's attraction." Instead of focusing on "sin management," he writes, Exodus strives "to make the Church famous for loving and serving people as Jesus would and pointing them to Him," assisting those who experience same-sex attractions (though still not "gay/lesbian" people) and wish to live a life defined by their commitment to faith rather than by their surrender to fleshly desires.[104] Though such a modification seems infinitesimal from the perspective of the gay-affirming progressive left, Chambers's statement and Exodus's continued moderation led to a number of affiliate SOCE organizations disassociating with Exodus.[105]

The most profound changes, however, came just as *Preaching to Convert* was undergoing final edits. On June 19, 2013, Chambers released a lengthy public statement to the international LGBTQ community in which he apologizes for a range of past actions: for his promotion of SOCE, for his failure to stand up to virulent anti-gay rhetoric, for his lack of openness about his own continuing same-sex attractions, and for his denigration of LGBTQ people. "More than anything," he writes, "I am sorry that so many have interpreted this religious rejection by Christians as God's rejection. I am profoundly sorry that many have walked away from their faith and that some have chosen to end their lives." Although clarifying that he does not apologize about his beliefs regarding the proper boundaries of sexuality and marriage, Chambers promises, "My beliefs about these things will never again interfere with God's command to love my neighbor as I love myself."[106] Later that day, in his opening speech to Exodus's Freedom Conference, Chambers announced that Exodus International was disbanding, to be replaced by an as-yet-unknown organization whose goals are "to reduce fear" and "come alongside churches to become safe, welcoming, and mutually transforming communities."[107]

Conclusion

Few areas of evangelical culture have shifted as radically during my writing process as Exodus and SOCE have. The ground continues to move, making it difficult to establish any clear kind of map. Shockwaves from Chambers's apology and Exodus's dissolution continue to spread. Several high-profile SOCE individuals and organizations that had previously separated from Exodus over Chambers's statements have recently converged to form a counter-Exodus organization, the Restored Hope Network (RHN).[108] In a prompt response to Exodus's announcement, RHN promotes its self-image as the best and most biblically sound SOCE, tut-tutting Exodus's end as the "the not-unexpected outcome of a cheap grace theology that severs the confession of Christ as Savior from the confession of Christ as Lord."[109] By all appearances, the RHN seems ready to combine a more hard-right condemnation of same-sex behavior with an unalloyed affirmation of SOCE's effectiveness. The organization includes representatives from NARTH, its rhetoric stands firm on unconditional sexual "transformation" as a goal of ministry/therapy, and a number of its "board of reference" members (for example, Robert Gagnon, Janet Parshall, and Matt Barber) come from the political pro-family right rather than from SOCE ministries.[110] On the political left, ex-gay watchdog groups and critics have greeted the closure with a mixture of "Good for them" and "It's not enough."[111] In terms of the next steps for those who share Chambers's nuanced take on sexual orientation and Christian living, researcher Mark Yarhouse poses some trenchant questions:

> Is there is room in a diverse and pluralistic culture for a Christian ministry to retain its beliefs and values about sexuality and marriage while moving away from the expectation of change (at least in the form of reparative therapy)? . . . [ellipses in original] A ministry would then have to ask: Is there an audience for that kind of ministry when many people (most?) who come to a ministry want the very change held out as normative in reparative therapy? All indications are that the message will be that of Christlikeness (or what Christians refer to as sanctification), and, I would guess, that the focus on sanctification will be independent of the question of whether attractions change.[112]

Yarhouse's comment on the post-Exodus organization's uncertain future touches on many of the issues I have identified in this chapter regarding present-day sexual orientation change efforts and the movements that act on their behalf. First, SOCE exist within a present-day US evangelicalism that sees itself as a community in crisis, losing members and cultural influence due in large part to its reputation for intolerance and homophobia. In response to this crisis, SOCE strives to move evangelical discourse to a less toxic, separatist position vis-à-vis LGBT people without also appearing to condone practices they consider unhealthy. Second, SOCE have fought to justify their existence in the face of a skeptical mental health establishment that seems ever on the verge of imposing outright prohibitions on SOCE. Their tactic on this front leapfrogs questions of efficacy to instead advance liberalist arguments regarding patients' right to self-determination and the indissociability of faith to an overall conception of mental health. Finally, the movement has begun to sharpen its rhetoric regarding what it is that SOCE actually do, exchanging a purely telic model of therapeutic cure (health as destination) for an ascetic model of spiritual life discipline (health as way or journey).

No complication on my part erases the real conflicts I have with the SOCE movement. Despite their moderating influence on evangelical rhetoric, Exodus and other SOCE-related entities remain political and cultural opponents of LGBT liberty movements. Moreover, SOCE ministries, while beneficial for some, have little to no empirical backing or regulatory standards like those that undergird most other mental health treatments. I join other critics in seeing queer inflections in their therapeutic/ascetic practices, but I also know that SOCE themselves believe strongly in normative, essential gender identities and roles. If they could, through some magic pill, exchange ascetics for simple heterosexuality, they would.[113] Finally, although I have strained to be critically generous with SOCE, I do not deny that many actions and words of SOCE have been harmful personally and politically to LGBT people and their families. Chambers's apology aside, the negative (to LGBT people) legacy of Exodus continues in organizations like the Restored Hope Network. That group's stances and alliances call into question their stated intention to be authentic and loving to all people. It remains to be seen if or how the RHN, Chambers, and the post-Exodus organization might exist within and alongside the conservative evangelicalism.[114]

I do not want to underplay the links between SOCE and more stridently anti-gay attitudes among some right-leaning evangelicals, particularly as the RHN appears dedicated to reinforcing those links. Yet the fact remains that most present-day SOCE ministries do not fit comfortably into a simple "anti-gay" box. By the time it closed, Exodus had ceased to be (if it ever was) merely a proxy for the Christian Coalition or the Family Research Council. And despite its hardline castigation of Exodus for having strayed from the straight and narrow, the Restored Hope Network retains some of the same internal tensions that eventually resulted in Exodus's transformation. Like Exodus had tried for some years, the RHN attempts to bundle together politically expedient assurances of a "gay cure" with an appealing ministry to people with same-sex attractions. The former involves a gesture of retrenchment, withdrawing behind clearly demarcated culture war lines. The latter involves outreach beyond those lines and, eventually, deep engagement with individuals' complicated desires and life struggles. Similarly, the same therapy-versus-discipline conflict that dogged Exodus remains unresolved in the Restored Hope Network. The umbrella organization overtly promises total reorientation to heterosexuality while member ministries often tacitly redefine success as holiness without necessarily attractional change. I would not be surprised, therefore, to see the RHN years from now rehearsing some of Exodus's own struggles as the contradictions between political boilerplate and ascetic nuance intensify.

SOCE ministries' risky, complicated outreach poses a challenge for me as a left-progressive critic. In my research into this and other areas of evangelical life, I have been surprised at the extent to which SOCE ministries are willing to engage in non-dismissive ways people they consider political and cultural enemies—people like me, in other words. The very first statement of the "Love Won Out" conference was a word of welcome from Melissa Fryrear, a psychologist and former lesbian working for Focus on the Family. Speaking to the huge audience that morning, she greeted various groups she knew would be in attendance: parents, spouses, pastors, concerned church members, friends, family, and people who themselves are struggling to find a way to reconcile their faith and their sexuality. "And," she added, "I know some of you may be here because you disagree with us. Perhaps you are angry or upset at Focus on the Family or Exodus. We welcome you, too." Without discounting for a moment the considerable theological and political differences that divide the mainstream pro-LGBT left from the ex-gay right, consider how likely it is that one would hear a similar welcome to ex-gays or conservative evangelicals from a spokesperson for the Human Rights Campaign or the National Gay and Lesbian Taskforce.

I am troubled, then, that my research into evangelicals reveals that they are often much more willing and able to imagine political difference with complexity and respect (if not always with accuracy). I have to wonder which side really is the more ideologically blinkered when my quickest reaction to the mention of an ex-gay person is to make a joke. After all, to deny the legitimacy of someone's understanding of their own identity, to declare as off-limits certain technologies of self or certain avenues of being because they threaten the stability of our own identities—such acts leave precious little daylight between the LGBT left and those it critiques. It strikes me that seeing SOCE as an ascetic or queer operation that multiplies a range of identities could prove as unsettling—and perhaps just as productive—for the LGBT left as for the ex-gay right. "Sex is not fatality," counsels Foucault, "it's a possibility for creative life."[115] Perhaps taking seriously ex-gays'/former homosexuals' struggle to perform their conversions from homosexuality to holiness on a day-to-day basis can provoke LGBT people toward more creative innovations in their own identities and politics.

Conclusion

American Grace and Evangelical True Believers

I have ended with an especially profound, intimate, and therefore scandalous model of evangelical conversion, describing ministries and people dedicated to transforming *homosexuality* (seen as a desire-based identity) into *holiness* (a faith-based practice of self). As Exodus's ongoing struggles and recent dissolution demonstrate, such a nuanced transformation proves difficult to realize and communicate, let alone promote. To an increasingly gay-tolerant popular culture, as well as to the LGBT-affirming progressive left, the notion of living a life of self-denial and holy chastity seems bizarre and oppressive. To a hyper-partisan religious right, acknowledging limits to the mutability of same-sex desires—dispensing with the language of "cure" and "re-orientation"—seems like capitulation to a godless cultural tide.

Discovering if and how post-Exodus SOCE groups navigate their place between risky nuance and political/theological rigidity must wait until a future project. I am presently more interested in the sense from those beyond conservative evangelicalism that organizations like Exodus, post-Exodus, and the Restored Hope Network would be better off disappearing from existence altogether. To be sure, such sentiments originate in part from the experience of harm that ex-gay survivors (and former ministers) attribute to Exodus and other SOCE initiatives. Still more criticism comes from those who have examined SOCE clinical claims and found them wanting. But, apart from those personally burned by SOCE ministries or well-versed in research about them, much of the bias against groups like Exodus exists on the level of the pop-cultural subconscious. It circulates, for example, as the trope of the snooty, hypocritical homosexual-in-denial or in the late-night talk-show barbs launched at self-avowed strugglers like Ted Haggard. Such humor depends less on personal experiences or rational conclusions and more on a tacit consensus that it is silly or improper to suggest that someone *try not to be gay or lesbian.* From this perspective, even Exodus's attenuated, non-cure, non-coercive version of sexual orientation counseling offends. An unspoken assumption exists that advocating holy celibacy as the best course of action for LGBT people—not just *being* celibate yourself but actually *recommending* to LGBT people that they be celibate—is bad form. It violates a sense of decency, a twenty-first-century US sensibility that, so long as no one is being physically hurt, people should be able to like who they like without being nagged about it. It's a private matter, none of Exodus's business.

To varying degrees, many of the cases I have examined in this book inspire a similar sense of violation. The act of religious proselytization itself implies a double—and, in present-day culture, doubly offensive—assumption: (1) *Your deepest religious beliefs are wrong,* and (2) *It's my business to try to change them.* What presumption! Can't I walk down the street without having some stranger push a Bible tract at me? Does this friendly chat really have to veer awkwardly into a conversation about whether I'm aware that God loves me and has a wonderful plan for my life? Do they really need not just a Creation Museum but a fully sized Ark? Must we have hell houses? Or, in words attributed to Jimmy Durante, "Why can't everybody leave everybody else the hell alone?"

Evangelicals fascinate me precisely because of their eponymous insistence on *not* leaving everyone else alone. They are compelled instead by what British missionary Lesslie Newbigin calls "the logic of mission." For Christians, he writes, "the true meaning of the human story has been disclosed. Because it is the truth, it must be shared universally. It cannot be private opinion."[1] One insight I hope readers have garnered from my study is that debates about how to follow this missional logic remain varied and contentious. Evangelicals ask themselves some of the very same questions about evangelism—regularly, sincerely, exasperatedly—as annoyed non-evangelicals do. Hell houses, seeker-sensitive services,

Answers in Genesis, and more all endure some of their sharpest criticism from other evangelicals. Evangelical critics like Mark A. Noll have leveled devastating diagnoses of evangelicalism's all-too-common anti-intellectualism.[2] Evangelical scientists and think tanks like the BioLogos Foundation regularly contest Ken Ham's narrow creationism. Evangelical philosophers like Elmer John Thiessen elaborate complex ethical bases for distinguishing legitimate proselytization from immoral coercion, turning these tools to critique hell houses and other suspect productions.[3] Younger evangelicals like Rachel Held Evans strive to put distance between their faith and culture war skirmishes over homosexuality.[4] And entire outreach strategies have been premised upon Christians' embarrassment at and desire not to be lumped in with the always-be-Christianizing, everyone-is-a-potential-prospect conversationalist or the homophobic street preacher haranguing mourners at a funeral. Indeed, so great is the desire to "leave everybody else alone," so painful the self-inflicted wounds of awkward/offensive/presumptive evangelism, that most self-identified evangelicals rarely evangelize at all, at least not with any frequency. Certainly most don't engage in the kinds of performances I have studied here. That all evangelicals *should* engage in outreach but that only a minority actually *do* serves as cause for alarm among a broad cross-section of the evangelical spectrum. Such a gap between profession and action, argue those sounding the alarm, indicates a malaise in the US Church more generally, an ailment brought on in part by evangelical maladaptation to twentieth- and twenty-first-century culture.

Many of those outside of evangelicalism, of course, shed no tears about the dearth of proselytization. In their bestselling overview of religion in the United States, *American Grace,* Robert Putnam and David Campbell give a thorough and generally sunny assessment of US religious plurality. Paralleling Peter Berger's insights, Putnam and Campbell find that faith in the twenty-first century has not dwindled but diversified. In contrast to occasional pronouncements of the end of religion, the United States now sees more and more types of religious identifications appearing every day, including a growing (though by no means majority) segment of "nones" (i.e., people who express no particular religious affiliation).[5] Of particular interest to Putnam and Campbell is how such religious diversity occurs without extreme, violent interfaith tension. Although they note partisan culture war frictions in the name of religion, for the most part the authors conclude that the United States handles plurality rather well. The ubiquity and intermixing of faith positions, they suggest, means that—more than ever before in US history—just about everyone has some close relationship with someone not of their faith. This they christen the "Aunt Susan Principle." They explain thus:

> We all have an Aunt Susan in our lives, the sort of person who epitomizes what it means to be a saint, but whose religious background is different from your own. Maybe you are Jewish and she is a Methodist. Or perhaps you are Catholic and Aunt Susan is not religious at all. But whatever her religious background (or lack thereof), you know that Aunt Susan is destined for heaven. And if she is going to heaven, what does that say about other people who share her religion or lack of religion? Maybe they can go to heaven too.[6]

Closely related is the "My Friend Al Principle," where, after establishing a relationship with "Al" in one context (e.g., he shares your profession, hangs out at your coffee shop), you learn that he is in fact a member of a faith/non-faith group not your own.[7] In both the Aunt Susan and Friend Al scenarios, the strangeness of other faith positions versus the familiarity of the people involved produces cognitive dissonance. More often than not, this dissonance resolves in favor of interpersonal relations rather than interfaith prejudice. If I'm suspicious of atheists, but Aunt Susan/Friend Al is an atheist, then I am likely to alter my level of suspicion rather than my level of friendship. In other words, the United States' religiously diverse society enables (and to a certain extent mandates) peaceful and respectful experiences of coexistence, collaboration, and even friendship or kinship with otherwise unfamiliar faith/non-faith positions. It makes the strange more familiar, acclimatizing people to the fact of ever-broader religious plurality. It infuses the secular age with "American Grace," an ability to be faithful but tolerant.

Integral to this American grace, in Putnam and Campbell's configuration, is the discovery that most believers in the United States of whatever faith are not "fanatics." That is, only about a tenth of adults in the United States qualify as what the authors term "true believers," coupling a high degree of religious involvement with stalwartly exclusivist views. In contrast to most other US adults, for example, true believers hold that that one religion (theirs) is true and others are not, that premarital sex and homosexuality are wrong, and that religious pluralism is worrisome rather than welcome. Crucially, these believers disagree with the consensus in the United States that "everyone should leave everyone else alone." They evangelize at much higher rates than is the norm. The Aunt Susan Principle does not obtain with them. For Putnam and Campbell, such true believers provide a grim portrait of what US life could be without the grace granted by religious diversity and tolerance.[8]

Though, as I have stressed, evangelicalism embraces a wide and conflicting range of belief profiles, I have dealt with quite a few people and groups who fit Putnam and Campbell's definition of the fanatical "true believer." I concur that the experience of encountering militant faith-based intolerance is unpleasant. For what it's worth, I am grateful that most US adults—including most US evangelicals—do not endorse the hard-line stances of Steven Anderson, Ray Comfort, Americans for Truth About Homosexuality, or Answers in Genesis. Whatever criticisms I may level at a politics of tolerance, I cannot deny that I find certain modes of intolerance themselves intolerable for various ethical, political, and theological reasons. In this feeling I would be joined by many, perhaps even most, evangelicals in the United States.

At the same time that they would aver that militancy or rudeness is wrong, however, few of the evangelical ministers and thinkers I have examined here would accept that theirs is but one truth among many or that they needn't move themselves to share their faith publically and even persuasively. Even Jim Henderson, perhaps the most irenic and anti-confrontational of the evangelists I have surveyed, might in the last analysis qualify as one of *American Grace*'s true believers. He *seems* non-fanatical. His model of Ordinary Attempts challenges Christians to give up manipulative salesmanship techniques in favor of forging authentic, long-term relationships with "the people Jesus misses most." He encourages everyday kindness and simple politeness as reparative, or perhaps repentant, modes of effective evangelism. Indeed, it would not be inaccurate to say that Henderson bases his approach on something like the Aunt Susan Principle, encouraging evangelicals to make themselves a positive example of Christianity to those in their social circles. But, unlike Putnam and Campbell's Aunt Susan, Henderson would insist that, at least eventually, evangelical Aunt Karen must incorporate into her witness of self her convictions regarding the capital-T Truth of Christ. Evangelical pastor Trevin Wax sounds a similar note about relational evangelism, observing, "Our identity in Christ should be such an integral part of our lives that it is impossible for someone to know us well without understanding how our Christian faith informs our lives."[9] Evangelical Christians, in other words, should not merely be nice people who hold some deep, private beliefs about God. If an evangelical does not evangelize, if she does not make it her business to proclaim the Truth of sin, sacrifice, and redemption, then something has gone wrong.

In the course of my examinations, I have touched on several evangelical explanations of this "something wrong." Soul-winners explain the problem as simple disobedience, the heretical inaction of so-called Christians who somehow rationalize a refusal to go door-to-door, Bible in hand, proclaiming the gospel. For meta-kerygmatic evangelists, evangelicals' reticence to share lies in the damaged reputation of the Church due in part to its own missteps. Other evangelicals see the problem as a mismatch between outdated methods and twenty-first-century audiences; hell houses, the Creation Museum, and seeker-sensitive services each strive in part to repackage the good news in slick, exciting new formats, (post)modernizing the medium without losing the message.

For still others, however, the crisis of evangelicalism stems from too much consonance between secular culture and the Church. From this perspective, the evangelistic desire to make disciples of all the world has morphed into a numbers- and surface-based ministry style. The church marketing movement in particular has been credited with making some versions of Christianity very popular while at the same time lowering the bar for what a successfully evangelized disciple looks like. To many evangelicals, the megachurch seeker service, the outreach mode that a majority of churchgoing US Protestants encounter, has encouraged a lowest-common-denominator, consumer-friendly version of Christianity. Critics point out that the high-production, low-demand service crafted to appeal to Unchurched Harry or Saddleback Sam bears a disturbing resemblance to the Moralistic Therapeutic Deism that Christian Smith and his colleagues detect in young adults' religious beliefs.[10] God is all about what's best for you personally. God is content to remain respectfully distant until needed. God wants humans to be nice, which includes not being overly pushy (or, in seeker services' case, "churchy") about matters of faith.

To be clear, I do not claim that every seeker-sensitive service model waters down evangelical convictions, and I trust that most ministry teams that produce megachurch seeker services do so in the hopes of facilitating a much deeper and more complicated spirituality. Yet it is the case that, despite such good clergy intentions, a significant number of megachurch attendees—and thus a significant number of churchgoers in the United States generally—appear to make do with the seeker-sensitive worship experience and little else. The seeker service provides just enough "religion" to meet felt needs but not so much as to define them as fanatical "true believers." It does not surprise me, then, to learn that, although most of Putnam and Campbell's true-believing 10 percent are evangelical (52 percent), most evangelicals overall (75 percent) fit more comfortably into the non-fanatical, grace-filled (and therefore less frequently proselytizing) 90 percent.[11] I argue that this strain of MTD-flavored Christianity dovetails with Putnam and Campbell's pleasingly tolerant, faithful-but-non-fanatic portrait of America. Consider, for instance, how megachurch pastor Joel Osteen serves simultaneously as (1) the ultimate expression of seeker-sensitive production, (2) the embodiment of MTD-style Christianity, and (3) perhaps the most American Grace-full of Christians.[12] Relentlessly positive, emotionally moving, and perfectly inoffensive, the Smiling Preacher presents God as conveniently interested in helping you achieve your best life now—without any exclusivist demands about lifestyle or theology and without the expectation that believers spread a truth beyond "be your own, nice self." Osteen *believes,* certainly, but the mode of belief he champions resembles a lifestyle essentially indistinguishable from the generic "American" way of being in the twenty-first century. And he leads the most popular church by attendance in the country.

Granted, one can do a lot worse than Joel Osteen as an exemplar of religious belief. Better a grace-full, tolerant moralistic-therapeutic-deism than a nation built around "God hates fags," right? But of course putting things in that way plays into a false dichotomy. Positing the either/or switch of "tolerant grace or pathological fanaticism" shuts down a wide range of alternatives, options for deep and evangelizing convictions that do not result in totalitarian dystopias. Though I am far from endorsing many of the outreach strategies I have covered, I would hope that in this book I have at least multiplied possibilities for imagining what a deeply held, profoundly felt, and imperatively shared evangelical faith can look like. Moreover, I hope I have opened a way for seeing evangelicalism in the United States as a heterogeneous collection of communities and individuals who unite in constantly seeking out, innovating, defining, theorizing, criticizing, reacting to, refining, combining, experimenting with, discarding, and realizing this ever-expanding, ever-deepening repertoire of techniques for changing the hearts, minds, and souls of those around them. Even given their most disastrous or ill-conceived or commercially compromised experiments, evangelicals—the evangelicals who evangelize, I mean—inspire me as a scholar and sometime practitioner of activist performance. Just as I am grateful that their most extreme members do not define the ideological norm in the United States, so too am I glad that so many of them act in defiance of that norm.

To return to a theme I outlined in my first chapter, I have difficulty celebrating the fact that American grace takes as one of its preconditions the Durante Principle of everyone leaving everyone else alone in favor of a purely private religion of self-fulfillment. I worry that, in avoiding the specter (and occasional reality) of faith-based coercion and bigotry, we have internalized a general suspicion toward the very idea of persuasive endeavors in the service of deep convictions. What does it mean to expect evangelicals to censor their evangelizing? Or, to shift registers slightly, what does it mean to sanction strong beliefs of any sort—but only insofar as someone holding such deep and abiding convictions agrees to keep them to herself? Though I have no wish to assert a point-by-point homology between evangelical outreach and left-progressive activist performance (e.g., "What's the 'hell house' of left-progressive activism?"), I do contend that, mutatis mutandis, the two face a similar set of challenges. The danger of the secular age, from an evangelical perspective, lies not primarily in the possibility that the true faith (i.e., biblicist-crucicentric-conversionist-activist Protestant Christianity) might lose market share to any of the ever-increasing number of competitors. Christianity has at many times and places survived and thrived as a minority practice in a plural context. The threat, rather, comes from the distortion field generated by the mentality of the supermarket of ideas. The gracefully tolerant, pluralist frame for religious faith, where every faith becomes one more or less equally legitimate option among many (including non-faith), alters what it means to believe. Within such a frame, evangelicalism morphs from a Truth that imposes belief-based demands to a lifestyle option that offers mainly private benefits to individuals. In a similar way, critics like Stanley Fish and Wendy Brown warn about the silent meta-principle of liberal tolerance that underwrites much of twenty-first-century US culture. Let a thousand flowers bloom, provided none tries to crowd others out of the garden. As I have suggested in concert with a variety of critics, such a view circumscribes the imaginative potential for changing the world for the better. Some ideals, after all—some values, some beliefs—are better than others, worth breaching the conventions of polite society to say *You're wrong* and *You should believe this instead.*

Veterans at making just this sort of audacious recommendation, performance activists on the progressive left have developed a rich and ever-expanding variety of techniques, debates, and considerations about persuading and activating audiences. I seek to enhance this discourse with my modest survey of some evangelical strategies. Again, my point is not to draw an equation between left-progressive strategies and evangelical techniques. Proselytization is after all only one possible activist endeavor. Activist causes and performers are rarely *only* concerned with spreading a gospel. I have left relatively untouched the wider range of activisms beyond outreach, acts such as protest, civil disobedience, or direct-action disruption. In such instances, winning or reviving converts isn't a central goal. The aim involves standing up for something noble, spotlighting an intolerable process, or putting a stop to a perceived injustice. Evangelical examples of such non-conversion-centered activisms are easy to find.

Yet I think that the evangelicals I have studied here offer some valuable lessons to predominantly secular left-progressive activist performers and scholars. First, evangelicalism's outreach-oriented activists insist that, ultimately, even the most vital social justice protests must participate with and bow to evangelicals' eponymous goal of making disciples. These evangelists argue that Christians' action in the world is not—at least from a human perspective—a winner-take-all battle between allies and enemies but a day-to-day, moment-to-moment, living invitation to a better way, a better worldview. While part of this witness may involve taking a stand or protesting, it must also (for the evangelicals I have focused on here) involve attentiveness to the impact of that witness on outsiders and bystanders. It isn't enough to demonstrate for or against a cause; evangelical outreach demands that activists commit to explaining and discussing their stance and the values that motivate it, inviting bystanders into the worldview of those values.

To put it another way, an activism that does nothing more than aim for opponents' defeat or eradication ceases to be properly evangelical. Evangelicals frame moments of proselytization not as holier-than-thou gestures of conquest but as acts of love, acknowledgments of the dignity of the other. Outreach flows, at least in part, from a genuine belief that the evangelical way of life would be in the other's best interests. Now, I will be the first to concede that such loving regard for opponents can be difficult to locate in many popular instances of stances and demonstrations produced in the name of evangelical Christianity. Nor can I simply, credulously affirm that the good intentions of, say, Exodus and other SOCE ministries mitigate the real harm that ex-gay survivors attest to. Evangelicals' struggle between maneuvering against culture war foes and extending a hand in love to those same enemies is just that—a struggle, one of the definitive contests that defines evangelicalism as a concept. Yet it strikes me that this struggle recapitulates, mutatis mutandis, struggles of citizens within agonistic liberal democracy generally. That is, within democratic space, partisans for just about any vital cause that puts them in contention with other citizens have to balance "winning against" opponents with "winning over" opponents—that is, provided the parties involved are willing to maintain at least some level of democratic co-existence.[13] Evangelicalism's conversionist orientation—imperfectly realized as it may be—offers a reminder that democratically minded activism must always include an element of attraction and empathy with the enemy.

Yet neither do evangelicals shy away from the danger of alienating others. In stark contrast to the Durante Principle, where respect equals leaving others' beliefs alone and unknown, evangelicals declare, *I respect your deep convictions enough to challenge them with my own.* Moreover, they are unafraid to incorporate acts of challenge—whether overt (knocking on your door) or subtle (asking a question)—into their everyday lives as a discipline of activist outreach. The evangelists I examine in chapters three and four especially provide images of activism conceived not as a once-in-a-while, exceptional event but as a life vocation of engaging in and altering others' beliefs. To be sure, some iterations of this vocational activism risk seeming pre-packaged, annoying, and fake on the one hand (the kerygmatic, confrontational evangelisms) or covert to the point of meaninglessness on the other (the meta-kerygmatic evangelisms). The evangelicals I study, however, affirm that the labor of navigating these risks is well worth the results in terms of actual effects on others' lives.

I am also fascinated that, in initiating their challenge to others' beliefs (others' *non*-belief), the evangelicals I have studied readily assume the task of understanding of their target audiences. They accept the hard truth that evangelism is necessary rather than automatic, that due to the fallen creation, the gospel they share may initially seem counter-intuitive, counter-cultural, or even foolish to non-believers. Evangelicals engaged in outreach, especially those working from Schaefferian or worldview-based assumptions, thus make an effort to learn about the systems of sense-making in which their audiences live. They go out into the world, into other worldviews, rather than simply waiting for others to enter theirs. Evangelicals recognize that, however unimpeachable and self-evident their core truths may seem to them, others may not see it the same way. They are called upon to be polite, winsome, patient—but also honest and true to their convictions. For some, convincing unbelievers of the Truth may require some kind of moral shock: a fire-and-brimstone mini-lesson, a "good person test," or a Judgement House scene where Saint Peter calls you—yes, you!—and asks if your name is in the Book of Life. For others, making disciples may require long-term, open-ended relationships consisting of conversation after conversation: *Tell me about yourself. What leads you to believe that? Can I tell you my story?* For still others, evangelism may mean market research that helps a church know what kind of service might attract or repel visitors. Although some of these attempts turn out better than others—ideological empathy is, after all, fiendishly difficult—at the best of times evangelicals strive to maintain a spirit of openness even in the midst of scorn or failure. Conversion is, after all, a miraculous act of the Spirit rather than a work of humans, and lucky (or blessed) are those evangelists who see their efforts bear fruit.

I am, of course, describing the best-case examples of evangelism (as defined by evangelicals themselves), not necessarily the actual examples you may have encountered. From both personal experience and the input of countless friends and colleagues as I have worked on this book, I know that for every saintly Aunt Susan there is an equal and opposite member, "Uncle Derek," who is *one of those kind of Christians.* "Derek" broadcasts membership in a conservative evangelicalism and exhibits its worst features. Perhaps he spouts tired rhetoric about gays going to hell. Or he rails against Obama because of that pastor Jeremy Wright (or because of Obama's secret Muslim religion). Or he simply *pesters,* awkwardly, insistently, maddeningly about whether you'd like to talk about Jesus or go to church or read this tract. If Aunt Susan makes other faiths palatable, Uncle Derek (or "Co-worker Maria" or "Mom") contributes to the de-churching impulse that Kinnaman and Lyons credit with pushing people away from faith.

So yes: such people exist. Like any large group, evangelicalism has its better and lesser angels. I suppose, also, that in looking past such bad examples and insisting on a critically generous examination of evangelicals, I open myself to charges that I am advocating the same kind of tolerance and grace-fullness I have just criticized. To make a few final points, then, let me say that I am, most of the time, a fan of tolerating other faiths and ideologies—within limits—as a last-ditch alternative to violence. And, lest I give the concept short shrift, in some contexts a grit-your-teeth-and-bear-it tolerance *is* a desirable alternative to a real and present danger of violence. What I object to is tolerance's becoming a political or social end in itself, a goal we achieve and settle on. I also object to the notion that tolerance necessarily means *a prohibition of disagreement or persuasive overtures.* In no way do I believe that tolerating evangelicals, even understanding them deeply, means that one must never disagree with them, and disagree strongly, loudly, and boldly. Nor do I think they should have a monopoly on evangelizing. My own Christian faith—the realities it affirms, the ethics it espouses, and the demands it imposes—is something I share, though not generally through the techniques of my evangelical youth. I would like to see more performances from the progressive left that similarly share affirmative visions of How Things Ought To Be or What Is To Be Done in ways that audiences not already on board with activists can hear and be persuaded by. We're well-versed at protest, utopian performatives, and facilitation. How about persuasion? Acts of distinction? Microdramas of decision presented to audiences of one or two? Life disciplines of commitment to counter-cultural causes? Performances designed especially to attract neophytes to the cause?

Finally, I want to emphasize that for the progressive left to reassess its views toward and relationships with US evangelicals seems to me a necessary and long-overdue rehearsal for the real show, the deepening actuality of the globalized twenty-first century. The secular age disrupts everything, even positions ostensibly comfortable with secularism. It means *more* and *more diverse* faith/non-faith positions. The time when religious conviction could be dismissed as an endangered species in the face of regnant secularism has long passed. The present and future are incontestably religious. We see this in the changing demographics of evangelicalism in the United States. We see this in the vibrant and strikingly different evangelicalisms exploding in places like Africa, southern and eastern Asia, Latin America, and the Caribbean. We see this in the increasing and often tense intermixing of Islamic faiths and post-Christendom secularity in Europe. The secular age requires thoughtful modes of religious interaction. American Grace will likely be (or attempt to be) one of those modes, but so too will evangelical outreach. Within this secular age, it is incumbent upon everyone—evangelicals and non-evangelicals alike—to become better preachers and more curious listeners.

Notes

Introduction

1. Penn Jillette, "A Gift of a Bible," *Penn Says,* webcast, August 2008, Crackle.com, http://www.crackle.com/c/Penn_Says/A_Gift_of_a_Bible/2415037.

2. I should clarify, however, that not every group or Christian sect that *evangelizes* is *evangelical* in the sense of the groups I study. As I use the term in this book, *evangelicalism* names a distinct (though essentially contested) subset of Christianity, one that does not necessarily include any Christian group that engages in proselytizing outreach. See chapter two for a more detailed analysis of US evangelicalism.

3. Lance Gharavi, "About[/]Doing: Religion and Theater in the Academy," in *Religion, Theater, and Performance: Acts of Faith,* ed. Lance Gharavi, 210–24 (New York: Routledge, 2011).

Chapter 1

1. Stanley Fish, "One University, Under God?" *Chronicle of Higher Education* 51, no. 18 (2005).

2. Alain Badiou, *Saint Paul: The Foundation of Universalism,* trans. Ray Brassier (Stanford: Stanford University Press, 2003).

3. Žižek has published several engagements with faith and Christianity. As a starting point, see Slavoj Žižek, *The Fragile Absolute: Or, Why the Christian Legacy Is Worth Fighting For* (New York: Verso, 2000).

4. Jürgen Habermas, *An Awareness of What Is Missing: Faith and Reason in a Post-Secular Age,* trans. Ciaran Cronan (Cambridge: Polity Press, 2010).

5. Terry Eagleton, "Lunging, Flailing, Mispunching," Review of *The God Delusion* by Richard Dawkins, *London Review of Books* 28, no. 20 (2006), http://www.lrb.co.uk/v28/n20/terry-eagleton/lunging-flailing-mispunching. Eagleton expands on these arguments in *Reason, Faith, and Revolution: Reflections on the God Debate* (New Haven: Yale University Press, 2009).

6. Richard Schechner, *Performance Studies: An Introduction,* 2nd ed. (New York: Routledge, 2007), 2.

7. A broad discourse already exists exploring the historical and phenomenological links between theater and religious ritual. See, e.g., Victor Turner, *From Ritual to Theater: The Human Seriousness of Play* (New York: PAJ Publications, 2001), and Eric Csapo and Margaret C. Miller, eds., *The Origins of Ancient Theater in Ancient Greece and Beyond* (Cambridge: Cambridge University Press, 2007). Evangelicalism also boasts a growing body of work about theater, mainly in the form of how-to drama guides and collections of skit scripts for use in worship. For a more in-depth exploration, see Todd E. Johnson and Dale Savidge, *Performing the Sacred: Theology and Theater in Dialogue* (Grand Rapids, MI: Baker Academic, 2009).

8. To point out the obvious: I am playing mainly in the sandbox of the twentieth and twenty-first centuries when I discuss the umbrella of "activist performance" and scholarship about the same. I justify my temporal restriction partially in the knowledge that the terms *activist/activism* are of recent vintage. The *OED* reports that the first instance of *activism/activist* being used as I mean them occurs in 1920. I take *activism* thus to be a notion more historically specific than a generic person who behaves with political goals. A study like mine of activist performance thus differs from a more general inquiry into the politics of, say, Elizabethan history plays. Certainly one can research the political subtexts at work in *Richard II,* but to describe Shakespeare and the Lord Chamberlain's Men as *activist* in the same sense as an Occupy Wall Street protester forces an anachronistic frame onto a past event. Shakespeare would not have understood himself as "an activist" in the same way that a Tea Party demonstrator in the present does.

9. Jan Cohen-Cruz, "Motion of the Ocean: The Shifting Face of Theater for Social Change in the US since the 1950s," *Theater* 31, no. 3 (2001): 96.

10. Doug Paterson, "To For With: Some Observations on Community-Based Theater," in *ReImaging America: The Arts of Social Change,* ed. Mark O'Brien and Craig Little (Santa Cruz: New Society, 1990), 237–43.

11. For the standard study of Cornerstone and an excellent introduction to community-based performance more generally, see Sonja Kuftinec, *Staging America: Cornerstone and Community-Based Theater* (Carbondale: Southern Illinois University Press, 2003).

12. The proper degree of political engagement with community-based practices proves a tricky subject. Cohen-Cruz, writing elsewhere about community-based theater, quotes artist Linda Burnham, who characterizes the community-based crowd as split between "the people who see everything as a struggle against oppression" and "the people who believe creativity is an essential part of being human and a necessity for everyone." Jan Cohen-Cruz, "A Hyphenated Field: Community-Based Theater in the USA," *New Theater Quarterly,* Winter 2001: 373.

13. Tim Miller and David Román theorize this political tingle, writing specifically about the charge of queer community-based art in "Preaching to the Converted," *Theater Journal* 47, no. 2 (1995): 169–88.

14. Paulo Freire, *Pedagogy of the Oppressed,* trans. Mayra Bergman Ramos (New York: Continuum, 1997 [1970]).

15. In one of the most common TO activities, forum theater, one group of spect-actors will replay a scene of oppression taken from someone's life experience. After an initial performance, the scene repeats. In the repetitions, however, the joker invites spect-actors to attempt interventions. A spect-actor may freeze a scene, replace one of the performers, and try out different strategies for handling or reacting to the

oppression. Boal wrote a number of books explaining and refining his arsenal. Two good places to start are Augusto Boal, *The Theater of the Oppressed,* trans. Charles A. McBride (New York: Theater Communications Group, 1979), and Jan Cohen-Cruz and Mady Schutzman, eds., *Playing Boal: Theater, Therapy, Activism* (New York: Routledge, 1994).

16. Edward Hallett Carr, *What Is History?* (New York: Alfred A. Knopf, 1967), 9; Michel de Certeau, *Heterologies: Discourse on the Other,* trans. Michael Massumi (Minneapolis: University of Minnesota Press, 1997), 203.

17. In this project, I prefer *left-progressive/progressive left* to the adjective *liberal,* reserving the latter to refer to the broader political-philosophical tradition of human rights that values individual autonomy within social orders.

18. Baz Kershaw, *The Radical in Performance: Between Brecht and Baudrillard* (New York: Routledge, 1999), 16.

19. Ernesto Laclau and Chantal Mouffe, *Hegemony and Socialist Strategy: Towards a Radical Democratic Politics* (New York: Verso, 1985).

20. For more on radical democracy and radical democratic thought, see Chantal Mouffe, ed., *Dimensions of Radical Democracy: Pluralism, Citizenship, Community* (New York: Verso, 1992), and Lars Tønder and Lance Thomassen, eds., *Radical Democracy: Politics between Abundance and Lack* (New York: Manchester University Press, 2005).

21. Étienne Balibar, "Is a Philosophy of Human Civic Rights Possible? New Reflections on Equaliberty," *South Atlantic Quarterly* 103, no. 2–3 (2004): 311. Balibar specifically refers to the historically novel construction of *citizenship* within modern liberal democratic theory, where the rights of the citizen—the right to have rights, essentially—are considered universal: "[Equaliberty] poses, in the characteristic form of a double or simultaneous negation, that equality is impossible without liberty and liberty impossible without equality, and therefore that liberty and equality stand in a relation of mutual implication. It thus equates in principle generic humanity and citizenship, implying a juridical adequation of the 'rights of man' and the 'rights of the citizen.' It is thus, if you will, the principle of democratic constitution of the constitution in its typically modern universalist conception" (313). Balibar poses a friendly critique of equaliberty's problems, a critique that informs my own in this chapter.

22. I draw the redistribution/recognition dyad from Nancy Fraser and Axel Honneth, *Redistribution or Recognition: A Political-Philosophical Exchange* (New York: Verso, 2003).

23. Influential as they are, Laclau and Mouffe's work and radical democratic theory more generally are not without their critics. Many of the theorists I mentioned earlier (e.g., Žižek and Badiou) currently define themselves against some of the more prominent versions of radical democracy, seeing these as inextricable from a corrupt global capitalist system. Whether one can be radically democratic and revolutionarily anti-capitalist at once remains a point of contention. Nevertheless, I argue that, as a rule of thumb, most endeavors of the progressive left can be more or less fairly described as aligned with the radical democratic impulse to maximize equaliberty while eschewing the authority of a singular vision or program. Many (though not all) criticisms of radical democracy themselves rehearse the same basic values as the object of their criticism. The call to radicalize radical democracy remains within the ambit of Mouffe and Laclau's model.

24. See, for instance, the opening chapter to Jill Dolan's *Geographies of Learning: Theory and Practice, Activism and Performance* (Middletown, CT: Wesleyan University Press, 2001).

25. David Román, *Acts of Intervention: Performance, Gay Culture, and AIDS* (Bloomington: Indiana University Press, 1998), xxvi–xxviii.

26. Cohen-Cruz, "A Hyphenated Field," 372–75.

27. Eve Kosofsky Sedgwick, "Paranoid Reading and Reparative Reading, or You're So Paranoid, You Probably Think This Essay Is About You," in *Touching Feeling: Affect, Pedagogy, Performativity* (Durham: Duke University Press, 2003), 123–51.

28. Sedgwick, "Paranoid," 130.

29. Susan Leigh Foster, "Choreographies of Protest," *Theater Journal* 55, no. 3 (2003): 395–412.

30. "The obligation to protect the traditions and sovereignty of this state is my obligation and will be fulfilled by me," Wallace explained to the *Southern School News*. "I embody the sovereignty of this state." "Wallace, Aide Differ on Admissions," *Southern School News* 9, no. 12 (1963): 7. For a comprehensive study of this event, see E. Culpepper Clark, *The Schoolhouse Door: Segregation's Last Stand at the University of Alabama* (New York: Oxford University Press, 1993).

31. Foster, "Choreographies of Protest," 410.

32. Foster, "Choreographies of Protest," 397.

33. I do not mean that scholarship about non-left-progressive movements or performances does not exist; only that it is limited within conversations about *activist theater*. In disciplines such as social movement sociology, ethnography, or cultural anthropology, by contrast, in-depth research about, e.g., white supremacist movements or separatist enclaves is relatively common. Even in these fields, though, a left-progressive tint to the critical lens often obtains. See Kathleen M. Blee, "Ethnographies of the Far Right," *Journal of Contemporary Ethnography* 36, no. 2 (2007): 119–28. Within theater studies, performance historians do write about plays or performances that would not pass muster today as inclusive or tolerant, e.g., National Socialist *Thingspiele* from the 1930s, anti-Mormon melodramas of the 1800s, or North Korean propaganda performances. See, respectively, Erica Fischer-Lichte, *Theater, Sacrifice, Ritual: Exploring Forms of Political Theater* (New York: Routledge, 2005), chapter five; Megan Sanborn-Jones, *Performing American Identity in Anti-Mormon Melodrama* (New York: Routledge, 2009); and Suk-Young Kim, *Illusive Utopia: Theater, Film, and Everyday Performance in North Korea* (Ann Arbor: University of Michigan Press, 2010). But such nonprogressive performances are rarely if ever considered within the same rubric as activism or "theater for social change."

34. See, e.g., Kershaw, *The Politics of Performance*, 21; Janelle Reinelt, "Notes for a Radical Democratic Theater: Productive Crises and the Challenge of Indeterminacy," in *Staging Resistance: Essays on Political Theater*, ed. Jeanne Colleran and Jenny S. Spencer (Ann Arbor: University of Michigan Press, 1998), 286–87; Jan Cohen-Cruz, ed., *Radical Street Performance: An International Anthology* (New York: Routledge, 1998), 2.

35. Cohen-Cruz's anthology itself contains only one example of conservative or right-wing performance, David Welch's study of a Nuremburg Rally in 1934, "From *Triumph des Willens (Triumph of the Will, 1935)*," in Cohen-Cruz, *Radical Street*, 169–78.

36. One exception—I am sure there are others I have missed—would be a working-group session, "Vanguards of the Right," in the 2009 meeting of the American Society for Theater Research. I am heartened to learn that this session is the basis for a forthcoming anthology from the University of Michigan. Still, the singularity of such a session and its anthology hints at a lacuna in the field. Some key examples of the elision or marginalization of activist work from non-left perspectives might include articles in the 2001 special issue of *Theater* on Theater and Social Change; Cohen-Cruz, *Radical*

Street Performance (which, as noted, includes one example of non-left theater); Colleran and Spenser, *Staging Resistance* (which also includes only one article dealing tangentially with right-wing, anti-abortion demonstrations, Linda Kuntz's analysis of *Keely and Du*); Tim Prentki and Sheila Preston, eds., *The Applied Theater Reader* (New York: Routledge, 2008), and Susan Haedicke and Tobin Nellhaus, eds., *Performing Democracy: International Perspectives on Community-Based Performance* (Ann Arbor: University of Michigan Press, 2001). I hasten to add that all of these are valuable resources. It's just that they are more valuable for critics and activists operating within left-progressive perspectives.

37. For example, David Schlossman concedes that activism may occur on both the right and the left, but (citing his familiarity with and participation in left-leaning activisms) he restricts his study of activist performance "to refer specifically to non-violent, progressive activism." David A. Schlossman, *Actors and Activists: Performance, Politics, and Exchange among Social Worlds* (New York: Routledge, 2002), 27.

38. For Dubin's original distinction, see Steven C. Dubin, *Arresting Images: Impolitic Art and Uncivil Actions* (New York: Routledge, 1992), 227, 353n.3. Dubin draws on the work of Howard S. Becker's notion of "moral crusaders" and deals mainly with left-inclusive/right-exclusive distinctions as they relate to the production, reception, and censorship of offensive art. Dubin notes that the left (or "some zealots on the left") can be at times exclusionary and censorious, but that in the long run left-leaning activists tend to push for more inclusion.

39. For an example of interpositionist rhetoric, see James Kilpatrick, *The Southern Case for School Segregation* ([New York]: Crowell-Collier, [1962]). For secondary sources, see Garrett Epps, "The Littlest Rebel: James J. Kilpatrick and the Second Civil War," *Constitutional Commentary* 10 (1993): 19–36; and Numan V. Bartley, *The Rise of Massive Resistance: Race and Politics in the South during the 1950's* (Baton Rouge: Louisiana State University Press, 1969).

40. See, for instance, Stephan Lesher, *George Wallace: American Populist* (Reading, MA: Addison-Wesley, 1994), 162–63.

41. Historian Jeff Frederick neatly punctures any notion that Wallace was innocent of stoking the fires of racial unrest for his own political benefit. See Frederick, *Stand Up for Alabama: Governor George Wallace* (Tuscaloosa: University of Alabama Press, 2007), 57–63.

42. In this matter Wallace was more lucky than brilliant; it was Nicholas Katzenbach (the deputy attorney general) who actually decided (with the best intentions) that he and not the students should physically confront Wallace, an action that played into Wallace's desired framing. See Dan T. Carter, *The Politics of Rage: George Wallace, the Origins of the New Conservatism, and the Transformation of American Politics,* 2nd ed. (Baton Rouge: Louisiana State University Press, 2000), 147–48.

43. "I am going to stand for you at the University of Alabama," Wallace assured his constituents by television in a statewide announcement before the protest. "You can stand up for Alabama and stand up for me by standing up at your home or your workbench on that day." Claude Sitton, "Alabama Guardsman in Tuscaloosa as Wallace Plans to Defy U.S. Court," *New York Times,* June 10, 1963, 20.

44. As I have argued elsewhere, Phelps and his band are uninterested in winning converts. They proclaim that God hates fags not because they expect anyone will find their arguments convincing—they do not expect that anyone will—but because their beliefs impel them to act as physical manifestations of God's wrathful conviction of temporal depravity. See John Fletcher, "Ten-Foot Pole Historiography: Lib-

eral Democracy, Ideological Difference, and Despicable Acts," in *Querying Difference in Theater History,* ed. Scott Magelssen and Ann Haugo, 16–24 (Newcastle: Cambridge Scholars Publishing, 2007).

45. *Snyder v. Phelps* et al. 562 U.S. __ (2011), http://www.supremecourt.gov/opinions/10pdf/09-751.pdf.

46. Nor, it should be remembered, did all those protesting against the WTO align behind a radically anti-capitalist position. For a study of some of the tensions between some 1999 WTO protest groups (especially direct-action protesters and labor unions), see Margaret Levi and Gillian H. Murphy, "Coalitions of Contention: The Case of the WTO Protests in Seattle," *Political Studies* 54 (2006): 651–70.

47. Often forgotten in accounts of present-day nonviolent protests is the multiplicity of ways in which *violence* is defined. As Foster documents, Martin Luther King Jr.'s nonviolent philosophy elaborated strictly defined guides for nonviolent behavior. Foster, "Choreographies," 399. The WTO protesters, being a movement of many movements, held diverse understandings of nonviolence. Some post-anarchist groups, for example, argue that property damage is *not* violence since it does not physically harm human beings, or that such violence is nothing compared to police violence or the "violence" of capitalism. For an overview of this perennial debate about violence on the anti-globalization left, see Chris Hurl, "Anti-Globalization and the 'Diversity of Tactics,'" *Upping the Ante* 1 (2005), http://uppingtheanti.org/journal/article/01-anti-globalization-and-diversity-of-tactics/. One does not have to be hyper-conservative to see how such a debate troubles the descriptor *nonviolent* for officers charged with preventing violence.

48. I am indebted to Sonja Kuftinec for helping me to arrive at this insight.

49. This is not to say that the police were uniformly innocent of abuses of power. Nor does my generous reading of the police here negate the fact that, in terms of sheer force, the police had (and in many cases realized) incomparably greater and more damaging tools than were available to the protesters and that the use of that force in response to a real or imagined "anarchist" minority is often disproportional in the extreme. That factor alone renders a simple equation between protesters and police impossible. My point is not that the police and the protesters were equal partners, only that they were in fact both engaged as dancers in the activist space.

50. Timothy Burke, "A Scholar, an Expert, an Intellectual," *Easily Distracted,* blog, August 21, 2012, http://blogs.swarthmore.edu/burke/2012/08/21/a-scholar-an-expert-an-intellectual/.

51. Michael Walzer, *On Toleration* (New Haven: Yale University Press, 1997), 8–9.

52. "Politics exists," writes Rancière, "because those who have no right to be counted as speaking beings [the 'part with no part'] make themselves of some account, setting up a community by the fact of placing in common a wrong that is nothing more than this very confrontation, the contradiction of two worlds in a single world: the world where they are and the world where they are not, the world where there is something 'between' them and those who do not acknowledge them as speaking beings and the world where there is nothing." Jacques Rancière, *Disagreement: Politics and Philosophy,* trans. Julie Rose (Minneapolis: University of Minnesota Press, 1999), 27.

53. Such a vision, in much more attenuated articulation, resembles that of Carl Schmidt, the interwar German theorist that Mouffe draws on. For Schmidt, politics essentially concerns dividing the world into friends and enemies. His critique of parliamentary democracy emphasized (as Mouffe does) that system's tendency to place

a premium on consensus at the expense of actual conflict. Mouffe steps away from Schmidt (and, it must be said, away from several other present-day, non-Schmidtian theorists) in seeking a mode of conflict that preserves the bite of committed difference without also necessitating the destruction of one's foes.

54. The next few paragraphs summarize arguments I make in different form in "Performing Coexistence with Good Faith Intolerance," in *Religion, Theater, and Performance: Acts of Faith,* ed. Lance Gharavi, 225–40 (New York: Routledge, 2011).

55. Wendy Brown, *Regulating Aversion: Tolerance in the Age of Identity and Empire* (Princeton: Princeton University Press, 2007), 86–88.

56. Stanley Fish, *The Trouble with Principle* (Cambridge: Harvard University Press, 1999), 249.

57. Swaine refers to such positions as "heteronomous" to distinguish them from the ideal "autonomous" citizen of liberal democracy whose ideas are theoretically always open to reassessment and change. See Lucas Swaine, "Deliberate and Free: Heteronomy and the Public Sphere," *Philosophy and Social Criticism* 35, no. 1–2 (2009): 184–88.

58. Brown, *Regulating Aversion,* 40.

59. Žižek: "The much-praised 'proliferation of new political subjectivities,' the demise of every 'essentialist' fixation, the assertion of full contingency, occur against the background of a certain silent *renunciation* and *acceptance:* the renunciation of the idea of a global change in the fundamental relations of our society . . . and, consequently, acceptance of the liberal democratic capitalist framework which *remains the same.*" See Slavoj Žižek, Judith Butler, and Ernesto Laclau, *Contingency, Hegemony, Universality: Contemporary Dialogues on the Left* (New York: Verso, 2000), 321.

60. Josh McDowell and Bob Hostetler, *The New Tolerance: How a Cultural Movement Threatens to Destroy You, Your Faith, and Your Children* (Carol Stream, IL: Tyndale, 1998), 18–20.

61. Sociologist Bradley R. E. Wright points out that surveys indicate that US evangelicals tend to assume that other groups view them more negatively than those groups actually do. See his *Christians Are Hate-Filled Hypocrites . . . And Other Lies You've Been Told* (Minneapolis: Bethany House, 2010), 204.

62. See, e.g., Glenn Gentry, "Rawls and Religious Community: Ethical Decision Making in the Public Square," *Christian Bioethics* 13 (2007): 171–81.

63. Ola Sigurdson, "Beyond Secularism? Towards a Post-Secular Political Theology," *Modern Theology* 26, no. 2 (2010): 184.

64. Stendahl's three rules of religious understanding are both infamously unwritten (he delivered them at a press conference in 1985) and ubiquitously quoted. For one source, see the obituary by the Tanenbaum Center for Interreligious Understanding, "Remembering Bishop Krister Stendahl," April 16, 2008, http://www.bc.edu/dam/files/research_sites/cjl/pdf/Tanenbaum_Stendahl.pdf.

Chapter 2

1. Spencer, it should be noted, was not merely a random blogger but one of the most visible figures in the Christian blogosphere. See his obituary in the *Associated Baptist Press:* Bob Allen, "'Internet Monk' Michael Spencer, acclaimed religion blogger, dead at 53," *Associated Baptist Press,* April 6, 2010, http://www.abpnews.com/content/view/5019/53/. His Internet Monk blog continues under others' management.

2. For a page that preserves all three original posts, see Michael Spencer, "The

Original Coming Evangelical Collapse Posts," Internet Monk, blog, March 2009, http://www.internetmonk.com/archive/the-original-coming-evangelical-collapse-posts. For the article (which condenses the posts), see Michael Spencer, "The Coming Evangelical Collapse," *Christian Science Monitor,* March 10, 2009, http://www.csmonitor.com/2009/0310/p09s01-coop.html. My quotes here reference the online posts.

3. Allen's *Associated Baptist Press* obituary for Spencer makes special mention of the article (Allen). For examples of podcasts dealing with the article, see the following: William Lane Craig, "The Coming Evangelical Collapse," *Reasonable Faith Podcast,* June 22, 2009, http://www.reasonablefaith.org/podcast/Reasonable_Faith.xml; Tony Campolo, "Campolo—Discussion of the Coming Evangelical Collapse Part I," *Tony Campolo Podcast,* July 30, 2009, http://www.tonycampolo.org/podcast/tonycampolo_podcast.xml (this website also has Parts II and III of Campolo's discussion, Aug. 8, 2009, and Sept. 3, 2009, respectively); and Craig Donofrio and William M. Cwirla, "Episode 43: Michael Spencer," *The God Whisperers* (podcast), March 30, 2009, http://itunes.apple.com/us/podcast/the-god-whisperers/id286040700.

4. I draw Berger's assessments from two sources: Peter Berger and Anton Zijderveld, *In Praise of Doubt: How to Have Convictions without Becoming a Fanatic* (New York: HarperOne, 2009), 2–7; and R. Albert Mohler Jr., "Rethinking Secularization: An Interview with Peter Berger," *Thinking in Public* (podcast), Oct. 11, 2010, http://www.albertmohler.com/2010/10/11/rethinking-secularization-a-conversation-with-peter-berger/. For Berger's early work on religion and secularization, see Peter L. Berger, *The Sacred Canopy: Elements of a Sociological Theory of Religion* (New York: Anchor Books, 1967).

5. Berger and Zijderveld, *In Praise,* 4.

6. Indeed, such anti-politicization arguments form part of his diagnosis of evangelicalism's malaise.

7. Taylor defines faith via two criteria: "the belief in transcendent reality, on the one hand, on the connected aspiration to a transformation which goes beyond ordinary human flourishing on the other." Charles Taylor, *A Secular Age* (Cambridge: Belknap Press, 2007), 510.

8. Taylor, *Secular Age,* 513–14. Taylor also cautions that secularity in this sense unfolds unequally in different times and places. Some contexts insist upon conformity to belief more strongly than others. The secular age, Taylor clarifies, does not mean that there exists now a "level playing field" between belief and unbelief "since what we really have is not a playing field at all, but a very accidented terrain; there are lots of tilts, but they don't all slide in the same direction. The tilt of the Bible Belt is not that of the urban university" (531).

9. Donald W. Dayton, "Some Doubts about the Usefulness of the Category 'Evangelical,'" in *The Variety of American Evangelicalism,* ed. Donald W. Dayton and Robert K. Johnston (Knoxville: University of Tennessee Press, 1991), 245–51. Reflecting on his own anthology of essays about evangelicalism, Dayton concludes that (to give the full quote) "I find myself unable to make the common label 'evangelical' describe the range of movements covered in this volume. I, therefore, avoid the word wherever possible and even regret that it must be used in the title of the book. I would rather call for a moratorium on the use of the term, in the hope that we would be forced to more appropriate and useful categories of analysis" (251). Frequently cited as it is, Dayton's call remains largely unheeded. I follow this trend in my present project.

10. Jon R. Stone, *On the Boundaries of American Evangelicalism: The Postwar Evan-*

gelical Coalition (New York: St. Martin's, 1997), 4–5. Stone quotes the kaleidoscope metaphor from historian Timothy Smith.

11. "Parachurch" refers to faith-based (and in this context evangelical) organizations that operate outside of the aegis of a specific congregation or denomination. The Campus Crusade for Christ (now called "Cru"), which I discuss in detail in the next chapter, is an example of a parachurch organization.

12. D. G. Hart, *Deconstructing Evangelicalism: Conservative Protestantism in the Age of Billy Graham* (Grand Rapids, MI: Baker, 2004), 125.

13. Reviews of Hart in scholarly journals tend to mirror my own reaction: Hart's criticisms are probing and his historiographic critique strong, but his conclusion—evangelicalism's constructed nature renders it untrue—doesn't convince. See, for instance, Timothy Larsen, Review of *Deconstructing Evangelicalism, Journal of Religion* 85, no. 1 (2005): 120–21, and Stephen Tuck, "Deconstructing Evangelicalism. Conservative Protestantism in the Age of Billy Graham/Wonderful Words of Life. Hymns in American Protestant History and Theology," *Journal of Ecclesiastical History* 56, no. 3 (July 2005): 633–35. It does not help Hart's case that he himself used the term in previously published work. In any case, *evangelicalism* remains a term of choice for many (at least academic) evangelicals. See, e.g., the lively conversations in Stanley Gundry, Andrew David Naselli, and Collin Hansen, eds., *Four Views on the Spectrum of Evangelicalism* (Grand Rapids, MI: Zondervan, 2011).

14. I take a cue from Robert K. Johnston's entry on evangelicalism from the *Oxford Companion to Christian Thought,* ed. Adrian Hastings, Alistair Mason, and Hugh Pyper (New York: Oxford University Press, 2000), 217–20. There Johnston offers history, sociology, and theology as possible modes of defining the term. R. Albert Mohler Jr. more recently has suggested investigating evangelicalism through historical, phenomenological, and normative lenses. See his entry on "Confessional Evangelicalism" in Gundry, Naselli, and Hansen, *Four Views,* 68–96.

15. I am not the first to consider evangelicalism as such. While discussing the slipperiness of *evangelical,* Robert K. Johnston and Donald W. Dayton both mention essentially contested concepts (though without giving much in the way of explanation). See, e.g., Johnston, "American Evangelicalism: An Extended Family," in Dayton and Johnston, 253–54; Dayton, "The Limits of Evangelicalism: The Pentecostal Tradition," in Dayton and Johnston, 36–56, 47; and Mohler, "Confessional Evangelicalism," 69–70. For Gallie's initial discussion about essentially contested concepts, see W. B. Gallie, "Essentially Contested Concepts," *Proceedings of the Aristotelian Society,* n.s., 56 (1955–56): 167–98. A useful investigation and expansion of Gallie's theories is David Collier, Fernando Daniel Hidalgo, and Andra Olivia Maciuceanu's article "Essentially Contested Concepts: Debates and Applications," *Journal of Political Ideologies* 11, no. 3 (2006): 211–46.

16. Gallie himself refers to essentially contested concepts as positively valued (Gallie, "Essentially," 171). Subsequent theorists have since expanded the term to include negatively valued concepts as well (e.g., obscenity, fascism, bigotry) (Collier, Hidalgo, and Maciuceanu, "Essentially," 216). Gallie specifies seven criteria for approaching a concept as essentially contested. They are (in his original order) as follows: appraisiveness, internal complexity, diverse describability, persistent openness, reciprocal recognition of the concept's contestedness by parties, reference to an exemplar or core that anchors the concept, and the progressiveness of the continued contestation (Gallie, "Essentially," 171). All of these easily apply to the term *evangelicalism.*

17. David W. Bebbington, *Evangelicalism in Modern Britain: A History from the 1730s to the 1980s* (New York: Routledge, 1989), 1. There Bebbington notes one use of "Evaungelicalles" to refer to adherents to the Reformation by Thomas More in 1531, but this appears to be an anomaly rather than a common practice.

18. See George M. Marsden, *Fundamentalism and American Culture: The Shaping of Twentieth-Century Evangelicalism, 1870–1925* (New York: Oxford University Press, 1980), 44–45. Throughout this historical overview, I rely heavily on Marsden's influential account of the rise of fundamentalism and the mid-1900s advent of neo-evangelicalism. For the rise of neo-evangelicalism, see Marsden's *Reforming Fundamentalism: Fuller Seminary and the New Evangelicalism* (Grand Rapids, MI: Eerdmans, 1987). Marsden's *Understanding Fundamentalism and Evangelicalism* (Grand Rapids, MI: Eerdmans, 1991) summarizes and elaborates on elements from both of these latter works. Supplementing Marsden's history are some other key works. For complementary accounts of evangelicalism's history in the nineteenth and twentieth centuries, see Ernest Sandeen, *Roots of Fundamentalism: British and American Millenarianism, 1800–1930* (Chicago: University of Chicago Press, 1970), and Dayton and Johnston, *Variety*. Robert E. Webber provides both a cogent summary of evangelicalism's early twentieth-century phases as well as a very detailed account of US evangelicalism's transformations from the late 1960s on in his book *The Younger Evangelicals: Facing the Challenges of the New World* (Grand Rapids, MI: Baker Books, 2002). Dayton's contributions to evangelical historiography are especially important as a balance to Marsden's marked preference for the Reformed (i.e., Calvinist) tradition as central to evangelicalism. See, in addition to the previously cited volume he edited with Johnston, Dayton's own history of the (decidedly non-Reformed) Pentecostal tradition, *The Theological Roots of Pentecostalism* (Peabody, MA: Hendrickson Publishers, 1991). Wheaton College's Institute for the Study of American Evangelicals (ISAE) hosts an excellent website with a thorough overview of evangelicalism's history, theology, and presence in the United States. See Homepage, Institute for the Study of American Evangelicals, http://isae.wheaton.edu/. Finally, for a recent overview of evangelicalism's past and present, one that incorporates a broader perspective (geographically, temporally, and theologically) than the individual historians I've mentioned, see Mark Russell et al., *Routes and Radishes and Other Things to Talk About at the Evangelical Crossroads* (Grand Rapids, MI: Zondervan, 2010), 13–31, 33–50.

19. For detailed studies of the shift in biblical (and especially evangelical and fundamentalist) scholarship in the United States from the eighteenth to the twentieth centuries, see Nathan O. Hatch and Mark A. Noll, eds., *The Bible in America: Essays in Cultural History* (New York: Oxford University Press, 1982).

20. Timothy P. Weber, "The Two-Edged Sword: The Fundamentalist Use of the Bible," in Hatch and Noll, *Bible,* 103.

21. This strengthening occurred on two levels—academic and popular. Academically, theologians like B. B. Warfield and A. A. Hodge at Princeton Seminary proposed a formal theology of biblical inspiration as verbal (i.e., every word inspired by God), inerrant (i.e., factually correct in all truth-statements), infallible (i.e., internally consistent in all theological propositions), and plenary (i.e., complete in all respects). On a popular level, preachers such as Dwight L. Moody helped to spread a "plain sense" hermeneutic, stressing that the Bible is trustworthy and complete in translated English, available for interpretation to any person regardless of academic/theological training or ecclesiastical station. For the spread of the "every man an interpreter" doctrine, see Nathan O. Hatch, "Sola Scriptura and Novus Ordo Seclorum," in Hatch

and Noll, *Bible*, 59–78. For the roots and rise of the "common sense" hermeneutic, see George M. Marsden, "Everyone One's Own Interpreter? The Bible, Science, and Authority in Mid-Nineteenth-Century America," in Hatch and Noll, *Bible*, 79–100. For the rise of the influential Princeton arguments for biblical inerrancy, see Marsden, *Fundamentalism*, 109–18. Grant Wacker's "The Demise of Biblical Civilization," Hatch and Noll, 121–38, continues the story of Princeton Theology that Marsden begins, where twentieth-century critics within Warfield and Hodge's own tradition began disputing their doctrines.

22. See Marsden, *Fundamentalism*, chapter ten, for more about fundamentalists' "Great Reversal" from prior engagements with social activism. In part these prior engagements included a general push against perceived decadence of industrialized urban culture (drinking, theater, gambling, card-playing, etc.). Also in the air—though not universal—was a rise in millenarian thinking, which emphasized the imminent return of Christ in judgment of the wicked world. In preparation for this soon-to-occur Second Advent, believers were to withdraw from society and prepare themselves for the apocalypse. For a detailed, well-regarded study of this influence on fundamentalism, see Sandeen, *Roots*, and Timothy P. Weber, "Premillennialism and the Branches of Evangelicalism," in Dayton and Johnston, *Variety*, 5–21.

23. See Sandeen, 188–207, for a thorough discussion of these publications, their origins, and their effects. *The Fundamentals* are available online in their entirety in several locations. See, e.g., Russell A. Torrey, ed., *The Fundamentals of the Christian Faith, The Fundamentals Homepage*, R. W. Nadeau, December 23, 2005, http://www.xmission.com/~fidelis/.

24. Quoted in Marsden, *Fundamentalism*, 159. The term *fundamentalist* seems to have come not merely from *The Fundamentals* but also from lists of "fundamental doctrines," which included such things as the literalist view of scripture, the material reality of miracles, and substitutionary atonement. Marsden stresses that the battle in question was primarily doctrinal rather than social. Sandeen stresses that the lists of fundamentals typically cited by fundamentalists represented not a restatement of previously held or traditional beliefs but a novel collage of beliefs from a variety of strands. See Sandeen, *Roots*, 192.

25. See J. Gresham Machen, *Christianity and Liberalism* (Grand Rapids, MI: Eerdmans, 1991 [1923]). For more on Machen, see Marsden, *Understanding*, chapter seven.

26. Webber, *The Younger Evangelicals*, 26–30.

27. I revisit this controversy and its aftermath in greater detail in my chapter on the Creation Museum. Here, as there, I rely heavily on Ronald L. Numbers, *The Creationists: From Scientific Creationism to Intelligent Design*, expanded ed. (Cambridge: Harvard University Press, 2006), chapter five.

28. For information on these failed overtures and subsequent splits, see Marsden, *Fundamentalism*, chapters twenty and twenty-one.

29. Carl F. H. Henry, *The Uneasy Conscience of Modern Fundamentalism* (Grand Rapids, MI: Eerdmans, 1947), 19.

30. See Marsden, *Reshaping*, for a detailed account of this institution and its impact on evangelicalism.

31. Marsden, *Understanding*, 73.

32. Each of these entities has a well-developed web presence and is articulate about its own founding and history. See Homepage, National Association of Evangelicals, March 7, 2011, http://www.nae.net/; Homepage, Campus Crusade for Christ

International, http://www.ccci.org/; and Homepage, *Christianity Today,* http://www.christianitytoday.com/ct/. I examine Campus Crusade for Christ in detail in the next chapter.

33. Webber, *Younger,* 30–32.

34. See Webber, *Younger,* 33–46, for a detailed review of evangelicalism during the late twentieth century.

35. For a study of the US Christian right as it relates to conservatism more generally, see Martin Durham, *The Christian Right, the Far Right, and the Boundaries of American Conservatism* (New York: Manchester University Press, 2000).

36. See Webber, *Younger,* 36. Webber notes that this pragmatism simultaneously dehistoricized the Christian message, stripping it of direct ties to religious tradition.

37. For a lively study of this trend, see Heather Hendershot, *Shaking the World for Jesus: Media and Conservative Evangelical Culture* (Chicago: University of Chicago Press, 2004).

38. Evangelicalism has even made certain overtures—to a limited extent—to Roman Catholicism such that one can speak reservedly of a kind of Catholic evangelicalism. For a study of the evangelical-Catholic encounter (as well as some other opening-up moments), see chapter four of Gary Dorrien, *The Remaking of Evangelical Theology* (Louisville, KY: Westminster John Knox Press, 1998).

39. For a history of African American Protestantism as it relates to white evangelicalism, see Milton G. Sernett, "Black Religion and the Question of Evangelical Identity," in Dayton and Johnston, *Variety,* 135–47.

40. Sociologist Christian Smith, in his *Christian America? What Evangelicals Really Want* (Berkeley: University of California Press, 2000), finds 12.8 percent of the US population identifies as fundamentalist (17).

41. Mohler, "Confessional Evangelicalism," 75–77.

42. Keven T. Bauder, "Fundamentalism," in Gundry, Naselli, and Hansen, *Four Views,* 21n5.

43. Conrad Hackett and D. Michael Lindsay, "Measuring Evangelicalism: Consequences of Different Operationalization Strategies," *Journal for the Scientific Study of Religion* 47, no. 3 (2008): 499. Hackett and Lindsay's work receives a useful expansion and explanation in Bradley R. E. Wright's *Christians Are Hate-Filled Hypocrites . . . And Other Lies You've Been Told* (Minneapolis: Bethany House, 2010). A sociologist, Wright speaks to a popular, mainly evangelical audience, and his main purpose involves a critique of shoddily used survey data by and about evangelicals. Nevertheless, his book helpfully and accurately explains for the layman key methods and debates used by sociologists of religion to gauge attitudes of and about evangelicals in the United States. His bibliography, though not as extensive or advanced as Hackett and Lindsay's, proved most useful to me.

44. Brian Steensland et al., "The Measure of American Religion: Toward Improving the State of the Art," *Social Forces* 79, no. 1 (2000): 291–318.

45. The General Social Survey (GSS) is a bi-annual, extensive survey of Americans. Wright describes the GSS as "the Cadillac of national studies because it has been collected every year or two since 1972, and thus it allows us to track changes in religious beliefs, attitudes, and affiliation." Wright notes that the GSS's dataset (several thousand), while adequate for measuring a majority US religion like Christianity, proves less useful for gauging other faiths. See Wright, *Christians,* 30, 228.

46. "Other" here would include not only minority faiths such as Islam, Buddhism, and Hinduism but also Christian-variant religions such as the Church of Jesus Christ

of Latter-Day Saints and the Jehovah's Witnesses. For a general discussion of faith families and research divisions within the United States, albeit one pitched toward a more popular rather than scholarly audience, see Robert D. Putnam and David E. Campbell, *American Grace: How Religion Divides and Unites Us* (New York: Simon and Schuster, 2010), chapter one. Putnam and Campbell tend to use a schema similar to the RELTRAD system.

47. As I will discuss, strict distinctions between the Black Church and evangelical churches are troubled, especially as a large percentage of Black Christians readily self-identify as evangelical and hold to conservative evangelical theologies. Sociologists often preserve (or even—as in the case with Gallup—impose) a distinction, however, due to the fact that many Black Churches feature a unique emphasis on African American culture, issues, and traditions, blending these into evangelical theological praxis in ways that set them apart from predominantly white or mixed-race evangelical congregations. Still, debate persists about when and how to categorize certain churches or pastors as evangelical rather than or in addition to "Black." See Putnam and Campbell, *American Grace,* 15, 573 n19 and Steensland et al., "Measure," 294. For a more careful investigation into Black theology and denominations, albeit with an emphasis on televangelism, see Jonathan L. Walton, *Watch This! The Ethics and Aesthetics of Black Televangelism* (New York: New York University Press, 2009). Walton discusses the history of categorizing African American Christianity on 26–33.

48. Hackett and Lindsay, "Measuring," 505.

49. Steensland et al., "Measure," 312n16; Putnam and Campbell, *American Grace,* 15, 573n19.

50. For an enlightening study of T. D. Jakes's ministry and theology, see Walker, *Watch This!,* chapter four. Walker points out that Jakes's theological affiliation, Apostolic Pentecostalism (also known as "Oneness" or "Jesus Only" Pentecostalism) technically denies the existence of the Trinity, a distinction that most within evangelicalism and on the religious right gloss over (Walker, *Watch,* 77, 104). At the very least, putting Jakes's Pentecostalism and Wright's liberation-theology UCC Christianity together into the same category makes for a strained maneuver.

51. Steensland et al., "Measure," explain that research suggests the nondenominational or no denominational movement is primarily an evangelical rather than mainline phenomenon, though they admit their conclusions in this area are tentative (298–99). For their detailed list of denominations and affiliations, see the appendix to their article (314–16).

52. Hackett and Lindsay helpfully present a table with yearly reports from Gallup's measurements on 502.

53. For this reason, Gallup at times couples its self-identification question with two others based on belief and action: whether the person has encouraged others to believe in Jesus Christ and whether the person believes the Bible to be the actual word of God. Furthermore, Gallup also excludes from the category "evangelical" any nonwhites and non-Catholics (though either of these groups may self-identify as evangelical or born-again). See Frank Newport, "Who Are the Evangelicals?" Gallup, June 24, 2005, http://www.gallup.com/poll/17041/Who-Evangelicals.aspx.

54. Hart, *Deconstructing,* 176.

55. David Kinnaman and Gabe Lyons, *UnChristian: What a New Generation Really Thinks About Christianity . . . And Why It Matters* (Grand Rapids, MI: Baker, 2007), 46.

56. Kinnaman and Lyons, *UnChristian,* 249–50.

57. See Barna Group, "Survey Explores Who Qualifies as an Evangelical," *The*

Barna Group, January 18, 2007, http://www.barna.org/barna-update/article/13-culture/111-survey-explores-who-qualifies-as-an-evangelical?q=evangelical. George Barna, quoted in the "Call for Clarity" subsection of the article, suggests even this small number may overestimate the real number of authentic evangelicals.

58. Hackett and Lindsay, "Measuring," 500.

59. Smith, *Christian,* 9. Smith's first chapter provides an admirable diagnosis of major fallacies common to writing about evangelicals, fallacies I strive in various ways to avoid here. His project also provides a valuable, nuanced examination of just what evangelicals mean by imagining a "Christian nation." I depart slightly from Smith mainly in that (at least in this work) he largely defines evangelicals as a subset of conservative (in a theological sense) Protestants, whereas my study touches on sectors of evangelicalism that aren't necessarily conservative.

60. Newport, "Who Are the Evangelicals?"

61. Many evangelicals formally repudiate creeds per se as vestiges of restrictive Catholicism. I use the Nicene Creed here, however, because most evangelicals—even those opposed to creeds—would affirm its tenets as basic (if not comprehensive) orthodoxy. For a conversation about evangelical attitudes about creeds, see Michael Spencer, "The Evangelical Liturgy 15: The Creeds," *The Internet Monk,* blog, Oct. 9, 2009, http://www.internetmonk.com/archive/the-evangelical-liturgy-15-the-creeds. For the text and history of the Creed, see John H. Leith, ed., *Creeds of the Churches: A Reader in Christian Doctrine from the Bible to the Present* (Garden City, NY: Anchor Books, 1963), 31–33. In Leith's text, the Creed is called the Constantinopolitan Creed, or the Creed of the 150 Fathers of Constantinople, in reference to the fact that, despite its name, the Creed comes not from the 325 Council of Nicaea but (according to the records from the 451 Council of Chalcedon) from the 381 Council of Constantinople.

62. See Bebbington, *Evangelicalism,* 2–17. Bebbington's quadrilateral, as it's sometimes called, is widely cited by evangelical theologians as useful (if necessarily incomplete and general). See, for example, Mark Russell et al., *Routes and Radishes and Other Things to Talk about at the Evangelical Crossroads* (Grand Rapids, MI: Zondervan, 2010), 13–31, 18–20. For an enlightening interview wherein Bebbington reflects on the longevity of his fourfold description, see Mohler, "Evangelical Identity Revisited: A Conversation with Historians David Bebbington and Gregory Wills," *Thinking in Public* (podcast), September 13, 2010, http://www.albertmohler.com/2010/09/13/evangelical-identity-revisited-a-conversation-with-historians-david-bebbington-and-gregory-wills/.

63. For an extremely useful guide to some of the major areas of evangelical disagreement, see Gregory A. Boyd and Paul R. Eddy, *Across the Spectrum: Understanding Issues in Evangelical Theology* (Grand Rapids, MI: Baker Academic, 2007). Dorrien, *Remaking,* provides a much more detailed, historical-chronological account of twentieth-century evangelical debates over theology. Gundry, Naselli, and Hansen, *Four Views,* likewise lay out some key intra-evangelical tensions.

64. Recently, sociologist (and self-proclaimed "evangelical Catholic") Christian Smith has issued a combination study of and jeremiad against evangelical biblicism. There he outlines ten assumptions about the Bible that, taken together, create the constellation of beliefs that is biblicism. These are as follows: (1) Divine Writing—the Bible represents the direct, literal words of God; (2) Total Representation—the Bible (the Protestant canon of sixty-six books contained in two testaments) is God's complete and final word; (3) Complete Coverage—directly or indirectly, the Bible

contains all that God has to say about any human issue imaginable; (4) Democratic Perspicacity—the Bible is understandable by any intelligent person when presented in that person's own language; (5) Commonsense Hermeneutics—the Bible is best understood in its "plain sense," that is, in the literal, obvious meaning of the words; (6) Solo Scriptura—scripture can and should be read apart from extra-biblical sources like creeds, confessions, and other such traditional writings; (7) Internal Harmony—everything scripture says about any topic is coherent and self-consistent when properly understood; (8) Universal Applicability—a proposition or normative teaching in scripture remains fully in effect for Christians today except in cases where subsequent scripture specifically revokes or overrules that teaching (e.g., Jewish dietary laws); (9) Inductive Method—the proper path to any conclusion about Christian belief or practice starts by determining "what the Bible says" about the topic or belief through careful (solo scriptura) study; and (10) Handbook Model—the assumption (rarely made explicit) that the Bible more or less comprises a handbook for living that Christians any and everywhere can consult to structure their lives. See Smith, *The Bible Made Impossible: Why Biblicism Is Not a Truly Evangelical Reading of Scripture* (Grand Rapids, MI: Brazos, 2011), 4–5. I find Smith's list a valuable catalogue of extant evangelical beliefs, and my briefer overview of biblicism here (written prior to the publication of Smith's book) mirrors Smith's take on biblicism. I hasten to underline, however, that almost no evangelical would endorse each and every one of these assumptions as Smith states them. Very few evangelicals, for instance, believe that God literally dictated scripture to biblical writers, nor do evangelicals crack open the Bible when flummoxed about how to operate iTunes. I restrict my use of this source in my main text. In contrast to Smith's more straightforwardly scholarly work (e.g., *Christian America*), his biblicism book takes an explicitly polemical tone (though much, much fairer than many secular critiques of evangelicalism). Smith opposes the version of biblicism he describes and wants to convince other Christians of his case. While my own theological views make me sympathetic to Smith's arguments, and although I find his list extremely useful, I hesitate to attribute his assumptions (particularly as presented in his clear-but-tendentious phrasing, e.g., "solo scriptura") to my evangelical subjects.

65. For this reason (there are others), evangelicals tend to define members of the Church of Jesus Christ of Latter-Day Saints as non-Christian, since Mormons revere additions to the Protestant canon.

66. For evangelical debates about biblical inspiration, see chapter one of Boyd and Eddy, *Across the Spectrum.*

67. See, for example, A. William Merrill, "Bibliolatry—A Fraudulent Accusation," *Baptist2Baptist.net,* Southern Baptist Convention, October 2000, http://www.baptist2baptist.net/b2barticle.asp?ID=54.

68. Perhaps the most widely cited statement of this doctrine is the 1978 "Chicago Statement on Biblical Inerrancy." Reacting to one of evangelicalism's perennial battles over orthodoxy, a broad coalition of evangelical traditions united to produce a document that clarifies some common assumptions. The Statement, for example, specifies that the Bible is inerrant "in its autographs"—the original writings of the authors (which are unavailable today), allowing for a small degree of wiggle room in accounting for clear transcription errors in scripture. International Council on Biblical Inerrancy, "The Chicago Statement on Biblical Inerrancy," *Dallas Theological Seminary,* 1978, http://library.dts.edu/Pages/TL/Special/ICBI_1.pdf.

69. The Pledge of Allegiance to the Bible as I learned it (and any internet search will confirm): "I pledge allegiance to the Bible, God's Holy Word. I will make it a lamp

unto my feet, a light unto my path, and hide its words in my heart that I might not sin against God."

70. Smith, *Bible,* 17.

71. See, for example, Kevin DeYoung's review of Smith's biblicism argument, "Christian Smith Makes the Bible Impossible," Review of *The Bible Made Impossible, Gospel Coalition,* August 2, 2011, http://thegospelcoalition.org/blogs/kevindeyoung/2011/08/02/christian-smith-makes-the-bible-impossible/.

72. Penal substitution is not the only evangelical view of atonement, but it is the most widespread one. For an overview of alternative atonement theologies (e.g., the Christus Victor model), see chapter eight of Boyd and Eddy, *Across the Spectrum.*

73. Debate exists as to whether a Christian needs to be able to identify this specific moment. Many evangelicals convert at very young ages and/or do not remember an exact instance of conversion, yet they still consider themselves to have been saved.

74. The amount of agency any human has in conversion lies at the heart of one of the deepest divisions within Protestantism—that between the Calvinist (Reformed) tradition and the Arminian tradition (this debate is itself a continuation of long-standing Christian arguments about soteriology). Briefly: the Reformed tradition of John Calvin, which maintains a strong influence in many sectors of evangelical higher education, insists that God alone determines who converts and who does not. In this view, God has predestined from the beginning of time a portion of humanity (the elect) who will be saved, determining that the rest of humanity is irredeemably doomed (reprobate). The elect ultimately have no choice but to accept salvation, since (for Calvinists) God's grace is all-powerful and irresistible. The non-elect have no recourse from the doom of their depravity. For strict Calvinists, then, Jesus died not for everyone but only for the elect; atonement is limited rather than universal. After all, Calvinists argue, if God died for all but only some are saved, then Jesus died in vain, and his grace is less than totally effective. Calvinist theology famously uses the acronym TULIP to name its key tenets: Total depravity, Unconditional election, Limited atonement, Irresistible grace, and Perseverance of saints. Countering this tradition, and more widespread on a popular level, is the Arminian tradition (after Jacobus Arminius [Jakob Hermanszoon], a Dutch critic of Calvinism). This argues that Christ did die for everyone, that God's grace extends to all, but that humans have the ability to refuse this invitation. Not all evangelicals participate in this debate, nor are all Calvinists or Arminians equally strict in their interpretation of each tradition. Indeed, except for extreme cases, Calvinists and Arminians alike affirm the necessity of conversion and evangelism. Significant as these distinctions are in some contexts (such as how one describes conversion—do you *accept* Christ or do you *submit* to God's grace?), the differences between Reformed evangelicals and others are often invisible at the level of activism. Both sides insist that Christians must spread the gospel to everyone, everywhere. The literature about Calvinism and Arminianism is too vast to summarize here, but as a start see chapters two, three, and nine of Boyd and Eddy, *Across the Spectrum.* For a classical statement of how Calvinist predestination jibes with the imperative to evangelize, see J. I. Packer, *Evangelism and the Sovereignty of God* (Grand Rapids, MI: IVP Academic, 1991).

75. Although the notion of hell as eternal torment for the unconverted remains predominant, there exists some disagreement as to the nature of hell and the ultimate fate of the unsaved among evangelicals. Some reject the notion of a literal hell altogether, instead interpreting scripture as counseling that everyone is eventually saved (a liberal position in evangelicalism). Others see hell as a real possibility but

deny that God's invitation ends at death; in this view even those in hell (generally not seen here as unending, fiery torture) can convert. Finally, still others see the unsaved not as existing in eternal torment but as being annihilated; hell is not eternal punishment but a one-time destruction by fire. See chapter twelve of Boyd and Eddy, *Across the Spectrum*.

76. See David J. Bosch, *Transforming Mission: Paradigm Shifts in Theology of Mission* (Maryknoll, NY: Orbis Books, 2005 [1991]), 10–11.

77. In her dissertation on volunteer tourism, Jennifer Erdely conducts an ethnographic study of a group of missionaries from the UCC working in post-flood New Orleans. There the volunteers discuss how they understand their mission work, distinguishing it sharply from evangelizing initiatives. See Jennifer Erdely, "When the Saints Go Marching In: An Ethnography of Volunteer Tourism in Post-Hurricane Katrina New Orleans" (PhD diss., Louisiana State University, 2011), 81–82.

78. I hasten to note that evangelicalism does not differ in this respect from other large groups or labels. The number of people in the United States identifying as "American citizens" would doubtless be huge. But in terms of deep civic literacy, significantly fewer of these pass muster. Andrew Romano reports that a Newsweek/Daily Beast poll found that 38 percent of US citizens failed a ten-question version of the citizenship test given to immigrants wishing to become US citizens. See Andrew Romano, "How Dumb Are We?" *Newsweek,* March 20, 2011, http://www.newsweek.com/2011/03/20/how-dumb-are-we.html.

Chapter 3

1. Steven Anderson, *Basic Soul-Winning Demonstration Video (witnessing, gospel),* YouTube video, 10:00, posted by sanderson1611, March 8, 2008, http://www.youtube.com/watch?v=BXMA4xOS5BY&feature=channel_video_title.

2. Daniel Ball, *Backwards and Forwards* (Carbondale: Southern Illinois University Press, 1983), 22–23.

3. Steven Anderson, "Soul-Winning Training," MP3 sermon, Faithful Word Baptist Church (Tempe, AZ), May 1, 2011, 1:20:40, http://www.faithfulwordbaptist.org/page5.html.

4. The Southern Baptist Convention, the largest evangelical denomination, recently played out this contention in its debate over a resolution affirming the value of the sinner's prayer in SBC theology. Some Calvinist Baptists (a growing segment of the SBC) dislike how attention to the sinner's prayer seems to overemphasize human action in the process of justification. They also point out that the sinner's prayer as such does not appear in scripture. See Ted Olson, "Southern Baptists Debate Sinner's Prayer," *Christianity Today* (web only), June 20, 2012, http://www.christianitytoday.com/ct/2012/juneweb-only/baptists-sinners-prayer.html.

5. Hank Willenbrink III, "Scaring the Jesus into You: American Hell Houses in Performance" (PhD diss., University of California–Santa Barbara, 2009), 153.

6. In the SBC debate about the sinner's prayer, supporters of the pro-prayer resolution included language stressing that the sinner's prayer is not an incantation. The words themselves are not efficacious. See Olsen, "Southern Baptists."

7. For Faithful Word's weekly soul-winning schedule (as well as an embedded video of his soul-winning demonstration), see "Soul-Winning," Faithful Word Baptist Church website, Faithful Word Baptist Church, n.d., http://www.faithfulwordbaptist.org/page7.html.

8. Some clarification is in order. "Baptist" is a fairly common appellation across US Christendom. Most often, the term is shorthand for one of two large denominations, the Southern Baptist Convention (or the SBC, the largest Protestant denomination in the United States) or the American Baptist Church. But apart from these formal bodies, "Baptist" can describe a wide array of denominations, associations, or even individual congregations. Churches that identify as Independent Fundamental Baptist generally affirm a similar set of "Baptist distinctives," including restrictions on ecumenical activity, insistence upon believers' baptism (as opposed to infant baptism), and a strict separation of church and state. For the IFB's own explanation of its beliefs and history, see Cooper P. Abrams III, "A Brief Survey of Independent Fundamental Baptist Churches . . . What They Are and What Is Their History," Baptistinfo. org., http://www.baptistinfo.com/define.shtml. Though by definition Abrams's portrait of IFB beliefs is not normative for other IFB churches, Anderson appears to align with the beliefs and distinctives Abrams lists. A link to Faithful Word Baptist Church and to Anderson's sermons appears on the Baptistinfo website. Fred Phelp's church, though called "Westboro Baptist," has nothing to do with the IFB.

9. For this reason, I will use the King James Version for scriptures quoted in this section. For a sample of Anderson's views on Bible versions, see his "Correcting the King James Bible," Faithful Word Baptist Church website, http://www.faithfulwordbaptist.org/kingjamesbible.html.

10. Anderson expounds on his views on homosexuals in a number of sermons. For an outline of his theological grounding for such views, see Anderson, "The Truth About Homosexuals," Faithful Word Baptist Church website, http://faithfulwordbaptist.org/truth_about_homosexuals.html. Like many other Christians with similarly anti-gay views (e.g., Fred Phelps), Anderson stresses that he does not condone personal violence toward gay people.

11. The sermon that got so much attention is Steven Anderson, "Why I Hate Barack Obama," MP3 sermon, Faithful Word Baptist Church (Tempe, AZ), 1:06:20, August 16, 2009, http://www.faithfulwordbaptist.org/081609p.mp3. It was not the first time Anderson had applied Psalm 58 to Obama. See Anderson, "Barack Obama Melting as a Snail," MP3 sermon, Faithful Word Baptist Church (Tempe, AZ), 1:03:20, January 18, 2009, http://www.faithfulwordbaptist.org/011809p.mp3. A welter of articles and op-eds condemning Anderson appeared soon after the August 16 sermon. Pace many of these articles, I would resist describing Anderson as an extreme specimen of the political religious right. True to IFB doctrine and the Baptist tradition more generally, Anderson eschews direct political-partisan advocacy. On the relatively rare occasions in which his sermons deal with political issues specifically, he exhibits little interest in endorsing any political candidate or party, displaying instead a general distrust of human government institutions generally. Nor could his extreme social views be easily reconciled with even the most conservative national politicians or platforms. Indeed, Anderson tends to find the religious right's leaders so insufficiently orthodox (not using the King James Version only, colluding with unrepentant sinners, etc.) as to make any degree of serious support for them unimaginable. He is sui generis, not hyper-Pat Robertson.

12. See, for instance, Corey Hodges, "Preacher's Anti-Obama Sermon Goes Against the Bible," *Salt Lake Tribune,* September 11, 2009.

13. Like many soul-winning evangelists, Anderson stresses a difference between believing *in* Jesus (which even demons do) and believing *on* Jesus as savior and Lord. See Anderson, "Basic Soul-Winning Demonstration."

14. Steven Anderson, "Soul-Winning Training."

15. Anderson, "Soul-Winning Training." Anderson actually has a number of sermons on soul-winning techniques, all available on the Faithful Word Baptist Church website.

16. See, e.g., Anderson, "Why Bible College Is Unscriptural," MP3 sermon, Faithful Word Baptist Church (Tempe, AZ), February 10, 2008, http://www.faithfulwordbaptist.org/021008p.mp3. Anderson's animosity toward Hyles-Anderson appears to relate in part to his dislike of Jack Schaap, its current chancellor. See Anderson, "Dr. Jack Schaap's Perverted Teachings Exposed," Faithful Word Baptist Church website, http://www.faithfulwordbaptist.org/schaap.html.

17. See "Doctrinal Statement," Hyles-Anderson College website, n.d., http://hylesanderson.edu/about/doctrinal-statement/. There appears to be no relation between Steven Anderson and the "Anderson" in the college name.

18. See Anderson, "Why Bible."

19. Jack Hyles, *Let's Go Soul Winning* (Murfreesboro, TN: Sword of the Lord Foundation, 1962).

20. C. S. Lovett, *Soul-Winning Made Easy (The Encounter Method)* (Baldwin Park, CA: Personal Christianity, 1959).

21. Hyles, *Let's Go,* 13–14.

22. Hyles, *Let's Go,* 25–26; Anderson, "Soul-Winning Training."

23. Though Hyles endorses the straightforward "Are you a Christian?" question at some points, he calls the "If you died" tactic "the best question I have ever used." Hyles, *Let's Go,* 33.

24. Hyles, *Let's Go,* 27.

25. Anderson, *Basic.*

26. Lovett, *Soul-Winning,* 46.

27. Lovett, *Soul-Winning,* 48.

28. Lovett, *Soul-Winning,* 50.

29. Anderson, "Soul-Winning Training."

30. Hyles, *Let's Go Soul Winning,* 38.

31. Lovett, *Soul-Winning,* 19.

32. Hyles, *Let's Go Soul Winning,* 14.

33. Hyles, *Let's Go Soul Winning,* 33.

34. Lovett, *Soul-Winning,* 29–32. Here and throughout, Lovett includes several photos that feature a soul-winner and a prospect posed in the most effective positions and illustrating particular gestures to accompany certain parts of the pitch.

35. Anderson, "Basic Soul-Winning Video."

36. Lovett, *Soul-Winning,* 46.

37. Anderson, "Soul-Winning Training."

38. Hyles, *Let's Go Soul Winning,* 27.

39. Lovett, *Soul-Winning,* 20, 22, capitalization in the original.

40. Lovett, *Soul-Winning,* 20.

41. Lovett, *Soul-Winning,* 23.

42. Anderson, "Soul-Winning Training."

43. Anderson, "Soul-Winning Training."

44. Lovett, *Soul-Winning,* 22.

45. Lovett, *Soul-Winning,* 22, 23.

46. Throughout this section, I rely heavily on the history laid out by John G. Turner, *Bill Bright and the Campus Crusade for Christ: The Renewal of Evangelicalism in Postwar America* (Chapel Hill: University of North Carolina, 2008).

47. Turner, *Bill Bright,* 18–22.

48. Turner, *Bill Bright,* 41–42. See also Campus Crusade for Christ, "About Us," campuscrusadeforchrist.com, Campus Crusade for Christ, Inc., http://campuscrusadeforchrist.com/about-us.

49. Cru's decision to rechristen itself occurred subsequent to the start of my research, and materials from the organization refer to both the Campus Crusade for Christ and Cru. For this chapter, I tend to use Cru to refer to the organization's present-day orientations and "Campus Crusade for Christ" to refer to the organization's past actions and positions. That said, the two terms are essentially interchangeable.

50. Campus Crusade for Christ, "About Us."

51. Frank Bettger, *How I Raised Myself from Failure to Success in Selling* (New York: Prentice-Hall, 1947).

52. A recreation of the "Four Spiritual Laws" tract is "Exhibit 12" in Campus Crusade for Christ. *How to Make a Mark That's Hard to Erase: A Manual for Evangelism and Discipleship* (n.p.: Campus Crusade for Christ, 1982), 330–38. The Law presentation (now called the four "Principles" but retaining some of the classical illustrations) are also presented on Campus Crusade's website. "How to Know God Personally," Campus Crusade for Christ Web Page, Campus Crusade for Christ International, http://www.ccci.org/how-to-know-god/would-you-like-to-know-god-personally/index.htm.

53. Turner, *Bill Bright,* 100.

54. Campus Crusade itself boasts that the tract has enjoyed a printing run of about 2.5 billion since the 1950s. Campus Crusade for Christ, "History," campuscrusadeforchrist.com, http://campuscrusadeforchrist.com/about-us/history.

55. Turner, *Bill Bright,* 100–102.

56. I am grateful to Neil Downey, an editor at Cru Press and one of the developers for many of Cru's current evangelism and discipleship materials, for outlining Cru's shift away from a purely Four Laws approach. Neil Downey, e-mail message to author, January 4, 2013.

57. Centerfield Productions, "The Compass—The Four Laws," PDF document, http://www.centerfieldproductions.com/members/content/compass/thefourlaws.pdf, 3.

58. Centerfield Productions, "Four Laws Script," PDF document, http://www.centerfieldproductions.com/members/content/compass/fourlawsscript.pdf. For an earlier CCC script/guide to *Four Laws* Booklet-based evangelism, see Campus Crusade for Christ, *How to Make a Mark,* 95–110.

59. Centerfield Productions, "Four Laws Script," 4.

60. For a similar script constructed around *Would You Like to Know God Personally,* see Cru Press, "The Big Six Questions: Clarifying 'Knowing God Personally,'" PDF document, 2010, Cru Press Green, http://crupressgreen.com/wp-content/uploads/2012/03/The-Big-Six-Questions.pdf.

61. Centerfield Productions, "Four Laws Script," 2.

62. I should note that Cru now provides resources and training materials for such apologetics through the Cru Press Green website.

63. For two sets of CCC instructions about testimonies, see Campus Crusade for Christ, *How to Make a Mark,* 125–32, and Centerfield Productions, "Sharing Your Story," PDF document, Compass Curriculum, http://www.centerfieldproductions.com/members/content/compass/sharingyourstory.pdf.

64. Centerfield Productions, "Sharing Your Story," 1.

65. Centerfield Productions, "Sharing Your Story," 2.

66. Campus Crusade for Christ, *How to Make a Mark,* 125.

67. Quoted in Turner, *Bill Bright,* 220.

68. See, for example, Cru Press Green, Cru's online clearinghouse for outreach and discipleship resources, at http://crupress.campuscrusadeforchrist.com/green/.

69. For more about Centerfield, see Tim Henderson, "About Us," centerfieldproductions.com, Centerfield Productions, n.d., http://www.centerfieldproductions.com/about.

70. The theological performative operating in the CCC approach represents a slight shift from Anderson's soul-winning model. Anderson takes pains to stress that belief on Christ produces eternal salvation. The Four Laws approach (borrowing from Henrietta Mears's Keswick theology) clarifies that this belief is at once repentance (turning away from Self toward Jesus) and surrender.

71. The website for Living Waters Publications contains information about Comfort's life and ministry as well as links to the organization's related ministries and publications. See Living Waters Ministries, *Living Waters,* 2011, http://www.livingwaters.com/.

72. See Last Words Ministries, *Last Words Radio* (Podcast series), last updated December 27, 2009, http://itunes.apple.com/podcast/last-words-radio/id291651675; Trisha Ramos, *Fish with Trish* (website), 2011, http://www.fishwithtrish.com/; and Todd Friel, *Wretched with Todd Friel* (website), 2011, http://www.wretchedradio.com/.

73. Though he does not foreground his own church affiliations, Comfort has long-standing links to Calvary Chapel, a California-based association of nondenominational evangelical churches founded by evangelist Chuck Smith. Living Waters produced a website dedicated to educating Calvary Chapel pastors about Comfort and his work. According to that website, Comfort is himself an ordained Calvary Chapel minister, and it was Calvary Chapel that initially brought Comfort over to the United States. See "Home," *Calvary Chapel Free Gift,* http://www.calvarychapelfreegift.com/index.shtml. For information about Calvary Chapel, see the organization's website at "Home," *Calvary Chapel,* 2010, http://www.calvarychapel.com/. Calvary Chapel's theology features something of a mix between light fundamentalism (espousing strict biblical inerrancy and dispensationalism) and Pentacostalism (recognizing continuing gifts/manifestations of the Holy Spirit, e.g., speaking in tongues). Comfort himself tends to avoid strongly endorsing such potentially divisive doctrinal stances in public, preferring to focus on Living Waters's outreach focus.

74. Ray Comfort, *180* (Online Film), 33:03, http://www.180movie.com/.

75. My quotations reference Comfort's own PDF transcripts of these sermons, which he makes available online. N.b., Comfort writes the title as Hell's "Best Kept Secret" (not "Best-kept Secret"). See Ray Comfort, "Hell's Best Kept Secret," PDF, *Living Waters Publications,* http://www.livingwaters.com/helps/HellsBestKeptSecret.pdf and "True and False Conversion" (PDF document), *Living Waters Publications,* http://assets.livingwaters.com/pdf/TrueAndFalseConversion.pdf.

76. "Evangelical Frustration" was the initial title for "Hell's Best Kept Secret."

77. In "True and False Conversion," Comfort credits his statistic to an article from a major denomination's publication that compared the number of decisions for Christ made in 1991 (294,000) with the number added to church membership (14,000) (1). If accurate, these figures suggest a drop-off rate of more like 95 percent. In a subsequent publication, Comfort provides more exact details. The magazine is the March/April 1993 issue of *American Horizon* (not, as Comfort's sermon puts it,

American Horizons), published by the Assemblies of God; the numbers are 294,784 conversions and 14,337 converts. See Ray Comfort, *The Way of the Master* (Alachua, FL: Bridge-Logos, 2006), 98. In both sources, Comfort leaves unasked questions such as whether these figures are accurate, whether the discrepancies in decisions made and church attendance necessarily indicate false conversion, and whether the magazine's figures can apply to Christianity as a whole. The effect of the "90 percent" statistic, ubiquitous throughout Living Waters ministry materials, functions more as impressive-sounding rhetoric than as sociologically accurate evidence.

78. Comfort, "Hell's Best Kept Secret," 1.

79. Comfort, "Hell's Best Kept Secret," 6.

80. Although Comfort does not explicitly espouse Calvinist tenets in his writing, his underlying theology is strongly Reformed, and the list of recommended readings in his *School of Biblical Evangelism* slants toward Reformed writers (e.g., Charles Spurgeon, John Piper, R. C. Sproul). See Kirk Cameron and Ray Comfort, *The School of Biblical Evangelism* (Orlando: Bridge-Logos, 2004), 761.

81. Comfort, "Hell's Best Kept Secret," 2.

82. Cameron and Comfort, *School,* 117.

83. See, e.g., *Way of the Master TV, Wretched with Todd Friel,* and *Last Words Radio.* The latter, a podcast series (now cancelled but still available through iTunes), featured a regular live evangelism segment. The hosts would contact an evangelist on the street, who in turn convinces a passerby to speak over the phone with the hosts on the podcast. The hosts then take the prospect through a typical WotM presentation, providing in-depth analysis and color commentary after the evangelizing phone call ends.

84. Anderson, "Soul-Winning Training."

85. Cameron and Comfort, *School,* 104.

86. Cameron and Comfort, *School,* 21.

87. Comfort, "Hell's Best," 9.

88. Cameron and Comfort, *School,* 125.

89. Steven Anderson, *Epic Soul-Winning FAIL—Living Waters University (Ray Comfort & Kirk Cameron) Way of the Master,* YouTube video, 2:22, posted by sanderson1611, November 7, 2010, http://www.youtube.com/user/sanderson1611#p/search/30/xu6PCexvZI4.

90. Cameron and Comfort, *School,* 118.

Chapter 4

1. Randy Newman, *Questioning Evangelism: Engaging People's Hearts the Way Jesus Did* (Grand Rapids, MI: Kregel, 2004), 22.

2. For a description, see Kinnaman and Lyons, *UnChristian,* 55–56. See also Zachary Gale, "Confessions of a Sinful Church," *New University,* April 25, 2005, http://www.newuniversity.org/2005/04/features/confessions_of_a_sinful113/, and Wyatt Buchanan, "SOUTHERN CALIFORNIA; Conservative Colleges Visited by Gay Christians; Response Differs Strongly as Group Buses across Nation," *San Francisco Chronicle,* April 5, 2006.

3. For titles and links to audio/video files of each sermon in this series, see Kensington Community Church, "Confessions of a Sinful Church," http://kensingtonchurch.tv/play.php?id=15.

4. Kensington Community Church, "Confessions Series Promo," Vimeo Video, 2:28, October 12, 2008, http://kensingtonchurch.org/arts/video.php?id=5.

5. Kinnaman and Lyons, *UnChristian,* 17.

6. Kinnaman and Lyons, *UnChristian,* 27.

7. Kinnaman and Lyons, *UnChristian,* 69.

8. Kinnaman and Lyons, *UnChristian,* 31–32.

9. Kinnaman and Lyons, *UnChristian,* 74. In their qualitative interviews with people who have left Christianity, Wright et al. find explanations that reinforce Kinnaman and Lyons's arguments. "Push" factors that repel people from faith tend to play a greater role than do "pull" factors (e.g., non-Christians who influence or recruit people into apostasy). See Wright et al., "Explaining Deconversion from Christianity: A Study of Online Narratives," *Journal of Religion and Society* 13 (2011): para. 67.

10. See, e.g., Drew Dyck, *Generation Ex-Christian: Why Young Adults are Leaving the Faith . . . And How to Bring Them Back* (Chicago: Moody, 2010); Ken Ham and Britt Beemer, *Already Gone: Why Your Kids Will Quit Church and What You Can Do to Stop It* (Green Forest, AR: Master Books, 2009); and David Kinnaman, *You Lost Me: Why Young Christians Are Leaving Church . . . And Rethinking Faith* (Grand Rapids, MI: Baker, 2011). A number of recent studies outside of the evangelical press (but consulted by many evangelicals) also deal with the issue of younger generations' drift away from traditional Christianity. See Kendra Creasy Dean, *Almost Christian: What the Faith of Our Teenagers Is Telling the American Church* (New York: Oxford, 2010); Christian Smith with Melinda Lundquist Denton, *Soul Searching: The Religious and Spiritual Lives of American Teenagers* (New York: Oxford, 2005); Christian Smith with Patricia Snell, *Souls in Transition: The Religious and Spiritual Lives of Emerging Adults* (New York: Oxford, 2009).

11. "Bait and Switch (episode 394)," *This American Life,* podcast audio, This American Life From WBEZ, MP3, 58:28, November 9, 2009, http://www.thisamericanlife.org/radio-archives/episode/394/bait-and-switch.

12. Jim Henderson, "I'm on This American Life (This Weekend)," *Off the Map,* blog, Off The Map, November 6, 2009, http://offthemap.com/2009/11/06/im-on-this-american-life-this-weekend/. Italics in original.

13. Jim Henderson, *Evangelism Without Additives: What if Sharing Your Faith Meant Just Being Yourself?* (Colorado Springs: Waterbrook, 2007), 11.

14. Henderson, *Evangelism Without Additives,* 2.

15. Henderson, *Evangelism Without Additives,* 117.

16. Jim Henderson, Todd Hunter, and Craig Spinks, *The Outsider Interviews: A New Generation Speaks Out on Christianity* (Grand Rapids, MI: Baker, 2010), 18.

17. Henderson, *Evangelism Without Additives,* 18–19.

18. Henderson, Hunter, and Spinks, *The Outsider Interviews,* 18–19.

19. See Jim Henderson, *Off the Map* (web page), 2011. http://offthemap.com/people/jim-henderson/. Off The Map has since ended in favor of Henderson's new site, *Jim Henderson Presents* (web page), 2011, http://jimhendersonpresents.com/; and Randy Siever, *Doable Evangelism* (web page), 2011, http://doableevangelism.com/.

20. Henderson, *Evangelism Without Additives,* 115–16. For a description of the organization's workshop offerings (including the "Interview with Three Lost People" segment), see Randy Siever, "The DE Seminars and Workshops," *Doable Evangelism* (website), Doable Evangelism, September 1, 2011, http://doableevangelism.com/seminars/.

21. See, for example, Siever, "The Lost Interviews," *Doable Evangelism* (website). Doable Evangelism, 2011, http://doableevangelism.com/the-lost-interviews/.

22. Henderson, *Evangelism Without Additives,* 15.

23. Henderson, *Evangelism Without Additives,* 60–61.

24. Henderson, *Evangelism Without Additives,* 37.

25. Henderson, *Evangelism Without Additives,* 129.

26. Henderston, *Evangelism Without Additives,* 25.

27. Henderson's list: "'quiet time';'I felt a peace about it'; hand of the Lord; put out a fleece; 'I felt a real burden'; anointing; a word from the Lord; 'I covet your prayers'; 'I just feel so blessed'; 'the Lord convicted me'; 'I felt led to . . .'; 'the Lord spoke to me'; 'I sought the Lord's face.' And here's my all-time favorite: 'If he opens the door . . .'" *Evangelism Without Additives,* 61.

28. Henderson, *Evangelism Without Additives,* 130.

29. Henderson, *Evangelism Without Additives,* 11.

30. Henderson, *Evangelism Without Additives,* 71.

31. Henderson, *Evangelism Without Additives,* 26

32. Henderson, *Evangelism Without Additives,* 95.

33. Henderson, *Evangelism Without Additives,* 73.

34. Siever bases his arguments on a study by an organization called Vision New England, which focuses on Christian evangelism in the Northeast. A 2007 survey of conversion by VNE found that only 14 percent of Christians surveyed experienced the "one moment in time" decision prized by kerygmatic approaches. The remainder described their decision as the result of months or years of consideration. See Vision New England, "Vision New England Recent Convert Study," Vision New England, January 23, 2008, http://www.efcneda.org/pubs/Vision%20New%20England%20Recent%20Convert%20Study.pdf.

35. Randy Siever, "Busting the Myth of Pre-Evangelism" (blog entry), *Doable Evangelism,* Doable Evangelism, June 1, 2008, http://doableevangelism.com/2008/06/01/busting-the-myth-of-pre-evangelism/.

36. Henderson, Hunter, and Spinks, *The Outsider Interviews,* 88–89.

37. Henderson, Hunter, and Spinks, *The Outsider Interviews,* 92–93.

38. Henderson, Hunter, and Spinks, *The Outsider Interviews,* 94.

39. Joe Aldrich, *Lifestyle Evangelism: Learning to Open Your Life to Those Around You* (Colorado Springs: Multnomah, 1999 [1981]), 73–74.

40. Henderson, *Evangelism Without Additives,* 131.

41. Cathy Lynn Grossman, "For Many, 'Losing My Religion,' Isn't Just a Song; It's Life," *USA Today,* December 25, 2011, http://www.usatoday.com/news/religion/story/2011-12-25/religion-god-atheism-so-what/52195274/1.

42. Troy Anderson, "A New Day for Apologetics," *Christianity Today,* July 2, 2008, http://www.christianitytoday.com/ct/2008/july/14.29.html.

43. I discuss Craig's debate career elsewhere. See Fletcher, "Performing Coexistence," 236–37.

44. Chris Norton, "Apologetics Makes a Comeback among Youth," *Christianity Today,* August 31, 2011, http://www.christianitytoday.com/ct/2011/september/apologetics-return-youth.html.

45. Stan Guthrie, "Interview: Douglas Groothuis on Good Apologetics," Interview with Stan Guthrie, *Christianity Today,* September 11, 2011, http://www.christianitytoday.com/ct/2011/october/douglas-groothuis-good-apologetics.html.

46. The L'Abri community still exists. See "Official Homepage for the L'Abri Fellowship International," L'Abri Fellowship International, 2011, http://www.labri.org/.

47. Francis Schaeffer, *The God Who Is There* (Downers Grove, IL: Intervarsity, 1998 [1968]), 26–27.

48. Schaeffer, *God,* 76–77, 218.

49. Schaeffer, *God,* 105.

50. I should clarify that Schaeffer is no blinkered prude standing in disapproval of modern art and music. Indeed, he recognizes and even admires the virtuosity and "genius" of several of the figures whose work he critiques. It is the genius of artists like Picasso or John Cage that makes their work such honest, sobering indictments of the ramifications of the meaning/rationality split.

51. Schaeffer, *God,* 119.

52. Schaeffer, *God,* 66. Schaeffer here references Paul in I Corinthians chapter 15.

53. Schaeffer, *God,* 72–75.

54. For Pearcey's full argument, see Nancy Pearcey, *Total Truth: Liberating Christianity from Its Cultural Captivity* (Wheaton, IL: Crossway, 2004).

55. For a more comprehensive overview of and comparison between different apologetics strands, see Steven B. Cowen, ed., *Five Views on Apologetics* (Grand Rapids, MI: Zondervan, 2000). Cowen's collection contains extended dialogue and debate between representatives of various apologetic traditions in evangelicalism.

56. See Josh McDowell, *The New Evidence that Demands a Verdict* (Nashville: Thomas Nelson, 1999) and Lee Strobel, *The Case for Christ: A Journalist's Personal Investigation of the Evidence for Jesus* (Grand Rapids, MI: Zondervan, 1998).

57. Greg Bahnsen, a protégé of one of the founders of presuppositional apologetics (Cornelius Van Til), gives several concise explanations of presuppositionalist thinking. See Greg Bahnsen, "Evangelicalism and Apologetics," *Covenant Media Foundation,* http://www.cmfnow.com/articles/PA013.htm, and Bahnsen, "Presuppositional Procedure," *Covenant Media Foundation,* http://www.cmfnow.com/articles/pa210.htm. See also John Frame's defense of presuppositionalism, "Presuppositional Apologetics," in Cowan, *Five Views,* 208–31.

58. Schaeffer, *God,* 197.

59. Schaeffer, *God,* 155.

60. Schaeffer, *God,* 158.

61. Schaeffer, *God,* 171.

62. Gregory Koukl, *Tactics: A Game Plan for Discussing Your Christian Convictions* (Grand Rapids, MI: Zondervan, 2009), 19.

63. Koukl, *Tactics,* 38. Italics in original.

64. Koukl, *Tactics,* 26.

65. Koukl, *Tactics,* 49.

66. Koukl, *Tactics,* 108.

67. Koukl, *Tactics,* 95.

68. Koukl, *Tactics,* 27.

69. Koukl, *Tactics,* 40.

70. Koukl, *Tactics,* 95.

71. Contra Anderson, Koukl interprets scriptural warnings about argument to refer to pervasive dissention within the church, not to the hashing out of disagreements per se. *Tactics,* 31.

72. Koukl, *Tactics,* 38–39.

73. Dare 2 Share, "About Greg Stier," *dare2share.org,* Dare 2 Share Ministries International, n.d., http://www.dare2share.org/about/greg-stier/. Stier also maintains a personal web page and blog, *Gregstier.org,* Dare 2 Share Ministries International, 2012, http://www.gregstier.org/.

74. Dare 2 Share, "About Dare 2 Share Ministries," *Dare 2 Share.org,* Dare 2 Share

Ministries International, n.d., http://www.dare2share.org/about/overview/. See also Dare 2 Share, "Fact Sheet," *dare2share.org,* Dare 2 Share Ministries International, n.d., http://www.dare2share.org/about/fact-sheet/.

75. Dare 2 Share, "Statement of Faith," *dare2share.org,* Dare 2 Share Ministries International, n.d., http://www.dare2share.org/about/statement-of-faith/.

76. Bill Hybels and Matt Mittelberg, *Becoming a Contagious Christian* (Grand Rapids, MI: Zondervan, 1994), 46, quoted in Greg Stier, *Outbreak: Creating a Contagious Youth Ministry through Viral Evangelism,* 2nd ed. (Chicago: Moody, 2006), 29.

77. Stier takes the notion of an ideavirus from marketing guru Seth Godin, *Unleashing the Ideavirus* (Dobbs Ferry, NY: Do You Zoom, 2001).

78. Stier, *Outbreak,* 24–30.

79. The GOSPEL acronym is present throughout D2S ministries. For Stier's explanation of these points, see Greg Stier, "Sharing Your Faith Overview," video, 7:00, *dare2share.org,* Dare 2 Share Ministries International, http://www.dare2share.org/thecause/gospel-journey-tools/ and Greg Stier, *Dare 2 Share* (Carol Stream, IL: Tyndale House, 2006), 77–115.

80. Stier follows this advice with a sample script, a model dialogue of someone sharing the GOSPEL pitch. See Stier, *Dare 2 Share,* 115–20.

81. Stier, "Sharing Your Faith."

82. Stier, *Outbreak,* 30.

83. Stier, *Dare 2 Share,* 175–77.

84. Stier, *Outbreak,* 39.

85. Stier, *Outbreak,* 39–40.

86. Koukl, *Tactics,* 25.

87. Dare 2 Share, "THE Cause Circle," *dare2share.org,* Dare 2 Share Ministries International, n.d., http://www.dare2share.org/thecause/the-cause-circle/. This site includes a downloadable PDF version of the Pray-Pursue-Persuade strategy.

88. Stier, *Dare 2 Share,* 5; Dare 2 Share, "Deep & Wide Youth Ministry Overview," *dare2share.org,* Dare 2 Share Ministries International, 2008, http://www.dare2share.org/deepandwide/overview/.

89. See Dare 2 Share, "Culture Commission Archives," *dare2share.org.,* Dare 2 Share Ministries International, n.d. [2008], http://www.dare2share.org/culturecommission/archives/. More up-to-date articles about pop-culture-to-Christianity segues appear in Dare 2 Share, "Soul Fuel Archives," *dare2share.org,* Dare 2 Share Ministries International, 2012, http://www.dare2share.org/soulfuel/archives/.

90. Stier, *Dare 2 Share,* 179–261. These profiles are also available as separate, downloadable PDFs from the Dare 2 Share site. See Dare 2 Share, "How to Share Your Faith With . . . ," *dare2share.org,* Dare 2 Share Ministries International, n.d., http://www.dare2share.org/worldviews/.

91. Stier, *Dare 2 Share,* 230.

92. Stier, *Dare 2 Share,* 260.

93. Stier, *Dare 2 Share,* 183.

94. Stier, *Dare 2 Share,* 248.

95. A 2011 *Christianity Today* article, for example, analyzes statistical findings that evangelicals alone among US Christian groups surveyed register a majority opinion (60 percent) that Islam is "more likely" to encourage violence in its followers than other faiths are. The article also relates other evangelical groups and spokespeople who disagree strongly with that view. Tobin Grant, "Polling Evangelicals: Is Islam Violent?" *Christianity Today,* March 10, 2011, http://blog.christianitytoday.com/ctpolitics/2011/03/polling_evangel_1.html.

96. See, e.g., "Cults and Modern-Day False Prophets," Young Earth Creationist Club, http://www.creationists.org/cults.html.

97. See, e.g., Cameron and Comfort, *School,* 471–90, 516–56.

98. Steven Anderson, *Pentecostal Soul-Winning Demonstration Video (Baptist),* YouTube video, 18:48, posted by sanderson1611, March 9, 2009, http://www.youtube.com/user/sanderson1611#p/search/1/xBIR4xS6soU.

99. Of course, Anderson views the gospel as more than simply a get-out-of-hell-free card. I simply point out that in his soul-winning presentation, the gospel serves only this function.

Chapter 5

1. Here and throughout, I use the capitalized "Hell House" and "Hell Houses" to describe productions that use Keenan Roberts's Hell House Outreach Kit. Similarly, I use "Judgement House" to refer to productions that use Tom Hudgins's particular form. Since each Judgement House performance uses a specific script, I refer at times to the script by name (e.g., *59 Minutes* or *Land of the Free, Home of the Brave*). Other events like *Scaremare, Final Exit,* or *The 99* exist as discrete performances. I use lowercase "hell house" or "judgement house" to designate essentially bootleg or homegrown versions of the franchised forms.

2. Keenan Roberts, *The Hell House Outreach Manual* (Thornton, CO: Keenan Roberts, 2010), hereafter *Hell House Manual.* My thanks to Allan Davis for allowing me to consult his copy of the *Manual.*

3. To date, Jason C. Bevins provides the most comprehensive catalogue and description of such variants. He gives detailed accounts of Hell House, Judgement House, Tribulation Trail, Rapture House, and a traditional stage drama with similar eschatological themes, *Heaven's Gates and Hell's Flames.* See chapter five of his *Religion of Fear: The Politics of Horror in Conservative Evangelicalism* (New York: Oxford University Press, 2008).

4. George Ratliff (director), *Hell House,* DVD (Brooklyn: Plexifilm, 2001).

5. Cited by Bob Allen, "Popular 'Hell Houses' Draw Praise, Criticism," *Associated Baptist Press News,* October 19, 2000, www.abpnews.com/; Mary Hunt, quoted in National Gay and Lesbian Taskforce, "New Report Titled 'Homophobia at Hell House' Reveals How Right Wing Fuels Homophobia, Demonizes Lesbian and Gay Youth," October 27, 2006, www.thetaskforce.org/press/releases/pr996_102706. I discuss more recent criticism by evangelicals later in this chapter.

6. Brian Jackson, "Jonathan Edwards Goes to Hell (House): Fear Appeals in American Evangelism," *Rhetoric Review* 26, no. 1 (2007): 42–59; Bevins, *Religion of Fear.*

7. Ann Pellegrini, "'Signaling through the Flames': Hell House Performance and Structures of Religious Feeling," *American Quarterly* 59, no. 3 (2007): 911–35.

8. Allan Davis, "A Hell House Divided: Performing Identity Politics through Christian Medium of Proselytization," (MA thesis, Brigham Young University, 2011); Willenbrink, "Scaring."

9. Pellegrini, "Signaling," 912.

10. John Fletcher, "Tasteless as Hell: Community Performance, Distinction, and Counter-Taste in Hell House," *Theater Survey* 48, no. 2 (2007): 313–30.

11. Greg Hartman, "A Hell of a Ride," *Plain Truth Ministries,* PDF document, November–December 2003: 41–44, http://www.ptm.org/03PT/NovDec/hellRide.pdf, 42.

12. New Destiny Christian Center, "The Hell House Outreach Kit," *New Destiny Christian Center,* http://www.godestiny.org/hell_house/HH_kit.cfm.

13. Jackson, "Jonathan Edwards," 51.

14. Bevins, *Religion of Fear,* 132.

15. Ethan Blue, "National Trauma, Church Drama: The Cultural Politics of Fear," *Bad Subjects* 72 (2005): n.p., http://bad.eserver.org/issues/2005/72/blue.html. For more on Scaremare, see the production's web page: "Scaremare," *Liberty University Online,* 2008, http://www.scaremare.com/.

16. See Richard Schechner's now dated but still influential "6 Axioms for Environmental Theater," *TDR* 12, no. 3 (1968): 41–64. To be clear, I am less interested in classifying Hell Houses or Judgement Houses as specimens of environmental theater (their text-based status differentiates them from the performances Schechner has in mind) and more in using Schechner's model as a quick guide to distinguish them from more conventionally "theatrical" fare.

17. In many evangelical traditions, "rededication" or "recommitment" figures as a renewal of the theological performative, generally recommended in response to a perception of having backslid. Different traditions value rededication differently. Baptists, for instance, tend to uphold a "once saved, always saved" theology; provided a person has actually been saved in the past, rededication is meaningful but not salvific. Reformed traditions, minimizing human agency in favor of the irresistible divine act of salvation, similarly regard authentic salvation as a one-time, irreversible event. Many Pentecostal traditions, by contrast, operate from more Arminian bases and consider salvation as something relatively fragile. Though God is ever-faithful in saving the faithful, humans have the agency to turn away from God even after converting, essentially losing the salvation they received. Rededication therefore assumes a soteriological significance nearly on par with an initial commitment. For an explanation of impermanent grace from a theologically evangelical point of view, see Donald G. Bloesch, *Essentials of Evangelical Theology,* 2 vols. (San Francisco: Harper and Row, 1979), vol. I, 247.

18. Lance Meche (Youth Pastor), personal communication, Tallahassee, FL, March 22, 2004.

19. Ratliff, *Hell House,* focuses a bit on this phenomenon, interviewing several audience members waiting to get in who clearly desire only to gawk at the spectacle.

20. Roberts, *Hell House Outreach Manual,* 3.

21. Russell D. Moore, "Seven Reasons Halloween Judgment Houses Often Miss the Mark," *Moore to the Point,* blog, October 24, 2011, reposted from October 31, 2008, http://www.russellmoore.com/2011/10/24/seven-reasons-halloween-judgment-houses-often-miss-the-mark-2/.

22. Amy K. Hall, "Moore: Judgment [*sic*] Houses Miss the Mark," *Stand to Reason Blog,* October 26, 2011, http://str.typepad.com/weblog/2011/10/moore-judgment-houses-miss-the-mark.html. Hall's title and entry refers casually to Judgement House (presented as "Judgment House") and Hell House as more or less the same thing, an elision that is understandable but (as I will argue) inaccurate.

23. Tom Farr, "Fear Tactics: Scaring People toward Jesus," *Tom Farr: A Journey of Faith and Creativity,* blog, October 14, 2011, http://tom-farr.blogspot.com/2011/10/fear-tactics.html.

24. Shannon Dingle, October 25, 2011 (9:55 a.m.), comment on Moore, "Seven Reasons."

25. Nigel Goodnow, October 28, 2011 (10:49 a.m.), comment on Hall, "Moore: Judgment." One commenter registers a different theological qualm about Hell Hous-

es that indicates a tension in evangelical doctrines of the afterlife. Hell Houses err, this commenter argues, in presenting hell as a realm ruled by Satan and his demons whereas scripture (as interpreted by many evangelicals) describes Satan and the demons as in torment themselves. God, not Satan, provides the punishment and rules hell. See James Krikava, October 25, 2011 (9:30 a.m.), comment on Moore, "Seven Reasons."

26. Dustin Slatin, October 25, 2011 (10:16 a.m.), comment on Moore, "Seven Reasons."

27. Baz Kershaw, *The Politics of Performance: Radical Theater as Cultural Intervention* (New York: Routledge, 1992), 25–26.

28. See Adam B. Vary, "Hell House of the Stars," *Advocate,* October 12, 2004: 80–82; and Richard Rushfield, "Raising Hell," *New York Times,* August 29, 2004, sec. 2–3. How closely or sincerely the "Youth Group" actually attempted to live into the spirit of Roberts's Hell House is, of course, questionable. Newspaper reports suggest that Maher's portrayal of the demon guide included a great deal of tongue-in-cheek commentary. Jill Soloway, one of the codirectors, insists that their aim was "really about the literalism—not against religion, against Christianity" (Vary, 82).

29. Ben Brantley, "A Guided Tour of Hell, with an Appearance by Satan," *New York Times,* October 14, 2006, sec. B; Howard Kissel, "Scaring Up a Scene: Brooklyn Theatrical Haunt Stages a Halloween Horror," *New York Daily News,* October 8, 2006.

30. Kim Kozlowski, "Churches Use Pagan Day to Send Message," *Detroit News,* October 30, 2002, two dot ed., 1A.

31. John Moore, "'Hell House' Pastor Hopes N.Y. Gets Point," *Denver Post,* October 1, 2006, final ed., F08.

32. Lance Meche (Youth Pastor), personal communication, Tallahassee, FL, March 22, 2004.

33. Román and Miller, "Preaching," 177.

34. Jill Dolan, "Performance, Utopia, and the 'Utopian Performative,'" *Theater Journal* 53 (2001): 455–79. By "a better world," Dolan means that utopias suggest a "common future, one that's more just and equitable, one in which we can all participate more equally, with more chances to live fully and contribute to the making of culture" (455).

35. Anthony Cohen, *The Symbolic Construction of Community* (New York: Tavistock, 1985), 12.

36. Pierre Bourdieu, *Distinction: A Social Critique of the Judgment of Taste,* trans. Richard Nice (Cambridge: Harvard University Press, 1984). Specifically, Bourdieu argues, "Taste, the propensity and capacity to appropriate (materially or symbolically) a given class of classified, classifying objects or practices, is the generative formula of life-style, a unitary set of distinctive preferences which express the same expressive intention in the specific logic of each of the symbolic subspaces, furniture, clothing, language, or body hexis" (173).

37. Bourdieu, *Distinction,* 229.

38. Bruce L. Shelley and Marshall Shelley, *The Consumer Church: Can Evangelicals Win the World without Losing Their Souls?* (Downers Grove, IL: InterVarsity Press, 1992), 20.

39. Bourdieu, *Distinction,* 170–71.

40. Shelley and Shelley, *Consumer Church,* 49.

41. Virginia Culver, "Church's 'Hell House' to Feature Gay Wedding," *Denver Post,* September 29, 1999, 2nd ed., B05.

42. Bourdieu, *Distinction,* 56.

43. The actor appears in Ratliff's film.

44. Kozlowski, "Churches."

45. The production's version of the "conversion room" featured a live praise-and-worship band cheerily singing standard contemporary Christian music in place of a somber message about the gospel. A large pitcher of red Kool-Aid (a convention not included in actual hell house productions) unsubtly communicated the producers' judgment of Roberts's theology as destructive.

46. Pellegrini, "Signaling," 928.

47. I take the general outline and impressions of this performance from the production I saw: *59 Minutes,* Amite Baptist Church (Denham Springs, LA), October 24, 2009. Recording actual lines of dialogue, however, was impractical while watching the production. For direct quotes from the script (Judgement House scripts are rarer and more tightly controlled than Roberts's Hell House Outreach Kit), I thus rely on YouTube videos posted by other churches of their own productions of the same Judgement House script (*59 Minutes*) as was used at Amite Baptist. For this scene, I consulted "Judgement House—Scene 5: The Gates of Heaven," video clip, 7:36, October 4, 2011, posted by JesusFreak429, YouTube, http://www.youtube.com/watch?v=GIlSvz7PYrU&feature=related. As of June 2013, the user JesusFreak429 has posted most of that church's production online.

48. For an example of this scene, see "59 Minutes (Judgement House) Scene 3: Church Foyer," video clip, 4:43, posted October 31, 2010 by JesusFreak429, YouTube, http://www.youtube.com/watch?v=hBZywGDQQto&feature=related. In the YouTube scene Jake is a girl named "Lindsey," a divergence from the script I saw as well as from the script description in Tom Hudgins, *Judgement House Training Manual* ([Clearwater, FL]: New Creation Experiences, 2008), 13.

49. Though in scripture Jesus grants his disciple Peter the "keys of the kingdom," traditions identifying Peter as staffing the pearly gates are apocryphal—to say nothing of Roman Catholic.

50. Hudgins, *Judgement,* 66.

51. New Creation Evangelism, Inc., "How Is Judgement House Different?" *Judgement House,* New Creation Experiences, Inc., lasted updated December 2011, http://judgmenthouse.info/new-to-jh/how-is-judgement-house-different/.

52. Hudgins, *Judgement,* 66.

53. For a description of these requirements, see New Creation Evangelism, Inc., "Judgement House Annual Covenant Partner Agreement and Application Form," PDF document, last updated December 2011, available at http://judgmenthouse.info/become-covenant-partners/new-or-renew/.

54. Hudgins, *Judgement,* 58.

55. Hudgins, *Judgement,* 9.

56. By "muted" I mean that, although the script unproblematically presents support for the US military as a natural function of godly Christian lives, it bypasses references to, say, fighting Islamic terrorists in Afghanistan. *Land of the Free,* in other words, does not explicitly mobilize au courant pro–War on Terror jingoism in the same way that Hell House uses ripped-from-the-headlines issues.

57. For descriptions of Hell House scripts, see Hudgins, *Judgement,* 11–13, and also New Creation Experiences, Inc., "Our Scripts," *Judgement House,* New Creation Experiences, Inc., last updated December 2011, http://judgmenthouse.info/about/our-scripts/.

58. Hudgins, *Judgement,* 98.

59. Hudgins, *Judgement,* 72–73.

60. Hudgins, *Judgement,* 69–71.

61. Hudgins, *Judgement,* 72.

62. Hudgins, *Judgement,* 26. The *Manual* repeatedly implores the production's main director to make sure that cast members pray between tour groups (31).

63. Hudgins, *Judgement,* 73.

64. New Creation Experiences, Inc., "Why Judgement House?" *Judgement House,* New Creation Experiences, Inc., last updated December 2011, http://judgmenthouse.info/new-to-jh/why-judgement-house/.

65. To be specific, social movement theory affirms that social networks can be and often are implicated in recruitment into activist participation. But social network involvement does not guarantee such mobilization, nor does every activist participate as such due to social network affiliations. For an overview of the relevant literature, see Donatella della Porta and Mario Diani, *Social Movements: An Introduction,* 2nd ed. (Malden, MA: Blackwell, 2006), 117–31.

66. New Creation Experiences, Inc ., "What Is Judgement House?" *Judgement House,* New Creation Experiences, Inc., last updated December 2011, http://judgmenthouse.info/new-to-jh/what-is-judgement-house/.

67. New Creation Experiences, Inc., "Why Judgement House?"

68. Hudgins, *Judgement,* 71.

69. Hudgins, *Judgement,* 65.

70. Hudgins, *Judgement,* 75.

71. For information on *Final Exit,* see "The Final Exit . . ." *Life 101.9,* audio podcast, August 9, 2011, http://www.life1019.com/2011/08/the-final-exit/; "'Final Exit' Live and Ready to Travel," *Christian Film News,* last modified October 25, 2001, http://christianfilmnews.com/1013/final-exit/; and "'Final Exit' Dramatization Evangelizes Thousands," *AG* [Assemblies of God] *News,* last modified February 6, 2004, http://ag.org/top/News/index_articledetail.cfm?Process=DisplayArticle&targetBay=c97d4d5c-a325-4921-9a9e-e9fbddd9cdce&ModID=2&RSS_RSSContentID=3148&RSS_OriginatingChannelID=global&RSS_OriginatingRSSFeedID=3359&RSS_Source=search.

72. Ann Pellegrini expresses a similar sentiment. "One of the things that most interests me about Hell House," she writes, "is its faith in the power of theater to reach in and transform its audience." Pellegrini, "Signaling," 920.

73. As in all things, evangelicals disagree about the merits of the play. The (not entirely evangelical) group MassResistance articulates the view that the play represents anti-faith, pro-homosexual propaganda. See Ann Contrada, "'THE LARAMIE PROJECT' Undermines Parental Rights, Leads Students to Radical Groups," *MassResistance,* blog, October 25, 2007, http://www.massresistance.org/docs/issues/laramie_project/Play_violates_rights.html. In contrast, Bill Henson, a minister who works with "same-sex-attracted" people and generally adopts a view that homosexuality is sinful, relates that he feels the play portrays evangelicals fairly, even encouraging other evangelicals to attend. See Henson, "Laramie Project," *Lead Them Home,* blog, April 15, 2008, http://blog.leadthemhome.org/2008/04/laramie-project.html.

Chapter 6

1. The gar, explains the Museum's guidebook, were chosen for the exhibit due to their status as "living fossils," challenging evolutionary accounts of the history of

life. Answers in Genesis, *Journey Through the Creation Museum* (Green Forest, AR: Master Books, 2008), 14.

2. Mark Isaak cites several statistics to this effect, noting that many of the scientists who do profess anti-evolutionist beliefs do not in fact train or work in fields relevant to the study of biological science. See Isaak, *The Counter-Creationism Handbook* (Berkeley: University of California Press, 2007), 13.

3. Since, as I will explain, the general term *creationism* describes Christians who also endorse evolutionary theory, I use *anti-evolutionist* to name that subset of Christian creationism opposed to evolutionary theory and to other scientific theories that endorse timescales and processes that run counter to Genesis accounts of creation and the flood. For simplicity's sake I also restrict my discussion of creationism to the Christian variety active in the United States. For an overview of creationism from the perspective of other faiths and in other countries, see Numbers, *Creationists,* chapter eighteen.

4. Isaak's *Counter-Creationism Handbook* nicely catalogues such rebuttals. For a more focused criticism of the Creation Museum and AiG in particular, see the web page of Australian Skeptics, Inc., "No Answers in Genesis," last modified July 14, 2009, http://www.noanswersingenesis.org.au/.

5. Key court cases in the evolution and education debate include 1968's Epperson v. Arkansas, where the Supreme Court invalidated prohibitions against teaching evolutionary theory, and 1987's Edwards v. Aguillard, where the Supreme Court ruled that public schools cannot require creation science to be taught in science classes alongside evolution. See Epperson v. Arkansas. 393 US 87 (1968); and Edwards v. Aguillard. 428 US 578 (1987). I discuss another such case, Kitzmiller v. Dover Area School District, later in this article. See Kitzmiller v. Dover Area School District. No. 04cv2688 (2005).

6. I note here that mine is not the only performance-based work on the Museum. I highly recommend Jill Stevenson's in-depth analysis of the Creation Museum's affective strategies. Our work on the Museum and on evangelical performances more generally complement each other, and I very much appreciate her generosity and assistance in shaping my thoughts on AiG. See Jill Stevenson, "Embodying Sacred History: Performing Creationism for Believers," *TDR* 56, no. 1 (2012): 93–113.

7. For convenience's sake, I use a lower-case *m* when talking about museums in general and an upper-case *M* to name the Creation Museum specifically.

8. See Barbara Kirshenblatt-Gimblett, *Destination Culture: Tourism, Museums, and Heritage* (Berkeley: University of California Press, 1998), and Valerie Casey, "Staging Meaning: Performance in the Modern Museum," *TDR* 49, no. 3 (2005): 78–95.

9. Kirshenblatt-Gimblett, *Destination Culture,* 3.

10. Kirshenblatt-Gimblett, *Destination Culture,* 17–18. Kirshenblatt-Gimblett follows Judith Butler, among others, in extending Austin's theories to include non-speech actions that have performative (world-shaping) effects.

11. Kirshenblatt-Gimblett, *Destination Culture,* 31. She is quoting George Brown Good, a nineteenth-century ichthyologist and museum curator who in 1889 stressed the need for museums not to assume that objects speak for themselves.

12. Michael Ames, "Museology Interrupted," *Museum International* 57, no. 3 (2005): 44.

13. Casey, "Staging Meaning," 80.

14. Stacia McKeever, Gary Vaterlaus, and Diane King, *The Creation Museum: Behind the Scenes!* (Hebron, KY: Answers in Genesis, 2008), 32.

15. Kershaw, *Politics,* 25–26.

16. Readers interested in a more detailed walk-through of the Museum's main tour than I am able to give here may refer to the Museum's own *Journey Through the Creation Museum* (a photobook re-creation of the tour) and the *Creation Museum: Behind the Scenes!* volume. See Answers in Genesis, *Journey,* and McKeever, Vaterlaus, and King, *Creation Museum.* Both are available from AiG's website. Writing from a more skeptical point of view, Daniel Phelps provides a very descriptive account of the main tour, complete with photographs and his own often sardonic commentary in an article available on the National Center for Science Education's website. See Phelps, "The Anti-Museum: An Overview and Review of the Answers in Genesis Creation 'Museum,'" *National Center for Science Education,* last modified October 17, 2008, http://ncseweb.org/creationism/general/anti-museum-overview-review-answers-genesis-creation-museum. I have consulted these and other texts in addition to my own notes here.

17. Stevenson compellingly suggests that this creationist scientist (or, rather, the actor playing the scientist) provides Museum-goers with a "model creationist with whom they can identify and subsequently emulate." She points out that this "thoughtful, grandfatherly man," who bears more than a passing resemblance to Santa Claus ("complete with a twinkle in his eye"), provides the narration for nearly all the Museum's educational films, adding to the affects of trustworthiness and ideological/theological confidence the Museum seeks to infuse into its anti-evolutionist presentation. See Stevenson, "Embodying," 110.

18. Kirshenblatt-Gimblett, *Destination Culture,* 3.

19. The "Monkey Trial," famously (and, to creationists, inaccurately) dramatized in Jerome Lawrence and Robert Edmond Lee's *Inherit the Wind,* is widely seen as an early watershed for US fundamentalism. While John T. Scopes, the defendant charged with teaching biological evolution in public school, technically lost, the highly publicized trial itself was seen as an indictment of anti-evolutionists' ignorance and intolerance. For an eyewitness (though not exactly neutral) account, see Arthur Garfield Hays, "The Scopes Trial," in *Evolution and Religion: The Conflict between Science and Theology in Modern America,* ed. Gail Kennedy, 35–52 (Boston: D. C. Heath, 1957).

20. Judith Butler, *Bodies That Matter: On the Discursive Limits of "Sex"* (New York: Routledge, 1993), 224–25. Butler further argues, of course, that such authorizing entities themselves must cite other authorities, and so on, creating a citational chain.

21. Michael Behe's *Darwin's Black Box: The Biochemical Challenge to Evolution* (New York: Touchstone, 1996) serves as the one of the most popular texts from ID thinkers. The notion that nature displays the marks of a designer is not new. William Paley made similar arguments in 1802.

22. Specifically, the debate involved actions of the Dover County Board of Education, which had mandated that Dover science classrooms distribute statements questioning the validity of Darwinian theory and recommending that students consult an alternative text that ninth grade science classrooms were required to provide (*Of Pandas and People,* which included information about ID theory). Embarrassingly for the Board, the text was revealed to be a minimally revised version of an overtly religious creation science textbook from 1989. Indeed, the only change was the replacement of the words *creationism* and *creationist* with *ID.* See Kitzmiller v. Dover Area School District, 32.

23. The "wedge" refers to the "Wedge Document," a memo from the Discovery Institute's Center for Renewal of Science and Culture in which it outlined their goals

of using ID as a way to reintroduce religious elements into science classrooms. The text of the decision itself provides a thorough account of the Dover case and its history. See Kitzmiller v. Dover Area School District, 28–29. For more information, see Barbara Forrest (whose research informed the court's decision) and Paul R. Gross's exposé, *Creationism's Trojan Horse: The Wedge of Intelligent Design* (New York: Oxford University Press, 2004).

24. Significantly, the court itself specified that, while in this instance ID theory had been used duplicitously by religious creationists, many ID proponents are themselves innocent of deceptive motives (Kitzmiller v. Dover Area School District, 139).

25. Isaak, *Counter-Creationism Handbook,* xxiii.

26. Daniel Phelps, for instance, expresses bafflement about why the believer-turned-agnostic Charles Templeton earns so much attention and ire ("Apparently, AiG is REALLY PISSED at Rev. Templeton"), finding the whole defense-of-the-Bible section "a bit dull" (Phelps, "Anti-Museum," under "Biblical Authority and Biblical Relevance Rooms").

27. Perhaps the most well-established advocate of moderate, evolution-friendly creationism within the evangelical spectrum is the BioLogos Foundation, an evangelical coalition "committed to exploring and celebrating the compatibility of evolutionary creation and biblical faith, guided by the truth that 'all things hold together in Christ' [Col 1:17]." See BioLogos Foundation's website at http://biologos.org/.

28. Space prohibits me from exploring in detail the wide range of creationist beliefs. For contemporary surveys of key creationist viewpoints from an evangelical perspective, see Boyd and Eddy, *Across,* chapters four and five, and Baynard Taylor, *The Great Ape Debate* (Cincinnati: Standard, 2008).

29. Far more popular among anti-evolutionist/inerrancy-minded evangelicals throughout the entire creation/evolution have been "day-age" or "gap" theories. These preserve a more or less inerrant view of Genesis, but they either read the "days" of creation metaphorically (one "day" equaling an era of billions of years, for instance) or infer an indeterminate time-span (a gap) between Genesis 1:1 and 1:2. Numbers quotes a "frustrated fundamentalist" who, in 1980, lamented that no Christian denomination or organization had officially endorsed as exclusively orthodox the literal, six-day creation and flood. See Numbers, *Creationists,* 345.

30. Even the Martin Luther display communicates a subtle anti-Catholicism endemic to Protestant evangelical culture.

31. Thomas Reid, William Harrison, and Dugald Stewart are prominent spokespeople for this philosophy. For an overview of their beliefs and history, see Theodore Dwight Bozeman, *Protestants in the Age of Science: The Baconian Ideal and Antebellum American Religious Thought* (Chapel Hill: University of North Carolina Press, 1977), chapter one, and Terrence Martin, *The Instructed Vision: Scottish Common Sense Philosophy and the Origins of American Fiction* (Bloomington: Indiana University Press, 1961), chapter one. For a general guide to Common Sense notions from a key US interlocutor of the Scottish Realists during the late 1800s, see James McCosh, "Criteria of the Various Kinds of Truth," *Princeton Review* 56 (1880): 419–40.

32. Note the similarity between a Common Sense view of scripture reading with the "Bible-reading" techniques that emerged in the late 1800s. One reads the Bible as is, taking its verses and testimony as readily apparent facts and eschewing any interpretation (or hypothesis) that would corrupt or undermine the plain sense of scripture. For a detailed analysis of how Baconian assumptions about the world informed views of scripture, see George Marsden, "Everyone," 79–100.

33. Modern science, of course, would take issue with this silent (re)definition of science. For example, in its educational publication addressing evolution and creationism, *Science, Evolution, and Creationism* (Washington, DC: National Academies Press, 2008), the National Academy of Sciences (NAS) stresses the importance of seeing science as not just a matter of pure investigations but as a process of constructing "testable explanations and predictions of natural phenomena" (10). While most scientists trust that their investigations enable them to approach a progressively more accurate and useful model for reality, they stress that science views predictions and test results as provisional and revisable rather than infallible and eternal. For an excellent exploration of present-day understandings of scientific processes, including a careful criticism of "common sense" science, see A. F. Chalmers, *What Is This Thing Called Science?* 3rd ed. (Indianapolis: Hackett, 1999).

34. Bill Jack and Jeff Baldwin, representatives of "Worldview Academy" and hosts of *Radio Worldview,* devote two episodes of their podcast to the comparison/contrast of evidentialist and presuppositionalist apologetics. They explicitly link themselves and their worldview-based ministry to the presuppositionalist approach. See Worldview Academy, "Presuppositionalism vs. Evidentialism," podcast audio, *Radio Worldview,* 42:44, MP3, April 29, 2009, http://itunes.apple.com/us/podcast/radio-worldview/id83107754; and Worldview Academy, "Presuppositionalism vs. Evidentialism Part Two,"podcast audio, *Radio Worldview,* 45:27, MP3, May 19, 2009, http://itunes.apple.com/us/podcast/radio-worldview/id83107754.

35. See James W. Sire, *The Universe Next Door: A Basic Worldview Catalog,* 4th ed. (Downers Grove, IL: IVP Academic, 2004), and David Naugle, *Worldview: The History of a Concept* (Grand Rapids, MI: William B. Eerdmans, 2002). For more recent conceptions and criticisms of worldview analysis from evangelical perspectives, see J. Matthew Bonzo and Michael Stevens, eds., *After Worldview: Christian Higher Education in Postmodern Worlds* (Sioux Center, IA: Dordt College Press, 2009).

36. Ham has published his own worldview book, *War of the Worldviews,* focusing on creationist issues. See Becky Stelzer, Stacia McKeever, and Michael Matthews, eds., *War of the Worldviews* (Green Forest, AR: Master Books, 2005).

37. See the websites for Worldview Academy at http://worldview.org/index.php and Summit Ministries, http://www.summit.org/. For the textbook used by Summit Ministries, see David K. Noebel, *Understanding the Times: The Collision of Today's Competing Worldviews,* 2nd ed. (Manitou Springs, CA: Summit, 2006).

38. Ken Ham, *Why Won't They Listen? The Power of Creation Evangelism* (Green Forest, AR: Master Books, 2005), 67–68.

39. Ham, *Why,* 87.

40. Ham, *Why,* 97.

41. Ham, *Why,* 83.

42. Ham's divisions are reminiscent of but distinct from those of another interpretive scheme popular among conservative evangelicals, premillennial dispensationalism. See Marsden, *Fundamentalism,* 52–55, for a description of dispensational history and belief.

43. Central to AiG's version of young-earth creationism is the tenet that, prior to the Fall of Man, no death or disease of any kind existed. See Ken Ham and Stacia McKeever, *The Seven C's of History* (Hebron, KY: Answers in Genesis, 2007), 6–7. Thus all creatures were essentially vegetarian, acquiring predatory diets and habits only after the expulsion from the Garden.

44. Contrary to most depictions of the forbidden fruit, in the Museum's display

Adam and Eve appear to be eating grapes. The Museum's *Behind the Scenes* book explains this choice by referencing "Jewish teachings," which identify the fruit as "the grape from which wine is derived" (McKeever, Vaterlaus, and King, *Creation Museum,* 79).

45. Carl Kerby, "Demolishing Strongholds: Evolution in Pop Culture," podcast audio, March 18, 2006, http://www.sermonaudio.com/sermoninfo.asp?SID=11309951504. (N.b.: this is something of a stump speech for Kerby; several sources online feature various recordings of him delivering the speech.)

46. Here Kerby takes a jab at the Campus Crusade for Christ's "Four Spiritual Laws" approach to evangelism.

47. Curiously enough, Ham maintains that the most common stumbling-block question he encounters has less to do with the explanation of evil and instead concerns who Cain married. The Museum thus has a special text display dedicated to answering that question: Cain married one of Adam and Eve's daughters, i.e., his sister.

48. McKeeve, Vaterlaus, and King, *Creation Museum,* 82.

49. AiG stresses the distinction between *kind* and *species,* specifying that Noah took on board the Ark at least two of every *kind* of animal. Since AiG maintains that speciation occurred only after the flood, they believe the numbers of animals on the Ark were more manageable than would otherwise have been possible.

50. It is perhaps surprising that geology (in the form of catastrophism) and not biology has so served anti-evolutionist interests the most throughout the twentieth century. Since until recently most evidence for historical evolution existed in fossils dated via reference to rock layers, young-earth creationists like George McCready Price in the early 1900s saw an opening whereby "if [evolution's] geology were true, the rest would seem more or less reasonable"—and vice versa (Price quoted in Numbers, *Creationists,* 91). Building on Price's flawed but influential *The New Geology* (1923), a series of creationist geology works followed, most notably John C. Whitcomb and Henry M. Morris's *The Genesis Flood* in 1961 (Numbers, *Creationists,* 255). It is this latter work that AiG founder Ken Ham cites as one of the pivotal books shaping his convictions and persistent arguments against evolution (McKeever, Vaterlaus, and King, *Creation Museum,* 6). Numbers's *The Creationists* provides an exhaustive history of twentieth-century creation science.

51. In I Corinthians, Jesus is described as "the last Adam," whose act of sacrifice restores the divine-human relationship shattered by the original sin of the first Adam. For an overview of AiG's particular interpretation of that passage, see Ken Ham, *The Purpose and Meaning of Life: From Creation to the Cross* (Hebron, KY: Answers in Genesis, 2008).

52. Román and Miller, "Preaching," 177–78.

53. Critical museum reviewer Phelps has a point, however, when he notes how few of the Museum's displays use hands-on, discover-it-for-yourself features common to many secular discovery centers. He is not wrong in reading a degree of authoritarianism—we will *tell* you what the biblical worldview is—in this choice (Phelps, "Anti-Museum," under "Discussion").

54. Román and Miller, "Preaching," 177.

55. Jill Stevenson, "Embodying," 104–5.

56. For more information, see Answers in Genesis's Vacation Bible School web page at http://answersvbs.com/2012/.

57. Answers in Genesis takes the position that extraterrestrial life is likely an evolu-

tionist myth. See Jason Lisle, "Are ETs and UFOs real?" *Answers in Genesis,* December 6, 2007, http://www.answersingenesis.org/articles/nab/are-ets-and-ufos-real.

58. Randy Witt and Barb Witt, Operation Space *Assembly Guide* (Hebron, KY: Answers in Genesis, 2008), 19–20.

59. Witt and Witt, *Assembly Guide,* 21.

60. Witt and Witt, *Assembly Guide,* 70.

61. "What Makes an Answers VBS Program Different from Any Other Vacation Bible School?" *Answers in Genesis,* http://answersvbs.com/2012/about/incredi-world/.

62. See "Course Overview," *Answers in Genesis,* http://answersvbs.com/2012/about/course-overview/.

63. Karl Giberson, "A House of Sand and Fog," *BioLogos Forum,* blog, October 12, 2009, http://biologos.org/blog/a-house-of-sand-and-fog.

64. Harris, for instance, published a 2009 op-ed in the *New York Times* criticizing the Obama administration's nomination of Francis Collins, the well-respected former director of the Human Genome Project, to the directorship of the National Institutes of Health. Harris's reasoning: Collins is an avowed Christian, a theistic evolutionist, and is thus unfit to serve as national advocate for science. See Sam Harris, "Science is in the Details," *New York Times,* July 27, 2009, late ed., A21. Harris's implication, like that of AiG, was that religious worldviews and secular scientific practice are incompatible, that people must commit to one or the other.

65. Giberson, "House."

66. See The Ark Encounter website at http://arkencounter.com/.

67. Labov spoke at Louisiana State University, noting that Louisiana recently passed a law mandating that the flaws and controversies of evolutionary theory (code for anti-evolutionist counterattacks) be taught in public schools. See Jay Labov, "Science, Evolution, and Creationism: The Critical Need for Science as a Liberal Art in the 21st Century," Public Speech, Louisiana State University, January 7, 2009. The NAS's *Science, Evolution, and Creationism* is in fact a step toward re-thinking the presentation of pro-evolutionist views.

68. Michael Ruse, *The Evolution-Creation Struggle* (Cambridge: Harvard University Press, 2005), 287.

69. Ruse, *Evolution-Creation,* 284.

70. Mary Midgely, *Evolution as a Religion: Strange Hopes and Stranger Fears* (New York: Methuen, 1985), 3–4.

71. Jonathan Haidt, *The Righetous Mind: Why Good People Are Divided by Politics and Religion* (New York: Pantheon, 2012), 287–88.

Chapter 7

1. Beyond Relevance [Richard Reising], "What if Starbucks Marketed Like the Church? A Parable," YouTube Video, 5:33, posted by beyondrelevance, October 2008, http://youtu.be/D7_dZTrjw9I.

2. Richard Reising, "The Video: Marketing Is More than You Realize," *Beyond Relevance,* blog, November 13, 2008, http://www.beyondrelevance.com/index.cfm/pageid/913/postid/26/blogid/4/index.html#e5059.

3. Reising, "The Video."

4. Richard Reising, "The Next Level in Signage," *Artistry Labs,* http://www.artistrylabs.com/church-signage.

5. Donald A. McGavran, *Understanding Church Growth,* rev. ed. (Grand Rapids, MI: Eerdmans, 1980 [1970]), 6.

6. See, e.g., McGavran, *Understanding,* 26–30.

7. McGavran, *Understanding,* 24.

8. For a detailed overview of McGavran's ministry and the Church Growth Movement, see Elmer Towns et al., *Evaluating the Church Growth Movement: Five Views* (Grand Rapids, MI: Zondervan, 2004).

9. George Barna, *Marketing the Church* (Colorado Springs: NavPress, 1988), 42–43. Barna draws his "four Ps" from E. Jerome McCarthy's *Basic Marketing.*

10. George Barna, *A Step-by-Step Guide to Church Marketing: Breaking Ground for the Harvest* (Ventura, CA: Regal Books, 1992), 24.

11. Barna, *Marketing,* 50.

12. Barna, *Step-by-Step,* 24. Italics in original.

13. Barna, *Step-by-Step,* 25.

14. Barna, *Marketing,* 7–8.

15. In their 2011 report, Bird and Thumma allow a lower cutoff number of 1,800 per week. See Warren Bird and Scott Thumma, *A New Decade of Megachurches* (Hartford, CT: Leadership Network and the Hartford Institute for Religious Research, 2011), online at http://leadnet.org/resources/download/a_new_decade_of_megachurches_2011_profile_of_large_attendance_churches_in_t, 4.

16. Bird and Thumma, *New Decade,* 6.

17. Bird and Thumma, *New Decade,* 4.

18. Most of the top ten largest congregations listed in the Hartford Institute for Religion Research's searchable database of US megachurches, for example, feature services that incorporate the attractional worship elements I describe later. See Hartford Institute for Religion Research, "Database of Megachurches in the U.S.," Hartford Seminary, http://hirr.hartsem.edu/megachurch/database.html.

19. John Hagee's Cornerstone Church in San Antonio, for example, is a megachurch crafted around Hagee's signature blend of fundamentalist-leaning Christianity and politicized involvement—features typically eschewed by seeker-sensitive services.

20. Kimon Howland Sargeant, *Seeker Churches: Promoting Traditional Religion in a Non-Traditional Way* (New Brunswick: Rutgers University Press, 2000). Other good sources describing the seeker movement in its first flourishing include Michael G. Maudlin and Edward Gilbreath, "Selling Out the House of God? Bill Hybels Answers Critics of the Seeker-Church Movement," Interview with Bill Hybels, *Christianity Today* 38, no. 8 (1994): 20–26; and Donald E. Miller, "Postdenominational Christianity in the Twenty-First Century (Americans and Religions in the Twenty-First Century)," *Annals of the American Academy of Political and Social Science* 558 (1998): 196–211.

21. Maudlin and Gilbreath, "Selling Out," 23.

22. For more on the Willow Creek Association, see Willow Creek Association's website, "Our Story," Willow Creek Association, 2012, http://www.willowcreek.com/about/.

23. Warren relates the story of his ministry and details his plan for seeker-sensitive ministry in Rick Warren, *The Purpose Driven Church: Growth Without Compromising Your Message and Mission* (Grand Rapids, MI: Zondervan, 1995).

24. Warren, *Purpose Driven,* 169.

25. Warren, *Purpose Driven,* 280.

26. William Cowper, "There Is a Fountain," in *Baptist Hymnal,* 107 (Nashville: Convention Press, 1975).

27. For an in-depth history of Pentecostal/charismatic worship, see Don Williams, "Charismatic Worship," in Paul Zahl et al., *Six Views on Exploring the Worship Spectrum,* 131–52 (Grand Rapids, MI: Zondervan, 2004). Robert R. Redman also traces the Pentecostal/charismatic praise-and-worship tradition, coupling it with an exploration of seeker-sensitive worship, in his article "Welcome to the Worship Awakening," *Theology Today* 58, no. 3 (2001): 369–83.

28. For convenience's sake, I follow Kenneth Hull's lead in shortening "praise and worship songs" to "worship songs." Kenneth Hull, "Music Wars, Neuroscience, and Self Psychology," *Liturgy* 24, no. 4 (2009): 24. Redman notes, however, that some Pentecostal/charismatic theologies distinguish between *praise* (focused on the attributes of God) and *worship* (emphasizing the believer's relationship with God), though he observes that this distinction is somewhat loosely defined. Redman, "Welcome," 378.

29. Zahl et al., *Six Views,* 126.

30. Williams, "Charismatic Worship," 143.

31. Williams, "Charismatic Worship," 143.

32. David W. Stowe, *No Sympathy for the Devil: Christian Pop Music and the Transformation of American Evangelicalism* (Chapel Hill: University of North Carolina Press, 2011), 1. For more on the history and makeup of CCM, see Eric Gormly, "Evangelizing through Appropriation: Toward a Cultural Theory on the Growth of Contemporary Christian Music," *Journal of Media and Religion* 2, no. 4 (2003): 251–65. Discourse about the worship wars per se comes mainly from Christian sources, with topical overviews typically interwoven with authors' own normative recommendations (for one side, for the other, or for rapprochement). See, e.g., T. David Gordon, "Pop Goes the Worship," Interview with Mark Moring, *Christianity Today,* March 9, 2011, http://www.christianitytoday.com/ct/2011/march/popgoesworship.html, and Ed Stetzer, "Ending the Worship War without a Truce," *Ed Setzer: The Lifeway Research Blog,* October 15, 2009, http://www.edstetzer.com/2009/10/ending-the-worship-war-without.html. Of course, the "worship wars" frame simplifies the vast and variegated topography of Christian music into two basic camps. A host of other styles thrive in US churches, many of which do not fit well into the worship wars polarization scheme. For a sampling of such forms, see Steve Thorngate, "New Harmonies," *Christian Century,* March 29, 2011.

33. Hull, "Music Wars," 24.

34. Hull, "Music Wars," 25.

35. Chris Tomlin, Jesse Reeves, and Ed Cash, "How Great is Our God," *Arrival,* compact disc, sixsteps records/Sparrow Records, 2004.

36. Hull, "Music Wars," 28.

37. Redman, "Welcome," 378.

38. Hull, "Music Wars," 30.

39. Hull, "Music Wars," 26.

40. Warren, *Purpose Driven,* 256. Redmond points out that the Vineyard movement recommends a similar energetic-to-quiet-to-personal arc (invitation, engagement, exaltation, adoration, intimacy). See Redmond, "Welcome," 377.

41. Hull, "Music Wars," 27–28.

42. Warren, *Purpose Driven,* 295.

43. The first two are actually messages I heard firsthand at two seeker-friendly services in Baton Rouge (Bethany World Harvest Prayer Center and Healing Place Church, respectively). The "affair-proof marriage" sermon included an extended discourse on "five things men can do to make themselves irresistible to women," with each point drawn directly from a best-selling self-improvement book by William Har-

ley Jr., *His Needs, Her Needs: Building an Affair-Proof Marriage* (Grand Rapids, MI: Fleming H. Revell, 2001).

44. Warren, *Purpose Driven,* 299.

45. Warren, *Purpose Driven,* 300.

46. Warren, *Purpose Driven,* 296–98.

47. "Your best life now" is also the title of one of Osteen's best-sellers, *Your Best Life Now: Seven Steps to Living at Your Full Potential* (New York: Time Warner Book Group, 2004).

48. Quoted in Sargeant, *Seeker Churches,* 95.

49. Dean M. Kelley, *Why Conservative Churches Are Growing: A Study in Sociology of Religion* (New York: Harper and Row, 1972).

50. Kelley, *Why Conservative,* 35.

51. Kelley, *Why Conservative,* 35.

52. Ronald B. Flowers, Review of *Why Conservative Churches Are Growing,* by Dean M. Kelley, *Journal of Church and State* 50, no. 4 (2008): 700. See also Kelley, *Why Conservative,* 51–52.

53. Kelley, *Why Conservative,* 84.

54. It should be said that Kelley's argument rests on a statistical correlation (i.e., increasing membership rates and strictness seem to coincide) that makes intuitive sense, not on an ironclad demonstration of causation (i.e., strictness results in membership growth). Though many statistical studies in the 1980s appeared to reinforce Kelley's case, some present-day researchers have called his causative case into question. Such researchers credit the comparative birth rates of liberal/mainline and conservative demographics with the finding Kelley sought to explain. The populations peopling conservative churches, in other words, simply reproduced at higher rates than did those in liberal/mainline congregations. See, e.g., David A. Hollinger, "After Cloven Tongues of Fire: Ecumenical Protestantism and the Modern American Encounter with Diversity," *Journal of American History* 98, no. 1 (2011): 21–48.

55. See, for example, a post by Southern Baptist theologian R. Albert Mohler Jr., "Why Conservative Churches Are Growing: David Brooks and the Limits of Sociology," *Albertmohler.com,* blog, April 25, 2011, http://www.albertmohler.com/2011/04/25/why-conservative-churches-are-growing-david-brooks-and-the-limits-of-sociology/.

56. Warren, *Purpose Driven,* 80.

57. Warren, *Purpose Driven,* 132, 320. The Covenant itself is reprinted on 321–22.

58. Warren, *Purpose Driven,* 132.

59. Warren, *Purpose Driven,* 133.

60. Warren, *Purpose Driven,* 134.

61. Warren, *Purpose Driven,* 343–48.

62. Warren, *Purpose Driven,* 239–41.

63. For a brief overview of multisite churches, see Bennett Liles, "Satellite Churches," *Sound and Video Contractor* 28, no. 10 (2010): 56–59.

64. I draw these numbers from the Database of Megachurches sponsored by the Hartford Institute for Religion Research, n.d., http://hirr.hartsem.edu/cgi-bin/mega/db.pl?db=default&uid=default&view_records=1&ID=*&sb=3&so=descend. The Hartford Institute stresses that it depends upon church or denominational self-reports of weekly attendees.

65. For an interview with Gruenwald in which he explains many of the church's ministries, see Chris Norton, "Virtual Vitality," *Christianity Today* 55, no. 11 (2011): 104.

66. LifeChurch.tv's website is, of course, http://www.lifechurch.tv. Many megachurch websites now feature similar countdown clocks and online service options on their websites. See, e.g., Lakewood Church's "Watch Online" page at http://www.lakewood.cc/pages/watchonline.aspx.

67. The online church website for LifeChurch.tv is http://live.lifechurch.tv.

68. For another account of a LifeChurch.tv service, see James Byassee, "Synchronized Worship," *Christian Century*, January 26, 2010.

69. Healing Place Church, which I mentioned above, is likewise a multisite church. There I made sure to note the digital clock

70. Byassee, "Synchronized," 26.

71. I had watched—or is it attended?—the previous week's sermon, Renew, online.

72. I take quotes from the transcript of his sermon. Craig Groeschel, "Remain," n.d. [2011], LifeChurch.tv, http://open.lifechurch.tv/message_groups/1563-re.

73. Norton, "Virtual," 104. YouVersion also exists as an online website at http://www.youversion.com.

74. Jeffery L. Sheler, *Believers: A Journey into Evangelical America* (New York: Viking, 2006), 115–16.

75. Todd Johnson, "Heads Up: Tracing the Battle Lines in the Worship Wars," *Library* 19, no. 4 (2004): 34.

76. NetworkChurches.tv (web page), LifeChurch.tv, 2012, http://network.lifechurch.tv/index.html.

77. RawChurch.tv (web page), 2011, http://www.rawchurch.tv/index.php.

78. See Warren Bird and Kristin Walters, "Multisite is Multiplying," Leadership Network, 2010, online at http://leadnet.org/resources/download/multisite_is_multiplying_new_developments_in_the_movements_expansion, 2; and Greg Ligon, "Multisite Movement Gaining New Momentum in New Places," The Leadership Network, 2011, online at http://leadnet.org/resources/download/multisite_movement_gaining_new_momentum_in_new_places.

79. Bird and Walters, "Multisite," 21–23.

80. Maudlin and Gilbreath, "Selling Out," 23.

81. For more about Willow Creek's believers' worship and its differences from the seeker-sensitive service, see a piece by Willow Creek's music leader, Joe Horness, "Contemporary Music-Driven Worship," in Zahl et al., *Six Views*, 99–116.

82. Quoted in Sheler, *Believers*, 125.

83. See, e.g., Christine Wicker, *The Fall of the Evangelical Nation: The Surprising Crisis Inside the Church* (New York: HarperOne, 2008). She devotes a chapter to megachurches structured around the seeker-sensitive outreach model (or similar schemes), focusing especially on Lake Pointe Church in Texas.

84. Sheler, *Believers*, 116.

85. Jim Henderson and Matt Casper, *Jim and Casper Go to Church: Frank Conversation about Faith, Churches, and Well-meaning Christians* (Carol Stream, IL: BarnaBooks, 2007), 2.

86. Lauren Sandler, *Righteous: Dispatches from the Evangelical Youth Movement* (New York: Viking, 2006), 77.

87. Henderson and Casper, *Jim and Casper*, 38.

88. Pictures of this setup are at http://www.flickr.com/photos/worshipideas/5953248490/in/set-72157627229069362/.

89. Henderson and Casper, *Jim and Casper*, 4.

90. Henderson and Casper, *Jim and Casper,* 40.

91. Jeff Sharlet, "Soldiers of Christ: Inside America's Most Powerful Megachurch," *Harper's Magazine,* May 2005, 50.

92. Lois Romano, "'The Smiling Preacher' Builds on Large Following," *Washington Post,* January 30, 2005, A01.

93. For a non-faith-based analysis of Osteen's rhetorical style, see Helje Kringlebotn Sødal, "'Victor, Not Victim': Joel Osteen's Rhetoric of Hope," *Journal of Contemporary Religion* 25, no. 1 (2010): 37–50.

94. Al Mohler quotes extensively from and comments upon a 2005 interview Osteen had with Larry King in which Osteen expressed his discomfort with the s-word. See R. Albert Mohler Jr., "The Limits of Encouragement," *AlbertMohler.com,* blog, June 24, 2005, http://www.albertmohler.com/2005/06/24/the-limits-of-encouragement/.

95. Michael S. Horton, "Joel Osteen and the Glory Story," online article, Westminster Seminary California, October 1, 2007, http://wscal.edu/resource-center/resource/joel-osteen-and-the-glory-story.

96. I lack the space for a full analysis of the prosperity gospel tradition here. For a general introduction, see David Van Biema and Jeff Chu, "Does God Want You to Be Rich?" *Time,* September 10, 2006, http://www.time.com.libezp.lib.lsu.edu/time/magazine/article/0,9171,1533448,00.html. For a more scholarly account, see Stephen Hunt, "Dramatising the 'Health and Wealth Gospel': Belief and Practice of a Neo-Pentecostal 'Faith' Ministry," *Journal of Beliefs and Values* 21, no. 1 (2000): 73–86. Jonathan Walton addresses the Word and Faith tradition's considerable influence in the Black Church in Walton, *Watch This!,* 93–101.

97. Van Biema and Chu, "Does God."

98. Michael Spencer, "Outing Joel Osteen: A Challenge to the Evangelical Blogosphere," *Internet Monk,* blog, January 29, 2005, http://www.internetmonk.com/archive/outing-joel-osteen-a-challenge-to-the-evangelical-blogosphere. Italics in original.

99. Groeschel criticizes what he calls "name it and claim it, blab it and grab it" theology in the "Remain" sermon I saw him preach. "Baloney" is how Warren characterized the idea that God wants everybody rich. The idea, he continued, is "a false idol . . . I can show you millions of faithful followers of Christ who live in poverty. Why isn't everyone in the church a millionaire?" Quoted in Van Biema and Chu, "Does God."

100. Sally Morgenthaler, *Worship Evangelism: Inviting Unbelievers into the Presence of God* (Grand Rapids, MI: Zondervan, 1998).

101. Sally Morgenthaler, "Worship as Evangelism," *Rev!* May–June 2007: 48–53, http://nancybeach.typepad.com/nancy_beach/files/morgenthaler_article.pdf.

102. Morgenthaler, "Worship as Evangelism," 50.

103. Morgenthaler, "Worship as Evangelism," 50.

104. Morgenthaler, "Worship as Evangelism," 51.

105. Scott Thumma and Warren Bird, "Not Who You Think They Are: The Real Story of People Who Attend America's Megachurches," The Leadership Network and the Hartford Institute for Religion Research, 2008, http://hirr.hartsem.edu/megachurch/National%20Survey%20of%20Megachurch%20Attenders%20-final.pdf.

106. Thumma and Bird, "Not Who," 16–18.

107. Mark Chaves, Shawna Anderson, and Jason Byassee, *American Congregations at the Beginning of the Twenty-First Century,* PDF document, National Congregations Study,

2008, http://www.soc.duke.edu/natcong/, 2–3. Here the authors use "average" in the sense of "median." The NCS draws on and compares data from two surveys of US congregations: one carried out in 1998 and one carried out in 2006–7. Unlike Thumma and Bird's research, the NCS collects information on US Christian and Jewish congregations (though not, as far as I can tell, from Mormon groups), not just from Protestant churches.

108. Michael Bell helpfully unpacks the NCS findings (including the tricky difference between *mean* and *median* averages) in "Michael Bell: 'What Is an "Average Church?"'" *Internet Monk,* blog, July 13, 2009, http://www.internetmonk.com/archive/michael-bell-what-is-an-average-church.

109. The median church's attendance (75) times the number of weeks in a year (52) times five-and-a-half years (5.5) equals 21,450, which is still smaller than Saddleback's reported 22,418 attendees per week (op. cit.).

110. Chaves, Anderson, and Byassee, *American Congregations,* 3.

111. Chaves, Anderson, and Byassee, *American Congregations,* 20.

112. "Key Findings," *REVEAL Now,* Willow Creek Association, http://www.revealnow.com/key_findings.asp.

113. Adele Banks, "Willow Creek Finds Limits to Its Model," *Christian Century,* January 28, 2008: 16.

114. In his review of the *REVEAL* study, sociologist Bradley Wright suggests that Hybels's distress is unwarranted. Several features of the study's methodology, Wright observes, make it difficult to draw the kind of causal relationships between church activities and spiritual growth that Hybels and the study's authors do. See Bradley R. E. Wright, "What We Can and Can't Learn from Willow Creek's *REVEAL* Study," *Journal of Youth Ministry* 7, no. 1 (2008): 108.

115. Thumma and Bird, "Not Who," 10–11. The authors mention the *REVEAL* study, noting that their own findings alongside Willow Creek's suggest a general arc to spiritual growth patterns. Longer-term members across the board appear to experience a bit of plateau or decline in spiritual satisfaction.

116. Thumma and Bird, "Not Who," 7–8.

117. Thumma and Bird, "Not Who," 18–19.

118. Smith and Snell, *Souls in Transition,* 154. For the original description of MTD, see Smith and Denton, *Soul Searching,* 162–71.

119. See, for example, R. Albert Mohler Jr., "Moralistic Therapeutic Deism—the New American Religion," *Christian Post,* April 18, 2005, http://www.christianpost.com/news/moralistic-therapeutic-deism-the-new-american-religion-6266/, and Brian H. Cosby, "MTD: Not Just a Problem with Youth Ministry," *The Gospel Coalition,* blog, April 9, 2012, http://thegospelcoalition.org/blogs/tgc/2012/04/09/mtd-not-just-a-problem-with-youth-ministry/.

120. For an idea of how such an organic church works, see Brian Hofmeister, "The Dirt on Organic," *Christianity Today,* April 26, 2010, http://www.christianitytoday.com/le/2010/spring/dirtorganic.html. Hofmeister clarifies that his organic church experiences were not especially successful in the long run, replicating larger-church issues as they became more successful. For an outsider's perspective on a house church, see Henderson and Casper, *Jim and Casper,* 73–85.

121. See George Barna, *Revolution* (Carol Stream, IL: Barna Books, 2005). See also the Barna Group's clearinghouse of its research articles on the organic church movement at "Organic Church," *Barna Group,* n.d., http://www.barna.org/topics/organic-church.

122. For the following history of the Emerging Church, I rely heavily on Eddie Gibbs and Ryan K. Bolger, *Emerging Churches: Creating Christian Community in Postmodern Cultures* (Grand Rapids, MI: Baker, 2005).

123. Quoted in Gibbs and Bolger, *Emerging,* 32.

124. I adopt the convention I have used throughout regarding capitalization, i.e., one emerging church (like Mars Hill Bible Church) but the widespread Emerging Church as a movement or conversation.

125. Zahl et al., *Six Views,* 229.

126. For some of the better attempts at a description of Emergent characteristics as well as good additional sources for the history of the Emerging Church, see James Bielo, "The 'Emerging Church' in America: Notes on the Interaction of Christianities," *Religion* 39 (2009): 219–32, and Joshua M. Moritz, "Beyond Strategy, Towards the Kingdom of God: The Post-Critical Reconstructionist Mission of the Emerging Church," *Dialog: A Journal of Theology* 47, no. 1 (2008): 27–36. I rely especially on Bielo's four discursive practices of the Emerging Movement: postfoundationalism, ancient-future synthesis, missional focus, and de-conversional appeal. Gibbs and Bolger provide an often-quoted list of nine Emerging practices (*Emerging,* 45). See also Morgenthaler's description of Emerging worship in Zahl et al., *Six Views,* 217–30.

127. Gibbs and Bolger, *Emerging,* 69.

128. Zahl et al., *Six Views,* 224.

129. For representative criticisms of the Emerging Church, see Kevin DeYoung and Ted Kluck, *Why We're Not Emergent: By Two Guys Who Should Be* (Chicago: Moody, 2008), and D. A. Carson, *Becoming Conversant with the Emerging Church: Understanding a Movement and Its Implications* (Grand Rapids, MI: Zondervan, 2005).

130. Bell has since resigned from Mars Hill (though not due to pressure from the *Love Wins* controversy).

131. Rob Bell, *Love Wins: A Book about Heaven, Hell, and the Fate of Every Person Who Ever Lived* (New York: HarperOne, 2011).

Chapter 8

1. Today, "Exodus" can refer to a number of related SOCE ministries. The original organization formed in 1976 was known as "Exodus, International, North America." In 2004, some non-US Exodus affiliates formally became the "Exodus Global Alliance" and continue to operate under that name. See their website, http://exodusglobalalliance.org/, for a more detailed history and explanation. Somewhat confusingly, the US-based ministry led by Chambers—the ministry that sponsors Love Won Out conferences—continues to be known as "Exodus, International." Their website is http://exodusinternational.org/. My work here relates mainly to this latter organization.

2. The Love Won Out conference I attended was co-sponsored by Exodus International and Focus on the Family (James Dobson's organization). All quotes from speakers come from my notes taken there. Soon after the 2009 conference, Focus on the Family stepped back to let Exodus handle these conferences on its own. Focus representatives still sometimes appear as speakers for LWO meetings.

3. For examples of such allegations, see Wayne R. Besen, *Anything But Straight: Unmasking the Scandals and Lies behind the Ex-Gay Myth* (New York: Harrington Park Press, 2003).

4. Besen's monograph functions as a vitriolic but thorough entrée into his cru-

sade against SOCE. He currently sponsors a group called Truth Wins Out that criticizes SOCE organizations and rhetoric, often staging counter-events at Love Won Out conferences. See Truth Wins Out, March 5, 2012, http://www.truthwinsout.org/. Other sources for ex-ex-gay discourse would be the news-blogs Dave Rattigan et al., *Ex-Gay Watch,* blog, http://www.exgaywatch.com/wp/, and Jim Burroway, ed., *Box Turtle Bulletin,* blog, http://www.boxturtlebulletin.com/. Rattigan's and Burroway's sites, while adamantly opposed to SOCE and highly critical of Exodus, nevertheless reflect a more complex, informed view of SOCE ministries' history, makeup, and diversity than the pop cultural stereotype of the "ex-gay."

5. Peterson Toscano, "Peterson Toscano," *Beyond ExGay,* 2012, http://www.beyondexgay.com/who/Peterson. I saw *Doin' Time* when Toscano performed it at the 2003 "Witness Our Welcome" Conference in Philadelphia.

6. See, for example, Michael Bussee, "Statement of Apology by Former Exodus Leaders," *Beyond ExGay,* n.d. [2007], http://www.beyondexgay.com/article/busseeapology. Bussee added his endorsement to a statement released by a number of former Exodus ministers in which they repudiate SOCE ministries and apologize to the LGBT community for their participation in what they see as a harmful, fraudulent ministry. The Beyond ExGay website has links to other such statements.

7. "Ted Haggard Sex Scandal," *CNN Larry King Live,* CNN.com, January 29, 2009, http://transcripts.cnn.com/TRANSCRIPTS/0901/29/lkl.01.html.

8. To be sure, most SOCE ministry discourse addresses lesbian and gay identities specifically, with less focus on bisexual and transgender identities as such. To a greater extent than is the case in transgender discourse, evangelical SOCE ministries tend to blur issues of same-sex attraction and gender non-conformity. Transgender identities tend to figure in SOCE ministries as a species of homosexual deviance basically dealt with in similar ways.

9. Two Greek terms of note are used in such verses. The first is *arsenokoitai,* a neologism that combines terms for *male* and *bed* and gets translated *homosexual* by the New International Version. The other is *malakoi* (from *malaka,* meaning *soft* or *weak*), often rendered *effeminate.* Considerable debate exists about what specifically these terms refer to.

10. The most elaborate Bible-based arguments regarding the immorality of same-sex eroticism come from Robert Gagnon, an associate professor at Pittsburg Theological Seminary. Gagnon draws on extensive philological and archeological research to interpret and situate the key same-sex-eroticism-related texts, expanding the list to include practically every scriptural reference that could possibly be interpreted as referring to homosexual practice. Gagnon's massive study on the topic is *The Bible and Homosexual Practice: Texts and Hermeneutics* (Nashville: Abingdon, 2001). He maintains a website that hosts his blog and contains various articles and exchanges he has written (including extensive rebuttals to various biblical scholars who differ with his interpretations) at http://www.robgagnon.net/.

11. See, e.g., Anderson, "Truth ." Anderson recycles this argument in multiple sermons, e.g., "Sodomite Reprobates," MP3 sermon, July 7, 2006, http://hardpreaching.com/070906p.mp3.

12. Ralph Blair, "The Bible Is an Empty Closet," *Evangelicals Concerned,* http://www.ecinc.org/Scriptures/clbrpg.htm. Blair's site contains specific counter-readings of all of the main biblical anti-homosexuality texts. Blair's is only one such set of counter-readings. See, e.g., Justin Lee, *Torn: Rescuing the Gospel from the Gays-vs.-Christians Debate* (New York: Jericho Books, 2012), chapters 12 and 13. Other evan-

gelicals have criticized such LGBT-affirming counter-readings. See, e.g., Joe Dallas, *The Gay Gospel? How Pro-Gay Advocates Misread the Bible* (Eugene, OR: Harvest House, 2007). It is fair to say that, for many of those who have engaged in such debates fully, the scriptural argument has reached a state of deadlock in which each side knows full well the other side's standard set of arguments and rebuttals.

13. See "Fact Sheet for Metropolitan Community Churches," October 2011, found at Metropolitan Community Churches, "Who We Are," 2012, http://mccchurch.org/overview/.

14. The Dallas MCC congregation's statement of faith, for example, echoes evangelical reverence for the Bible as authoritative. Metropolitan Community Church of Greater Dallas, "Our Core Values," March 29, 2012, http://mccgd.org/our-core-values/. In her ethnographic study of ex-gay and gay Christians, Michelle Wolkomir notes a parallel biblicist view of scripture between evangelical ex-gay and gay-affirming MCC Christians, though the two groups reach opposing conclusions about what the Bible authoritatively says vis-à-vis homosexuality and gender. See Michelle Wolkomir, *Be Not Deceived: The Sacred and Sexual Struggles of Gay and Ex-Gay Christian Men* (Piscataway, NJ: Rutgers University Press, 2006), chapters 2 and 5.

15. This view, of course, minimizes, rationalizes, or otherwise ignores the multiple other models of licit sexual relationships found in scripture, e.g., polygamy, women as chattel, singleness, and concubinage.

16. See the Americans for Truth (about Homosexuality) website at http://www.americansfortruth.com and the National Organization for Marriage at http://www.nationformarriage.org.

17. Frank Newport, "For the First Time, Majority of Americans Favor Legal Gay Marriage," *Gallup.com,* May 20, 2011, http://www.gallup.com/poll/147662/First-Time-Majority-Americans-Favor-Legal-Gay-Marriage.aspx.

18. I harbor my own suspicions about the sincerity of religious right organizations who cry foul on tolerance measures. Nevertheless, some of the issues they raise dovetail with criticisms of left-progressive tolerance discourse from critics like Wendy Brown and Stanley Fish. For more on these criticisms and evangelical takes on them, see John Fletcher, "Performing Coexistence," 231–33.

19. A recently released 2009 strategy document from the National Organization for Marriage provides an eye-opening insight into NOM's strategies. Assessing the challenges of resisting legalized same-sex marriage, the document notes the need for sophisticated, multi-pronged initiatives to overcome the generally low priority most voters place on same-sex marriage initiatives (10). The document also highlights specific projects aimed at minority voting blocs (Latinos and blacks). One such project strives to intervene into the "process of assimilation" of Latinos into gay-friendly Anglo culture by "making support for [heterosexual] marriage a key badge of Latino identity—a symbol of resistance to inappropriate assimilation." Another seeks to "drive a wedge between gays and blacks" by highlighting African American spokespeople who disagree with the LGBT movement's mobilization of civil rights discourse (13). NOM earned widespread criticism from the left (including from the NAACP) for these strategies. See "NOM Deposition Exhibit 25: 'National Organization for Marriage Board Update 2008–2009,'" in National Organization for Marriage and American Principles in Action v. Walter F. Mckee, et al., 1:09-cv-00538, United States District Court for the District of Maine, http://www.hrc.org/nomexposed/entry/must-read#.T3z5itnwCV9.

20. In 2010, the Southern Poverty Law Center named AFTAH an anti-gay hate

group (along with groups like the American Family Association, the National Organization for Marriage, the Family Research Council, and Steven Anderson's Faithful Word Baptist Church). The SPLC cites LaBarbera's propagation of widely discredited "facts" about homosexuality that (e.g., linking LGBT identities to health risks and pedophilia). See Evelyn Schlatter, "18 Anti-Gay Groups and Their Propaganda," *Intelligence Report* 140 (2010), Southern Poverty Law Center, http://www.splcenter.org/get-informed/intelligence-report/browse-all-issues/2010/winter/the-hard-liners.

21. "About Americans for Truth and Peter LaBarbera," *Americans for Truth (about Homosexuality)*, 2011, http://americansfortruth.com/about/. LaBarbera is correct in registering Phelps's impatience with those who believe in the non-reprobate status of homosexuals. Indeed, Phelps himself operates as something of a necessary rhetorical adjunct to the anti-gay religious right, providing LaBarbera and other critics with a foil against which they can present themselves as reasonable and loving.

22. "Pro-Truth Resources on Homosexuality," *Americans for Truth (about Homosexuality)*, 2011, http://americansfortruth.com/pro-truth-resources/.

23. See Daniel Burke, "Splinter Churches Realign Mainline Protestantism," *Religion News Service*, February 27, 2012, http://www.religionnews.com/culture/social-issues/splinter-churches-realign-mainline-protestantism. Burke notes that such protest schisms face difficulties in terms of church monies and properties as well as demographic decline.

24. Not all conservative evangelicals interpret scripture as forbidding female clergy. Pentecostal traditions often take a more open stance toward women in ministry than do reformed traditions.

25. Dallas's descriptions are of course anecdotal and general. Nevertheless, judging from my research, Dallas's description jibes with the self-reports of other evangelicals who participate in SOCE ministries.

26. Joe Dallas and Nancy Heche, eds., *The Complete Christian Guide to Understanding Homosexuality* (Eugene, OR: Harvest House, 2009), 231.

27. Worthen and his wife, Anita, maintain a SOCE ministry in California, New Hope Ministries. The website for New Hope, which contains a number of writings by the Worthens, is at https://www.newhope123.org/. Following a great deal of controversy (which I will relate later in the chapter) Love in Action reformatted itself in early 2012 as a more general ministry for sexual purity called Restoration Path. See their website at http://restorationpath.org/ (Love in Action's former URL redirects to the Restoration Path home page). Restoration Path does not appear to have any direct connections with Frank Worthen.

28. Jay E. Adams, *Competent to Counsel* (Grand Rapids, MI: Zondervan, 1970), 41.

29. For Adams's introduction to nouthetic counseling, see Jay E. Adams, *The Christian Counselor's Manual* (Grand Rapids, MI: Zondervan, 1973). See also Adams's organization, The Institute for Nouthetic Studies, http://www.nouthetic.org/, as well as the National Association of Nouthetic Counselors, http://www.nanc.org/. In the 1980s and 1990s, counselors like David Powilson modified aspects of Adams's philosophy to found the modern biblical counseling movement. For an overview of this movement, which remains in many ways tied to nouthetic models, see Heath Lambert, *The Biblical Counseling Movement After Adams* (Wheaton, IL: Crossway, 2012).

30. Adams, *Christian Counselor's*, 406.

31. In her study *Straight to Jesus: Sexual and Christian Conversions in the Ex-Gay Movement* (Berkeley: University of California Press, 2006), Tanya Erzen provides an admirably even-handed, thorough history of the early ex-gay movement (22–42). The

APA's *Report* (discussed later in this paper) also sketches a history of SOCE research. See APA Task Force on Appropriate Therapeutic Responses to Sexual Orientation, *Report of the Task Force on Appropriate Therapeutic Responses to Sexual Orientation* (Washington, DC: American Psychological Association, 2009), http://www.apa.org/pi/lgbt/resources/therapeutic-response.pdf.

32. He relates his history with Exodus in Bussee, "Statement."

33. Elizabeth Moberly, *Homosexuality: A New Christian Ethic* (Cambridge: James Clarke, 1983).

34. Moberly, *Homosexuality,* 8.

35. Besen, *Anything But Straight,* 100.

36. Moberly, *Homosexuality,* 20.

37. Moberly, *Homosexuality,* 18, 21.

38. Moberly, *Homosexuality,* 47.

39. Erzen, *Straight to Jesus,* 145.

40. Chambers, *God's Grace,* 34.

41. See Sam R. Williams, "A Christian Psychology of and Response to Homosexuality," PDF document, October 2011, *The Gospel Coalition,* http://tgc-documents.s3.amazonaws.com/A%20Christian%20Psychology%20and%20Response%20to%20Homosexuality-1.pdf, 5–6.

42. Dallas introduces that distinction in Dallas and Heche, *Christian Guide,* 224.

43. Williams, "Christian Psychology," 6.

44. Williams, "Christian Psychology," 7.

45. For ethnographic studies of such processes, see Erzen, *Straight to Jesus,* and Michelle Wolkomir, *Be Not.* For evangelical descriptions of these processes, see Joe Dallas, *Desires in Conflict: Hope for Men Who Struggle with Sexual Identity* (Eugene, OR: Harvest House, 2003); Anita Worthen and Bob Davies, *Someone I Love Is Gay: How Family and Friends Can Respond* (Downers Grove, IL: Intervarsity Press, 1996); and Richard Cohen, *Gay Children, Straight Parents: A Plan for Family Healing* (Downers Grove, IL: IVP Books, 2007).

46. Dallas, *Complete Christian Guide,* 234.

47. Dallas, *Complete Christian Guide,* 236.

48. Dallas, *Complete Christian Guide,* 238.

49. Dallas, *Complete Christian Guide,* 241.

50. Dallas, *Complete Christian Guide,* 243.

51. See Andrew Comiskey, "Living Waters," *Desert Stream Ministries,* April 2012, http://desertstream.org/Groups/1000040175/Desert_Stream_Ministries/Who_We_Are/Affiliated_Programs/Living_Waters/Living_Waters.aspx.

52. Erzen's *Straight to Jesus* deals specifically with this sort of residential treatment.

53. Erzen, *Straight to Jesus,* 160.

54. Peterson Toscano, "How I Survived the Ex-gay Movement," *Doin' Time in the Homo No Mo Halfway House* web page, 2008, http://www.homonomo.com/History/Survivor.

55. Tim Cox, "My Journey into Manhood: Undercover at a Gay Conversion Camp," *Stinque.com,* April 2010, http://www.scribd.com/stinque/d/29771138-Ted-Cox-My-Journey-Into-Manhood. For People Can Change's own website, which includes information about their Journey into Manhood weekends, see http://www.peoplecanchange.com/. PCC is not overtly religious, though its guidelines note that "those who are able to yield to the will of a 'higher power'" or spiritual good may experience more success. See "Philosophy and Values," *People Can Change,* 2010, http://www.peoplecanchange.com/about/values.php.

56. Cox, "My Journey," 7–8.

57. Cox, "My Journey," 12.

58. Wolkomir, *Be Not Deceived,* 101–4.

59. Alan Chambers [ed.], *God's Grace and the Homosexual Next Door* (Eugene, OR: Harvest House, 2006), 31.

60. Scott Davis, "Developing a Christlike Attitude toward Homosexuals (Does God *Really* Hate Gays?)," in Chambers, *God's Grace,* 53.

61. It is, however, worth noting that the position of LGBT-identified and/or struggling adolescents can be somewhat complicated. Stories abound in which evangelical parents, convinced that homosexuality is both spiritually and physically fatal, take their children to SOCE ministries in the hopes of curing them. In such cases, the conservative biases of the parents can override their children's desires, and the issue of coercion becomes quite sticky. While many mainstream SOCE ministries insist on the adolescent's free participation (e.g., Dallas and Heche, *Complete Christian,* 227), some others have accepted youthful clients against those clients' wills. In 2005, for example, a fifteen-year-old youth, Zach Stark, blogged extensively about being subjected to a Love in Action camp. His blog—and his situation—attracted considerable national attention. For an overview of this incident (including a sampling of the camp's code of conduct), see Michael Airhart, "Zach Stark Speaks: Forced into Ex-Gay Boot Camp in 2005," *Truth Wins Out,* May 6, 2008, http://www.truthwinsout.org/blog/2008/05/627/.

62. See, e.g., People Can Change's "Philosophy and Values."

63. APA Task Force, *Report,* 11. Confusingly, both the American Psychological Association and the American Psychiatric Association have used the acronym APA, and both have a long and storied history of making proclamations relating to the non-pathology of homosexuality and the ethics/efficacy of SOCE. As a rule of thumb, the Psychological organization is much larger and its purview more general. The Psychiatric organization, though smaller, publishes the *DSM* and is therefore especially influential in determinations of what does or does not count as mental illness. In this chapter, I use APA to refer to the American Psychological Association alone.

64. The roundtable was a panel at the 2012 Gay Christian Network Conference in Orlando, Florida, which I will write about later in this chapter. For the YouTube video of the roundtable, see Gay Christian Network, "Ex-Gay Panel Discussion with Alan Chambers," YouTube video, 2:28:56, posted by jshkrueger, January 12, 2012, http://youtu.be/TXgA7_QRvhg.

65. See Erzen, *Straight to Jesus,* 142–45, for a history of NARTH. See also NARTH's home page at National Association for the Research and Therapy of Homosexuality, March 6, 2012, http://narth.com/.

66. Warren Throckmorton, "NARTH Is Not Primarily Composed of Mental Health Professionals," *Warren Throckmorton,* blog, October 24, 2011, http://wthrockmorton.com/2011/10/24/narth-is-not-primarily-composed-of-mental-health-professionals/.

67. A search for "NARTH" on the Exodus website reveals a few scattered references to NARTH research, none later than 2010.

68. The key move here would be the APA's 1997 "Resolution on Appropriate Therapeutic Responses to Sexual Orientation," which strongly affirmed consensus about the nonpathology of homosexuality and warned therapists about misleading clients (see APA Task Force, *Report,* 12, for a history).

69. In their work, Jones and Yarhouse generally do not align themselves explicitly with evangelical causes, though they are often based in evangelical colleges and universities (e.g., Stanton at Wheaton College, Yarhouse at Regent University). For

an example of their scholarship (which, while published with an evangelical press, scrupulously avoids association with NARTH), see Stanton L. Jones and Mark A. Yarhouse, *Ex-Gays? A Longitudinal Study of Religiously Mediated Change in Sexual Orientation* (Downers Grove, IL: IVP Academic, 2007). Throckmorton regularly reviews SOCE rhetoric and research on his blog, at http://www.wthrockmorton.com/.

70. Heather L. Brooke, "'Gays, Ex-Gays, Ex-ex-gays: Examining Key Religious, Ethical, and Diversity Issues': A Follow-up Interview with Douglas Haldeman, Ariel Shildo, Warren Throckmorton, and Mark Yarhouse," *Journal of Psychology and Christianity* 24, no. 4 (2005): 343–44.

71. For a more in-depth and sympathetic exploration of these questions, see Douglas C. Haldeman, "Gay Rights, Patient Rights: The Implications of Sexual Orientation Conversion Therapy," *Professional Psychology: Research and Practice* 33, no. 3 (2002): 260–64, and Haldeman, "When Sexual and Religious Orientation Collide: Considerations in Working with Conflicted Same-Sex Attracted Male Clients," *Counseling Psychologist* 32 (2004): 691–715. For treatments of these issues from a less sympathetic point of view, see Chuck Bright, "Deconstructing Reparative Therapy: An Examination of the Processes Involved When Attempting to Change Sexual Orientation," *Clinical Social Work Journal* 32, no. 4 (2004): 471–81, and Stephen C. Halpert, "'If It Ain't Broke, Don't Fix It': Ethical Considerations Regarding Conversion Therapies," *International Journal of Sexuality and Gender Studies* 5, no. 1 (2000): 19–35. It should be noted that NARTH also picked up the "patients' rights" banner and still uses that line of argument to justify itself. See, e.g., NARTH, "NARTH Statement on California SB 1172—Sexual Orientation Change Efforts," April 23, 2012, http://narth.com/2012/04/narth-statement-on-californis-sb-1172-sexual-orientation-change-efforts/.

72. Erzen stresses, however, that Spitzer had urged his fellow psychiatrists to retain some kind of classificatory category in the *DSM* so that therapists might be able to treat people who desired change (Erzen, *Straight to Jesus,* 142).

73. Robert L. Spitzer, "Can Some Gay Men and Lesbians Change Their Sexual Orientation? 200 Participants Reporting a Change from Homosexual to Heterosexual Orientation," *Archives of Sexual Behavior* 32, no. 5 (2003): 413.

74. For the full debate, see (in addition to Spitzer's initial article) "Peer Commentaries on Spitzer (2003)," *Archives of Sexual Behavior* 32, no. 5 (2003): 419–68, and Spitzer, "Reply: Study Results Should Not Be Dismissed and Justify Further Research on the Efficacy of Sexual Reorientation Therapy," *Archives of Sexual Behavior* 32, no. 5 (2003): 469–72. Besen spends considerable time relating a more anecdotal, first-hand account of this affair in which (true to his hotly anti-ex-gay stance) he presents Spitzer as well-intended but naïve about his being used by ex-gay political forces like NARTH, who provided Spitzer with much of his survey pool (Besen, *Anything but Straight,* 227–41).

75. Spitzer explicitly recanted in an article by Gabriel Arana, "My So-Called Ex-Gay Life," *American Prospect,* April 11, 2012, http://prospect.org/article/my-so-called-ex-gay-life. There Arana recounts his long-term therapy with Nicolosi, therapy he now sees as ineffective and wrongheaded. As part of his coverage of Nicolosi and NARTH, Arana interviews Spitzer (now in his eighties and weary from public controversies) about his infamous study. "In retrospect, I have to admit I think the critiques are largely correct," Spitzer tells Arana. "The findings can be considered evidence for what those who have undergone ex-gay therapy say about it, but nothing more." He asks Arana to publish a retraction "so I don't have to worry about it anymore."

76. APA Task Force, *Report,* 2–3.

77. See, e.g., "Psychologists Reject Gay 'Therapy,'" AP, *New York Times,* August 6, 2009, A16.

78. For NARTH's pre-report reaction to the announcement of the APA task force, see Mike Hatfield, "New APA Taskforce Lacks Reparative/Reorientation Therapists," *National Association for the Research and Therapy of Homosexuality,* March 23, 2007, http://www.narth.com/docs/lacks.html. For NARTH's subsequent responses to the report, see National Association for the Research and Therapy of Homosexuality, "NARTH Response to APA 2009 Task Force Report," n.d. [2009], http://www.narth.com/docs/apataskforcereportbroch.pdf, and Joseph Nicolosi, "The 2009 APA Task Force Report: Science or Politics?" *National Association for the Research and Therapy of Homosexuality,* January 10, 2011, http://narth.com/2011/01/dr-nicolosi-on-the-apa-task-force-report/.

79. APA Task Force, *Report,* 44–48.

80. APA Task Force, *Report,* v.

81. APA Task Force, *Report,* 30.

82. APA Task Force, *Report,* 60–61.

83. See, e.g., David Crary, "Psychologists Repudiate Gay-to-Straight Therapy," *Associated Press,* August 5, 2009.

84. The Paulks appeared on *Newsweek*'s cover as part of the story by John Leland and Mark Miller, "Can Gays 'Convert'?" *Newsweek,* August 17, 1998, 46–50. In May of 2013, as this book was in press, John Paulk and Anne Paulk announced their divorce. John Paulk repudiated SOCE ministries, apologizing to the LGBT community for his participation in them. See Melissa Steffan, "Former Ex-Gay Spokesman John Paulk Apologizes amid Divorce," *Christianity Today,* May 2, 2013, http://blog.christianitytoday.com/ctliveblog/archives/2013/05/former-exgay-spokesman-john-paulk-apologizes-amid-divorce.html.

85. Exodus's web page no longer hosts copies of these advertisements. Besen's anti-SOCE website Truth Wins Out has compiled copies of some of them, along with advertisements from PFOX. See "'Ex-Gay' Ads," *Truth Wins Out,* 2011, http://www.truthwinsout.org/ex-gay-ads/. For a description and analysis of Exodus's campaign, see Steve Boese, "Exodus Ad: Question Homosexuality," *Ex-Gay Watch,* blog, July 8, 2004, http://www.exgaywatch.com/wp/2004/07/exodus-ad-quest/.

86. John Smid, "I Acknowledge! Part One," *Grace Rivers,* blog, January 4, 2012, http://www.gracerivers.com/acknowledge-part-one/.

87. For PCC's press release regarding their survey, see Rich Wyler, "Turning Straight? 4 Out of 5 Program Participants Report Reduction in Unwanted Homosexual Attractions," PDF document, *People Can Change,* February 5, 2008, http://www.peoplecanchange.com/jim/2007survey_pr.pdf.

88. Dallas, *Desires,* 51–52; Dallas and Heche, *Christian Guide,* 232.

89. National Association for the Research and Therapy of Homosexuality, "NARTH Statement on Sexual Orientation Change," *National Association for the Research and Therapy of Homosexuality,* January 25, 2012, http://narth.com/2012/01/narth-statement-on-sexual-orientation-change/.

90. Justin [Lee], "What I Believe," *Gay Christian Network,* 2010, http://gaychristian.net/justins_view.php.

91. For the "Side B" argument, see Ron B., "Love That Does Not Count the Cost," *Gay Christian Network,* 2003, http://gaychristian.net/rons_view.php.

92. I would be remiss in my duties as a theater scholar if I did not cite *Straight to*

Heaven, a musical created and performed by GCN leadership about the plight of gay and lesbian Christians. Though it plays partially as a spoof (numbers include riffs on showtune standards, e.g., "One Gay More" and "Your Son'll Come Out Tomorrow"), the script effectively captures many of the spiritual struggles facing evangelical LGBT people. The show also reflects GCN's dim view of gay-to-straight ministries. A video of the performance exists on the GCN web page; see *Straight to Heaven,* online video, 1:00:45, *Gay Christian Network,* 2007, http://www.gaychristian.net/video/musical.php.

93. Warren Throckmorton and Mark A. Yarhouse, "Sexual Identity Therapy: Practice Framework for Managing Sexual Identity Conflicts," 2006, available at http://wthrockmorton.com/wp-content/uploads/2007/04/sexualidentitytherapyframeworkfinal.pdf.

94. Throckmorton and Yarhouse, "Sexual Identity Therapy," 4.

95. Throckmorton and Yarhouse, "Sexual Identity Therapy," 15.

96. APA Task Force, *Report,* 20. For another argument along Throckmorton and Yarhouse's lines, see Mark A. Yarhouse and A. Lee Beckstead, "Using Group Therapy to Navigate and Resolve Sexual Orientation and Religious Conflicts," *Counseling and Values* 56 (2011): 96–120.

97. Michel Foucault, *Ethics: Subjectivity and Truth,* ed. Paul Rabinow (New York: New York Press, 1997), 267.

98. The full quote, from his 1980 essay "About the Beginnings of the Hermeneutics of the Self," bears repeating: "I became more and more aware that there is in all societies, I think, in all societies whatever they are, another type of techniques: techniques which permit individuals to effect, by their own means, a certain number of operations on their own bodies, on their own souls, on their own thoughts, on their own conduct, and this in a manner so as to transform themselves, modify themselves, and to attain a certain state of perfection, of happiness, of purity, of supernatural power, and so on. Let's call this kind of techniques a techniques or technology of the self." Michel Foucault, *Religion and Culture,* ed. Jeremy R. Carrette (New York: Routledge, 1999), 162.

99. Foucault, *Religion,* 162–63.

100. Erzen, *Straight to Jesus,* 89. Jeffrey Bennett arrives at similar conclusions (i.e., the similarity between queer identities and ex-gay identities) in his article analyzing the rhetoric of ex-gay couple John and Anne Paulk's memoir. See Bennett, "Love Me Gender: Normative Homosexuality and 'Ex-gay' Performativity in Reparative Therapy Narratives," *Text and Performance Quarterly* 23, no. 4 (2003): 331–52.

101. See, for example, Parents, Friends, and Family of Ex-Gays and Gays (PFOX), "Tolerance for the Ex-Gay Community," *Parents, Friends, and Family of Ex-Gays and Gays,* http://pfox.org/Tolerance_Ex-Gay_Community.html.

102. Chambers, "Letter from Alan Chambers for April 2012," *Exodus International Blog,* April 10, 2012, http://exodusinternational.org/blog/.

103. Bob Ragan, "Made for Something More—Real Voices April 2012," *Exodus International Blog,* April 10, 2012, http://exodusinternational.org/blog/.

104. Alan Chambers, "Defining Exodus—Letter from Alan Chambers for June 2012," *Exodus International,* June 19, 2012, http://exodusinternational.org/2012/06/defining-exodus-letter-from-alan-chambers-for-june-2012/#more-9307.

105. See David Roberts, "Exodus International Has Lost Twenty Ministries," *Ex-Gay Watch,* blog, June 13, 2012, http://www.exgaywatch.com/wp/2012/06/exodus-international-has-lost-twenty-ministries/. Subsequent updates revise the number of ministries to eleven.

106. Alan Chambers, "I Am Sorry," *Exodus International,* June 19, 2013, http://exodusinternational.org/2013/06/i-am-sorry/, emphasis in original.

107. Exodus International, "Exodus International to Shut Down," *Exodus International,* June 19,2013, http://exodusinternational.org/2013/06/exodus-international-to-shut-down/.

108. For more information on the RHN, see Restored Hope Network, "Summary," *Restored Hope Network,* 2012, http://www.restoredhopenetwork.com/index.php/who-we-are/what-we-believe. See also Warren Throckmorton, "A Look inside the Restored Hope Network," *Warren Throckmorton,* blog, August 3, 2012, http://wthrockmorton.com/2012/08/03/a-look-inside-the-restored-hope-network/.

109. Restored Hope Network, "Response to the Announced Closure of Exodus," *Restored Hope Network,* June 20,2013, http://www.restoredhopenetwork.com/images/files/press/RHN%20Press%20release%206.20.13.pdf.

110. For a list of RHN's board members, see Restored Hope Network, "The Restored Hope Network Board of Reference," *Restored Hope Network,* 2012, http://www.restoredhopenetwork.com/index.php/who-we-are/board-of-reference.

111. See, for example, Tyler Gillespie, "Dan Savage on Exodus Closure: God Hates Fags, With Hugs," *Out,* June 21, 2013, http://www.out.com/entertainment/popnography/2013/06/21/dan-savage-exodus-closure and Jeremy Hooper, "On Alan Chambers' Big Announcement," *Good As You,* blog, June 20,2013, http://www.goodasyou.org/good_as_you/2013/06/on-alan-chambers-big-announcement.html.

112. Melissa Steffan, "After Exodus: Evangelicals React as Ex-Gay Ministry Starts Over," *Christianity Today,* June 21, 2013, http://www.christianitytoday.com/ct/2013/june-web-only/exodus-international-alan-chambers-apologize-for-exgay-past.html?start=2

113. In the conference I attended, Chambers baldly stated to his audience that any LGBT person, if given the opportunity to take a "straight pill," would gladly do so. I am uncertain whether Chambers would stand behind such a sentiment today. Many SOCE advocates, however, would continue to support Chambers's initial assertion.

114. Besen concludes his analysis/attack on ex-gay ministries by outlining several steps that Exodus under Chambers could take to demonstrate its commitment to a different kind of politics. Many of these—disassociating from NARTH, encouraging standardization and transparency in its affiliated ministries—make good sense. Besen, *Anything but Straight,* 253–59.

115. Foucault, *Ethics,* 163.

Conclusion

1. Lesslie Newbigin, *The Gospel in a Pluralist Society* (Grand Rapids, MI: Eerdmans, 1989), 125.

2. Noll's work remains influential in discourse about evangelical higher education and scholarship. Mark A. Noll, *The Scandal of the Evangelical Mind* (Grand Rapids, MI: Eerdmans, 1994). First sentence: "The scandal of the evangelical mind is that there is not much of an evangelical mind" (1).

3. Elmer John Thiessen, *The Ethics of Evangelism: A Philosophical Defense of Proselytizing and Persuasion* (Downers Grove, IL: IVP Academic, 2011). Thiessen briefly examines hell houses. He stresses that such productions are borderline-leaning-toward-shady but not clearly wrong; though he personally finds hell houses "offensive," he underlines that fear-based appeals and appeals to younger audiences are not ipso facto unethical (176–78).

4. Rachel Held Evans, "How to Win a Culture War and Lose a Generation," *Rachel Held Evans,* blog, May 9, 2012, http://rachelheldevans.com/win-culture-war-lose-generation-amendment-one-north-carolina.

5. Putnam and Campbell stress that "nones" very rarely identify as atheist or agnostic. Most report having some religious beliefs but prefer not to associate with any one formal faith. Putnam and Campbell, *American Grace,* 126.

6. Putnam and Campbell, *American Grace,* 526–27.

7. Putnam and Campbell, *American Grace,* 531.

8. Putnam and Campbell, *American Grace,* 542–47. Putnam and Campbell attribute true believers' exclusivism largely to the fact that most tend to live in "religiously monochromatic social environments." They do not experience the religious bridging that comes from knowing Aunt Susans and Friend Als and are thus able to maintain unchallenged beliefs about other groups.

9. Trevin Wax, "Building Deep Relationships before Sharing Christ? Impossible!" *Kingdom People: Living on Earth as Citizens of Heaven,* blog, November 9, 2010, http://thegospelcoalition.org/blogs/trevinwax/2010/11/09/building-deep-relationships-before-sharing-christ-impossible/.

10. Horton, "Joel Osteen," draws the MTD-Osteen parallel.

11. Putnam and Campbell, *American Grace,* 547.

12. I do not suggest that Osteen's congregants are themselves MTD, inoffensive, self-oriented Christians. My argument here is based on Osteen's most public performances as a megachurch seeker-sensitive pastor. The inner lives and spiritual health of Lakewood Church attendees is beyond my purview.

13. I recognize that many causes past and present have rejected co-existence with opponents. At this point, I would suggest, the situation passes from the performance of activism into a theater of warfare.

Bibliography

Abrams, Cooper P., III. "A Brief Survey of Independent Fundamental Baptist Churches . . . What They Are and What Is Their History." Baptistinfo.org. http://www.baptistinfo.com/define.shtml.

Adams, Jay E. *The Christian Counselor's Manual.* Grand Rapids, MI: Zondervan, 1973.

Adams, Jay E. *Competent to Counsel.* Grand Rapids, MI: Zondervan, 1970.

Airhart, Michael. "Zach Stark Speaks: Forced into Ex-Gay Boot Camp in 2005." *Truth Wins Out,* May 6, 2008. http://www.truthwinsout.org/blog/2008/05/627/.

Aldrich, Joe. *Lifestyle Evangelism: Learning to Open Your Life to Those Around You.* Colorado Springs: Multnomah, 1999 [1981].

Allen, Bob. "'Internet Monk' Michael Spencer, acclaimed religion blogger, dead at 53." *Associated Baptist Press,* April 6, 2010. http://www.abpnews.com/content/view/5019/53/.

Allen, Bob. "Popular 'Hell Houses' Draw Praise, Criticism." *Associated Baptist Press News.* October 19, 2000. www.abpnews.com.

Ames, Michael. "Museology Interrupted." *Museum International* 57, no. 3 (2005): 44–51.

Anderson, Steven. *Basic Soul-Winning Demonstration Video (witnessing, gospel).* YouTube video. 10:00. Posted by sanderson1611, March 8, 2008. http://www.youtube.com/watch?v=BXMA4xOS5BY&feature=channel_video_title.

Anderson, Steven. "Correcting the King James Bible." Faithful Word Baptist Church Website. http://www.faithfulwordbaptist.org/kingjamesbible.html.

Anderson, Steven. "Dr. Jack Schaap's Perverted Teachings Exposed." Faithful Word Baptist Church Website. http://www.faithfulwordbaptist.org/schaap.html.

Anderson, Steven. *Epic Soul-Winning FAIL—Living Waters University (Ray Comfort & Kirk Cameron) Way of the Master.* YouTube video. 2:22. Posted by sanderson1611, November 7, 2010. http://www.youtube.com/user/sanderson1611#p/search/30/xu6PCexvZI4.

Anderson, Steven. *Pentecostal Soul-Winning Demonstration Video (Baptist).* YouTube video. 18:48. Posted by sanderson1611. March 9, 2009. http://www.youtube.com/user/sanderson1611#p/search/1/xBIR4xS6s0U.

Anderson, Steven. "Sodomite Reprobates." MP3 sermon. Faithful Word Baptist Church (Tempe, AZ), July 7, 2006. http://hardpreaching.com/070906p.mp3.

Anderson, Steven. "Soul-Winning Training." MP3 sermon. Faithful Word Baptist Church (Tempe, AZ), May 1, 2011. 1:20:40. http://www.faithfulwordbaptist.org/page5.html.

Anderson, Steven. "The Truth about Homosexuals." Faithful Word Baptist Church Website. http://faithfulwordbaptist.org/truth_about_homosexuals.html.

Anderson, Steven. "Why Bible College Is Unscriptural." MP3 sermon. Faithful Word Baptist Church (Tempe, AZ), February 10, 2008. http://www.faithfulwordbaptist.org/021008p.mp3.

Anderson, Steven. "Why I Hate Barack Obama." MP3 sermon. Faithful Word Baptist Church (Tempe, AZ), January 18, 2009. 1:06:20. http://www.faithfulwordbaptist.org/081609p.mp3.

Anderson, Troy. "A New Day for Apologetics." *Christianity Today,* July 2, 2008. http://www.christianitytoday.com/ct/2008/july/14.29.html.

Answers in Genesis. *Journey through the Creation Museum.* Green Forest, AR: Master Books, 2008.

APA Task Force on Appropriate Therapeutic Responses to Sexual Orientation. *Report of the Task Force on Appropriate Therapeutic Responses to Sexual Orientation.* Washington, DC: American Psychological Association, 2009. http://www.apa.org/pi/lgbt/resources/therapeutic-response.pdf.

Arana, Gabriel. "My So-Called Ex-Gay Life." *American Prospect,* April 11, 2012. http://prospect.org/article/my-so-called-ex-gay-life.

Badiou, Alain. *Saint Paul: The Foundation of Universalism.* Translated by Ray Brassier. Stanford: Stanford University Press, 2003.

Bahnsen, Greg. "Evangelicalism and Apologetics." *Covenant Media Foundation.* http://www.cmfnow.com/articles/PA013.htm. Originally published in Synapse 3 (Fall 1974).

Bahnsen, Greg. "Presuppositional Procedure." *Covenant Media Foundation.* http://www.cmfnow.com/articles/pa210.htm. Originally published in Penpoint 7, no. 8 (September 1996).

"Bait and Switch (episode 394)." *This American Life.* Podcast audio. This American Life from WBEZ. MP3. 58:28. November 9, 2009. http://www.thisamericanlife.org/radio-archives/episode/394/bait-and-switch.

Balibar, Étienne. "Is a Philosophy of Human Civic Rights Possible? New Reflections on Equaliberty." *South Atlantic Quarterly* 103, no. 2–3 (2004): 311–22.

Ball, Daniel. *Backwards and Forwards.* Carbondale: Southern Illinois University Press, 1983.

Banks, Adele. "Willow Creek Finds Limits to Its Model." *Christian Century,* January 28, 2008.

Barna, George. *Marketing the Church.* Colorado Springs: NavPress, 1988.

Barna, George. *Revolution.* Carol Stream, IL: Barna Books, 2005.

Barna, George. *A Step-by-Step Guide to Church Marketing: Breaking Ground for the Harvest.* Ventura, CA: Regal Books, 1992.

Barna Group. "Survey Explores Who Qualifies as an Evangelical." *The Barna Group,* January 18, 2007. http://www.barna.org/barna-update/article/13-culture/111-survey-explores-who-qualifies-as-an-evangelical?q=evangelical.

Bartley, Numan V. *The Rise of Massive Resistance: Race and Politics in the South during the 1950's.* Baton Rouge: Louisiana State University Press, 1969.

Bauder, Keven T. "Fundamentalism." In Gundry, Naselli, and Hansen, *Four Views,* 19–49.

Bebbington, David W. *Evangelicalism in Modern Britain: A History from the 1730s to the 1980s.* New York: Routledge, 1989.

Behe, Michael. *Darwin's Black Box: The Biochemical Challenge to Evolution.* New York: Touchstone, 1996.

Bell, Michael. "Michael Bell: 'What Is an "Average Church?"'" *Internet Monk.* Blog. July 13, 2009. http://www.internetmonk.com/archive/michael-bell-what-is-an-average-church.

Bell, Rob. "Drop the Jawbone." Mars Hill Bible Church, Grand Rapids, MI, June 13, 2009. Audio at http://castroller.com/Podcasts/MarsHillBible/1149125.

Bell, Rob. *Love Wins: A Book about Heaven, Hell, and the Fate of Every Person Who Ever Lived.* New York: HarperOne, 2011.

Bennett, Jeffrey. "Love Me Gender: Normative Homosexuality and 'Ex-gay' Performativity in Reparative Therapy Narratives." *Text and Performance Quarterly* 23, no. 4 (2003): 331–52.

Berger, Peter L. *The Sacred Canopy: Elements of a Sociological Theory of Religion.* New York: Anchor Books, 1967.

Berger, Peter, and Anton Zijderveld. *In Praise of Doubt: How to Have Convictions Without Becoming a Fanatic.* New York: HarperOne, 2009.

Besen, Wayne R. *Anything But Straight: Unmasking the Scandals and Lies behind the Ex-Gay Myth.* New York: Harrington Park Press, 2003.

Bettger, Frank. *How I Raised Myself from Failure to Success in Selling.* New York: Prentice-Hall, 1947.

Bevins, Jason C. *Religion of Fear: The Politics of Horror in Conservative Evangelicalism.* New York: Oxford University Press, 2008.

Beyond Relevance [Richard Reising]. "What if Starbucks Marketed Like the Church? A Parable."YouTube Video. 5:33. Posted by beyondrelevance, October 2008. http://youtu.be/D7_dZTrjw9I.

Bielo, James. "The 'Emerging Church' in America: Notes on the Interaction of Christianities." *Religion* 39 (2009): 219–32.

Bird, Warren, and Scott Thumma. *A New Decade of Megachurches.* Hartford, CT: Leadership Network and the Hartford Institute for Religious Research, 2011. Online at http://leadnet.org/resources/download/a_new_decade_of_megachurches_2011_profile_of_large_attendance_churches_in_t.

Bird, Warren, and Kristin Walters. "Multisite Is Multiplying." Leadership Network, 2010. Online at http://leadnet.org/resources/download/multisite_is_multiplying_new_developments_in_the_movements_expansion.

Blair, Ralph. "The Bible is an Empty Closet." *Evangelicals Concerned.* http://www.ecinc.org/Scriptures/clbrpg.htm

Blee, Kathleen M. "Ethnographies of the Far Right." *Journal of Contemporary Ethnography* 36, no. 2 (2007): 119–28.

Bloesch, Donald G. *Essentials of Evangelical Theology.* 2 vols. San Francisco: Harper and Row, 1979.

Blue, Ethan. "National Trauma, Church Drama: The Cultural Politics of Fear." *Bad Subjects* 72 (2005): n.p. http://bad.eserver.org/issues/2005/72/blue.html.

Boal, Augusto. *The Theater of the Oppressed.* Translated by Charles A. McBride. New York: Theater Communications Group, 1979.

Boese, Steve. "Exodus Ad: Question Homosexuality." *Ex-Gay Watch.* Blog. July 8, 2004. http://www.exgaywatch.com/wp/2004/07/exodus-ad-quest/.

Bonzo, Matthew J., and Michael Stevens, eds. *After Worldview: Christian Higher Education in Postmodern Worlds.* Sioux Center, IA: Dordt College Press, 2009.

Bosch, David J. *Transforming Mission: Paradigm Shifts in Theology of Mission.* Maryknoll, NY: Orbis Books, 2005 [1991].

Bourdieu, Pierre. *Distinction: A Social Critique of the Judgment of Taste.* Translated by Richard Nice. Cambridge: Harvard University Press, 1984.

Boyd, Gregory A., and Paul R. Eddy. *Across the Spectrum: Understanding Issues in Evangelical Theology.* Grand Rapids, MI: Baker Academic, 2007.

Bozeman, Theodore Dwight. *Protestants in the Age of Science: The Baconian Ideal and Antebellum American Religious Thought.* Chapel Hill: University of North Carolina Press, 1977.

Brantley, Ben. "A Guided Tour of Hell, with an Appearance by Satan." *New York Times,* October 14, 2006, sec. B.

Bright, Chuck. "Deconstructing Reparative Therapy: An Examination of the Processes Involved When Attempting to Change Sexual Orientation." *Clinical Social Work Journal* 32, no. 4 (2004): 471–81.

Brooke, Heather L. "'Gays, Ex-Gays, Ex-ex-gays: Examining Key Religious, Ethical, and Diversity Issues': A Follow-up Interview with Douglas Haldeman, Ariel Shildo, Warren Throckmorton, and Mark Yarhouse." *Journal of Psychology and Christianity* 24, no. 4 (2005): 343–51.

Brown, Wendy. *Regulating Aversion: Tolerance in the Age of Identity and Empire.* Princeton: Princeton University Press, 2007.

Buchanan, Wyatt. "SOUTHERN CALIFORNIA; Conservative Colleges Visited by Gay Christians; Response Differs Strongly as Group Buses across Nation." *San Francisco Chronicle,* April 5, 2006.

Burke, Daniel. "Splinter Churches Realign Mainline Protestantism." *Religion News Service,* February 27, 2012. http://www.religionnews.com/culture/social-issues/splinter-churches-realign-mainline-protestantism.

Burke, Timothy. "A Scholar, an Expert, an Intellectual." *Easily Distracted.* Blog. August 21, 2012. http://blogs.swarthmore.edu/burke/2012/08/21/a-scholar-an-expert-an-intellectual/.

Bussee, Michael. "Statement of Apology by Former Exodus Leaders." *Beyond ExGay.* [2007]. http://www.beyondexgay.com/article/busseeapology.

Butler, Judith. *Bodies That Matter: On the Discursive Limits of "Sex."* New York: Routledge, 1993.

Byassee, James. "Synchronized Worship." *Christian Century,* January 26, 2010.

Cameron, Kirk, and Ray Comfort. *The School of Biblical Evangelism.* Orlando: Bridge-Logos, 2004

Campolo, Tony. "Campolo—Discussion of the Coming Evangelical Collapse Part I." *Tony Campolo Podcast,* July 30, 2009. http://www.tonycampolo.org/podcast/tony-campolo_podcast.xml.

Campus Crusade for Christ. *How to Make a Mark That's Hard to Erase: A Manual for Evangelism and Discipleship.* N.p.: Campus Crusade for Christ, 1982.

Carr, Edward Hallett. *What Is History?* New York: Alfred A. Knopf, 1967.

Carson, D. A. *Becoming Conversant with the Emerging Church: Understanding a Movement and Its Implications.* Grand Rapids, MI: Zondervan, 2005.

Carter, Dan T. *The Politics of Rage: George Wallace, the Origins of the New Conservatism, and the Transformation of American Politics.* 2nd ed. Baton Rouge: Louisiana State University Press, 2000.

Casey, Valerie. "Staging Meaning: Performance in the Modern Museum." *TDR* 49, no. 3 (2005): 78–95.

Centerfield Productions. "The Compass—The Four Laws." PDF document. http://www.centerfieldproductions.com/members/content/compass/thefourlaws.pdf.

Centerfield Productions. "Four Laws Script." PDF document. http://www.centerfieldproductions.com/members/content/compass/fourlawsscript.pdf.

Centerfield Productions. "Sharing Your Story." PDF document. http://www.centerfieldproductions.com/members/content/compass/sharingyourstory.pdf.

Chalmers, A. F. *What Is This Thing Called Science?* 3rd ed. Indianapolis: Hackett, 1999.

Chambers, Alan. "Defining Exodus—Letter from Alan Chambers for June 2012." *Exodus International.* June 19, 2012. http://exodusinternational.org/2012/06/defining-exodus-letter-from-alan-chambers-for-june-2012/#more-9307.

Chambers, Alan [ed.]. *God's Grace and the Homosexual Next Door.* Eugene, OR: Harvest House, 2006.

Chambers, Alan. "I Am Sorry." *Exodus International.* June 19, 2013. http://exodusinternational.org/2013/06/i-am-sorry/.

Chambers, Alan. "Letter from Alan Chambers for April 2012." *Exodus International Blog.* April 10, 2012. http://exodusinternational.org/blog/.

Chaves, Mark, Shawna Anderson, and Jason Byassee. *American Congregations at the Beginning of the Twenty-First Century.* PDF document. National Congregations Study, 2008. http://www.soc.duke.edu/natcong/.

Clark, E. Culpepper. *The Schoolhouse Door: Segregation's Last Stand at the University of Alabama.* New York: Oxford University Press, 1993.

Cohen, Anthony. *The Symbolic Construction of Community.* New York: Tavistock, 1985.

Cohen, Richard. *Gay Children, Straight Parents; A Plan for Family Healing.* Downers Grove, IL: IVP Books, 2007.

Cohen-Cruz, Jan. "A Hyphenated Field: Community-Based Theater in the USA." *New Theater Quarterly,* Winter 2001: 364–78.

Cohen-Cruz, Jan. "Motion of the Ocean: The Shifting Face of Theater for Social Change in the US since the 1950s." *Theater* 31, no. 3 (2001): 95–107.

Cohen-Cruz, Jan, ed. *Radical Street Performance: An International Anthology.* New York: Routledge, 1998.

Cohen-Cruz, Jan, and Mady Schutzman, eds. *Playing Boal: Theater, Therapy, Activism.* New York: Routledge, 1994.

Colleran, Jeanne, and Jenny S. Spencer, eds. *Staging Resistance: Essays on Political Theater.* Ann Arbor: University of Michigan Press, 1998.

Collier, David, Fernando Daniel Hidalgo, and Andra Olivia Maciuceanu. "Essentially Contested Concepts: Debates and Applications." *Journal of Political Ideologies* 11, no. 3 (2006): 211–46.

Comfort, Ray. *180.* Online film. 33:03. http://www.180movie.com/.

Comfort, Ray. "Hell's Best Kept Secret." PDF document. *Living Waters Publications.* http://www.livingwaters.com/helps/HellsBestKeptSecret.pdf.

Comfort, Ray. "True and False Conversion." PDF document. *Living Waters Publications.* http://assets.livingwaters.com/pdf/TrueAndFalseConversion.pdf.

Comfort, Ray. *The Way of the Master.* Alachua, FL: Bridge-Logos, 2006.

Cosby, Brian H. "MTD: Not Just a Problem with Youth Ministry." *The Gospel Coalition.*

Blog. April 9, 2012. http://thegospelcoalition.org/blogs/tgc/2012/04/09/mtd-not-just-a-problem-with-youth-ministry/.

Cowen, Steven B., ed. *Five Views on Apologetics.* Grand Rapids, MI: Zondervan, 2000.

Cowper, William. "There Is a Fountain." In *Baptist Hymnal,* 107. Nashville: Convention Press, 1975.

Cox, Tim. "My Journey into Manhood: Undercover at a Gay Conversion Camp." *Stinque.com.* April 2010. http://www.scribd.com/stinque/d/29771138-Ted-Cox-My-Journey-Into-Manhood.

Craig, William Lane. "The Coming Evangelical Collapse." *Reasonable Faith Podcast,* June 22, 2009. http://www.reasonablefaith.org/podcast/Reasonable_Faith.xml.

Csapo, Eric, and Margaret C. Miller, eds. *The Origins of Ancient Theater in Ancient Greece and Beyond.* Cambridge: Cambridge University Press, 2007.

"Cults and Modern-Day False Prophets." Young Earth Creationist Club. http://www.creationists.org/cults.html.

Culver, Virginia. "Church's 'Hell House' to Feature Gay Wedding." *Denver Post,* September 29, 1999, 2nd ed., B05.

Dallas, Joe. *Desires in Conflict: Hope for Men Who Struggle with Sexual Identity.* Eugene, OR: Harvest House, 2003.

Dallas, Joe. *The Gay Gospel? How Pro-Gay Advocates Misread the Bible.* Eugene, OR: Harvest House, 2007.

Dallas, Joe, and Nancy Heche, eds. *The Complete Christian Guide to Understanding Homosexuality.* Eugene, OR: Harvest House, 2009.

Davis, Allan. "A Hell House Divided: Performing Identity Politics through Christian Medium of Proselytization." MA thesis, Brigham Young University, 2011.

Davis, Scott. "Developing a Christlike Attitude toward Homosexuals (Does God *Really* Hate Gays?)." In Chambers, *God's Grace,* 41–57.

Dayton, Donald W. "The Limits of Evangelicalism: The Pentecostal Tradition." In Dayton and Johnson, *Variety,* 36–56.

Dayton, Donald W. "Some Doubts about the Usefulness of the Category 'Evangelical.'" In Dayton and Johnston, *Variety,* 245–51.

Dayton, Donald W. *The Theological Roots of Pentecostalism.* Peabody, MA: Hendrickson Publishers, 1991.

Dayton, Donald W., and Robert K. Johnston, eds. *The Variety of American Evangelicalism.* Knoxville: University of Tennessee Press, 1991.

Dean, Kendra Creasy. *Almost Christian: What the Faith of Our Teenagers Is Telling the American Church.* New York: Oxford, 2010.

de Certeau, Michel. *Heterologies: Discourse on the Other.* Translated by Michael Massumi. Minneapolis: University of Minnesota Press, 1997.

della Porta, Donatella, and Mario Diani. *Social Movements: An Introduction.* 2nd ed. Malden, MA: Blackwell, 2006.

DeYoung, Kevin. "Christian Smith Makes the Bible Impossible." Review of *The Bible Made Impossible. Gospel Coalition,* August 2, 2011. http://thegospelcoalition.org/blogs/kevindeyoung/2011/08/02/christian-smith-makes-the-bible-impossible/.

DeYoung, Kevin, and Ted Kluck. *Why We're Not Emergent: By Two Guys Who Should Be.* Chicago: Moody, 2008.

Dolan, Jill. *Geographies of Learning: Theory and Practice, Activism and Performance.* Middletown, CT: Wesleyan University Press, 2001.

Dolan, Jill. "Performance, Utopia, and the 'Utopian Performative.'" *Theater Journal* 53 (2001): 455–79.

Donofrio, Craig, and William M. Cwirla."Episode 43: Michael Spencer." *The God Whis-*

perers (podcast), March 30, 2009. http://itunes.apple.com/us/podcast/the-god-whisperers/id286040700.

Dorrien, Gary. *The Remaking of Evangelical Theology*. Louisville, KY: Westminster John Knox Press, 1998.

Dubin, Steven C. *Arresting Images: Impolitic Art and Uncivil Actions*. New York: Routledge, 1992.

Durham, Martin. *The Christian Right, the Far Right, and the Boundaries of American Conservatism*. New York: Manchester University Press, 2000.

Dyck, Drew. *Generation Ex-Christian: Why Young Adults Are Leaving the Faith . . . And How to Bring Them Back*. Chicago: Moody, 2010.

Eagleton, Terry. "Lunging, Flailing, Mispunching." Review of *The God Delusion* by Richard Dawkins. *London Review of Books* 28, no. 20 (2006). http://www.lrb.co.uk/v28/n20/terry-eagleton/lunging-flailing-mispunching.

Eagleton, Terry. *Reason, Faith, and Revolution: Reflections on the God Debate*. New Haven: Yale University Press, 2009.

Epps, Garrett. "The Littlest Rebel: James J. Kilpatrick and the Second Civil War." *Constitutional Commentary* 10 (1993): 19–36.

Erdely, Jenn. "When the Saints Go Marching In: An Ethnography of Volunteer Tourism in Post–Hurricane Katrina New Orleans." PhD diss., Louisiana State University, 2011.

Erzen, Tanya. *Straight to Jesus: Sexual and Christian Conversions in the Ex-Gay Movement*. Berkeley: University of California Press, 2006.

Evans, Rachel Held. "How to Win a Culture War and Lose a Generation." *Rachel Held Evans*. Blog. May 9, 2012. http://rachelheldevans.com/win-culture-war-lose-generation-amendment-one-north-carolina.

Exodus International. "Exodus International to Shut Down." *Exodus International*. June 19, 2013.

Farr, Tom. "Fear Tactics: Scaring People Toward Jesus." *Tom Farr: A Journey of Faith and Creativity*. Blog. October 14, 2011. http://tom-farr.blogspot.com/2011/10/fear-tactics.html.

"59 Minutes (Judgement House) Scene 3: Church Foyer." Video clip. 4:43. October 31, 2010. Posted by JesusFreak429. YouTube. http://www.youtube.com/watch?v=hBZywGDQQt0&feature=related.

"The Final Exit . . ." *Life 101.9*. Audio podcast. August 9, 2011. http://www.life1019.com/2011/08/the-final-exit/.

"'Final Exit' Dramatization Evangelizes Thousands." *AG* [Assemblies of God] *News*. Last modified February 6, 2004. http://ag.org/top/News/index_articledetail.cfm?Process=DisplayArticle&targetBay=c97d4d5c-a325-4921-9a9e-e9fbddd9cdce&ModID=2&RSS_RSSContentID=3148&RSS_OriginatingChannelID=global&RSS_OriginatingRSSFeedID=3359&RSS_Source=search.

"'Final Exit' Live and Ready to Travel." *Christian Film News*. Last modified October 25, 2001. http://christianfilmnews.com/1013/final-exit/.

Fischer-Lichte, Erica. *Theater, Sacrifice, Ritual: Exploring Forms of Political Theater*. New York: Routledge, 2005.

Fish, Stanley. "One University, Under God?" *Chronicle of Higher Education* 51, no. 18 (2005): C1–C4.

Fish, Stanley. *The Trouble with Principle*. Cambridge: Harvard University Press, 1999.

Fletcher, John. "Performing Coexistence with Good Faith Intolerance." In Gharavi, *Religion*, 225–40.

Fletcher, John. "Tasteless as Hell: Community Performance, Distinction, and Counter-Taste in Hell House." *Theater Survey* 48, no. 2 (2007): 313–30.

Fletcher, John. "Ten-Foot Pole Historiography: Liberal Democracy, Ideological Difference, and Despicable Acts." In *Querying Difference in Theater History,* edited by Scott Magelssen and Ann Haugo, 16–24. Newcastle: Cambridge Scholars Publishing, 2007.

Flowers, Ronald B. Review of *Why Conservative Churches Are Growing,* by Dean M. Kelley. *Journal of Church and State* 50, no. 4 (2008): 699–701.

Forrest, Barbara, and Paul R. Gross. *Creationism's Trojan Horse: The Wedge of Intelligent Design.* New York: Oxford University Press, 2004.

Foster, Susan Leigh. "Choreographies of Protest." *Theater Journal* 55, no. 3 (2003): 395–412.

Foucault, Michel. *Ethics: Subjectivity and Truth.* Edited by Paul Rabinow. New York: New York Press, 1997.

Foucault, Michel. *Religion and Culture.* Edited by Jeremy R. Carrette. New York: Routledge, 1999.

Frame, John. "Presuppositional Apologetics." In Cowan, *Five Views,* 208–31.

Fraser, Nancy, and Axel Honneth. *Redistribution or Recognition: A Political-Philosophical Exchange.* New York: Verso, 2003.

Frederick, Jeff. *Stand Up for Alabama: Governor George Wallace.* Tuscaloosa: University of Alabama Press, 2007.

Freire, Paulo. *Pedagogy of the Oppressed.* Translated by Mayra Bergman Ramos. New York: Continuum, 1997 [1970].

Gagnon, Robert. *The Bible and Homosexual Practice: Texts and Hermeneutics.* Nashville: Abingdon, 2001.

Gale, Zachary. "Confessions of a Sinful Church." *New University,* April 25, 2005. http://www.newuniversity.org/2005/04/features/confessions_of_a_sinful113/.

Gallie, W. B. "Essentially Contested Concepts." *Proceedings of the Aristotelian Society,* n.s., 56 (1955–56): 167–98.

Gay Christian Network. "Ex-Gay Panel Discussion with Alan Chambers." YouTube video. 2:28:56. Posted by jshkrueger, January 12, 2012. http://youtu.be/TXgA7_QRvhg.

Gay Christian Network. *Straight to Heaven.* Online video. 1:00:45. *Gay Christian Network.* 2007. http://www.gaychristian.net/video/musical.php.

Gentry, Glenn. "Rawls and Religious Community: Ethical Decision Making in the Public Square." *Christian Bioethics* 13 (2007): 171–81.

Gharavi, Lance. "About[/]Doing: Religion and Theater in the Academy." In Gharavi, *Religion,* 210–24.

Gharavi, Lance, ed. *Religion, Theater, and Performance: Acts of Faith.* New York: Routledge, 2011.

Gibbs, Eddie, and Ryan K. Bolger. *Emerging Churches: Creating Christian Community in Postmodern Cultures.* Grand Rapids, MI: Baker, 2005.

Giberson, Karl. "A House of Sand and Fog." *BioLogos Forum.* Blog. October 12, 2009. http://biologos.org/blog/a-house-of-sand-and-fog.

Gillespie, Tyler. "Dan Savage on Exodus Closure: God Hates Fags, With Hugs." *Out.* June 21, 2013.

Gordon, David T. "Pop Goes the Worship." Interview with Mark Moring. *Christianity Today,* March 9, 2011. http://www.christianitytoday.com/ct/2011/march/popgoesworship.html.

Gormly, Eric. "Evangelizing through Appropriation: Toward a Cultural Theory on the

Growth of Contemporary Christian Music." *Journal of Media and Religion* 2, no. 4 (2003): 251–65.

Grant, Tobin. "Polling Evangelicals: Is Islam Violent?" *Christianity Today,* March 10, 2011. http://blog.christianitytoday.com/ctpolitics/2011/03/polling_evangel_1.html.

Groeschel, Craig. "Remain." [2011]. LifeChurch.tv. http://open.lifechurch.tv/message_groups/1563-re.

Grossman, Cathy Lynn. "For Many, 'Losing My Religion' Isn't Just a Song; It's Life." *USA Today,* December 25, 2011. http://www.usatoday.com/news/religion/story/2011-12-25/religion-god-atheism-so-what/52195274/1.

Gundry, Stanley, Andrew David Naselli, and Collin Hansen, eds. *Four Views on the Spectrum of Evangelicalism.* Grand Rapids, MI: Zondervan, 2011.

Guthrie, Stan. "Interview: Douglas Groothuis on Good Apologetics." *Christianity Today,* September 11, 2011. http://www.christianitytoday.com/ct/2011/october/douglas-groothuis-good-apologetics.html.

Habermas, Jürgen. *An Awareness of What Is Missing: Faith and Reason in a Post-Secular Age.* Translated by Ciaran Cronan. Cambridge: Polity Press, 2010.

Hackett, Conrad, and D. Michael Lindsay. "Measuring Evangelicalism: Consequences of Different Operationalization Strategies." *Journal for the Scientific Study of Religion* 47, no. 3 (2008): 499–514.

Haedicke, Susan, and Tobin Nellhaus, eds. *Performing Democracy: International Perspectives on Community-Based Performance.* Ann Arbor: University of Michigan Press, 2001.

Haidt, Jonathan. *The Righteous Mind: Why Good People Are Divided by Politics and Religion.* New York: Pantheon, 2012.

Haldeman, Douglas C. "Gay Rights, Patient Rights: The Implications of Sexual Orientation Conversion Therapy." *Professional Psychology: Research and Practice* 33, no. 3 (2002): 260–64.

Haldeman, Douglas C. "When Sexual and Religious Orientation Collide: Considerations in Working with Conflicted Same-Sex Attracted Male Clients." *Counseling Psychologist* 32 (2004): 691–715.

Hall, Amy K. "Moore: Judgment [*sic*] Houses Miss the Mark." *Stand to Reason Blog.* October 26, 2011. http://str.typepad.com/weblog/2011/10/moore-judgment-houses-miss-the-mark.html.

Halpert, Stephen C. "'If It Ain't Broke, Don't Fix It': Ethical Considerations Regarding Conversion Therapies." *International Journal of Sexuality and Gender Studies* 5, no. 1 (2000): 19–35.

Ham, Ken. *The Purpose and Meaning of Life: From Creation to the Cross.* Hebron, KY: Answers in Genesis, 2008.

Ham, Ken. *Why Won't They Listen? The Power of Creation Evangelism.* Green Forest, AR: Master Books, 2005.

Ham, Ken, and Britt Beemer. *Already Gone: Why Your Kids Will Quit Church and What You Can Do to Stop It.* Green Forest, AR: Master Books, 2009.

Ham, Ken, and Stacia McKeever. *The Seven C's of History.* Hebron, KY: Answers in Genesis, 2007.

Harley, William, Jr. *His Needs, Her Needs: Building an Affair-Proof Marriage.* Grand Rapids, MI: Fleming H. Revell, 2001.

Harris, Sam. "Science Is in the Details." *New York Times,* July 27, 2009, late ed., A21.

Hart, D. G. *Deconstructing Evangelicalism: Conservative Protestantism in the Age of Billy Graham.* Grand Rapids, MI: Baker, 2004.

Hartman, Greg. "A Hell of a Ride." PDF document. *Plain Truth Ministries,* November/December 2003: 41–44. http://www.ptm.org/03PT/NovDec/hellRide.pdf.

Hatch, Nathan O. "Sola Scriptura and Novus Ordo Seclorum." In Hatch and Noll, *Bible,* 59–78.

Hatch, Nathan O., and Mark A. Noll, eds. *The Bible in America: Essays in Cultural History.* New York: Oxford University Press, 1982.

Hatfield, Mike. "New APA Taskforce Lacks Reparative/Reorientation Therapists." *National Association for the Research and Therapy of Homosexuality.* March 23, 2007. http://www.narth.com/docs/lacks.html.

Hays, Arthur Garfield. "The Scopes Trial." In *Evolution and Religion: The Conflict between Science and Theology in Modern America,* edited by Gail Kennedy, 35–52. Boston: D. C. Heath, 1957.

Hendershot, Heather. *Shaking the World for Jesus: Media and Conservative Evangelical Culture.* Chicago: University of Chicago Press, 2004.

Henderson, Jim. *Evangelism Without Additives: What if Sharing Your Faith Meant Just Being Yourself?* Colorado Springs: Waterbrook, 2007.

Henderson, Jim. "I'm on This American Life (This Weekend)." *Off the Map.* Blog. Off The Map. November 6, 2009. http://offthemap.com/2009/11/06/im-on-this-american-life-this-weekend/.

Henderson, Jim, and Matt Casper. *Jim and Casper Go to Church: Frank Conversation about Faith, Churches, and Well-meaning Christians.* Carol Stream, IL: BarnaBooks, 2007.

Henderson, Jim, Todd Hunter, and Craig Spinks. *The Outsider Interviews: A New Generation Speaks Out on Christianity.* Grand Rapids, MI: Baker, 2010.

Henry, Carl F. H. *The Uneasy Conscience of Modern Fundamentalism.* Grand Rapids, MI: Eerdmans, 1947.

Hodges, Corey. "Preacher's Anti-Obama Sermon Goes against the Bible." *Salt Lake Tribune,* September 11, 2009.

Hofmeister, Brian. "The Dirt on Organic." *Christianity Today,* April 26, 2010. http://www.christianitytoday.com/le/2010/spring/dirtorganic.html.

Hollinger, David A. "After Cloven Tongues of Fire: Ecumenical Protestantism and the Modern American Encounter with Diversity." *Journal of American History* 98, no. 1 (2011): 21–48.

Hooper, Jeremy. "On Alan Chambers' Big Announcement." *Good As You* blog. June 20, 2013.

Horness, Joe. "Contemporary Music-Driven Worship." In Zahl et al., *Six Views,* 99–116.

Horton, Michael S. "Joel Osteen and the Glory Story." Online article. Westminster Seminary California. October 1, 2007. http://wscal.edu/resource-center/resource/joel-osteen-and-the-glory-story.

Hudgins, Tom. *Judgement House Training Manual.* [Clearwater, FL]: New Creation Experiences, 2008.

Hull, Kenneth. "Music Wars, Neuroscience, and Self Psychology." *Liturgy* 24, no. 4 (2009): 24–31.

Hunt, Stephen. "Dramatising the 'Health and Wealth Gospel': Belief and Practice of a Neo-Pentecostal 'Faith' Ministry." *Journal of Beliefs and Values* 21, no. 1 (2000): 73–86.

Hurl, Chirs. "Anti-Globalization and the 'Diversity of Tactics.'" *Upping the Ante* 1 (2005). http://uppingtheanti.org/journal/article/01-anti-globalization-and-diversity-of-tactics/.

Hybels, Bill, and Matt Mittelberg. *Becoming a Contagious Christian.* Grand Rapids, MI: Zondervan, 1994.

Hyles, Jack. *Let's Go Soul Winning.* Murfreesboro, TN: Sword of the Lord Foundation, 1962.

International Council on Biblical Inerrancy. "The Chicago Statement on Biblical Inerrancy." *Dallas Theological Seminary.* 1978. http://library.dts.edu/Pages/TL/Special/ICBI_1.pdf.

Isaak, Mark. *The Counter-Creationism Handbook.* Berkeley: University of California Press, 2007.

Jackson, Brian. "Jonathan Edwards Goes to Hell (House): Fear Appeals in American Evangelism." *Rhetoric Review* 26, no. 1 (2007): 42–59.

Jillette, Penn. "A Gift of a Bible." *Penn Says.* Webcast. August 2008. Crackle.com. http://www.crackle.com/c/Penn_Says/A_Gift_of_a_Bible/2415037.

Johnson, Todd. "Heads Up: Tracing the Battle Lines in the Worship Wars." *Library* 19, no. 4 (2004): 33–38.

Johnson, Todd E., and Dale Savidge. *Performing the Sacred: Theology and Theater in Dialogue.* Grand Rapids, MI: Baker Academic, 2009.

Johnston, Robert K. "American Evangelicalism: An Extended Family." In Dayton and Johnston, *Variety,* 252–72.

Johnston, Robert K. "Evangelicalism." In *Oxford Companion to Christian Thought,* edited by Adrian Hastings, Alistair Mason, and Hugh Pyper, 217–20. New York: Oxford University Press, 2000.

Jones, Stanton L., and Mark A. Yarhouse. *Ex-Gays? A Longitudinal Study of Religiously Mediated Change in Sexual Orientation.* Downers Grove, IL: IVP Academic, 2007.

"Judgement House—Scene 5: The Gates of Heaven." Video clip. 7:36. October 4, 2011. Posted by JesusFreak429. YouTube. http://www.youtube.com/watch?v=GIl Svz7PYrU&feature=related.

Kelley, Dean M. *Why Conservative Churches Are Growing: A Study in Sociology of Religion.* New York: Harper and Row, 1972.

Kensington Community Church. "Confessions Series Promo." Vimeo Video. 2:28. October 12, 2008. http://kensingtonchurch.org/arts/video.php?id=5.

Kerby, Carl. "Demolishing Strongholds: Evolution in Pop Culture." Podcast audio. March 18, 2006. http://www.sermonaudio.com/sermoninfo.asp?SID=11309951504.

Kershaw, Baz. *The Politics of Performance: Radical Theater as Cultural Intervention.* New York: Routledge, 1992.

Kershaw, Baz. *The Radical in Performance: Between Brecht and Baudrillard.* New York: Routledge, 1999.

"Key Findings." *REVEAL Now.* Willow Creek Association. http://www.revealnow.com/key_findings.asp.

Kilpatrick, James. *The Southern Case for School Segregation.* [New York]: Crowell-Collier, [1962].

Kim, Suk-Young. *Illusive Utopia: Theater, Film, and Everyday Performance in North Korea.* Ann Arbor: University of Michigan Press, 2010.

Kinnaman, David. *You Lost Me: Why Young Christians Are Leaving Church . . . And Rethinking Faith.* Grand Rapids, MI: Baker, 2011.

Kinnaman, David, and Gabe Lyons. *UnChristian: What a New Generation Really Thinks about Christianity . . . And Why It Matters.* Grand Rapids, MI: Baker, 2007.

Kirshenblatt-Gimblett, Barbara. *Destination Culture: Tourism, Museums, and Heritage.* Berkeley: University of California Press, 1998.

Kissel, Howard. "Scaring Up a Scene: Brooklyn Theatrical Haunt Stages a Halloween Horror." *New York Daily News,* October 8, 2006.

Koukl, Gregory. *Tactics: A Game Plan for Discussing Your Christian Convictions.* Grand Rapids, MI: Zondervan, 2009.

Kozlowski, Kim. "Churches Use Pagan Day to Send Message." *Detroit News,* October 30, 2002, two dot edition: 1A.

Kuftinec, Sonja. *Staging America: Cornerstone and Community-Based Theater.* Carbondale: Southern Illinois University Press, 2003.

Labov, Jay. "Science, Evolution, and Creationism: The Critical Need for Science as a Liberal Art in the 21st Century." Public Speech at Louisiana State University, January 7, 2009.

Laclau, Ernesto, and Chantal Mouffe. *Hegemony and Socialist Strategy: Towards a Radical Democratic Politics.* New York: Verso, 1985.

Lambert, Heath. *The Biblical Counseling Movement after Adams.* Wheaton, IL: Crossway, 2012.

Larsen, Timothy. Review of *Deconstructing Evangelicalism. Journal of Religion* 85, no. 1 (2005): 120–21.

Lee, Justin. "What I Believe." *Gay Christian Network.* 2010. http://gaychristian.net/justins_view.php.

Lee, Justin. *Torn: Rescuing the Gospel from the Gays-vs.-Christians Debate.* New York: Jericho Books, 2012.

Leith, John H., ed. *Creeds of the Churches: A Reader in Christian Doctrine from the Bible to the Present.* Garden City, NY: Anchor Books, 1963.

Leland, John, and Mark Miller. "Can Gays 'Convert'?" *Newsweek,* August 17, 1998, 46–50.

Lesher, Stephan. *George Wallace: American Populist.* Reading, MA: Addison-Wesley, 1994.

Levi, Margaret, and Gillian H. Murphy. "Coalitions of Contention: The Case of the WTO Protests in Seattle." *Political Studies* 54 (2006): 651–70.

Ligon, Greg. "Multisite Movement Gaining New Momentum in New Places." Leadership Network, 2011. Online at http://leadnet.org/resources/download/multisite_movement_gaining_new_momentum_in_new_places.

Liles, Bennett. "Satellite Churches." *Sound and Video Contractor* 28, no. 10 (2010): 56–59.

Lisle, Jason. "Are ETs and UFOs real?" *Answers in Genesis.* December 6, 2007. http://www.answersingenesis.org/articles/nab/are-ets-and-ufos-real.

Lovett, C. S. *Soul-Winning Made Easy (The Encounter Method).* Baldwin Park, CA: Personal Christianity, 1959.

Machen, J. Gresham. *Christianity and Liberalism.* Grand Rapids, MI: Eerdmans, 1991 [1923].

Marsden, George M. "Everyone One's Own Interpreter? The Bible, Science, and Authority in Mid-Nineteenth-Century America." In Hatch and Noll, *Bible,* 79–100.

Marsden, George M. *Fundamentalism and American Culture: The Shaping of Twentieth-Century Evangelicalism, 1870–1925.* New York: Oxford University Press, 1980.

Marsden, George M. *Reforming Fundamentalism: Fuller Seminary and the New Evangelicalism.* Grand Rapids, MI: Eerdmans, 1987.

Marsden, George M. *Understanding Fundamentalism and Evangelicalism.* Grand Rapids, MI: Eerdmans, 1991.

Maudlin, Michael G., and Edward Gilbreath. "Selling Out the House of God? Bill Hybels Answers Critics of the Seeker-Church Movement." Interview with Bill Hybels. *Christianity Today* 38, no. 8 (1994): 20–26.

McDowell, Josh. *The New Evidence that Demands a Verdict.* Nashville: Thomas Nelson, 1999.

McDowell, Josh, and Bob Hostetler. *The New Tolerance: How a Cultural Movement Threatens to Destroy You, Your Faith, and Your Children.* Carol Stream, IL: Tyndale, 1998.

McGavran, Donald A. *Understanding Church Growth.* Rev. ed. Grand Rapids, MI: Eerdmans, 1980 [1970].

McKeever, Stacia, Gary Vaterlaus, and Diane King. *The Creation Museum: Behind the Scenes!* Hebron, KY: Answers in Genesis, 2008.

Merrill, A. William. "Bibliolatry—A Fraudulent Accusation." *Baptist2Baptist.net.* Southern Baptist Convention, October 2000. http://www.baptist2baptist.net/b2barticle.asp?ID=54.

Midgely, Mary. *Evolution as a Religion: Strange Hopes and Stranger Fears.* New York: Methuen, 1985.

Miller, Donald E. "Postdenominational Christianity in the Twenty-First Century (Americans and Religions in the Twenty-First Century)." *Annals of the American Academy of Political and Social Science* 558 (1998): 196–211.

Moberly, Elizabeth. *Homosexuality: A New Christian Ethic.* Cambridge: James Clarke, 1983.

Mohler, R. Albert, Jr. "Confessional Evangelicalism." In Gundry, Naselli, and Hansen, *Four Views,* 68–96.

Mohler, R. Albert, Jr. "Evangelical Identity Revisited: A Conversation with Historians David Bebbington and Gregory Wills." *Thinking in Public.* Podcast. September 13, 2010. http://www.albertmohler.com/2010/09/13/evangelical-identity-revisited-a-conversation-with-historians-david-bebbington-and-gregory-wills/.

Mohler, R. Albert, Jr. "The Limits of Encouragement." *AlbertMohler.com.* Blog. June 24, 2005, http://www.albertmohler.com/2005/06/24/the-limits-of-encouragement.

Mohler, R. Albert, Jr. "Moralistic Therapeutic Deism—the New American Religion." *Christian Post,* April 18, 2005. http://www.christianpost.com/news/moralistic-therapeutic-deism-the-new-american-religion-6266/.

Mohler, R. Albert, Jr. "Rethinking Secularization: An Interview with Peter Berger." *Thinking in Public.* Podcast. Oct. 11, 2010. http://www.albertmohler.com/2010/10/11/rethinking-secularization-a-conversation-with-peter-berger/.

Mohler, R. Albert, Jr. "Why Conservative Churches Are Growing: David Brooks and the Limits of Sociology." *Albertmohler.com.* Blog. April 25, 2011. http://www.albertmohler.com/2011/04/25/why-conservative-churches-are-growing-david-brooks-and-the-limits-of-sociology/.

Moore, John. "'Hell House' Pastor Hopes N.Y. Gets Point." *Denver Post,* October 1, 2006, final edition, F08.

Moore, Russell D. "Seven Reasons Halloween Judgment Houses Often Miss the Mark." *Moore to the Point.* Blog. October 24, 2011, reposted from October 31, 2008. http://www.russellmoore.com/2011/10/24/seven-reasons-halloween-judgment-houses-often-miss-the-mark-2/.

Morgenthaler, Sally. "Worship as Evangelism." *Rev!* May–June 2007: 48–53. http://nancybeach.typepad.com/nancy_beach/files/morgenthaler_article.pdf.

Morgenthaler, Sally. *Worship Evangelism: Inviting Unbelievers into the Presence of God.* Grand Rapids, MI: Zondervan, 1998.

Mouffe, Chantal, ed. *Dimensions of Radical Democracy: Pluralism, Citizenship, Community.* New York: Verso, 1992.

National Academy of Sciences. *Science, Evolution, and Creationism.* Washington, DC: National Academies Press, 2008.

National Association for the Research and Therapy of Homosexuality. "NARTH Response to APA 2009 Task Force Report." PDF document. [2009]. http://www.narth.com/docs/apataskforcereportbroch.pdf.

National Gay and Lesbian Taskforce. "New Report Titled 'Homophobia at Hell House' Reveals How Right Wing Fuels Homophobia, Demonizes Lesbian and Gay Youth." October 27, 2006. www.thetaskforce.org/press/releases/pr996_102706.

Naugle, David. *Worldview: The History of a Concept.* Grand Rapids, MI: Eerdmans, 2002.

New Creation Experiences, Inc. "How Is Judgement House Different?" *Judgement House.* New Creation Experiences, Inc. Last updated December 2011. http://judgmenthouse.info/new-to-jh/how-is-judgement-house-different/.

New Creation Experiences, Inc. "Judgement House Annual Covenant Partner Agreement and Application Form." PDF document. Last updated December 2011. http://judgmenthouse.info/become-covenant-partners/new-or-renew/.

New Creation Experiences, Inc. "Our Scripts." *Judgement House.* New Creation Experiences, Inc. Last updated December 2011. http://judgmenthouse.info/about/our-scripts/.

New Creation Experiences, Inc. "What Is Judgement House?" *Judgement House.* New Creation Experiences, Inc. Last updated December 2011. http://judgmenthouse.info/new-to-jh/what-is-judgement-house/.

New Creation Experiences, Inc. "Why Judgement House?" *Judgement House.* New Creation Experiences, Inc. Last updated December 2011. http://judgmenthouse.info/new-to-jh/why-judgement-house/.

New Destiny Christian Center. "The Hell House Outreach Kit." *New Destiny Christian Center.* http://www.godestiny.org/hell_house/HH_kit.cfm.

Newbigin, Lesslie. *The Gospel in a Pluralist Society.* Grand Rapids, MI: Eerdmans, 1989.

Newman, Randy. *Questioning Evangelism: Engaging People's Hearts the Way Jesus Did.* Grand Rapids, MI: Kregel, 2004.

Newport, Frank. "For the First Time, Majority of Americans Favor Legal Gay Marriage." *Gallup.com,* May 20, 2011. http://www.gallup.com/poll/147662/First-Time-Majority-Americans-Favor-Legal-Gay-Marriage.aspx.

Newport, Frank. "Who Are the Evangelicals?" Gallup, June 24, 2005. http://www.gallup.com/poll/17041/Who-Evangelicals.aspx.

Nicolosi, Joseph. "The 2009 APA Task Force Report: Science or Politics?" *National Association for the Research and Therapy of Homosexuality.* January 10, 2011. http://narth.com/2011/01/dr-nicolosi-on-the-apa-task-force-report/.

Noebel, David K. *Understanding the Times: The Collision of Today's Competing Worldviews.* 2nd ed. Manitou Springs, CA: Summit, 2006.

Noll, Mark E. *The Scandal of the Evangelical Mind.* Grand Rapids, MI: Eerdmans, 1994.

"NOM Deposition Exhibit 25: 'National Organization for Marriage Board Update 2008–2009.'" In National Organization for Marriage and American Principles in Action v. Walter F. Mckee, et al., 1:09-cv-00538, United States District Court for the District of Maine. http://www.hrc.org/nomexposed/entry/must-read#.T3z5itnwCV9.

Norton, Chris. "Apologetics Makes a Comeback among Youth." *Christianity Today,* August 31, 2011. http://www.christianitytoday.com/ct/2011/september/apologetics-return-youth.html.

Norton, Chris. "Virtual Vitality." *Christianity Today* 55, no. 11 (2011): 104.

Numbers, Ronald L. *The Creationists: From Scientific Creationism to Intelligent Design.* Expanded ed. Cambridge: Harvard University Press, 2006.

Olson, Ted. "Southern Baptists Debate Sinner's Prayer." *Christianity Today* (web only), June 20, 2012. http://www.christianitytoday.com/ct/2012/juneweb-only/baptists-sinners-prayer.html.

Osteen, Joel. *Your Best Life Now: Seven Steps to Living at Your Full Potential.* New York: Time Warner Book Group, 2004.

Packer, J. I. *Evangelism and the Sovereignty of God.* Grand Rapids, MI: IVP Academic, 1991.

Paterson, Doug. "To For With: Some Observations on Community-Based Theater." In *ReImaging America: The Arts of Social Change,* edited by Mark O'Brien and Craig Little, 237–43. Santa Cruz: New Society, 1990.

Pearcey, Nancy. *Total Truth: Liberating Christianity from Its Cultural Captivity.* Wheaton, IL: Crossway, 2004.

"Peer Commentaries on Spitzer (2003)." *Archives of Sexual Behavior* 32, no. 5 (2003): 419–68.

Pellegrini, Ann. "'Signaling through the Flames': Hell House Performance and Structures of Religious Feeling." *American Quarterly* 59, no. 3 (2007): 911–35.

Phelps, David. "The Anti-Museum: An Overview and Review of the Answers in Genesis Creation 'Museum.'" *National Center for Science Education.* Last modified October 17, 2008. http://ncseweb.org/creationism/general/anti-museum-overview-review-answers-genesis-creation-museum.

Prentki, Tim, and Sheila Preston, eds. *The Applied Theater Reader.* New York: Routledge, 2008.

Putnam, Robert D., and David E. Campbell. *American Grace: How Religion Divides and Unites Us.* New York: Simon and Schuster, 2010.

Ragan, Bob. "Made for Something More—Real Voices April 2012." *Exodus International Blog.* April 10, 2012. http://exodusinternational.org/blog/.

Rancière, Jacques. *Disagreement: Politics and Philosophy.* Translated by Julie Rose. Minneapolis: University of Minnesota Press, 1999.

Ratliff, George, director. *Hell House.* DVD. Brooklyn: Plexifilm, 2001.

Redman, Robert R. "Welcome to the Worship Awakening." *Theology Today* 58, no. 3 (2001): 369–83.

Reinelt, Janelle. "Notes for a Radical Democratic Theater: Productive Crises and the Challenge of Indeterminacy." In Colleran and Spencer, *Staging Resistance: Essays on Political Theater,* 284–300.

Reising, Richard. "The Next Level in Signage." *Artistry Labs.* http://www.artistrylabs.com/church-signage.

Reising, Richard. "The Video: Marketing Is More than You Realize." *Beyond Relevance.* Blog. November 13, 2008. http://www.beyondrelevance.com/index.cfm/pageid/913/postid/26/blogid/4/index.html#e5059.

Restored Hope Network. "Response to the Announced Closure of Exodus." *Restored*

Hope Network. June 20,2013. http://www.restoredhopenetwork.com/images/files/press/RHN%20Press%20release%206.20.13.pdf.

Restored Hope Network. "The Restored Hope Network Board of Reference." *Restored Hope Network*. 2012. http://www.restoredhopenetwork.com/index.php/who-we-are/board-of-reference.

Restored Hope Network. "Summary." *Restored Hope Network*. 2012. http://www.restoredhopenetwork.com/index.php/who-we-are/what-we-believe.

Roberts, David. "Exodus International Has Lost Twenty Ministries." *Ex-Gay Watch*. Blog. June 13, 2012. http://www.exgaywatch.com/wp/2012/06/exodus-international-has-lost-twenty-ministries/.

Roberts, Keenan. *The Hell House Outreach Manual*. Thornton, CO: Keenan Roberts, 2010.

Román, David. *Acts of Intervention: Performance, Gay Culture, and AIDS*. Bloomington: Indiana University Press, 1998.

Román, David, and Tim Miller. "Preaching to the Converted." *Theater Journal* 47, no. 2 (1995): 169–88.

Romano, Andrew. "How Dumb Are We?" *Newsweek*, March 20, 2011. http://www.newsweek.com/2011/03/20/how-dumb-are-we.html.

Romano, Lois. "'The Smiling Preacher' Builds on Large Following." *Washington Post*, January 30, 2005.

Ron B. "Love That Does Not Count the Cost." *Gay Christian Network*. 2003. http://gaychristian.net/rons_view.php.

Ruse, Michael. *The Evolution-Creation Struggle*. Cambridge: Harvard University Press, 2005.

Rushfield, Richard. "Raising Hell." *New York Times*, August 29, 2004, sec. 2–3.

Russell, Mark, Allen Yeh, Michelle Sanchez, Chelle Stearns, and Dwight Friesen. *Routes and Radishes and Other Things to Talk About at the Evangelical Crossroads*. Grand Rapids, MI: Zondervan, 2010.

Sanborn-Jones, Megan. *Performing American Identity in Anti-Mormon Melodrama*. New York: Routledge, 2009.

Sandeen, Ernest. *Roots of Fundamentalism: British and American Millenarianism, 1800–1930*. Chicago: University of Chicago Press, 1970.

Sandler, Lauren. *Righteous: Dispatches from the Evangelical Youth Movement*. New York: Viking, 2006.

Sargeant, Kimon Howland. *Seeker Churches: Promoting Traditional Religion in a Non-Traditional Way*. New Brunswick: Rutgers University Press, 2000.

Schaeffer, Francis. *The God Who Is There*. Downers Grove, IL: Intervarsity, 1998 [1968].

Schechner, Richard. *Performance Studies: An Introduction*. 2nd ed. New York: Routledge, 2007.

Schechner, Richard. "6 Axioms for Environmental Theater." *TDR* 12, no. 3 (1968): 41–64.

Schlatter, Evelyn. "18 Anti-Gay Groups and Their Propaganda." *Intelligence Report* 140 (2010). Southern Poverty Law Center. http://www.splcenter.org/get-informed/intelligence-report/browse-all-issues/2010/winter/the-hard-liners.

Schlossman, David A. *Actors and Activists: Performance, Politics, and Exchange among Social Worlds*. New York: Routledge, 2002.

Sedgwick, Eve Kosofsky. "Paranoid Reading and Reparative Reading, or You're So Paranoid, You Probably Think This Essay Is About You." In *Touching Feeling: Affect, Pedagogy, Performativity*, 123–51. Durham: Duke University Press, 2003.

Sernett, Milton G. "Black Religion and the Question of Evangelical Identity." In Dayton and Johnston, *Variety,* 135–47.

Sharlet, Jeff. "Soldiers of Christ: Inside America's Most Powerful Megachurch." *Harper's Magazine,* May 2005: 41–54.

Sheler, Jeffery L. *Believers: A Journey into Evangelical America.* New York: Viking, 2006.

Shelley, Bruce L., and Marshall Shelley. *The Consumer Church: Can Evangelicals Win the World without Losing Their Souls?* Downers Grove, IL: InterVarsity Press, 1992.

Siever, Randy. "Busting the Myth of Pre-Evangelism." *Doable Evangelism.* Blog. Doable Evangelism. June 1, 2008. http://doableevangelism.com/2008/06/01/busting-the-myth-of-pre-evangelism/.

Sigurdson, Ola. "Beyond Secularism? Towards a Post-Secular Political Theology." *Modern Theology* 26, no. 2 (2010): 177–96.

Sire, James W. *The Universe Next Door: A Basic Worldview Catalog.* 4th ed. Downers Grove, IL: IVP Academic, 2004.

Sitton, Claude. "Alabama Guardsman in Tuscaloosa as Wallace Plans to Defy U.S. Court." *New York Times,* June 10, 1963, 1+.

Smid, John. "I Acknowledge! Part One." *Grace Rivers.* Blog. January 4, 2012. http://www.gracerivers.com/acknowledge-part-one/.

Smith, Christian. *The Bible Made Impossible: Why Biblicism Is Not a Truly Evangelical Reading of Scripture.* Grand Rapids, MI: Brazos, 2011.

Smith, Christian. *Christian America? What Evangelicals Really Want.* Berkeley: University of California Press, 2000.

Smith, Christian, with Melinda Lundquist Denton. *Soul Searching: The Religious and Spiritual Lives of American Teenagers.* New York: Oxford, 2005.

Smith, Christian, with Patricia Snell. *Souls in Transition: The Religious and Spiritual Lives of Emerging Adults.* New York: Oxford, 2009.

Sødal, Helje Kringlebotn. "'Victor, Not Victim': Joel Osteen's Rhetoric of Hope." *Journal of Contemporary Religion* 25, no. 1 (2010): 37–50.

Spencer, Michael. "The Coming Evangelical Collapse." *Christian Science Monitor,* March 10, 2009. http://www.csmonitor.com/2009/0310/p09s01-coop.html.

Spencer, Michael. "The Evangelical Liturgy 15: The Creeds." *The Internet Monk.* Blog. Oct. 9, 2009. http://www.internetmonk.com/archive/the-evangelical-liturgy-15-the-creeds.

Spencer, Michael. "The Original Coming Evangelical Collapse Posts." Internet Monk. Blog. March 2009. http://www.internetmonk.com/archive/the-original-coming-evangelical-collapse-posts.

Spencer, Michael. "Outing Joel Osteen: A Challenge to the Evangelical Blogosphere." *Internet Monk.* Blog. January 29, 2005. http://www.internetmonk.com/archive/outing-joel-osteen-a-challenge-to-the-evangelical-blogosphere.

Spitzer, Robert L. "Can Some Gay Men and Lesbians Change Their Sexual Orientation? 200 Participants Reporting a Change from Homosexual to Heterosexual Orientation." *Archives of Sexual Behavior* 32, no. 5 (2003): 403–17.

Spitzer, Robert L. "Reply: Study Results Should Not Be Dismissed and Justify Further Research on the Efficacy of Sexual Reorientation Therapy." *Archives of Sexual Behavior* 32, no. 5 (2003): 469–72.

Steensland, Brian, Jerry Z. Park, Mark D. Regnerus, Lynn D. Robinson, W. Bradford Wilcox, and Robert D. Woodberry. "The Measure of American Religion: Toward Improving the State of the Art." *Social Forces* 79, no. 1 (2000): 291–318.

Steffan, Melissa. "After Exodus: Evangelicals React as Ex-Gay Ministry Starts Over."

Christianity Today. June 21, 2013. http://www.christianitytoday.com/ct/2013/june-web-only/exodus-international-alan-chambers-apologize-for-exgay-past.html?start=2.

Steffan, Melissa. "Former Ex-Gay Spokesman John Paulk Apologizes amid Divorce." *Christianity Today*. May 2, 2013. http://blog.christianitytoday.com/ctliveblog/archives/2013/05/former-exgay-spokesman-john-paulk-apologizes-amid-divorce.html.

Stelzer, Becky, Stacia McKeever, and Michael Matthews, eds. *War of the Worldviews*. Green Forest, AR: Master Books, 2005.

Stetzer, Ed. "Ending the Worship War without a Truce." *Ed Setzer: The Lifeway Research Blog*. October 15, 2009. http://www.edstetzer.com/2009/10/ending-the-worship-war-without.html.

Stevenson, Jill. "Embodying Sacred History: Performing Creationism for Believers." *TDR* 56, no. 1 (2012): 93–113.

Stevenson, Jill. *The Performative Culture of Evangelical Devotion: Affect, Cognition, and Evangelical Dramaturgy*. Ann Arbor: University of Michigan Press, 2013.

Stier, Greg. *Dare 2 Share*. Carol Stream, IL: Tyndale House, 2006.

Stier, Greg. *Outbreak: Creating a Contagious Youth Ministry through Viral Evangelism*. 2nd ed. Chicago: Moody, 2006.

Stier, Greg. "Sharing Your Faith Overview." Video. 7:00. *dare2share.org*. Dare 2 Share Ministries International. http://www.dare2share.org/thecause/gospel-journey-tools/.

Stone, Jon R. *On the Boundaries of American Evangelicalism: The Postwar Evangelical Coalition*. New York: St. Martin's, 1997.

Stowe, David W. *No Sympathy for the Devil: Christian Pop Music and the Transformation of American Evangelicalism*. Chapel Hill: University of North Carolina Press, 2011.

Strobel, Lee. *The Case for Christ: A Journalist's Personal Investigation of the Evidence for Jesus*. Grand Rapids, MI: Zondervan, 1998.

Swaine, Lucas. "Deliberate and Free: Heteronomy and the Public Sphere." *Philosophy & Social Criticism* 35, no. 1–2 (2009): 183–213.

Tanenbaum Center for Interreligious Understanding."Remembering Bishop Krister Stendahl." April 16, 2008. http://www.bc.edu/dam/files/research_sites/cjl/pdf/Tanenbaum_Stendahl.pdf.

Taylor, Baynard. *The Great Ape Debate*. Cincinnati: Standard, 2008.

Taylor, Charles. *A Secular Age*. Cambridge: Belknap Press, 2007.

"Ted Haggard Sex Scandal." Transcript. *CNN Larry King Live*. CNN.com. January 29, 2009. http://transcripts.cnn.com/TRANSCRIPTS/0901/29/lkl.01.html.

Thiessen, Elmer John. *The Ethics of Evangelism: A Philosophical Defense of Proselytizing and Persuasion*. Downers Grove, IL: IVP Academic, 2011.

Thorngate, Steve. "New Harmonies." *Christian Century*, March 29, 2011.

Throckmorton, Warren. "A Look Inside the Restored Hope Network." *Warren Throckmorton*. Blog. August 3, 2012. http://wthrockmorton.com/2012/08/03/a-look-inside-the-restored-hope-network/.

Throckmorton, Warren. "NARTH Is Not Primarily Composed of Mental Health Professionals." *Warren Throckmorton*. Blog. October 24, 2011. http://wthrockmorton.com/2011/10/24/narth-is-not-primarily-composed-of-mental-health-professionals/.

Thumma, Scott, and Warren Bird. "Not Who You Think They Are: The Real Story of People Who Attend America's Megachurches." The Leadership Network and the

Hartford Institute for Religion Research, 2008. http://hirr.hartsem.edu/megachurch/National%20Survey%20of%20Megachurch%20Attenders%20-final.pdf.

Tomlin, Chris, Jesse Reeves, and Ed Cash. "How Great Is Our God." *Arrival.* Compact disc. Sixsteps Records/Sparrow Records, 2004.

Tønder, Lars, and Lance Thomassen, eds. *Radical Democracy: Politics between Abundance and Lack.* New York: Manchester University Press, 2005.

Torrey, Russell A., ed. *The Fundamentals of the Christian Faith. The Fundamentals Homepage.* R. W. Nadeau. Last modified December 23, 2005. http://www.xmission.com/~fidelis/.

Towns, Elmer, Craig Van Gelder, Charles Van Engen, Gailyn Van Rheenan, and Howard Snyder. *Evaluating the Church Growth Movement: Five Views.* Grand Rapids, MI: Zondervan, 2004.

Tuck, Stephen. "Deconstructing Evangelicalism. Conservative Protestantism in the Age of Billy Graham/Wonderful Words of Life. Hymns in American Protestant History and Theology." *Journal of Ecclesiastical History* 56, no. 3 (2005): 633–35.

Turner, John G. *Bill Bright and the Campus Crusade for Christ: The Renewal of Evangelicalism in Postwar America.* Chapel Hill: University of North Carolina, 2008.

Turner, Victor. *From Ritual to Theater: The Human Seriousness of Play.* New York: PAJ Publications, 2001.

Van Biema, David, and Jeff Chu. "Does God Want You To Be Rich?" *Time,* September 10, 2006. http://www.time.com.libezp.lib.lsu.edu/time/magazine/article/0,9171,1533448,00.html.

Vary, Adam B. "Hell House of the Stars." *Advocate,* October 12, 2004, 80–82.

Vision New England. "Vision New England Recent Convert Study." Vision New England. January 23, 2008. http://www.efcneda.org/pubs/Vision%20New%20England%20Recent%20Convert%20Study.pdf.

"Wallace, Aide Differ on Admissions." *Southern School News* 9, no. 12 (1963).

Walton, Jonathan L. *Watch This! The Ethics and Aesthetics of Black Televangelism.* New York: New York University Press, 2009.

Walzer, Michael. *On Toleration.* New Haven: Yale University Press, 1997.

Warren, Rick. *The Purpose Driven Church: Growth without Compromising Your Message and Mission.* Grand Rapids, MI: Zondervan, 1995.

Wax, Trevin. "Building Deep Relationships before Sharing Christ? Impossible!" *Kingdom People: Living on Earth as Citizens of Heaven.* Blog. November 9, 2010. http://thegospelcoalition.org/blogs/trevinwax/2010/11/09/building-deep-relationships-before-sharing-christ-impossible/.

Webber, Robert E. *The Younger Evangelicals: Facing the Challenges of the New World.* Grand Rapids, MI: Baker Books, 2002.

Weber, Timothy P. "Premillennialism and the Branches of Evangelicalism." In Dayton and Johnston, *Variety,* 5–21.

Weber, Timothy P. "The Two-Edged Sword: The Fundamentalist Use of the Bible." In Hatch and Noll, *Bible,* 101–20.

Welch, David. "From *Triumph des Willens (Triumph of the Will, 1935).*" In Cohen-Cruz, *Radical Street,* 169–78.

Wicker, Christine. *The Fall of the Evangelical Nation: The Surprising Crisis inside the Church.* New York: HarperOne, 2008.

Willenbrink, Hank, III. "Scaring the Jesus into You: American Hell Houses in Performance." PhD diss., University of California–Santa Barbara, 2009.

Williams, Don. "Charismatic Worship." In Paul Zahl et al., *Six Views,* 131–52.

Williams, Sam R. "A Christian Psychology of and Response to Homosexuality." PDF document. *The Gospel Coalition.* October 2011. http://tgc-documents.s3.amazonaws.com/A%20Christian%20Psychology%20and%20Response%20to%20Homosexuality-1.pdf.

Witt, Randy, and Barb Witt. Operation Space *Assembly Guide.* Hebron, KY: Answers in Genesis, 2008.

Wolkomir, Michelle. *Be Not Deceived: The Sacred and Sexual Struggles of Gay and Ex-Gay Christian Men.* Piscataway, NJ: Rutgers University Press, 2006.

Worldview Academy. "Presuppositionalism vs. Evidentialism." Podcast audio. *Radio Worldview.* 42:44. MP3. April 29, 2009, http://itunes.apple.com/us/podcast/radio-worldview/id83107754.

Worldview Academy. "Presuppositionalism vs. Evidentialism Part Two." Podcast audio. *Radio Worldview.* 45:27. MP3. May 19, 2009. http://itunes.apple.com/us/podcast/radio-worldview/id83107754.

Worthen, Anita, and Bob Davies. *Someone I Love Is Gay: How Family and Friends Can Respond.* Downers Grove, IL: Intervarsity Press, 1996.

Wright, Bradley R. E. *Christians Are Hate-Filled Hypocrites . . . And Other Lies You've Been Told.* Minneapolis: Bethany House, 2010.

Wright, Bradley R. E. "What We Can and Can't Learn from Willow Creek's *REVEAL* Study." *Journal of Youth Ministry* 7, no. 1 (2008): 101–14.

Wright, Bradley R. E., Dina Giovanelli, Emily G. Dolan, and Mark Evan Edwards. "Explaining Deconversion from Christianity: A Study of Online Narratives." *Journal of Religion and Society* 13 (2011): n.p.

Wyler, Rich. "Turning Straight? 4 Out of 5 Program Participants Report Reduction in Unwanted Homosexual Attractions." PDF document. *People Can Change.* February 5, 2008. http://www.peoplecanchange.com/jim/2007survey_pr.pdf.

Yarhouse, Mark A., and A. Lee Beckstead. "Using Group Therapy to Navigate and Resolve Sexual Orientation and Religious Conflicts." *Counseling and Values* 56 (2011): 96–120.

Zahl, Paul, Harold Best, Joe Horness, Don Williams, Robert Webber, and Sally Morgenthaler. *Six Views on Exploring the Worship Spectrum.* Grand Rapids, MI: Zondervan, 2004.

Žižek, Slavoj. *The Fragile Absolute: Or, Why the Christian Legacy Is Worth Fighting For.* New York: Verso, 2000.

Žižek, Slavoj, Judith Butler, and Ernesto Laclau. *Contingency, Hegemony, Universality: Contemporary Dialogues on the Left.* New York: Verso, 2000.

Index

activism: as evangelical distinctive, 64, 70–73, 109. *See also* missions; performance; and performance activism
activist performance. *See* performance activism
Adams, Jay E., 279, 287
AiG. *See* Answers in Genesis (AiG)
Alabama, University of, 30
Aldrich, Joe, 135
Ambassador model of apologetics, 124, 145–47. *See also* apologetics: conversational; Koukl, Greg
American Baptist Church, 59
American Family Association, 271, 273
American Methodist Episcopal Church, 59
American Methodist Episcopal Zion Church, 60
American Psychiatric Association, 288
American Psychological Association (APA), 267, 288, 290–92, 296–97
Americans for Truth about Homosexuality (AFTAH), 271, 273–74, 307,
Ames, Michael M., 194
Amite Baptist Church, 175. *See also* Judgement House: *59 Minutes*
Anderson, Steven, 11, 74, 77, 79, 83, 109, 112; as evangelical, 85–88; homosexuality and, 86–87, 269–71, 273, 307; soul-winning and, 88–94, 97–100, 101–3, 105, 106, 108–10, 114–20, 125, 132, 133–34, 145, 147–50, 152–55, 226
Andrews, Steve, 126
Anglican Church in North America, 276
Answers in Genesis (AiG): 73, Ark Encounter, 216; creationist theology, 199–201; culture war and, 73, 192–93, 199–200, 206–7, 215–19; evangelicalism and, 201, 215, 305, 307; Vacation Bible School curricula, 212–16; worldview apologetics and, 203–9, 211–12, 214–17
anti-evolutionism, 192–93, 196, 199–201, 203, 211, 215–16, 218. *See also* Answers in Genesis (AiG); creationism, young-earth
apagogy, 206–7
apologetics, 98, 106, 109, 153; conversational-tactical, 9, 124, 136, 145–47, 149–50, 154;definition, 136–38 ;evidential, 142–43 Francis Schaeffer and, 139–44, 149, 203–4, 214, 312; presuppositional, 143–44, 193, 203–4, 211; renaissance in, 138–39, 144–45; worldview, 146, 203–9, 211–12, 214–17
Assemblies of God, 59, 157, 271

atheism, 1–2, 49, 109, 138, 149, 151–52, 212, 247–48, 306; new atheists, 15, 138, 216
attractional church service, 10, 223, 230, 245, 251–52, 256–57, 259–60, 301. *See also* seeker-sensitive church service
Aunt Susan Principle, 306–7; versus "Uncle Derek," 313
Austin, J. L., 83. *See also* performative (general)

Bacon, Francis, 202–3
Badiou, Alain, 15, 41, 43–44
Balibar, Étienne, 25
Baptist (Protestant tradition), 54, 87–88. *See names of specific denominations*
Barber, Matt, 299
Barna, George: Barna Research Group and, 61; church marketing and, 228–29, 239–40, 257
Barna Research Group: defining evangelicalism, 61–62, 72; Kinnaman and Lyons, 127
Bauder, Kevin T., 58
Bebbington, David: on history of evangelicalism, 53; quadrilateral definition of evangelicalism, 64–72
Behe, Michael, 199
Bell, Rob, 259
Berger, Peter, 47–49; 305
Besen, Wayne, 281
Bettger, Frank, 102
Bevins, Jason C., 159, 161
Bible. *See* biblicism
biblical counseling, 279–80, 295
biblicism, 64–68, 71, 72, 88, 99, 109, 147, 198, 236, 310; creationism and, 200–203, 205–7, 212, 214; homosexuality and, 269, 271, 276, 278, 279, 294
BioLogos Foundation, 305
Bird, Warren, 229, 252–55
Black Church, 57, 59–62, 74
Blair, Ralph, 270
Blue, Ethan, 161
Boal, Augusto, 20–21, 286
born-again: as sociological category, 61–62, 73. *See also* conversion
Bosch, David J., 70–71
Bourdieu, Pierre, 172–73, 188
Bozeman, Theodore Dwight, 202–3
Bright, Bill, 8, 101–4, 107, 112, 118, 120, 222
Bright, Vonette, 101
Brown, Wendy, 6, 16, 40–41, 43, 310
Burke, Timothy, 36–37
Burns, Elizabeth, 168
Bussee, Michael, 266, 280
Butler, Judith, 84, 199, 264–65

Cameron, Kirk, 109. *See also* Comfort, Ray; Way of the Master
Campbell, Bruce E., 60, 305–7, 309
Campus Crusade for Christ (CCC; Cru), 8, 56, 79, 117, 271; Bill Bright and, 101–3; criticisms of, 110–15, 123, 125, 128–32, 209, 260–61; Four Spiritual Laws, 102–8, 118, 148, 222; personal testimony and, 106–8
Carr, Edward, 22
Casey, Valerie, 193
Casper, Matt, 247–48
CCM. *See* Contemporary Christian Music (CCM)
Certeau, Michel de, 22
Chambers, Alan: apology for SOCE, 298–301; at Love Won Out conference, 262–64, 274, 289; criticizing antigay evangelicalism, 274, 286–87; Exodus International and, 266–67, 288–89, 298–301; Gay Christian Network roundtable, 288–89, 294–95, 298; SOCE and, 267, 282–83, 292–99, 301
charismatic tradition. *See* Pentecostalism
Church Growth Movement, 223, 227–28, 240–41, 251, 257
Church of Christ—Disciples (Disciples of Christ), 59
Church of God in Christ, 60
Church of Jesus Christ of Latter-Day Saints (Mormons), 51, 72, 98, 137, 149, 151–52, 282, 285
church marketing movement, 223, 228–29, 240, 256, 308
Cohen, Anthony, 171–72
Cohen-Cruz, Jan, 18, 28, 36

Cohen, Richard, 281
Colson, Charles, 142
Comiskey, Andrew, 284–85
Comfort, Ray: signature sermons, 110–13, 260; theology, 112–13, 167, 307; Way of the Master and, 8, 52, 74, 79, 108–10, 113–17, 118–20, 122, 125, 132, 134, 145, 148–50, 152–55, 237, 264
community-based performance, 19–21, 26, 28, 210; hell houses as, 163, 170–75, 200
Contemporary Christian Music (CCM), 57, 234–35
conventions, theatrical, 19, 162, 176, 224; authenticating, 168–69, 184–85; rhetorical, 168–69, 184–85, 195, 208
conversion: as aim of activism, 45, 311; as aim of evangelism, 8, 35, 70–71, 81, 153, 205; as evangelical distinctive, 3–7, 69–72, 147, 310, 312; in hell house and Judgement House, 162, 167–68, 170, 177, 187, 227; kerygmatic evangelism and, 1–3, 80, 89, 93, 102, 105, 109, 122; meta-kerygmatic evangelism and, 124, 132–35, 153; Miller and Román, 170–71, 211; personal testimony and, 106–7, 289; queer (Erzen), 297; Ray Comfort on108, 110–16; seeker-sensitive church services and, 236, 261; SOCE and, 10, 263–64, 267, 279, 296–97, 302–3; theology of, 69; 81–85, 93, 313
conversionism, 69–72, 109, 147, 162, 236, 310, 312
conversion therapy. *See* SOCE
Cooper, Gary, 280
Cornerstone Theater Company, 20
countertaste, 173–75
Cox, Tim, 285–86
Craig, William Lane, 138–39
creationism, young-earth, 9, 67, 192–93, 195–97, 199, 202–3, 205, 209, 211–16, 218, 305; versus Intelligent Design, 199–201, 216; versus other creationist views, 201. *See also* Answers in Genesis (AiG); Creation Museum
Creation Museum, 9, 227, 304, 308; culture war and, 73, 192–93, 198–200, 206–7, 215–19; creationism and, 198, 200–202, 206–7; criticisms of, 192–93, 215–16; features and displays, 191–92, 194–98, 207–10, 212; history of, 192; Intelligent Design and, 199–200; performativity and, 193–94, 196, 198–99, 207; preaching to the converted, 210–11;science and, 196–97, 200, 202–3, 207; theology of, 207–9; Vacation Bible School and, 212, 215; worldview apologetics and, 203–6, 211–12
critical generosity, 8, 10, 13, 28–29, 32–34, 36–37, 183, 188, 300–301, 313
Cru (Campus Crusade for Christ; CCC), 8, 56, 79, 117, 271; Bill Bright and, 101–3; criticisms of, 110–15, 123, 125, 128–32, 209, 260–61; Four Spiritual Laws, 102–8, 118, 148, 222; personal testimony and, 106–8
crucicentrism, 64, 68–69, 72, 86, 109
culture war, 3, 57, 73, 109, 146, 158, 180, 182, 216, 264, 267, 272, 278, 301, 305, 311. *See also* evangelicalism: religious right and; homosexuality: culture war and

Dallas, Joe, 274, 277–81, 283, 289, 293; ROUTE model and, 284
Dare 2 Share Ministries International (D2S), 124, 147–53, 154–56
Darwinism, 54, 192, 202, 217. *See also* creationism, young-earth; evolution, theory of
Davis, Allan, 159
Davis, Scott, 287
Dawkins, Richard, 15, 138, 216
Dayton, Donald W., 50–51
democratic paradox, 37–40
Derrida, Jacques, 84, 199, 205
Dickerson, Dave, 128–29
discipleship, 73, 82, 104, 107, 116–17, 128, 225, 239, 253, 255–56, 260, 294
Disciples of Christ (Church of Christ—Disciples), 59
Discovery Institute, 199
Doable Evangelism, 124, 128, 130, 133, 135–36

Dolan, Jill, 27, 32, 36; utopian performative, 171, 174–75, 189
Dubin, Steven C., 32
Durante Principle, (Jimmy), 304, 310, 312

Eagleton, Terry, 15, 43–44
Emerging Church, 258–59
environmental theater, 161–62
Episcopal Church, 59, 65, 276,
equaliberty, 25–26, 37, 39–40
Erzen, Tanya, 281, 285, 297
essentially contested concept, 8, 51–52, 79, 323n16
evangelicalism: as essentially contested concept, 8, 51–52, 79; attitudes toward, 5–6, 43–45, 50, 62, 304–5, 313; boundaries of, 58, 215; Black Church and, 57; complexity of, 13–14, 44, 50–53, 79; crisis in, 46–48, 122—28, 192–93, 300, 308; definition, 3, 56, 72–75, 319n2; fundamentalism and, 25, 57–58; future of, 314; history, 53–58, 324n18; homosexuality and, 268–78; other denominations and, 56, 63–64, 73, 326n38; performance activism and , 3–7, 311; religious right and, 51, 57, 72–73; secular age and, 48–49; scholarship about, 11–12, 50–51, 62; science and, 202–3; SOCE and, 266, 300; sociological assessments, 59–63, 255–57; theological beliefs, 63–72; tolerance and, 76, 87, 153, 173, 189, 238, 272–73, 300, 307
Evangelical Lutheran Church in America (ELCA), 59, 276
Evangelicals Concerned, 270, 294
evangelism, 8–10, 17, 76, 78, ; as performance activism, 3–7, 311; definition, 53, 70–71 (*see also* missions, Christian); centrality to evangelicalism, 53, 81, 311; hard-sell versus soft-sell, 121, 171–72, 232, 237, 246. *See also specific evangelistic tactics*
evangelism, friendship, 135, 147
evangelism, kerygmatic, 8, 78, 79, 85, 100, 103, 117–21, 136, 180, 182, 312; criticisms of, 122–23, 124–27, 130, 133, 138 152–53; definition, 78; dramaturgical analysis, 79–81; theological performative and, 84–85. *See also* evangelism; Four Spiritual Laws; soul-winning; Way of the Master
evangelism, lifestyle, 135, 148
evangelism, meta-kerygmatic, 8, 148, 218, 308, 312; criticisms of, 154; definition, 124; left-progressivism and, 155–56; versus kerygmatic, 124–27, 131–32, 152–55; *See also* apologetics, conversational; Dare2Share; Doable Evangelism
evangelism, personal. *See* evangelism, kerygmatic; evangelism, meta-kerygmatic
evangelism, soul-winning: compared with alternatives, 101–3, 106, 108–11, 114, 116, 122, 135, 136, 148, 150, 152, 154, 167, 170, 228, 232; description, 85–86, 88–100; Steven Anderson and, 8, 11, 77, 79, 85, 86–94, 97–100, 101–3, 105, 106, 108–10, 114–20, 125, 132, 133–34, 145, 147–50, 152–55, 226; versus left-progressive activism, 94, 118–20
Evans, Rachel Held, 305
evidentialism (apologetics). *See* apologetics: evidential
evolution, theory of. *See* anti-evolutionism; creationism, young-earth
ex-ex-gay. *See* ex-gay survivor
ex-gay (identity label), 267, 293, 295, 297, 302
ex-gay movement. *See* SOCE
ex-gay survivor, 10, 263, 265, 288, 295, 303, 311. *See also* SOCE: criticisms of
Exodus International, 73, 262–63; Alan Chambers and, 266–67, 288–89, 298–301; antigay evangelicalism and, 266–68, 273–75, 278, 286–87; criticisms of, 265–66, 287–88, 294, 311; dissolution and aftermath, 298–304; founding and history, 278–80, 292–94; Gay Christian Network and, 294—96, -idea of "change," 292–96, 298; NARTH and, 282, 290, 294; SOCE and, 262–68, 277–82, 286–87,

288–89, 291–304; testimonials and, 289–90

Faithful Word Baptist Church, 77, 85
Family Research Council, 271, 301
Falwell, Jerry, 57, 160–61
Farr, Tom, 167–68, 182
Final Exit, 158, 186–90
Fish, Stanley, 6, 15–16, 40–41, 43–44, 310
Focus on the Family, 57, 271, 273, 289, 301–2
Foster, Susan Leigh, 29–31, 33, 36
Foucault, Michel, 205, 302; ascesis, 297
Four Spiritual Laws (Campus Crusade for Christ presentation), 8, 79, 101–3, 106–8, 110, 118, 222; criticisms of, 110–15, 123, 125, 132, 209, 260–61; Four Laws script, 104–6
Freire, Paulo, 20–21, 215
Freres Corbusier, Les, 169, 175, 187
Friel, Todd, 109
Fryrear, Melissa, 301–2
fundamentalism, Christian: and Steven Anderson, 86–88; as epithet, 4, 35, 98, 116, 157, 158, 160, 169, 215; definition, 58; history, 54–56, 101; homosexuality and, 10, 86, 269–70, 275, 287; Independent Fundamental Baptist Church, 86, 88; relation to evangelicalism, 52, 57–58, 72–73, 152, 201, 202, 205, 211, 238
fundamentalist. *See* fundamentalism, Christian
Fundamentals, The, 54

Gagnon, Robert, 299, 359n10
Gallie, W. B., 51–52
Gallup Poll, 60, 62, 272
Gay Christian Network (GCN), 271, 294–95, 298. *See also* Chambers, Alan: Gay Christian Network roundtable
General Social Survey (GSS), 59
Gharavi, Lance, 12
Giberson, Karl, 215–16
Glass, Ira, 128–29, 133–34
God (Christian), 7, 12, 30, 34, 35, 53, 61, 76, 81, 86, 223, 227, 232–33, 235—36, 304, 308–9; apologetics and, 141–44; creationism and, 201, 203–4, 206–9, 211–14; hell house and Judgement House and, 166–72, 174, 177–78, 183, 185–86, 189; in evangelical theology, 63, 65–66, 68–71, 78–79, 81–84, 237, 240–41, 243, 249–51; interpersonal evangelism and, 90–94, 97–104, 107, 110–19, 123–25, 132, 139, 148–50, 153, 155; Moralistic Therapeutic Deism and, 255–59; SOCE and, 262–65, 268–71, 274, 284, 286–87, 291, 296, 298–99; Word of God (*see* biblicism)
Graham, Billy, 55–56, 101, 228
Great Commission (Matthew 28:19–20a), 81
Groeschel, Craig, 241–45, 251, 256, 260. *See also* Lifechurch.tv; multi-site church; seeker-sensitive church service
Gritter, Wendy, 295
Groothuis, Douglas, 139
Gruenwald, Bobby, 242

Habermas, Jürgen, 15
Hackett, Conrad, 59–60, 62
Haggard, Ted, 248, 266, 304
Haidt, Jonathan, 218–19
Hall, Amy K., 167—68, 182
Ham, Ken, 192, 206–7, 209, 216, 305
Harris, Sam, 15, 138, 216
Hart, D. G., 51, 61
Healing Place Church (Baton Rouge), 226
Hegel, Georg Wilhelm Friedrich, 139
hell house, 9, 22, 74, 83, 157, 190, 191, 213, 222, 227, 232, 237, 308; as community-based performance, 163, 170–75, 200; as environmental theater, 161–62; compared to *Final Exit*, 186–87; compared to Judgement House, 176–84, 186; critiques of, 167–69, 304–5; history of, 160–63; ironic productions, 169–70, 175, 187; Keenan Roberts and, 158–61, 170; studies of, 158–59, 175; Tallahassee production, 157–58, 164–67; variants and related forms, 158, 160

Henderson, Jim, 9, 124, 128–36, 145–47, 149–50, 153–56, 218, 247–48, 307
Henry, Carl, 55—56
Hitchens, Christopher, 15, 138
holy envy, 44–45
Holy Spirit, 63, 65, 68–71, 78, 81, 84, 99–100, 105, 117–18, 122, 124, 147, 150, 153–54, 167, 170, 183, 186, 188, 227
homiletics. *See* sermon
homosexuality: anti-gay views, 34, 74, 125, 127–28, 190, 263, 266–78, 281, 287, 298, 301, church debates and, 74, 276–77; culture war and, 3, 44, 57, 68, 73, 125, 127–28, 171, 180, 264, 267, 271–77, 302, 305–7, 313; Fred Phelps and, 30, 34–35, 190; hell houses and, 157–58, 169, 173, 180; identification as, 277–78, 297–98, 304; LGBT-affirmative Christianity, 270–71, 276, 287; progressive tolerance and, 23, 25–27, 33, 41, 174, 189–90, 266, 304, 313; Román and Miller on, 170–71; SOCE and, 10, 74, 262–63, 265, 266–68, 273–304 (*see also* SOCE); Steven Anderson and, 86–87, 269–71, 273, 307; theology and, 74, 86–87, 268–78
Hood, James, 30
Horton, Michael S., 250
Hostetler, Bob, 42–43
house church, 257
Hudgins, Tom, 160, 180, 189
Hull, Kenneth, 234–35
Hunter, Todd, 258
Hybels, Bill, 148, 223, 229–32, 237–38, 244–47, 254, 256–57, 260
Hyles-Anderson Bible College, 88
Hyles, Jack, 88–89, 93–94, 98, 100

ID. *See* Intelligent Design
ideavirus, 9, 148. *See also* Stier, Greg
IMPACT model of music, 236, 242. *See also* seeker-sensitive church service: music in
Independent Fundamental Baptist Church (IFB), 86, 88, 98, 332n8. *See also* fundamentalism
inerrancy, biblical, 54, 65, 66, 86, 270; creationism and, 200–203, 205–7, 214. *See also* biblicism
infallibility, biblical. *See* biblicism; inerrancy
Intelligent Design (ID), 199–201, 216,

Jackson, Brian, 159–60
Jehovah's Witnesses, 72, 98, 137
Jesus (Christ), 53, 61, 63, 66–69, 78, 81, 83, 87, 91–92, 102–5, 112, 125, 130, 132, 141, 148–49, 171, 173, 176, 209–10, 228, 243, 247, 251, 270, 287, 298, 307, 313; crucicentrism and, 64, 68–69, 72, 86, 109; in hell house and Judgement House, 165–66, 168, 169, 179, 182, 186–87
Jesus Movement, 233, 278
Jillette, Penn, 1–3
Jones, Stanton, 290–91
Journey into Manhood (SOCE program), 285–86, 293
Judgement House, 9, 158, 160, 213, 313; as community-based performance, 163; compared to *Final Exit,* 186–87; compared to Hell House, 176–84, 186; *59 Minutes* production, 175–80; history, 160–62, 180; prayer in, 183–86; scripts, 181–83
justification (salvation), 69, 82, 91, 117, 136–37. *See also* conversion: theology of

Kelley, Dean M., 237–40,
Kensington Community Church, 125–26
Kerby, Carl, 209
Kershaw, Baz: 24, 36; theatrical conventions 168–69, 195
kerygmatic evangelism. *See* evangelism: kerygmetic
Kinnaman, David, 127–30, 267, 274, 313
Kirshenblatt-Gimblett, Barbara, 193–94, 196
Koukl, Greg, 9, 124, 144–47, 149, 150, 153–56, 167, 218

LaBarbera, Peter, 273

Labov, Jay, 216–18
Laclau, Ernesto, 37–40
Laws, Curtis Lee, 54
Lee, Justin, 294–95. *See also* Gay Christian Network
left-progressivism: features of, 23–26
Lindsay, D. Michael, 59–60, 62
LifeChurch.tv, 241–45, 247, 254, 257. *See also* multisite church
literalism, biblical. *See* biblicism
Living Waters (Ray Comfort), 109–10, 113. *See also* Comfort, Ray; Way of the Master
Living Waters (SOCE ministry), 282, 284–85
Lovett, C. S., 88–89, 92–100
Love in Action, 265–65, 278, 282, 285, 293, 295
Love Won Out conference, 262, 274, 301; Alan Chambers and, 262–64, 274, 289. *See also* Exodus International
Lutheran Church (Evangelical Lutheran Church in America), 59, 276
Lyons, Gabe, 127–30, 267, 274, 313

Machen, J. Gresham, 54–55
mainline Protestant, 59–60, 63–64, 71, 224, 238, 252, 270, 271, 276–77, 294
Malone, Vivian, 30
Marsden, George M., 53
Mars Hill Bible Church, 259
Marsh, Patrick, 194–95
Matlock, Josh, 125
Marks, Jeremy, 295
McDowell, Josh: apologetics, 138, 142—43, tolerance critique, 42–43
McDowell, Sean, 139
McGavran, Donald, 227–29, 231–32, 261
Mears, Henrietta, 101
megachurch, 10, 74, 223, 226, 231, 237, 239, 251; and seeker-friendly services, 223–24, 229–30; complexities of, 240; criticisms of, 245–49, 252–56, 308–9; definition (Bird and Thumma), 229–30, membership and, 226, 253–55; multisite churches as, 240–41, 243–45; successes and failures of, 251–55
Mehta, Hemant, 138
Meredith, James, 34
meta-kerygmatic evangelism. *See* evangelism: meta-kerygmatic
Methodist. *See* United Methodist Church
Metropolitan Community Church (MCC), 271
Midgely, Mary, 217
Miller, Tim, 170–71, 175, 185–86, 210–11
missio Dei, 70, 222
missions, Christian, 70—71, 77, 81, 85, 137, 223, 228. *See also* activism: as evangelical distinctive; evangelism
Moberly, Elizabeth, 280–82, 285, 287
modernity, 43, 47, 54, 258; Francis Schaeffer on, 139–40. *See also* secular age
Mohler, R. Albert Jr., 58
Moody, Dwight L., 160
Moore, Russell D., 167–68, 182
Moralistic Therapeutic Deism (MTD), 255–56, 259–60, 308–9
Morgenthaler, Sally, 251–53, 258
Mouffe, Chantal, 6;democratic paradox, 37–40; radical democracy, 24–26
multisite church, 10, 125; criticisms of, 248; description, 241, 243–45; LifeChurch.tv and, 241–45, 247; research on, 245; seeker-sensitive services and, 240–45
music, 12, 139, 159, 165, 171, 205, 213; Contemporary Christian, 57, 234–35; criticism, 247–49; in services, 224–25, 226, 228, 230, 231, 232–36, 241–42, 244, 246, 249, 257, 258. *See also* worship song

NARTH (National Association for the Research and Therapy of Homosexuality), 282, 290–91, 294, 299
National Congregations Study (NCS), 253, 257
National Organization for Marriage (NOM), 271–72
Naugle, David, 204
Neel, John, 186–89

neo-evangelicalism, 55–56. *See also* evangelicalism: history
new atheists, 15, 138, 216
new paradigm church. *See* seeker-sensitive church service
Newbigin, Lesslie, 304
Newport, Frank, 62
New Thomas Road Baptist Church, 161
Newman, Randy, 123–24, 145
Nicene Creed, 63, 83
Nicolosi, Joseph, 281–82, 285, 290–91
Noll, Mark A., 305
nouthetic counseling, 279–80, 287, 295

Obama, Barack, 60, 86, 313
Off The Map, 130
Oneness Pentecostalism, 60
Ordinary Attempts, 9, 132–36, 153, 155, 307
organic church, 257
Osteen, Joel, 230, 237, 241; criticisms of, 249–51, 256, 309; theology of, 250, 259

paranoid stance, 28–29, 33, 35, 36, 159
Parents, Friends, and Families of Ex-Gays and Gays (PFOX), 297
Parshall, Janet, 299
Paterson, Doug, 20
Paulk, Ann, 293, 365n84
Paulk, John, 293, 365n84
Pearcey, Nancy, 141–42
Pellegrini, Ann, 159, 175
Pentecostalism, 13–14, 56, 57, 98, 152, 164, 271; Oneness Pentecostalism, 60; Third Wave, 233; Word of Faith, 250; worship music and, 224, 233, 235, 236, 249
People Can Change (PCC), 285–86, 293
performance, 16–17
performance activism: definitions and types, 2, 18–22, 31–32, 311, 316n8; evangelical outreach as, 3–7, 311; progressive versus non-progressive, 3, 23–26, 29–37, 118–20, 155–56; scholarly tendencies and, 5, 8, 12–13, 26–33, 49–50; tensions in, 4–7, 37–44
performative (general), 83–85, 264; in Creation Museum, 193–94, 196, 199, 202, 207, 212; prayer as, 185–86; sexuality and, 264–65
performative, theological, 83–85, 86, 93, 106, 116, 124, 264
performative, utopian, 36, 171–72, 174–75, 189, 314
Perkins, Tony, 273
Perry, Tory, 271
personal evangelism. *See* evangelism, kerygmatic; evangelism, meta-kerygmatic
Pervasive Interpretive Pluralism (PIP), 67
Phelps, Fred, 30, 34–36, 190, 270, 273, 287
Philpott, Kent, 278
postmodernism, 24, 119, 135, 143, 146, 149, 150, 153, 154, 157, 216, 218; worldview analysis of, 204–5; worship styles and, 257–59
praise and worship music, musicology of, 234–36; history, 233–34; seeker-sensitive services and, 236. *See also* music; seeker-sensitive church service: music in
prayer, 3, 67, 70, 86, 89, 133; Jim Henderson and, 133, 135, 150; Judgement House and, 177, 180, 182, 183–86, 189; sinner's, 82–84, 92–93, 103, 105, 109, 111, 115–16, 135, 167, 177, 180, 243; SOCE and, 275, 277, 279—80, worship services and, 224, 233, 235, 236, 242, 243, 257, 259
preaching to the converted: article by Román and Miller, 170–71, 210–11;Creation Museum and, 200, 210–11; hell house and, 163, 170–72, 190; Judgement House and, 183, 185–86, 190; worship services and, 260
Presbyterian Church, 53, 59, 270, 276
presuppositionalism. *See* apologetics: presuppositional
progressive left. *See* left-progressivism
proselytization. *See* evangelism.
prosperity gospel, 250–51
Putnam, Robert D., 60, 305–7, 309

Qur'an, 43, 44

radical democracy, 7, 16, 24–27, 39, 41, 50
Ragan, Bob, 298
Ramos, Trisha, 109
Rancière, Jacques, 6, 38, 41
Ratliff, George, 158
RawChurch.tv, 245. *See also* LifeChurch.tv; multisite church
Redman, Robert R. Jr., 235
Reising, Richard, 221–23, 225, 228, 239, 260
religious right: and homosexuality, 271–78, 290–92; criticisms of, 48, 272; culture war and, 3, 57, 62, 152, 275, 311; representatives of, 57, 60, 109; relation to evangelicalism, 51, 57, 72–73
RELTRAD (Religious Tradition), 59–60, 62
reparative therapy, 267, *See also* SOCE
Restored Hope Network (RHN), 299–301, 303
REVEAL study. *See* Willow Creek Church: REVEAL study and
Riley, Mike, 278
Ringer, Bob, 102
Roberts, Keenan, 158–61, 167, 169–70, 173, 175, 177–80, 187, 189
Robinson, Gene, 276
Roman Catholic Church, 51, 52, 56, 59, 61–65, 73, 83, 98, 137, 152, 224, 270, 282, 306, 326n38
Román, David: critical generosity, 28–29, 36; preaching to the converted, 170—71, 175, 185–86, 210–11
Rowe, Maggie, 169
Ruse, Michael, 217

Saddleback Church, 223, 239, 252; as multisite, 240–41, 244; as seeker-sensitive, 229–30, 257; criticisms of, 245–48; history, 231; membership and, 239–41, 253–54; worship services, 231, 235, 236–37
Saddleback Sam, 231, 235, 308
salvation. *See* conversion
same-sex-attracted/same-sex attraction (SSA), 265–67, 277–78, 280, 282–87, 289, 293, 295–98, 301, 303
sanctification, 82, 91, 117, 279, 300. *See also* discipleship
Sargeant, Kimon Howland, 230
saved. *See* conversion
Sexual Identity Therapy (SIT) Framework, 296–97
Schaeffer, Francis: core views, 139–44, 152; legacy, 144–47, 149, 151–55; total truth and, 139, 142, 154–56, 214, 218; worldview analysis and, 9, 154, 203–5, 214, 218, 312
Schechner, Richard, 16–17, 161–62
Schlossman, David A., 31–32
Scopes Trial, 55, 192, 198
Scottish School of Common Sense, 202–4
secular age, 8, 48–49, 192, 255, 259, 306; book (*A Secular Age*) 48–49; challenges posed by, 10, 14, 49, 75–76, 137–38, 141, 150, 155, 160, 257, 310, 314; definition, 48–49, 138; secular-age evangelicalism, 172, 193, 222–23, 268
Sedgwick, Eve Kosofsky, 28–29, 36
seeker-sensitive church service, 10, 74, 223, 304, 308; criticisms of, 223–24, 245–57, 308–9; definition, 229–30; history, 230–32; Lakewood Church as, 230, 249–51, 257; multisite churches and, 240–45; music in, 232–36, 249; Saddleback Church as, 229–30, 257; sermons (homiletics) in, 226, 229, 231, 236–37, 243, 249; theology and, 226, 232, 236–40; versus alternative models, 257–59; versus worship services, 240; Willow Creek Church as, 229–30, 252, 257
seeker service. *See* seeker-sensitive church service
sermon, 3, 17, 50, 66, 70, 125, 164 175, 204, 209, 211–12, 224, 258; fire-and-brimstone/turn-or-burn, 47, 115, 157, 159–60, 162, 229; Joel Osteen and, 249–50; multisite church and, 241–45, 247–48; Ray Comfort and, 110–13, 260; revival (*see* preaching to the converted); seeker-sensitive

sermon (*continued*)
services and, 226, 229, 231—33, 236–37, 243, 249; Steven Anderson and, 86–87, 88
"Seven C's of History," 207–8
Sexual Orientation Change Efforts. *See* SOCE
Sharlet, Jeff, 248
Shelley, Bruce, 172–73
Shelley, Marshal, 172–73
Siever, Randy, 130–31, 133–36, 145, 153
Sigurdsen, Ola, 43–44
Sire, James W., 204
Smid, John, 266, 293, 295, 298
Smith, Christian: biblicism, 328n64; defining evangelicalism, 62–63, 273; Moralistic Therapeutic Deism, 255–57, 308; Pervasive Interpretive Pluralism, 67;
SOCE (Sexual Orientation Change Efforts): as ascesis, 296–97; criticisms of, 74, 281, 288–92, 294–96, 298–300; evangelicalism and, 10, 266–68, 298–302; Exodus International and, 262–68, 277–82, 286–87, 288–89, 291–304; future, 298–304; history, 278–82, 288–96, 298–300; theories behind, 279–86, 292–9
Soloway, Jill, 169
soul-winning: compared with alternatives, 101–3, 106, 108–11, 114, 116, 122, 135, 136, 148, 150, 152, 154, 167, 170, 228, 232; description, 85–86, 88–100; Steven Anderson and, 8, 11, 77, 79, 85, 86–94, 97–100, 101–3, 105, 106, 108–10, 114–20, 125, 132, 133–34, 145, 147–50, 152–55, 226; versus left-progressive activism, 94, 118–20
Southern Baptist Convention (SBC), 59, 74, 137, 167, 271; author's childhood in 5, 13, 164
So Whats, 138
Spencer, Michael: criticisms of Joel Osteen, 250–51; "The Coming Evangelical Collapse," 46–49
Spitzer, Robert, 291
Stand To Reason, 144–45, 167
Starbucks, 134–35; church marketing video, 220–22, 260, Dare 2 Share skit, 149–50; Exodus as, 288
Stendahl, Krister, 44–45
Stevenson, Jill, 212
Stier, Greg, 9, 124, 147–53, 154–56, 218
Strobel, Lee, 138, 142–43
Stone, Jon R., 50, 56
Summit Ministries, 204–5

taste (Pierre Bourdieu), 172–75, 188
Taylor, Charles, 8, 14, 48–49, 138. *See also* secular age
televangelism, 44, 60, 250
testimony, personal, 106–8, 110
theater, 16–17
theater for social change. *See* performance activism
Theater of the Oppressed (TO), 20–21, 189, 286
theological performative, 83–85, 86, 93, 106, 116, 124, 264
Thomas, Randy, 293
Throckmorton, Warren, 290, 296–97
Thumma, Scott, 229, 252–55
Timbers, Alex, 169
Theissen, Elmer John, 305
tolerance: as left-progressive value, 3–4, 6, 24–27, 307; evangelicalism and, 76, 87, 153, 173, 189, 238, 272–73, 300, 307; Moralistic Therapeutic Deism and, 256; tensions concerning, 25, 40–46, 49–50, 310, 313
Toscano, Peterson, 265–66, 285
truth: capital-T, 1, 120, 307—10; total (Schaefferian), 139, 142, 154–56, 214, 218 (*see also* Schaeffer, Francis)

unchurched Harry, 230, 235, 252, 308
United Church of Christ, 59, 60, 71
United Methodist Church, 5, 59, 60, 65, 164, 226, 249, 263, 271, 306
utopian performative, 36, 171–72, 174–75, 189, 314

Vacation Bible School (VBS), 212–13; Answers in Genesis and, 213—16
Van Til, Cornelius, 143, 203

VBS. *See* Vacation Bible School (VBS)
Vineyard Association, 233

Wallace, George, 30, 32, 33–36
Walzer, Michael, 38
Warren, Rick, 223, 229—32, 236–47, 250–51, 256–57, 260; founding of Saddleback, 231; on church membership, 239–40; on music, 232, 236; on preaching (homiletics), 236–37
Wax, Trevin, 307
Way of the Master, 8, 52, 74, 79, 80,122, 152–55, 237, 264; description, 108–20. *See also* Comfort, Ray
Webber, Robert E., 55–57
Westboro Baptist Church. *See* Fred Phelps
Willenbrink, Hank III, 83–84, 159
Williams, Sam R., 283
Willow Creek Church, 223, 240; as multisite, 241; as seeker-sensitive, 229–30, 252, 257; criticism of, 245–48; history, 230–31; membership and, 239, 241; REVEAL study and, 254
Wimber, John, 233–34
wonderful plan. *See* Four Spiritual Laws
Word of Faith movement, 250–51
worldview, 3, 11, 13, 311; Creation Museum/Answers in Genesis and, 9, 193, 203–19; evangelicalism's, 45, 159, 169, 172, 174, 264, 283, 291; Francis Schaeffer and, 9, 154, 203–5, 214, 218, 312; 204–6, 312; versus non-evangelical, 5–7, 84, 175, 189, 279; Moralistic Therapeutic Deism, 256, 259; worldview analysis, 9, 146, 203–7, 209, 211, 214–17
Worldview Academy, 204–5
worship evangelism, 223, 230, 242, 245, 251–52, 254. *See also* seeker-sensitive church service
worship songs: musicology of, 234–36; history, 233–34; seeker-sensitive services and, 236. *See also* music; seeker-sensitive church service: music in
Worthen, Anita, 281
Worthen, Frank, 278
Wright, Jeremiah, 60, 313
Wyler, Rich, 285

Yarhouse, Mark, 283, 290–91, 296–97, 299–300
young-earth creationism. *See* creationism, young-earth
Youth Group, The, 169

Zijderveld, Anton, 47, 49
Žižek, Slavoj, 15, 41, 43–44, 156

Made in the USA
Las Vegas, NV
07 March 2021

19000898R30240